EDUCATIONAL MEDIA AND TECHNOLOGY YEARBOOK

EDUCATIONAL MEDIA AND TECHNOLOGY YEARBOOK

Michael Orey, V. J. McClendon, and Robert Maribe Branch, Editors

2008 Edition Volume 33

Published in cooperation with the Association for Educational Communications and Technology

Education Media Yearbook

A Member of the Greenwood Publishing Group

Westport, Connecticut • London

Educational media and technology yearbook.—Westport, CT : Libraries Unlimited,
A Member of the Greenwood Publishing Group, Inc. 1985–
     p. v.
Annual
2008–   vol. 33
Published in cooperation with the Association of Educational Communications and
Technology, 1985–
Continues: Educational media yearbook
ISBN 978–1–59158–647–0
LB1028.3.E372   2008   85643014

British Library Cataloguing in Publication Data is available.

ISBN: 978–1–59158–647–0

First published in 2008

Libraries Unlimited, 88 Post Road West, Westport, CT 06881
A member of the Greenwood Publishing Group, Inc.
www.lu.com

Printed in the United States of America

The paper used in this book complies with the
Permanent Paper Standard issued by the National
Information Standards Organization (Z39.48–1984).

10 9 8 7 6 5 4 3 2 1

Contents

Part Three: Leadership Profiles

Part Four: Organizations and Associations in North America

Part Five: Graduate Programs in North America

Part Six: Mediagraphy—Print and Non-Print Resources

Preface

This is the seventh year for which I have been an editor and the fifth where I am the senior editor. I have decided to try something different in this issue of the *Educational Media and Technology Yearbook* (EMTY). I usually try to capture the essence of what is going on in the field each year. I do this by going over the AECT program and look for emergent themes and then identify specific authors and papers to invite to write a chapter for the EMTY. Instead, this year I asked one faculty member from each of the top programs to identify one paper written by some individual(s) within their program to include in the EMTY. The paper ought to represent the current thinking in the department. I realize that there is a great deal of diversity of thinking within departments, so this may have been an impossible task, but it gets worse.

This plan has a major flaw in it. It requires that there be a recognized list of the top programs. I know of none. So, I have asked around and have casually come up with these programs. For definition purposes, these would be the top programs in an organization like AECT, not necessarily ISTE or ISLS (International Society of the Learning Sciences). Here is the list of these nine schools: UGA, Virginia Tech, Florida State, Penn State, Indiana, Utah State, San Diego State, Arizona State, and Syracuse.

So, I sent out this list to a person I have either corresponded with in the past or found their e-mail address online. I asked them to do two things. One was to nominate someone from their department to be a contributor to this year's EMTY. The other thing I asked them to do was to validate my list by either agreeing with the list or making suggestions for deletions and additions. I received three responses that addressed the top programs question. Two people said that it was more or less accurate. The other person decided to divide and add. That is, this person took my original 9 and divided into a top group and then a second-tier level. This second tier would also include the addition of the University of Twente and Wayne State. Others outside my list of 9 suggested adding Northern Illinois, Memphis, South Alabama, Brigham Young, George Mason, and East Carolina. If we ignore a first- and second-tier orientation and we assume we have not left off others who have good quality programs, that brings my list up to 17 top schools. While I needed to go with the original 9 to get manuscripts, perhaps for the next issue I can look to all these 17 and others if people contact me to let me know that their program ought to be on this top Instructional Technology Program list.

The audience for the *Yearbook* consists of media and technology professionals in schools, higher education, and business contexts. Topics of interest to professionals practicing in these areas are broad, as the Table of Contents demonstrates. The theme unifying each of the following chapters is the use of technology to enable or enhance education. Forms of technology represented in this volume vary from traditional tools such as the book to the latest advancements in digital technology, while areas of education encompass widely ranging situations involving learning and teaching.

As in prior volumes, the assumptions underlying the chapters presented here are as follows:

- Technology represents tools that act as extensions of the educator.

- Media serve as delivery systems for educational communications.

- Technology is *not* restricted to machines and hardware, but includes techniques and procedures derived from scientific research about ways to promote change in human performance.

- The fundamental tenet is that educational media and technology should be used to:

  1. achieve authentic learning objectives,

  2. situate learning tasks,

  3. negotiate the complexities of guided learning,

  4. facilitate the construction of knowledge,

  5. support skill acquisition, and

  6. manage diversity.

The *Educational Media and Technology Yearbook* has become a standard reference in many libraries and professional collections. Examined in relation to its companion volumes of the past, it provides a valuable historical record of current ideas and developments in the field. Part One, "Trends and Issues," presents an array of chapters that develop some of the current themes listed above, in addition to others. Part Two, "Library & Information Science," concentrates upon chapters of special relevance to K-12 education, school learning resources, and school library media centers. In Part Three, "Leadership Profiles," authors provide biographical sketches of the careers of instructional technology leaders. Part Four, "Organizations and Associations in North America," and Part Five, "Graduate Programs in North America," are, respectively, directories of instructional technology-related organizations and institutions of higher learning offering degrees in related fields. Finally, Part Six, the "Mediagraphy," presents an annotated listing of selected current publications related to the field.

The Editors of the *Yearbook* invite media and technology professionals to submit manuscripts for consideration for publication. Contact Michael Orey (mikeorey@uga.edu) for submission guidelines.

Michael Orey, V. J. McClendon, and Robert Maribe Branch

Contributors

Denice Adkins

B. J. Berquist

Elizabeth Boling

Abbie Brown

Katherine S. Cennamo

Christa Harrelson Deissler

Ileana de la Teja

Sheetal Janubhai Desai

Linda Esser

Lesley S. J. Farmer

Theodore W. Frick

Chad Galloway

Barbara Grabowski

Tim Green

Pei-Hsuan Hsieh

Wen-Min Hsieh

Wendi Arant Kaspar

James D. Klein

Barbara B. Lockee

Terrance S. Newell

Julie Moore

Jamal Olusesi

Drew Polly

Priya Sharma

J. Michael Spector

Susan L. Stansberry

Kenneth R. Thompson

Diane L. Velasquez

Ying Xie

Suhyun Yoo

Part One
Trends and Issues

Introduction

Michael Orey

This is the seventh edition of this book where I have served as the editor of the Trends section. I have used a variety of strategies for organizing this section. As noted in the preface, I have asked some of the top programs in the United States to help me out this year. Having come up with a list of top programs (regardless of how unscientific this list was generated), I asked each program to provide me with a chapter that would be representative of the research being done by their department. Thinking about my own department where we have twelve faculty members with diverse interests and over 40 doctoral students also with diverse research interests it is nearly impossible to select one chapter that would represent the entire group. My own process was to send an e-mail to everyone and tell them about some of the research for which I had firsthand knowledge. One other faculty provided me with a few more studies. I then looked for similarities between these studies. My conclusion was that all of them either studied the impact of an instructional strategy or they looked for an explanatory framework that included an instructional strategy. For example, one researcher might use what we already know about setting up learning communities to study how this strategy can be used to foster a learning community in an online class. On the other hand, another researcher might take a look at an online class that has a reputation for fostering learning communities and try to determine what strategies were employed to develop these communities. I sent out my conclusions via e-mail for confirmation (remember, I only had one out of twelve faculty actual reply to the first e-mail) and was told that this characterization of research from our department does not cover all research in the department. Rejected! I share this story here not to reveal how dysfunctional my department is (I actually believe that we all get along pretty well), but to point out how complicated is the process of selecting one paper to represent an entire department to indicate trends within our field. In the end, I chose a dissertation project that looked at teacher epistemological belief change through the dual lenses of transformative learning and conceptual change. The bottom line is that I did what I think others did, we tried to do the best we could, but no matter how well we did, the single chapter will not be a perfect indication of trends from that one department.

In addition to the chapters from the top departments, I also had several chapters that were included because of the open invitation I have for contributors to this book. Some of these fit into helping to see the trends. One of them is continuation of the work Michael Molenda has provided to this book for several years. Every year, Michael would contribute a data-driven assessment of what is going on in the field of Instructional Technology. He has now retired, but Abbie Brown and Tim Green have volunteered this year to write this chapter. I also have a thoughtful piece on the evolution of a doctoral program in our field and several other papers that ought to be representative of trends in our field. I turn now to a discussion of each chapter.

After one year without a trends chapter, Brown and Green have brought it back with their chapter entitled, "Issues and Trends in Instructional Technology: Making the Most of Mobility and Ubiquity." As the title implies, all three primary sectors of Instructional Technology (K-12 schools, Higher Education, and Business and Industry) have taken advantage of both "mobility" and "ubiquity." Businesses are leading the way with mobility by making use of mobile, wireless devices for delivery of training. All sectors are continuing to make use of eLearning or Online Learning in various ways. However, with all of these technologies including the wireless ones, there are still many cautions about the limited impact of these technologies on outcomes of learning.

The cautions continue in the Polly and Moore chapter entitled, "The Great Divide: Preparing Pre-Service Teachers to Integrate Technology Effectively." In this chapter, they blend two of the sectors of the Brown and Green chapter: K-12 Schools and Higher Education. They do this by focusing on how university students who are learning to be classroom teachers are learning how to integrate technology into their future classrooms. While they found a great deal of rhetoric, they found very little data. When they found successes, they came from a lot of hard work. The usual model for helping pre-service teachers learn how to use technology in the classroom is to have them take one course on this topic. The better solution is to not only provide this class, but also provide many models of effective integration in other classes where they are learning and to provide them with mentors (practicing teachers), either in person or via video, that can model expert integration examples. As implied in the first chapter, technology is now ubiquitous in the schools and in higher education. Not surprisingly, it is not enough to just provide the technology hardware, but the technology (soft skills) to be able to masterfully use the hardware.

When I had sent out the e-mails to the "top" Instructional Technology programs, I was seeking research articles that would help me to define the trends in the field, but what I had not thought about was that the recipients of my e-mails would think that what I wanted was a paper about their programs. Elizabeth Boling wrote such a paper and while I did not think of this, I do think that it is a very good idea and her chapter entitled "From Students to Scholars: Revision of the Doctoral Program in Instructional Systems Technology at Indiana University" is important for understanding some of the trends in our field. One of the courses I teach is an introduction to our field. As part of the introduction, I try to help my students understand that technology is more than devices, that technology is also the knowledge about how to help learners achieve their learning goals. It is interesting that this latter form of technology is the centerpiece of the doctoral program revision at Indiana University. It is more about mentoring and scaffolding and building powerful relationships between students and professors and less oriented to, say a computer. While the latter can mediate the dossiers, it is the former that allows the students actually build a meaningful dossier that will support that student as they become colleagues in our field.

Interestingly, Cennamo and Lockee also had the same interpretation and they choose to write about how a Performance Technology framework was used to revise their curriculum. While many instructional technology programs incorporate the human performance technology (HPT) movement into their curriculum, the IDT faculty at Virginia Tech made a conscious decision to apply HPT principles to revise the design of their own graduate program. As practitioners of HPT, the faculty team based the revised design on established processes and considerations grounded in HPT theory. The result is a curriculum that is more reflective of the needs of our constituents—program graduates and those who hire them.

The next group of papers is the actual research papers that I requested from the "top" programs in the United States. Before talking about them individually, I do want to point out that I did not have a very high return rate. Two of the top universities that I contacted never replied to my e-mails. Two others replied and promised a paper, but it did not arrive in time to include in this book. One of the universities decided to send me a paper with three authors, each of whom was from one of the top research programs (Arizona State University, Penn State University, and Florida State University). Other than this paper, of the "top" programs, I got papers from Indiana University, Penn State University, and the University of Georgia. Let's look at the individual contributions.

I will begin with the paper by faculty from three of the top programs. This paper was written by Klein, Grabowski, Spector, and Teja and the chapter is entitled, "Competencies for Instructors: A Validation Study." The competencies are for both face-to-face instructors as well as online instructors, the latter having an emerging need. In trying to capture a trend from this chapter, it is perhaps how our field often gets swept away with a new "hot" topic, but always there is a substantial basis that this new trend can rest upon. In this case, the hot topic is online learning and more specific online instructors. The basis is the International Board of Standards for Training, Performance, and Instruction (ibstpi) competencies for instructors, which continue to be important regardless of the trend.

Frick and Thompson have described an interesting development project that may help address a long-standing issue we face in our field, how to bring about successful educational change. The development project involves a collection of tools that allow for the simulation of change in order to make predictions of change. These sets of tools can help teachers to understand the answers to the Frick and Thompson's key three questions of: "Change what? Change how? and How do you know the change is working?" As they point out, education has seen many attempt change, but few or no changes have occurred in education in the past 200 years. It is through these safe simulation tools that teachers can see the benefits of changing and making sure that they actually participate in the real change, not some superficial understanding of the change. The nice thing about this chapter as a trend in our field is that it is using simulations, computers, and systems theory as the basis for achieving their goals.

From Penn State University, Sharma, Xie, Hsieh, Hsieh, and Yoo contribute a chapter entitled, "Student Learning Outcomes in Technology-Enhanced Constructivist Learning Environments: What Does Research Show?" In this paper, they were looking to review all the research that has been done on constructivist learning, but only if it was enhanced with technology. Surprisingly, with these three criterion (research outcome, constructivist learning, technology-enhanced) they were able to find only 10 articles that they could use for their review! As for its relevance for assessing the trends in the field, I return to my introductory class. This paper fits nicely because it looks at both the soft technology (constructivist learning) and the hard technology (computers). It suggests a trend in that what they and others are seeking are good powerful outcomes. They did find good powerful outcomes when the constructivist learning environment used what I what call the methods of Cognitive Apprenticeships—Modeling, Scaffolding, Coaching, Articulation, and Reflection.

Finally, in Deissler's chapter from the University of Georgia entitled "Changing Beliefs versus Changing Concepts: Transformational Learning as a Tool for Investigating and Encouraging Teacher Belief Change," we see the soft technologies of Conceptual Change being contrasted with Transformational Learning. From a trends view, we see another paper concerned about bringing about change in the schools. At the heart of that change is using technology, but it has the equally important view of seeing technology used for higher-order thinking and problem solving. While Frick and Thompson looked at this kind of change from a systemic view, this view of change looks at epistemological change within an individual and how that major change in view can impact change in the classroom and change in the use of technology.

Issues and Trends in Instructional Technology: Making the Most of Mobility and Ubiquity

Abbie Brown
East Carolina University

Tim Green
California State University, Fullerton

We are indebted to Barbara Bichelmeyer and Michael Molenda, the authors of this chapter in previous editions of the yearbook; we have benefited greatly from their advice and counsel and have used a format and approach similar to theirs (Bichelmeyer and Molenda, 2006; Molenda and Bichelmeyer, 2005) in reporting on this year's trends and issues. This chapter comprises four sections: Overall Developments, Corporate Training and Development, Higher Education, and K-12 Settings.

OVERALL DEVELOPMENTS

In the two years since the previous review was written (Bichelmeyer and Molenda, 2006), the United States economy has continued to see improvement. Although the current economic outlook is mixed due to concerns over the housing market, oil prices, and the war in Iraq, the increased economic growth in the last quarter of 2006 and into the first quarter of 2007 seemed to settle fears that an economic downturn was inevitable. For public K-12 and higher education, the financial support provided through tax revenue generated at the state level grew over previous years. This translated into state funding for education being restored in many parts of the country (U.S. Department of Education, 2006).

Laptop Computers Continue to Gain in Popularity

Laptop computers have continually risen in popularity as users seek greater mobility and flexibility (Ferguson, 2006). Increasing numbers of undergraduates own and use laptops at school (Salaway et al., 2006). In 2007, the computer industry saw demand for laptop or notebook computers continue to increase. According to Ferguson (2006), "In 2000, notebooks held 18.7 percent of the PC market, according to Merrill Lynch. Now, notebook shipments make up 36 percent of the market and could capture 44 percent by 2008." The preference for light, powerful, and portable computing devices is undoubtedly a trend that will maintain or gain momentum.

Online Learning Continues to Grow

According to the Sloan Consortium's fourth annual study of online learning, *Making the Grade: Online Education in the United States* (2006), online learning continues to grow. According to the Sloan Consortium report, the number of students taking online courses increased 35%, the largest annual increase measured to date (Allen and Seaman, 2006). Of the 3.1 million students learning online, more than half (51.5%) are studying at two-year Associates institutions (Allen and Seaman, 2006).

The larger educational institutions tend to be developing and providing the greatest amount of online instruction. The vast majority of Chief Academic Officers surveyed by the Sloan Consortium believe that online education serves those students who would not otherwise be served by the institution. They believe online offerings and face-to-face offerings are serving different populations.

Although the majority of academic leaders continue to believe online programs are as good as or better than face-to-face (Allen and Seaman, 2006), employers seem to take a different view. At least one study indicates that employers prefer applicants with degrees from traditional, brick-and-mortar institutions (Carnevale, 2007). A separate survey conducted by publisher Vault Inc. (2006) indicated that online graduate degrees were more acceptable to employers than online undergraduate degrees.

Information Security Remains a Cause for Concern

Data breaches continue to remain a problem for all organizations that aggregate personal information from a large number of people (e.g., employees, students). However, universities seem to be having the greatest amount of trouble. An article in the December 18, 2006, issue of *The New York Times* states, "... educational institutions were twice as likely to report suffering a breach as any other type of entity, with government, general businesses, financial service and healthcare companies pulling up behind" (Zeller, 2006). Unfortunately this trend will probably continue, even as large organizations develop improved security procedures.

Copyright and Fair Use Are the Subject of Continued Debate

U.S. Representatives Rick Boucher (D-VA) and John Doolittle (R-CA) introduced the Freedom And Innovation Revitalizing U.S. Entrepreneurship Act of 2007 (FAIR USE Act) in February of that year. The bill is intended to protect the fair use rights of users of copyrighted material and would allow customers to circumvent digital copy restrictions in six limited areas when copyright owners' business models are not threatened. Fair use doctrine allows customers of copyright works to make limited numbers of copies, particularly for reviews, news reporting, teaching, and research. The Recording Industry Association of America (RIAA) opposed this bill, referring to it as one that would "legalize hacking" (Gross, 2007; The Online Office of Congressman Rick Boucher, 2007). Copyright and Fair Use continue to be hotly debated topics and the trend seems to be continued argument between those who wish to protect the rights of the artists and owners of copyright and those who wish to promote creative use of media for nonprofit endeavors.

CORPORATE TRAINING AND DEVELOPMENT

As had been done in previous issues and trend chapters of the yearbook (Molenda and Bichelmeyer, 2005; Bichelmeyer and Molenda, 2006), this chapter's authors continue to track corporate application of instructional technologies primarily by referring to the *State of the Industry in Leading Enterprises: ASTD's Annual Review of Trends in Workplace Learning and Performance* (Rivera and Paradise, 2006), a publication of the results of an annual survey that has been reported in *Training* magazine since 1997. The current ASTD annual report is based on data collected from the Benchmarking Forum (BMF) organizations and ASTD BEST award winners alongside historical Benchmarking Survey (BMS) data. Essentially, the report describes the activities of organizations that are recognized as exemplary in their approach to workplace learning and performance.

Learning Investments

Within ASTD's sample of large organizations the average annual expenditure for employee learning increased by approximately 4% from the previous year, and the average number of hours of formal learning per employee in BMF organizations increased from 35 to 41 (Rivera and Paradise, 2006). The average cost per learning hour fell for members of the BMF sample, but the cost increased among those organizations designated as BEST by ASTD (Rivera and Paradise, 2006). Overall, the trend seems to be modest increases in the annual expenditure for employee learning as well as an increase in the amount of time employees spend receiving formal instruction. The average cost per learning hour is declining, except within those organizations that have received ASTD BEST awards.

Use of Technology: E-Learning on the Rise

E-learning (instruction delivered via networked computing devices) continued to gain in popularity (Rivera and Paradise, 2006). ASTD reports that organizations are using technology to deliver learning almost 40% of the time; that 60% of technology-based learning was delivered as online instruction; and close to 90% of this online instruction was self-paced (Rivera and Paradise, 2006). The trend is unquestionably an increased use of e-learning, particularly for self-paced learning activities.

Use of External Services (Outsourcing)

Organizations surveyed by ASTD (Rivera and Paradise, 2006) indicate an overall decline in expenditure for external services. Outsourcing has diminished approximately 25% in the past year. Rivera and Paradise (2006) attribute this in part to the conservative stance many companies now take regarding the outsourcing of "areas of the learning function that may contain knowledge that leads to a competitive advantage" (p. 4). The trend is a marked decrease in use of external services and greater reliance on in-house production.

Measurement

Measurement of the organizational impact of learning activity remains an elusive goal for most businesses. The ability to manage and report on learning activities has increased dramatically and many companies are developing proprietary methods of measurement. According to the ASTD report, "Most BMF and BEST organizations either had or were in the process of developing dashboards and scorecards to monitor the results of the enterprise learning function" (Rivera and Paradise, 2006, p. 4). The trend is a continued effort to increase the reliability of metrics to better understand the impact of instructional activities on the organization.

Globalization

According to Rivera and Paradise (2006), "Globalization has emerged as a significant challenge for organizations that want to expand their learning functions outside their home countries" (p. 5). Challenges both technological and cultural are preventing global expansion of domestic learning functions. Technological challenges include hardware and networking deficits and problems with standardization. Cultural challenges include adapting to the local culture, language barriers, territorialism, and inconsistent learning objectives across regions (Rivera and Paradise, 2006). The trend is toward a focus upon the development of specific learning function elements, particularly learning management systems (Rivera and Paradise, 2006).

HIGHER EDUCATION

This chapter's authors examined universities' information technology use primarily by referring to the *EDUCAUSE Core Data Service Fiscal Year 2005 Summary Report*.

Nine hundred thirty-three institutions submitted the 2005 survey; the data set was frozen in June 2006 to prepare the analysis for the summary report released in November 2006. Undergraduate trends in particular are examined primarily by referring to *The ECAR Study of Undergraduate Students and Information Technology, 2006*. This is a study of 96 two-year and four-year institutions; 28,724 students responded to the ECAR survey.

Information Technology Staffing and Planning

A number of functional areas showed a significant increase from the previous year in reporting to the top information technology (IT) administrator for all schools surveyed by the EDUCAUSE Core Data Service. These areas include Student Computing, Academic Computing, Enterprise Infrastructure/Identity Management, Research Computing, Multimedia Services, Distance Education, Telephony, Technology R&D/Advanced Technology, IT Policy, and Administration of IT Organization (Hawkins and Rudy, 2006). This may indicate a trend toward placing a greater value on these functional areas within the university system; this may be particularly significant to instructional technology specialists who are most likely to take a leadership role within Academic Computing, Multimedia Services, Distance Education, and Technology R&D.

Technology Support for Faculty

Offering faculty training upon request and offering training through scheduled seminars were the two most common methods of assisting faculty according to the EDUCAUSE Core Data Service survey. Ninety-five percent of all campuses surveyed provided training upon request and 90% offered training through seminars. Faculty were also supported by student assistants and by instructional technologists who were discipline specialists. The use of discipline specialist/instructional technologists occurred mostly in doctoral degree-granting institutions, and there has been a significant rise in this practice based on reports from the previous year. The use of instructional designers and faculty teaching/excellence centers increased a small amount, with a decrease in the use of designated instructional technology centers (Hawkins and Rudy, 2006). The trend among all institutions is to support faculty through requested training and scheduled seminars. A trend to watch for is the use of discipline specialist/instructional technologists.

Student Computing

Student ownership of computers continues to rise (the median increasing from 80% to 85% between 2004 and 2005) according to Hawkins and Rudy (2006). Students at private institutions are more likely to own computers than students at public institutions. The ECAR study (Salaway et al., 2006) reports that nearly all survey respondents reported owning a computer. As many as 38.3% of 18- and 19-year-olds begin their undergraduate experience owning both a desktop and laptop computer; 72.8% of the freshmen at four-year institutions who responded to the survey own a laptop computer (Salaway et al., 2006). Students born between 1980 and 1994 (occasionally referred to as "Millenials") tend to use digital media for communication and recreation (*The Chronicle of Higher Education*, 2007). Over 95% of BA, MA, and doctoral degree-granting institutions reported providing high-speed network access in undergraduate residence halls (Hawkins and Rudy, 2006). The trend is a rise in the number of student-owned computers on campuses and continued institutional support of high-speed networks for these computers.

Course Management Systems

According to the EDUCAUSE Core Data Survey, over 91% of all responding campuses report supporting one or more course management systems (CMS) such as Blackboard or eCollege. Nearly 70% of all responding campuses support a single commercial CMS (Hawkins and Rudy, 2006). Although faculty use of course management systems continues to be selective and far from ubiquitous, the Core Data Survey indicates a significant increase in faculty CMS use overall (Hawkins and Rudy, 2006). The trend is increased faculty use of CMS as well as a general reliance on the use of commercial CMS.

Campus Networking

Network bandwidth for on-campus computers continues to increase significantly at almost all institutions. Remote access (internal modem pools) continued its precipitous decrease, indicating that campuses are moving away from this form of remote access support (Hawkins and Rudy, 2006). Wireless network access increased significantly at almost all institutions surveyed by the EDUCAUSE Core Data Service. Wireless network access in campus libraries is up 28% over the last two years (Hawkins and Rudy, 2006).

E-Learning

E-learning or online education continues to be a popular topic on college campuses. There are pros and cons to e-learning: it overcomes limits of time and space, makes new markets for institutions, and improves institutional flexibility; at the same time it requires more academic support to help students succeed, limits its own use by people who are not comfortable with the technology, and increases work for faculty members (*Chronicle of Higher Education*, 2006). In the wake of Hurricane Katrina, many administrators are also viewing e-learning technologies as critically important components in academic continuity and emergency planning (Maloney, 2007).

Integrating Information Technology in College Courses

Advances in information technologies, such as the ability to write to the Web without specialized Web page creation skills, continue to open the Web as a communication tool to more people, and options for creating technologically rich and instructionally sound class activities abound (Maloney, 2007); students are not expecting (or hoping) to see much of this in the traditional college classroom.

According to the ECAR study results, although most undergraduates are enthusiastic users of computing tools, they are only moderately interested in seeing these technologies integrated into their courses. Over half of the students responding to the ECAR survey indicated they would prefer only a "moderate" amount of information technology in their courses; younger students and female students in particular seem to prefer less technology in their courses (Salaway et al., 2006). Salaway et al. (2006) suggest this finding indicates that students may arrive on campus with many information technology tools and skill in using them for communication and recreation, but they are comparatively unskilled in making use of information technology to support academic activity. ECAR respondents do favor CMS; 75.6% who use these systems report positively about their use and only 4.5% of those using CMS report an overall negative experience. Students particularly value the ability to keep track of assignments and grades using CMS (Salaway et al., 2006). The trend is toward less use of information technology for instruction and greater use of it for administration and communication. Students continue to develop technological proficiencies for purposes of communication and recreation. However, using similar technologies for academic purposes is something students currently shy from.

K-12 EDUCATION

The issues related to the use of technology in K-12 education have not significantly changed since the previous issues and trend review appeared in the 2006 yearbook. In their review, Bichelmeyer and Molenda (2006) focused on three broad issues: use of technology-based media for delivery of instruction, constraints on acceptance and use of technology, and challenges to existing paradigms. While the issues have remained the same since the last review, the trends have not. In examining the trends, we focused primarily on two comprehensive reports—*Education Week*'s (2005) 9th Annual Technology Counts 2006 issue and *America's Digital Schools 2006: Mobilizing the Curriculum (ADS 2006)* (Greaves and Hayes, 2006).

The *Education Week*'s Technology Counts 2006 issue focuses on a survey of state education representatives conducted by the Editorial Projects in Education Research Center that assesses the status of K-12 educational technology across the nation by tracking state progress in critical areas of technology policy and practice. The three major areas are access to technology, the use of technology, and the ability of teachers to use technology effectively. A new feature of the Technology Counts 2006 issue was the assigning of letter grades for all fifty states indicating how well the states were performing in these major areas. As a whole, the nation earned a C-plus, with West Virginia and Virginia leading the nation with grades of A and A-minus while Nevada earned the lowest grade with a D-minus (*Education Week*, 2006).

ADS 2006, sponsored by Discovery Education and Pearson Education, is a comprehensive report of the results of a survey administered to over 900 school administrators (superintendents, curriculum directors, and technology directors). The key trends identified in this report are a continued shift to mobile computing from desktop computing, movement to 1:1 computing, increased bandwidth use, growth in online learning, increased professional development, and managing the total cost of ownership of computers.

Funding

With state tax revenues remaining stable or on the slight increase over the past two years throughout much of the United States, K-12 public education budgets have benefited. According to the Denver-based National Conference of State Legislatures, during the 2006–2007 budget year schools were expected to spend nearly 8% more on K-12 education than in the previous year. For twelve states, double-digit increases were predicted. This increase is in addition to the 7% average states provided K-12 public education during the 2005–2006 budget year (McNeil, 2007). On the surface, this may seem like K-12 public schools should be adequately financed. It is important to remember, however, that from 2000 through 2004 most states leveled off or in most cases cut funding to schools—both K-12 and higher education.

With the resurgence of funding for K-12 education, where is the money being budgeted and spent? It is often hard to find detailed data showing how districts and schools allocate new revenue. A few states, like Arkansas and Wyoming, have begun to analyze and track spending. They are hoping this data will allow states to make more informed decisions on whether money being spent on programs is actually helping students achieve (McNeil, 2007).

Despite the lack of crystal-clear clarity on where money is being spent, we can report technology spending priorities as reported by the Technology Counts 2006 survey. The report identifies the top five priorities within technology budgets. State education representatives were asked to report their two highest priorities. The top reported priority for technology spending was professional development. Thirty-one states reported this as their high priority for spending, followed by Internet connectivity/networking (19 states), data management systems (15 states), hardware (15 states), and curriculum/instruction/assessment (11 states) (*Education Week*, 2006).

Using Technology for Student Assessment: Data Management Systems

The use of technology for student assessment continues to dominate the K-12 technology landscape. This use of technology is due primarily to the reoccurring theme in K-12 education of accountability—through standardized testing and the initiatives of the No Child Left Behind (NCLB) Act. To this end, states have heavily invested in data management systems to collect and manage student assessment data. Despite the investment in these systems, electronic information is not consistently available in a form that teachers can easily use to inform their teaching to improve student learning (*Education Week*, 2006).

Virginia B. Edwards, editor and publisher of *Education Week* and Technology Counts 2006, writes, "While progress has been made in bolstering computerized data systems in K-12 education, states are not consistently making the critical connection between information and learning" (*Education Week*, 2006). Only twenty-eight states provide current student state assessment results through a centralized data system that teachers can access. Almost half (24 states) of the states do not provide systems that allow teachers to track student progress on a year-to-year basis. Only twenty states have systems that allow teachers to compare their school with other similar schools (*Education Week*, 2006). It is evident that student assessment data is being collected, but just as evident is the lack of accessibility for teachers to this data.

The trend we see is tremendous pressure placed on improving the data management systems schools have invested significant amounts of money to develop. Teachers need to be able to easily access student data in order to make informed decisions about how to improve student learning. To make the data more accessible to teachers, there will need to be a move to interactive database-driven Web portals that allow teachers to access and manipulate current student data to track progress over time. With increased access to data, keeping data secure will also be a high priority. As Bichelmeyer and Molenda predicted in 2006, we make a similar prediction—there will be continued opportunities for companies to provide schools with assistance in managing and securing the dearth of student data schools must collect in order to conform to the mandates of NCLB.

Computer-Based Media: The Ubiquity of Computers and Networks

The increase in the ubiquity of computers and networks continues to be a major trend in K-12 education. The percentage of public schools using wireless networks during 2001 to 2005 increased by four times (Market Data Retrieval Service, 2005). In 2005, 45% of public schools had wireless networks (Borja, 2006). This percentage is likely to increase as the newer generation of wireless protocols and devices allow for faster data transmission and become more secure. This trend is acknowledged by technology companies such as Sunnyvale, California-based Meru Networks, a leading producer of wireless networks. Meru Networks reported that its K-12 requests for proposals for new wireless networks increased from 10% to 50% over the past year and a half (Borja, 2006). To further support this trend, the Technology Counts report states that 42% of state technology representatives surveyed indicated that Internet connectivity and networking was one of their top two priorities for technology spending during the 2006–2007 school year (*Education Week*, 2006).

With the increase in wireless connectivity, mobile computing devices are becoming even more popular in schools. *ADS 2006* indicated that 19% of all student devices are mobile, and by 2011 this percentage will increase to 50% (Greaves and Hayes, 2006). Schools are moving away from traditional desktop computers to mobile, wireless devices. This trend is reflected in the computer market where it is estimated that by 2008 laptops will generate nearly 50% of the revenue gained from the sale of computers—this is up from 41.6% in 2006 (Ferguson, 2006). The *ADS 2006* reported that 52% of state technology directors surveyed were very likely (26%) or somewhat likely (26%) to adopt a student appliance for every student by 2011 (*Education Week*, 2006). The *ADS 2006* defines a student appliance as "[a] newly emerging category of computing device designed specifically between a traditional business laptop and a handheld device." The tablet-PC was documented to be the most likely purchased student appliance (Greaves and Hayes, 2006). The available data strongly suggests the continued trend of the purchase and use of mobile, wireless computing devices in K-12 education.

Emerging Digital Technologies: Collaborative Digital Tools and Personal Broadcasting

A rising trend that has emerged since the last review is the use of collaborative digital tools—primarily by students to stay connected with friends and peers. Blogs, wikis, instant messaging, peer-to-peer networks, and social networking spaces are examples of some of the most popular tools students are using—for better or worse. The promise of these tools for education lies in their ability to allow students to generate and share knowledge, collaborate, and learn together (The Horizon Report, 2006; Richardson, 2006). Collaborative digital tools and mobile computing devices combine to create a perfect match that allows students the opportunity to learn anywhere, anytime, and with anyone.

Another emerging technology trend we have observed is personal broadcasting. Personal broadcasting is the creation and distribution of audio and video content of personal experiences, information, and events (The Horizon Report, 2006). This trend has seen a tremendous surge in K-12 education over the past two years, as the process for creating and distributing audio and video has become relatively easier and as low-cost tools to create and distribute audio and video have become more widely available. Through personal broadcasting technologies, students are able to share media they have created as well as access media created by others.

One of the most popular applications of personal broadcasting is podcasting. Brown and Green (2006) write that "[a] podcast is an audio or video file placed on the Web for individuals to subscribe and listen to or watch using a computer or a portable digital media player such as the Apple iPod." Since the introduction of podcasting in late 2004, podcasting has grown significantly. Seventeen million podcasts were downloaded in November 2006—this was an increase of ten million downloads over the number of downloads reported in April 2006 (Madden, 2006; Miller, 2006). This number will no doubt continue to increase.

We see the continued use of collaborative digital tools and personal broadcasting by students, and an increase of their integration into the curriculum by teachers. We also see a movement toward making content more available and mobile by taking advantage of the capabilities of devices like Apple iPods, the Sony PSP, and cellular phones. In addition to viewing content on these devices, as the technology improves, students will be able to use the devices to create and distribute content they have produced—virtually anytime, anywhere.

Teacher Access to and Use of Technology

Reliable data that describes teacher access to technology is not as readily available as is data describing student access to technology. Despite this lack of reliable data, it could be inferred that teacher access to technology can be equated with student access to technology—in other words, the more access students have to technology, the more likely it is that teachers would have access to similar technology. With the student-to-computer ratio significantly decreasing over the past seven years, it would seem that teachers have benefited. However, according to the Teachers Talk Tech Report (Quality Education Data, 2006), 55% of teachers surveyed indicated that access to computers was their most significant obstacle to integrating technology into the daily curriculum. This percentage increases slightly when isolating the responses from middle school (59%) and high school teachers (57%).

Unlike data regarding teacher access to technology, there is a plethora of data depicting the use of technology by teachers. Fifty-four percent of teachers surveyed for the 2006 Teachers Talk Tech Report indicated that technology is having a profound impact on the classroom and how they teach. Veteran teachers (ten or more years teaching) reported seeing the greatest impact on their professional practice. Sixty-seven percent of the teachers reported that they integrate technology into their classroom instruction at least a couple of times a week. Of this 67%, 37% indicated integrating technology on a daily basis. At the elementary school level, daily use of technology is 44%, while at the middle school and high school levels the percentages are lower—33% and 34% respectively. This may be due to where teachers are able to have their students access computers. At the elementary school level, students most often access computers in the classroom, while at the middle and high school levels students access computers in a media center or a computer lab (Quality Education Data, 2006).

When asked to rate the importance of computer technology personally in four different areas (administrative functions such as attendance and grading; communications with other teachers, administrators, parents, and students; research information for preparing lessons; and as a teaching tool for students), 88% of teachers reported administrative functions as very or somewhat important to their teaching. This area received the highest percentage of responses out of the four areas. Although receiving the lowest overall percentage of responses with 79%, the area of computers as a teaching tool for students saw the greatest percentage gain (14%) during the last three years (Quality Education Data 2006).

Overall, teachers seem to be embracing technology and feel that technology can have a positive impact on their teaching and student learning. Eighty-two percent of teachers strongly or somewhat agree that computers help engage their students in the learning process. Sixty-five percent strongly or somewhat agree that their students' academic performance improves with the use of classroom computers (Quality Education Data 2006). Both percentages have increased over the previous year's responses. We see this trend continuing as computing tools become increasingly mobile and are moved into the classroom where teachers and students can more conveniently use them.

Student Access to and Use of Technology

Student access to computers has significantly improved over the past seven years. The ratio of students per instructional computer was 5.7:1 in 1999 as compared to 3.8:1 in 2005 (Market Data Retrieval Service, 2005). Although new data has not been made available for the past two years, in looking at the trends from 2002 to 2005 the ratio has remained relatively stable. We predict that the ratio will, at the minimum, remain stable if not decrease. One trend that could have a significant impact on this is the move to 1:1 computing (also referred to as 1:1 learning). The idea behind 1:1 computing is to provide each student and teacher with 24/7 access to an Internet-connected wireless computing device that can be used in the classroom and at home (Greaves and Hayes, 2006). Although this may seem more like fantasy than possible reality, 24% of school districts are in the process of transforming to 1:1 computing. This is an increase of 20% since 2004 (*E-School News*, 2006). As prices of computing tools continue to decrease and the quality improves—especially with the emergence of projects such as MIT's $100 laptop program, the Intel Eduwise laptop, and the Microsoft Ultra-Mobile PC—the trend toward 1:1 computing being adopted by schools district will most likely remain.

Delivery of Instruction Online

With twenty-two states having established statewide virtual schools and sixteen states with cyber charter schools (*Education Week*, 2006), delivering instruction through online education has certainly been a key trend over the past two years. The *ADS 2006* survey indicates that the number of students taking an online course will grow to 15.6% by the year 2011. This is a compound annual rate increase of 32.6%. This is an estimated 8 million students! If this estimate is accurate, or even close to being accurate, K-12 education will have significant challenges to address. Teachers will need training and professional development to help work in the new teaching and learning environment. In most schools, technology infrastructure will have to be upgraded to handle the increased demand placed on current systems. In addition to these issues, there will be—without a doubt—many unforeseen issues that school leaders will have to wrestle with. Despite the challenges, online education holds a great deal of promise for K-12 education. One such promise is in creating equity among schools where students in rural and urban districts will be able to tap into advanced placement courses that they currently do not have access to. Another promise is in providing a learning environment that may better meet the needs of certain student populations. We see online education continuing to be a key trend in K-12 education in the years to come.

Teacher Licensure Requirements and Professional Development

In their last review, Bichelmeyer and Molenda (2006) stated that the good news according to the Technology Counts 2004 survey was that forty states have technology standards for teachers. The bad news, according to this same survey, was that many states did not have enforcement policies to ensure that teachers could meet these standards. Has the landscape changed since this survey was conducted? The simple answer is that not much has changed. The Technology Counts 2006 survey indicated that the number of states with technology standards for teachers remained at forty. However, most states have not adopted licensure policies to ensure that teachers are able to meet these standards. Thirty states have no technology requirements. Before receiving an initial teaching license, twenty-one states require that teachers take one or more technology courses or pass a technology exam (four of these states require both coursework and a test). Only nine states require teachers to demonstrate ongoing competence in technology or to complete professional development related to technology before being recertified. Despite this, we believe it is important to note, as we did in the section on funding, that professional development was rated as the highest priority for where technology budgets would be spent (*Education Week*, 2006). This could indicate that more states are beginning to recognize the importance of helping teachers keep current with technology and their technology skills. Whether this spending priority turns into a trend remains to be seen.

Overall, we believe that the numbers related to teacher expectations will generally remain consistent. However, we are hopeful that with the updated International Society for Technology in Education (ISTE) technology standards released in June 2007, states will view this as an opportunity to reevaluate their own teacher technology standards and the technology requirements they have for teacher licensure.

CONCLUSION

During the period covered in this review, K-12 schools, higher education institutions, and businesses were continuing to recover from the tremendous budget reductions that took place during the economic downturn of 2000–2003. Although technology budgets have not recovered to the levels seen in the late 1990s, there is cautious optimism that as state tax revenues and corporate revenues increase, or remain at the minimum plateau, current technology budgets will continue to remain stable. This cautious optimism has led K-12 schools and higher education institutions to continue to invest in information technology. Businesses continue to invest in and make use of computing tools, focusing their instructional capabilities on e-learning, doing more in-house production, and grappling with the challenges of effective measurement and globalization. The adoption of emerging technologies, such as mobile, wireless computing devices, led the way. In K-12 education, the impact of NCLB mandates has led to a disproportionate amount of technology budgets being spent on student data management systems. We are yet to see positive learning results from the implementation of these systems. In higher education we see a consistent trend toward employing computing technologies in the classroom, but without the support of undergraduates, the majority of whom prefer a "moderate" amount of technology use during class time. University e-learning efforts have increased students' options and opened the university to students who might not otherwise be able to attend.

Although corporate training, higher education, and K-12 schools face a number of challenges, they are all currently benefiting from the advances made in computing mobility and ubiquity. Perhaps unsurprisingly, greater mobility and ubiquity of computing tools will inevitably lead to their increased use for teaching and learning in all sectors. We predict this use will be further amplified by the greater control individuals have over the media they are able to produce and distribute. One of the most important and intriguing trends we see in every sector is movement away from educators' reliance upon highly specialized instructional media production personnel and toward the production of instructional media by content specialists and the educators themselves.

REFERENCES

Allen, I. E. and Seaman, J. (2006). *Making the Grade: Online Education in the United States, 2006.* Needham, MA: The Sloan Consortium.

Bichelmeyer, B. and Molenda, M. (2006). Issues and Trends in Instructional Technology: Gradual Growth Atop Tectonic Shifts. Submitted for publication in Fitzgerald, M. A., Orey, M., and Branch, R. M. (eds.), *Educational Media and Technology Yearbook 2006.* Westport, CT: Libraries Unlimited.

Borja, R. R. (2006, October 27). Technology Upgrades Prompt Schools to Go Wireless. *Education Week, 26*(9), 10.

Brown, A. and Green, T. (2006). *Podcasting and Vodcasting: When, Where, and How They Are Currently Used for Instruction.* Proceedings from the annual conference of the Association of Educational and Communication Technologies, Dallas, TX.

Carnevale, D. (2007, January 5). Employers Often Distrust Online Degrees. *The Chronicle of Higher Education.*

E-Learning: Successes and Failures. (2006). *The Chronicle of Higher Education 53*(8), B20.

E-School News. (2007, March 22). Parents, Teachers, Kids Speak Up on Ed Tech. Retrieved on March 26, 2007, from http://www.eschoolnews.com/news/showStory.cfm?ArticleID=6951

E-School News. (2006, March 1). 1-to-1 Computing on the Rise in Schools. Retrieved on March 26, 2007, from http://www.eschoolnews.com/news/showstory.cfm?ArticleID=6278

Ferguson, S. (2006). Will the Notebook Market Hit a Tipping Point in '07?. *eWeek Enterprise News and Reviews*. Retrieved on December 19, 2006, from http://www.eweek.com/print_article2/0,1217,a=196750,00.asp

Greaves, T. W. and Hayes, J. (2006). *America's Digital Schools 2006: Mobilizing the Curriculum*. Retrieved from the Web on March 26, 2007, from http://www.ads2006.org/ads2006/index.php

Gross, G. (2007, February 28). RIAA Opposes New Fair Use Bill. *InfoWorld*. Retrieved on November 29, 2007, from http://www.infoworld.com/archives/emailPrint.jsp?R=printThis&A=/article/07/02/28/HNriaaopposesfairuse_1.html

Hawkins, B. L. and Rudy, J. A. (2006). *EDUCAUSE Core Data Service Fiscal Year 2005 Summary Report*. Boulder, CO: EDUCAUSE.

The Horizon Report. (2006). Retrieved on March 25, 2007, from http://www.nmc.org/pdf/2006_Horizon_Report.pdf

How the New Generation of Well-Wired Multitaskers Is Changing Campus Culture. (2007). *The Chronicle of Higher Education 53*(18), B10.

Madden, M. (2006, November). Pew Internet Project Data Memo. Pew Internet and American Life Project.

Maloney, E. J. (2007). What Web 2.0 Can Teach Us About Learning. *The Chronicle of Higher Education, 53*(18), B26.

Market Data Retrieval Service. (2005). K-12 Technology Review. Retrieved on November 29, 2007, from http://www.schooldata.com/

McNeil, M. (2007, March 23). As Budgets Swell, Spending Choices Get New Scrutiny. *Education Week, 26*(29), 1, 19.

Miller, S. (2006, November 23). For the Podcaster in the Field, A More Advanced Recorder. *The New York Times*, p. C8.

Molenda, M. and Bichelmeyer, B. (2005). Issues and Trends in Instructional Technology: Slow Growth as Economy Recovers. In Fitzgerald, M. A., Orey, M., and Branch, R. M. (eds.). *Educational Media and Technology Yearbook 2005*. Westport, CT: Libraries Unlimited.

Online Graduate Degrees Are More Accepted Than Online Bachelor's Degrees, Says Vault Survey. (2006). Retrieved on October 16, 2006, from http://www.thevault.com/nr/printable.jsp?ch_id=420&article_id=28540309

The Online Office of Congressman Rick Boucher (2007, February 27). Reps. Boucher and Doolittle Introduce the FAIR USE Act of 2007. Press Release. Retrieved on November 29, 2007, from http://www.boucher.house.gov/index.php?option=com_content&task=view&id=1011&Itemid=75

Quality Education Data (2006). Teachers Talk Tech conducted by Quality Education Data (QED), a subsidiary of Scholastic, Inc. Retrieved on November 29, 2007, from http://newsroom.cdwg.com/features/feature-06-26-06.html

Richardson, W. (2006). *Blogs, Wikis, Podcasts, and Other Powerful Web Tools for Classrooms*. Thousand Oaks, CA: Corwin Press.

Rivera, R. J. and Paradise, A. (2006). *State of the Industry in Leading Enterprises: ASTD's Annual Review of Trends in Workplace and Learning Performance*. Alexandria, VA: American Society of Training and Development.

Salaway, G., Katz, R. N., and Caruso, J. B., with Kvavik, R. B. and Nelson, M. R. (2006). *The ECAR Study of Undergraduate Students and Information Technology, 2006*. Boulder, CO: EDUCAUSE.

Technology Counts 2006. (2005, May 4). *Education Week, 25*(35).

U.S. Department of Education (2006, September). *Projections of Education Statistics to 2015.* Retrieved on March 26, 2005, from http://nces.ed.gov/pubs2006/2006084.pdf

Zeller, T. (2006, December 18). LINK BY LINK; An Ominous Milestone: 100 Million Data Leaks. *The New York Times.* Retrieved on November 29, 2007, from http://query.nytimes.com/gst/fullpage.html?res=9F07E1DC1331F93BA25751C1A9609C8B63

The Great Divide: Preparing Pre-Service Teachers to Integrate Technology Effectively

Drew Polly
University of North Carolina at Charlotte

Dr. Julie Moore
University of Georgia

INTRODUCTION

The availability of technology for both teacher and student use has exploded in schools over the past 20 years. While technology differences still exist between some schools and school districts, on average, American schools have more access to technology than ever before. In 2001, 99% of public schools in the United States had access to the Internet, up from only 35% in 1994 (NCES, 2002). The latest reports regarding technology access (Editorial Projects in Education Research Center, 2007) cite that the ratio between students and instructional computers is an all-time low of 3.6 to 1. Further, the report states about 95% of schools have high-speed Internet access. Both of these statistics meet the suggestion of the 1997 President's Committee of Advisors on Science and Technology (PCAST) that there should be a ratio of 4 or 5 students to each computer to achieve the effective use of computers in schools.

However, the picture isn't entirely positive. Access to computers alone does not ensure that they will be used or integrated effectively. For the past decade, teachers have reported feeling unprepared to use technology in their teaching (NCES, 1999, 2002, 2004). Becker and Ravitz (2001) surveyed secondary teachers and found that less than 25% of them were using computers on a weekly basis to enhance instruction. In most cases the technology was used for drill and practice rather than promoting process or higher-order thinking skills (Becker, 2001).

This paper aims to hold a critical lens up to the current status of technology integration in America's schools, colleges, and departments of education (SCDEs), a venue with the potential to have great influence in promoting technology integration into schools. Included herein are analyses of national reports, recent research, as well as initiatives designed to support technology integration in SCDEs.

TECHNOLOGY'S PLACE IN TEACHER EDUCATION

The need to integrate technology fully into teacher education programs has been stressed for nearly a decade by educational researchers (Cuban, 2001; Bransford, Brown,

Thanks to I-Mei Ma, Ben Deaton, Ernise Singleton, and Feng Wang for assistance in the early preparation of this manuscript.

Table 1. Evolution of Technology Use in the School and Classroom

1970s	1980s	2000s
Technology as subject: • Study the machine. • Learn specific skills to make the technology work. • Study the social implications.	• Supplement to teaching and learning. Curriculum-based software. • Teacher and student tools.	• Infused across the curriculum. • Integral to student learning. • Seamless integration.

& Cocking, 2000; Jonassen & Reeves, 1996) national organizations (International Society for Technology in Education [ISTE], 2000a, 2000b) and policy makers (No Child Left Behind, 2001).

Leaders in both teacher education and educational technology have posited that pre-service teachers' success in integrating technology into their classroom is dependent on both their technology skills, as well as the experiences they have observing effective modeling and practicing the integration of technology into instruction (Mishra & Koehler, 2006; Office of Technology Assessment, 1995; Panel of Educational Technology, 1997; Schrum, 1999). The responsibility of teacher education programs, therefore, is twofold: (1) provide adequate hands-on experience for pre-service teachers to develop their technology skills and (2) present effective models of technology integration in methods courses (Hargrave & Hsu, 2000).

However, many instructors in SDCEs are still not comfortable with technology and, thus, provide few models of technology integration during pre-service teachers' coursework (Stetson & Bagwell, 1999). Since teacher education programs train nearly half a million future teachers annually, SDCE faculty members have tremendous potential to influence the future of education in America. It is not realistic to expect pre-service teachers leaving SDCEs to be able to integrate technology effectively in their professional career if they have little to no experience of modeling with it in their preparation experience.

Perhaps surprisingly, this focus on technology integration is actually a fairly recent phenomenon. The next section highlights our historical understanding of the role of technology education in order to provide some context to the current state of technology integration in SCDEs.

HISTORY OF TECHNOLOGY IN SCDEs

The evolution of technology in teacher education mirrors our changing understanding of the role of technology in schools (Glenn, 2002). In his look at the background that laid the foundation for today's environment, Glenn (2002) characterized technology use in schools by decade.

As Table 1 indicates, our understanding of the role of technology has shifted in the last 30 years, which in turn shifted technology's role in teacher education practices. Original concerns with computer programming, computer parts, and learning the skills to use the machines have evolved into viewing technology as a tool to enhance student learning and be an integrated, seamless part of the curriculum. During the same time, research and policy has also had significant impact as standards have evolved that now shape our expectations for students, practicing teachers, and teachers coming out of SCDEs (see Table 2).

The focus on technology integration in teacher education began in the 1990s when several organizations produced standards documents that attempted to define what students

Table 2. Technology and Teacher Education Timeline

Year	Event	Impact
1983	A Nation at Risk released	Recommended that students be required to take a computer course in high school
1980s–1990s	National Council for Accreditation of Teacher Education (NCATE) begins to include technology in its standards	Pre-service institutions now required to show technology used to support pedagogical practices
1988	Office of Technology Assessment (OTA) releases *Power On!*	Provided the first national look at technology use
1990s	Apple Classroom of Tomorrow studies	Identified challenges associated with technology infused classrooms
1993	NCATE endorses International Society for Technology in Education (ISTE) recommendations	ISTE's partnership with NCATE begins
1995	OTA's *Teachers and Technology: Making the Connection* released	Emphasized shortcomings of pre-service education
1997	American Association of Colleges for Teacher Education Study	Looked at capacity in SCDEs and identified areas of concern
1997	NCATE releases *Technology and the New Professional Teacher: Preparing for the 21st Century Classroom*	Report on technology that makes recommendations about integration of technology in schools of teacher education
1998	*National Educational Technology Standards (NETS)* for students released by ISTE	As of June 2003, 48 of the 51 states (incl. District of Columbia) have "adopted, adapted, aligned with, or otherwise referenced at least one set of standards" in official state documents
1999	Preparing Teachers to Use Technology (PT3) program initiated within U.S. Department of Education	Provided funding for reconceptualizing and restructuring pre-service experiences with technology
2000	ISTE releases *NETS for Teachers (NETS-T)*	32 states have adapted, adopted, or aligned with NETS-T and 3 states have referenced
2000	CEO Forum *Teacher Preparation School Technology and Readiness (StaR Chart)* developed	Instrument by which teacher educators can measure progress toward program-level technology integration
2001	*National Educational Technology Standards for Administrators* (TSSA) released by ISTE	29 states have adapted, adopted, or aligned with TSSA and 7 states have referenced it
2001	NCATE Standards Revised	Added technology components to two indicators and fully endorsed ISTE's three sets of technology standards (students, teachers, and administrators
2003	All program report submissions must use ISTE/NCATE Standards for advanced/specialist programs	

Figure 1. Conceptualization of teacher technology competencies and benchmarks (Moore et al., 1998).

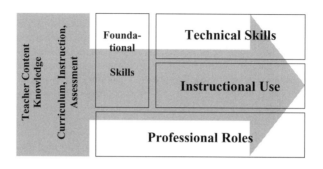

and teachers should be able to do with technology. During this time the Milken Family Foundation (Coughlin & Lemke, 1999), the North Central Regional Technology in Education Consortium (NCRTEC, 1997), and the International Society for Technology in Education (ISTE) (ISTE, 2000a) each developed a set of competencies or benchmarks for students and/or teachers. Moore et al. (1999) examined these early competency sets and identified four primary areas: Foundational skills, technical skills, instructional use, and professional roles. Figure 1 provides a graphic representation how these skill sets relate to one another. Moore et al. (1999) argue that a relative few number of foundational skills must be mastered prior to actual use and integration of technology, and that teacher content and pedagogical knowledge should play a role throughout.

The National Council of Accreditation of Teacher Education's (NCATE) endorsement of the ISTE's National Educational Technology Standards (NETS) in 1993 helped make the ISTE standards the most visible of all of the sets to come out of the early mid-1990s and a document of great impact (Glenn, 2002). ISTE's release of National Educational Technology Standards for Teachers (NETS-T) in 2000 and the National Educational Technology Standards for Administrators (TSSA) in 2001 has served to increase their influence on SCDEs, schools, and state policies. According to ISTE, "At the state level, 48 of the 51 states have adopted, adapted, aligned with, or otherwise referenced at least one set of standards in their state technology plans, certification, licensure, curriculum plans, assessment plans, or other official state documents" (ISTE, 2003).

With NCATE embracing technology as part of their accreditation standards, it now becomes imperative, not just from a teacher preparation standpoint but as a political necessity, for SCDEs to take seriously the integration of technology in their programs. The next section will review research on how SCDEs are currently incorporating technology into their programs.

CURRENT LITERATURE ABOUT TECHNOLOGY IN SCDEs

Unfortunately, very few national studies exist that explore the use of technology in SCDEs. In their literature review on information technology (IT) and teacher education in 1996 (as quoted by Moursand & Bielefeldt, 1999), Willis and Mehlinger (1996) found that most teachers were taking some coursework in IT, but that for the most part this was not tied to other course work, field experiences, or student teaching. Willis and Mehlinger summarized the state of technology and teacher education in the following way:

Most pre-service teachers know very little about effective use of technology in education and leaders believe there is a pressing need to increase substantially the amount and quality of instruction teachers receive about technology. The idea may be expressed aggressively, assertively, or in more subtle forms, but the virtually universal conclusion is that teacher education, particularly preservice, is not preparing educators to work in a technology-enriched classroom. (p. 978)

Two recent large-scale research studies indicate much the same.

In response to various calls to SCDEs to improve their training of future teachers, the American Association of Colleges for Teacher Education (AACTE) initiated a study to understand how technology was being taught across the country. In this study, Persichitte, Tharp, & Caffarella (1997) surveyed numerous SCDE faculty that were experimenting with technology integration into their courses. Study results indicate that while classrooms were generally well-equipped, use of the technology lagged behind. As a whole, students were not expected to use technology in their classroom settings or access course information using the Web. Despite this, the study did identify numerous adopters of information technologies nationwide. They found that the most critical factor was training for faculty at all levels and in all disciplines that developed their personal and pedagogical skills related to technology. Persichitte et al. (1998) also found that faculty responded well to the use of incentive plans, which reward faculty for the significant knowledge, time, and initiative required for reaching high levels of technology integration within instruction.

A 1998 study conducted by ISTE on behalf of the Milken Exchange on Education Technology surveyed teacher education institutions across the country (Moursund & Bielefeldt, 1999). Approximately one third of U.S. SCDEs participated, representing approximately 90,000 graduates per year. The results of the study indicate that despite most SCDEs belief that their IT infrastructure was adequate, integration of that technology by faculty lagged behind.

The Moursand and Bielefeldt (1999) study found that while faculty had IT skills similar to their students, most did not model those skills in their teaching. As a result, most student teachers did not routinely use technology during their student teaching even though technology was available in their placement classrooms. About half of pre-service teachers' technology instruction occurred in methods and curriculum courses. These integrated experiences proved to be more important than stand-alone IT courses as findings indicated the number of hours that technology instruction was integrated into other courses correlated more highly with other variables than the number of hours of formal IT instruction. As the authors indicate, "The most important finding of the survey is that formal stand-alone IT coursework does not correlate well with scores on items dealing with technology skills and the ability to integrate IT into teaching" despite such courses being cited as important features of teacher education programs. Moursund and Bielefeldt (1999) recommended the following as a result of their study:

1. IT instruction should be integrated into other courses and SCDE activities rather than just in stand-alone classes.

2. Technology planning at the institution level should focus not just on facilities but on the integration of IT in teaching and learning.

3. Student teachers need more opportunities to use IT during field experience and under supervision.

4. Faculty should be encouraged to model and integrate technology.

5. Models for integration should be disseminated widely.

Table 3. Issues Confronting Schools, Colleges, and Departments of Education (Dervied from Fulton et al., 2003)

School, Colleges, and Departments			
Faculty	**Institutional**	**Pre-service**	**In-service**
• Initial technology skills • Ability to use various tools and software programs • Creating a learning environment infused with technology • Linking to student standards • Assessing student learning outcomes • Examining beliefs about teaching and learning • Continuing to acquire new skills • Lessening the anxiety about learning new skills and program delivery	• Acquiring technologies • Staffing issues • Classroom configuration • Distance education issues • Linking with PK-12 schools • Budgets • Accreditation	• Initial technology skills • Ability to use various tools and software programs • Creating a learning environment infused with technology • Linking to student standards • Assessing learning student outcomes • Examining beliefs about teaching and learning • Continuing to acquire new skills	• Initial technology skills • Ability to use various tools and software programs • Creating a learning environment infused with technology • Linking to student standards • Assessing student learning outcomes • Examining beliefs about teaching and learning • Continuing to acquire new skills

FACTORS AFFECTING TECHNOLOGY INTEGRATION IN SCDEs

As the previous section discusses, moving beyond stand-alone IT courses is now recognized as important and valued. However, this shift is not easy as there are many barriers to integrating technology into courses and activities in SCDEs.

Fulton, Glenn, and Valdez (2003) identified a variety of issues confronting SCDEs and teachers (see Table 3). While initial skills and access to technology are still important, preparing teachers to use technology effectively now also includes more complex teacher behaviors such as linking to standards, assessing student outcomes, and examining beliefs about teaching and learning. These complex skill sets are not just needed by pre-service teachers but, perhaps more importantly, by university faculty as well.

Individual skills are not developed in a vacuum, however. From an institutional point of view, Spodark (2003) discusses five obstacles to technology integration at an SCDE at a small mid-Atlantic college. He summarized the most critical factors as (1) lack of a clear vision, (2) lack of leadership, (3) lack of critical mass, (4) lack of incentive, and (5) lack of faculty participation.

Clearly, attention to both individual factors outlined by Allen (2003) and institutional factors outlined by Spodark (2003) are needed if technology integration is to be successful in SCDEs. Beginning in 1999, the U.S. Department of Education started the Preparing Tomorrow's Teachers to Use Technology (PT3) program to address the factors discussed above. The PT3 initiative provided ample resources for projects to better prepare pre-service teachers' ability to integrate technology in their curriculum. Initiatives funded by PT3 grants have become models for non-PT3 SCDEs nationwide. The following section shares experiences of reforms SCDEs have employed in an attempt to increase pre-service teachers' ability to integrate technology effectively.

INITIATIVES TO IMPROVE TECHNOLOGY INTEGRATION IN SCDEs

Recognizing the need for change, many SCDEs have modified their programs in an effort to improve the technology integration capability of their students. The primary changes in SCDEs have involved course redesign, faculty development, the use of electronic portfolios, creative applications of technology tools, and the use of video technologies. Below are descriptions and examples of each.

Course Redesign

Redesigning courses in SCDEs is an extensive task, and requires a strong partnership between faculty members and "experts" in technology integration. SCDEs must provide ample technologies, training for faculty about how to integrate technologies into their courses, as well as on-site support for faculty when they integrate technology into their course.

Most of the redesigned courses are based on both the NCATE and ISTE's NETS-T standards (2000), and provide pre-service teachers with both hands-on practice, as well as opportunities to integrate technology into their field experiences and student teaching. For example, Sonoma State University's Bridge program enabled faculty to identify courses that they wanted to redesign and to select what skills they wanted to develop, giving faculty an added incentive to participate (U.S. Department of Education, 2006a). Following training, graduate students and faculty members collaborated with them to design and integrate these new technologies into their course. As a result, 85% of Sonoma State's faculty revised their courses and infused technology into education courses (U.S. Department of Education, 2006a).

Faculty Professional Development

SCDEs have also provided professional development opportunities to increase the level of technology proficiency in their faculty. While most faculty training incorporated some sort of workshop, various incentives were used to motivate the faculty to participate. The literature in technology integration has been consistent citing the difficulty in getting well-seasoned instructors to integrate new technologies into their instruction (Becker & Ravitz, 2001; Stetson & Bagwell, 1999). Table 4 shows the various incentives used to motivate faculty to participate in technology training at their respective SCDEs.

At Purdue University, researchers have structured a learner-centered, problem-based approach to technology integration, in which School of Education instructors use the Internet and other technologies to address instructional problems that they face in trying to infuse technology in their courses. Instructors participate in a two-day workshop and a yearlong one-on-one mentoring program with graduate students to refine their technology skills and design technology-rich activities that can be used to enhance their methods courses. Ninety-five percent of the faculty participated in this workshop (Lehman et al., 2003). Combined professional development approaches that employed workshops and mentoring were associated with faculty infusing technology more frequently in methods

Table 4. Incentives Provided for Faculty to Participate in Technology Training

Incentive	Description
Money to purchase technologies	Participants receive a stipend to purchase software or technology equipment.
One-on-one mentoring	Participants have the opportunity to collaborate with a faculty member or graduate student, who will facilitate the planning and integration of technology-rich activities into their courses.
Release time	Participants are released from part of their teaching or research time in order to receive training, observe exemplar models of technology integration and redesign courses. Most models pay for summer training, when most faculty are "off."
On-site support	Participants have access to faculty or graduate students that will assist them with integrating technology during their courses.
Money to travel	Participants receive release time and funding to travel to other universities to collaborate with other faculty, or attend conferences to share and gain ideas on how to better integrate technology in their courses.

courses, teacher candidates creating more technology-rich products during course activities and more positive attitudes toward the benefit of technology in K-12 schools (Howland & Wedman, 2004; Nave, 2004; Strudler et al., 2003).

E-Portfolios and Performance-based Assessments

Portfolio assessment has been a standard in teacher education for over a decade. The use of e-portfolios allows students to develop their technology skills within the context of displaying evidence of teacher practice. E-portfolios provide evidence of qualification for instructors and employers, as well as an indication of students' current strengths and weaknesses as an instructor (Delandshere & Arens, 2003). Portfolios vary in their contents, including student work samples, lessons, and assessments that teachers have developed and integrated into their classroom. Storing such documents allows pre-service teachers to reflect on their own teaching practice, as well as demonstrate proficiency in their teaching.

Numerous teacher education programs have instituted portfolios, where teacher candidates add artifacts as they progress through their courses and field experiences (Andrews et al., 2002). The use of e-portfolios increased the number of technology-rich activities that students completed during their courses, which in turn influenced increases in their technology skills, attitudes toward technology, and vision for technology in schools (Bahr et al., 2004; Wentworth, Waddoups, & Earle, 2004).

Technology Tools

In addition to the purchase of software and computers, some SCDEs have chosen how to investigate if hand-held technologies can enhance their curriculum, as well as local PK-12 schools. The University of Virginia purchased these handheld devices and trained faculty, pre-service teachers, and in-service teachers how to use them. All three groups received training with the handheld technologies before collaborating on the design and implementation of technology-rich activities. The faculty and pre-service teachers favorably responded to this project, because it gave both groups the chance to experience technology integration in a PK-12 setting, and the in-service teachers enjoyed having on-site support with the handhelds in their classroom (U.S. Department of Education, 2003b).

Video Tools

The increased access of video technologies has led teacher educators to use video to help assess pre-service teachers' experiences. Some teacher education instructors require pre-service teachers to videotape a lesson and self-reflect on their performance, while some instructors use the video tapes to provide feedback to the pre-service teachers. Videos are also starting to find their way into e-portfolios. Video-taped lessons can also be archived in the e-portfolios, providing richer evidence of teacher practice than a lesson plan or a sample of students' work.

Videos also provide models of exemplar teaching practices. Northern Iowa's In-Time project (http://www.intime.uni.edu) provides over 500 exemplary teaching vignettes of technology integration lessons in PK-12 classrooms (Krueger et al., 2004). InTime and other similar projects are using technology to provide models of exemplar technology integration use. For pre-service teachers who have a limited amount of time in a PK-12 classroom, these models provided ample access to concrete examples of technology integration in K-12 classrooms.

Video conferencing is also being used by SCDEs to assess and communicate with pre-service teachers in the field. Video-based conferences allow supervisors and faculty to observe and communicate with pre-service teachers without taking time to travel to various schools (Lehman et al., 2003; Lehman & Richardson, 2007). For SCDEs that have hundreds of student teachers, this technology lets pre-service teachers receive more feedback on an ongoing basis without much inconvenience to the supervisors or faculty.

MEASURING THE EFFECTIVENESS OF THESE REFORMS

While the anecdotes and narratives of these reforms are promising and show new ways of integrating technology in SCDEs, there is very little empirical data to date relating to the effectiveness of these projects (Mims et al., 2006; Moore & Duffield, 2006). While anecdotal evidence helps to get a description of each endeavor, empirical data is needed in order to distinguish the best practices for preparing teachers to integrate technology effectively.

Arizona State University is one of the few SCDEs that collected empirical data after course redesign (Brush et al., 2003). Pre-service teachers finished their sequence of courses by designing and implementing technology-rich lessons in a PK-12 classroom with their mentor teacher. A post-survey of 100 pre-service teachers showed that after completing the training and the field experience 86% of them felt confident about integrating technology into a lesson in a content area such as language, arts, science, or math, and 92% felt able to develop ideas for integrating technology, given a learning goal for a lesson. Further questions revealed that the implementation activity had a positive impact, as 53% of the participants rated themselves as inadequately prepared to integrate technology prior to the field experience (Brush et al., 2003).

TRENDS ACROSS TECHNOLOGY INTEGRATION SUCCESSES

Earlier, we stated that teacher education programs had two primary responsibilities with regard to preparing teachers to integrate technology effectively: (1) provide adequate hands-on experience for pre-service teachers to develop their technology skills and (2) present effective models of technology integration in methods courses (Hargrave & Hsu, 2000). The literature provides evidence that pre-service teachers benefit from hands-on practice with technologies. Stand-alone technology courses have provided a venue for students to use technology, as well as contemplate how they could be integrated into a PK-12 classroom. However, it is obvious that similar experiences are lacking in most methods courses. Without such hands-on technology use in courses couched in specific disciplines or age levels, little will be gained (Schrum, 1999).

Second, successful efforts have incorporated models of effective technology use into their courses. These models come in the form of an expert, usually the instructor, or a video clip of a technology-enhanced lesson in a PK-12 classroom. The models provide an ideal performance for pre-service teachers to aim for as they learn technologies and design technology-enhanced activities, and, if facilitated well, provide a catalyst for in-depth discussions about teaching, learning, and the role of teachers in the learning process.

Another common factor of successful endeavors was that they occurred over a sustained period of time. Course redesign, faculty development, and other attempts to integrate technology in SCDEs were not overnight changes, but rather modifications that occurred over time. This is consistent with professional development literature, which stresses the importance of ongoing and continuous support for instructors (e.g., Hawley & Valli, 1999; Loucks-Horsley et al., 2003). Future efforts to further technology integration in SCDEs must continue to involve long-term support for instructors.

ISSUES IN NEED OF FURTHER ATTENTION

While initiatives to integrate technology into SCDEs have had success, there are certain issues that still need to be addressed. One of these is the disconnection between higher education and PK-12 education, in terms of both access to technology and the manner in which technology is used. Even if pre-service teachers experience technology integration in their methods courses, they lack a sense of what technology integration looks like in a PK-12 setting. This dilemma can be overcome by providing field experiences for pre-service teachers that allow them to view teachers who are proficient at integrating technology.

Instructors in SCDEs struggle to infuse technology in their own courses, as well to learn technologies common in PK-12 settings. Using technology in their own courses does not necessarily mean instructors have a strong sense of technology's role in PK-12 classrooms. As with the previous issue, pre-service teachers need to have adequate experiences observing and participating in technology-rich activities in PK-12 classrooms.

With increasing emphasis on accountability in our schools, we must help new teachers understand how to navigate the complex world of curriculum standards, test scores, and student work in order to modify and adjust their teaching. Situating the exploration of technology integration in such contexts would provide opportunities to not only understand how technology might best be used in instructional settings, but would also help pre-service teachers develop much needed skills of curriculum alignment, interpretation of student data, and formulation of interventions.

Lastly, it is unclear whether or not many current initiatives tackle the complex issue of creating a shared vision of the role of technology in teaching and learning. While it may be possible to impact the practice of individual faculty members with incentive programs and individual course redesign, without some sort of cohesive vision for the role and use of technology, such efforts may prove to be short-lived or isolated as faculty move or change teaching assignments and new teaching assistants become methods courses instructors.

While this chapter has looked at SCDEs' efforts to improve technology integration, the overall focus should be preparing pre-service teachers to adequately integrate technology into K-12 classrooms. This requires researchers of SCDEs to extend their thinking and closely examine teacher induction and the support of new teachers. Literature on induction has concluded that most new teachers tend to ignore what they learned in their SCDEs and teach in methods that resemble their own educational experiences in PK-12 settings (Kilpatrick et al., 2002).

WHERE TO NOW?

In the past two decades, technology has become common in schools, and is emphasized as a vital tool in education. While access to both computers and the Internet is at an all-time high, pre-service teachers are not receiving the necessary training on how to use and integrate technology into their instruction. A myriad of research studies, funding initiatives, and reform efforts have been described here to show that endeavors to infuse technology into SCDEs are yielding many positive benefits, such as faculty with proficient technology skills, methods courses that model technology integration, and pre-service teachers who are more comfortable using technology when they enter the classroom. Yet, much of the data that has been presented is either in anecdotal form or is based on personal perceptions of preparedness. To increase our understanding of the current state of teacher education, further studies are needed to determine the "best practices" in the field of teacher education so that each pre-service teacher will be adequately prepared to infuse technology into their instruction. Additionally, it is vital that we follow our graduates into the field to truly understand their preparedness and actual use of technology as a tool for teaching and learning.

WORKS CITED

Andrews, S. P., Ducharme, A., & Cox, C. (2002). Development and use of electronic portfolios in preservice education. Paper presented at the *2002 Society for Information Technology and Teacher Education International Conference*, Nashville, TN.

Bahr, D. L., Shaha, S. H., Farnsworth, B. J., Lewis, V. K., & Benson, L. F. (2004). Preparing tomorrow's teachers to use technology: Attitudinal impacts of technology-supported field experience on pre-service teacher candidates. *Journal of Instructional Psychology, 31*(2), 88–97.

Becker, H. J. (2001). How are teachers using computers in instruction? Paper presented at the annual meeting of the American Educational Research Association, Seattle, WA.

Becker, H. J. & Ravitz, J. L. (2001). Computer use by teachers: Are Cuban's predictions correct? Paper presented at the annual meeting of the American Educational Research Association, Seattle, WA.

Bransford, J. D., Brown, A., & Cocking, R. (Eds.). (2000). *How people learn: Mind, brain, experience and school*, expanded edition. Washington, DC: National Academy Press.

Brush, T., Glazewski, K., Rutowski, K., Berg, K., Stromfors, C., Van-Nest, M. H., Stock, L., & Sutton, J. (2003). Integrating technology into a field-based teacher training program: The PT3@ASU project. *Journal of Educational Technology Research and Development, 51*(1), 57–72.

Coughlin, E. D. & Lempke, C. (1999) *Professional development continuum*. Santa Monica: CA: Milken Family Foundation.

Cuban, L. (2001). *Oversold and underused*. Cambridge, MA: Harvard University Press, pp. 2–10.

Delandshere, G. & Arens, S. A. (2003). Examining the quality of evidence in preservice teacher portfolios. *Journal of Teacher Education, 54*(1), 57–73.

Editorial Projects in Education Research Center (2007). *Technology Counts: A digital decade*. Washington, DC: Author.

Fulton, K., Glenn, A. D., & Valdez, G. (2003). Three preservice programs preparing tomorrow's teachers to use technology: A study in partnerships. Retrieved November 30, 2007, from; http://www.learningpt.org/pdfs/tech/preservice.pdf.

Glenn, A. D. (2002). Emergence of technology standards for preservice teacher education North Central Regional Educational Laboratory, Oak Brook, IL [On-line]. Available at http://www.ncrel.org/tech/standard/.

Hargrave, C. P. & Hsu, Y. (2000). Survey of instructional technology courses for preservice teachers. *Journal of Technology and Teacher Education, 8*(4), 303–314.

Hawley, W. D. & Valli, L. (1999). The essentials of effective professional development. In Darling-Hammond, L. & Sykes, G (eds.), *Teaching as the learning profession: Handbook of policy and practice*. San Francisco: Jossey-Bass.

Howland, J. & Wedman, J. (2004). A process model for faculty development: Individualized technology learning. *Journal of Technology and Teacher Education, 12*(2), 239–263.

International Society for Technology in Education (2000a). National educational technology standards for students (NETS-S). Eugene, OR: Author.

———— (2000b). National educational technology standards for teachers (NETS-T). Eugene, OR: Author.

———— (2001). National educational technology standards for administrators (TSSA). Eugene, OR: Author.

———— (2003). *Use of NETS by state*. Retrieved on October 20, 2003, from http://www.iste.org/

Jonassen, D. H. & Reeves, T. C. (1996). Learning with Technology: Using Computers as Cognitive Tools. In Jonassen, D. H. (Ed.), *Handbook of research on educational communications and technology* (pp. 693–719). New York: Macmillan.

Kilpatrick, J., Swafford, J., & Findell, B. (2002). *Adding it up: Helping children learn mathematics*. Washington, DC: National Academy Press.

Krueger, K., Boboc, M., Smaldino, S., Cornish, Y., & Callahan, W. (2004). InTime impact report: What was InTime's effectiveness and impact on faculty and preservice teachers? *Journal of Technology and Teacher Education, 12*(2), 185–210.

Lehman, J. D. & Richardson, J. (2007). Linking teacher preparation programs with K-12 schools via video conferencing: Benefits and limitations. Paper presented at the annual meeting of the American Educational Research Association, Chicago, IL.

Lehman, J. D., Richardson, J., Bai, H., & White, P. (2003). Connections in teacher education: Lessons from electronic portfolios, videoconferencing, and distance field experiences. Paper presented at the annual meeting of the American Educational Research Association, Chicago, IL.

Loucks-Horsley, S., Love, N., Stiles, K. E., Mundry, S., & Hewson, P. W. (2003). *Designing professional development for teachers of science and mathematics*, 2nd ed. Thousand Oaks, CA: Corwin Press.

Market Data Retrieval (2002). *Technology in education* [On-line]. Available at http://www.schooldata.com/publications3.html

Mims, C., Polly, D., Shepherd, C., & Inan, F. (2006). From campus to the field: Examining PT3 projects designed to improve preservice teachers[1] methods courses and field experiences. TechTrends. 50(3), 16–24.

Mishra, P. & Koehler, M. J. (2006). Technological pedagogical content knowledge: A framework for teacher knowledge. *Teachers College Record, 108*(6), 1017–1054.

Moore, J. A. & Duffield, J. A. (2006). Lessons learned from PT3. *Tech Trends*, *50*(3), 54–58.

Moore, J. A., Knuth, R., Borse, J., & Mitchell, M. (1999) Teacher technology competencies: Early indicators and benchmarks. Presentation at the *1999 Society for Information Technology and Teacher Education Conference*, San Antonio, TX.

Moursand, D. & Bielefeldt, T. (1999). *Will new teachers be prepared to teach in a digital age?: A national survey on information technology in teacher education*. Washington, DC: Milken Exchange on Educational Technology.

National Center for Education Statistics (NCES) (1999). *Teacher quality: A report on the preparation and qualifications of public school teachers*. Washington, DC: U.S. Department of Education.

―――― (2002). *Internet Access in U.S. Public Schools and Classrooms: 1994–2001*. Washington, DC: U.S. Department of Education.

Nave, B. (2004). *Boston University preparing tomorrow's teachers for technology (BU-PT3) Final summative report*. Boston, MA: School of Education, Boston University.

No Child Left Behind (NCLB) Act of 2001 (2002). Pub. L. No. 107–110, 115 Stat. 1425.

North Central Regional Technology in Education Consortium (NCRTEC) (1997). *NCRTEC portfolio: Training and professional development—curricular strands (draft)*. Oak Brook, IL: Author.

Office of Technology Assessment (1995). *Teachers and technology: Making the connection* (Report no. OTA-HER-616). Washington, DC: U.S. Government Printing Office.

Panel on Educational Technology (1997). *Report to the President on the use of technology to strengthen PK-12 education in the United States*. Washington, DC.

Persichitte, K. A., Tharp, D. D., & Caffarella, E. P. (1997). *The use of technology by schools, colleges, and departments of education: 1996*. Washington, DC: American Association of Colleges for Teacher Education.

―――― (1998). Pre-service teacher preparation and interactive information technologies critical mass. Paper presented at the Annual Meeting of the Association for Educational Communications and Technology. St. Louis, MO.

Powell, J. V. (1999). Computers and early childhood inservice teachers: A ten-year follow-up study. *Information Technology in Childhood Education Annual*, 1999 (1), 193–209.

Schrum, L. (1999). Technology professional development for teachers. *Educational Technology Research and Development*, *47*(4), 83–90.

Spodark, Edwina (2003). Five obstacles to technology integration at a small liberal arts university. *T H E Journal*, *30*(8), 14–19.

Stetson, R. & Bagwell, T. (1999). Technology and teacher preparation: An oxymoron? *Journal of Technology and Teacher Education*, *7*(2), 145–153.

Strudler, N., Archambault, L., Bendixen, L., Anderson, D., & Weiss, R. (2003). Project THREAD: Technology helping restructure educational access and delivery. *Educational Technology Research and Development*, *51*(3), 41–56.

University of Northern Iowa (2003). InTime overview [On-line]. Available at http://www.intime.uni.edu

U.S. Department of Education (2002).

U.S. Department of Education (2006a). Building the digital bridge: Sonoma State University links dozens of partners in drive to restructure teacher ed programs [On-line]. Retrieved on December 3, 2006, from http://www.pt3.org/stories/sonoma.html

———— (2006b). Technology tools: Digital handhelds [On-line]. Retrieved on December 3, 2006, from http://www.pt3.org/stories/digital_handhelds.html.

Wentworth, N., Waddoups, G. L., & Earle, R. (2004). Technology integration into a teacher education program. *Computers in the Schools, 21*, 1–14.

Willis, J. W. & Mehlinger, H. D. (1996). Information technology and teacher education. In Sikula, J., Buttery, T.J., & Guyton, E. (Eds.). *Handbook for research on teacher education*, 2nd edition (pp. 978–1029). New York: Simon & Schuster.

From Students to Scholars: Revision of the Doctoral Program in Instructional Systems Technology at Indiana University

Elizabeth Boling
Indiana University

In 2004 the faculty of the Instructional Systems Technology (IST) program at Indiana University Bloomington (IUB) started the process of revising our doctoral program. We had made an unsuccessful attempt to do so several years earlier by charging a committee to develop a plan for revision, and it is my observation that this attempt probably failed because a comparatively full-blown plan emerging from a committee tends either to be accepted or not accepted by the full faculty; it is not perceived to be the property of the entire group (regardless of the committee's intention) and therefore not perceived to be open to radical reinterpretation after it is presented to the group (regardless of the committee's openness to change). Consequently, our subsequent efforts were carried out from the earliest discussions through detailed revisions by the faculty as a whole, a process that took two years from start to finish, since we had no single model that was clearly applicable in its entirety from which to work.

This chapter will describe the perceived need for revising our program, the goals we held for the new program, strategic decisions we made that underlie the new program, design tensions we faced and our resolution of them, major features of the new program, our design process, and the open issues we face as we begin implementation of the new design.

WHAT WAS THE PERCEIVED NEED FOR REVISION?

Although many capable and well-prepared scholars have graduated from this program over the years, and done so in what might be considered good time for a 90-hour Ph.D. (5–6 years from matriculation to degree awarded), we were also aware that a number of emerging scholars of great potential were bogging down on the way to their degrees. There were two main profiles in these cases: individuals who made it past the qualifying exam and then never put forward a viable dissertation research proposal or failed to follow through on an accepted proposal, and individuals who struggled either with the qualifying exam or the dissertation research process, or both, and did not take the doctoral degree before running out of the time allowed (at IUB, seven years from oral quals to successful defense and submission of the dissertation) or required an inordinate amount of time and attention in order to design and complete dissertation research. An additional, sometimes overlapping, group of students caused us concern, and these were the ones for whom degree completion was taking more than 5–6 years (IUB allows 7 years to complete coursework before requiring revalidation, plus the 7 years to complete dissertation research post-quals). Possibly of even greater concern was that some students who graduated in good time were not actually as well prepared to be researchers and scholars as they could have been since they may or may not have had available, or have taken advantage of, opportunities for productive interaction with the faculty and with senior student researchers during their programs of studies.

Setting aside those instances in which life circumstances (severe illness, family crisis) or shifting goals (change in career, rethinking the major area of study) interrupted people's progress, we diagnosed some clear barriers to successful, timely completion of the Ph.D. that we believed could be addressed through redesign of the program. Chief among these were: students could put off the courses and experiences most relevant to their becoming scholars until late in their programs; the dissertation was for many, if not most, an event separate from, and profoundly different from, the coursework phase of their programs; opportunities for apprenticeship experiences were not always available for students since the faculty did not uniformly participate in making them available, and when such opportunities were available they could be ignored by students with no immediate penalty; it was possible to pass the qualifying exam and simply not take the next step (prospectus and research committee formation) because there was no programmatic mechanism for bridging these two events; and the faculty had limited opportunities to gauge accurately a student's readiness for dissertation research (qualifying exams notwithstanding) until preparations for the dissertation were underway. Our perception of these barriers was reinforced by an open meeting with the student body in which we invited their input on the existing doctoral program. The students were forthcoming then and in less public venues, and the reports they gave of their own experiences paralleled our observations.

GOALS FOR THE REVISED PROGRAM

Our primary goal for the revised program was to graduate world-class scholars ready for research-oriented positions in which they would rise to leadership roles by virtue of their exceptional preparation in the dimensions of inquiry, teaching or training, and sustained service to individual organizations and to their field of practice. While we pride ourselves on having graduated many such scholars under previous designs for the doctoral program, our aim in the recent redesign was to ensure this outcome for more of our students and to do it in a timely fashion. To accomplish this we wanted to provide students with an awareness of their roles as scholars-in-training from their earliest days in the program, and construct the program so that they had both clear opportunities to act on this awareness and the clear requirement to act on it.

STRATEGIC DECISIONS

In reviewing our goals and the barriers inherent in our then current program, we decided that apprenticeship qualities needed to characterize the program in order to get students involved early and repeatedly in research activities, ensure that much of their effort went toward authentic scholarship experiences (versus scholarship manufactured in and for the classroom), and leave them post-quals poised to carry out, and capable of completing, dissertation research. Although we discussed, and even fleshed out, some plans for course sequences aimed at accomplishing our larger goals, those plans carried two major drawbacks that we could foresee. The first drawback was that we could not be confident students moving from course to course in such a plan would connect those experiences together in the seamless way that we hoped for them to work. The second drawback was that any version of a course-oriented plan called for a measure of top-down coordination and curriculum control that we did not deem sustainable, if it was even possible—or desirable, in the university environment.

Our second major strategic decision was to replace the qualifying examination with a professional dossier based on the tenure and promotion dossier model. Although we know that graduates of our doctoral program do not all seek tenure track faculty positions in colleges and universities, we decided that assembling indicators of developing scholars' capabilities in key areas (research, teaching or training, and service) would serve three functional goals at once: (1) provide the awareness of the activities expected of students from the start of the program and the clear requirement to engage in those activities; (2)

lend authenticity to many activities carried out by students; and (3) provide an evolving means whereby faculty might gauge students' preparedness for dissertation research and professional performance.

We had revised the qualifying exam about ten years previously, moving from a timed, proctored event at which students responded to multiple questions sampling their knowledge of the field, to a three-papers-in-three-weeks format in which students answered fewer questions but drew more broadly on their knowledge of the field and demonstrated more fully their abilities to construct arguments, marshal appropriate evidence, and express themselves as scholars. This shift was seen at the time it was made as a move toward authentic assessment of readiness to conduct doctoral research, and it was a legitimate shift in that direction. However, it came too late in the program for any effective developmental intervention in the event that the student turned out not to be prepared and far, far too late for anyone, student or advisory committee, to feel less than demoralized at the very least. The dossier we envisioned would be developed and reviewed iteratively, thereby reducing or eliminating the surprise factor at the moment of "qualification."

Our third strategic decision was to require a substantial portion of credits in the major to be taken as seminar credits, and to use the seminar as a structuring vehicle for students to assist them as they developed their dossiers, and as a vehicle for crediting faculty as they shifted their doctoral teaching focus from numbered courses to apprenticeship mentoring in their research groups. The seminars would meet, and teaching them would carry specific responsibilities, but they would no longer be—as they had been—topical courses covering only the subject matter or projects brought to them by an individual member of the faculty.

DESIGN TENSIONS

As happens in any design project, we faced several situations in which two functional requirements, both positive and necessary, suggested design moves that were not necessarily compatible and had to be reconciled or required us to examine parts of the program outside the literal boundaries of the program description.

Research Group Structure and Faculty Research Programs

We agreed that an apprenticeship model for the program required identifiable re-search groups, similar to labs in science programs, that incoming students would join as novices and participate in with progressively more responsibility until they were collab-orating directly with faculty and eventually mentoring students junior to themselves. We could not, however, dictate the format or rhythm of research programs faculty members already had underway, and we faced the additional problem of how faculty members who were not currently engaged in a full program of research might establish such a research group. This design tension was addressed through several design moves. First, while we mandated dossier deliverables that could best be satisfied through research group activities (indicators of in-depth knowledge, evidence of independent research), we left flexible the specific method by which those deliverables could be satisfied. Next, we agreed that faculty members would set their own requirements for entry to a research group; any model from an all-comers-accepted to prerequisite course required and/or application-only or a vacancy/no vacancy model would be acceptable, and students would not be led to expect uniformity in the structure of these groups. Third, we trusted the structure of the program itself to provide inherent incentives for faculty to establish research groups since the available pool of research assistance at the doctoral level would be most accessible to members of the faculty best able to attract and support students.

Sufficient Program Structure and the Freedom to Explore

Perhaps the most difficult design tension we wrestled with throughout the process was the need to structure the new program sufficiently to support novice scholars but leave it flexible enough to allow individuals just entering this field of study the freedom to explore. In an analogous set of tensions, we wanted to structure the program enough to make students aware of the capabilities they need to acquire, and the means available for acquiring those capabilities, without reducing the program to a checklist format that might make students feel they only needed to accumulate a certain number of checkmarks in order to graduate. We addressed this tension in part through keeping an eye on the tenure and promotion model in use at IUB, which sets general standards for the indicators of scholarly achievement but does not specify certain numbers or types of publications, teaching experiences, and so on for the individual dossier. In addition, we required exploration of multiple research groups early in the program and planned for research groups to present their work in the doctoral seminars so that students had as many chances as possible to examine their options. We made the policy decision that students could switch their primary group membership as late as the third dossier review, although they would need to be aware that such a switch would come at a cost of time and effort on their part.

Early Involvement in Research and Foundation Building in Knowledge and Skills

With an equally strong perceived need to involve students in research experiences early in the program and to ensure that they were building foundational knowledge and skills quickly enough to profit from those research experiences, we faced the problem of making students wait until they knew what they were doing, thereby delaying their meaningful involvement in research, or immersing them quickly in experiences that they might not appreciate or absorb and thereby frustrating them and ourselves. We addressed this tension via the doctoral core, a set of three courses required at the beginning of the program and covering foundational readings in research across the field, guided research in the field, and seminar-format discussions of the dimensions, requirements, and practicalities of scholarship. This core overlaps by one semester with the requirement to join a research group, which bridges the early foundation experience to early responsibilities in a functioning research program. For students entering the doctoral program without an MS in the field, we also decided to require completion of the applicable courses from our four MS core sequence.

MAJOR FEATURES OF THE PROGRAM DESIGN

While there are details of policy and logistics not included in this chapter, the major features of the program can be described to give a fairly complete picture of the program design. Each component of this program is intended to support and be supported by the others.

Doctoral Core Courses

At the beginning of the program, doctoral students complete three core courses:

- Readings course covering major areas of research in the field, in which students both read and write about key works in the field and discuss those works; the student chooses a best paper from this course to include in the dossier.

- Inquiry course requiring both analysis of published research in the field and a series of focused activities providing hands-on tools skills in research applicable to common projects in the field.

- Doctoral seminar that the first-year students experience as a specialized extension of the seminar series described below. Special sessions of the seminar are devoted to topics applicable to first-year doctoral students (the nature of scholarship, types of knowledge building, choosing a research area, deciding authorship, the nature and pursuit of grants, and so on), while they also attend general sessions at which faculty and more advanced scholars present and discuss their work.

"Bullseye" Courses

Faculty members offer topical seminars, structured independent study experiences or hybrid MS/doctoral courses that do into depth in the areas addressed by their research. These courses may be, and generally are, identical to traditional doctoral-level topics courses. Some research groups require one of these courses as a pre- or corequisite to joining the group, so that new members of a research group are brought up to speed in the area where the group is working and so that students and faculty have a chance to explore the fit between their interests—a factor not always considered in the decision to pursue certain paths of research but one we have observed to be important nevertheless.

Doctoral Seminar Series

The doctoral seminar series is taken over four consecutive semesters, barring personal crisis or illness that necessitates skipping a semester, beginning with the first seminar taken during the first year of the program as part of the doctoral core. The seminars are taught concurrently; that is, one seminar meets each term and includes students from the first through the fourth years in the same classroom. Each of these seminars requires deliverables, most of which are expected to be satisfied through research group activities and some of which are related to the seminar itself (specifically, participation and presentation). In general, students in the first seminar are expected to produce literature reviews in their chosen area(s) of research focus; in the second, a proposal for independent research and presentation of that proposal for discussion at the seminar; in the third, completion of that research; and in the fourth a submitted publication resulting from the research. These key deliverables will appear in the dossier and, although they may be undertaken in collaboration with one or more other students and may grow out of work happening within a research group, they are expected to be conceived and carried out as the first steps toward independent research at the dissertation level. Faculty of record organize and chair the seminars, assess the in-seminar performance of the students, and solicit input from faculty members heading research groups on the performance of students in those groups and on their primary deliverables.

Research Groups

As described above, each member of the faculty (and in some cases, more than one in collaboration with others, both inside and outside the university) heads a research group that may be tightly or loosely structured and may be pursuing one or many lines of research. Faculty decide on the requirements for membership and continued participation in a research group, and on the nature of the opportunities available within the group. We have agreed to make these opportunities as compatible with the seminar requirements as possible, but have also agreed that students will share much of the responsibility for defining their opportunities in the event that an ongoing program of interest to them is not naturally synchronized with their current standing in the program. As an example of the flexibility and shared responsibility built into the seminar/research group model, a student may get involved in a research project outside the department and seek sponsorship in a departmental research group best related to that external project. The student is responsible for keeping the departmental research group informed about the external project, for seeking advice on aligning that external project with seminar and dossier requirements, and for contributing to the sponsoring research group at a mutually satisfactory level. The faculty member in this instance will have agreed to keep current with the student's external work and to communicate with the external faculty member about the student's performance, to reduce barriers for that student to make contributions to the work of the departmental group and to advise the student about her dossier. Or a student may participate more or less equally in two research groups, making sure to coordinate communications about his activities between them and understanding that input to his seminar grade will be negotiated between the faculty leaders of both groups.

Dossier and Dossier Reviews

Each student begins to assemble a dossier during the first semester of the program. The dossier serves as an organized collection of indicators that the student is acquiring capabilities required by the program. The dossier is reviewed three times: (1) the semester of the second doctoral seminar by the student's advisory committee; (2) the semester of the student's third or fourth seminar by a panel of the entire faculty with an oral defense by the student open to the full department; (3) the semester in which the student takes the dissertation proposal preparation course, or the semester immediately following, by the student's advisory committee. The first review of the dossier yields developmental feedback only. The second review results in a pass/fail decision and corresponds to the written qualifying exam, which at IUB is one of two parts to the exam required for admission to candidacy. A student failing this review may try again the semester immediately following, but if that review is also judged as a fail the student will either opt to pursue a lesser degree (MS, if applicable, or specialist degree) or leave the program. The third review corresponds to the "oral exam," which is the second part of the exam leading to candidacy. Candidacy commences from the date of this exam and expires seven years from this date.

The basic structure of the dossier is as follows:

    I.   Candidate's statement (updated for each review)

    II.   Précis of feedback from previous reviews verified by committee (reviews 2 and 3)

    III.   Progress in academic program

        1.   Undergraduate and any pre-IU graduate transcripts (copies acceptable)

        2.   Program of Studies

        3.   Current transcripts from IU (informal online report showing grades, current GPA and highlighted to show residency requirement met)

    IV.   Evidence of research competencies

    V.   Evidence of teaching competencies

VI.   Evidence of service competencies

VII.   Draft of dissertation proposal (review 3)

VIII. List of dissertation committee members (review 3)

IX.   Curriculum vitae (dated)

As with a tenure dossier, the student provides a statement, revised and expanded at each review, explaining the focus, trajectory, and integration of her activities and connecting those activities in a meaningful way with the deliverables, or indicators, included in the dossier. At the second review, the student makes a short presentation to the full faculty and any students attending, which summarizes his intellectual development to date, his integration of research, teaching and service activities, and his professional goals. Two faculty readers, not members of this student's advisory committee, ask the student questions based on a close reading of the dossier. Following the oral defense sessions, the full faculty panel makes pass/fail decisions for each student under review.

A *Dossier Handbook* provides detail to students on the types of indicators considered appropriate for evidence of competencies in research, teaching, and service. In each category we describe "baseline indicators," which are the minimum required, and "target indicators," which are a range of additional deliverables that might be applicable to a student's profile as a scholar and experiences in the program. It is not possible to pass a dossier review on the baseline indicators alone, but no amount of target indicators will substitute for the baseline indicators. The *Handbook* also outlines the guidelines followed by the faculty for reviewing the dossier. These include the specific requirement that the student's efforts exhibit growth in capabilities, increasing focus and integration in scholarship, and increasing integration of research, teaching, and service activities across the pre-dissertation semesters of study.

Additional Program Requirements

As with any doctoral program, requirements outside the major constitute a major feature of the design. These are not very much different than they were in the previous design. They include required inquiry (research design and methods) courses, a 12-credit doctoral minor, educational foundations requirements, and elective credits. In addition, the dissertation proposal course, or its equivalent, and 12 dissertation credits are required.

DESIGN PROCESS

With a faculty membership of nine FTE (small compared to some departments in the IUB School of Education and large compared to many programs in the field), we carried out the design of our doctoral program largely as a committee of the whole. We held faculty meetings every other week for most of the two years of design, and devoted a large part of those meetings in one way or another to the issues involved in the design. In addition, we met monthly during the summer 2004 term, prior to launching the program since this is the point at which all of us realized keenly the necessity of working out the logistical and supporting details of the program. We achieved buy-in to the program largely through inclusion of all members of the faculty in the design process. We have had two faculty members join us subsequent to the main effort of design, and have incorporated them into ongoing review and revision of the design partly to continue the process of buy-in.

During this extended period, we found ourselves iterating discussions about the goals for the program, the capabilities and knowledge we expect our graduates to possess, and other fundamental aspects of the design. To some extent this was necessary because individual members of the faculty might or might not have been able to participate in all discussions and we needed to bring everyone along in the shared agreements about where we were going with the design. In part these repeated discussions also prevented us from focusing on one part of the design to the exclusion of others, a tendency we succumbed to more than once. A discussion of course sequence might begin to grow and grow until we had an unwieldy list of classes, objectives, and requirements on the white board, at which point we would draw back and remind ourselves of the program features that were intended to fulfill functions we had been trying to cover solely through coursework.

We also engaged in what might be termed conceptual prototyping. We produced program descriptions in various formats—visual diagrams, text-based diagrams, narrative descriptions, and others. Each of these allowed for new understandings of the implications of major program features, and many of them exposed areas in which we had not understood each other during previous discussions. We did not engage in a fully participatory process with the students in the program, and because we did not, we also did not share all iterations of the evolving design with the student body anticipating that to do so might raise unwarranted fears and/or expectations about the future program. Later in the process we did share program descriptions with students to get their perspective on the clarity, feasibility, and usability of the design.

Not all of the work done during the design of the program was completed by the committee of the whole. Each individual member of the faculty at one time or another took a portion of the work to flesh out in detail and/or develop as a proposal that was then shared with and shaped by the entire group. We were fortunate that enough trust and common desire to achieve a high-quality workable result existed in the group to allow us to work this way. We worked through both conceptual and logistical concerns as we envisioned and reenvisioned the program, with issues of the design's practicality constantly grounding our more fanciful and convoluted prototype designs. At a certain point we recognized that the design had reached the point at which we could implement it; we forwarded it to the appropriate committees for approval and put it into place. At the time of this writing, we are maintaining the previous program design for students far enough along in their studies not to be able, or in some cases, willing, to switch to the new program.

EARLY REVISIONS TO THE PROGRAM

Our first several semesters of implementation have resulted in revisions to the design as originally conceived. In particular, we simplified the dossier guidelines and seminar deliverables radically when we saw that the details we had provided as "helpful structure" were being perceived as a terrifying overload of requirements and as unhelpful constraints by students who were achieving the competencies we wanted, but experiencing an unacceptable and unwonted level of distress in the process. In addition, some of the specific requirements seemed to be placing a burden of intense supervision on the leaders of research groups, thereby interfering with the natural conduct of their research programs and introducing a kind of false mentoring relationship into the groups. Simplification of those requirements, with the resulting flexibility, seems to be addressing this problem.

The members of the faculty who volunteered to teach the seminar series first have found themselves refining what turned out to be a somewhat conceptual portion of the design as they go, and with input from the students and the rest of the faculty have been busy differentiating the first year seminar experience from the subsequent three and establishing norms for how research groups and individual students will participate in presentation/discussion sessions during seminar. We also realized that the conversion of topical seminars into a single course that serves as the vehicle for building scholarly community and for structuring research group experiences had eliminated a primary mechanism whereby students and faculty found shared interests in research and explored topics of research in depth. We have therefore instituted the "bullseye" course feature of the program, which is at the moment an advisory requirement rather than a programmatic one and is one of the issues we are watching as the program evolves. We also revised the research class in the doctoral core so that hands-on experiences in data collection and analysis, usability methods, and other research skills precede analysis and discussion of published research since this sequence seems to support students' understanding better than engaging in the more abstract experience first.

These early revisions have actually been conducted as a quasi-participatory design process because the students in seminar have been invited to reflect on their experiences in the program and have also taken the initiative to comment on the program as they experience it and to suggest thoughtful improvements—sometimes quite pointedly.

OPEN ISSUES

At the time of this writing we are four semesters into the implementation of this program. We have held two first dossier reviews and one second dossier review so far; taught two iterations of the doctoral core and four iterations of the seminar. We have yet to make final decisions on the requirements for students majoring in other doctoral programs and taking minors in IST, including the required courses they may need to take, the format of their qualifying exam with us, and the way in which seminar requirements may apply to them. We do not yet know whether three types of dossier reviews, all of which need to be conducted once each term, are going to be a heavier burden in the long run than our previous qualifying exam process with all its attendant complexities of developing questions, administering the exams, and dealing with the aftermath for students who did not pass (although we do expect to reap more benefits from the reviews than we did from the old exam). The consistency and sustainability of the seminar, when it is passed from one member of the faculty to another, and the articulation of seminar with the research programs of individual faculty are both issues that we anticipate as challenges to be addressed in the inevitable refinement of the program.

CONCLUSION

We do anticipate that the new doctoral program will achieve the goals we set for it to a greater extent than did the previous program design. We are already finding ourselves having different conversations with our doctoral students, and addressing issues relevant to their eventual performance as scholars earlier in their programs and in more focused ways. We expect to see our students arriving at the point of dissertation research better prepared for it, and graduating with a stronger, more integrated set of capabilities as researchers and a greater appreciation of their professional identities as scholars.

ACKNOWLEDGMENTS

While I was elected to write this chapter, the entire core faculty of our program participated substantially in revision of the IST doctoral program at Indiana University. They are (in alphabetical order and by category) Robert L. Appelman, Barbara A. Bichelmeyer, Elizabeth Boling, Thomas A. Brush, Theodore W. Frick, James A. Pershing, Charles M. Reigeluth; (emeriti members) Ivor K. Davies and Michael Molenda; (recently joining members) Curtis J. Bonk and Anne Leftwich. A special thanks goes to Charlie Reigeluth for reviewing this chapter.

AUTHOR BIO

Elizabeth Boling is Associate Professor of Education and joined the Instructional Systems Technology Department, Indiana University, Bloomington in 1992. She holds her

B.F.A. (Texas Tech University) and M.F.A. (Indiana University) in Printmaking. She worked as interface designer and production manager for educational software development under contract to Macmillan Publishing (1983–1987), then as Graphics and Animation Manager for Instructional Products at Apple Computer, Inc. from 1988 to 1992. Her research interests include visual design for interactive information and instruction, and design process and methods. She served as Editor-in-Chief for *TechTrends* from 2004 to 2006, and has served as President of AECT's Design and Development Division.

Applying Human Performance Technology Principles for IDT Program Improvement

Katherine S. Cennamo and Barbara B. Lockee
Virginia Tech

IDT AT VIRGINIA TECH

For over 30 years, the Instructional Design and Technology (IDT) program at Virginia Tech has successfully prepared academic professionals, as well practitioners in the theory and practice of our field. However, in recent years, our program has encountered a variety of challenges that have impacted the potential success of our doctoral students in particular. In an effort to provide the most productive and supportive learning experience possible, our program faculty engaged in a significant program re-design effort to ensure the future quality of our program and therefore, of our graduates.

WHY HPT

The human performance technology (HPT) movement has had a tremendous impact on the field of IDT, moving beyond a current trend to an essential skill set for IDT practitioners (Dick & Wager, 1995; Larson & Lockee, 2004). IDT academic programs have addressed the need to develop such a skill set in their students by adding relevant coursework and practical experiences within their graduate program curricula (Larson, 2005). Therefore, when performance needs were evident within the program at VT, we, the IDT faculty, naturally turned to an HPT process to resolve our own programmatic issues. The issues we faced were both instructional and noninstructional; therefore, the HPT approach was a natural choice for developing a solution to the challenges we faced.

Like many terms in our field, HPT has been defined in multiple ways. For our purposes, we found the most applicable definition to be offered by Harless (as cited in Stolovich & Keeps, 1999, pp. 8–9), stating that "human performance technology is the process of selection, analysis, design, development, implementation, and evaluation of programs to most cost-effectively influence human behavior and accomplishment." This definition parallels the design process with which we were familiar while providing the breadth necessary to address our performance issues in a comprehensive and holistic manner.

While many models for HPT exist (see Gilbert, 2007; Rosenberg, 1990; Rummler & Brache, 1995), we based our program revision process on a widely adopted model created by Van Tiem, Moseley, and Dessinger (2004), and endorsed by the International Society for Performance Improvement (ISPI). This model follows a general five-step process, reflecting a systematic approach to resolving human performance problems. The first step, performance analysis, involves identifying the gap in performance, that is, the difference between current and desired performance outcomes. The second step, cause analysis, focuses on identifying the causes for the performance gap. During the third step, intervention selection/design, a plan is created to address the performance deficiency, and the intervention implementation occurs during the fourth step. Finally, the fifth step, evaluation, determines how effectively the desired outcomes are being accomplished as a result of the new intervention (Van Tiem, Moseley, and Dessinger, 2004).

PERFORMANCE ANALYSIS: THE NEED FOR CHANGE

As stated by Rossett (1999, p. 139), "analysis provides the foundation for HPT, a profession and a perspective that demands study before recommendations, data before decisions, and involvement before actions." The IDT faculty realized that we needed to step back to analyze our context through a variety of lenses to determine both the extent of the performance problems and the cause behind these issues. We collected data through formal and informal mechanisms, including observations, surveys, focus groups, and benchmarking activities. The combination of data sources helped clearly define the performance issues, as well as the reasons behind them.

To summarize the challenges we faced, some background information is useful. Virginia Tech has had a well-established IDT program in the field for many years, enrolling approximately 35 full-time doctoral students at any one time. Almost all of our students are supported by assistantships with funding generated by our faculty. In addition, the program provides significant funding for students to attend professional conferences. Though our curriculum has been successful in the past and the support of our students is substantial, the need for programmatic changes became apparent over the past few years. From an instructional perspective, student performance problems were becoming more frequent in our doctoral exams, enough so to become a notable trend. It was clear that students were not demonstrating the skills necessary to analyze and synthesize research literature. Also, there seemed to be a lack of awareness regarding expectations for the processes related to successful completion of the exams and the program in general. It appeared as if students needed a greater amount of structure and guidance in order to be successful.

The program also faced difficulties that were noninstructional in nature. The student body, once renowned for its cohesive and collegial nature, had become disconnected and was lacking as a social support mechanism. Both faculty and students noted this phenomenon and both expressed the need to rebuild community among all stakeholders in the program.

CAUSE ANALYSIS: REASONS FOR CHANGE

After extensive discussion and analysis, the IDT program faculty determined that the aforementioned challenges developed as a result of four converging factors. During the past several years, our program faculty had changed significantly with the retirement and promotion of several key faculty members, and the hiring of several others. In addition, our faculty offices had been moved. Whereas we had once been housed in the midst of our student lab, faculty offices were reassigned to distribute faculty throughout the building. Unintentionally, that made us less accessible to students. Additionally, other programs in our School of Education had similar staffing changes, programs on which we depend for foundational courses for our students. Due to this shift in the faculty base, the content of several of the required courses also changed to the extent that we could no longer count on students gaining the prerequisite skills for our classes. Many times, classes that our students needed were not available to them.

At the same time, our student body had changed significantly. While at one time, our student body consisted primarily of domestic students, such students currently make up only about one-quarter of our doctoral student population. The remainder of the doctoral student population comes from a variety of other countries including China, Korea, Turkey, and Malawi. The international students, unfamiliar with the U.S. educational system that stresses self-directed learning, seemed to need more structure in navigating the doctoral program requirements. In many countries, students are rewarded for their ability to repeat information verbatim and this trend has been the case with much of our student population. Although these students were comfortable with the coursework requirements, they were less familiar with the self-directed learning required to complete a dissertation.

The need for change was felt by the students as well as faculty. In the spring of 2004, the students conducted a series of focus groups within the Professional seminar, which at that time was conducted by senior students. Students were asked to suggest ways in which the program could be improved. Focus groups were followed by extensive online discussions. The focus group and online discussion data were categorized and summarized by one of the senior students.

The suggestions clustered in five areas: dissertations and exams, research and networking, advising, mentoring, and leadership. Specific suggestions in the area of *dissertations and exams* included having socials at the beginning of each semester, mentoring as a second-year residency requirement, and conducting mock exams; however, students who had been through a number of exams expressed that they would not feel comfortable creating a mock exam experience for newer students because of the individual nature of each exam. New students were concerned about what to expect in each exam and what the standards were for acceptable performance. However, experienced students recommended resources that were already available such as the IT Web site and a session in ProSem offered each semester on exam preparation.

In the area of *research and networking*, new students expressed concerns about finding research participants and choosing research methods. Experienced students thought that these needs were typically met within courses required by the program. Specific suggestions for research and networking included coordinating with other departments to gain access to public schools and other sources of research participants, creating "tracks" in ProSem to cater to the research needs of the students, and including students in more faculty research projects.

In the area of *advising*, students expressed a need to talk with their advisors more. Specific suggestions included having a suggested number of meetings per semester between a student and his or her advisor, creating environments for informal chats with advisors, such as over lunch or at more regular social gatherings, having regular meetings with an advisor and all of his or her advisees, and including students in more faculty research projects.

In the area of *mentoring*, newer students expressed needs for mentoring from students who were farther along in the program. Specific suggestions included: having regular meetings with an advisor and all of his or her advisees, having more social events, implementing a formal mentoring program, and keeping informal mentor/protégé relationships that have been developing naturally. Students acknowledged that the structure of a two-year residency requirement within a doctoral program requiring at least three years to complete creates logistical problems for a formal mentoring program.

In addition, senior students felt overburdened by their *leadership responsibilities* within the IT student association and the Professional Seminar. Specific suggestions focused on clarifying leadership responsibilities in ways such as documenting previous semester ProSem programs, developing a syllabus for ProSem, developing a list of objectives and general requirements for ProSem planning, creating incentives for ProSem leadership, and including a student from all stages in the program in the ProSem leadership.

INTERVENTION DESIGN AND IMPLEMENTATION

At this point in the HPT process, the intervention is designed and developed and then implemented (ISPI, 2004). For purposes of discussion, the design and implementation of our programmatic changes are addressed in a combined format as follows:

We began the design of our intervention with a discussion of the student focus group data. From this data, we identified the set of needs that we believed were reflected in the student's feedback. Although much of the focus group data presented specific suggestions for program improvement, we looked beyond the explicit suggestions to tease out the needs of the students that we believed were inherent in the data.

After we identified the needs of the students, we embarked on an extensive program revision process. We examined the programs of several peer institutions in depth. With knowledge of our student's needs and the benchmarks provided through examining other programs, we engaged in a serious discussion of who we were and who we wanted to be.

We agreed that the emphasis of our program should be on preparing university faculty members and staff. Virginia Tech is located in a rural area and students have little access to corporate settings for internships and course experiences. At the same time, we identified our strengths historically in preparing future faculty members. There are many opportunities on campus for students to gain experience in faculty support roles. Thus, after revising our strengths, we chose to continue to focus on the preparation of faculty and support personnel for higher-education positions.

Revisions were comprehensive, encompassing everything from changing our name (from Instructional Technology to Instructional Design and Technology), altering our admission process to a cohort-based approach, establishing an expanded set of required courses, modifying our exam structure, and revising our Professional Seminar. A substantial re-design of our program Web site was conducted as well, providing explicit details on the processes and procedures required for every stage of the doctoral program, as well as other relevant program information regarding curriculum, faculty, and student resources.

Cohort System and Course Sequence

Recognizing the needs of our students for additional structure, we changed from a system where we accepted applications for admission in the fall, spring, or summer semesters, we changed our admission policies to a cohort system. Students are admitted once a year, in the fall semester. During their first semester, students are required to enroll in three core courses that serve as the foundation for our field. The Instructional Design course introduces them to the skills of instructional design, Learning Theories for Instructional Design introduces them to the foundational learning theories of behaviorism, cognitivism, and constructivism, and Foundations of Technology Tools introduces them to principles in the application of technology to solve problems (instructional and noninstructional). Students also enroll in two hours of dissertation credit and one hour of Professional Seminar credit.

During their second semester, students begin to become immersed in the research in the field. They are required to take a course called Trends in Instructional Technology in which they develop knowledge related to the history of IDT, related research themes and designs, and skills in the critique of empirical studies. In this course, they identify a research topic of interest and begin to develop a literature review under the supervision of the course faculty member. During the second semester, they also begin their required qualitative and quantitative research sequence. All students are required to take two courses in either qualitative or quantitative methods, and one course in the other methodology. For example, students who choose to take two quantitative courses are required to take one course in qualitative methods. At this point, they also enroll in one elective course, two hours of dissertation credit, and one hour of Professional Seminar credit. During their third and forth semesters, students continue to enroll for two hours of dissertation credit each semester, one hour of Professional Seminar credit, and one elective course. They also complete their two-semester research sequence in the second year. During the fall semester, students are expected to enroll in Applied Theories in Instructional Design. In this course, students' knowledge of learning theories, instructional design, and technology tools courses cone together to inform the design and development of instructional materials based on a firm foundation of learning theories. In their fourth semester, students enroll in our Research in Instructional Technology course in which they learn to prepare a research proposal. As students enter the third year, their schedules become more flexible. They can choose electives based on their specific areas of interest, as well as engage in internship experiences where they can apply course-related skills and knowledge. Much of the third year Plan of Study is designated for research and dissertation credit hours, as well.

Dissertation Credit and Exam Structure

In reorganizing the program to provide more structure, we established a set series of activities for students to perform while enrolled for dissertation credit. Typically, students enroll in two hours of dissertation credit each semester their first two years. Dissertation hours are tightly tied to our exam sequence and thus, the exam structure will be discussed in the context of dissertation hour credit. The exam sequence consists of a qualifying exam, a prelim exam, a prospectus exam, and a dissertation defense. We also hold informal, but required, committee meetings prior to the preliminary exam (pre-prelim meeting) and the prospectus (pre-prospectus meeting) to provide guidance to students in preparing for those major exam experiences.

In the past, students were expected to develop the shell for a professional portfolio for their qualifying exam, based on the Association for Educational Communication and Technology's (AECT, 2000) Standards for Education Technology Specialist Programs. The qualifying exam was primarily diagnostic in nature, in that we hoped to identify potential areas of concern before students progressed very far in the program. Our intent was to review the professional portfolio during each scheduled exam. However, once students began their dissertation research, meetings were focused on conceptual issues and students were heavily involved in preparing for these exams and it seemed extraneous to ask the students to update their professional portfolios while immersed in the stress of their other exam preparation. We found it difficult to find a time in which it seemed logical to have students present their updated portfolios. It did not seem to fit with the literature review we focused on during the preliminary exam. It did not fit with the research methods discussion that occurred during the prospectus exam. And it seemed to be unnecessarily stressful to ask students to present it during their final defense. Thus, we eliminated the professional portfolio as a requirement. Instead, students are expected to complete a "checklist of competencies," based on the AECT indicators, as part of the paperwork that must be completed before they are awarded their degree.

Currently, students are provided with a reading list of seminal publications in the field during their first semester of enrollment. Readings were selected to expose the students to key articles and books in (1) instructional design, (2) learning theories, and (3) research methods, as well as (4) foundational articles in the field such as "The Science of Learning and the Art of Teaching" (Skinner, 1954). During the second semester, students continue their readings and form study groups to discuss their readings. Their readings culminate in a qualifying exam administered in the middle of the spring semester. In the qualifying exam, they are expected to demonstrate their knowledge of these four areas and their writing skills during a five-hour written exam on the readings. Questions focus on synthesis and application and are primarily diagnostic in nature. The written qualifying exam is followed by an oral exam with the student's examination committee. During the qualifying oral, students also present their proposed Plan of Study. Although students can (and sometimes do) fail the qualifying exam, it remains primarily diagnostic in nature. We seek to determine the extent of the student's understanding of key concepts in order to judge the adequacy of the student's Plan of Study. Based on the knowledge demonstrated during the exam, we often recommend additional courses to complement those selected by the students. We also make an initial assessment of the student's writing ability and may recommend remediation when skills are lacking.

Once students pass the qualifying exam, they are expected to begin planning for their preliminary exam. Previously, students were expected to conduct a literature review for their prelim exam. In the pre-prelim meeting, students would propose an area of study and an outline for the literature review. Once the outline was approved by the committee, students were expected to prepare the literature review without assistance. However, we discovered that, for many students, it was too much of a leap from the research papers that they were used to completing in their classes to completing "the" literature review without support from faculty. Thus, we took several steps to support students through that process. During their second semester, they are expected to enroll in our Trends in Instructional Technology course. In this course, they are exposed to current research in the field and begin to identify an area of interest. They also begin to review and synthesize research within an area of interest. In addition, we revise our preliminary examination to consist of a series of four "papers," much like the papers that they should have written in the past. However, when students have adequately focused their area of interest, they should be able to synthesize these four papers into a literature review with the support of their advisor. Granted, students are often required to conduct additional reviews of the literature once they have narrowed their research focus; likewise, they may also discard sections from the preliminary exam document if it no longer fits their focus.

Following their qualifying exam, current students are expected to begin reading in preparation for their "pre-prelim" planning meeting, in cooperation with their major professor. The intent of the pre-prelim planning meeting is to enter into a contractual relationship between the student and his or her examining committee. The outcome of the pre-prelim is a clear set of agreed upon expectations for the prelim exam. In their pre-prelim, students are expected to propose a general area of study. During an hour-long meeting with their examining committee, students make a brief proposal that outlines their area of research interest and topics in which they need additional information. Based on the presentation provided by the student, each member of the committee develops one question, the answer to which will move the students closer to a dissertation study. Typically, students assemble a four-member examining committee, which would result in four questions to which the student is expected to respond. The questions are designed to immerse students in the literature that faculty judge as necessary to fully understand the student's area of interest. Students have five months from the time in which they receive their prelim questions to the completion of the written portion of the prelim exam. Students are expected to complete the written portion of this exam without assistance. Upon completion, students deliver their written prelim exam to their committee two weeks prior to their oral preliminary exam.

The prelim exam is judged on a set of explicit criteria, presented to the student along with the exam questions. Written responses are judged on the adequacy with which the students presented the relevant literature and the quality of written expression. During the oral exam, students are required to make a brief presentation to the committee that summarizes their written responses. Students are further questioned on their responses and provided with a chance to elaborate on areas that are unclear. In the oral exam, students are judged on the quality of their presentation and oral expression.

After the successful completion of the preliminary exam, students are encouraged to work closely with their major professor to design a research study. Once the student and his or her advisor has agreed upon a study, the student schedules a pre-prospectus meeting with his or her advisory committee. In the pre-prospectus meeting, the student makes a brief oral presentation outlining his or her research methods. The intent of the pre-prospectus meeting is to reach agreement on the research methods prior to the preparation of the prospectus document and to assist students in planning the best possible research study. As in the pre-prelim planning meeting, the outcome of the pre-prospectus meeting is a contractual agreement between the student and his or her committee as to the content and focus of the prospectus. After this planning meeting, the student continues to work with his or her advisor to prepare a research proposal. Students receive further support and guidance in preparing their prospectus in their Research in Instructional Technology course. The focus of this course is on a review of research methods, as they are applied in the field of instructional design and technology, and the preparation of a research proposal. Once students have prepared a prospectus that meets the approval of their major professor, they must participate in an oral exam in which all committee members are present. Students are expected to provide faculty with their written prospectus two weeks prior to the oral exam. During the oral exam, students are expected to make a brief presentation of the proposed study. Faculty then question students on their proposed methods, as well as the conceptual and logistical details of the research plan. The prospectus is judged on the quality and completeness of the written prospectus, as well as the quality of the student's oral presentation and ability to respond to questioning.

Once the prospectus exam is completed successfully, students are free to conduct their research study. Students may consult committee members and faculty at any time during this process. Further, students are expected to work closely with his or her major professor to prepare an acceptable dissertation document. As is true in most programs, the student's academic career culminates in an oral defense of their dissertation document.

ProSem

At one time, the Professional Seminar was a highlight of the program. Students looked forward to the regular Friday afternoon gatherings, typically followed by a social outing. It was a time to reconnect with their peers and discuss topics that were not addressed in their coursework. Over time, this spirit had dissipated to the point that attendance in the sessions was light. Although 30 people might be enrolled in the pass/fail course, attendance at many sessions would drop to 5 or 6 people. Attempts by the ProSem leadership to require attendance were met resentfully. Students frequently negotiated for other experiences that might "count" as ProSem attendance. Attendance at the social gather that followed ProSem was almost nonexistent. Clearly, as faculty, we knew something was wrong.

At that point, ProSem was managed by senior students who had passed their preliminary examination. At the time this strategy was initiated, students viewed it as an honor to assume responsibility for ProSem. They looked at it as an opportunity to positively influence the culture of the program. However, in recent years the leadership of ProSem had suffered. Senior students increasingly looked at it as a burden.

At that time, students were expected to enroll in ProSem for their entire time in the doctoral program. Students typically enrolled for three years. As they progressed through the program, they moved from session participants to assume leadership for planning and conducting the ProSem sessions. Many times, the same topics were addressed each semester. Although the specific presentations varied, the general topics remained the same. Sessions typically focused on exam preparation, job searches, tours of campus facilities, and guest speakers. Senior students expressed general boredom with the topics. They frequently looked for guest speakers that would align with their personal research topic; more frequently, they simply looked for anyone who could fill a session.

In order to address concerns about the leadership responsibilities of the senior students, faculty assumed responsibility for ProSem in order to allow senior students to focus on the Instructional Technology Student Association (ITSA). Since our senior students were feeling overburdened with the needs of ITSA and ProSem, we looked at the chance to assume responsibility for ProSem as an opportunity to address many of the students' needs. We began by our developing expectations for ProSem.

ProSem expectations

The expressed purpose of ProSem is to develop a common culture within the IDT program area and to address topics that are not addressed in typical coursework. It is a forum in which students learn about the expectations of the doctoral program and the work world beyond the program. The intent is to establish a supportive community among all doctoral students and faculty.

Specific objectives include:

1. To develop skills needed to succeed in the program (doctoral exams, ethical behavior, leadership skills, writing skills, oral communication skills, etc.).

2. To develop skills needed to succeed in the profession (job search skills, professional ethics, networking, professional associations, grant writing, publishing, awareness of trends in fields, etc.).

3. To develop an awareness of the research conducted by peers, faculty, and others in the field.

Each week, ProSem begins with small group advisee meetings for the first half-hour of each session. During these meetings, students report their progress to their peers. During the remaining class time, we schedule sessions that include student and faculty conference presentations, encore exam presentations, and discussions around the theme of the semester.

Advisee groups

At the beginning of each ProSem, students break up into "advisee groups" where the students of each advisor meet together with the student's advisor. Students are asked to report on progress since the last meeting, outline goals for the next two weeks, and bring up any issues of concern. Students who are further along in the program provide advice for the new students on exam preparation, course selection, and other program related issues. Advisors have a chance to convey information to the entire group that may be of use to all of them. In this way, we encourage students to use each other as resources, while at the same time, faculty are present to prevent misconceptions that may arise when peers advise each other. In fact, when faculty are not present, students continue to meet, serving as peer mentors for each other. Students who are no longer required to attend ProSem are encouraged to attend the advisee group sessions in order to mentor newer students.

Encore exams

Students who successfully complete an oral exam are invited to make "encore exam" presentations in our Professional Seminar. This allows students to model a successful exam performance. ProSem students are further exposed to the research in the field and begin to develop their conceptions of the nature of a successful research project.

Conference presentations

Students who plan to present at a conference are required to practice their presentation during ProSem. Just as at a conference, students are expected to conform to time limitations. Students and faculty in attendance provide them with written feedback to improve their presentations. If necessary, faculty work with the students to revise their presentations prior to the conference. Students receive direct instruction on preparing conference proposals and presentations within our "Career preparation" strand in ProSem.

ProSem themes

Required enrollment in ProSem was reduced to only the first two years in the program. This reduced the responsibilities of the senior students, while at the same time allowing us to develop a two-year curriculum of topics and activities.

- *Career planning* Includes activities such as developing a five-year plan, job searches, presenting at conferences, and preparing a vita.

- *Professional ethics* Students explore issues of plagiarism, authorship, collaboration, attribution of credit, and ownership of knowledge using case studies.

- *Professional Writing* Includes practice in selecting a topic for publication, locating publication outlets, using models to develop scholarly articles, APA style, and small group writing critiques.

- *Faculty Research* Students are introduced to the research interests of the IDT faculty.

Using a rotating schedule whereby each topic is addressed once during a two-year period, we avoid the problem with repetition of topics, while at the same time, ensuring that all students would receive exposure to each topic. Essential topics such as exam preparation and conference presentations occur each semester, but rather than address them in didactic presentations, as had been done in the past, students develop skills in exam preparation and research skills through observation and questioning of successful models. Exam preparation and research skills are also discussed in the context of the informal advisee group sessions.

ProSem is a one credit-hour class that meets every other week for two-hours. Beginning the first week of class, ProSem meets eight times each semester. One session is devoted to introductions. During this session, students typically update each other on their progress through the program and their current employment status. As is typical in course, the course professor reviews the syllabus and course expectations. Students then break into extended advisee group sessions. The remaining of the semester consists of two sessions for encore exams and one session for practice conference presentations. This leaves four two-hour sessions each semester in which to address the semester theme.

Annual Reviews

In addition to our new courses, cohort-based admissions approach, revised doctoral exam procedures, and Professional Seminar changes, we also instituted an annual review process for our students. Modeled after the annual review process that is often required of faculty, the annual review process was designed to prepare students to consider their performance in light of the criteria used to hire and promote university faculty. Students are required to prepare a self-evaluation report that includes documentation of (a) academic progress, (b) research and scholarship activities (such as research progress, presentations, publications, grant activity, etc.), (c) teaching related activities (such as classes taught, workshops led, courses developed, course grading, workshops attended to improve teaching skills, etc.), and (d) service and outreach activities such as assistantship status and performance and professional service to fellow students, the program, school or university, and the profession. Students are also expected to provide a list of goals for the coming academic year.

The IT program area faculty meet as a graduate advisory committee once each spring semester to conduct an annual review of each graduate student. This review enables the faculty and the student to determine if appropriate progress is being made toward successful program completion and to determine potential areas for improvement/advancement. During the spring meeting, the faculty consider a variety of performance indicators including a student's self-evaluation of progress as well as observations of course, exam, and assistantship performance. Students are judged according to the following scale: (1) fails to meet expectations, (2) meets expectations, or (3) exceeds expectations, in each of the four aforementioned areas. After the faculty review meeting, students are informed of the outcomes of the review as well as advised of recommended next steps.

Addressing Student Needs

The previously described changes reflect our attempt to design and implement a comprehensive plan for the effective preparation of our graduates, particularly from an academic perspective. Above all, however, we wanted to enhance students' experiences in the program. We wanted to focus on community-building, clarifying exam expectations, and exposing our students to model research projects, while addressing professional development topics of importance that are not addressed in their other coursework. These changes reflect the needs specifically articulated by students and we felt it was imperative for both academic and motivational reasons to address these needs.

In order to address concerns about building community, we moved ProSem to Friday mornings to make it easier for those who want to leave town to attend. We moved the social event following ProSem from a local restaurant to a lunchtime gathering at a campus food court in order to be easily accessible and affordable. In order to address needs for mentoring, we established opportunities to make it easier for new students to connect with other students and faculty. We initiated beginning-of-semester social gatherings to supplement our traditional end-of-semester party. Faculty and students were encouraged to go to lunch together following ProSem. Other ProSem activities such as advisee group sessions and encore exam presentations further supported the mentoring of new students. In order to address our students' needs for more contact with their advisors, we formalized "advisee group sessions" within our ProSem structure.

We have addressed student's need to become aware of exam expectations through several means. Students observe a successful exam performance during the "encore exam" presentations in our Professional Seminar. In addition, the question and answer session often includes advice on exam preparation and organization. Further, discussions during the advisee group sessions often focus on advices on exam preparation and clarification of exam expectations. And finally, we have developed documents, readily available on our Web site, that describe our exam expectations and evaluation criteria.

In order to address student's needs for more involvement in program area research projects, we schedule one semester in which faculty present their research within ProSem and students are invited to join various projects. In addition, we further expose students to program area research through "encore exam" presentations and practice conference presentations.

EVALUATION

Two years have passed since the initial intervention was implemented. Formative evaluation data was collected upon the end of the first year through analysis of student performance on exams, as well as a survey of students to collect their feedback on program revisions. Regarding student performance, the added structure within the preliminary exam, along with the additional foundational coursework has made a positive impact on students' ability to successfully complete the preliminary examination. Student survey feedback also indicates that the changes made to ProSem (the addition of encore exams and the advisee group meetings), as well as the extensive program Web site re-design have helped address the lack of awareness about program-related procedures and expectations regarding doctoral exams. Specific supporting comments from the survey reflect this outcome, including, "I now understand the requirements of the program from the Professional

Seminar, the IDT Web site, and my advisor. Now I know what I should do to fulfill the requirements of the program," and "especially helpful have been our classmates' sharing of their exam experiences through encore presentations and friendly advice during advisee meetings."

Student feedback from the survey also indicated the effectiveness of the strategies employed to rebuild the sense of community within the IDT program. One student stated, "I feel very connected to the IDT community now. Especially the advisory groups helped me a lot to keep in touch with my peers. I really like the way the ProSem course has been presented. It was more collaborative than the previous one." Another student echoed this sentiment, stating that "[t]he ProSem has been enormously helpful in creating a sense of community, not only among the students, or between the students and faculty (although these are genuinely important and beneficial), but with the community of IDT professionals in the field. Classmates sharing with each other and faculty sharing their professional experiences and anecdotes have made the greatest contribution in this area."

Current evaluation efforts are focusing on the effectiveness of other aspects of our intervention, such as the cohort-based admissions process and the annual reviews. Anecdotal feedback suggests that students are leveraging the cohort approach to prepare for the qualifying exam together, which reflects our intended outcome of increasing community and collegiality among students.

Working through the process of program revision guided by an HPT framework took a great deal of effort on the part of the IDT faculty team, but the positive outcomes indicate that the effort was worthwhile. The systematic, data-driven nature of the process fit well within our IDT perspective. For other academic programs in our field looking to resolve challenges (instructional or not), our successful utilization of the HPT approach to performance improvement within our graduate program reflects the efficacy of this model for such purposes.

REFERENCES

Association for Educational Communications and Technology. (2000). *Standards for the accreditation of school media specialist and educational technology specialist programs.* Bloomington, IN: AECT. Available at http://www.aect.org

Dick, W., & Wager, W. (1995). Preparing performance technologists: The role of the university. *Performance Improvement Quarterly, 8*(4), 34–42.

Gilbert, T. (2007). *Human competence: Engineering worthy performance.* New York: McGraw-Hill.

Larson, M., & Lockee, B. (2004). Instructional design practice: Career environments, job roles, and a climate of change. *Performance Improvement Quarterly, 17*(1), 22–40.

Larson, M. (2005). Instructional design career environments: Survey of the alignment of preparation and practice. *TechTrends, 49*(6), 22–33.

Rosenberg, M. J. (1990). Performance technology: Working the system. *Training, 27*(2), 42–48.

Rossett, A. (1999). Analysis for human performance technology. In H. D. Stolovich & E. J. Keeps (Eds.), *Handbook of human performance technology* (pp. 139–162). San Francisco, CA: Pfeiffer.

Rummler, G. A., & Brache, A. P. (1995). *Improving performance: How to manage the white space on the organization chart,* 2nd ed. San Francisco, CA: Jossey Bass.

Skinner, B. F. (1954). The science of learning and the art of teaching. *Harvard Educational Review, 24,* 99–113.

Stolovich, H. D., & Keeps, E. J. (1999). What is human performance technology? In H. D. Stolovich & E. J. Keeps (Eds.), *Handbook of human performance technology* (pp. 3–23). San Francisco, CA: Pfeiffer.

Van Tiem, D., Moseley, J., & Dessinger, J. (2004). *Fundamentals of performance technology: A guide to improving people, process, and performance*, 2nd ed. Washington, DC: International Society for Performance Improvement.

Competencies for Instructors: A Validation Study

James D. Klein
Arizona State University

Barbara Grabowski
Pennsylvania State University

J. Michael Spector
Florida State University

Ileana de la Teja
Tele-universite, Universite du Quebec a Montreal

COMPETENCIES FOR INSTRUCTORS: A VALIDATION STUDY

The International Board of Standards for Training, Performance and Instruction (ibstpi) is dedicated to advancing the capability of individuals and organizations in the training, instruction, and performance improvement professions through the development of competency-based standards. The board consists of fifteen professionals elected to broadly represent academia, businesses, consultancies, and government agencies throughout the world. Currently, directors are from Asia, Australia, Europe, and North America (see http://www.ibstpi.org for more information about the board's mission and its directors).

Over the past 20 years, ibstpi has developed competencies for instructors (Hutchison, Shepherd, & Stein, 1988; Klein, Spector, Grabowski, & De la Teja, 2004), instructional designers (ibstpi, 1986; Richey, Fields, & Foxon, 2001), training managers (ibstpi, 1989; Foxon, Richey, Roberts, & Spannaus, 2003) and evaluators (Russ-Eft, Bober, De la Teja, Foxon, & Koszalka, in press). Ibstpi regards a competency as a set of related skills, knowledge and attitudes that enable an individual to adequately perform a task or fulfill a job function. Competency statements are intended to reflect requisite knowledge, skills, and attitudes. These competency statements are individually elaborated in terms of specific performance statements that indicate observable means of determining whether or not an individual has the indicated competency. The entire set of competencies and supporting performance statements for a job function or position comprises the standards for that position.

The construction of a valid set of competency standards is based on a large-scale research and development process. With respect to the ibstpi standards, each recent project entailed rigorous work by a team of researchers, involvement of the entire board, and input of practitioners and academics representing organizations worldwide (see Klein & Richey, 2005, for a description of ibstpi's approach to competency development and validation).

In this article, we focus on the development and validation of a set of competencies for instructors in face-to-face and online settings. We begin with a brief history of the instructor competencies developed by ibstpi since 1988. This is followed by a discussion of the results of a validation study that offers empirical evidence regarding the usefulness, criticality, and appropriateness of the ibstpi competencies for instructors in various settings.

INSTRUCTOR COMPETENCIES: A BRIEF HISTORY

In 1988, ibstpi published its first set of instructor competencies (see Hutchison, Shepherd, & Stein, 1988). These standards were identified via extensive review and testing by a group of practitioners and academics in the training and instructional design field. The competencies focused on the contemporary view of an instructor's role (e.g., working with students by delivering lectures, giving demonstrations, facilitating discussions, and administering tests and assessments). When the 1988 ibstpi competencies were developed, instructors mainly worked with learners who were located in the same place, learning at the same time. Thus, the original instructor competencies addressed the standards for trainers in face-to-face classroom settings.

During the last two decades, more emphasis on the active role of learners and the use of technology for teaching and learning have changed how we view what competent instructors know and do. A learner-centered perspective reminds us that students bring knowledge, experiences, personal meaning and perspectives to learning that can benefit everyone in the setting. Furthermore, while much instruction still takes place in classrooms, online learning and other computer mediated methods have become commonplace in schools, higher education, and training settings. Because these trends have changed our expectations of teaching and learning, ibstpi has updated its set of competencies to reflect how instructors in face-to-face, online, and blended settings plan, implement, manage, and assess teaching and learning. Below, we discuss how these updated competencies were identified and validated.

IDENTIFYING COMPETENCIES FOR INSTRUCTORS

The original set of instructor standards published by ibstpi included 14 competencies that focused on instruction as it relates to preparation, delivery, evaluation, and follow-up in face-to-face settings. At the time of their development, the statements were based on ibstpi's understanding of the decisions, actions, and behaviors that competent instructors must demonstrate. While current knowledge about learning and technology has advanced in recent years, some fundamental tenets of instruction have not changed. These views are reflected in the updated instructor competencies.

In addition to the previous competencies developed by ibstpi, the updated instructor standards were influenced by theory, research, and practice related to teaching and learning. Over 200 theoretical, conceptual, and empirical studies found in books, journal articles, and conference proceedings were examined to provide a foundation for the updated instructor competencies (see Ganesan, 2004; Klein, et al., 2004; Spector & De la Teja, 2001). Furthermore, materials from several train-the-trainer courses used in corporate and educational settings were reviewed to examine current practice. Instructor and facilitator guides, as well as participant materials were obtained and reviewed from the following areas: banking, financial services, a for-profit online university, manufacturing, and pharmaceuticals.

The ibstpi board also cohosted a meeting of experts in the distance education field (see Goodyear et al., 2001) and served as an expert panel to identify instructor competencies. Members of ibstpi also conducted six focus groups with individuals from business, academia, and professional organizations to obtain further input on the competencies identified by the board.

These strategies led to the identification of updated competency statement applicable for instructors in both face-to-face and online settings. Table 1 shows how these updated instructor competencies compare with the original ibstpi standards. Six competency statements that were not in the original list are now in the updated standards. Another six statements from the earlier set were expanded to reflect the changing roles of instructors and the use of technology for teaching and learning. Four other competencies were worded differently to update terminology and two competencies in the updated list were stated exactly as they were in the original list. Furthermore, a competency from the earlier set—*Use instructional methods appropriately*—was elevated to include eight competency statements related to the use of instructional methods and strategies to promote learning and performance.

Table 1. A Comparison of Updated and Original Ibstpi Instructor Competency Statements*

Updated Competencies	Original Competencies	Changes to Competencies
Communicate effectively	Demonstrate effective communication skills	Minor change
Update and improve one's professional knowledge and skills	—	New competency
Comply with established ethical and legal standards	—	New competency
Establish and maintain professional credibility	Establish and maintain instructor credibility	No change
Plan instructional methods and materials	Analyze course materials and learner information	Expanded concept
Prepare for instruction	Assure preparation of the instructional site	Expanded concept
Stimulate and sustain learner motivation and engagement	Provide positive reinforcements and motivational incentives	Expanded concept
Demonstrate effective presentation skills	Demonstrate effective presentation skills	No change
Demonstrate effective facilitation skills	—	New competency
Demonstrate effective questioning skills	Demonstrate effective questioning skills and technique	Minor change
Provide clarification and feedback	Respond appropriately to learners' needs for clarification or feedback	Minor change
Promote retention of knowledge and skills	—	New competency
Promote transfer of knowledge and skills	—	New competency
Use media and technology to enhance learning and performance	Use media effectively	Expanded concept
Assess learning and performance	Evaluate learner performance	Minor change
Evaluate instructional effectiveness	Evaluate delivery of instruction	Expanded concept
	Report evaluation information	
Manage an environment that fosters learning and performance	Manage the learning environment	Expanded concept
Manage the instructional process through the appropriate use of technology	—	New competency

*The ibstpi instructor competencies are copyrighted by the International Board of Standards for Training, Performance & Instruction and used with permission. All rights reserved.

WORLDWIDE VALIDATION STUDY

Purpose and Scope

A worldwide validation study was conducted to gather empirical evidence about the set of updated competency statements approved by ibstpi. The purpose of the study was to determine the level of criticality of the competencies in the initial list for instructors in face-to-face and online settings and to gather comments on each. Another purpose was to refine the language used in the competency statements to reflect an international audience in diverse settings and to insure that no critical area of work had been overlooked.

By asking respondents with experience in either face-to-face or online instruction to rate the criticality of the competencies for that setting, we were able to test the assumption drawn by the board that there was a basic set of competencies for instructors that did not differ by instructional setting. Therefore, we believed that differences in perceived criticality between face-to-face and online instructor competencies would be minimal.

Procedures and Instrumentation

A validation instrument was developed and made available via the Internet and on paper. Respondents were recruited and data were collected over a three-month period. Data were summarized by face-to-face and online setting and were used by ibstpi to develop a final list of competency statements.

The validation instrument was created, pilot tested, and refined. The pilot instrument included demographic questions and criticality statements. Twenty-seven responses were collected during the pilot test. The length of the instrument was found to be problematic for many online respondents. To address this problem, the instrument was clustered into four separate parts so that the respondents would submit the survey when each part was completed. The final instrument consisted of a section with respondent background characteristics and three competency sections, along with a scale to indicate the criticality of specific statements and enter additional comments about the statements or the survey as a whole. While the primary means for distribution of the survey was in a Web-based form, a paper-based version was also available. By far, most responses came via the Internet—the ratio was about 35 Internet responses for every paper-based response.

Eighteen demographic questions were asked to collect extensive background data on the respondents to establish a rationale for the level of generalizability of data. We sought data on the respondents in three general areas: Personal profile (including gender, age, educational background, and field of expertise); Experiential profile (including number of years of experience in face-to-face, blended and online settings, perceived level of instructor and technology expertise, experience as an online student, frequency of computer use, and experience developing a Web page); and Job profile (including geographic location of job, type of organizational setting, focus of the job, percentage of time devoted to instruction or training, and major language used on the job).

Respondents were asked to rate the level of criticality of the competencies for instructors in face-to-face and online settings. A scale of 1 to 5 was used, with 5 being very highly critical to their job, and 1 having no criticality to their job. Individuals were asked to rate the criticality of competency statements in a particular setting only if they had teaching experience in that setting. A section for comments was also included. Four open-ended questions were asked regarding any additional skills, suggestions for rewording, comments comparing online versus classroom teaching, and any general comments.

Following approved University Human Subjects Institutional Review Board procedures, the ibstpi research team sent requests for participation in the validation study to training institutions, professional organizations, professional electronic mailing lists, conference participants and other worldwide contacts in training, teaching, and distance education. These sources were identified through extensive Internet searches and board member contacts. Trainers and instructors were contacted via e-mail, phone, and newsletter announcements. The URL containing the Informed Consent and a link to the valida-tion instrument and the address to acquire a paper-based version was provided in each communiqué. The paper-based version of the survey was mailed to any individual who requested it. In addition, a link to the instrument was included on the ibstpi Web site. The instrument, therefore, was available to anyone visiting the site on his or her own accord. Since the sample was not selected on a random basis, the profile data cannot be assumed to be representative of the entire population of instructors or trainers. The intent was to solicit responses from experienced instructors and trainers worldwide.

Participants

A large, diverse sample ($N = 1327$) responded to the request to participate in the validation study. Not every respondent, however, answered every question. Percentages represent the proportion of those who responded to each individual question. These are summarized by the three profiles of personal, experiential, and occupational.

Respondent personal profile

More than half (55.3%) of respondents were male (613 of 1109) while 44.7% were female (496 of 1109). The average age of respondents was 41.1 years old, ranging from age 20 to 70. The majority was between 30 and 49 years old. Many respondents had either a master's degree (24.5%, 271 of 1107) or an undergraduate degree (22.6%; 250 of 1107). Respondents came from diverse fields of expertise. The majority considered themselves experts in Training and Development (57%, 625 of 1097), Adult Education (47.3%, 519 of 1097), or Education (39.1%, 429 of 1097).

Respondent experiential profile

Almost all of the respondents had experience as an instructor or trainer in face-to-face settings (98.8%, 1089 of 1102, $M = 10.9$ years). Less than half had experience teaching in online (40.9%, 452 of 1105, $M = 3.5$ years) or blended settings (39.8%, 433 of 1087, $M = 3.2$ years). Because there were high numbers of respondents with online and blended experience, we were able to compare their responses credibly with those having only face-to-face experience. A large percentage of respondents (87.9%) rated their expertise as an instructor or trainer as either high or very high (975 of 1110). Expertise with technology to support learning was also rated high or very high (74.5%, 826 of 1109). Three-fourths (75.1%) of the respondents (832 of 1108) had created a Web page, and 68.9% (759 of 1101) had experience as a student in an online course. Finally, 72.7% (806 of 1109) indicated that they use the computer and information technologies often or very often.

Respondent job profile

Most respondents (73%; 808 of 1107) listed instructor or trainer as their job focus. Others noted classroom teacher as their focus (37.4%; 414 of 1107). Design, development, facilitation, and management were each listed by at least one fourth of the respondents. In addition, many respondents (58.1%; 633 of 1089) devote at least half of their time on the job to instruction or training. Many respondents work in educational settings (60.7%; 677 of 1115) followed by high-tech organizations (23%; 257 of 1115). Furthermore, most respondents were from North America (75.5%; 836 of 1107) followed by Western Europe (9.8%; 108 of 1107). The low number of participants from other geographic locations was

Table 2. Summary of Revisions to the Updated Instructor Competency Statements

Initial Competency Statement	Final Decision about Statement
Communicate effectively	Retained
Update and improve one's professional knowledge and skills.	Retained
Establish and maintain professional credibility	Retained
Comply with established ethical and legal standards	Retained
Prepare for instruction	Retained
Adapt instructional methods and materials	Revised to—Plan instructional methods and materials
Organize the learning environment	Deleted
Recognize and accommodate learner diversity*	Included in performance statement
Stimulate learner motivation and engagement	Revised to—Stimulate and sustain learner motivation and engagement
Demonstrate effective presentation skills	Retained
Demonstrate effective facilitation skills	Retained
Demonstrate effective questioning skills	Retained
Provide clarification and feedback	Retained
Promote retention of knowledge and skills	Retained
Promote transfer of knowledge and skills	Retained
Use media and technology to enhance learning and performance*	Retained
Assess learning and performance	Retained
Evaluate instructional effectiveness	Retained
Document and report evaluation data*	Included in performance statement
Manage the learning environment	Revised to—Manage a learning environment that fosters learning and performance
Use technology to manage information, learning and performance*	Revised to—Manage the instructional process through appropriate use of technology

*Competency statement rated less than 4.0 by respondents.

counterbalanced by international representation on the ibstpi board when data from the validation study were analyzed and the competency statements were refined.

Findings from the Validation Study

Data obtained from the individuals who participated in the validation study were used to establish the usefulness and appropriateness of the competencies for instructors in face-to-face and online settings. Open-ended comments made by the respondents were also used to revise statements for meaning and clarity. Using the criticality data and the open-ended comments, ibstpi analyzed, debated, and acted upon each statement in one of three ways: (a) retain as stated, (b) revise, or (c) delete. Using this process, an initial set of 21 competencies was refined to include 18 competency statements. Table 2 shows the comparison between the initial competencies and improvements made as a result of the validation study.

Table 3 provides the average criticality ratings for the competencies. In nearly all cases, the final list of competencies included statements that received a rating of 4.0 or above on a 5-point scale for both face-to-face and online settings. Competencies related to Professional Foundations were among the most highly rated of all statements. For statements related to Planning and Preparation, one competency remained unchanged, one was reworded for clarity, and one was deleted. These decisions were based on open-ended comments made by respondents and the board's belief that the initial statements provided support for other competencies. One competency related to Instructional Methods and Strategies—*Recognize and accommodate learner diversity*—was deleted. This statement was the only one rated below 4.0 by instructors with experience in both face-to-face and online settings. Even though it was not included in the final list of competencies, the board decided the concept was important and retained for use a performance statement to further explain the actions required of a competent instructor. Another competency—*Use media and technology to enhance learning and performance*—was retained despite a lower rating for face-to-face settings (3.96). The rating for online settings was high (4.54) and the board concluded this competency was critical for all instructors, especially when the future vision of an instructor is considered.

Turning to Assessment and Evaluation, two of the three competencies were retained. The third competency—*Document and report evaluation data*—was rated at 3.93 for face-to-face settings and 4.04 for online settings. Furthermore, open-ended comments suggested that many instructors who completed the validation survey are not responsible for these tasks. While the competency was deleted, the board felt the idea was important and decided to include it as a performance statement to support the competency—*Evaluate instructional effectiveness*. Both competencies related to Management were revised for clarity and meaning. One was reworded to link the concept of management to learning and performance in instructional settings. The other competency—*Use technology to manage information, learning and performance*—was reworded to be—*Manage the instructional process through the appropriate use of technology*. The ibstpi board defines technology broadly and changed the emphasis in this competency by moving management to the first part of the statement.

Discussion

The results of the validation study provide empirical evidence that the instructor competencies identified and validated by ibstpi apply to a wide range of settings. The competency—*Communicate effectively*—was ranked the highest by respondents with experience in both face-to-face and online settings (4.71 and 4.64, respectively). The most compelling evidence to support our conclusion comes from comparing the difference between means, and the ranking of the criticality ratings by setting. In the first case, 15 of the initial 21 competencies were within 0 to 0.1 points. Three were within 0.11 to 0.16 points. Of those, two were deleted from the final list, and for the third, both ratings were above 4.0.

A few differences were observed between face-to-face and online instructors. For example, the lowest ranked competency for the face-to-face setting was—*Use technology to manage information, learning and performance*. This statement was rated 0.70 points higher for the online setting. In addition, the competency—*Use media and technology to enhance learning and performance*—was rated 0.58 points higher for the online setting. These results suggest differences in the way instructors in face-to-face and online settings perceive the integral nature of technology and the specifics about how it is used differently depending on setting.

One other difference is worth noting. The criticality rating for statement—*Demonstrate effective presentation skills*—was 0.47 points higher for the face-to-face setting. While both groups rated it above 4.0, this is another example of the difference in

Table 3. Criticality of Ibstpi Instructor Competencies in Face-to-Face and Online Settings

Competency Statement	Face-to-Face Setting				Online Setting			
	Average Rating	SD	N	Rank	Average Rating	SD	N	Rank
Communicate effectively	4.71	0.58	822	1	4.64	0.72	330	1
Update and improve ones professional knowledge and skills	4.49	0.74	803	3/4	4.59	0.65	320	2
Establish and maintain professional credibility	4.36	0.86	797	8	4.32	0.89	314	11
Comply with established ethical and legal standards	4.45	0.81	787	5	4.51	0.77	314	6
Prepare for instruction	4.61	0.64	787	2	4.57	0.75	313	3
Adapt instructional methods and materials	4.16	0.82	778	15	4.24	0.88	307	16
Organize the learning environment	4.12	0.85	775	16/17	4.28	0.95	302	13
Recognize and accommodate learner diversity	3.96	0.91	616	18/19	3.92	0.94	237	21
Stimulate learner motivation and engagement	4.38	0.72	602	7	4.38	0.81	231	8/9
Demonstrate effective presentation skills	4.49	0.70	600	3/4	4.02	1.01	229	20
Demonstrate effective facilitation skills	4.23	0.84	583	13	4.19	1.04	220	17
Demonstrate effective questioning skills	4.28	0.77	586	11	4.25	0.89	224	15
Provide clarification and feedback	4.43	0.67	582	6	4.52	0.74	221	5
Promote retention of knowledge and skills	4.35	0.77	577	9	4.37	0.83	214	10
Promote transfer of knowledge and skills	4.30	0.82	571	10	4.38	0.81	214	8/9
Use media and technology to enhance learning and performance	3.96	0.95	574	18/19	4.54	0.68	213	4
Assess learning and performance	4.12	0.94	555	16/17	4.27	0.87	205	14
Evaluate instructional effectiveness	4.25	0.85	548	12	4.29	0.88	204	12
Document and report evaluation data	3.93	1.05	540	20	4.04	1.03	200	19
Manage the learning environment	4.19	0.87	535	14	4.16	1.00	197	18
Use technology to manage information, learning and performance	3.76	1.02	539	21	4.46	0.79	200	7

execution of the skills by setting, however, retaining the importance generally for both settings. Despite these few differences, ibstpi maintains the position that a core set of competencies exists for instructors in all settings.

CONCLUSION

The mission of ibstpi is to improve individual and organizational learning and performance and, in doing so, promote the quality and integrity of professional practice. Consistent with this mission, the ibstpi competencies for instructors reflect a continuing commitment to improve professional practice. While the standards developed by ibstpi have stood the test of time for two decades, it is likely that additional updates will be required in the future to keep pace with rapid changes in the Instructional Design and Technology field.

REFERENCES

Foxon, M., Richey, R.C., Roberts, R., & Spannaus, T. (2003). *Training manager competencies: The standards* (2nd ed.). Syracuse, NY: ERIC Clearinghouse on Information and Technology.

Ganesan, R. (2004). Perceptions and practices of expert teachers in technology-based distance and distributed learning environments. Unpublished dissertation, Syracuse University, Syracuse.

Goodyear, P., Salmon, G., Spector, J. M., Steeples, C., & Tickner, S. (2001). Competences for online teaching: A special report. *Educational Technology Research & Development, 49*(1), 65–72.

Hutchison, C., Shepherd, J., & Stein, F. (1988). *Instructor competencies: The standards*, Vol. I. Chicago: International Board of Standards for Training, Performance and Instruction.

International Board of Standards for Training, Performance and Instruction. (1986). *Instructional design competencies: The standards.* Batavia, IL: ibstpi

———. (1989). *Training manager competencies: The standards.* Batavia, IL: ibstpi

Klein, J. D., & Richey, R. C. (2005). Improving individual and organizational performance: The case for international standards. *Performance Improvement, 44*(10), 9–14.

Klein, J. D., Spector, J. M., Grabowski, B., & De la Teja, I. (2004). *Instructor competencies: Standards for face-to-face, online, and blended settings.* Greenwich, CT: Information Age Publishing.

Richey, R. C., Fields, D. F., & Foxon, M. (with Roberts, R. C., Spannaus, T., & Spector, J. M.). (2001). *Instructional design competencies: The standards* (3rd ed.). Syracuse, NY: ERIC Clearinghouse on Information and Technology.

Russ-Eft, D., Bober, M., De la Teja, I., Foxon, M., & Koszalka, T. (in press). *Evaluator competencies: The internationally validated standards.* San Francisco: Jossey-Bass.

Spector, J. M., & De la Teja, I. (2001, December). *Competencies for online teaching.* ERIC Digest EDO-IR-2001-09. Syracuse, NY: ERIC Information Technology Clearinghouse. Available at http://www.ericit.org/digests/EDO-IR-2001-09.shtml

Predicting Education System Outcomes: A Scientific Approach

Theodore W. Frick
Indiana University Bloomington

Kenneth R. Thompson
System-Predictive Technologies Columbus, Ohio

OVERVIEW

Many well-intentioned people want to improve education. So do we. We believe that education could be far more effective, efficient, and satisfying than it is in our current educational systems—both K-12 and higher education.

Educators who have taught for a while have seen several widely talked about changes come and go. For example, some of the innovations have been referred to as: site-based management, constructivist classrooms, technology integration, school restructuring, and yes, even systemic change. Educators have correctly observed that not much has really changed from what they can see. They view new calls for change with a certain detachment and skepticism. We find these attitudes understandable, given the history of numerous innovations that have largely failed to make significant improvements in education. Many think: "Just another buzzword. Just another fad. Ho hum."

Why? We believe that the following questions have not been adequately addressed:

- Change what?

- Change how? and

- How do you know the change is working?

We must know *what* to change in order to know *how*. We must know whether the change accomplishes the goal and that the change does not have negative, unintended effects. Change for the sake of change is nonproductive. And, without knowing what to change, the "how" is irrelevant.

As an analogy, consider an old bridge that is failing—it is structurally weak and is impeding the flow of traffic. If the bridge is not fixed, it will collapse and vehicles will plunge into the river. When engineers design a new bridge, they utilize adequate scientific theories. No one in modern times would consider designing a new bridge by trial and error.

Up until the present, we have had no *valid* way of predicting that new educational system designs will work any better than what we now have. We have had no valid way of describing the elements of any educational system or of evaluating the effects of change throughout the system. New designs and curricula have been patches—much like fixing rust spots on an old car with body filler and paint, putting on new seat covers, or getting new tires. The overall structure remains unchanged.

Many researchers have focused on the change *process*. We believe it is equally important to focus on the outcomes of change—that is, how well the new system is

We want to acknowledge two people who helped with preparation of this chapter. Joyce Koh, a doctoral student in Instructional Systems Technology at Indiana University, was instrumental in creating Figures 1–8. They are even more interesting when animated in PowerPoint, as she created them originally for making conference and class presentations. Kathleen Brophy Frick, a lifetime teacher of young children up through adults, served as an editor who helped us write in a language that is less technical. She made us see gaps that needed to be filled for explaining our ideas more clearly.

predicted to work and how well it does work. We need both approaches—process and outcomes: they are complementary. The change process could be effective, *but* the resulting new system may not have the desired outcomes. The new system may be effective, *but* the change process may leave staff and families, teachers and students bitter and exhausted. For best results, both processes and outcomes must be satisfactory. This has not been predictable.

We are working squarely on the problem of predicting education system outcomes. The predictions must be based on scientific theory, its implications, and data to support the theory. If the predictions are not based on scientific theory, then how can we justify expending great effort and resources, only to end up with something that is no better—or possibly even worse—than what we now have? It is no wonder that educational practitioners often distrust, resist, and undermine the efforts of educational reformers. The stakes are very high. The consequences of mistakes can be devastating—particularly when changing a whole system of education.

Understanding systemic change is not a simple matter. Educators will need to learn new thinking patterns. Hart (1993) has noted that the vast majority of individual belief patterns do not contain dynamic cycles. Cognitive maps of belief structures tend to be linear with few, if any, feedback loops. Hart indicated that exceptions occurred with those people in professions that taught them to think in dynamic cycles (e.g., ecologists, systems engineers). Similarly, Senge (1990) has provided insight into business organizations by identification of archetypal patterns of *dynamic* cycles. These patterns are not easily described or understood through static print and diagrams. To address this problem of understanding, Senge and his colleagues have developed role-playing activities and computer simulations in order to help business people understand these patterns of dynamic relationships—some of which run counter to individual intuitions about how systems such as business organizations grow and change.

For these reasons, we believe that it will be very helpful to educators, if they can use computer software that will help them to design new educational systems. The software must be usable, flexible, portable, and user friendly. If the computer programs are not user friendly, then the change process will not be adopted by busy education professionals. The products we are developing must be rigorous and usable, generalizable and adaptable.

SimEd TECHNOLOGIES

SimEd Technologies consist of four parts:

1. The "Get Ready, SET, Go!" change model,

2. The theory model options set called Axiomatic Theories of Intentional Systems (*ATIS*),

3. Computer software: Analysis of Patterns in Time and Configuration (*APT&C*), and

4. Computer software: Predicting Education System Outcomes (*PESO*).

Designed to work together, SimEd Technologies use computer technology to help describe educational systems, predict system changes, and document the outcomes of change.

We will describe the Get Ready, SET, Go! model to predict educational system outcomes to guide the change process. This inquiry-based change model will utilize adequate theory and computer programs that are currently under development. Then we will go into a more detailed discussion of other parts of the SimEd Technologies. The model is outlined below.

Get Ready, SET, Go!

- **Phase 1: Get Ready**

  - Identify the specific current education system to be improved.

  - Over some interval of time, measure system properties using our computer software *ATP&C* (more below).

  - Predict outcomes under existing conditions *if nothing is changed in the system* using our computer modeling tool *PESO* (more below).

  - If these outcomes are what are wanted, then do not modify the system. However, if the outcomes are not desired, then the system must be changed so that the desired outcomes can be obtained. If change is desired, proceed to Phase 2.

- **Phase 2: SET**

  - Use *PESO* software to model newly envisioned educational system designs, the desired feasible changes.

  - Run *PESO* predictions out far enough in time to make sure all the consequences of the newly designed system would be acceptable. This iterative process will determine the outcomes of the system under the conditions defined by the changes. Are these the wanted outcomes? If yes, proceed to Phase 3.

- **Phase 3: Go!**

  - Implement the new design chosen in Phase 2 in the education system.

  - After the new education system has been established, then over some interval of time, measure system properties with *APT&C* software.

  - Verify that the measures confirm the predicted system outcomes. If not, then analyze both the Phase-2 and Phase-3 processes to determine what modifications are required.

PESO Simulation

We are building a software simulation called *PESO: Predicting Education System Outcomes*. *PESO* will model system concepts and allow educators to focus on the predictions. *PESO* is a logic-based simulation.

The most familiar simulations are scenario-based programs that provide "scripts" to determine outcomes. A familiar example is SimCity (see http://simcity.ea.com/). Scripts for simulations can be narrative or quantitative. Narrative scripts characterize the qualitative parameters of a system—that is, the social, philosophical, and individual descriptions and the uncertainty of future outcomes. Quantitative scripts define the scientific facts, known or credible data, and quantitative models that are used to determine future outcomes. However, in both narrative and quantitative scripts the content is closed. There are a limited number of possible outcomes, and the scripts predetermine the outcomes.

If the script lacks fidelity, then users may learn the wrong things. For example, consider what might happen *if* modern flight simulators that are used to train military and commercial pilots lacked fidelity. A pilot in the simulator might discover, when encountering something called "wind shear" while trying to land the plane on the runway, that if she or he pulls hard on the yoke, this would keep the plane from crashing in the simulator. However, in reality such an action will not work and the real plane would crash. There would be devastating consequences for making the wrong decision. The better course of action is to not attempt to land the plane under such conditions, and wait until the storm passes. Thus, a simulation script that lacks fidelity could be misleading and dangerous.

Friedman (1999) recognizes these kinds of problems with scenario-based models in his report, "The Semiotics of SimCity," when he states:

> Of course, however much "freedom" computer game designers grant players, any simulation will be rooted in a set of baseline assumptions. SimCity has been criticized from both the left and right for its economic model. It assumes that low taxes will encourage growth while high taxes will hasten recessions. It discourages nuclear power, while rewarding investment in mass transit. And most fundamentally, it rests on the empiricist, technophilic fantasy that the complex dynamics of city development can be abstracted, quantified, simulated, and micromanaged. (np)

On the other hand, *logic-based* models depend on the logic of a theory that has been shown to be valid for the targeted empirical system, in this case, an education system. The theory describes the empirical system in terms of its affect relations, properties, and axioms. The theory is then used to project outcomes founded on the theory with respect to input parameters. The instantiated axioms would generate a set of outcomes, which become input parameters that instantiate yet more axioms. Unlike scenario-based models that are closed due to the limited number of scripts, logic-based models potentially have an infinite number of outcomes. Such models are more flexible.

PESO is a logic-based software tool that makes predictions for a specific educational system, based on current conditions. One must first observe properties of that system and determine how the values of those system properties change over some time period. Properties may increase, decrease, remain constant, or increase to some value then decrease. When those changes in system property values are entered into *PESO*, the software finds relevant axioms and theorems that match those conditions, and then executes the logic of Axiomatic Theories of Intentional Systems (*ATIS*: Thompson, 2005). *PESO* effectively applies relevant parts of the theory in order to make predictions of what will happen in the system.

Significant progress has been made on *PESO* software. The current prototype is built in Flash using a programming language called ActionScript. Each of the axioms, antecedents, consequents, properties, and property attributes are treated as "objects." What this technical capacity of software means is that the software can be easily extended and modified as the theory is further developed and validated. In effect, *PESO* handles the complexity of the theory by carrying out the reasoning according to the theory and the specific conditions that are typed into the software. The examples and figures below illustrate how *PESO* does the reasoning—based on the axioms and theorems of *ATIS*.

AN EXAMPLE OF PESO: PREDICTING EDUCATION SYSTEM OUTCOMES

In the United States, all public schools are affected by No Child Left Behind (2001) legislation. NCLB requires schools annually to assess student achievement at numerous grade levels. Based on average test scores, schools are identified as succeeding or failing. Schools that repeatedly fail to meet current state standards for student achievement are held accountable. Parents have the opportunity to send their children to different schools, if their present school is not succeeding.

Figure 1. *ATIS* **Axiom 13: If system input decreases, then filtration increases.**

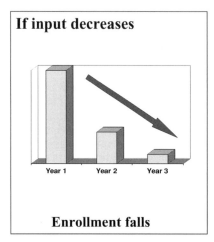

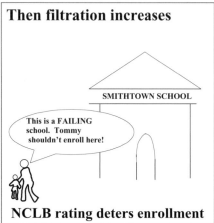

Consider school #9 in Smithtown, USA, a fictitious school created for our example. Smithtown #9 has been identified as a failing school. If a particular school is identified as failing according to state standards, NCLB permits parents to move their children to a different school. What would happen as a consequence of falling enrollment? Student enrollments are a type of *input* in a school system. Axiom 13 predicts that decreasing input implies increasing filtration. *Filtration* is a system property. A filter is something that allows certain things into a system but not others. One may not think of a label of "failure" according to state standards as a filter, but it is (see Figure 1).

In this example, we are using systems language that is not familiar to most educators. In each graphic, the system property (such as "filtration") and its value (e.g., increases) are listed for an educational system. Each axiom is an "if . . . , then . . . " statement that is part of the theory. These "if . . . , then . . . " statements are called logical implications. Axiom 13 states that—If system input decreases, then filtration increases. This is not a temporal

Figure 2. Axiom 11: If system input decreases, then storeput decreases.

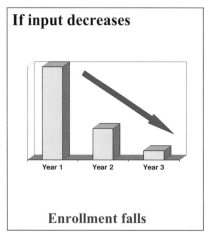

Figure 3. Axiom 10: If system input decreases, then fromput decreases.

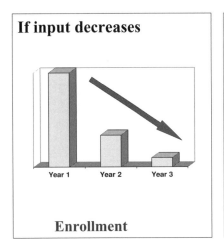

If input decreases

Enrollment

Then fromput decreases

Hmm...there aren't as many diplomas to print this year!

ADMINISTRATION

Fewer students to graduate

relationship, but a logical relationship. If it is true that input decreases, then it is also true that filtration increases. It does not matter which occurs first.

Does the systems theory make any other predictions? Yes, *PESO* identifies axioms 11, 10, and 16 as relevant. See Figures 2–4.

The predictions, pictured in Figures 2–4, tell this story. If enrollments are decreasing, then the overall number of students in the school will go down, and eventually fewer will be eligible to graduate and leave this school.

But wait—there's more! In fact, this is one of the most significant features of the *PESO* simulation: chains of implications. These chains are based on the premise: If A implies B, and if B implies C, then A implies C. To continue the example, Axiom 28 is triggered by Axiom 13. See Figure 5.

How could Smithtown School #9 adapt? Given the prediction that the NCLB label of "failing school" will result in a lower student enrollment, actions can be taken to prevent that

Figure 4. Axiom 16: If system input decreases, then feedout decreases.

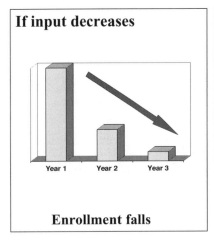

If input decreases

Enrollment falls

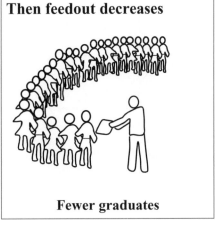

Then feedout decreases

Fewer graduates

Figure 5. Axiom 28: If system filtration increases, then adaptability increases.

from occurring. System theory embedded in the *PESO* software offers Smithtown School options for actions that could prevent lower enrollment. Smithtown could consider actions *increasing system strongness with respect to instructional affect relations*. If strongness of instructional affect relations is increasing, what does *ATIS* predict?

> 055: If *strongness increases*, then hierarchical order decreases.
> 056: If *strongness increases*, then flexibility increases.
> 106: If *strongness increases*, then toput increases.
> 107: If *strongness increases*, then input increases.
> 108: If *strongness increases*, then filtration decreases.

Figure 6. Axiom 56: If system strongness increases, then hierarchical order decreases.

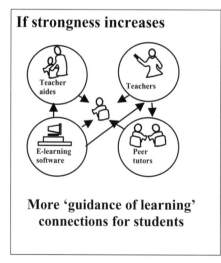

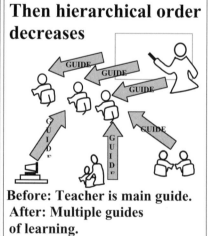

Figure 7. Axiom 55: If system strongness increases, then flexibility increases.

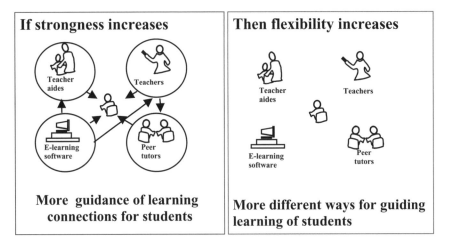

How could Smithtown increase strongness of instructional affect relations? The school could offer more guidance of student learning by bringing in teaching aides, either paid or volunteer, or by providing more instructional technology that can actually guide learning. Peer tutoring programs in which more advanced students could tutor less advanced students would increase the guidance of learning. As can be seen above, the theory predicts that quite a few things would change in the system if strongness were increased. See Figures 6–8.

In Figure 7, it can be seen that if strongness increases, then flexibility increases. Flexibility means here that there are more different kinds of alternative paths through which guidance can occur. For example, the teacher could be guided himself or herself by e-learning materials and then guide students, and likewise for teacher aides. Or the teacher can instruct some students, who then in turn instruct others, etc. In Figure 8, filtration is

Figure 8. Axiom 108: If system strongness increases, then filtration decreases.

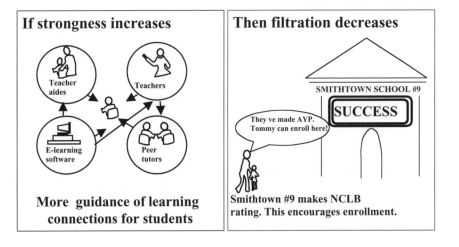

decreased by removal of the "failure" rating by meeting NCLB criteria for annual yearly progress. Axiom 108 predicts that if strongness increases, then filtration decreases.

There are additional axioms and theorems that are triggered by increasing strongness of affect relations, but space precludes discussion here.

ATIS: THE BASIC CONCEPTS

ATIS (Axiomatic Theories of Intentional Systems) is a theory model options-set that is designed to construct scientific theory for certain types of behavioral systems. In particular, it is used to develop behavioral predictive theories and technologies.

ATIS is founded on a basic principle that we all rely on day-to-day to make decisions about what we do. The principle is based on Jerome Bruner's (1990) conclusion about how we derive meaning from our cultural contexts—that is, the systems in which we live:

> We will be able to interpret meanings in a principled manner only in the degree to which we are able to specify the structure and coherence of the larger contexts in which specific meanings are created and transmitted. (pp. 64–65)

We normally do this interpretation and integration of observed phenomena intuitively. If in fact our world were not well-organized and intuitively predictable, we would not be able to function in our daily lives. We know that if we show up for work and do what we are supposed to do, our job will still be there the next day—assuming that the larger context in which we work does not change.

Students know that if they study their text assignments, listen in class and comprehend what the instructor is saying, and work the problems for the class in such a manner that they get the correct answers, they will receive a grade that reflects the quality of their work. That is, if a student consistently receives an "A" on quizzes, tests, reports, etc., then that student expects to receive an "A" for the course. If such students end up with a "C" for the course, they know that there is "something wrong." Why is there something wrong? The continual integration of data into their thinking gave rise to a new structure that reaffirmed their perceptions that they were doing well. When they received a "C," it was not consistent with the principles upon which they had been relying. Their immediate reaction—the instructor really messed up! They will go and get the grade changed because it does not reflect the structure of the system that they had come to expect.

ATIS relies on the observable fact that our lives are more predictable than not. If the outcomes are not what we expected, then we did not have full knowledge. The behavioral sciences are distinct from the physical sciences mainly in terms of what we actually know about any particular event. If we knew more about an event, our prediction may have been correct. We all believe that events are predictable—if we only knew more. That our lives are more predictable than not is the basic tenant of *ATIS*.

If we did not know that, if we treat our children in a certain way, they will respond predictably, then child rearing and education would be impossible. The slogan that "all children are different" is a platitude, but, if they were, education itself would not be possible. Children are all "different" in that we know that we must treat them and recognize them individually if we want them to achieve, but we also know that children learn by just such attention.

Are different outcomes predictable for educational systems? Of course they are. Differing outcomes can be attributable to a variety of conditions including "attention of the child," "teaching skills of the teacher," "intellect of the child," "intellect of the teacher," and "physical surroundings." The question is not whether an event is predictable, but whether we know what we need to know in order to make the prediction. *ATIS* helps to focus attention on what one needs to know, and provides the structure to make a reasoned decision concerning the outcomes.

BACKGROUND OF ATIS: GENERAL SYSTEMS THEORY

The concept of general systems theory (GST) was first introduced by Ludwig von Bertalanffy in 1949. Bertalanffy (1968) argued that there exists a general theory that could characterize the behavior of systems, regardless of whether these are scientific, natural, or social; and he proposed GST as an interdisciplinary theory that could contribute to the unity of science. System behavior results from the relationships between its components, and is not just a simple summation of its parts. The characteristics of each system component therefore cannot adequately explain how the system itself behaves.

Since then, there have been extensive contributions by others in the development of GST as a logical and mathematical theory to provide an "exact language permitting rigorous deductions and confirmation (or refusal) of theory" (Bertalanffy, 1972, p. 30). Others have also contributed well-developed descriptive theories (e.g., Wymore, 1967; Cornacchio, 1972; Mesarović & Takahara, 1975; Lin, 1987; Lin, 1999; Bar-Yam, 2003). In education, GST has been used by researchers to discuss educational systems design and systemic change, but these approaches have not been grounded in scientific theory about educational systems (Banathy, 1991; Caine & Caine, 1997; Duffy, Rogerson, & Blick, 2000; Senge, Cambron-McCabe, Lucas, Smith, Dutton, & Kleiner, 2000). Rather these approaches largely describe processes through which organizations can change, not whether those changes are likely to result in desired outcomes.

The *SIGGS* theory model provided the first extensive formalization of a GST model for educational theorizing (Maccia & Maccia, 1966; Steiner, 1988). Through the synthesis of four theories: Set, Information, di-Graph, and General Systems, *SIGGS* provided a logical description of general system properties, which enabled retroduction of 201 hypotheses in a theory of school systems. Frick, Hood, Kirsch, Reigeluth, Walcott, and Farris (1994) extended Maccia and Maccia's work by classifying the system properties into basic, structural, and dynamic properties. This classification recognized that some *SIGGS* properties were structural as they described the connectedness between system components (*SIGGS* Web site, 1996a). Yet, others were dynamic and described how patterns of relationships between system components are altered due to changes within the system or between the system and its environment (*SIGGS* Web site, 1996b). Thompson (2005) recognized that the structural properties essentially defined the system topology.

To provide a theory that is logically and mathematically sound, a system-descriptive axiom set is needed. Although *SIGGS* was fairly comprehensive, there was no attempt to analyze the 201 hypotheses for consistency or to finalize an axiom set that would be the underlying axioms for a GST. Thompson has since been developing *ATIS*, which is a logico-mathematical theory model for analyzing and predicting behavior of systems that are goal-directed or intentional. Using the original *SIGGS* hypotheses, Thompson developed a nomenclature to define system properties, which improved the precision with which *SIGGS* properties could be used (Thompson, 2005). Thompson also identified an initial list of approximately 100 axioms (subject to change, as this work is ongoing), and extended the 73 SIGGS general system properties to 136 in *ATIS* (*APT&C* Web site, 2005).

USING GENERAL SYSTEM PROPERTIES TO DESCRIBE AN EDUCATIONAL SYSTEM

The following are a few examples of the basic, structural, and dynamic properties formulated in *ATIS* as applied to educational systems. For greater detail, the reader is referred to extensive reports by Thompson (*APT&C* Web site, 2005): http://www.indiana.edu/~aptfrick/reports/.

Basic Properties

Basic properties define the initial attributes required to identify and analyze a system. In *ATIS*, there are only three Basic properties—complexness, general system state, and size. For example, a system consists of at least two components that are connected by an affect relation. Understood in the context of an education system, one example would be teachers and students, who are components that are connected together by a "guidance of learning" affect relationship. These affect relations determine the complexness of the system. The formal definition and logico-mathematical typology of "complexness" is:

> **Complexness,** $X(S)$, $=_{df}$ the connectedness of an affect relation.
>
> $$X(S), =_{df} (A_m \in A)|(x, y) \in A_m \supset x \in_C C$$

Complexness is measured by the number of connections.

Structural Properties

"Strongness" is an example of a structural property that describes relationships between system components. "Strongness" is defined formally:

> **Strong system (strongness),** $_s S$, $=_{df}$ a system with affect relation sets characterized by strongly connected components.

$$_s S =_{df} S|\exists A_i(_s C)$$

"Strongly connected components" means that all components in the affect relation set are connected to each other, but at least one of the connections is unilateral (one or more is not bidirectional; otherwise the components would be completely connected).

Assume that we are examining the affect relation "guidance of learning" in a classroom. If classroom instruction is solely from the teacher, for example, demonstrating, explaining, questioning, prompting, and evaluating student responses, then such "guidance of learning" is defined by the unilateral connectedness from the teacher to the students. Strongness can be increased if there were more connections between system components. For example, when students work in project groups, "guidance of learning" connections can be created among students as they share what they know with each other. Such affect relations become "completely connected" when all of them have bidirectional connections with each other. "Completely connected" components are defined formally:

> **Completely connected components set,** $_{cc} C$, $=_{df}$ a set of system components that are pair-wise path-connected in both directions.

$$_{cc} C =_{df} X = \{x|x \in R \subset S_0 \wedge \exists y \in R[x \neq y \wedge (x, y) \in_{cc} E]\}$$

Dynamic Properties

"Adaptableness" is an example of a dynamic property that describes how the relationship between system components changes over time. It is defined formally:

Adaptable system (adaptableness), $_A S$, $=_{df}$ a system compatibility change within certain limits to maintain stability under system enviornmental change.

$$_A S =_{df} \Delta S'_{t(1),t(2)} \Vdash \Delta C_{t(1),t(2)} < \alpha \Vdash_{SB} S_{t(1),t(2)}$$

For example, a school system has high adaptability if its graduation rates do not vary significantly when the standards for passing state examinations are raised.

"Filtration" is another example of a dynamic property. It describes the criteria a system uses to determine which toput qualifies as input to the system. The criteria for selecting its applicants act as a filter for entry to the school (e.g., students who are less than 5 years old are typically not allowed to enter K-12 schools). "Filtration" is defined formally:

Filtration, $F(S)$, $=_{df}$ the set of *toput system-control qualifiers* that control *feedin* of *toput*.

$$F(S) =_{df} \{P(x)|P(x) \in_{TP} L_C \wedge A^{filtration} \sigma_x(\sigma_x : T_P \times_{TP} L_C \rightarrow (T_P, I_P))$$

THIS IS GETTING PRETTY TECHNICAL—HOW CAN IT BE MANAGED?

The busy education professional may wonder, "Do I have to be a mathematician to benefit from these concepts in my work?" The short answer is: No, you don't have to. We don't have to be engineers to drive our cars or use our microwave ovens. We can use devices built on scientific theories without knowing all the details.

ATIS is quite complex and very detailed. It is difficult, even for the present authors, to keep track of all the detail. This is where we believe that computer technology can help us. We are building a software simulation, called *PESO*: Predicting Education System Outcomes. *PESO* will keep track of all the details, allowing us to focus on the predictions.

HOW PESO MAKES LOGIC-BASED PREDICTIONS

Even though there are over 200 axioms and theorems in ATIS as of this writing (APT&C Web site, 2005), only 5 axioms apply under the condition: input decreases. Axioms 10, 11, and 13 predict three outcomes of decreasing input. However, Axiom 11 predicts a decrease in storeput, which triggers Axiom 16. Similarly, Axiom 13 triggers Axiom 28. This kind of chaining illustrates how the inference engine that is built into *PESO* works. *PESO* actualizes the logical implication of transitivity—for example, if A implies B, and if B implies C, then A implies C.

PESO will carry out the implications, as illustrated in Figures 1–8 above. First, the user must enter the specific conditions that currently exist for a particular school system or district. *PESO* then finds all the relevant axioms and theorems from *ATIS* and uses them to make predictions about this particular system—not other systems, not all systems, but *this* system under these conditions.

How will you know, for example, whether input is increasing, flexibility is decreasing, or filtration is increasing in your particular education system? You will need to *measure* these system properties. This means you will need to observe, collect data, and/or use existing data about your education system. You will be able to use *APT&C* software to assist in the data collection and analysis. This will help you identify the temporal and structural patterns in your education system, and it will do the calculations for you.

SimEd TECHNOLOGIES WILL INCLUDE APT&C SOFTWARE

Analysis of Patterns in Time and Configuration, *APT&C,* is a different kind of measurement paradigm. *APT&C* is a mixed-mode research methodology and software tool to help create knowledge of education systems that is directly linked to practices and changes in practices. *APT&C* bridges the gap between traditional linear models in quantitative research and qualitative research findings that lack generalizability (Frick, 1990, 2005). *APT&C* builds on work done by Frick (1990) on *APT* and by Thompson (2005).

APT&C is different from the widely used Statistical Package for the Social Sciences. *SPSS* uses the traditional approach to measurement and statistics that requires you to measure things *separately*, and enter numbers for each variable such as a student's test score, age, or grade in school. Then you analyze the data by using statistics such as correlation, analysis of variance, regression analysis, etc. This is referred to as a linear models approach by statisticians. Linear models statistically *relate separate measures* of things.

In contrast, *APT&C* directly *measures the relation*. The difference is significant. In the linear models approach, you will get an *r* value or the results of an *F* test, for example, to tell you whether a relation between or among measures is statistically significant. In *APT&C* you will get different kinds of values that are measures of temporal or structural patterns. For example, you could predict student engagement when direct instruction is or is not occurring as Frick (1990) did. He found that students were 13 times more likely to be off-task when direct instruction was not occurring during academic activities. This is a temporal pattern. In his study, students were observed to be engaged about 97 percent of the time during direct instruction, but only 57 percent of the time during nondirect instruction. These percentages are measures of the temporal relation, and are based on probability theory and set theory.

This kind of *APT&C* finding is similar to epidemiological findings in medicine. For example, heavy cigarette smokers are 5–10 times more likely to have lung cancer later in their lives (Kumar et al., 2005), and if they quit smoking, the likelihood decreases. While causal conclusions cannot be made in the absence of controlled experiments, nonetheless one can make practical decisions based on such epidemiological evidence. You can do likewise with *APT&C*. The practical conclusion of Frick's study is that direct instruction engages students. If a teacher wants students to learn, direct instruction is more likely to produce student engagement.

In addition to temporal properties, *APT&C* will allow you to measure structural properties of educational systems. Examples of structural properties were listed in Figures 1–8 above, such as *strongness* and *flexibility*. You will enter data into what are called "affect relation matrices" to indicate the structure or configuration of your educational system. Then the software will "crunch the numbers" and provide the values for properties such as strongness and flexibility. This is how you will determine whether *strongness* or *flexibility* is increasing or decreasing over some period of time.

Once you have measured and analyzed these dynamic and structural patterns in your education system, then you can identify the specific conditions that exist regarding those property values of your educational system. You use the *PESO* program to then make predictions of educational outcomes for your system under these specific conditions. If, for example, strongness of instructional affect relations is *decreasing* in your system, *PESO* will apply different axioms than if it is *increasing*.

Further information on *APT&C* and additional references are found in: http://education.indiana.edu/~frick/proposals/apt&c.pdf.

NEXT STEPS

SimEd Technologies are theories, methodologies, and software tools to describe complexity in educational systems. *PESO* will need to be tried out and validated in real educational systems, whether schools or school districts, charter schools, alternative schools, or school to work programs. When it is established that *PESO* adequately describes and predicts educational system outcomes, educators can use *SimEd Technologies* to model the consequences of educational systems changes. *SimEd Technologies* will show educators all the consequences, even the unintended consequences, of changing one part of the complex educational systems they direct. Better changes and better predictions of outcomes will result.

REFERENCES

APT&C (2005). Research reports. Retrieved on January 21, 2006, from http://www.indiana.edu/~aptfrick/reports/.

Banathy, B. (1991). *Systems design of education*. Englewood Cliffs, NJ: Educational Technology Publications.

Bar-Yam, Y. (2003). *Dynamics of complex systems*. Boulder, CO: Westview Press.

Bertalanffy, L. von (1968). *General system theory: Foundations, development, applications*. New York: George Braziller.

———. (1972). The history and status of general systems theory. In G.J. Klir (Ed.), *Trends in general systems theory*. New York: Wiley-Interscience.

Bruner, J. (1990). *Acts of meaning*. Cambridge, MA: Harvard University Press.

Caine, R. & Caine, G. (1997). *Education on the edge of possibility*. Alexandria, VA: Association for Curriculum Supervision and Development.

Cornacchio, J. V. (1972). Topological Concepts in the Mathematical Theory of General Systems. In G.J. Klir (Ed.), *Trends in general systems theory*. New York: Wiley-Interscience, 303–339.

Duffy, F., Rogerson, L., & Blick, C. (2000). *Redesigning America's schools: A systems approach to improvement*. Norwood, MA: Christopher-Gordon Publishers.

Frick, T. (1990). Analysis of Patterns in Time (APT): A method of recording and quantifying temporal relations in education. *American Educational Research Journal, 27*(1), 180–204.

———. (2005). Bridging qualitative and quantitative methods in educational research: Analysis of Patterns in Time and Configuration (APT&C). Retrieved on January 21, 2006, from http://education.indiana.edu/~frick/proposals/apt&c.pdf.

Frick, T.W., Hood, P., Kirsch, K., Reigeluth, C., Walcott, A., & Farris, H. (1994). *Simulosophy Group Report: Sixth International Conference on the Design of Social Systems*. Retrieved on September 15, 2005, from http://www.indiana.edu/~tedfrick/simulosophy.pdf.

Friedman, T. (1999). The Semiotics of SimCity. *First Monday, 4*(4). Retrieved on September 15, 2005, from http://www.firstmonday.dk/issues/issue4_4/friedman/.

Hart, J. (October, 1993). Cognitive maps. Presentation at the Cognitive Science Colloquium Series, Indiana University, Bloomington.

Lin, Y. (1987). A model of general systems. *Mathematical modeling, 9*(2), 95–104.

―――. (1999). *General systems theory: A mathematical approach.* New York: Kluwer Academic/Plenum.

Maccia, E.S., & Maccia, G.S. (1966). *Development of educational theory derived from three theory models.* Washington, DC: U.S. Office of Education, Project No. 5-0638.

Mesarović, M.D., & Takahara, Y. (1975). General systems theory: Mathematical foundations. In R. Bellman (Ed.), *Mathematics in science and engineering,* Vol. 113. New York: Academic Press.

Senge, P. (1990). *The fifth discipline: The art and practice of the learning organization.* New York: Doubleday/Currency.

Senge, P., Cambron-McCabe, N., Lucas, T., Smith, B. Dutton, J., & Kleiner, A. (2000). *Schools that learn.* New York: Doubleday/Currency.

SIGGS Web site. (1996a). *SIGGS structural properties.* Retrieved on September 15, 2005, from http://www.indiana.edu/~tedfrick/siggs3.html.

―――. (1996b). *SIGGS dynamic properties (temporal change).* Retrieved on September 15, 2005, from http://www.indiana.edu/~tedfrick/siggs4.html.

Steiner, E. (1988). *Methodology of theory building.* Sydney: Educology Research Associates.

Thompson, K.R. (2006). "General System" defined for predictive technologies of A-GSBT (Axiomatic-General Systems Behavioral Theory). Manuscript accepted for publication, *Scientific Inquiry, 7*(1), 1–11.

Wymore, A.W. (1967). *A mathematical theory of systems engineering: The elements.* New York: Wiley.

Student Learning Outcomes in Technology-Enhanced Constructivist Learning Environments: What Does Research Show?

Priya Sharma, Ying Xie, Pei-Hsuan Hsieh, Wen-Min Hsieh, and Suhyun Yoo
The Pennsylvania State University

INTRODUCTION

Constructivism is generally viewed as a description of how individuals construct knowledge and meaning. Despite consistent debate on the ontological and epistemological bases of constructivism, as well as its nomenclature as a theory or a philosophy, constructivism has been widely embraced in the educational community. In the past decade, an increasing number of researchers and educators have attempted to integrate constructivist designs to empower student learning (Jonassen et al., 1999). These different learning environments, although all based on constructivist premises, have different philosophical and theoretical underpinnings and thus differ in their design and implementation.

Philosophically, constructivism can be broadly classified as individual or social constructivism by the context within which meaning making occurs. Individual constructivism focuses on describing how knowledge is assimilated and accommodated within the individual. This camp includes Piaget's cognitive constructivism and Glasersfeld's (1995) radical constructivism, where the emphasis is on identifying how individuals encounter new information and organize it within their existing knowledge schemes. The second camp of constructivism deals with the role of social discourse and interaction in circumscribing individual knowledge, specifically in terms of acknowledging cultural and social norms. Vygotsky and Cole (1978), often cited as a social constructivist, emphasized the agency and mediation of community and culture in cognition and meaning making. Vygotsky and Cole's propositions on the mediatory role of semiotics in learning and interaction emphasize the notion of dialogue and discussion as a mechanism to create a shared understanding of experience. The underlying notion in constructivism is that individuals are responsible for their own learning, which can be supported by providing access to new information and new perspectives that cause disequilibrium. Disequilibrium causes learners to consider the viability of new information within their existing schema, which in turn can result in changing mental schema. Bereiter (1994) suggests that individual constructivism focuses on the mental activities of the learner, while social constructivism focuses on cultural practices in the learner's environment.

Many educators and thinkers have theorized that the growth of the personal computer and Internet technologies spurred an increased interest in constructivist learning environments (Perkins, 1991; Salomon et al., 1991). Computers and Internet technologies can have fundamental impacts on the way we think about teaching and learning, especially if we conceptualize the role of the teacher and learner differently. In some sense, these technologies have provided the ability to more easily implement teaching that is less based on direct instruction or transfer of knowledge and more based on guiding social exploration in information-rich environments (Salomon, 1991). There is an increasing amount of dialogue that indicates that computer-mediated learning environments can be easily used to support constructivist learning (Jonassen et al., 1999; CGTV, 1993). For example, from a social constructivist perspective, the computer can provide access to a multitude of information and collaboration possibilities. Students can access information pertinent to their interests in a variety of forms and media, thereby allowing for a number of virtual experiences as well as opportunities to examine multiple viewpoints (Rice & Wilson, 1999) and to allow for individual interaction within rich social contexts that support peer and expert scaffolding.

Technology in Constructivist Learning Environments

Jonassen et al. (1999) briefly compared the two views on technology, traditional instructional vs. constructivist view. They point out that technology has in the past largely been used in education to learn *from*, in the belief that technology programs could convey information more effectively than teachers, but constructivists are interested in using technologies as tools to construct knowledge *with*, since they believe that learners construct understanding by themselves, instead of receiving information through technology. Therefore, the interest of most constructivists is on the use of technology to create rich learning environments, not on technology itself. This notion was supported by the media effect debates (Clark, 1994; Kozma, 1994), which suggest that technology or media in itself cannot affect learning—the design makes the difference.

However, the increasing interest in constructivism is unaccompanied by sufficient empirical evidence pointing to the utility of constructivism as a philosophy and basis of design for learning. Much of the literature on constructivism deals with conceptual and design explanations, but there is little evidence indicating operationalization of constructivist concepts and the subsequent evidence for learning. This lack of evidence further aggravates criticisms of constructivism (Chadwick, 2004). For example, Kirschner et al. (2006) suggest that having individuals construct their own solutions to problems may not be the best method to promote learning, especially in the context of minimally guided instruction, of which constructivist learning environments are a part. Kirschner et al. also point to the lack of empirical research that supports the adequacy of constructivist and other minimally guided types of instruction. Despite various fallacies in the argument linking constructivism to minimally guided instruction, we agree with the suggestions of Kirshner et al. about the need to identify what empirical research suggests about effectiveness of constructivist learning environments for individual learning. The current lack of evidence also poses difficulties for educators and researchers who wish to adopt constructivism in the design for learning.

Our focus in this paper is to examine empirical research in the area of constructivist learning and design, specifically within those environments that are technology enhanced. We begin by identifying our research process and focus and then present results of the analysis. In an attempt to identify and validate the impact of constructivist designs on student learning, we intend to examine only studies that report on design and provide empirical evidence of student learning within the constructivist environment. We end by identifying implications for designers and researchers interested in effective design and evaluation of constructivist learning.

RESEARCH PROCESS

We began our process by searching for peer-reviewed articles that specifically addressed the design of constructivist environment for learning. Our search targeted articles from 1995 to 2006 in three major databases, PsyINFO, ERIC, and Google Scholar. At the initial stage, 236 article abstracts were found by using the following combination of the keywords: Constructivis* in Abstract and Learner/Learning in Title. We also used a combination of other keywords such as Environment*, Online, Technology, Design, Web-based, Internet, Research, and Instruction* in addition to Constructivis*. To provide substantial evidence of effective constructivist learning environment designs, we excluded articles that only posed conceptual models or stands and did not offer any empirical data related to learning and design. At the next level of review, we examined 103 articles to find research that reported detailed design implementations and data supporting learning outcomes. In our final count, we identified 79 articles that fit our requirements and created detailed summaries focusing on environment design, research design, and learning outcomes. However, only 17 articles of the 79 (that is, 22% or less than a quarter of the articles) used technology in the design of the environment. The other 62 articles involved face-to-face or classroom settings in designing constructivist learning environments, and did not use any technology.

FINDINGS

As stated above, the purpose of this article is to identify the impact of technology-enhanced constructivist learning environments on individual student learning. In addition to the design of the environment, we also looked for empirical evidence that addresses students' learning gains. After careful examination of the 17 articles, seven articles were identified as not being in line with this purpose. However, since we realized that some studies provided useful information regarding design and technology use for constructivist design, we provide a brief description of these studies while excluding them from our main analysis. These articles were excluded because they—combined objectivist and constructivist designs (Bellefeuille, 2006), reported data about student perceptions (Bostock, 1998; Lester et al., 1999), lacked clear design principles (Choi & Johnson, 2005), provided no empirical evidence (Forster, 1999; Murphy et al., 2005), or focused on areas other than student knowledge gain (Lavonen et al., 2002). Short descriptions of some of the relevant articles focus on the implications for constructivist design. We found that despite the lack of focus on student learning, use of constructivist learning environment design resulted in positive perceptions of and positive attention gains toward the content.

Positive Impact on Student Perceptions

Bostock (1998) and Lester et al. (1999) both explored student perceptions within a constructivist learning environment and found that students enjoyed engaging in authentic and problem-solving environments. Bostock (1998), for example, described the implementation of constructivist learning environment, whose design principles included: (1) authentic assessment, (2) student responsibility and initiative, (3) generative learning strategies, (4) authentic learning contexts, and (5) cooperative supports. Computer technologies such as the World Wide Web, e-mail, and video were adopted for the course design. Data was collected through five Web-form questionnaires and one structured interview. The first and the last questionnaires were partly duplicated with the intent to detect attitude changes during the course. Sample questions asked in the initial and final questionnaires focused on overall attitude toward the course, the comparison of traditional instruction with computer assisted learning, and which types of deliverables students preferred. Results from 300 enrolled students suggested that they viewed the authentic assessment methods positively. Students liked the ownership of their learning, and enjoyed the assigned tasks. However, an unexpected result was a significant drop in preference for group work in favor of individual assessed work due to the timetable and physical layout of the course. Bostock suggested that due to different learner styles, partial implementation of constructivist principles might be optimal for the majority of students.

Lester et al. (1999) used a radically different design and used life-like pedagogical agents for mixed-initiative problem solving in a constructivist learning environment. In their design, as learners traveled with Herman (the life-like pedagogical agent) from planet to planet, they solved design problems in DESIGN-A-PLANT environments. Specifically, learners were confronted with problems of varying levels of difficulty: from very simple, involving only a single constraint to very complex, requiring learners to address multiple constraints simultaneously. As they designed plants for a variety of environmental conditions, the agent introduced problems, explained concepts in botanical anatomy and physiology, provided problem-solving advice, and interjected congratulatory and off-the-cuff remarks. The evaluation was conducted through an informal experiment in which approximately twenty focus group learners interacted with the agent for forty-five minutes to one hour. The results suggested that life-like pedagogical agents whose behaviors are selected and assembled with a well-designed sequencing engine can effectively guide learners through a complex subject in a manner that exhibits both pedagogical and visual coherence. This study also indicated that learners found the problem-solving environment to be engaging and likeable.

Positive Impact on Student Attention

Choi and Johnson (2005) adopted sociocultural learning theories and construc-tivist approaches as theoretical assumptions and suggested the following principles: (1) real-world context and engaged experiences can make the best learning environments, (2) knowledge cannot be simply transmitted from the instructor to the learners, and (3) context-based learning through technology will be very effective for the enhancement of learner's knowledge construction, transfer, or application. Moreover, they assumed that video is a powerful tool that engages learners in active learning. Based on these theoreti-cal assumptions, they investigated the effect of context-based instruction on learning and motivation in online courses and in this study. The authors attempted to gather empirical evidence when technology was used under constructivist learning environment by compar-ing video-based with text-based learning environments. The results indicated that there was a statistically significant difference in attention between video-based instruction and tradi-tional text-based instruction. However, there were no differences in perceived learning and in relevance, confidence, and satisfaction of the model defined as four major motivations conditions.

Although these studies didn't mention if the constructivist's environments helped stu-dents to improve their performance in the courses, such environments proved to be appealing and engaging. From the reports of these studies, we can conclude that the major factors identified by students as important to engaging in the processes included: (1) authentic contexts, (2) authentic assessment—allowing students to take ownership of their learn-ing, and (3) providing pedagogically sequenced scaffolds to address authentic problems (e.g., using the life-like pedagogical agent). These findings are important for future design because it was found that students learn the best in a positive and engaging environment.

Types of Technology-Enhanced Constructivist Learning Environments

We describe the empirical studies we analyzed within two categories—individual and collaborative. We derived this distinction based on the selected research articles. In the 10 articles that presented empirical evidence for learning outcomes, technology was used in two specific ways that are loosely based on the earlier theoretical distinctions between individual and social constructivism. Table 1 presents an overview of the studies, their classification as individual or collaborative, and the main guidelines for design based on empirical evidence.

Individual constructivist environments

In individual constructivist environments, technology tends to be used to create rich and contextualized learning environments enabling knowledge construction wherein indi-vidual learners interact with technology by themselves, whereas collaborative constructivist learning environments focus on supporting students' collaborative work using technology.

Table 1. Design Guidelines and Technology Used

Design Guideline	Author (Year)	Classification	Technologies Used
Allowing students to view information in multiple contexts	Cobb (1999)	Individual	• CD-ROM based multimedia dictionary
Providing guidance to navigate the learning content	Windschitl & Andre (1998)	Individual	• Computer-based simulations
	Harskamp & Suhre (2004)	Individual	• Two computer interactive programs
Engaging students in dialogue to promote knowledge co-construction	Puntambekar (2006)	Collaborative	• CoDE (Constructivist, Distributed learning Environment) • Reflective notebooks • Discussion tool (WebBoard)
	Schellens & Valcke (2005)	Collaborative	• Web Crossing conferencing server • Discussion board
Engaging students in exploring resources and creating artifacts of learning	Gilbert and Driscoll (2002)	Collaborative	• Computer Supported Intentional Learning Environments (CSILE)
	Bonk, Hay, & Fischler (1996)	Collaborative	• Multimedia to create artifacts • Online resources, including access to a community of practice
	Juniu (2006)	Collaborative	• Classroom instruction • Multimedia technologies • World Wide Web
Engaging students in accessing multiple, authentic resources	Murphy et al. (2005)	Collaborative	• Internet access to a remote-controlled telescope • CD-ROM with PowerPoint slides, imaging processing software, and image gallery • Website for communication

We were able to identify only three studies that reported data on using technology for designing individual constructivist learning environments (Cobb, 1999; Harskamp & Suhre, 2006; Windschitl & Andre, 1998). All three studies focused on creating technology-based learning environments within which individual students could interact with the learning environment itself instead of other learners or their instructors.

Allowing students to view information in multiple contexts

Cobb (1999) and Windschitl and Andre (1998) designed very different learning environments but one key element in each was the provision of context—allowing students to put new information within the context of authentic situations. Cobb (1999), for example, tried to apply constructivist principles to language acquisition. His assumption was that, as constructivist learning theory suggests, knowledge encoded from data by learners themselves would be more flexible, transferable, and useful than knowledge encoded for them by experts and transmitted to them by an instructor or other delivery agent. In this study, he attempted to establish conditions in which the prediction could be operationalized and tested in the domain of second language vocabulary acquisition. The PET (Preliminary English Test) 2000 program was developed to provide first-year college students with a contextual learning environment for English vocabulary acquisition. The program interface allowed students to view to-be-learned words in several contexts in a short time by providing a zoom lens on a large amount of distributed data per word. The program contained a list of 2,387 words and the students were assigned approximately 200 words to be learned every week and most students worked individually. Analysis of variance (ANOVA) for the pre- and posttest indicated that the experimental group that used the PET scored higher on the posttest although both control and experimental were equal at the pretest. Cobb concluded that learning was enhanced because the program allowed the students to work with each word individually through the various interfaces and by using the various contextual cues present for each word.

Similarly, Windschitl and Andre (1998) used simulations to allow students to situate and view information within various contexts. They conducted a comparison study of the use of simulations in constructivist and nonconstructivist conditions to facilitate conceptual change in college students. The researchers suggested that simulations could provide students with a chance to create and evaluate their hypotheses in rich and contextualized environments, especially when used in a constructivist manner. The group of students that used the constructivist simulation was provided with an initial orientation on the use of the simulation software. Students were then provided a set of 12 questions to answer and they used a thematic instructional guide to hypothesize about and test the answers to the questions. To aid them in answering the questions, a computer simulation that modeled the functioning of the human heart was used and two windows were accessible to the user. One window allowed selection of dynamic information representation forms including different charts. The second window contained an electrocardiograph type of display plus transparent frontal views of the circulatory system and the human heart. Thus, students could immediately view the impact of different hypotheses on these external representations of understanding. The confirmatory group used the same simulation but they were asked to perform procedures in a lockstep fashion and use the simulation to follow instructions. A one-way ANOVA found that for two of the six questions in the pretest where misconceptions were apparent, the constructivist group performed significantly better than the confirmatory group. Also a regression on the posttest indicated that high levels of epistemological sophistication in the constructivist group led to higher posttest performance and in the confirmatory group epistemological belief was negatively related to performance. Thus, this study suggests that constructivist approaches to simulations could be more effective in altering learners' misconceptions and that provision of overly detailed instructions could be detrimental to conceptual change.

Providing guidance to navigate the learning content

Guidance is of paramount importance in helping students to interact and navigate within any learning environment, especially when they are confronted with problem situations. In Windschitl and Andre's (1998) study students in the constructivist situation were provided with an initial orientation session on how to interact with the program, however no other guidance was provided as they engaged in the learning interaction. The researchers mentioned that providing additional guidance might positively affect student interaction within the environment. Harskamp and Suhre (2006) provided an example of the importance of student guidance within a constructivist environment. They conducted a quasi-experimental study to compare the learning effects based on traditional instruction and two kinds of interactive computer programs (direct instruction and cognitively guided instruction) by observing and analyzing secondary-level students' mathematical problem-solving procedures. The students in the traditional class followed normal procedures to learn a formula or equation with at least one problem but no hints. In the direct instruction (DI) environment, the students received instructional hints in a fixed sequence of curriculum topics as long as they incorrectly answered a problem. In the cognitively guided instruction (CGI) environment, the students could freely access instructional hints at any time to answer problems in their own preferred sequences. At the end of the instruction, the students in the DI environment viewed a formal solution to the problem. The students in the CGI environment could answer the problem by inspecting several solution procedures. Both instructional programs employed the same 35 mathematical problems and had different interfaces for students and teachers. The study results showed that both types of computer instruction were effective in improving the quality of students' analysis and verification skills through the implementation of the instructional hints during problem-solving procedures. The students' levels of understanding for problems were improved by interacting with the CGI and the DI. However, students were much more encouraged to actively engage in the learning process under the CGI condition than under the DI. An enduring effect on student problem-solving behaviors, especially student analytical skills, was also found in the CGI environment. Different effects of the instructional hints were also found on different problem-solving abilities between weak and strong students. Based on their findings, Harskamp and Suhre (2006) suggested incorporating some forms of obligatory instructional hints to help both weak and strong students improve mathematical problem-solving abilities.

In the studies cited above, Cobb (1999) and Windschitl and Andre (1998) were interested in creating rich and contexualized learning environments and their comparison studies indicate that these environments can allow individual students to engage in the learning process and effectively transfer or externalize knowledge to novel situations. In these environments, technology was effectively used to provide learners with information that could be viewed within multiple contexts and in multiple forms to support contextualization of knowledge. Beyond providing an authentic contextual learning environment, Windschitl and Andre (1998) also allowed students to "explore" in this environment—allowing students to actively interact with the learning materials—a very important factor for individual constructivism. However, even when based on premises of individual constructivism, the design doesn't warrant a secluded environment where students simply fumble through the environment on their own. All three study results underscored the importance of providing guidance for students in order for them to learn more effectively.

Collaborative constructivist learning environments

Six studies explored the use of technologies for students learning through collaboration. Except for one study (McKinnon et al., 2002) that did not provide detailed information about the use and design of the educational environment and materials, and which was therefore excluded, most studies found that technologies could benefit group learning but only through careful design. One design method is to support students in constructing knowledge through dialogue. For example, Puntambekar (2006) and Schellens and Valcke (2005) both used Web-based discussions to enhance individual learning, but they also provided authentic situations on which students based their discussions. A second design involves the creation of environments within which students use technology to explore information and resources and collaboratively create artifacts to demonstrate their learning. This design is exemplified in Gilbert and Driscoll's (2002) research, where students used computer supported collaborative learning environments (CSILE) to supporting group idea construction. A similar design is also visible in the research of Bonk et al. (1996) and Juniu (2006), where students acted as consumers and creators of knowledge using various technological tools. The third design is a scaled-down version of the previous design theme, where technology becomes a means of providing access to rich and authentic resources for supporting learning, as in the case of McKinnon et al. (2002). The following details the design of the technologies and their effects for learning based on three common themes.

Engaging students in dialogue to promote knowledge co-construction

Both Schellens and Valcke (2005) and Puntambekar (2006) studied the effect of Web-based discussion activities based on authentic problems on students' collaborative learning processes. Schellens and Valcke (2005) studied the effects of Web-based asynchronous discussions on students' cognitive processing. Two hundred thirty freshmen enrolled in an online course were randomly assigned into different discussion groups, resulting in 23 different discussion groups in parallel for four months. Every three weeks a new discussion case was introduced and authentic situations (e.g., case studies) were provided as the basis of the discussion. Each student posted at least one reaction to solve the case and replied to another peer's work at least once. Moderators provided structural feedback to scaffold the discussions instead of providing concrete content feedback. Discussion transcripts of eight groups were randomly selected and analyzed for cognitive processing activities (e.g., presentation of new information, explicitation or elaboration of earlier ideas, evaluation) and for different learning phases at the individual and social level. Results indicated that proportions of communication behavior mirror different phases of knowledge construction. At the end of the research study, for example, there was significantly less communication related to presentation of new facts (or lower level of cognitive processing) and significantly higher numbers of higher levels of cognitive processing and knowledge construction, evidenced by communication that reflected negotiation, co-construction, and evaluation. Results also indicated that more phases of higher knowledge construction appeared in the groups with more discussion activities. Groups with intensive discussion (characterized by large numbers of messages) performed at a qualitatively higher level of knowledge construction than those groups with relatively less discussion. The researchers concluded that the amount of discussion activity affected the nature and quality of discussions and the phases of knowledge construction.

Puntambekar (2006) designed an online learning environment called CoDE (Constructivist Distributed learning Environment) to understand how collaborative interactions develop over time. Similar to Schellens and Valcke's (2005) study, the environment was completely online with a few face-to-face meetings. And as in Schellens and Valcke design, Puntambekar's (2006) study included several real-world problems, authentic context, and discussion boards. Beyond these common elements, reflective notebooks were provided for the students. Seven problems were used during the course, and for each problem, students first brainstormed in their reflective notebooks using textbooks and Web resources. They then participated in a whole-class discussion of the selected problem on the WebBoard. The discussion consisted of three stages, including initial discussion of issues, raising issues important to the problem, and discussion of solutions for the problem based on theories.

At the end of each problem, students wrote a final individual reflective essay. Twenty-six students enrolled in the course and data from 24 students was used for analysis. Seven sets of discussions on the WebBoard and essays were analyzed. Each problem had an average of 134 WebBoard responses and 24 reflective essays. Students' responses indicated evidence of: (1) divergence of new perspectives (that is, the frequency with which students raised new issues), (2) shared understanding, and (3) internalization, that is, students were applying what they had learned in their practice as professionals.

Both of these studies used discussion boards to engage students in knowledge-construction through dialogue with their classmates and reflections by themselves. Despite the positive effects that were found, including evidence of emergence of new perspectives, shared understanding, and internalization of learning content (Puntambekar, 2006), and higher level of cognitive processing and knowledge construction with higher levels of group discussion (Schellens and Valcke, 2005), the process of co-constructing knowledge with peers did not seem to occur naturally for some students. End of course interviews in Puntambekar's (2006) study showed that 54% of the students wanted feedback on their responses from the instructor and that some of the students did not regard the discussion as a forum to construct knowledge based on peer responses. Another interesting finding was that 66% of the students said that the constructivist approach was a challenge because they expected that the instructor would go over the theories before students were asked to solve the problem, indicating a more authoritative acceptance of content.

Engaging students in exploring resources and creating artifacts of learning

Technology can provide many opportunities for students to interact with each other to share and build their knowledge. All of the studies cited in this section allow students to use technological tools as consumers of knowledge despite different levels of involvement with these tools. Technologies could also be used to create artifacts either collaboratively or individually.

One method of supporting such knowledge building is illustrated through Gilbert and Driscoll's (2002) case study, which aimed to determine necessary learning conditions for collaborative knowledge-building communities. Collaborative knowledge building means that students share thoughts to solve problems and to establish a knowledge base. In this study, 20 graduate students were situated in a CSILE (Scardamalia & Bereiter, 1992) environment by providing four learning conditions (Gilbert & Driscoll, 2002, p. 63): (1) having a collective and authentic goal to support collaboration and engagement in the community, (2) using cooperative groups to provide for social negotiation and to promote multiple perspectives, (3) personally selecting course readings and group decision-making to encourage ownership and responsibility in learning, and (4) employing technology tools to archive the work of the community and facilitate communication. Each condition addressed different community learning effects.

In the first stage, the students were enrolled in the Altviews course to discuss a real charter school design project. Then, the students moved on to the second stage by forming six learning groups to discuss necessary tasks related to planning, learning objectives and curricula, learning environment, community integration, apprenticeship and extra curricula. The students also had to develop a concept map by using Inspiration software to picture the relations among those tasks. In the discussion process, every student was responsible for selecting empirical, conceptual, or theoretical reading articles to support their proposed task activities. Each student had to submit a reflection paper for evaluating the instructional effects in Altviews course. Finally, in the fourth stage, students created artifacts or objects on the Construe Web site, a kind of knowledge database. In the study period of over fifteen weeks, ten sources of data were collected from the students and the coding schemes included student reflection, referencing, and higher-order-thinking categories. Study results showed the advantages of using technology, such as Inspiration and Construe software, to store and to integrate students' collaborative knowledge building events toward the end of learning condition. In CSILE, the students were motivated to share ideas in groups. The researcher could also clearly identify different positive instructional effects (e.g., providing scaffolds and motivation) among different conditions by viewing the codes with the coding scheme. Based on the results, Gilbert and Driscoll proposed that future learning environments should use scaffolds, track the learning process, balance tension, promote relevance and motivation, promote a shared vision, and promote the acquisition of knowledge.

In the Indiana Weather Project (IWP), Bonk et al. (1996) investigated the application of situated learning and constructivist theory to support fifth- and sixth-grade elementary school students' understanding of weather systems. Specifically, by using technological and community resources, the IWP attempted to create a learning environment that blended both individual and collaborative philosophical approaches to allow for individual knowledge construction and social interaction. A variety of resources, including hardware and software tools, and experts, both teacher and professional meteorologists, were made available to the students. The design aimed to transform the role of students from knowledge consumers to knowledge producers by incorporating multimedia composition tools for the students. Students utilized computer hardware and software to generate and synthesize knowledge about weather. In one task, students were assigned the role of weather forecaster, while in another more successful task, students needed to select the best U. S. city to live in and defend their selection in a multimedia project. Other optional projects included writing weather reports, vacation advice, and newspaper articles for students' selected cities. During the process of knowledge generation, teachers used software tools such as MediaText and HyperStudio to offer young children writing and multimedia support. In addition, students were introduced to authentic learning by combining multimedia tools with electronic connection to an existing community of practice, that is, meteorological professionals. Concept maps, similarity judgment triads, and open-ended metacognitive reflection questions were used to measure students' knowledge structure. The results showed a significant cognitive gain after students completed the weather unit. However, one recommendation of the researchers was that when introducing technology to the classroom, the design should concentrate on introducing a single tool that works best instead of exposing teachers and students to a variety of devices. The introduction of several tools at the same time caused some confusion for the students and might have therefore impeded their knowledge construction and articulation ideas.

Apart from the provision of resources, another important aspect addressed by Bonk et al. (1996) is the need to design engaging tasks for the students, especially those that involve real-world connections. Juniu (2006) combined classroom instruction with multimedia technologies and the World Wide Web for a project-based learning activity in physical education. Computers and software were used as mindtools (Jonassen et al., 1999) to support an interactive, collaborative, and student-centered classroom. Within the overall project, the class engaged in three overall stages: (1) planning and preparation, which included instructor-initiated discussion to elicit inquiries, group brainstorming, using concept map software to organize ideas and organize actions, and gathering information; (2) tasks and action, which included collecting data by searching the Web, conducting interviews, mapping national statistics, administering health-related physical fitness tests, analyzing data by using Excel for summarizing data, and engaging in collaborative work to recognize pattern and answer questions; and (3) presentation stage, where students designed their final presentations using tools including PowerPoint and Dreamweaver. The instructor's coaching was provided through the learning process. Formative assessments of student learning throughout the project-based learning activity, final projects of the group projects, and students' and instructors' journals were used to analyze results. Although data analysis methods were not described, it was reported that the project-based learning process was a successful experience. Students were able to explore new information, reflect on their own learning, visualize their thinking, incorporate feedback into planning, and explain changes to meet their goals. The challenging task for the instructor was to create a context that resembles an authentic environment with social, cultural, and physical characteristics.

Engaging students in accessing multiple, authentic resources

The studies above used technology as a medium (e.g., discussion boards, CSILE) for students to build knowledge collaboratively and also to exhibit that knowledge by constructing numerous artifacts. A variation of this design is to provide access for students to explore various rich resources, without necessarily providing options for externalizing the knowledge. For example, McKinnon et al. (2002) studied the social constructivist design and use of a project called *Journey through Space and Time* with 5–6 graders. The program consisted of Internet access to a remote-controlled telescope with guidance of educational materials, learning activities that address the key learning areas, a CD-ROM containing PowerPoint slides showing step-by-step procedures, image processing software and a gallery of celestial images, and a Web site for communication. Students spent four hours a day for each of the work in a 10-week period on using this program. Seventy-four students from four schools participated in the 4-month study. The same pretest and post-test were administered at the beginning and the end of the study. The test consisted of multiple-choice questions with justification for choices. Students from all schools increased their mean scores over time on general knowledge about astronomy, general knowledge learning outcomes, spatial astronomical knowledge, and spatial observed learning outcome, however, with a different gradient of increase. The differences of the mean score increases could be explained by students' prior knowledge—students with higher prior knowledge didn't improve as much as students with low prior knowledge.

DISCUSSION AND CONCLUSION

Our exploration of the literature for the past ten years, focusing on technology-enhanced constructivist learning environments, indicates that designs are focused either on individual or collaborative processes. It is evident that the design of technology-enhanced learning environments for collaborative learning takes precedence in the literature when compared with the design of individual learning environments. Especially in the case of constructivist learning environments, the ability of technology to afford access to multiple static and dynamic resources is utilized as one of the key design components. For individual learning, technologies are advantageous primarily when they afford detailed exploration of a content area to address an individual student's prior knowledge or conceptions (e.g., Windschitl & Andre, 1998). The ability to simultaneously provide multiple representations and interpretations of content (e.g., Cobb, 1999) tailored to students' varying needs is an affordance of technology that could not be easily duplicated. Both these types of individual designs allow learning to occur by accounting for a learner's prior schemata.

In a collaborative learning environment, learners are confronted with multiple human and content resources to support new knowledge construction. For example, peers have different experiences and different prior knowledge, and thus can serve to challenge and build individual thinking. This type of co-construction occurs by providing opportunities to engage peers in dialogue with each other around authentic topics (e.g., Puntambekar, 2006; Schellens & Valcke, 2005) and also encouraging creation of artifacts that represent tentative understanding of knowledge (e.g., Gilbert & Driscoll, 2002). However, a finding that emerged across many collaborative studies is students' lack of confidence in the role of peers in knowledge construction. This suggests that within constructivist and collaborative learning environments, there is need to provide orientation and explanations on the utility and processes of peer feedback to get buy-in from individual students. Another option is for instructors to comment on quality of outcomes achieved through collaboration. For example, in Schellens and Valcke's (2005) study, it was shown that high levels of discussion resulted in high levels of thinking and discussion. If the quality of such outcomes is made public and communicated to students, they may likely engage more enthusiastically in group processes. Especially, when assessment is factored into the equation, students are likely to baulk at working with others (e.g., Forster, 1999) without assurance that group work can result in positive outcomes.

The assessment of individual and group learning is also one that needs to be addressed more clearly in research in collaborative constructivist learning environments. In most of the studies cited above, evidence of higher levels of knowledge construction was based on analyses of group discussions and artifacts; however, hypotheses or analyses to support evidence of individual learning are missing. This evidence is important to identify the specific areas in which individual reflections and group dialogue might complement and support each other, and how they might be appropriately employed within a learning environment. Thus, research and practice descriptions should focus on which strategy is most useful for specific types of knowledge constructions, and also identify which tools or designs are most appropriate. The need for appropriate technologies and tools is important in any environment, as identified by Bonk et al. (1996). They suggest that technology tools must be appropriately selected and designed so as not to overwhelm students with too many choices. Bonk et al. (1996) used technology as a method to provide resources and allow students to construct artifacts; however, they did not identify which media or tools proved most effective for different types of activities. This area of research is one that can lead to important implications on selection of software and hardware tools. Although instructors can provide some guidance on the utility of tools, even they may be overwhelmed with trying to deal with multiple technologies and no clear understanding of the benefits and detriments associated with each tool.

The studies described in this paper indicate that guidance in some form is essential within constructivist learning environments to help orient students to the technology and its use (e.g., Windschitl & Andre, 1998), to help with the learning process (e.g., Juniu, 2006) and provide hints on uses of specific tools and technologies during the instruction (e.g., Harskamp & Suhre, 2006). The role of guidance is explicit in the social cognitivist views of Vygotsky and Cole (1978), where the expert guides a learner to attain full learning and performance potential. While many studies in our analysis mentioned guidance, more descriptive details on technological tools and designs that support peer and expert support can be useful. In many studies, expert and peer support was provided within an authentic problem setting; however, the exact method of interaction of individual learners with their peers and experts was not described. Descriptions of interaction and support prompts that help learners would be useful for designing constructivist learning environments. Especially, descriptions of the role of guidance in supporting individuals with less sophisticated epistemological beliefs would be helpful. In Windschitl and Andre's (1998) study, individuals with more sophisticated beliefs did better with constructivist learning situations than epistemologically less mature students. In such cases, it would be important for sufficient guidance to be embedded within less structured content to support students with more fixed views of knowledge.

In summary, technology-enhanced constructivist learning environments offer many opportunities to engage students in authentic, complex, and guided learning interactions and in this paper, we have attempted to identify empirical evidence of successful design structures to enhance student learning. These guidelines include: allowing students to view information in multiple contexts, providing appropriate guidance to navigate information appropriately, engaging students in dialogue to promote knowledge co-construction, engaging students in exploring resources and creating artifacts of learning, and engaging students in accessing multiple, authentic resources. Additional areas of investigation include focusing on differentiating individual and group learning outcomes, describing peer and expert guidance interaction patterns, and explicating specific tools and designs to support specific learning activities.

REFERENCES

Bellefeuille, G. L. (2006). Rethinking reflective practice education in social work education: A blended constructivist and objectivist instructional design strategy for a Web-based child welfare practice course. *Journal of Social Work Education (Special Section: Innovations in Gerontological Social Work Education)*, *42*(1), 85–103.

Bereiter, C. (1994). Constructivism, socioculturalism, and Popper's world 3. *Educational Researcher*, *23*(7), 21–23.

Bonk, C. J., Hay, K. E., & Fischler, R. B. (1996). Five key resources for an electronic community of elementary student weather forecasters. *Journal of Computing in Childhood Education*, *7*(1/2), 93–118.

Bostock, S. J. (1998). Constructivism in mass higher education: A case study. *British Journal of Educational Technology*, *29*(3), 255–240.

Cognition and Technology Group at Vanderbilt (CGTV) (1993). The Jasper series: Theoretical foundations and data on problem solving and transfer. In L.A., Penner, G. M. Batsche, H. M. Knoff, & D. L. Nelson (Eds.). The challenges in mathematics and science education: Psychology's response (pp. 113–152). Washington, DC: American Psychological Association.

Chadwick, C. (2004). Why I am not a constructivist. *Educational Technology*, *5*, 46–49.

Choi, H. J., & Johnson, S. D. (2005). The effect of context-based video instruction on learning and motivation in online courses. *American Journal of Distance Education*, *19*(4), 215–227.

Clark, R. E. (1994). Media will never influence learning. *Educational Technology Research and Development*, *42*(2), 21–29.

Cobb, T. (1999). Applying constructivism: A test for the learner-as-scientist. *Educational Technology Research and Development*, *47*(3), 15–31.

Forster, P. (1999). Applying constructivist theory to practice in a technology-based learning environment. *Mathematics Education Research Journal*, *11*(2), 81–93.

Gilbert, N. J., & Driscoll, M. P. (2002). Collaborative knowledge building: A case study. *Educational Technology Research and Development*, *50*(1), 59–79.

Glasersfeld, E. V. (1995). *Radical constructivism: A way of knowing and learning*. London: Falmer Press.

Harskamp, E. G., & Suhre, C. J. M. (2006). Improving mathematical problem solving: A computerized approach. *Computers in Human Behavior*, *22*(5), 801–815.

Jonassen, D. H., Peck, K. L., & Wilson, B. G. (1999). *Learning with technology: A constructivist perspective*. Upper Saddle River, NJ: Merrill.

Juniu, S. (2006). Use of technology for constructivist learning in a performance assessment class. *Measurement in Physical Education and Exercise Science 10*(1), 67–79.

Kirschner, P., Sweller, J., & Clark, R. (2006). Why minimal guidance during instruction does not work: An analysis of the failure of constructivist, discovery, problem-based, experiential, and inquiry-based teaching. *Educational Psychologist*, *41*(2), 75–86.

Kozma, R. B. (1994). Will media influence learning? Reframing the debate. *Educational Technology Research and Development*, *42*(2), 7–19.

Lavonen, J., Meisalo, V., & Lattu, M. (2002). Collaborative problem solving in a control technology learning environment, a pilot study. *International Journal of Technology and Design Education, 12*(2), 139–160.

Lester, J. C., Stone, B. A., & Stelling, G. D. (1999). Lifelike pedagogical agents for mixed-initiative problem solving in constructivist learning environments. *User Modeling and User-Adapted Interaction, 9*(1/2), 1–44.

McKinnon, D. H., Geissinger, H., & Danaia, L. (2002). Helping them understand: Astronomy for Grades 5 and 6. *Information Technology in Childhood Education Annual, 14*, 263–275.

Murphy, K. L., Mahoney, S. E., Chen, C.-Y., Mendoza-Diaz, N. V., & Yang, X. (2005). A constructivist model of mentoring, coaching, and facilitating online discussions. *Distance Education, 26*(3), 341–366.

Perkins, D. N. (1991). Technology meets constructivism: Do they make a marriage? *Educational Technology, 31*(5), 18–23.

Puntambekar, S. (2006). Analyzing collaborative interactions: Divergence, shared understanding and construction of knowledge. *Computers and Education, 47*(3), 332–351.

Rice, M. L., & Wilson, E. K. (1999). How technology aids constructivism in the social studies classroom. *Social Studies, 90*(1), 28–33.

Salomon, G. (1991). Learning: New conceptions, new opportunities. *Educational Technology, 31*(6), 41–44.

Salomon, G., Perkins, D. N., & Globerson, T. (1991). Partners in cognition: Extending human intelligence with intelligent technologies. *Educational Researcher, 20*(3), 2–9.

Scardamalia, M., & Bereiter, C. (1992). An architecture for collaborative knowledge-building. In E. D. Corte, M. Linn, H. Mandl, & L. Verschaffel (Eds.), *Computer-based learning environments and problem solving* (pp. 41–46). Berlin: Springer-Verlag.

Schellens, T., & Valcke, M. (2005). Collaborative learning in asynchronous discussion groups: What about the impact on cognitive processing? *Computers in Human Behavior, 21*(6), 6–28.

Vanderbilt, C. a. T. G. a. (1993). Designing learning environments that support thinking: The Jasper series as a case study. In T. M. Duffy, J. Lowyeh, & D. H. Jonassen (Eds.), *Designing environments for constructive learning* (pp. 9–36). Berlin: Springer-Verlag.

Vygotsky, L. S., & Cole, M. (1978). *Mind in society: The development of higher psychological processes*. Cambridge, MA: Harvard University Press.

Windschitl, M., & Andre, T. (1998). Using computer simulations to enhance conceptual change: The roles of constructivist instruction and student epistemological beliefs. *Journal of Research in Science Teaching, 35*(2), 145–160.

Changing Beliefs versus Changing Concepts: Transformational Learning as a Tool for Investigating and Encouraging Teacher Belief Change

Christa Harrelson Deissler
University of Georgia

INTRODUCTION

Much of what is done in the name of professional development for K-12 teachers is intended to influence teachers' practice with an ultimate goal of improving student learning. In order to encourage teachers to change their practice, professional developers should be aware of the epistemology that supports whatever practices they are recommending for use. Furthermore, much of the literature on epistemology points to the need for understanding the process of belief change and development when attempting to encourage a change in epistemology. In this paper, I will discuss the literature that has led me to the conclusion that epistemological change is most appropriately investigated through the use of Transformational Learning theory and how this particular theory is a more sensitive tool for investigating such a change compared to other theories such as Conceptual Change.

EPISTEMOLOGICAL CHANGE

Perry (1970) was one of the first researchers to investigate the nature of epistemological development with his study of college students, which resulted in a leveled view of personal epistemology. The resulting model from Perry's longitudinal studies includes nine epistemological positions at which a student might find him or herself, and as Hofer and Pintrich (1997) point out, these positions are similar to Piaget's developmental schemes. In fact, Hofer and Pintrich go on to compare Perry's model with epistemological perspectives of Belenky et al. (1986) in "women's ways of knowing," Baxter Magolda's (1992) ways of knowing in epistemological reflection, King and Kitchener's (1994) reflective judgment stages, and Kuhn's (1970) epistemological views in argumentative reasoning. In these models of epistemological development, the epistemologies range from "absolute truth" views of knowledge at the earliest stages of development to "relative/contextual views of knowledge" in the later stages.

Another developmental view of epistemological beliefs that Hofer and Pintrich (1997) could add to their comparison above is the model proposed by Qian and Alvermann (1995). They have conducted research into the specific relationship of students' epistemological beliefs and conceptual change in science. They found that students who had a "simple-certain" view of scientific knowledge were less likely to experience conceptual change. This simple-certain view of knowledge in their model is in comparison to "complex and tentative." In this study, they investigate the influence of existing epistemological beliefs on new learning, but they do not investigate the development of epistemological beliefs or recommend strategies to encourage epistemological belief change. It simply acknowledges that existing beliefs have an influence on learning specific concepts.

While Qian and Alvermann do not specifically recommend strategies to facilitate epistemological development, many researchers (King & Kitchener, 1994; Schön, 1987; Bushnell & Henry, 2003) have emphasized the importance of reflection in the process of epistemological change. Schön's (1983) model of reflective practice advocates three forms of reflection that must be employed to facilitate change in practice. Those three forms are reflection-in-action, reflection-on-action, and reflection-for-action. In fact, the works of both Schön and King and Kitchener are taught in the curriculum of the class that was the focus of my study on which I am basing my thoughts presented here in this paper.

Finally, Brownlee et al. (2001) have discussed the direct impact that teachers' own epistemological beliefs have on the types of learning opportunities that they design for their students. They designed a specific intervention to address pre-service teachers' epistemological beliefs. Elements of the intervention include: situating student learning experiences, an atmosphere of mutual respect, and regular opportunities for reflection. The result of this intervention is that students did "become more meta-cognitive" (p. 263) and the authors argue that this happened as a result of having the students reflect on epistemological beliefs.

In summary, it seems that most educational researchers with an interest in epistemology recognize that there are levels of epistemological beliefs, and these beliefs have a significant influence on learning. I would argue that for a teacher, these personal epistemological beliefs are of utmost importance since the beliefs of the teacher influence the design of any lesson or learning activity that is implemented. Therefore, it is important that teacher educators and professional developers encourage epistemological development and design learning activities of their own that model the application of a "relative/contextual" epistemology. The use of Transformational Learning Theory is one way to investigate the change process that teachers are likely to experience.

POSSIBLE LENSES FOR THE INVESTIGATION OF EPISTEMOLOGICAL BELIEF CHANGE

Given my interest in encouraging teachers' epistemological belief change, I turned to the literature on educational theories that have been proposed as an explanation for the process of changing one's beliefs. This led me to the theories of conceptual change and transformational learning. In this section I will discuss each of these two theories that served as a lens for investigation into the change process that I witnessed in educators in a study that I recently conducted (Deissler, 2007), and will end with an argument for the use of transformational learning theory.

Conceptual Change

Conceptual change can be broadly defined as learning that facilitates the change of an existing concept or idea. While I have focused specifically on beliefs, which are often more emotional and less logical than concepts, there is a large part of the conceptual change literature that addresses the fact that concepts are not always based on factual information, and further, there is a suggested relationship between the affective domain and the conceptual change process (Pintrich et al., 1993; Chinn & Samarapungavan, 2001; Hofer & Pintrich, 1997). There are multiple versions of conceptual change theory, and below I summarize and synthesize the main works that have informed my understanding of conceptual change.

Pintrich et al. (1993) provided a comprehensive summary of conceptual change research and pointed toward Piaget as the originator of the notion of conceptual change with his thoughts of disequilibrium and accommodation. They summarize Posner et al. (1982) and the four conditions that must exist for a learner to make accommodations in their existing concepts for new information and ideas. Those four conditions are that (1) the learner must be *dissatisfied* with their existing concept; (2) the new concept must be *intelligible*; (3) the new concept must be *plausible*; and (4) the new concept must seem *fruitful*. Notice two of the conditions of this model appeal to the logical constructs of intelligibility and plausibility. However, the classification of concepts as being satisfactory

Table 1. Conceptual Change Observation Tool

Observed Category of Conceptual Change	Conditions for Conceptual Change
a. Ignore the data b. Reject the data c. Profess uncertainty about the validity of the data d. Exclude the data e. Hold the data in abeyance f. Reinterpret the data g. Accept the data and make peripheral theory changes h. Accept the data and change theories	• The learner was *dissatisfied* with their existing concept • The learner felt the new concept was *intelligible* • The learner felt the new concept must be *plausible* • The learner felt the new concept was *fruitful*

or fruitful appeals to the affective domain. So even in this early model of conceptual change, there was some consideration of more subjective issues.

Chinn and Brewer (1993, 1998) created a taxonomy of the conceptual change process (see, Table 1). Their original work in 1993 in which they studied students' responses to anomalous data, led to the original taxonomy. At that time they proposed seven categories of responses that learners exhibit when presented with anomalous data. Those categories of responses are to

a.   ignore the data

b.   reject the data

c.   exclude the data

d.   hold the data in abeyance

e.   reinterpret the data

f.   accept the data and make peripheral theory changes

g.   accept the data and change theories.

Upon further studies in 1998, they determined that there is an eighth category of response that was not found in the original studies. That category of response is to *profess uncertainty about the validity of the data*. This eighth response category falls between categories b and c above. While this taxonomy provides a continuum of responses that might be observed in the conceptual change process, it does not suggest reasons why a learner might respond to a new concept in any of the particular ways. However, when Chinn and Brewer's taxonomy is combined with the conditions of Posner et al., the result is a much more productive framework for investigation of the conceptual change process. The result of the combination is represented below in a sort of analysis checklist that allows an investigator to look for the logical stages of conceptual change while still considering elements of the affective domain.

However, even if we view the model proposed by Posner et al. to be inclusive of the affective domain, and we overlap their conditions with Chinn and Brewer's taxonomy, Pintrich et al. (1993) still argue that these models are "cold," rational models that do not allow for the consideration of the role played by motivation and context in the conceptual change process. They discuss the role of beliefs of all sorts, including epistemological

Table 2. Conceptual Change Observation Tool—*Expanded*

Observed Category of Conceptual Change	Observed Conditions for Conceptual Change	Observed Elements of the Conceptual Change Instructional Model
a. Ignore the data b. Reject the data c. Profess uncertainty about the validity of the data d. Exclude the data e. Hold the data in abeyance f. Reinterpret the data g. Accept the data and make peripheral theory changes h. Accept the data and change theories	• The learner was *dissatisfied* with their existing concept • The learner felt the new concept was *intelligible* • The learner felt the new concept must be *plausible* • The learner felt the new concept was fruitful	• Reveal student preconceptions • Discuss and evaluate preconceptions • Create conceptual conflict with those preconceptions • Encourage and guide conceptual restructuring.

beliefs, on the conceptual change process. They go on to say that as long as learning is situated within the design of traditional classrooms and schools, and not authentic environments in which concepts can be applied and utilized, conceptual change is very unlikely.

While the works above focus on conceptual change of grade-school students within specific disciplines, Davis (2001) argues that conceptual change is relevant when studying the professional development of teachers (see, Table 2). She argues that conceptual change could be considered in any discipline and at any level. Further, in order to facilitate conceptual change, an educator should employ the specific instructional model that she outlines. The elements of the conceptual change instructional model are:

1. Reveal student preconceptions

2. Discuss and evaluate preconceptions

3. Create conceptual conflict with those preconceptions

4. Encourage and guide conceptual restructuring.

With this in mind, the observation tool expands to include one more column.

My goal in using conceptual change theory is as a lens for examining change in the epistemological beliefs of teachers. While much has been written on conceptual change (Chinn & Brewer, 1993, 1998; Posner et al., 1983; Pintrich et al., 1993; Davis, 2001), and much has been written on epistemological beliefs and belief change (see above), the literature that specifically addresses the relation of epistemological beliefs to conceptual change (Qian & Alvermann, 1995, 2001) investigates only the influence of epistemological beliefs on learning, not on teaching. Further, the literature discussed above focuses on conceptual change in relation to subject-specific concepts, rather than epistemological beliefs as a concept. Therefore, the specific gap in the literature related to conceptual change is to investigate the theory's application to the development of epistemological concepts and beliefs.

However, there is an area of the literature in the field of Adult Education that has addressed the issue of belief change, and that is transformational learning. In this next section, I will discuss the theory of transformational learning, and will then present the final complied theoretical framework that I created. Finally I will discuss the advantages of adding the use of transformational learning, as it is a more sensitive tool for the investigation of something as intangible as personal beliefs.

Transformational Learning Theory

Another theory that is relevant to the investigation of teacher belief change is transformational learning theory. Transformational learning is an adult learning theory that is used as a lens to investigate certain transformations adults experience when a change in perspective is taking or has taken place (Mezirow, 1991). Through that lens of transformational learning theory, professional development must encourage a transformation in epistemological beliefs.

There are ten phases of transformational learning theory (or "transformative" as it is used interchangeably in the literature). Those original ten phases reported by Mezirow are:

1. A disorienting dilemma

2. Self-examination with feelings of guilt or shame

3. A critical assessment of epistemic, sociocultural, or psychic assumptions

4. Recognition that one's discontent and the process of transformation are shared and that others have negotiated a similar change

5. Exploration of options for new roles, relationships, and actions

6. Planning of a course of action

7. Acquisition of knowledge and skills for implementing one's plans

8. Provisional trying of new roles

9. Building of competence and self-confidence in new roles and relationships

10. A reintegration into one's life on the basis of conditions dictated by one's new perspective (Mezirow, 1991, pp. 168–169).

In Taylor's (1997) and Wilson and Kiley's (2002) reviews of the literature on transformational learning, they point out that the studies that they reviewed confirm to some degree what Mezirow has been arguing about transformative learning—the revision of meaning structures seems to be initiated by a disorienting dilemma followed by a series of learning strategies involving critical reflection, exploration of different roles and options, and negotiation and renegotiation of relationships. But they both also argue that the ideal practice for fostering transformative learning is theoretically based, with little support from empirical research.

King (1999, 2002, 2004) has written extensively on the topic of transformational learning. In 1999, she studied Adult Basic Education teachers who were in a professional development class learning to use technology in their teaching practices. Then in 2002, she conducted another study with K-12 teachers who were also in a professional development class learning to use technology in their teaching practices. In both of these studies she found that a majority of educators in the situation had experienced a perspective transformation, and that critical reflection was central to their transformation process. Finally, in 2004 she studied the transformational effects of an introduction to adult education class on the beliefs of adult educators. In this study, King addresses the issues that educators who are encouraging a transformation face and the responsibilities that they have. So we see that King has applied the stages of transformational learning in multiple studies in which she investigates the teachers' pedagogical beliefs, or beliefs about the process of teaching.

This is encouraging when considering transformational learning as a lens for investigating changes in teachers' epistemological beliefs.

Though all of King's studies are informative and help to validate the components of transformative learning theory, and offer support for the idea of using transformational learning as a lens to investigate teachers' epistemological belief change, they mimic the situation that Taylor (1997) and Wilson and Kiley (2002) describe, as cited above. The situation being that there is little empirical research that challenges or further develops the theory. It only uses the theory to investigate a situation. Therefore, I combined my understandings of conceptual change theory with transformational learning theory to create a modified framework for the investigation of epistemological belief change in teachers participating in a recent study that I conducted (Deissler, 2007).

A FRAMEWORK FOR INVESTIGATION OF EPISTEMOLOGICAL BELIEF CHANGE

In employing the framework that I developed, I looked for evidence of the conditions of conceptual change (Posner et al., 1982) and elements of Davis' (2001) conceptual change instruction within the activities of the class that was being studied. Among the participants, I watched for Chinn and Brewer's (1998) categories of conceptual change. In conjunction with the various elements and conditions of conceptual change theory, I also looked for evidence of the stages of transformational learning during the conceptual change process among the study participants. The use of transformational learning theory is particularly important because it is much more inclusive of the affective domain that Pintrich et al. (1993) insist is central to the theory of conceptual change.

Table 3 represents what I perceive to be an overlap of the two theories. The stages of transformational learning have been removed from the original order in which Mezirow proposed them, but as he points out in his writings (1991), the stages of transformational learning are rarely linear in their occurrence, and certain stages of transformation may be experienced multiple times within the transformation process.

CONCLUSION

By combining these two theories, I blended two areas of the literature that until the time of my study had remained fairly isolated in the literature. This new model served as a framework for the design of my study, and was a lens for analysis and interpretation of the data after it was collected. If it were not for the inclusion of transformational learning, I would not have been able to detect the subtle nuances of belief change as opposed to conceptual change. Transformational learning encouraged me to look for emotions such as guilt and self-doubt that I likely would have overlooked if I were focused specifically on conceptual change. It also prompted me to included questions in my interviews and use specific forms of data such as participants' reflections that helped me understand the internal processes that my participants were experiencing. These forms of data are more indicative of belief change than other forms of data (such as work products and participants' answers to questions about their teaching practice) that are more relevant to conceptual change.

In closing, I would suggest that researchers and designers of professional development for teachers remain cognizant of the importance of teachers' beliefs, and not just their practice. Furthermore, I would recommend that they become familiar with the theory of transformational learning to make use of it as an invaluable tool for investigation into the process of belief change and the design of experiences for teachers that encourage such a change.

Table 3. Conceptual Transformation

Observed Category of Conceptual Change	Conditions for Conceptual Change with Corresponding Stages of Transformational Learning	Observed Elements of the Conceptual Change Instructional Model
a. Ignore the data	• The learner was dissatisfied with their existing concept	• Reveal student preconceptions
b. Reject the data	• A disorienting dilemma	• Discuss and evaluate preconceptions
c. Profess uncertainty about the validity of the data	• Recognition that one's discontent and the process of transformation are shared and that others have negotiated a similar change	• Create conceptual conflict with those preconceptions
d. Exclude the data	• Exploration of options for new roles, relationships, and actions	• Encourage and guide conceptual restructuring
e. Hold the data in abeyance	• The learner felt the new concept was intelligible	
f. Reinterpret the data	• Self-examination with feelings of guilt or shame	
g. Accept the data and make peripheral theory changes	• Acquisition of knowledge and skills for implementing one's plans	
h. Accept the data and change theories	• The learner felt the new concept must be plausible	
	• A critical assessment of epistemic, sociocultural, or psychic assumptions	
	• Planning of a course of action	
	• Provisional trying of new roles	
	• The learner felt the new concept was fruitful	
	• Building of competence and self-confidence in new roles and relationships	
	• A reintegration into one's life on the basis of conditions dictated by one's new perspective	

REFERENCES

Baxter Magolda, M. B. (1992). Knowing and Reasoning in College: Gender Related Patterns in Students' Intellectual Development. New York: Jossey-Bass.

Belenky, M. F.; McVicker Clinchy, B.; Rule Golberger, N.; Mattuck Tarule, J. (1986). Women's ways of knowing: The development of self, voice, and mind. New York: Basic Books.

Brownlee, Joanne and Purdie, Nola and Boulton-Lewis, Gillian (2001) Changing epistemological beliefs in pre-service teacher education students. *Teaching in Higher Education 6*(2), 247–268.

Bushnell, M., and S. E. Henry. 2003. The role of reflection in epistemological change: Autobiography in teacher education. *Educational Studies, 34*, 38–61.

Chinn, C. A. & Brewer, W. F. (1993). The role of anomalous data in knowledge acquisition: A theoretical framework and implications for science instruction. *Review of Educational Research, 63*(1), 1–49.

——— (1998). An empirical test of a taxonomy of responses to anomalous data in science. *Journal of Research in Science Teaching, 35*(6), 623–654.

Chinn, C. A. & Samarapungavan, A. (2001). Distinguishing between understanding and belief. *Theory Into Practice, 40*(4), 235–241.

Davis, J. (2001). Conceptual change. In M. Orey (Ed.), *Emerging perspective on learning, teaching, and technology.* Available at http://www.coe.uga.edu/epltt/conceptualchange.htm.

Deissler, C. H. (2007). Educators' belief change in a situated learning environment. Unpublished dissertation, University of Georgia, Athens.

Hofer, B. K. & Pintrich, P. R. (1997). The development of epistemological theories: Beliefs about knowledge and knowing and their relation to learning. *Review of Educational Research, 67*(1), 88–140.

King, K. P. (1999). Unleashing technology in the classroom: What adult basic education teachers and organizations need to know. *Adult Basic Education, 9*(3), 162–176.

——— (2002). Educational technology professional development as transformative learning opportunities. *Computers & Education, 39*, 283–297.

——— (2004). Both sides now: Examining transformative learning and professional development of educators. *Innovative Higher Education, 29*(2), 155–174.

King, P. M. and Kitchner, K. S. (1994). Developing Reflective Judgment: Understanding and Promoting Intellectual Growth and Critical Thinking in Adolescents and Adults. San Francisco: Jossey-Bass Publishers.

Kuhn, D. (1991). *The skills of argument.* Cambridge, UK: Cambridge University Press.

Kuhn, T. (1970). *The structure of scientific revolutions.* Chicago: University of Chicago Press.

Mezirow, J. (1991). *Transformative dimensions in adult learning.* San Francisco, CA: Jossey-Bass.

Perry, W. G., Jr. (1970). *Forms of intellectual and ethical development in the college years: A scheme.* New York: Holt.

Pintrich, P. R., Marx, R. W., & Boyle, R. A. (1993). Beyond cold conceptual change: The role of motivational beliefs and classroom contextual factors in the process of conceptual change. *Review of Educational Research, 63*(2), 167–199.

Posner, G. J., Strike, K. A., Hewson, P. W., & Gertzog, W. A. (1982). Accommodation of a scientific conception: Toward a theory of conceptual change. *Science Education, 66*, 211–227.

Qian, G. & Alvermann, D. E. (1995). The role of epistemological beliefs and learned helplessness in secondary school students' learning science from text. *Journal of Educational Psychology, 87,* 282–292.

Schön, D. A. (1987). *Educating the reflective practitioner.* San Francisco, CA: Jossey-Bass.

Taylor, E. W. (1997). Building upon the theoretical debate: A critical review of the empirical studies of Mezirow's transformative learning theory. *Adult Education Quarterly, 48*(1), 34–59.

Wilson, A. L. & Kiley, R. C. (2002, May). Towards a critical theory of adult learning/education: Transformational theory and beyond. Paper presented at the annual meeting of the Adult Education Research Conference, Raleigh, NC.

Part Two
Library and Information Science

Introduction

V. J. McClendon

As indicated by the name change, this year continues the push to bring greater breadth to *Educational Media and Technology Yearbook's* (EMTY) library section. Since beginning editorship of the School Library Media section, I have attempted to span the interests of K-12, public, and academic libraries, as well as library education. The new section title, Library & Information Science, is more representative of most library schools encompassing all of areas of library service, technology and information literacy, and library professional education.

To celebrate that, this issue runs the gamut of those areas. Broad issues have begun to command our attention this year in libraries and technology including educational policy, information literacy, extending access and services to underserved populations, reflections on teaching, learning, and the future education of teacher librarians. As library professionals, we ubiquitously use the Internet for work, continuing education, and entertainment. It can also be a method of stimulating our own creativity and productivity.

There are few who do not recall the 2006 *Time* magazine's Person of the Year: You (Grosman, L., Dec. 13, 2006). As computer use becomes more seamlessly integrated into ever greater levels of our lives, users are responding by personalizing Internet content in some amazing ways. Most notably, blogs and YouTube videos (http://www.youtube.com) bring opportunities for new collaboration and fresh ideas far from traditional centers of power. This media diversity represents a dramatic democratic shift. It can not only provide a *hook* to get ourselves involved in today's issues, but for patrons as well—engaging and empowering!

A quick search locates hundreds of library-related blogs, including Frontier Librarian from Australia (http://frontierlibrarian.blogspot.com/), Bibliotecários sem Fronteiras (Librarians without Borders, http://biblio.crube.net/index.php), a Brazilian discussion of digital resources, BlogWithoutaLibrary (http://www.blogwithoutalibrary.net/) on library user experience, Librarian Activist (http://www.librarianactivist.org/), the Rambling Librarian of Singapore (http://ramblinglibrarian.blogspot.com/), and Gadgets blog (http://www.handheldlib.blogspot.com/) focusing on handheld technology use in libraries among others. No longer are librarians, IT, and LIS students reading only the comments of researchers and deans, but we are sounding off, pushing ideas and operations to places the old (*and not so old*) guard never imagined. Bloggers are bringing new realities, not simply as entertainment, but functional core job concepts as well. An excellent example comes from *BlogWithoutaLibrary* where Amanda Etches-Johnson, blogger/librarian, and librarian/commenter Michael Stephens, St. Joseph County Public Library, discuss "No Lists," times we say no to patrons and why, as a way of investigating and improving user experience (*BlogWithoutaLibrary*, July 3, 2007). What a great, functional idea!

Some may be wagging your heads, thinking this newfound democratic voice is only for the digital-well-to-do. Indeed, the digital divide is a continuing concern worldwide. Fortunately, libraries are poised to help bridge that divide by providing public computers and Internet access. While public libraries have traditionally hosted youth programs, *Library Journal* (July, 2007) demands to know what baby boomers want. Affluent boomers from 40 to 60 are considering retirement, volunteering, child rearing, and travel; according to *LJ,* we should be listening to boomer needs through Reader's Advisory (RA) groups (Wyatt, pp. 40–43).

The year's chapter lineup begins with a rigorous look at the romance novel, placement, and RA as an evaluative tool. In *The Red Dot District*, Esser, Adkins, and Velasquez take us inside public libraries to the dimly lit nooks of romance literature. Part of an extended two-year national study, the writers examine practitioners' attitudes toward *pink* literature and their extension to notions regarding romance readers. They provide us with a truly eye-opening reflection of our response as an industry. Statistics provided by the authors not only suggest that Americans love a little romance, to the tune of $1.2 billion annually (Romance Writers of America, 2005), but that we as librarians may be marginalizing our romance-reading patrons by systematically deselecting, omitting, and red-dot districting such literature. If other popular fiction genres are generally accepted, why is romance literature hidden? The Red Dot District begs the question—as a largely pink-collar industry, are we characterizing women readers as misguided and ill-informed?

The second chapter, *aRt, the 4th R: Arts and Communication across the Curriculum* by B. J. Berquist, represents a two year odyssey. Ms. Berquist is an art teacher who uses media, technology, and a kaleidoscope of resources to inspire and intrigue her students. Not only is she different, so are her students at Loysville Youth Development Center, a lockdown facility outside of Harrisburg, Pennsylvania. Despite frustrations over Adequate Yearly Progress (AYP) and NCLB, Berquist finds the time for everything from resource-based learning (Hill & Hannafin, 2001) to multiple intelligences (Gardner, 1993). Besides writing prose and poetry, she also pens a blog, *Between the Lines* (http://voicesfromloysville.blogspot.com/), where she and other educators wrestle with the issues of childhood detention and consider ways to break the revolving cycle of disappointment and violence in youthful offenders' lives. Berquist also serves as a host and helpdesk staffer at *TappedIn*, an "online workplace of an international community of education professionals where K-12 teachers and librarians, professional development staff, teacher education faculty and students, and researchers engage in professional development programs and informal collaborative activities with colleagues" (TappedIn, 1997). Ever the challenging type, she offers up ways to use cultural identity boxes, digital storytelling, rap poetry, as well as a conscience-rattling dose of graphic reality on living, learning, and teaching behind bars.

In this year's academic library chapter, we look at a major university's effort to promote greater use of an investment-heavy resource: microforms. For years microforms represented a technological advance and, in truth, still provide a great, compact, stable resource for our users to access older materials—if we can only get users to look at them! In *Digitizing Microforms on-Demand: Reviving Access to a Dead Collection?*—Desai and Kaspar detail libraries' growing awareness in providing the kind of content and access today's user demands. They discuss how one major university library developed *deliverEdocs* program to rejuvenate this historically underutilized collection by digitizing microforms on-demand. Desai & Kaspar not only provide an excellent review of the history of microforms and their use, but the transition of this typically non-portable resource to the digital environment. In fact, according to Crow (2002) many major universities have extensive, unique collections of microform data, and there is a growing trend to digitize these materials illustrating the quality research standing of their materials. Key to the usefulness of this chapter is its attention to the fine details of moving the digitization from concept to institutionalized process. The authors provide step-by-step instructions, illustrations, faculty notification, processing documentation, and feedback survey models (see Appendices A–C) for others who wish to duplicate their method.

Moving on to educational theory and practice, Terrance Newell discusses the theoretical underpinnings of Immersive Information Literacy Approach (I^2LA). Newell's work is based on the creation of authentic learning experience through the use of computer and Internet technologies for information literacy training. His chapter seeks to examine the professional discourse and perceptions of information literacy which then directly impact practice in the field of school library media. Information literacy, or the learner's ability to access, evaluate, and organize information for problem solving, is closely tied to the broader concepts of lifelong learning and critical thinking (Bruce, 1997). Newell's theory is that this interweaving of immersive technologies and information studies in the K-12 environment can create new best-practices for teacher-librarians. Based on Gee's (2003) work, Newell explains the connection between reading and reconceptualizing information for new purposes. It is in this space of defining literacy based on information manipulation that practitioners vary. In an attempt to study and solidify these concepts, Newell has created the VILLAS project (Virtual Reality Information Literacy Learning and Assessment Space), which serves as a model of such immersive online learning. Newell invites us to consider how we teach information literacy and how new technologies may stimulate students' desire to know and repackage information that is presented in a form particularly suited toward tech-savvy learners.

The 2007American Association of School Librarians hosted Daniel Pink. His book, *A Whole New Mind* (2005), discusses how divergent, lateral thinkers excel in our rapidly changing, outsourcing world. Few people are as well qualified to translate worldwide concerns such as lateral problem solving to the school library world as Dr. Lesley Farmer. Respected author, editor, teacher, and scholar, Dr. Farmer received the DEMCO Research Award in 2002 and in 2007 the Distinguished Scholarly and Academic Activity Award at California State University, Long Beach. Her EMTY contribution this year, entitled *Predictors for Success: Experiences of Beginning and Expert Teacher Librarians,* compares the developmental practice skills and global thinking of a California study group with representative populations around the world. Concerned with the success of Teacher Librarians (TL), their perceptions of self efficacy, persistence, and stress, the study identifies universally and culturally determined practices. Farmer's research illustrates the movement from an outside locus of control to a growing self-confidence, broader critical thinking, program development, student achievement planning, and school leadership roles among TLs over time. Overall, Farmer provides a well paved bridge between competency theory (Van Manen, 1977; Dreyfus, 2004; Ambrose & Bridges, 2005), and SLM program development, linking conceptual framework, practice, evaluation, and professional development. This chapter is a must read for other SLM program directors providing critical learning experiences needed to foster success among new and developing TLs.

The last chapter by Susan Stansberry is an excellent pairing to follow Farmer's work, as it illustrates the potential for SLM specialists to influence schools and districts on organizational levels. *Using Organizational Culture to Frame Discussions of the Disciplinary Field of School Library Media* encourages the professional teacher librarian to understand the potential for change, student achievement, and teacher collaboration by understanding the school as a culture. Understanding the corporate culture, and the social nature of our educational environments ensures the teacher librarian focuses on larger, global issues and becomes part of the community discussion on problem solving and program development. Stansberry charges the SLM specialist to engage others in the success of the library, jointly planning broad strokes for a stronger, collaborative future.

In sum, the authors of the Library and Information Science chapters recognize the challenges of the future, the critical role of technology, communication, and the position of theory and research to help tease out more creative, less traditionally centered solutions. Become a part of our community of practice through blogging, commenting, or traditional publishing to share in the democratic discussion.

REFERENCES

Ambrose, S., & Bridges, M. (2005). Becoming a master teacher. *Advocate, 22*(3), 5–8.

Berquist, B.J. (2007). Between the lines. *Blogger.* Retrieved on May 23, 2007, from http://voicesfromloysville.blogspot.com/.

Bruce, Christine. (1997). *The seven faces of information literacy.* Adelaide, Australia: Auslib Press.

Crow, R. (2002). The case for institutional repositories: A SPARC position paper. Washington, DC: SPARC. Retrieved on July 15, 2007, from http://www.arl.org/sparc/bm%7Edoc/ir_final_release_102.pdf.

Dreyfus, S. (2004). The five-stage model of adult skill acquisition. *Bulletin of Science, Technology & Society, 24*(3), 177–181.

Etches-Johnson, A. (2007, July 3). *Culture of "no" to a culture of "why?".* Blog Without a Library. Retrieved on July 15, 2007, from http://www.blogwithoutalibrary.net/?p=280#comment-17546.

Gardner, Howard. (1993). *Multiple intelligences: The theory into practice.* New York: Basic Books.

Gee, J. (2003). *What video games have to teach us about learning and literacy.* New York: Palgrave Macmillan.

Grossman, L. (2006, December 13). Time's person of the year: You. *Time Magazine, 167*(51), 38–41.

Hill, J. R., & Hannafin, M. J. (2001). The resurgence of resource-based learning. *Educational Technology, Research and Development, 49*(3), 37–52.

Pink, D. H. (2005). *A whole new mind: Why right-brainers will rule the future.* New York: The Berkeley Publishing Group.

Romance Writers of America. (2005). Market research study on romance readers. https://www.rwanational.org/eweb/dynamicpage.aspx?webcode=StatisticsAuthor. Accessed on May 25, 2007.

TappedIn. (1997). TappedIn: A community of education professionals. Accessed on May 23, 2007, from http://tappedin.org/tappedin/.

Van Manen, M. (1977). Linking ways of knowing with ways of being practical. *Curriculum Inquiry, 6*, 208–225.

Wyatt, N. (2007). An RA big think. *Library Journal, 132*(12), 40–43.

"The Red Dot District": Uncommon Ground in Reader Advisory Education and Professional Practice

Linda Esser, Denice Adkins, and Diane L. Velasquez
University of Missouri

Michael H. Harris, in *No Love Lost: Library Women vs. Women Who Use Libraries* (1992) suggests public librarians have yet to come to terms with the "unflinching conclusion" (p. 1) they are endowed with some special knowledge that enables them to distinguish between high and low culture; between good books and bad. Scholarship on cultural positioning parallels Harris's view. Librarians frequently assume a high culture perspective that marginalizes some categories of popular fiction (Bold, 1980; Harris, 1992; Mosley, Charles, & Havir; 1995; Scott, 2002). While public librarians may appear to be increasingly tolerant of readers' choices, recent research indicates remnants of the high culture/low culture distinction are deeply embedded in professional practice. While public librarians express opinions that are professionally palatable, in practice they continue to make judgments and comments based on patrons' reading choices (Adkins, Esser, & Velasquez, 2006). Romance fiction, in particular, is both categorized and marginalized in public libraries. Unfortunately, both the good/bad categorization and the marginalization sometimes overflow from the books to engulf library users who choose to read the kinds of genre fiction often relegated to the low culture trash pile.

THE VIEW FROM THE BOTTOM OF THE HIERARCHY OF TASTE

Modleski (1982) describes three attitudes often adopted toward women's popular fiction: " . . . dismissiveness; hostility—tending unfortunately to be aimed at the consumers of the narrative; or most frequently, a flippant kind of mockery" (p. 14). As Beth Rapp Young (1997) succinctly states, " . . . popular romance lies at the bottom of our hierarchy of taste" (p. 30). In the 1980s, a scene was played out at the Louisville Free Public Library (LFPL) that illustrates how these attitudes translate into professional practice. A former LFPL Director eliminated all standing subscriptions to series romance fiction paperbacks. These books were immensely popular with women readers, many of whom regularly checked library shelves and paperback racks for new books at the beginning of each month. The Director reallocated the funds to purchase additional titles for the fine arts collections held at the Main library. Fine arts books were of value to the community; paperback romance fiction was at the bottom of the Director's hierarchy of taste. Romance fiction readers quickly noticed the lack of new titles on the paperback racks and voiced their displeasure to librarians throughout the system. The librarians suggested patrons contact the Library Director. Within weeks, the subscriptions had been reinstated and back issues had been added to the system's collections for each branch library.

Alison Scott (2002) describes the more recent collection development practices of the Tulsa Public Library (TPL). TPL determined to limit funds for genre fiction, citing its mission as "cultural guardian" (Scott, 2002, p. 217) as the reason for the decision. TPL decided "merely satisfying patrons' immediate cravings" (p. 218) was secondary to its assumed role as cultural guardian, even though the decision disenfranchised a substantial number of TPL's romance fiction readers. According to Scott, "No other category of popular fiction is singled out for exclusion [at TPL], and the librarians feel no need to justify their deliberate alienation of a significant part of the reading public from the aims of a public library" (p. 218).

Publishing and reader statistics for the romance fiction industry in the United States are staggering. In 2004, 2,285 romance titles were released. Market sales share for romance fiction was 54.9% and accounted for nearly one-half of all paperback fiction sold resulting in $1.2 billion in sales. Romance fiction represents 39.3% of all fiction sold; Mystery/Thrillers are a close second at 29.6%. Science Fiction, a genre that seems to have an accepted place in public library collections, garners 6.4% of total market sales (Romance Writers of America, 2007).

There are an estimated 64.6 million romance fiction readers in the United States; 78% (50.4 million) are women. Forty-two per cent of romance fiction readers (27 million) hold a bachelor's degree or higher. Thirty-two per cent (25.2 million) purchased the last romance they read as a new book; 43% (27.7 million) received the last romance novel they read as a gift, borrowed the book from a friend, bought a used book or used other sources. Twenty-five per cent of romance fiction readers (16.1 million) checked out the last romance novel they read from the public library. This figure represents an 11% increase over the 14% reported in 2002 (Romance Writers of America, 2007).

EXPLORING THE RED DOT DISTRICT

The research team members are long-term romance readers. Individual subgenre preferences are diverse and range from suspense/thriller to historical fiction, regency, paranormal and contemporary. Two team members have work experience as public librarians; all have experience as women readers of the romance genre who have, at one time or another, checked romance fiction out of a public library. Informal, shared reminiscences about lived experiences as both romance consumers and professional librarians led to questions about the place of romance fiction in public libraries and current reader advisory practice. The result of these discussions was a pilot study focused on the attitudes of Missouri public librarians toward romance fiction and its readers. The Missouri study, conducted in 2005, surveyed a purposive sampling of 126 public library service agencies (main libraries and branches) in geographically distributed rural, suburban, and urban locations in the state. Seventy-seven surveys were returned for a 61% response rate. Results of the study provided a snapshot of romance acquisitions processes, cataloging practices, and attitudes of Missouri librarians toward romance fiction and its readers (Adkins, Esser, & Velasquez, 2006).

Some aspects of the data from the Missouri study proved tantalizing. To explore further the results of the Missouri study and to address some of its limitations, a broadly based mixed methods study is being conducted during 2006–2007 funded by a grant from the Romance Writers of America. Statistical data was gathered in late 2006 through a survey of 1,020 public librarians from across the United States to gather information regarding demographics, collections, and reader advisory practices. There were 396 usable returns for a 39% return rate. Responses came from libraries in 48 states. The survey included open-ended questions to elicit respondents' attitudes toward romance fiction and their perceptions of its readers. Survey data was examined using both statistical and qualitative analysis methods. The open-ended responses were coded and categorized based on common emergent themes.

Focus groups were conducted with public librarians at national, state, and regional conferences to discuss questions about course work related to reader advisory, and perceptions of readers based on reading preferences. Verbatim transcripts of focus group discussions were analyzed and coded to identify common themes. Preliminary results parallel those of the Missouri study.

The survey produced quantitative and qualitative results that were simultaneously interesting and frustrating. Statistical analysis indicates that many of the public libraries surveyed collect and promote romance fiction. Responses indicate 63% of the libraries have romance fiction collections and that 56% offer romance reader advisory services; 23% carry romance-specific reader advisory tools. Forty-one per cent of the libraries have romance displays; 13% host romance author visits. A few libraries (8%) carry romance-oriented journals such as *Romantic Times* and 6% host romance discussion groups.

These findings suggest that public libraries may be taking the path of least resistance toward romance novels and romance promotion. There is relatively little pain in making romance-specific reader advisory service available in addition to standard reader advisory service, providing general reader advisory tools or putting up romance fiction displays. However, as romance promotion becomes more time- and labor-intensive, libraries' commitment to those services appears to decline.

The source of frustration with the results of the data analysis can be attributed to clear indications that the good/bad categorization of romance fiction and the marginalization of its readers is alive and well in public libraries. Several respondents indicated women who read romance fiction are somehow intellectually less capable, intellectually exhausted, or self-identified as pseudo-intellectuals. The following verbatim comments, excerpted from the survey data, represent what Modleski (1982) refers to as "dismissiveness" and "hostility" toward women's popular fiction and its readers (p. 14).

> The ones who make excuses for their selection are often teachers or those who aspire to be intellectuals. My community has an extremely high percentage of college graduates and many of them look upon romance as escape literature.

> I personally am not real fond of Romance novels however I recognize that many people love them. If a person wants to read a book just for pure pleasure (doesn't want to be scared or learn anything) romance is a good choice.

Other survey respondents view romance fiction as a way to lead its misguided readers from the depths of the reading hierarchy to its pinnacle.

> I... will voice my viewpoint that some books are better than others. As librarians, I believe we walk a fine line: we need to accept all reading as good reading and build collections for a range of readers, but at the same time we can take an active role of guiding those interested in guidance to the best of entertainment, literary merit, and accurate information. How's that at being elitist and egalitarian at the same time?

> I've heard the comments (negative) [sic] about romance books, but I'm tolerant. Just really glad that people read at all; and, we're not all cut out to read Literature all the time.

Some public librarian survey participants consider the genre a means of educational inspiration for emergent literates and imply that literate readers do not choose to read romance fiction.

> A well written romance novel can catch the interest of a person who is typically a non-reader and help broaden their ability to read, their vocabulary, and other topics addressed in the book ... One novel like this can pique the interest of a reader to research topics they discover in the novel.

In some circumstances, categorization may, in fact, make explicit the marginalization of romance fiction collections in public libraries. What librarians regard as humor, readers might interpret as a kind of derision or flippant mockery (Modleski, p. 14).

> I have put the paperback romances into a hallway with flowers across the top. I call it my "Romance Bower."

> We put red dots on all of our paperback romances, then place them on a rack at the back of the library. Some of the staff refer to it as the "Red Dot District."

There are, however, public librarians who believe readers have a right to go slumming in the Red Dot District if they choose to do so. One public librarian who responded to the survey comments:

> My previous position was at a library at which the director (male) made extremely insulting comments about our patrons who read romance novels & refused to purchase any for the library (despite the fact that the majority of our patrons were women who checked out mostly romances). Now that I am the director of my own library, I make sure that the patrons have the kinds of books they want. I do not allow anyone to disparage romance novels or their readers. I find those who dismiss romances as "cheap" or "illiterate" to be unbearably pretentious & think that their elitist snobbery is a smokescreen to hide their own intolerance.

UNCOMMON GROUND IN READER ADVISORY PRACTICE AND EDUCATION

Comments from survey respondents present two very different perspectives in reader advisory services: (1) librarians as cultural guardians (Scott, 2002), which locates power and control over what patrons read with librarians, and (2) librarians as guardians of patrons' rights to choose which, in stark contrast, locates power and control with readers. Wayne Wiegand (1997) vehemently argues for the second perspective. Summarizing scholarship in library science, cultural studies and reading theory, Wiegand writes, " . . . the 'give 'em what they want' philosophy of collection development takes on a whole new meaning. Instead of considering patrons merely as 'consumers,' this alternative perspective of a traditional library service not only respects the readers' right to assign values to their reading, it also honors their ability to make reasoned decisions based on their own sociocultural circumstances" (p. 322). This is, as Wiegand often describes it, "the library in the life of the user" rather than "the user in the life of the library" (Wiegand, 2003). This is the argument Harris, Modleski, Scott, and other scholars have made and continue to make in an attempt to persuade librarians to trust and respect readers and their reading choices.

If librarians who work in public libraries are to respect readers and their reading choices, it seems that some understanding of reader advisory services, culture, readers, and/or reading theory should be part of their theoretical and practical education. An informal review of course descriptions at 50 out of 56 American Library Association (ALA) accredited library and information science programs indicates the majority of ALA accredited schools offer a class that is either explicitly oriented toward reader advisory or includes reader advisory as a significant element. Thirty of the 50 programs listed course offerings dealing with reader advisory or reader advisory-related topics. Eleven courses were specifically titled "Reader Advisory." Thirty-eight were reader advisory-related courses with titles similar to "Materials and Services for Adults" or "History of the Book." The heartening news is that 60% of LIS programs offer a course dealing with reader advisory. The disturbing results of the informal review is that those 48 courses, when placed in a larger context, comprise less than 2% of the 3,176 master's level courses listed by those 50 schools.

Content in reader advisory and reader advisory-related courses appears to take two directions: practical and theoretical. Several course descriptions mention the reader advisory interview, reader advisory resources, and unspecified *techniques and processes* for reader advisory work. Theoretical constructs include *reading theory, popular culture* and *the role of fiction* in libraries and for readers.

The results of the informal review of library science reader advisory-related courses provide a framework from which to consider additional results from the romance fiction study. More than half (61%) of study respondents indicated they held degrees in library science. Another 31% had different educational backgrounds, ranging from high school diplomas to master's and doctoral degrees in other fields. Library science master's degree holders were more likely to answer questions regarding attitudes toward romance fiction and its readers in a favorable way than those who did not hold the degree.

There is, however, a caveat. Library science master's degree holders were more likely than the nonlibrary science degree holders to not answer at all. In a few instances, the library science degree holders were twice as likely to leave a response blank as happened with the statement in the survey, "Romance novels are pornography for women." Research team members have ruminated over this particular finding, speculating about the possible meaning of the silences. Perhaps the gendered nature of the topic and the fact that survey respondents are primarily women (93%) plays a role in the lack of response. There may be discomfort in the admission that romance fiction may indeed be a kind of pornography for women. Faust (1980) comments that the *Sweet-Savage* subgenre is a clear example of romance fiction as genuine pornography for women. "Sweet Savagery legitimizes a wide range of sexual experience for women. The heroes may feel momentary jealousy but they admit that is irrational: the heroines are entitled to their sex lives just as the heroes are. . . . Sweet Savagery is a clear example of the genuine pornography of women. It thus fulfills a very simple function of providing titillation and escape" (p. 146, 155). Cultural guardians cannot be complicit in putting a genre that titillates women on public library shelves. If these guardians were found complicit, they would no longer control the high ground as arbiters of what is good/bad. If public librarians, most of whom are women, can keep romance fiction on the periphery, isolated in Red Dot Districts, there is no need to confront the sexual questions they may pose.

REVISITING THE RED DOT DISTRICT

What began as casual conversations about romance fiction and its readers over coffee has evolved into a pilot research project that grew into a study with national scope. Each set of research results generates additional questions. Some questions relate to library science education and what it teaches about readers' rights to assign value to their reading. Others revolve around women as romance fiction readers and the place of the public library in their reading lives.

How many of the survey respondents who were enrolled in classes either directly or indirectly related to reader advisory practice during their graduate programs? Do these kinds of classes make a discernable difference in how public librarians view readers' choices, regardless of the location of their choices on librarians' hierarchy of taste? If 61% of the respondents hold master's degrees in library science, why did so many open-ended responses evidence aspects of disdain for, and criticism of, readers and their reading choices? Why does romance fiction continue to be singled out for a particular kind of disdain not accorded any other fiction genre? During a casual conversation about the public library as a source of romance fiction, a reader explained she prefers to buy books so she can add them to her personal collection. Are romance fiction readers conservators of the genre as well as consumers? While other genres of popular fiction have found acceptance in academic library research collections, this has not been the case with romance fiction. Early mass-market romance fiction paperbacks, in particular, are difficult to find making research in the genre challenging. There are, however, romance fiction readers who have amassed substantial collections of the genre based on series, author, or subgenre reader preferences.

Is there uncommon ground between reader advisory education and professional practice? If there is common ground, there appears to be precious little of it. Reader advisory practice in public libraries seems to be largely self-taught. Evidence indicates library science students interested in reader advisory services have limited choices in related course work. There is every indication of a continuing disconnect between what is taught regarding reader advisory service and the construction of everyday professional practice.

One focus group participant described how she acquired skills in reader advisory theory and practice. The participant does not recall any courses offered during her master's program dealing with reader advisory or reading theory. What she knows about reader advisory services was acquired on the job. Program faculty appeared to place public librarianship at the bottom of the hierarchy of careers in the field.

> When I was in library school, the professors did not encourage anyone to work in public libraries. That was really second-rate. We were all encouraged to go into academic libraries. I don't remember much of anything that was practical at all [about reader advisory].

Asked how reader advisory services are handled in the public library where she works, the participant commented,

> There's people who love readers' advisory and think that's what we're there for, and the people who think, "Oh, not another [romance]?" I don't think that we've had anybody that's been persuaded that readers' advisory is important to them, to their job.

If reader advisory service is viewed as unimportant by library school faculty, as the participant's comments suggest, how can students who have chosen careers in public libraries acquire the necessary theoretical knowledge about readers and reading that provides the understandings necessary to translate theory into professional practice?

Public librarians' reader advisory practices toward romance fiction and its readers continue to be an area for conflict between public librarians who view themselves as guardians of the intellectual high ground and readers who would rather be slumming in a fully stocked Red Dot District. Perhaps what library educators are failing to teach students is respect for individuals as readers, and readers' rights to assign their personal meanings to the texts they read. A book does not have to be culturally worthy to be worthwhile.

Dr. Mary Bly, Associate Professor and Director of Graduate Studies, Department of English at Fordham University shares a personal story that makes the distinction between culturally worthy and worthwhile glaringly clear. Bly, a respected Shakespearean scholar, recounts the endless hours spent at her daughter's bedside and the company provided by a romance fiction novel.

> I fell into this book the way a starving person falls on a loaf of bread. I read it every moment my daughter wasn't sleeping. I read it to drown out the beeps from the monitors, and the results of blood tests I couldn't control, and the crying of babies in other rooms . . .

> Moments of clarity descend on us in the oddest moments, whether they have to do with how we feel as moms, or how we feel as wives, or how we feel as writers. Sometimes I have to remember why I'm a writer—and it's not just for the pure pleasure of creating stories. Part of the reason I'm a writer is that I get so much joy from taking people out of bad situations, if only for a few hours—and I know that pleasure so well because romances give it to me" (Garman, 2006).

Whether or not public librarians consider Dr. Bly's reading choice to be at the bottom of the hierarchy of reading is immaterial. Public librarians must come to understand that readers have the right to choose, as Dr.Bly did, to make reasoned decisions about their reading needs based on personal circumstances. What should Mary Bly have read while she sat at her daughter's bedside, seeking distraction from her child's life and death struggle? She knew what she needed as a reader at that moment in her life. Public librarians must learn to honor readers' choices and learn to trust that readers know what they need, regardless of the direction readers choose to take—even if they choose to stroll through the Red Dot District.

REFERENCES

Adkins, D., Esser, L., & Velasquez, D. (2006, July/August). Relations between librarians and romance readers: A Missouri survey. *Public Libraries*, 66–75.

Bold, R. (1980, May 15). Trash in the library. *Library Journal*, 1138–1139.

Faust, B. (1980). *Women, sex and pornography: A controversial study*. New York: Macmillan Publishing.

Garman, E. (2005, January 17). Love's labors: A Shakespeare professor confesses a terrible secret: She writes romance fiction, pseudonymously. http://www.newhourmetro.com/nymetro/arts/books/10870/. Accessed on May 2, 2006.

Harris, M. H. (1992). No love lost: Library women vs. women who use libraries. *Progressive Librarian*, *5*(Summer), 1–18.

Modleski, T. (1982). *Loving with a vengeance*. New York: Routledge.

Mosley, S., Charles, J., & Havir, J. (1995, May). The librarian as effete snob: Why romance? *Wilson Library Bulletin*, *69*, 24–25.

Romance Writers of America. (2005). Market research study on romance readers. https://www.rwanational.org/eweb/dynamicpage.aspx?webcode=StatisticsAuthor. Accessed on May 25, 2007.

Scott, A. E. (2002). Romance in the stacks; or, popular romance fiction imperiled. In L. C. Schurman & D. Johnson (Eds.), *Scorned literature: Essays on the history and criticism of popular mass-produced fiction in America* (pp. 213–224). Westport, CT: Greenwood Press.

Wiegand, W. A. (1997). Out of sight, out of mind: Why don't we have any schools of library and reading studies? *Journal of Education for Library and Information Science*, *38*(4), 313–327.

———. (2003, June). What American studies can teach the library and information sudies community about the library in the life of the user. *ASA Newsletter.* http://www.georgetown.edu/crossroads/AmericanStudiesAssn/newsletter/archivesarticleswiegand.htm

Young, B. R. (1997, March). Accidental authors, random readers, and the art of popular romance. *Paradoxa*, *3*, 29–45.

aRt, the 4th R: Arts and Communication across the Curriculum

B. J. Berquist

Loysville Youth Development Center, Harrisburg, Pennsylvania

Dedicated to Dawn Clouse, my daughter

INTRODUCTION

The 4th R, aRt, is a powerful and adaptive tool for engaging our struggling learners (see Ohler, 2000). This chapter will demonstrate, through the use of cultural identity boxes, digital storytelling, and other techniques, how all educators, especially those in correctional settings, can use individual learning styles to promote cross-curricular connections using art, literature, language arts, and communication skills.

The following strategies have been developed primarily through trial and error over 24 years of teaching at the Loysville Youth Development Center, a juvenile correctional facility in south central Pennsylvania. While there is no "one size fits all" method of teaching for any educator, the most important strategy I have found is that no one can do it alone. The four C's of Colleagues, Collaboration, Courage and Compromise are the quartet needed to survive stress, burnout, and a mind-numbing routine.

Communication, including writing, graphic art, music, and multimedia, provides a way for incarcerated juveniles to make connections with the outside world and facilitate transition back to their community. Often, alternative and correctional education is a "last chance" or a punitive approach to behavioral difficulties in the public school. Alternatives should be positive, proactive responses to the social, emotional, and educational needs of the child. Alternative education that includes the arts can promote excellence and high expectations within a nontraditional school setting. Research by Ezell and Levy (2003) found that the academic, vocational, and behavioral goals of the arts workshops were accomplished to "a very high degree" (p. 10).

In order to meet the learning styles of every student, it is important to offer a variety of assessment opportunities. Drawing, music, poetry, literature, photography, video are all tools that can be utilized to enable students to construct meaning from classroom lessons across the curriculum. The topics presented are meant to serve as guidelines for using your own creativity to offer similar experiences through Gardner's Multiple Intelligences (Gardner, 2007) for your students.

SETTING

Imagine that in order to enter your workplace each day, you walk past a 10-foot high chain-link fencing topped by rolls of razor wire. After presenting an ID card and perhaps a walk through a metal detector and a search through your personal items, you are buzzed through two security gates, walk to your school building, punch in a pass-code on a keypad, enter the building, retrieve a set of keys from the lockbox and enter your classroom so you can get ready for teaching classes to the people who live behind that chain-link fence.

On your desk sits a wooden block with 12 drilled holes filled with 12 numbered pencils. At the end of the class period, each pencil must be accounted for and at the end of each day, a form is filled out that verifies that all supplies and tools have been accounted for on that day. This is just one example of the *accountability* issues in addition to open public education facility curricula requirements for No Child Left Behind (NCLB) and the Individuals with Disabilities Education Act (IDEA) that working in a correctional facility presents. The Individuals with Disabilities Education Act (IDEA; originally the Education for all Handicapped Children's Act) is a landmark civil rights legislation that guarantees a free appropriate public education for all eligible children and youth with disabilities through age 21. IDEA has applied to public schools and state-operated programs, including juvenile detention and confinement facilities, since its passage in 1975.

Correctional education settings vary from institution to institution. Much depends on the type of student/offender residing in the facility, the purpose of the facility, and the administrative leadership. Settings can range from guards in every classroom, all classroom doors locked during sessions, and guard supervision in all hallways when students move from classroom to classroom, to open classrooms where the teacher is completely in charge of classroom management, no guards are in the hallways or classrooms, and students move independently from class to class at a bell.

Another factor that determines the atmosphere within an institution is the collaboration or lack thereof between the education faculty and administration and the institution administration. Some schools, under contract to local school districts, are a separate entity within the correctional facility. This situation requires a collaborative agreement between the school staff and the institution staff, who are, in effect, *in loco parentis*. Some schools are private and are under the rules and regulations of the governing body that can be the state, federal government, or an independent organization. The result of this is that all the parts of the whole are under the same authority. This may lead to an atmosphere that may be entirely punitive or rehabilitative or therapeutic, but often places less emphasis on the educational needs of the residents. Either setting risks alienating educational staff from institution staff. Administration is paramount in maintaining collaborative cooperation and positive results for the students. Teachers must meet the needs of the individuals in order for learning to take place. These individual needs can be complicated by social, emotional, cognitive, and psychological handicaps. This often requires educators to use teaching methods that may be discouraged or severely hampered by the rules and regulations of the institution. "On a systems level, collaboration between child-serving agencies, including juvenile justice, is widely acknowledged as a critical element in reform initiatives geared to improving outcomes for high-risk populations" (Meisel, Henderson, Cohen, & Leone, 1998).

WHO ARE THE TEACHERS?

Who are the people who enter these institutions to teach this hard-to-reach population of learners? Mostly, they are selfless, generous souls who, in their wildest dreams, never pictured teaching in a correctional facility when they were planning their lives. They are former public school teachers, social workers, and correctional officers who saw beyond the chain link and the locked doors to the wounded, discarded, troubled people inside and felt they had something to contribute to their healing, their self-esteem, their hopes and dreams. Teaching in a correctional facility is certainly not for everyone. It is emotionally draining, can be risky at best and downright dangerous at worst, and requires the skills of a comedian, nurse, social worker, actor, and consummate storyteller and script writer. A sense of humor is a primary survival skill. These requirements appear on the surface to be very similar to those needed to teach in an inner city public school. The difference is that for many of the students who have been in and out of institutions for many years, they are "institutionalized." These at-risk students have lost the ability to make decisions, solve problems, and think independently.

WHO ARE THE STUDENTS?

At-risk students are often described as the result of poverty, single-parent families, physical and mental abuse, neglect, teen pregnancy, incarcerated parent(s), and substance abuse. Students in correctional facilities fall off the at-risk charts with the additional descriptors of mental health issues, learning disabilities, and behavior issues. The National

At Risk Education Network (NAREN) defines "at-risk" youth as at risk of dropping out of school and at risk of not succeeding in life due to being raised in unfavorable circumstances (http://www.atriskeducation.net/). However one might describe them or explain their presence in a youth prison, students are needy in many ways and are often hungry for attention in any form. They may be drug dealers or drug users, may be streetwise but possess few social skills, have been abused physically and mentally and consequently are often abusers themselves, usually have one or more parent in prison, and have one or more children. And they are adolescents: child-like mentality in adult bodies, who often never had the opportunity to be "kids" because they were too busy just trying to survive from day to day.

A large percentage of students are classified as special education and have Individual Education Plans (IEP). An IEP outlines any special adaptations to a classroom curriculum that must be provided so that the student will be successful.

> Each public school child who receives special education and related services must have an Individualized Education Program (IEP). Each IEP must be designed for one student and must be a truly *individualized* document. The IEP creates an opportunity for teachers, parents, school administrators, related services personnel, and students (when appropriate) to work together to improve educational results for children with disabilities. The IEP is the cornerstone of a quality education for each child with a disability. To create an effective IEP, parents, teachers, other school staff—and often the student—must come together to look closely at the student's unique needs. (Price-Ellingstad, Reynolds, Ringer, Ryder, Sheridan, Haumann, et al., 2000)

OBSTACLES TO LEARNING AND TEACHING

"Prison education programs and the prison system are at odds: The goal of the educator is to bring up or draw out, to develop mental and moral growth, while the goal of the prison system is to close in and contain. Werner says, 'To teach in a prison is to compromise'" (Spencer, 1997). To meet educational and institutional requirements lessons are often disrupted by social workers, dentist and doctor visits, drug and alcohol counseling, IEPs, and state-mandated testing and evaluation. Because of the nature of the students' physical, mental, and emotional states, school attendance can also be interrupted by acting-out behaviors that require temporary isolation from the main student population. In this sporadic environment of school participation the arts are a powerful tool in which to build and sustain bridges for enhancing student communication skills.

ARTS AND COMMUNICATION

Communication is an expression of feelings, thoughts, ideas, viewpoints, and opinions. To communicate effectively, you must be actively engaged in the process. The students in a correctional setting have not had many successful experiences with communication. Society and role models offer more negative than positive ways in which to communicate. Movies, video games, music videos, music lyrics all tend to glorify violence, misogynistic behavior, and power and control actions (gangs, physical abuse, etc.). By exposing students to a variety of experiences and applying differentiated learning by using Howard Gardner's Multiple Intelligences, pathways are opened to learn new ways of communicating.

Obstacles to developing effective communication tools include numerous prior failures in educational settings (student is "programmed for failure"), visual, auditory, and/or fine motor skill learning disabilities, mental health issues, organization skills, and the institutionalization of the learners.

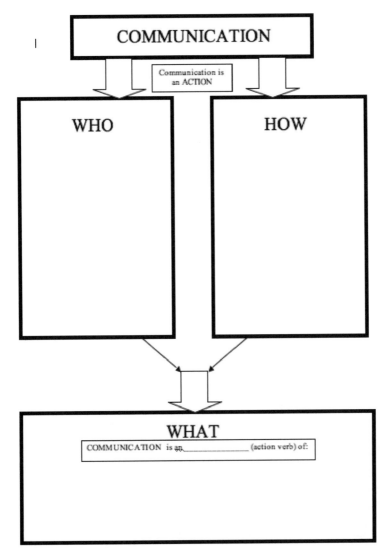

PROJECT AND LESSON IDEAS

Trade Books/Picture Books

Picture books are a wonderful bridge between using words and pictures to construct meaning. Illustrations are also a nonthreatening way to develop visual literacy or the ability to "read" an illustration, painting, or other graphic artwork. Although many picture books are designed for elementary audiences, they are a way to introduce a topic in a way that makes the students feel safe in a learning environment. By presenting a variety of books on the same topic, for example Three Little Pig stories, you can teach several literary elements. The first book I share when using this lesson is the Golden Books version. This stimulates prior knowledge in those fortunate enough to be familiar with fairy tales. I then introduce Jon Scieszka's *True Story of the 3 Little Pigs!* This book is a terrific way to explain a point of view while sharing some excellent illustrations. Another example of truly superb drawing is David Wiesner's *The Three Pigs*. Wiesner adds elements to the story to provide an example of how the plot of a story can be altered. *The Three Little Javelinas* by Susan Lowell places the setting in the southwestern United States and adds Spanish influences to provide a cultural diversity to the lesson.

Do not underestimate the power or the age-appropriate level of picture books. *Rose Blanche* (Holocaust) and *Hiroshima No Pika* (bombing of Hiroshima) are two books that deal with the very adult themes. Find picture books that appeal to you, and that apply to your lesson themes. When you teach with passion, the students are more likely to understand "voice" in a story and take an interest in what is being presented.

CULTURAL IDENTITY BOX

Choose 4 values that identity you from the Cultural Identifiers list.

Create/design one symbol to represent each of the identifiers you've chosen. Make 2" sketches of the symbols in your journal. Then make 4" finished drawings from your sketches on copy paper. Cut out and glue the four 4" cultural identity symbols to the 4 sides of the box.

Have the teacher take your digital portrait.

Attach the "What lies behind us" quote from Emerson or the I Am poem to the inside top of the 4" box provided by the teacher.

Glue your photo to the top of the box.

Put your name and cottage on the bottom of the box.

Family	Dad, Mom, grandmother, Uncle, Brother, Sister, Child
Love	Self, Family, Community
Life	Work Ethic, Socially Responsible, Goals
Respect	Clean, Personal Appearance, Kind, thoughtful, Considerate of Others, Share/Help Others, Listener
Education	Communication, Goals, Life-long Learner
Culture	African American, Hispanic American, Native American, European American, Asian American
Interests	Art, Music, Electronics, Cars, Sports, Girls
Peace	Inner Peace, Racial Harmony, Friendship, Family, Community, National, World

What lies behind us

And what lies before us

Are tiny matters

Compared to what lies

Within us.

Ralph Waldo Emerson

I AM (Model)
I am (two special characteristics you have)
I wonder (something you are actually curious about)
I hear (an imaginary sound)
I see (an imaginary sight)
I want (an actual desire)
I am (the first line of the poem repeated)

I pretend (something you actually pretend to do)
I feel (a feeling about something imaginary)
I touch (an imaginary touch)
I worry (something that really bothers you)
I cry (something that makes you very sad)
I am (the first line of the poem repeated)

I understand (something you know is true)
I say (something you believe in)
I dream (something you actually dream about)
I try (something you really make an effort about)
I hope (something you actually hope for)
I am (the first line of the poem repeated)

What does the Emerson quotation mean? How does it relate to the box?

No matter what you did before or what you will do in the future, they're just little things to what we have in us. Because of what we have in us we can do anything.

Some projects slowly evolve over a number of years and then suddenly all the pieces fall together. This is what happened with the Cultural Identity Box project. Boxes had always intrigued me as a vehicle for storytelling. Reading Johanna Hurwitz's *Birthday Surprises: Ten Great Stories to Unwrap* was one of the inspirations for my box journey. In each story, a person receives a box as a gift. The boxes contain memories, artifacts, and may actually be empty but for the recipient's imagination. Another inspiration was Empty and Meaningless, The Box Project by Adrienne Fritz. The final key arrived when I read a quotation from Ralph Waldo Emerson, "What lies behind us and what lies before us are tiny matters compared to what lies within us." My box project became symbolic of a past, a future, and a "heart" or what makes a person able to face the challenges they must.

The first question asked of the student when explaining this project is, "How do you get your 'heart'?" "Heart" is derived from biological, social, and cultural life experiences. Symbolism is introduced and students search for and design symbols for their choices of the four most significant cultural identifiers they feel influenced their "heart." Love, family, music, and sports are some of the most frequently chosen cultural identifiers. On completion of the project, reflective writing is used to evaluate comprehension, introspection, and application.

The Box Project (Berquist, 2006) can be adapted to a variety of topics or disciplines and involve more or less student writing, storytelling, and introspection. The box can be a how-to-do-something experience using instructions and diagrams. The box shape itself can be altered, repeated flattened, used to teach three-dimensional drawing.

BLANKET THE WORLD WITH PEACE PROJECT

The Peace Project is a wonderful example of collaboration. It is not a garden variety collaboration, but one that took place entirely online among teachers from several different states. I first met Anna Martin in Tapped In (www.tappedin.org), an online community of practice for educators. A high school art teacher, Anna had been very moved by stories from children who had lived in countries at war. She felt a need to address these children of conflict and wondered if a group from Tapped In would be able to come up with some ideas. Several art teachers started meeting in a group room that, as members of Tapped In, we were able to create, and after much discussion, decided that the theme for the project would be "peace through the resolution of conflict." This topic would allow participants to address war, abuse, gangs, racial issues, etc. as conflict. Anna created the Web page (http://www.cedarnet.org/emig/peace) for the project and members of the group submitted images and ideas. This site is still open to submissions. Submissions may be one site deep, meaning that the submitted image may be linked to a school or art homepage where more examples of work can be included. Projects based on the theme can be multimedia and include dance, poetry, music, video, and graphic art.

My students' contribution to this project was the Hats Off to Peace Project. Tapped In has provided a Web page where the project and step-by-step directions are posted. (http://ti2data.sri.com/info/teachers/hatsoff/) This page can be accessed by selecting the patriotic top hat on the Peace Blanket page.

BLOG—VOICES FROM LOYSVILLE

In an attempt to encourage more reflective writing I decided to create a blog (http://voicesfromloysville.blogspot.com/) for my students. Because of the safety and security issues that a correctional facility faces, we are not permitted to allow the students to access the Internet. My solution to this problem was to have the students write entries to weekly topics in their journals. I would then take those entries and post them to the blog. Blogs have two major appealing features: they provide an authentic audience for our writers and they give our writers a reason to write. My biggest obstacle so far has been finding classes who have been willing to reply to my student posts. Many correctional educators do not have access to the Internet at school and are not willing to do posts after school hours.

When I used the Robert Frost poem "The Road Not Taken" (Frost, 1964) that was narrated in video on Next Vista (Selman, 2006), I was able, through an LCD projector connected to my computer, to provide an audio and a visual component to the poem that allowed more opportunities for comprehension and reflection. The few examples of positive feedback for some of the posts were enough to sustain both me and the students. I had given the students a voice and someone was listening.

It's very moving to read these heartfelt reflections. I hope that the young man who wants his brother to stop hustling can open real communication with his brother, so that his message will be heard. What will his alternative be? Where can we find the hope that will sustain us all? Things are so difficult for so many people in this life, it is essential to find and nurture the wellspring of hope that I know each of us can tap within us.

Congratulations to teacher and students for an important and worthwhile project.

Thank you for publishing the writings of young men who don't always have a voice in the larger world. To me the theme of these writings is love. We all want to love and to feel loved, and in this way we are all one. We are not so separate from each other as we sometimes imagine. I think publishing this writing in a blog can help all of us who read it remember that. Thank you.

BJ

Would you please pass the following onto the young people you are working with on Between the Lines:

Thanks for taking the time to answer the question 'what are you going to do to make your dream come true?' which I posed recently on your weblog—your responses were enlightening and inspiring.

I recently used your weblog in some training to a group of youth professionals to illustrate how young people can communicate their thoughts to the wider world. Everyone was really impressed and thought it was a great thing you guys are doing.

Keep it going as people are reading ... thanks.

Thank you and thanks to all your students for posting these assignments. I so appreciate your ability to give these students a public voice. I do a lot of presentations on using blogs in adult education, and I always try to show this one, and to encourage people to go here and read the student work and post a comment! Marian

---

Greetings from California! It is so powerful to read what you wrote about the poem—thank you all for sharing. Many of you talk about the choice between good and bad paths, and how you are focused on following a good path for your future. One idea that I wanted to share is that while our choices do limit our possibilities, they also can create new opportunities for us as well. The choices that give us the chance to find happiness and meaning are the ones that allow us to explore the best of who we are. Sometimes that wonderful piece of ourselves is hard to see (like the end of the paths in the woods), but that piece is there, without a doubt. Your friend on the west coast, Rushton

---

This is a wonderful blog! The class topics, and responses are very thoughtful, and thought provoking! I am the principal at the juvenile detention center in Lincoln, Nebraska, sometimes I fill in for teachers when they are absent. Would it be ok if I were to show this blog to some of our students, and leave some of their comments, or responses to your topics in the comments?

Hello from a correctional educator. I teach at a prison for adult men, but I do not want to share specific information about where we are located. I gave a small group of my students, all adult men incarcerated at the institution where I teach, an assignment to respond to your posts. I asked them to respond to a specific person (identified by your initials). Their responses are coded with AO (for adult offender), their initials and their age. These are the responses:

CS, I have read your response to the poem and I'm not sure how to answer, but, I don't really think there is a right or wrong road to travel. I believe that the path we choose is the right path for each of us, as an individual, and the choices we make along that path is what makes it right or wrong. It would be nice if it were possible to look ahead and see the path before we choose, but, that is not a reality we have available for our benefit. What we do have is the ability to learn from our mistakes and move forward on our journey knowing that we don't have to make those mistakes again. Live and learn but try not to regret life. AOPL45

MP I read your response to the poem "The Road Not Taken". I think that you have started making good decisions that definitely play a major role in the future. I also can relate to the poem in similar ways. I was a person that didn't really have a difficult life but at one point and time I made my life difficult by making wrong decisions. I had to learn how to not involve myself with people that do not have similar goals as myself, or do not make an effort to stop walking the other road. When I read the poem, the message that I received is before making the choice of which road to take, he first analyzed both of his options. Therefore basing this poem to life sometimes before making impulsive choices you have to think about the future outcome and the people your decisions affect. AOGLB23

SS I read your response that you gave on the poem "The Road Not Taken", and I agree with you completely. I, too, was forced with that choice of hustling, or leading a straight productive life. But at that time, hustling was the road that I followed. It led me to a place where I didn't want to be. Today, I understand the life that I chose and I'm cool with it because by being locked up, I see the other road is still there and is waiting to be explored. AOJA26

SS I read your response to "The Road Not Taken" and I understand what you're going through. I, too, could've been involved in sports when I was younger and was pretty good. My people weren't involved in the lifestyle I chose to live; I wanted to have all the material things and get all the girls. I chose to hustle instead of waiting and staying in school. The path I chose led me in and out of jail my whole life, too. Now that I'm older, I wish I could've chose a different road and done things differently. You're still young and still have a chance to do something positive with your life. You're right about your past helping you make a better future but its up to you to use what you've learned and not go backwards when you get out. There'll be a lot of times when you want to give up but struggling only makes you stronger. You'll see all your friends getting money the easy way when you're doing the right thing; working for your money. This is the road that's "less traveled", like you said. It's real easy to sell drugs and be a "thug" but you know where that'll lead you, believe me there's a lot of people in jail for trying to be a hustler; crying about wanting to go home to their family but, you can't be a family person and a hustler, too. It takes a strong person to do the right thing and stay home with their family. So, no matter what your friends call you for doing the right thing, it's cooler being a square at home taking care of your family then being a thug locked up, depending on your family to take care of you or even worse: your family abandoning you. I pretty much got the same thing out of the poem as you did. You sound like you know what you want and you're all ready headed in the right direction. I just hope you stay on the right road. AOGF28

Topics used for the Between the Lines blog (Berquist, 2007) have so far included acrostic poems on education, a collaborative effort among the librarian, computer teacher, and myself on raps for Black History, reflections on colors for Dr. Seuss' birthday, political cartoons, reflections after viewing the documentary *A Hard Straight* (Toshima, 2004), cultural history, and music.

One of the features of a blog is that you can embed podcasts, videos, and artwork. My own personal learning curve has not reached that level yet, but it helps the students when they see that the teacher does not have all the answers and is willing to work to find out how to problem solve.

POLITICAL CARTOONS

Political Cartoons are an excellent source for discussion and for determining whether a topic is fact or opinion and what the cartoonist's point of view is. I have found that the Cagle Cartoonists Index (http://www.cagle.com) is a rich resource on a variety of topics from birth control to sports controversies. (One of our blog entries used the NBA controversy to discuss violence in sports (see Cagle, 2006).) There are other sites that provide resources for history and social issues. One example is HarpWeek Web site "Abraham Lincoln Cartoons: Comic Portraits of His Presidency" (http://www.abrahamlincolncartoons.info/). Careful observation nurtures visual literacy through comparing, contrasting, and use of symbols.

GRAPHIC NOVELS

Graphic novels put a story in a comic book format that is very appealing to students of all ages. This kind of storytelling is nonthreatening and has a sense of the familiar. This does not mean that the stories themselves are necessarily superficial. Art Spiegelman's *Maus* and *In the Shadow of No Towers* are excellent examples of this. A lesson that can be done with graphic novels is to have the students write their own story and create their own illustration/cartoon panels. This becomes an exercise in how to "build" a story by creating it a segment at a time. Graphic novels can be accessed through Web, print, television, and other communication media.

POETRY, MUSIC, RAP, AND HIP-HOP

Teaching Communication and Vocabulary

Teaching vocabulary necessary for content areas like science and social studies can get very boring if it is always the same (look up word, write the definition, use it in a sentence, etc.). Designing a strategy for teaching a set of vocabulary words helps to emphasize oral techniques and usage, not written ones, through the use a song, a dance, a rap, a choral response, etc. A good resource for integrating music into SAT and History lessons is *Flocabulary: Hip-Hop in the Classroom* (Harrison & Rappaport, 2006). Flocabulary has CDs and books to support lessons. There are also several online examples on the Flocabulary Web site of the music and lyrics used (http://www.flocabulary.com/).

Another wonderful resource for teaching literature is Baba Brinkman's *The Rap Canterbury Tales* (2007) that couch Chaucer's tales in contemporary language that remains faithful to the original stories and uses rap as a presentation tool to engage our learners. Brinkman has several publications that expand on the use of literature and rap. His work is available in CD, book, and download format (http://www.babasword.com/writing/rapcantales.html).

Students are eager to demonstrate their own prowess as hip-hop artists and will become actively engaged in writing their own lyrics. An example of this was the Black History Raps on the Between the Lines blog cited earlier. The Communication Rap, written by this author, was designed to teach communication, use pattern and rhythm, repetition, and rhyming, and include definitions of the seven elements of art.

COMMUNICATION RAP © By B. J. Berquist

Pound out the rhythm, strong and loud
Tell my message clear and proud:
I'm a CLaSS act dude with a very short fuse,
I bleed when I'm cut and hurt when I'm bruised.
My feelings are the rainbow, many COLORed like the days
One day blue, another day green,
I'm a CLaSS act dude—an individual teen.

Keep my heart on my sleeve and my thoughts in my head
One step two step, looking up and down; Misstep, fall down, full of dread.
Dot walks forward, moves up and down. Life's direction twists like a vine
I'm a CLaSS act dude on a tightrope LINE.

Some days are sharp and some are round,
My days have SHAPES that are full of sound.
The flatness of the days runs together in my mind.
I'm a CLaSS act dude making circles intertwined

Blow up balloons and let them fly,
3D SHAPEs rise up into the sky.
Hundreds of balloons mark a PATTERN that sails free
I'm a CLaSS act dude floating thoughts that are me

Smooth talk, rough talk sweet talk, laws
Sandpaper TEXTUREs scrape me raw.
Scratch through the paper till you see a hole
I'm a CLaSS act dude with a vulnerable soul.

White fades to grey if I'm ignored
Shadows creep in when I am bored.
SHADEs of color can light a spark
I'm a CLaSS act dude gonna make my mark!

STORYTELLING AND VIDEO

Storytelling is a powerful tool for teaching communication and literacy skills. Formats can range from digital storytelling using simple PowerPoint or the more complex iMovie or PhotoStory to graphic novels, to live or video recorded theater. There are vast resources online and in print for storytelling. The common thread among all storytelling is the integration of words and images. Stories can be the retelling of a familiar story from a different point of view, a step-by-step demonstration of how to do something, a video explaining a math or science concept, or the recounting of a personal experience. The story can be in narrative format, poetry, song, or images. The teacher can use a video story as a teaching tool or use a video from a source such as Next Vista to enhance a lesson.

Education is becoming more and more student centered and problem based. The students entering our correctional facilities have not had many, if any, experiences in using higher order thinking skills to develop sophisticated and effective communication skills. By engaging the students in a variety of sensory experiences using visual art, sound, video, music, we help the students become active participants in their learning. This results in the students taking ownership for a product, pride in accomplishing an educational goal, and the affirmation that they can learn.

CONCLUSION

Educators in all disciplines will scaffold success for their learners if lessons are presented that include the fourth R, aRt. Trade books, graphic novels, fine art, graphic art, literature, poetry, and writing are all ways in which to entice struggling students to become engaged in their learning. Video and audio used as either a presentation or evaluation tool can enhance lessons and draw on individual learner strengths.

To paraphrase John Donne (1624), no classroom is an island. In our flat world, educators have access to information and ideas from many cultures, disciplines, and viewpoints. Learners can construct meaning and engage in problem-based curriculum to solve real-life situations. Students can also learn that there may be no "right" or "wrong" answer to some problems and mistakes are part of real-life problem solving. Educators and students do not need to be online to use many of the resources discussed in this chapter, but educators do need to be able to be lifelong learners who seek professional development opportunities.

The topics presented, meant to serve as guidelines for using your own creativity, are merely scratching the surface of what we as educators can do for our students. Incarcerated juveniles, isolated, alienated, and struggling learners that they are, are basically the same as any other juvenile. They thrive on authentic success. They have dreams and goals that may or may not be realistic. The "C" in this conclusion that is of primary concern is Collaboration. Adapting and manipulating lesson ideas to fit the needs of your students is what educators do best. Join online special interest groups to collaborate with peers. For correctional educators the Correctional Education Association has many such groups available at their website (http://www.ceanational.org). A free online collaborative community that I have found supportive and nurturing is Tapped In (http://www.tappedin.org). Tapped In has a monthly calendar of events that presents online real-time text chats for many disciplines and grade levels. Being a lifelong learner is paramount to being a successful educator, and when you have an opportunity to collaborate with peers, you'll find that it can be an enriching and fun experience.

REFERENCES

Berquist, B. J. (2006). Cultural identity cubed. *School Arts, 105*(5), 28–29.

———. (2007). Between the lines. *Blogger.* Retrieved on April 8, 2007, from http://voicesfromloysville.blogspot.com/

Cagle, D. (2006). Violence in the NBA. *Daryl Cagle's Professional Cartoonists Index.* Retrieved on April 8, 2007, from http://cagle.com/news/NBAViolence

Donne, J. (1624). *Meditation XVII.* Retrieved on May 28, 2007, from http://www.global-language.com/devotion.html

Ezell, M. & Levy, M. (2003). An evaluation of an arts program for incarcerated juvenile offenders. *Journal of Correctional Education, 54*(3), 108–114.

Fritz, A. What is "empty & meaningless"? *Empty and meaningless: The box project.* Retrieved on March 24, 2007, from http://www.urbanesque.com/empty/what-is.html

Frost, R. & Williams, O. (1952). The road not taken. In O. Williams (Ed.), *Immortal Poems of the English Language.* New York: Washington Square Press.

Gardner, H. Howard Gardner's multiple intelligence theory. Retrieved on March 24, 2007, from http://www.ed.psu.edu/insys/esd/gardner/MItheory.html

Harrison, B. & Rappaport, A. (2006). *Flocabulary: The hip-hop approach to SAT – level vocabulary building.* Kennebunkport, ME: Cedar Mill Press.

Hurwitz, J. (1997). *Birthday surprises: Ten great stories to unwrap.* New York: HarperTrophy.

Innocenti, R. (2003). *Rose blanche.* New York: Creative Editions.

Küpper, L. (Ed.) (2000). My child's special needs. *A guide to the individualized education program.* Retrieved on April 21, 2007, from http://www.ed.gov/parents/needs/speced/iepguide/index.html

Lowell, S. & Harris, J. (ill). (1992). *The three little javelinas.* Flagstaff, AZ: Northland Company.

Martin, A. (2003). EMIG/peace quilt. *Blanket the world with peace.* Retrieved on March 24, 2007, from http://www.cedarnet.org/emig/peace/

Maruki, T. (1982). *Hiroshima no pika.* New York: HarperCollins.

Meisel, S., Henderson, K., Cohen, M., & Leone, P. (1998). *Collaborate to educate: Special education in juvenile correctional facilities.* Article retrieved on May 7, 2007, from http://www.eric.ed.gov/ERICDocs/data/ericdocs2/content_storage_01/0000000b/80/25/ef/91.pdf

Ohler, J. (2000). Art becomes the 4th R. *Educational Leadership, 58*(2), 39–44.

Scieszka, J. & Smith, L. (ill). (1999). *The true story of the three little pigs.* New York: Penguin Group.

Selman, L. (2006). Robert Frost's the road not taken. *Next Vista.* Retrieved on April 8, 2007, from http://www.nextvista.org/2006/09/10/traveling-robert-frosts-the-road-not-taken/

Spencer, S. (1997). Preconceptions and misconceptions of teaching composition to the incarcerated. Paper presented at the Annual Meeting of the Conference on College Composition and Communication. Article retrieved on May 7, 2007, from http://www.eric.ed.gov/ERICDocs/data/ericdocs2/content_storage_01/0000000b/80/22/b7/4e.pdf

Spiegelman, A. (1991). *Maus: A survivor's tale.* New York: Pantheon.

———. (2004). *In the shadow of no towers.* New York: Pantheon.

Toshima, G. (director). (2004). A hard straight [motion picture]. Harriman, NY: New Day Films.

Wiesner, D. (2001). *The three pigs.* New York: Clarion Books.

Digitizing Microforms on-Demand: Reviving Access to a Dead Collection?

Sheetal Janubhai Desai and Wendi Arant Kaspar
Texas A&M University Libraries

INTRODUCTION

"Are microforms dead?" Sridhar (2002, p. 139) posed this question in his article of the same title and argued that they are far from dead. He cited the following reasons why microforms are an optimal format:

- economical benefits of getting large research collections
- space saving
- speedy acquisition
- file integration
- ease of automation
- low cost on demand dissemination
- ease of archiving and security
- ease of handling and retrieving
- paperless.

Librarians and researchers advocate that "[a] good microform collection can play a central part in providing students and faculty with research materials, but its value depends as much upon its accessibility as it does upon choice of materials" (Manzo, 1997, p. 73). With this said, individual libraries have invested millions of dollars in dedicated staff, space, and technology to purchase and maintain them. Additionally, some publishers produced materials in this format exclusively for ease of availability for readers. Despite all this effort and expense, the microform collection has been undergoing a drop in usage thus risking becoming "*a dead collection.*"

LITERATURE REVIEW

Publications by Eichhorn (1984), Alexander & Page (1990), Arthur (2004), Edelstein (1993), Okerson (1985), Yang (2004), and Yang (2005) helped to build support for the new service we were trying to initiate known as "Digitizing Microforms on-Demand." Each author presented points indirectly favoring this new service.

Eichhorn's 1984 article provided the following fundamental standards for providing service to microform collections:

* a microform management policy
* a dedicated position for the support and management as a Microforms Librarian
* standards for environment and equipment
* bibliographic control and access
* promotion of microforms as a resource.

In 1990, Alexander and Page built on the above fundamental standards and described the impact of library automation on the usage and circulation of a microform collection. Specifically, their study examined the implementation of an Online Public Access Catalog (OPAC) and the creation of cataloging records as access points for microform collections. This illustrated the expectations of patrons (and library staff) with regard to the use of technology in accessing this format.

Arthur (2004) discussed the digitization of materials as a preservation solution, particularly digitizing paper as an alternative to putting it in microform, because of the following benefits:

* increased capture abilities with large format, color, and media materials
* no degradation of the original digitized image
* secure masters with adherence to standards
* higher user satisfaction
* increased distribution and access possibilities
* increased functionality
* incorporated easily into the desktop environment.

Edelstein discussed how the proliferation of electronic information has revived microform collection: "Not only is the decline of microfilm not inevitable, but the technology may be poised for a new spurt of growth. Ironically, the future success of microfilm was tied to the spread of electronic imaging at the individual workgroup and enterprise level" (Edelstein, 1993, p. 34).

Okerson (1985) detailed a microform digitization project that was systematic in the approach to microform conversion of materials. This was being considered in an effort to reclaim physical library space for more interactive services. She concluded by asking "[w]ill future (online) developments render not only our hardcopy but also our newly acquired microforms redundant . . . ?" (Okerson, 1985, p. 161).

In 2004, Yang described a service that literally provided on-demand electronic access of print materials to the patron. However, popular as this service was, deliverEdocs expressly omitted microform materials from this service.

AN UNDERUTILIZED COLLECTION

Texas A&M University Libraries houses a considerable microform collection of over four million pieces in microfiche, microfilm, microprint, and microcard. This collection is a rich source of information, including documents, primary sources, data, and literature that may no longer be readily available. According to the Association of Research Libraries

(ARL) statistics, the microform collection grows by about 60,000 items per year, which is a strong indication that some information is still being sold only in this format and that the format is not, in fact, "dead" at least as far as the publishers are concerned.

So, is the microform collection obsolete? Why is this collection underutilized and what are the usage and access barriers according to the users? The Texas A&M University Libraries service desks collected data from patrons via a survey administered by ARL measuring library service quality called LibQual+ to seek the patrons' views of the microform collection. The 2005 LibQual+ results revealed the following reasons why the patrons did not favor the microform collection:

- lack of familiarity with how to search for or access materials in this collection including not knowing which indexes to use

- difficulty in locating and retrieving specific information or items within a microform

- the lack of ease of access and usage so one could carry the material anywhere and have the convenience of making notes on the item

- complaints of physical discomfort with using the required equipment (i.e., microform readers, printers) leading to headaches, eyestrains, or dizziness.

In addition to the comments that patrons made about using microforms regarding convenience and satisfaction, other issues about the format included limited access to the material due to the building hours, functionality, distribution, and degradation of the microformat.

Additional patron comments from past LibQual+ surveys revealed a consistent pattern demand for online access:

- "Great electronic journal resources. Need all back issues when available. You have the text I require for a course this term online; I wish all texts were available online" (TAMU LibQual+, 2005).

- "Put all microfiche resources online" (TAMU LibQual+, 2006).

- "In general, I am pleased. The archival electronic retrieval needs to be extended back further in time. The government documents and government laboratory reports need to be available in another format than microfilm, preferably electronic such as PDF" (TAMU LibQual+, 2003).

Taking a closer look at the microform collection, we realized that there were many useful sources in microform but the format was not so appealing. If patrons were more interested in information in an electronic format, why not give it to them? Many libraries make a proactive effort to provide additional access to their singular microform holdings by systematically digitizing them and serving them up in institutional collections or repositories. A number of libraries have made concerted efforts in this direction, realizing that such repositories "[h]ave the potential to serve as tangible indicators of a university's quality and to demonstrate the scientific, societal, and economic relevance of its research activities, thus increasing the institution's visibility, status, and public value" (Crow, 2002, p. 4). This is a noble effort and to an extent, certainly achieves its aim: to increase the use of this often overlooked collection. However, with a microform collection the size of the Texas A&M University Libraries, the above-mentioned "just-in-case" model is not sustainable. Since library priorities are driven by patron demand and feedback, there was already a model in place known as deliverEdocs that could be augmented to accommodate this concern about an underutilized collection.

Texas A&M University Libraries' deliverEdocs retrieved, scanned, and delivered book material that was owned by the Libraries to the desktop. There were, of course, some limitations (i.e., format, length, and guidelines set in place by Interlibrary Loans Services (ILS)) but these did not seem to detract from the usage of the service. Yang (2004) discussed the implementation of the deliverEdocs services at Texas A&M University where the priority was "to get the materials for our patrons, no matter where the material resided, either in the Texas A&M University Libraries or anywhere in the world" (Yang, 2004, p. 80). Yang (2005) revisited the service a few years later to report on the customer satisfaction—where 84.1% of respondents cited their satisfaction with deliverEdocs because the "documents are delivered electronically" and 62.8% submitted more ILS request because of this service (Yang, 2005, p. 84).

ENHANCING ON AN ALREADY-SUCCESSFUL SERVICE

It was a natural progression to leverage the deliverEdocs service to include providing more access and usage of the microforms collection. The Course Reserves/Current Periodicals Department (CRCP) within the Access Services unit, as custodians and information support of the microforms collection, approached ILS in an effort to discover whether such a service (digitizing microforms on-demand) might be viable. At that time, ILS indicated that they were cancelling about ten requests for microform items per week. This led to discussions about the possibility of quietly expanding deliverEdocs to include microforms, whereby the request would come through the established channels and be funneled to CRCP personnel who would scan the requested documents in microform and save them to the appropriate system drive. Due to some hesitancy to commit to this service without evidence that it would be sustainable and that it would not build patrons expectations too high, it was decided by ILS and CRCP to not implement this new service in a formal way just yet. At that point, CRCP staff decided that a trial period with selected microform users would allow the opportunity to define policies, shakedown processes, and identify the necessary resources.

PREPARATION AND RESOURCES

Due to the fact that there was no protocol already set, much freedom was given to CRCP as far as what equipment to use and possibly purchase, a workflow process, what training guidelines to implement, how to train the students, what end-product to arrive at, and the turnaround time. The following preparatory steps were taken in order to meet the anticipated demand:

- a fully functioning workstation (scanner reader and a computer)
- a working training manual
- a processing slip (see Appendix B) created to keep track of the processing steps.

Additionally, CRCP selectively chose Texas A&M University faculty and staff from various areas of disciplines who heavily utilized the microform collection for research and classroom purposes. Those who agreed were from the following departments: Anthropology, Engineering, English, History, NASA, Texas Parks & Wildlife, and Texas Transportation Institute as well as faculty within the main Library and the Medical Science Library on campus. These individuals were sent an e-mail letter (see Appendix A) soliciting their participation and then were requested to submit microform requests. When the former were all set up, CRCP conducted a summer trial run that went from June 6 to August 5,

2005. Overall, a total of 20 requests were submitted and processed with 65 hours of total processing hours noted.

LIBRARY STAFF AND PATRON FEEDBACK

During the trial run, a survey (see Appendix C) was created to provide feedback to gauge the interest and success of the service. The survey was sent to all the faculty who participated and the responses (see Appendix D) received were very insightful and gave a good indication of what might be needed if the project were to be formally implemented as a regular service (i.e., better labeling, closer eye to detail, etc.).

As you can see, the majority of the comments were positive. However, because of it being summer, a few of the faculty were out of town so not everyone contacted replied to participate. Additionally, one faculty did not grasp exactly what the trial was about even though it was explained in e-mails and either never responded or gave a request that was too large or incomplete. Realizing this, it was discovered that more effort was needed to clarify the criteria and publicizing the service. For the most part, faculty found this service appealing since it helped them obtain material that was otherwise not readily available.

Feedback was also sought from the library student workers who were involved in the processing. As this project was a summer trial, there was no established training or manual: the student workers learned on the fly. So, the student workers helped create a working training manual and address any obstacles as they appeared and how to troubleshoot them. These student workers were very enthusiastic and helpful in getting this project running. Some took on more time than scheduled at some points of this project and willingly continued completing the tasks when required. This attitude motivated the others to get involved in this project in the event that this became a regular service. A comprehensive training manual was finally derived so that the requests could be uniformly processed with minimal error and attention to detail.

The student workers became very well-trained and did not hesitate to troubleshoot issues as they occurred including the following:

- some pages too large to scan so had to change lenses
- some pages were not the same as the others so had to adjust page layout (vertical, horizontal, etc.)
- some fiche only had the abstract and no body
- machine in use by patrons: had to make a schedule for both patron and student worker usage
- no page numbers on film pages or any indicators as such
- material illegible (i.e., faint, fuzzy font on microform)
- material in another language so could not comprehend where to end or start
- too many film to complete (need to contain to just one reel per request by individuals in a certain number of weeks)
- some pages on film were duplicated
- some pages on film were upside down or very faint especially with manuscripts
- microform item being copyright protected
- workstation equipment failure.

REVIEWING THE TRIAL AND TROUBLESHOOTING OPERATIONS

The feedback from the patrons and student workers indicated some areas of improvement to help streamline operations and provide better, more consistent service:

- labeling completed material in e-mails
- limiting the number of pages from film can do per request
- limiting the number of pages from fiche can do per request
- setting up a student worker schedule to work on the requests
- if ILS is willing to work with CRCP, then faculty can get access to material that is not readily available
- investing in new equipment since the current equipment does not scan well and is used by the patrons during times when work is needed to be done.

This implementation necessitated a streamlined workflow and a team-based approach to handle peaks and changes. Yang (2005) details on the following five key factors based on the original print policy to making deliverEdocs a success, factors that were no less important for digitizing microforms:

- the support of library administration, with regard to staff, equipment, and other resources
- a committed staff
- careful oversight of the processes
- additional support with well-trained student workers
- expert and responsive technical support.

As part of the effort to maintain consistent quality and track workflow, the above mentioned processing slip (see Appendix B) was revised to include a review section to act as the quality control. This will be discussed in the next section.

In the end, the feedback collected proved vital in revealing if this was a potentially user-friendly and user-inviting service. After the faculty and student worker comments were analyzed, it was clear that this was a service highly favored by the majority of the participants and manageable by the CRCP staff.

LEVERAGING ON AN EXISTING LIBRARY SERVICE

This service addition was well received and collaboration efforts were underway between ILS and CRCP. Point persons were delegated from both ILS and CRCP and a mutual system derived including constant communication between the units' point persons, uniformly agreed procedures on handling problem requests, adhering to restrictions aligning with ILS's book policies, and a mutually-accessible storage drive.

EQUIPMENT & PROCEDURES

CRCP requested library administration's support in purchasing a new scanner reader. Once this was delivered and set up, a document imaging software was installed on the staff CRCP workstation by the Libraries' Systems Department. Systems also helped in making sure both machines were talking to one another and assisted in deriving basic instructions on how to make the workstation operational. Training continues to be updated to maintain smooth and efficient processing. All these proved to improve processing and shortened the time it took to complete requests and were well received by the student workers.

An optimal process for digitizing the microforms was developed. The processing steps were derived as follows:

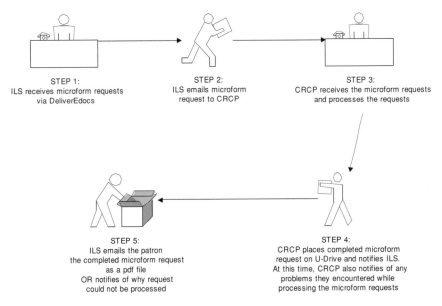

STEP 1:
ILS receives microform requests
via DeliverEdocs

STEP 2:
ILS emails microform
request to CRCP

STEP 3:
CRCP receives the microform requests
and processes the requests

STEP 5:
ILS emails the patron
the completed microform request
as a pdf file
OR notifies of why request
could not be processed

STEP 4:
CRCP places completed microform
request on U-Drive and notifies ILS.
At this time, CRCP also notifies of any
problems they encountered while
processing the microform requests

First, ILS receives microform requests via deliverEdocs from patrons. CRCP NEVER accepts requests at the desk UNLESS if it is from an ILS staff or is approved by CRCP. This helps to prevent the flooding of requests from patrons over the counter as well as from ILS. Secondly, ILS e-mails this request to CRCP. Thirdly, CRCP prints out the requests for the student worker to process. The student worker locates the microform and begins to process by taking a processing slip, the request slip, and the microform and sits at the CRCP staffside workstation to begin the scanning step:

- the microform to be loaded onto the scanner reader and the request located and positioned until there is a clear image

- the student then logs into the computer and pulls up the software imaging software where the scanning takes place

- when at the end of the request, the scanned images are saved as a pdf file with the Transaction Number file name (provided by the request form). This helps to keep track of what item is where.

After scanning is complete, the next step is the digitizing that entails the cropping and text recognition. These two clean and compress the pdf file and make it keyword searchable. Finally, the review also known as the quality control step ensures that:

- the correct microform is found

- the correct article is found

- all pages are processed (cropped, text captured, etc.)

- all of the pages in correct order
- all pages are rotated so look upright and in proper order
- any extra pages deleted or missing pages added
- all of the pages look clear and contain the entire page
- the entire pdf file looks like something that could be presented at a conference and/or submitted for a grade.

This step is performed by the student worker who gets done with the processing followed by a review check by the supervisor for quality control. When the review is finished, ILS is notified via e-mail or a log sheet. This is also the time when problem requests are reported to ILS who determine if it should be cancelled or processed. Some examples of problem requests are:

- guidelines set in place by ILS including requests that are over 50 pages
- item is not owned by library
- item is missing from shelf
- item is hard to scan or read (which is an issue with microformat)
- not enough information is provided by patron in helping to locate the microform or article
- wrong information is provided by the patron making it hard to locate the microform or article
- issues related to the content legibility and language format.

ILS notifies the patron and sends the pdf file or provides an explanation as to why the request was not processed. After this is done, the processing is then considered complete.

IMPLEMENTATION OF A REGULAR SERVICE MODEL

Beginning this service in full force December 2005, statistics were kept tracking the types of microform requested; how many per day, week, month; total pages per request; length of time in processing; any problems encountered, etc. This service varied in turnaround time primarily depending on these issues:

- item not locatable (missing, not owned by library, no longer in microform version)
- ILS guideline issues (i.e., over 50 pages, year published, etc.)
- item not scannable (very faint font, scratched up film or fiche)
- number of requests to be processed that day
- workstation problems.

For the most part, consistent with ILS print requirement guidelines, the requests are completed between one to three days (seven days maximum). To date, the longest a request had taken was two weeks, as a result of workstation problems, as well as the size of the request (200 pages). As of December 2006, a total of 1315 requests were submitted and 1099 processed and 216 unprocessed due to problems. This data revealed that this service definitely was a hit with patrons and the population stemming from students (including distance education students) to professors and other departments on campus. This was with minimal marketing effort. Once marketing is done for this service, the requests will predictably increase.

THE SCHOLARLY BY-PRODUCT: A DIGITAL COLLECTION

Finally, the possible creation of a repository of previously scanned files is actively being investigated. Currently, there is a digital collection created on Texas A&M University's institutional repository where scanned documents are uploaded. Though not publicly accessible, it is used as an internal resource to check against incoming deliverEdocs requests for scanner microforms.

Once this collection is reviewed for copyright compliance and after it gains critical mass, the intent is to make it a publicly available resource that would be searchable as any other electronic resource on the library Web page.

CONCLUSION

Digitizing microform on-demand to desktop delivery opened the doors to a jungle of microform that patrons were scared to venture into. With this service, more individuals are able to gain access to research material and receive it in easy-to-view pdf file format so it can be transformed into presentations and transparencies. Thus, material that was once lost or inaccessible has now been rediscovered and regaining popularity. Additionally, material can now be made available regardless of time and place as a result of its online nature. Also, with the push to a more ADA (Americans with Disabilities Association) compliant world, with digitized materials, there is an expectation that this material will be processed for the visually impaired or those with other access issues. Literally, this service helped to bring information on-demand to the user's fingertips to revive a once "dead collection" as characterized by McGeath (2006).

REFERENCES

Alexander, B. B., & Page, B. (1990). An overview of microform circulation in ARL libraries: Needs, statistics and the impact of automation. *Microform Review, 19,* 27–30.

Arthur, K. (2004). Recognizing digitization as a preservation reformatting method. *Microform & Imaging Review, 33*(4), 171–180.

Crow, R. (2002). The case for institutional repositories: A SPARC position paper. Washington, DC: SPARC. Retrieved on April 2, 2006, from http://www.arl.org/sparc/bm%7Edoc/ir_final_release_102.pdf.

Edelstein, H. A. (1993). The future of microfilm. *Inform, 7,* 34–50.

Eichhorn, S. (1984). Standards for public service of microform collections. *Microform Review, 13*(2), 103–107.

Manzo, B. (1997). Microform management in academic libraries. *Microform & Imaging Review, 26,* 73–80.

McGeath, K. (2006). Library services as commodity. *Texas Library Journal, 82*(2), 62–63.

Okerson, A. (1985). Microform conversion: A case study. *Microform Review, 14*(3), 157–163.

Smith, A. (1999). Why digitize? Council on Library Resources, Inc., 1–20.

Sridhar, M. S. (2002). Are microforms dead? *SRELS Journal of Information Management, 39*(2), 139–152.

Yang, Z. Y. (Lan). (2004). Customer satisfaction with interlibrary loan service—deliverEdocs: A case study. *Journal of Interlibrary Loan, Document Delivery & Electronic Reserve*, *14*(4), 79–94.

————. (2005). Providing free document delivery services to a campus of 48,000 library users. *Journal of Interlibrary Loan, Document Delivery & Electronic Reserve*, *15*(4), 49–55.

APPENDIX A: Faculty E-mail Letter of Request to Participate

To: (Faculty's Name)

From: Sheetal Desai
Date: June 14, 2005

RE: CRCP microform digitization service

The CRCP Department (Course Reserves / Current Periodicals: located at the back of the 2nd floor of Sterling C. Evans Library) houses a large number of microforms that are available for the public to utilize for curriculum and research support.

We are conducting a limited summer trial of a new service to increase access to the microforms. This trial involves allowing a select number of faculty to submit requests for copies of microform materials. CRCP would then digitize the requested material and, when possible, send the digitized document through email (or cd) to the faculty. Participants have been chosen on the basis of usage of the microforms heavily for classroom and/or research purposes.

You have been selected as a representative of your college to participate in this limited, trial run for the summer. Please submit your request of microfiche or microfilm that you would like to have our department scan and digitize. We are aware of copyright issues and thus there may be some restrictions that may surface. After your request has been delivered, we would appreciate feedback from on what you thought of the service, the end-product, and how we could improve it should it become a regularly-offered service.

If you are interested in participating in this trial run, please contact either myself or Wendi Arant Kaspar by June 30, 2005 for more details. If you have any questions, please free to contact us at (###) ###-####.

Thank you and we look forward to hearing from you.

Sheetal Desai
Wendi Arant Kaspar

Course Reserves/Current Periodicals (CRCP)
Texas A&M University Libraries
(###) ###-####

APPENDIX B: CRCP-ILS Digitizing Processing Slip

CRCP-ILS Digitizing Processing Slip

This processing slip is to help keep track of each digitizing request. Be sure this slip is completed and leave in the "Completed Request Slips" shelf on Sheetal's back table.

If you have any questions, please feel free to ask.

TN#: _____

Microform Type: Fiche   Film

Tasks To Complete	Staff Name	Begin Time	End Time
A) Retrieval of Item			
B) Scanning			
C) Digitizing:			
1) cropping			
2) text capturing			
3) save to S-drive			
D) Review			
E) Post to U-drive			

Problems encountered:

Date Request Received: _____ Date Request Processed:_____
Date Request Delivered: _____ Total Pages: _____ Total Time: _____

APPENDIX C: CRCP Microform Digitization Feedback Survey

Thank you for participating in CRCP's microform digitizing trial run. Please let us know how we did. Simply complete this survey and send it to the CRCP Department by emailing back this survey to (email). Your input is always important to us. If you have any future questions, please feel free to contact us at (###) ###-####.

Date(s) of request(s):

Number of microform requests submitted: _____		
Was the service clearly presented?	YES	NO
If no, how could it be more clearly defined?		
Were you contacted when request(s) were completed?	YES	NO
How was the end material delivered to you?	CD	Email
How would you have preferred the end material delivered to you?	CD	Email

Rate the following on a scale of 1 to 5
(1 = bad; 2 = fair; 3 = neutral; 4 = good; 5 = excellent)

How would you rate the quality of the request process?	_____
How would you rate the quality of the end material sent to you?	_____
How would you rate the readability of the end material (legible)?	_____
How would you rate the graphics of the end material (legible)?	_____

Would you like to see this type of processing continue?	YES	NO
Would you recommend this service to others?	YES	NO
Is there anything you'd like to see changed to better serve you?		

Any other feedback you would like to mention about the project?

APPENDIX D: CRCP Microform Digitization Feedback Survey Responses

Date(s) of Request(s):
June 16, 2005 - August 15, 2005   **Total Number of Jobs Submitted:** 19/20

Was the service clearly presented?
    Yes – 7 Comments: It was perfect!
    No - 0
    Yes & No - 1

If NO, how could it be more clearly defined?

Comments:

Including the original citation information on the email with the PDF attachment.

I will admit that I was confused for a while, but I guess that I am just dim-witted when it comes to technology.

Were you contacted when request(s) were completed?

Yes – 7

No - 1 Comments: Not until survey sent out.

Yes & No - 0

How was the end material delivered to you?

Email - 6

Cd - 2

How would you have preferred the end material delivered to you?

Email - 6

Cd - 2

Rate the following on a scale of 1 to 5: (1= bad; 2= fair; 3= neutral; 4= good; 5= excellent)

How would you rate the quality of the request process?

The following were the scores given for this question:

5 4 5 4 4 5 4 _I don't understand the question_

How would you rate the quality of the end material sent to you?

The following were the scores given for this question:

4 5 5 4 4 4 5 3

Comments:

Since I don't have "Office Imaging", the material is less useful to me now then it will be in "PDF".

The labeling of the different materials was not particularly useful.

How would you rate the readability of the end material (legible)?

The following were the scores given for this question:

4 3 5 4 2 4 5 3

Comments:

Materials which were upside down in the original microfilm are not usable when digitized. Other material which you can "zoom in" on was more legible than the original.

How would you rate the graphics of the end material (legible)?

The following were the scores given for this question:

3 2 5 4 4 4 2 1

Comments:

-Regarding the document received 8/1, I imagine that there was a problem with the original microfiche rather than the scanning process.

-I don't understand the question.

Would you like to see this type of processing continue?

Yes – 7

No – 0

Yes & No – 1 Comments: It is still hard for me to tell at this point how much more useful it will be once digitized. I have used microfilm for a long time, and while I have never been particularly fond of it, I am wondering whether it is worth the trouble.

Would you recommend this service to others?

Yes – 7

No - 0

Yes & No – 1 Comments: I am sure that some of my younger, techno-savvy colleagues would probably be more interested than I.

Is there anything you'd like to see changed to better serve you?

Comments:

-Include citation with completed request so the material is easy to identify. Most of the time it won't be a problem to figure out what journal (or other source) the material is from, but often faculty send multiple requests and it isn't always too easy to backtrack and ID the material if it comes w/o a citation.

-No.

-Would like to use a form on the web for placing a request.

-Workers need to give more thought to how to label the materials to make them more useful for researchers.

Any other feedback you would like to mention about the project?

Comments:

-I very much appreciate the availability of this service and hope it will continue.

-The legibility of some items isn't optional but it's readable enough to let me know whether I need to look at the actual film, and that itself is a big help. This is a great service and one that I hope can be continued.

-No, it was quick and well done, with care and in permanent contact with me via email.

-I process Document Delivery & Borrowing requests for 4500 TAMU patrons with MSL Interlibrary Loan and am forced to pay up to $25 per article request from non-TAMU source when an item is only held in microform at TAMU.

-To respond to your survey, I looked back at the documents received. The legibility of the first two reports I received is good. The legibility of the graphics in this one is not so good – probably because of the quality of the microfiche copy you started with.

Immersive Information Literacy: An Emerging Approach to K-12 Information Literacy Learning/Teaching

Terrance S. Newell

University of Wisconsin-Milwaukee

INTRODUCTION

This chapter emerges from K-12 information studies' (also known as school librarianship and school library media) constant concern with and attempt in developing information literate students. While the phrase *information literacy* is commonplace in many schools, the development of the concept is by no means a finished product, and much remains to be done as we move toward a more in-depth conceptualization of information literacy learning and an expansive range of instructional practices furthering information literacy within our schools. This chapter represents an attempt at recentering the concept of K-12 information literacy and instructional practices. The term *recentering* is used within this chapter to represent the move toward a more in-depth conceptualization and diverse instructional practice. Recentering does not refer to a unified movement from traditional information literacy conceptualizations/practices to radical ones; instead, it refers to an interrogation of concepts/practices from the center (tradition) to the margins (emerging thought). Such an interrogation is necessary because, across distinct educational environments, K-12 information specialists are interconnected by the information literacy narrative, and scholars have argued that there is a nexus between various conceptualizations within the narrative and different pedagogic approaches (e.g., Webber & Johnston, 2000). In other words, conceptualizations of information literacy inform teaching and learning, which situates the information literacy narrative as a critical site of struggle from which we can shift the center of thought/practice within the field.

Within the chapter, I begin to shift the center of thought/practice with a discussion of an emerging approach to information literacy learning/teaching entitled the *Immersive Information Literacy Approach* (I^2LA).

This emerging approach—that fuses a recentered view of information literacy, sociocultural learning theory, and immersive technology (e.g., virtual reality, computer simulations and video games) to create environments within which students can develop information literacy through authentic experiences, interactions, and communities of practice—emerges primarily from my own research studies and ideas rooted in fields such as K-12 information studies, critical studies, sociocultural psychology, gaming studies, anthropology, linguistics, and computer science. Furthermore, I²LA provides a new lens through which information educators—particularly school media specialists—can approach the development of information literate learners. The shift continues with an overview of the I²LA design framework, and concludes with a discussion of a three-dimensional, virtual reality, I²LA mode of instructional delivery to illustrate how the ideas derived from the (1) recentering of information literacy and (2) theoretical and technological coupling of I²LA can be applied in practice.

Information Literacy Conceptualizations

In a 1974 proposal submitted to the National Commission on Libraries and Information Science (NCLIS), Paul Zurkowski—a former president of the Information Industry Association—introduced the concept of information literacy (Eisenberg et al., 2004). Since the initial introduction of the concept, many scholars, professionals, and organizations have augmented the idea of information literacy. Presently, there are many conceptualizations of informational literacy; however, I will only overview five dominant constructions—information *literacy-as-skills*, information *literacy-as-attributes*, information *literacy-as-multimodal*, information *literacy-as-relational* and information *literacy-as-process*. The concept of information *literacy-as-skills* is a major conceptualization. This conceptualization presents information literacy as the teaching/learning of skills such as location (e.g., Hyland, 1978), information use (e.g., Hyland, 1978; ALA Presidential Committee, 1989), needs recognition (e.g., ALA Presidential Committee, 1989), information evaluation (e.g., ALA Presidential Committee, 1989), using technology (e.g., Shapiro & Hughes, 1996), formulating questions using analytic skills (e.g., Lenox & Walker, 1993), evaluating information using critical skills (e.g., Lenox & Walker, 1993), communicating information results and managing information tools for information access (e.g., Irving, 1990). Another dominant conceptualization, which I will call information *literacy-as-attributes*, emerged as the result of a Delphi study conducted by Doyle (1994). This conceptualization extends the concept of information literacy to the construction of distinct personal attributes of information literate people (Webber & Johnston, 2000). Within this conceptualization, information literacy is the internalization of characteristics such as "recognizing accurate and complete information for the purpose of decision-making, recognizing the need for information, formulating question based on information needs, identifying potential sources of information, developing successful search strategies, accessing sources of information, evaluating information, organizing information for practical application, integrating new information into existing bodies of knowledge, and using information in critical thinking and problem-solving" (Eisenberg et al., 2004, p. 23). Like all conceptualizations, the construction of the information literacy-as-attributes view is not limited to the work of one scholar. Other professionals, organizations, and scholars have augmented this conceptualization with personal attributes such as: having the desire to know (Lenox & Walker, 1993); being competent and independent; critically reflecting on the nature of information, information infrastructure and context (Shapiro & Hughes, 1996); being persistent, attentive, and cautious (Breivik, 1985); having developed an information style; being comfortable in multiple answer situations; having values that promote information use; being flexible thinkers (Kuhlthau, 1993); and being able to perform both independently and in group situations (Callison, 1986). The construction of information *literacy-as-multimodal* is also a dominant conceptualization. Scholars such as Lenox and Walker (1993) have extended the conceptualization of information literacy by articulating its multiplicity. These scholars believe that "[w]hether information comes from a computer, a book, a government agency, a film, a conversation, a poster, or any number of other possible sources, inherent in the concept of information literacy is the ability to dissect and understand what you see on the page or the television screen, in posters, pictures, and other images, as well as what you hear. If we are to teach information literacy, we must teach students to sort, to discriminate, to select and to analyze the array of messages that are presented" (Eisenberg et al., 2004, p. 25). Furthermore, within this conceptualization, it is believed that other literacies such as visual literacy can be mastered via information literacy (Breivik, 1989). The information *literacy-as-relational* conceptualization constructs information literacy as something experienced by students in different ways. Bruce (1997) employed a qualitative research design to illuminate seven ways that students experience information literacy. It is important to note that the seven *ways* or *faces* within the relational construction can stand as independent conceptualizations. Moreover, within the information literacy-as-relational conceptualization, the view of information literacy as the (1) use of information technology, (2) seeking/location of information, (3) controlling of information, (4) personal construction of knowledge, (5) wise use of information to meet the needs of others, and (6) execution of a process (Bruce, 1997) could each stand independently as conceptualizations. For example, information *literacy-as-process*, which is a primary conceptualization within K-12 information studies, conceptualizes information skills as more than isolated incidents (Eisenberg et al., 2004). Moreover, information skills are conceptualized as connected activities that encompass a way of thinking about and using information (Eisenberg et al., 2004), and K-12 information literacy illuminates two major processes—information problem-solving and research.

Although all of the conceptualizations are currently operating within K-12 learning environments to some degree, the information *literacy-as-process* conceptualization dominates, and it is considered the best-practice view of information literacy. Using the information literacy-as-process conceptualization, library media specialists are currently employing "instructional practices that call for the 'contextualization' of skill lessons presented as the need for their use arises within ongoing classroom instruction" (Thomas, 2004, p. 105). Therefore, within current best-practices, information skills (such as access, evaluation, and use) are not taught until they are needed to fulfill a particular need within a core subject, classroom assignment, and those skills are usually taught using process models, which are frameworks (e.g., ISP, Big6, REACTS, Pathways, and I-Search models) that allow students to learn information skills through the cognitive *process* of fulfilling an information need.

The information literacy-as-process conceptualization and integrated process approach to teaching/learning has undoubtedly advanced the field's approach to active information literacy instruction during the last two decades; however, we are still facing a consciousness of our limits in educating students, which is reflected in studies that illuminate a lack of (1) instructional role fulfillment by information educators and (2) a lack of information literacy skills in entering college students. Studies show that K-12 information educators, while attempting to fulfill an instructional role in practice, are struggling with environmental complexities such as: a lack of time (e.g., Giorgis & Peterson, 1996; Van Deusen & Tallman, 1994; McCracken, 2001; Newell, 2004), role perception conflict (e.g., Dorrell & Lawson, 1995; Ceperley, 1991; Lai, 1995; Newell, 2004), lack of teacher interest in cooperation (e.g., Lewis, 1990; Jones, 1997; Kinder, 1995; Pickard, 1993; McCracken, 2001; Newell, 2004), too many students to serve (McCracken, 2001; Kinder, 1995; and Newell, 2004), a misconception of information literacy by teachers (Newell, 2004), a dissonance of core content objects and information objects (Newell, 2004) and teacher ambivalence toward information literacy instruction (Newell, 2004). These environmental impediments are restricting many information educators from providing structures and opportunities for learning within integrated process approaches. However, even when a systematic program of instruction is in place, students often lack transference to other information environments such as university settings. In fact, university faculties believe that incoming freshmen are poorly prepared in respect to information literacy, and that only two-thirds of entering students can adequately employ skills related to information literacy

(ICAS, 2002). Moreover, disturbing findings are emerging in relation to students' inability to access information (Dunn, 2002), evaluate information (Dunn, 2002; ICAS, 2002), generate and focus an information and/or research question (Dunn, 2002), analyze and synthesize information (ICAS, 2002) and to apply information (Dunn, 2002), which suggests a recentering of our conceptualizations and an expansion of instructional best-practices.

Immersive Information Literacy Instruction

The *Immersive Information Literacy Approach* (I^{2}LA) is an emerging approach, which fuses a recentered view of information literacy, sociocultural learning theory, and immersive technology (e.g., virtual reality, computer simulations and video games) to create environments within which students can develop information literacy through authentic experiences, interactions, and communities of practice. This weaving together of theory, immersive technology, and the K-12 information studies area is an opportunity to extend the field's best-practices at best or engender discussions on alternative instructional approaches at the very least. I^{2}LA emerges from my interrogations of scholarly texts, theoretical approaches, national guidelines, and new technologies. The approach is an attempt to shift the center of instructional thought/practice from a generally accepted and sanctioned position to a more critical existence.

I^{2}LA and information literacy

Within the, I^{2}LA information literacy is reconceptualized as a form of literacy tied to the semiotic domain of information. The term semiotic refers to the many different things that take on meanings (e.g., texts, images, objects, and people) within particular contexts such as situations, practices, and subject areas (Gee, 2003). A semiotic domain is any knowledge set and set of practices "that recruits one or more modalities (e.g., oral or written language, images, equations, symbols, sounds, gestures, graphs, artifacts, etc.) to communicate distinctive types of meanings" (Gee, 2003, p. 18). Therefore, information literacy—as conceptualized within I^{2}LA—is a particular *knowledge set* and *set of social practices* that employ multiple representational and communicative modes to produce and communicate distinct types of meanings (Gee, 2003), and like any semiotic domain, information literacy has sub-domains or particular literacies such as access, evaluation, location, use, retrieval, problem-solving and research. The phrase *knowledge set* refers to the typical content that is considered acceptable within the domain (Gee. 2003, p. 30). For example, within the sub-domain of information access, areas such as (1) information needs, (2) accurate and inaccurate information, (3) basis for decision making, (4) need-based questions, (5) initial sources identification, and (6) search strategies are all recognizable as typical content. Using Gee's logic, if a student only knows a list of information sources then s/he does not know the knowledge set tied to the sub-domain of information access, because knowing the knowledge set (or the underlying principles and patterns of information access) allows the student to make judgments about information sources and systems that they have never seen before and systems that are not currently in existence (Gee, 2003). The phrase *social practices* refers to "distinctive ways of acting, interacting, valuing, feeling, knowing, and using various objects and technologies associated with a given semiotic domain" (Gee, 2003, p. 30). To continue the example from above, people engaged in the social practice of information access—or practices within any of the other sub-domains—tend to think, act, interact, value, believe, and use in domain-specific ways (Gee, 2003). Moreover, a student knows the social practices tied to information access if s/he (1) "knows what counts as thinking, acting, interacting, and valuing" like someone who accesses information efficiently and effectively; (2) recognizes the sorts of identities such people take on when they are accessing information efficiently and effectively; (3) can "recognize what counts as valued social practices" to information-literate people accessing information; and (4) recognizes "what counts as behaving appropriately in these social practices" (Gee, 2003, p. 30).

What distinguishes this reconceptualization from traditional ideas is the broad and situated construction of information literacy. Moreover, information literacy is not simply a set of skills, a list of attributes, the ability to dissect and understand multimodal messages, the use of information technology, the use of information objects, the act of information seeking/location, the controlling of information, the personal construction of knowledge, the wise use of information to meet the needs of others, or the execution of a process. Instead, information literacy is both a semiotic domain and a family of literacies operating within other semiotic domains (e.g., math, history, science, etc.). Thinking in terms of semiotic domains allows K-12 information educators to "say that people are (or are not) literate (partially or fully) in the domain if they can recognize (the equivalent of *reading*) and/or produce (the equivalent of *writing*) meanings in the domain" (Gee, 2003, p. 18). This view transforms a semiotic domain such as information literacy from a set of skills (or string of skills) to a distinctive community of social practices (Gee, 2003). Moreover, this reconceptualization does not represent a unified movement from traditional information literacy conceptualizations and instructional practices to radical ones; instead, it recognizes the multiplicity of information literacy and situates it within domains of meaning making practices. The reconceptualization also places all of the current information literacy conceptualizations (e.g., set of skills, list of attributes, dissection of multimodal messages, use of information technology, use of information objects, act of information seeking/location, control of information, construction of personal knowledge, wise use of information for others, and various processes) within a cohesive and coherent vision that places them within a semiotic domain. For example, the information literacy-as-attributes conceptualization can now be tied to social practices and illuminated as distinct attributes within sub-domains such as information problem-solving.

I^2LA and learning theory

As mentioned above, scholars have argued that there is a nexus between conceptualizations of information literacy and pedagogic approaches (e.g., Webber & Johnston, 2000). This connection is largely due to the fact that different conceptualizations are better situated within various theories of teaching and learning, which materializes into instructional approaches. For example, conceptualization of information literacy-as-skills has often been situated within behaviorist theory (Webber & Johnston, 2000) and materialized as instructional approaches such as the *Source Approach* (Kuhlthau, 1987) on the K-12 level and the *Library Tool Approach* (Kuhlthau, 1987) on the postsecondary level. Another example is the information literacy-as-process conceptualization, which currently dominates K-12 information literacy thought. Due to the dominance of this conceptualization, K-12 information specialists are primarily employing *integrated approaches* to information literacy instruction, which are "instructional practices that call for the 'contextualization' of skill lessons presented as the need for their use arises within ongoing classroom instruction" (Thomas, 2004, p. 105). Moreover, within the integrated approach, information literacies such as problem-solving are usually taught using process models, which are frameworks (e.g., ISP, Big6, REACTS, Pathways, and I-Search models) that allow students to learn information knowledge and practices through the cognitive *process* of fulfilling an information need. The phrase "cognitive process" reflects the strong nexus between process models and constructivist learning-as-cognition or cognitive constructivism. Constructivist learning-as-cognition or cognitive constructivism, in the sense that it is used in this chapter, is a discourse of information literacy learning and a practice of information literacy teaching, shaped by the view of "cognition and learning that has dominated American psychological research—a view that focuses on individual knowers and learners who acquire knowledge and cognitive skills by adding small pieces incrementally to what they have learned previously" (Greeno, 1993, p. 154). A cognitive view of constructivism situates learning as resulting from rich mental processes and experiences within a stable and objective world (Kirshner & Whitson, 1997; Carey, 1998). That is, students actively create new understandings (through mental processes) based upon previous knowledge, experiences, and beliefs while interacting upon and within information objects and events (Jonassen, 1994).

The recentered view of information literacy within I²LA is tied to theories (e.g., sociocultural constructivism and situated cognition theory) that reflect the social realities of cognition and learning. These theories acknowledge the overarching views articulated across cognitive constructivists, which view learning within the mind of the student, yet draw from the works of scholars such as Vygotsky (1978), Leont'ev (1981), and Lave (1988), situating learning within social activity and communities of practice. I²LA does not subscribe to the historical conflict that exists between the views of learning-as-cognition and learning-as-sociocultural; instead, it focuses upon the multiple points of juncture that connect the cognitive and sociocultural views (Cobb, 1996). In other words, I²LA views information learning as both a process of active meaning making within the student's mind and as a process of enculturation into the social practices of information literate people (Cobb, 1996). Therefore, information literacy learning occurs in the mind of the student; that is, students actively create new understandings (through mental processes) based upon previous knowledge, experiences, and beliefs while interacting upon and within information objects and events (Jonassen, 1994). However, information literacy learning cannot occur outside of information contexts and participation in the social practices tied to the information domain; moreover, there is a "nexus between the mind at work, and the world in which it works" that stretches across the student's mind, activity, and settings (Lave, 1988, p. 1).

I²LA and immersive technology

Immersive computer-based technologies have the ability to transform student learning by generating environments that emphasize the context within which information literacy learning occurs. There are various types and forms of immersive computer-based technologies. I²LA promotes the use of desktop virtual reality, computer simulation, and computer games, and it is important to note that I²LA promotes the creation of immersive platforms by information educators. The previous statement is not meant to devalue the educational potential of commercially produced games and simulation environments; instead, it is meant to emphasize the need for information educators to become producers of immersive platforms that approach the knowledge set and social practices of information literacy as active content and represent various information contexts. Historically speaking, the terms virtual reality, computer simulation, and computer games have different meanings; however, they are used interchangeably within I²LA under the umbrella of immersive technology. Moreover, within I²LA they are all considered immersive computer-based technologies that allow participants to examine 3-D simulations from every perspective through a computer screen by navigating the simulated environment with a control device such as a mouse or a keyboard (McLellan, 1992; Focier, 1999). These technologies provide an immersive experience and they are not very expensive, making them highly valuable for library and classroom settings. Using immersive technology, a recentered view of information literacy and sociocultural theory, information educators could create immersive, three-dimensional, highly interactive, multisensory, computer-generated learning environments that represent (1) the learners and (2) the information contexts or settings wherein students construct knowledge of information social practices through experiences. Learners

Figure 1. Iterative design framework for the I²LA.

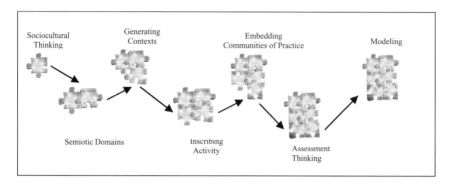

within these immersive learning environments interact with the environment, information objects (e.g., computers and books), and with each other through first-person views and/or avatars or virtual representations of themselves.

Designing Using the I²LA

The I²LA is designed to guide information educators as they construct learning environments that engender information literacy development through authentic experiences, interactions, and communities of practice. I²LA integrates learning theory, immersive technology, and the grammars of information literacy into an iterative design framework. This section overviews the design framework and its key phases (see Figure 1).

Phase 1: Sociocultural thinking

The first phase of the design framework for I²LA is sociocultural thinking, which is a critical reflection upon theories (sociocultural constructivism, situated cognition theory, etc.) that reflect the social realities of cognition and learning. As stated above, I²LA does not subscribe to any one social theory of learning, nor does it dismiss cognitive theories. Instead, I²LA encourages information educators to extend the site for learning and knowledge to social and cultural dimensions—which could take a number of forms. After reviewing different sociocultural theories of learning, information educators can take one of two approaches: (1) they can totally subscribe to one theory (e.g., situated cognition) and outline its characteristics; or (2) they can outline the multiple points of juncture across theories, without overly focusing upon differences within particular approaches. No matter what the approach, information educators are encouraged to create an outline of their learning theory (ies) that include the following minimum characteristics: goal of learning, view of learners, view of teachers, setting for learning, unit of analysis, what is produced during activity/interaction, and pedagogical implications within the learning theory. Table 1 represents an example outline of the minimum characteristics of situated learning.

Phase 2: Identifying semiotic domains

The second phase of the design framework involves semiotic domain identification. Within I²LA, information literacy is reconceptualized as both a semiotic domain with a family of sub-domains (e.g., research and problem-solving) and associated semiotic domains (e.g., math, history, science, everyday world, etc.). Information educators are encouraged to identify the primary sub-domain and/or the associated domain to be engaged as active

Table 1. Abridged Outline of Major Situated Learning Characteristics

Characteristics	Situated Learning
Goal of learning	To learn a semiotic domain by doing what literate people within the domain does, by engaging the social practices and content of the domain (Gee, 2003; Brown, Collins, & Newman, 1990; Schoenfeld, 1985). To generate knowing, thinking, understanding and identity in bodily (i.e., lived) experience and sociocultural eontext(s) (Lave, 1998; Kirshner & Whitson, 1997).
View of learners	Learners are active participants within learning communities (Lave & Wenger, 1991).
Setting for learning	Learning occurs in context(s)
Unit of analysis	Situated learning "shifts the focus from the individual as the unit of analysis towards the sociocultural setting in which activities are embedded" (Kirshner & Whitson, 1997, p. 5).
Purpose of activity/interaction	Develop meaning, knowledge, practices and identity within communities, context(s) and cultural tools.

content. Furthermore, educators are encouraged to outline the primary knowledge set and social practices of the identified domain to better construct learning environments that allows students to learn both content knowledge and practices. For example, information problem-solving is a particular type of literacy (or sub-domain) within the semiotic domain of information literacy, and it refers to a set of social practices that recruits one or more modalities to generate and communicate distinctive types of meanings and solutions within ill-structured, realistic problem situations. Information problem-solving has a particular knowledge set and social practices. The content knowledge (knowledge set) covers areas such as: problem identification, location, access, organization, evaluation, and use. The social practices focus on the ways that information literate people typically think, act, inter-act, and value during information problem-solving. To create content knowledge and social practices outlines of sub-domains, the information educator must review LIS literature and guidelines. When working within an associated domain (e.g., scientific research), information educators should work closely with educators in that domain as they generate content knowledge and social practices outlines because the association may transform content and practices. After generating an outline, the educator should reflect upon the first phase to ensure that the best theoretical selection was made in light of the content and practices that will be actively engaged.

Phase 3: Generating contexts

Information literacy learning should occur within information contexts and through participation in social practices. Context is not given in a physical setting (e.g., operating room) nor in types of people (e.g., doctors); instead, contexts are constituted in purpose-ful interactions among types of people within/across artifacts and environments (Erickson & Schultz, 1997). Within this phase, which focuses upon the physical part of context, immersive computer-based technologies are selected to generate environments that recreate the physical context(s) within which information literacy learning occurs, and information educators begin the process of design. Moreover, within this phase, information educators should identify immersive technologies (e.g., Second Life, Active Worlds, etc.) that allow them to create three-dimensional, highly interactive, multi-sensory, computer generated environments. Furthermore, they should identify various physical context(s) (e.g., libraries, homes, workplaces, community spaces, grocery stores, etc.) for information literacy learning, and create a 2-D layout of a larger environment that contains those contexts. Information educators are also encouraged to create a list of real world artifacts (e.g., computers, books, etc.) that are typically located in those environments so that their virtual counterparts can be generated in a later phase. Information educators should revisit phases 1 and 2 to determine if changes should be made due to context.

Phase 4: Inscribing activity

As stated above, contexts are constituted in purposeful interactions among types of people within/across artifacts and environments (Erickson & Schultz, 1997). During this phase, interactions and activity will be inscribed into the 2-D layout of the physical context. Moreover, information educators are using the learning theory, content knowledge, social practices, and contexts to generate stories, information problems, and roles for students and educators to fulfill.

During the previous phase, the educator designed a large physical context (experience space) with various contexts embedded within it. For example, the large physical context could be a small community with various contexts such as libraries, homes, and small businesses located within it. During this phase (phase 4), the educator must create a story for the experience space. For example, the various residents of the small community could be in desperate need of information knowledge and practices. Next, the information educator is encouraged to embed information problems throughout the experience space. For example, the information problems could be tied to characters (residents), artifacts, and contexts throughout the space. Finally, information educators should use learning theory to inscribe roles to students and other educators. For example, if the educator subscribes to situated learning theory, then students could be assigned the role of information literacy apprentices, and they would operate under the guidance of information educators to meet the needs of the community residents.

Phase 5: Embedding communities of practice

Information educators should identify the range of knowledge and practices that are required to solve all problems and prepare to embed them into the experience space as social practices that are communicated to support the learner's exploration. The knowledge and practices could be embedded in a number of ways depending on the applied learning theory and developed stories. For example, if the students were assigned the role of information literacy apprentices, then knowledge and social practices could be provided via an integrated combination of (1) live educators interacting with students face-to-face in a library and/or classroom setting, (2) live educators interacting with students using avatars within a virtual space, (3) preprogrammed environmental avatars interacting with students, and (4) just-in-time information that could take the form of pop-ups or databases that students access.

Phase 6: Assessment thinking

There are currently two dominant approaches to authentic assessment within K-12 information studies (portfolios and performances), and information educators are encouraged to integrate both approaches into immersive information learning environments. Portfolios are purposeful collections of students' work that illuminate their efforts, abilities, progresses, and understandings. Portfolios also provide a complex and comprehensive view of student performance in context (Turner, 1993; Paulson, Paulson & Meyer, 1991). Callison (1993) stated that school librarians naturally understand the characteristics of portfolio

Figure 2. Screen shot of the VIILAS community space.

assessment because school librarians are increasingly practicing some aspect of activity documentation in respect to the library collection and the curriculum. He encouraged school librarians to move beyond the use of records collection for showing the value of the school library toward the use of portfolios as a method for student assessment. Performance-based assessments are exercises that ask students to demonstrate their knowledge and skills by undertaking some type of performance (Rothman, 1996). They provide a basis for teachers to evaluate both the effectiveness of the process or procedure used and the product result-ing from performance of a task. These types of assessment usually require the student to demonstrate skills in a real-world environment or to complete a project by assuming the role of a real-life professional. These assessments are beneficial because they provide real incentives, drive instruction and learning in positive ways, and focus learning on higher order or complex thinking skills (Madaus & Tan, 1993; NCEST, 1992).

Immersive information learning environments naturally require students to demon-strate achievement through their performances; however, all of the performances can be designed to result in some type of product (portfolio) that reflects the student's processes and procedures.

Phase 7: Modeling

During this phase, information educators actually use immersive technology to create (prototype) and test their learning environments. I²LA strongly promotes the use of desktop virtual reality for the production of learning environment because it is inexpensive, serves as a meta-medium (able to support all other existing media), and because it can be used to generate sophisticated 3-D simulations environment with an easy learning curve.

After the prototype is created, the information educator should allow students (and other educators) to enter the development process as tester. Groups of students/educators should use the prototype and provide feedback, which will reshape aspects of the design.

Villas an I²LA Mode of Instructional Delivery

VILLAS stands for Virtual Reality Information Literacy Learning and Assessment Space, and it is an example of how the I²LA can be put into practice. In other words, if I²LA were a methodology then, VILLAS would be a method. VILLAS is a three-dimensional, virtual reality environment for learning and assessing information literacy within a socio-cultural learning approach (see Figure 2). VILLAS is constructed upon the I²LA pillars and

Figure 3. Personalized virtual representation.

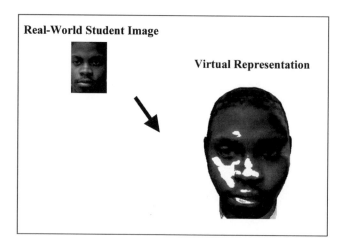

it serves as a space within which students can develop information literacy—particularly general information problem-solving—through authentic experiences, interactions, and communities of practice. The current version of VILLAS was designed for middle school students, and it is presently in a second round of real-world testing.

VILLAS interface

The VILLAS interface consists of three parts: world view window, toolbar, and chat window. The world view window displays the virtual environment. The toolbar is positioned below the world view window and it contains eight icons. The eight icons control features such as avatar visibility. The third part of the interface is the floating chat window. It is called a floating window because it can be easily moved across the screen for preferred positioning. The chat feature of VILLAS enables real-time communication; that is, typed messages appear immediately on the screen of other users.

The term virtual is often used in librarianship as a reference to increased flexibility of time and place constraints, and it usually refers to two-dimensional spaces such as Web sites. Web sites are considered 2-D because they only have height and width dimensions. Three-dimensional (3-D) virtual reality has height, width, and depth dimensions. It is the third dimension, depth, which allows learners to move within the space. VILLAS navigation occurs through mouse movements and/or keyboard arrow keys. Learners who are also video gamers will be very familiar with the concept of using a mouse to move through a virtual space. Moving the mouse forward, backwards, and sideways will move the avatar in the same directions. Other movements such as strafing, looking up/down, and kneeling are possible through combined mouse and keyboard strokes. The keyboard could also be used to navigate the world in place of the mouse. Keyboard navigation occurs via the arrow keys (e.g., left arrow moves the avatar left).

Learners within VILLAS are depicted as different characters, and these characters or virtual representations are called avatars. It is important to note that avatars, within VILLAS are designed to resemble students (see Figure 3), and these virtual representations provide learners with a virtual presence, which adds an extra dimension to collaboration because other learners can actually see, physically interact, and chat with each other (see Figure 4).

Figure 4. Virtual presence and collaboration in VILLAS.

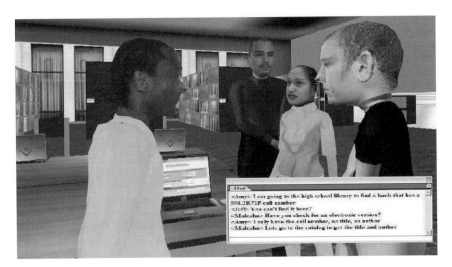

VILLAS context(s)

VILLAS aids students in the development of information literacy—particularly information problem-solving—by affording them opportunities to apply practices and knowledge in a real-world context and within a community of information practice. The real-world context is designed into the platform using 3-D virtual reality and authentic performance-based tasks. The real-world contexts consist of a middle school library (see Figure 5), a high school library (see Figure 6), informal information environments such as homes and businesses (see Figure 7), and electronic environments (see Figure 8). This design reinforces the idea that school library media centers are preparing students to navigate, evaluate, and use diverse print and electronic environments—some directly located within or linked to institutions and others independent from time and place constraints. Furthermore, it emphasizes the importance of context in information literacy development.

Figure 5. Screen shot of the VILLAS middle school library.

Figure 6. Screen shot of the VILLAS high school library.

The 3-D, immersive technology also enabled the construction of virtual information objects, artifacts, and resources such as books, computers, televisions, and people that appear real. Furthermore, these virtual objects and the virtual environment itself are interactive and respond to the participant's actions (e.g., the computers work and students can use the books within the space). Within the virtual information environments of VILLAS, students can: (1) move and interact freely and collaboratively using avatars; (2) communicate using chat features and gestures; (3) use a variety of information objects, artifacts, and resources to solve problems; (4) learn social practices via tutorials; and (5) consult virtual information educators (cybrarians) for tips, advice, and processes. The realistic contexts make problems more engaging and provide students with opportunities to think, reason, and use the knowledge and social practices of the information domain to problem solve within/across context.

Figure 7. Screen shot of a VILLAS informal information environment.

Figure 8. A student accessing the electronic environment.

Activity and community of practice within VILLAS

The learner begins her/his exploration of VILLAS within an area called Cybrarian Land. Cybrarian Land is the default environment that loads when students first enter VILLAS. Located within this environment are cybrarians, who are virtual information specialists. As students arrive to Cybrarian Land, they are (1) greeted by a cybrarian, (2) introduced to the concept of information problem-solving, (3) inducted as information literacy apprentices, (4) given their mission of helping the VILLAS community, and (5) provided with training on VILLAS navigation. The phases of information problem-solving introduction and apprenticeship induction are designed to draw students into the culture of information social practices. The introduction is designed to engender students' thinking of information-as-domain, and the apprenticeship is a way to enculturate students into domain-specific social practices through community interaction and authentic activity.

There are three communities represented in VILLAS: (1) the community of citizens located throughout VILLAS that need help; (2) the physical and virtual information community consisting of libraries, homes, databases, books, people, and the internet; and (3) a community of practice, which is composed of cybrarians and other information literate people that share knowledge, practices, and ways of being with students. Each authentic task emerges from a person in the community needing help with real-world information problems. The tasks are embedded with (a) subject matter ranging from daily life to academic work, (b) multiple sub-domain areas of focus such as access, evaluation, and use,

Figure 9. Screen shot of a student consulting a cybrarian.

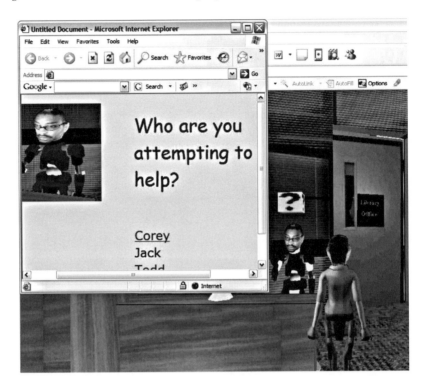

and (c) task structures ranging from well-structured problems to less-structured problems where problem identification, collection, organization, integration, evaluation, and use of information are emphasized. Students help community members through their role as information literacy apprentices. As information apprentices, students consult cybrarians and assist them in aiding the community using information knowledge and practices in a variety of information contexts.

As apprentices with a general understanding of information problem-solving, students enter the VILLAS community to help its citizens while mastering the social practices of the information domain. Upon their arrival to the VILLAS community, students are first greeted by the mayor. The mayor stresses the importance of the students' mission and reviews the VILLAS layout, navigation, and interface. He also briefs the students on the community of citizens needing help and provides them with a map indicating the citizens' locations. After the briefing, students are provided with a level of autonomy in directing their learning by assisting community members is any order. The information problems are solved by students employing social practices, interacting with the virtual environment/people, and acting upon information objects (e.g., print and electronic objects). Social practices are primarily delivered to students in a tutorial format. This type of information consists of knowledge, processes, and techniques that students need to solve the problems as information literacy apprentices. The tutorials are accessed through the cybrarians. For example, if an apprentice gets stuck then s/he can consult a cybrarian for tips and tutorials and/or collaborate within other students (see Figure 9). The cybrarian may be live (meaning that the information educator is chatting as the cybrarian), or the cybrarian will be an environmental avatar that can be accessed for tips and practices.

VILLAS assessment

The VILLAS assessment approach is a combination of numerical, graphic, and descriptive graphic scales used to assess learning. The numerical rating scale is simply a scale that raters use to indicate the degree to which a characteristic is achieved by marking a number. The graphic rating scales indicate degree of characteristic achievement along a horizontal continuum, and the descriptive graphic rating scales use descriptive phrases to identify degree of characteristic achievement along a horizontal graphic scale. The rating scales are designed to assess processes, procedures, and products. Moreover, many VILLAS tasks require students to demonstrate achievement through their performances; however, all of the performances result in some type of product and information educators can use the rating scales to assess the students' product as well as their processes and procedures. The rating scale serves the same purpose in product assessment that it does in process assessment. It helps raters assess the products of all students in terms of the same characteristics.

Summary

Within the last forty years, K-12 information studies has transitioned to an information literacy narrative and embraced an active approach to information literacy instruction. Currently, it is best-practice to use integrated instructional approaches—coupled with process models—to develop information literate students. Literature shows that integrated approaches are effective in ideal situations. However, research literature also reveals our limits in educating all students within integrated approaches outside of ideal conditions. This is not surprising if we realize that active, contextualized, and information instruction is a very recent revolutionary change, and that the field is still moving toward reliable forms of instruction. In other words, it is too early to *black-box* the instructional transition, and in light of K-12 information studies illuminating a lack of (1) instructional role fulfillment by information educators, (2) student skill transference across grades/environments, and (3) a lack of information literacy skills in entering college students, we must reexamine the monopoly status that integrated process approaches currently hold within the field. I believe that the way to reexamine our approach to educating information literate students is to (1) ask new questions about information learning environments, (2) rethink our learning theories, (3) reconceptualize our understanding of literacy and learning, (4) produce new learning approaches and modes of delivery that are constructed upon an in-depth knowledge of learning environments, learning theory, literacy, and technology, and (5) to examine the new approach's effectiveness as compared to current best-practices.

The I^{2}LA as an emerging approach, which fuses sociocultural theory, a recentered view of information literacy, and immersive technology to create environments within which students can develop information literacy through experiences, interactions, and communities of practice, is an attempt to shift the center of instructional thought and practice from a generally accepted and sanctioned position to a more critical existence. I^{2}LA learning environments may better aid information educators in developing students who can: (1) identify an information need; (2) access, evaluate, analyze, synthesize, and apply information; and (3) solve real-world problems in a variety of contexts using information literate processes (e.g., research process, information problem-solving processes and electronic searching processes). Moreover, these learning environments may transcend system impediments to the information educator's instructional role.

REFERENCES

American Library Association. (1989). *Presidential committee on information literacy, final report.* Chicago: American Library Association.

Breivik, P. (1985). Putting libraries back in the information society. *American Libraries, 16*(10), 723.

Breivik, P. & Gee, E. (1989). *Information literacy.* New York: Macmillan Publishing Co.

Bruce, C. (1997). *The seven faces of information literacy.* Adelaide, Australia: Auslib Press.

Callison, D. (1986). School library media programs and free inquiry learning. *School Library Media Quarterly, 15*(6), 20–24.

———. (1993). The potential for portfolio assessment. In C. C. Kuhlthau (Ed.), *Assessment and the school library media center* (pp. 121–130). Englewood, CO: Libraries Unlimited.

Carey, J. (1998). Library skills, information skills, and information literacy: Implications for teaching and learning. SLMQ Online. Accessed in March 2006 from http://www.ala.org/ala/aasl/aaslpubsandjournals/slmrb/slmrcontents/volume11998slmqo/carey.htm

Ceperley, P. E. (1991). Information needs 2000: Results of a survey of library media specialists. Charleston, WV: Appalachia Educational Lab. ERIC Document ED 340 393.

Cobb, P. (1996). Where is the mind? A coordination of sociocultural and cognitive constructivist perspectives. In C. T. Fosnot (Ed.), *Constructivism: Theory, perspectives, and practice* (pp. 34–54). New York: Teachers College Press.

Dorrell, L. D. & Lawson, L. V. (1995). What are principals' perceptions of the school library media specialist? *NASSP Bulletin, 79*(2), 72–80.

Doyle, C. (1994). Information-literate use of telecommunications. *DMLEA Journal,* 17(2), 17–20.

Dunn, K. (2002). Assessing information literacy skills in the California State University: A progress report. *Journal of Academic Librarianship, 30*(1/2), 26–35.

Eisenberg, M. B., Carrie, A., & Spitzer, K. L. (2004). *Information literacy: Essential skills for the Information Age.* Westport, CT: Libraries Unlimited.

Erickson, F. and Schultz, J. (1997). 'When is a context? Some issues and methods in the analysis of social competence', in Cole, M., Engeström, Y. and Vasquez, O. (Eds.) (1997). *Mind, Culture and Activity.* Cambridge: Cambridge University Press, 22–31.

Focier, R. C. (1999). *The computer as an educational tool: Productivity and problem solving.* Columbus, OH: Merrill.

Gee, J. (2003). *What video games have to teach us about learning and literacy.* New York: Palgrave Macmillan.

Giorgis, C. G. & Peterson, B. (1996). Teachers and librarians collaborate to create a community of learners. *Language Arts, 73*(8), 477–482.

Greeno, J. (1993). *Situativity and symbols.* (Response to Vera and Simon). Cognitive Science, *17,* 150–160.

Hyland, A. H. (1978). Recent directions in educating the library user: Elementary schools. In J. Lubans (Ed.), *Progress in educating the library user* (pp. 29–44). New York: Bowker.

Intersegmental Committee of the Academic Senates (ICAS). (2002). Academic literacy: A statement of competencies expected of students entering California's public colleges and universities. Retrieved June 5, 2005, from http://www.universityofcalifornia.edu/senate/reports/acadlit.pdf

Irving, A. (1990). *Wider horizons: Online information services in schools.* Library and Information Research Report 80. London: British Library.

Jonassen, D. (1994). Evaluating constructivist learning. *Educational Technology, 36*(9), 28–33.

Jones, A. C. (1997). An analysis of the theoretical and actual curriculum development involvement of Georgia school library media specialists. Doctoral dissertation, Georgia State University. *Dissertation Abstracts International, 58*(08A), 2890.

Kinder, S. J. (1995). Teacher-librarians' perceptions and priorities in regard to elementary school library programs and services. Unpublished master's thesis, University of Regina, Canada.

Kirshner, D. & Whitson, J. A. (1997). *Situated cognition: Social, semiotic, and psychological perspectives.* Mahwah, NJ: Lawrence Erlbaum Associates, 22–28.

Kuhlthau, C. C. (1993). Implementing a process approach to information skills: A study identifying indicators of success in library media programs. *School Library Media Quarterly, 22*(1), 11–18.

———. (1987). An emerging theory of library instruction. *School Library Media Quarterly, 16*(1), 23–27.

Lai, Y. (1995). The attitudes of public elementary school teachers and school library media specialists in three east Tennessee counties toward the instructional consultant role of the school library media specialist. Doctoral dissertation, University of Tennessee. *Dissertation Abstracts International, 56*(08A), 2986.

Lave, J. (1988). *Cognition in practice.* New York: Cambridge University Press.

Lenox, M. & Walker, M. (1993). Information literacy in the educational process. *The Educational Forum, 57,* 312–342.

Leont'ev, A. N. (1981). The problem of activity in psychology. In J. V. Wertsch (Ed.), *The concept of activity in Soviet psychology.* Armonk, NY: Sharpe.

Lewis, C. G. (1990). The school library media program and its role in the middle school: A study of the perceptions of North Carolina middle school principals and media coordinators. Doctoral dissertation, University of North Carolina at Chapel Hill. *Dissertation Abstracts International, 52*(01), 41.

Madaus, G. & Tan, A. (1993). The growth of assessment. In C. C. Kuhlthau (Ed.), *Assessment and the school library media center* (pp. 1–19). Englewood, CO: Libraries Unlimited.

McCracken, A. (2001). School library media specialists' perceptions of practice and importance of roles described in Information Power. *School Library Media Research, 4.* Retrieved on January 5, 2004, from http://www.ala.org/ala/aasl/aaslpubsandjournals/slmrb/ slmrcontents/volume42001/mccracken.htm.

McLellan, H. (1992). Virtual realities. Accessed on November 5, 2002, www.Aect.org/Intranet/Publications/edtech/15/index.html.

National Council on Education Standards and Testing (NCEST) (1992). *Raisingstandards for American education: A report to congress, the secretary of education, the national education goals panel, and the American people.* Washington, DC: NCEST.

Newell, T. S. (2004). Thinking beyond the disjunctive opposition of information literacy assessment in theory/practice. *School Library Media Research, 7.* Retrieved on August 5, 2005, from http://www.ala.org/ala/aasl/aaslpubsandjournals/slmrb/slmrcontents/volume72004/beyond.htm.

Pickard, P. W. (1993). The instructional consultant role of the school library media specialist. *School Library Media Quarterly, 21*(2), 115–121.

Rothman, R. (1996). Taking aim at testing. *Educational Psychology, 98*(13), 205–208.

Shapiro, J. and Hughes, S. (1996). Information literacy as a liberal art: Enlightenment proposals for a new curriculum. *Educom Review, 31*(2) [Online]. Available at http://www.educause.edu/pub/er/review/reviewarticles/31231.html [January 2000].

Thomas, N. P. (2004). *Information literacy and information skills instruction: Applying research to practice in the school library media center.* Westport, CT: Libraries Unlimited.

Turner, P. (1993). *Helping teachers teach: A school library media specialist's role.* Englewood, CO: Libraries Unlimited.

Van Deusen, J. & Tallman, J. I. (1994). The impact of scheduling on curriculum consultation and information skills instruction. *School Library Media Quarterly, 23*(1), 17–37.

Vygotsky, L. (1978). Mind in society: The development of higher psychological processes. Cambridge, MA: Harvard University Press.

Webber, S. & Johnston, B. (2000). Conceptions of information literacy: New perspectives and implications. *Journal of Information Science, 26*(6), 381–397.

Predictors for Success: Experiences of Beginning and Expert Teacher Librarians

Dr. Lesley S. J. Farmer
California State University, Long Beach

The current research examined the experiences of beginning teacher librarians (TL) and expert TLs to ascertain the factors that predict practitioner success. In the process, the study compares southern California TLs (and their academic preparation) with the experiences of TLs in other representative countries (e.g., Australia, Brazil, Canada, European Union, South Africa, Hong Kong, and Singapore). Factors were identified that link to TL preparation, with the intent of determining: (1) at what point in the academic-practice continuum identified skills, knowledge, and dispositions should be addressed; (2) what pre-service and in-service activities optimized learning. The investigator also uncovered universal and culturally determined practices.

PROBLEM STATEMENT

The teacher librarian preparation program has as its charge to prepare candidates to serve as successful teacher librarians in K-12 settings. While the intent is not to prepare them merely for their first job, the program does try to optimize the experiences of beginning practitioners. As such, part of that preparation may include field experience. Nevertheless, the first couple of years can be difficult, particularly if the TL's original expectations do not match the realities of day-to-day work or do not mesh with the school's existing values and norms.

Particularly since the profession predicts a surge of librarian retirements in the near future, it is imperative that those candidates who enter the profession will be successful, and will remain as TLs for the foreseeable future.

This study examined the academic preparation, predispositions, initial job experiences, and professional development opportunities of beginning TLs and expert TLs to ascertain possible predictive factors that can foster effective TLs.

LITERATURE REVIEW

The literature review drew upon the standards, academic preparation, career choice, and in-service experiences of TLs. Because their functions largely overlap those of classroom teachers and educational administrators, literature from these related fields were also examined.

Standards, Competencies, and Academic Preparation

Standards for pre-service librarians exist at state, national, and international levels. The International Federation of Library Associations and Institutions (2000) developed guidelines for library programs, which focus on the management and use of information within systems. In 2002, the National Council for Accreditation of Teacher Education, in collaboration with the American Association of School Librarians, established student outcomes for school library media preparation programs in the following areas: using information and ideas, teaching and learning, leading and collaboration, program administration. Most standards and library education programs incorporate theory, practice, and field experience.

Nevertheless, in reviewing the literature of the education and competencies of TLs in the United States, Shannon (2002) discovered a complex and sometimes conflicting picture; although resource management remained a constant, an increased need for technological and leadership skills became apparent, while instruction and collaboration skills were perceived unevenly. McCracken's 2000 survey indicated that TL's main roles were self-reported to be as information specialists and then as program administrators; instruction was less important, partly because of school community expectations. In surveying TL practitioners in Georgia, McCoy (2001) found that administration, information access and delivery, and collection development were core competencies; technology was less well defined. In a Northwest United States study of faculty, candidate, and administrator perceptions of ideal beginning TLs, the consensus was that the person should be able to work well with others, and have strong technical and managerial skills (Roys & Brown, 2004). Likewise, the summer 2006 issue of the *Journal of Education for Library and Information Science* included five papers about library education in Asia; the authors found that management and information /communication technologies were core elements, but great variability in education and other projected competencies existed; moreover, little attention was paid to TLs. Although academic experiences vary, several studies concur that prior successful academic librarianship preparation is the key for workplace success as a TL (Oberg, 1991; Shannon, 2002; Cochran-Smith, 2004).

Career Decisions and Dispositions

Certainly, individual attributes and situational realities impact career choice and subsequent actions. TLs bring a wide variety of career paths and expertise as do many classroom teachers. In their study of beginning teachers, Chin and Young (2007) created an ecological model of development, which captured factors related to choosing a teaching career and certificate program. Six distinct personnel clusters emerged from their analysis: compatible lifestylists (teaching fit their family lifestyle), working-class activists (first-generation college students with a strong sense of service), romantic idealists (younger, reform-minded, wanting self-fulfillment in their job), family tradition followers, second-career seekers, and career explorers (males seeking additional credentials). These clusters echo the attitudes of TLs, although it is not clear which cluster would reflect those TLs who worked in other library settings.

Independent of their career motivation, some librarians are more likely to be satisfied with their jobs than others. Williamson, Pemberton, and Lounsbury (2005) collected personal data from 1500 librarians to reveal that emotional resilience, work drive, and optimism were significant predictors of career and job satisfaction. Oberg (1995a) identified several personal attributes that were indicators of career success: leadership and collaborative skills to create and communicate a vision, self-confidence and self-knowledge for supervising, negotiating, and collaborating; ability to learn from role models; understanding of change processes; advocacy skills.

In-Service Experiences

Having realistic expectations of the job was another predictor for work and career satisfaction (Person, 1993; Johnson & Birkeland, 2003; Graziano, 2005). This understanding was largely dependent on prior experience working in libraries (Oberg, 1991; Macmillan, 1998; Domeracki, 2002; Yontz & McCook, 2003). While academic preparation programs intend to prepare TLs, on-the-job expectations can differ significantly from idealized ones (Kinard, 1991; Oberg, 1991; Person, 1993; Gwatney, 2001). TLs without prior work experience often had preconceptions about their work functions that reflected current professional standards, but found that their actual duties were less professional, which led to job dissatisfaction (McCracken, 2000; McCoy, 2001). Part of the problem resides in the school's expectations of TLs, which might not be informed based on current TL standards and best practices (Kinard, 1991; Kuhlthau, 1993; Cochran-Smith, 2004). That same phenomena happens in university settings, where teaching faculty value libraries more for their reference work than for their contributions to teaching (Manuel, Beck, & Molloy, 2005).

Little research about first year experiences of TLs has been conducted. Because the TL's job description has elements of a variety of other positions, the literature review was broadened to examine the experiences and challenges of first year classroom teachers and administrators. The induction activities (i.e., district-based in-service training for clear teaching credentials and library media teachers) described for these professional groups were also examined and adjusted to serve the purposes of supporting new library media teachers.

Cochran-Smith (2004) noted the importance of retention. While many people enter the teaching profession for idealistic reasons, such lofty goals will not keep them in the field without successful school conditions, site support, opportunities for professional learning communities, and advancement prospects. Johnson and Birkeland (2003) echoed this retention issue in their study of new teachers' career decisions. They mentioned the need for stable and orderly work environments, adequate resources, reasonable workload, and dependable advice and support from colleagues. In their review of recent empirical literature about teacher retention, Guarino, Santibanez, and Daley (2006) noticed that urban, low-performing schools had higher attrition rates. Schoolers with higher proportions of minority and low-income student populations also had higher attrition rates. In surveying TLs' perceptions of school climate throughout their first year, Domeracki (2002) discovered perceptions became less positive, as did job satisfaction.

In examining site-based factors, several indicators were identified as potential predictors of success. A professional school climate with a positive and focused vision was positively correlated with job performance and satisfaction (Oberg, 1991; Slygh, 2000; Vereen, 2002; Graziano, 2005). Peterson and Deal (2002) identified school cultural elements that foster positive thinking and action: norms of collegiality that encourage sharing issues and resources, norms of performance that encourage a strong work ethic, norms of improvement that encourage self-improvement, a shared sense of purpose and a shared sense of responsibility for student learning. In comparing beginning teachers in highly structured and "co-constructive" schools, Achinstein, Ogawa, and Speiglman (2004) found that a collaborative climate where beginning professionals are given autonomy and expected to be creative led to higher performance and greater job satisfaction. Similarly, Kuhlthau (1993) asserted that team-oriented, constructivist school climate led to success. In parsing school climate factors, Zhang, Verstegen, and Fan (2006) identified participation in decision-making as the strongest positive relationship with teacher job satisfaction. Gagnon (2004) noted that new TLs need a school climate in which they can express their feelings, thus reducing stress. In short, having a "voice" is important for beginning TLs.

Support by the principal and other personnel is also crucial to TL success. (Achinstein, Ogawa, & Speiglman, 2004; Graziano, 2005; Slygh, 2000; Vereen, 2002). Gagnon (2004) noted that principals organize and structure the school environment. Similarly, Oberg (1995a) asserted that principals help beginning TLs achieve by explaining library services to the school community, demonstrating personnel commitment to library services, and providing the resources and structures to facilitate library program success. It should be noted that beginning teachers sometimes perceive that the principal gave less support than the principals thought they gave (Oberg, 1995a; Ingram, 2002). Part of that support includes providing and encouraging professional development opportunities (Oberg, 1991; Dumas, 1994; Johnson, 2002; Hook, 2003; Achinstein, Ogawa, & Speiglman, 2004; Graziano, 2005). Clagg (2002) cautioned that staff development per se does not impact teacher retention; professional development needs to be immediately applicable to their practice; personal mentoring programs are more effective than standardized in-services. Smith and Ingersoll (2004) emphasized the need for collection induction activities such as planning and collaboration in these induction programs.

BACKGROUND THEORIES

Three theoretical strands provided valuable conceptual models for this investigation: competency theory, change theory, and contingency theory of socialization. The first focused on the individual's expertise, the second focused on decision-making and behavior, and the third focused on interpersonal relationships.

Competency Theory

Dreyfus (2004) posited five levels of adult skill acquisition, from notice to expert. The novice can follow directions, but cannot succeed independently; they need to understand the underlying principles and context of the skills. The advanced beginner practices skills, applying them to real situations, and is given additional examples in order to analyze new situations. Competent adults develop schema to help them decide how to apply their skills, identifying important elements for planning. Proficient adults leverage their emotional involvement to make situational decisions quickly rather than having to weigh each factor abstractly. Since situations may differ widely, with accompanying factors changing relative importance, competent and proficient adults may still make mistakes because they are unlikely to anticipate all consequences. Experts have a wide repertoire of skills and experiences, and can make discriminating decisions that take into account nuanced subclasses of situations. In their discussion of master teachers, Ambrose and Bridges (2005) asserted that, among things, expert faculty understand students "in multiple ways that represent the complex human beings they are," including their cultural and historical context (p. 5).

Van Manen's (1977) levels of reflectivity offered a developmental approach to teacher competency. Beginning teachers reflected technical rationality: technical application of skills; next, they reflected practical action: clarifying assumptions while addressing educational consequences; ultimately, they displayed critical reflection: concerned with knowledge and its context. Focusing on first-year teachers' experience, Short (2003) found that new teachers focused more on their own actions than on their students' learning, and Richardson (2003) noted how structured mentoring program helped first year teachers transition from self-concern to concerns about effective instruction, manifesting Van Manen's model.

In the process of learning, adults also tend to progress from passive receiver of information to engaged reflective learner (Ericsson & Charness, 1994). In his review of the literature on workplace learning, Smith (2003) concluded that skill development beyond the procedural level requires human guidance and opportunities for action learning. Nevertheless, scaffolding is needed to construct goals and strategies that will lead the beginning TL through a problem space. The need for timely feedback needs to be part of this socially contextualized experience in order to enable pre-service and beginning TLs to make appropriate changes. These findings reinforce the concept of structured service learning and field experience in TL preparation programs.

Belenky and Stanton (2000) focused on affective epistemologies of knowledge formation in relation to constructive teaching. They identified the following stages:

- silence: not seeing oneself as a learner, having a sense of powerlessness to change
- received knowledge: learning by listening to outside authority, a sense of one truth
- subjective knowers: learning by using procedures for finding the truth
- separate knowers: critical discernment, comprehending the affective domain, recognizing oneself in others
- connected knower: active construction of knowledge
- constructive knower: select and integrate a large repertoire of processes, cultivate range of abilities in others.

The researchers also recommended that pre-service academic faculty diagnose the stages of their teacher candidates, and provide developmentally appropriate learning activities to help candidates bridge to the next higher level.

Perrone's study of librarian expertise (2004) focused on the transition from competent to expert librarian, building on Berliner's 1994 research about exemplary performance. As librarians practice repeatedly, they need to exert less effort, but they also are less likely to be learning. It normally takes over 10,000 hours, or about five years, to optimize the opportunities of different situations to gain true domain-specific expertise that is manifested in flexible pattern-finding and quick, efficient problem-solving. However, if librarians focus on performance alone, they may well stay at the competent level. Dall-Alba and Sandberg (2006) echoed this possibility, defining two dimensions of professional development: improved skills (the competency level) and embodied understanding of practice (the "big picture"); beginners tend to focus on the former, but as they practice they may shift to the other perspective.

Dweck's 2006 research on self-theories offered one possible explanation for this gap between competency and expertise: a fixed mind-set vs. a growth mind-set. The former attitude assumes that intelligence is fixed; these individuals prefer lower-effort success and want to outperform others. The latter attitude assumes that intelligence is malleable and incremental; these individuals love learning, seek challenges, value effort, and persist despite obstacles. When faced with failure, the former are likely to think that results are out of their control and will try less; the latter want to master the situation, and will take a longer-term perspective.

Attribution theory is a related set of principles concerned with competency. In this theory, individuals attribute their success or failure to internal or external causes. If the cause is stable, there is little chance for change; if the cause is unstable, the outcome might be situational so that eventual change is possible. Likewise, the locus of control impacts success; if the individual feels that he or she can control the situation, then there is hope for eventual success even in the midst of immediate difficulties (Weiner, 1986).

Self-perception and self-confidence also impact competency. Bandura (1997) asserted that "perceived self-efficacy is concerned with judgments of how well one can execute courses of action required to deal with prospective situations" (122). Self-efficacy is reflected in one's choices of actions and situations, one's persistent efforts in overcoming obstacles, one's feelings of stress and anxiety (Schmidt, Kosmoski, & Pollack, 1998).

Individuals with high self-efficacy are likely to perform and cope better than individuals with low self-efficacy. For example, Nahl (2005) investigated the influence of affective variables in using the Internet. She found that high self-efficacy and optimism counteracted feelings of frustration and irritation in challenging Internet tasks; additionally, high affective coping skills led to lower uncertainty and greater acceptance of technology systems.

In a similar vein, Collins (2005), known for his work on helping institutions go from good to great, identified level 5 leadership (effective expert) as combining professional will and personal humility with ambition for their institution's success; these leaders set high standards for themselves and others toward that end, and find ways to produce long-term results. He asserts that level 5 leaders know and leverage their strengths, their motivations, and their passions.

Charter (1982) discovered that identified exemplary TLs were extroverted independent leaders and learners. Comparing beginning and experienced TLs, Oberg (1995b) found that experienced TLs had stronger professional networks, and were committed to ongoing professional education, mentoring, advocacy, and policy development.

Change Theory

Beginning TLs experience significant change as they transition from one role to another: either from a classroom teacher, other type of librarian, or a student to the role of a TL. They need to change both their behavior and their attitudes. This change involves both internal factors as well as interactions with external factors (e.g., school culture and norms).

Fiske (1980) focused on middle and later life changes, which applies to the career ladder of the majority of TLs. Fiske identified four dimensions of adult self-concept: interpersonal, altruistic, master, and self-protectiveness. Individuals differ in the attitudinal and behavioral degrees of commitment to these dimensions, and they change their priorities over time. Those central changes may be precipitated by role changes: becoming a teacher librarian, for instance. Self concerns and responses to external factors may be the impetus, but in either case, the subjective meaning of becoming a TL impacts one's changing self-concept. If, for instance, the new role of TL requires significant behavioral change, then the meaning of the role leads to greater consequence and requires more commitment. These changes can impact personal well-being along each dimension, and may result in abandoning the new role. Individual and external conditioning variables (i.e., personal resources, social support, social status, socialization experiences) all impact the individual's coping responses, interpretation of the change, and ultimate response to change (George, 1980). Brindley, Morton, and Williams (2006) reiterated the difficulties that second-career teachers faced. These mid-lifers come with precise career expertise that might not transfer well into educational culture, and they may have non-conforming habits that clash with their "new" organization. This situation can occur with classroom teachers entering school librarianship as well as noneducation librarians transitioning to K-12 settings.

Skinner's operant conditioning theory (1969) posited that individuals respond to discriminative stimuli; positive behaviors and effective reinforcers need to be identified. As the person performs appropriately, he or she can be reinforced intermittently until the old behavior is extinguished; furthermore, refinements of the desired behavior can be reinforced much in the way that teachers scaffold learning. Skinner's intent was purposeful external conditioning. However, operational conditioning might well occur on the unconscious level as new TLs respond to personally relevant institutional stimuli such as social inclusion or principal support. Additionally, an individual can purposely self-reinforce changing role expectations by substituting a new habit (e.g., seeking opportunities for collaboration) for an old one (e.g., depending completely on oneself to instruct) with the positive reinforcement of getting to work with more students (a positive past experience that might be harder to accomplish independently as a TL). In any case, for change to occur, the new behavior has to be more compelling and beneficial than the old one.

In her study of beginning TLs who had been paraprofessional library staffers, Oberg (1991) recognized the feelings of loss and dislocation that accompanied the abandonment of prior roles and the assumption of new roles. She counseled, "Awareness and acknowledgment of these feelings will go a long way in helping novice teacher-librarians deal with the challenges of their new role; in fact, such discomfort may be an indication that a real and necessary transformation is occurring" (p. 1).

One of the most important research-based models for change, the Concerns-Based Adoption Model, was developed at the University of Texas at Austin to address teacher resistance to innovation. It posited seven stages of concern, and asserted that change agents need to use a different approach at each point for people to advance to the next stage.

1. Awareness: briefly define the change and its benefits.

2. Information: provide factual information about how the change works.

3. Personal: link the change to the person, showing its impact and how the person will be supported.

4. Management: train the person, showing them how to manage the change.

5. Consequence: show concrete evidence that change impacts student learning.

6. Collaboration: provide opportunities to share experiences and leverage change's potential together.

7. Refocusing: provide opportunities for proactive improvement (i.e., more change) (Hord, 1987).

At the site level, the TL's role needs to be clearly delineated, communicated, and fit into a reasonable timeframe for development. Resources (human, material, space, time, money) need to be identified and allocated to insure the needed level of support. Stages of concern should be identified, with appropriate strategies determined to help the teacher librarian accept and implement the professional role. Monitoring and assessment need to be ongoing so plans can be modified as needed. As with operant conditioning, the Concerns-Based Adoption model may be proactively implemented on a conscious personal level. Indeed, academic preparation is the typical means of initial role acceptance; the individual becomes interested in teacher librarianship, gathers information and relates it to one's personal life, learns and practices the new skills with others, and refocuses his or her new role. If the stages are not successfully experienced, the potential TL is likely to drop the academic pursuit. On the other, if the final stage is reached successfully, the individual is certificated as a teacher librarian. In the new job, the beginning TL then has to revisit these adoption stages as he or she has to negotiate the TL role as expected by the school community.

A related theory focused on role development. More specifically, Toffler (1981) traced professional growth from the end of formal academic preparation and five months into employment, focusing on role-development stress. She noted two sources of role-development stress: role ambiguity where the role is unclear, and role conflict where expectations differ between employee and employer. Role development depends on both rational and emotional reactions; at the beginning, role stress tends to be more internal-based while over time the relational aspects of the job are the main predictors for successful role development.

It should be noted that the school community as much as the TL may need to grapple with change. Contemporary TLs are likely to have been taught newer instructional design approaches such as collaborative planning, newer learning strategies such as problem-based inquiry, and newer student learning issues such as information and technology literacy. When that new TL enters a preexisting school culture that expects a traditional TL role, the newcomer has to determine the extent that he or she will need to change self-expectations— or need to change the school community's expectations. Certainly, TLs should play an active role in school improvement so they can help shape change rather than be shaped by others. As TLs examine their own strengths and the contributions of the library media program, they can articulate those assets as a team player for systemic improvement. If the school community continues to do the same things in the same way, chances are that the library media program will not be optimized. Therefore, schools themselves have to change in order to improve. Even positive change requires disequilibrium and readjustment, which can threaten the existing structure of power and influence and can result in different reallocation of resources and priorities. Thus, the force for change needs to overcome resistance, and needs to benefit those who accept and spearhead change. Both social and functional aspects of change need to be addressed since the school culture as well as operations are affected.

Contingency Theory of Socialization

Contingency theory of socialization examines the interaction of a new employee and an organization in pursuit of attaining the goals of general satisfaction and mutual influence Four stages of socialization exist: anticipatory socialization (prior experience and pre-assessment of the job and the organization), encounter and accommodation (learning new tasks, establishing interpersonal relationships, clarifying the role within the organization, and evaluating congruence), role management (resolving personal and work conflicts), and outcomes (satisfaction, influence, distress, turnover) (Feldman, 1976). Feldman found that role-centric socialization was more impactful than social group initiation. However, personal resolutions of conflicts significantly impacted general satisfaction with the job.

Gott (1989) and Mezirow (1991) focused on socially constructed workplace learning. Gott asserted that three types of knowledge is required for real world tasks: procedural (reflecting Dreyfus's novice level), declarative (domain), and strategic (decision-making). Mezirow identified three types of workplace learning: instrumental (similar to Gott's procedural knowledge), dialogic (the organization and the person's role within it), and self-reflective (similar to Feldman's socialization stage of accommodation). Cunningham (1998) emphasized the effectiveness of workplace learning through interactions with other learners and experts, reinforcing social-interaction conceptualization.

In examining the emotional and cognitive stresses of organizational socialization, Nelson (1987) discovered a number of emotional factors that led to greater satisfaction: higher self-efficacy, open-mindedness, and greater risk-taking. Several studies showed how family support lowered stress (Cochran-Smith, 2004; Farmer, 2001; Johnson & Birkeland, 2003). In terms of knowledge, the more that individuals know about the job and the school, and have a strong library science background, the more likely that they will be able to handle stress, and will be successful and satisfied in their job.

Louis (1980) noted the inadequacies of organizational socialization, and identified key features of new employee experiences: surprise, contrast to assumptions, and need for change. Rather than trying to avoid all surprise or unexpected experiences, employers should help newcomers make sense of these surprises by facilitating relationships with knowledgeable peers, sharing information, and giving timely feedback. TL programs should also alert their pre-service students about possible assumptions and likely surprises when encountering the realities of the job and the organization.

Jones (1986) examined socialization tactics. He compared collective and formal initiations to individualized and informal ones. He also compared role models and self-identified situational action. Formal models tend to lower anxiety for newcomers with less self-efficacy (and likely to be associated with more routine jobs), while informal models lead to more differentiated responses to work situations, which is more reflective of TL positions. The implication is that self-efficacious professionals are more likely to be successful; organizations who want to help less confident beginning TLs need to focus on ways to reduce anxiety by providing targeted professional development opportunities and positive role models. In short, both organizational demands and personal self-efficacy impact the socialization process.

One specific perspective of this socialization theory focuses on work role transition. Nicholson (1984) posited three preconditions: the person's prior occupational socialization and motivational orientation, the organizational induction-socialization processes, and the role requirements. Three types of outcomes result: affective status and coping responses, identify changes, and behavioral changes. Depending on the nature and degree of personal and role development, four modes of adjustment are possible. *Replication* implies little significant change (an unlikely state for most TLs even if their prior job was in the same school). Absorption occurs as one gains the skills and knowledge to be successful and accepted; one could remain at this stage, which mirrors Dreyfus's competency level, or one can make further adjustment as follows. *Determination* is characteristic of mid-career change where the individual has a well-established self-identify and self-confidence in his skills, and desires control; as a result, the person tries to reshape the new work role and the environment. This adjustment is usually unstable; either the individual is successful and the rest of the school readjusts, or the individual makes personal changes in another direction. *Exploration* occurs with continual novelty of job demands or possibilities. This mode is more likely to happen in creative learning environments, which would match optimal TL work. If the new role offers more autonomy, the new TL is likely to absorb or follow expectations; with less autonomy, the TL is likely to determine the role differently or explore more. Likewise, if the new TL wants feedback, absorption or exploration will probably result.

One popular approach to socializing new personnel is the use of mentors. Mentorships by—and collaboration with—peers in the same subject domain result in job and career retention, although their impact is surprisingly not dependent on sociability (Clagg, 2002; Vereen, 2002; Pierce, 2004; Smith & Ingersoll, 2004; Australian Library and Information Association, 2005). Kardos (2004) reiterated the importance of matching subject-specific mentors with their beginning counterparts in order to positively impact teacher retention. Hein (2006) noted one limitation of mentorship: lack of joint available time. Nor is mentoring a natural activity for educators; making good practice explicit and crafting individualized learning activities for new peers requires training for mentors themselves (Feiman-Nemser, 2003). For mentors to be successful, Pierce (2004) asserted that several factors need to be in place: a sense that the mentor is the expert, a complementarity of needs between the beginner and expert (i.e., forming a professional identity and self-renewal), a willingness to nurture and to be nurtured. Monsour's (1998) recommendations for successful administrative mentoring programs included similar factors: mutually respectful pairs that met at least monthly and participated in various activities characterized by networking, emotional support and validation, resource sharing, site visits, and guidance. Kram (1985) identified four phases of mentorship: (1) initiation, with its sense of excitement and expectation as the relationship starts; (2) cultivation, when all mentoring functions are at their peak; (3) separation, which may be friendly or stressful; and (4) redefinition of the relationship. Thus, mentoring is in itself a microcosm of the contingency theory of socialization.

RESEARCH OBJECTIVES AND DESCRIPTION

The investigation examined the experiences of beginning and expert TLs to ascertain the factors, including role of employer-based induction programs, which impact their relative degree of success, particularly in implementing library media programs. It will also determine at what point in the academic-practice continuum identified skills, knowledge, and dispositions should be addressed, and what pre-service activities will optimize learning. This research compares southern California TLs (and their academic preparation) with the experiences of TLs in other representative countries (e.g., Australia, Brazil, Canada, European Union, South Africa, Hong Kong, and Singapore) in order to uncover possible universal and culturally determined practices.

Beginning and Expert TLs (defined as those who have been nationally certified or their equivalent in other countries) were interviewed in order to determine whether the nature of, and responses to, job demands change with experience.

A series of research questions were proposed:

- What are the critical differences between first/second year and expert TLs' behaviors in terms of: time management, challenges, sources of support, library program implementation, application of career-preparation skills/ knowledge/ dispositions?

- What are the critical differences between successful and unsuccessful first/second year TLs' behaviors in terms of: time management, challenges, sources of support, library program implementation, application of career-preparation skills/ knowledge/ dispositions?

- Is there a significant difference between successful and unsuccessful first/second year TLs in terms of demographics, prior teaching experience, status in TL preparation programs, school community, or district induction programs?

- What critical factors for success can be linked to TL academic preparation, including field experience?

- What critical factors for success are more effectively learned "on the job?"

- What information and activities would be most effective in helping TLs transition into their first/second years of school librarianship?

- To what extent do TL academic preparation and TL experiences reflect universal or culture-specific practices?

For the purposes of this study, "successful" was defined as those first/second year TLs who:

- have been retained by their school for a second year (or more),

- receive all satisfactory or better ratings in their evaluation,

- implement library media program principles (as defined by AASL) to at least the basic level, and

- choose to continue as an TL.

Successful TLs *may* also include those TLs who are retained, but choose to be transferred to another locale.

Unsuccessful TLs are defined as those TLs who:

- were *not* asked to remain at the school,
- were asked to leave the TL position, or
- chose for themselves to leave the profession.

RESEARCH METHODOLOGY

To address these issues, the investigator used a mixed methods approach to provide a rich dataset and to triangulate responses.

Findings from the literature review were compared to standards for incoming and proficient TLs (California Commission on Teacher Credentialing, National Council for Accreditation of Teacher Education, AASL, National Board of Professional Teaching Standards). In general, most standards for entering professionals focused on content knowledge and skills, with some attention to dispositions (e.g., ethical behavior, effective interpersonal skills, professional outlook). Proficient TLs were expected to play a leadership role within the educational setting and the community at large. On the other hand, professional success often depended on circumstantial factors, which called upon the TL's ability to negotiate personal and school community expectations.

As a pilot ethnographic exploratory study to determine appropriate criteria for assessment, thirty-nine beginning and expert TLs from the greater Los Angeles area were surveyed and interviewed. The subjects were recruited from the list of National Board for Professional Teaching Standards certified Library Media Teachers, and from two large school districts (Los Angeles and Long Beach) via their library services. The Interviews were conducted by the investigator via real-time or via online chat using a validated TL interview protocol instrument (Johnson & Birkeland, 2003). These interviews were followed by the administration and collection (via e-mail or print) of the following assessment instruments to gather specific data about the subjects:

- Library media program implementation and values rubric (Farmer): to assess the degree to which school library programs implemented AASL principles, and the degree to which TLs valued those principles;
- Library media teacher standards self-assessment (Farmer): to assess the degree to which TLs met professional standards;
- TL challenges and support survey (Bourke, 2003): to identify top-ranked challenges and support systems as self-reported by TLs;
- TL time management instrument (Farmer): to assess which major AASL principles were addressed throughout the work day;
- TL satisfaction survey (University of Alberta, 2005): to assess TL job satisfaction and work conditions.

The preliminary data validated the instruments, and the survey was adjusted to accommodate international TLs, who constituted the second level of the research. At this point, the data revealed significant differences between first- and second-year TLs, so both years were included in the ultimate study.

IASL regional directors were then contacted to identify first- and second-year TLs and expert TLs per country (Australia, Brazil, Canada, European Union, South Africa, Hong Kong, and Singapore). A follow-up message was sent to IASL members through the association's listserv. The same set of assessment instruments were administered to gather specific data about the subjects via e-mail and print.

FINDINGS

As of April 1, 2007, 125 responses were collected: 45 from the United States, 38 from Australia, 15 from Hong Kong, 10 from Canada, 5 from South Africa, 5 from Europe, and one each from Brazil and Singapore. Respondents ranged from their twenties (3) to their sixties (7) in age, with 45 % in their 50s, 30% in their 40s, and 17% in their 30s. Sixteen percent have never been married. Females constituted 89% of the respondents. Only 7% considered themselves to be a visible minority group member, and only 6% self-identified a disability. A third had dependent children; another 6% had dependent adults.

Academic Preparation

Two-thirds had education degrees, 47% had library/information science degrees, and another 31% are interested in earning a library/information science degree. Over 90% participated in field experience while enrolled in their pre-service academic programs.

In examining the responses of TLs, a few culture-specific factors were identified. Non-U.S. programs were slightly less satisfactory than U.S. ones, typically because of technology and collaboration elements. In a few Hong Kong cases (where TLs are re-quired for every site), individuals were assigned to become TLs, even though there was no self-identification of that role, which resulted in lower satisfaction of the academic preparation and site situation. The most frequent recommendations for program improvement included providing more technology and practical information (particularly textbooks in the United States, and human resource management in Australia and Canada).

Predispositions and Prior Experience

In stating the reason for becoming a TL, almost half mentioned their love of reading and sharing that interest. Longer-term TLs were more likely to mention loving libraries and books (newer TLs mentioned the act of reading more than simply books). The second most mentioned reason was working with people: students, teachers, and others. A close third was the interest in the research process, and helping others find and use information/materials (mentioned mainly by beginning U.S. TLs and U.S. nationally certified TLs). While a quarter liked teaching or working in education, almost that same number wanted an alternative to classroom teaching. About a fifth mentioned their love of libraries, and about an eighth were motivated to become TLs because of prior library work experience. About a tenth noted an interest in professional development or liked library working conditions.

Almost half had been classroom teachers before becoming TLs (TLs without a master's degree were more likely to have taught than TLs with a master's degree, and U.S. TLs were more likely to have been prior classroom teachers). Another quarter had been teachers on special assignment or other service personnel. About 40% had no prior library work experience; about 15% had worked in public libraries, and about 10% had work in university libraries. Nation Board certified TLs were less likely to have had field experience than first-year TLs. The main reasons people did not go into school librarianship initially were because they thought about teaching first or there were no librarian positions available.

Induction Experiences

During their professional induction period, about a quarter of respondents did not participate for any identified experience. Little training was experienced the first year, and not much more was given the second year; only by the third year did the majority of TLs participate in the majority of training options listed. Ninety percent did independent reading; they responded that they found this activity to be the most helpful method of training. The second most helpful training was library association conferences; the least helpful was district training (site-based faculty training was also not found to be very effective). Library and technology training sessions were found to be helpful. U.S. on-site training seemed to be more useful for non-U.S. TLs. On the other hand, non-U.S. TLs thought that professional workshops were more helpful for them than for U.S. TLs. More experienced TLs, particularly National Board certified TLs, stated that technology training and university courses were more helpful than what beginning TLs asserted.

Expectations of beginning TLs impacted their work. First-year TLs sometimes expected more collaboration. In some cases, they felt as if they had less control of their jobs than as a classroom teacher; in other cases, beginning TLs thought they had more autonomy. Expectations of the rest of the school community also influenced their work; if the prior TL was ineffective, the new TL was either welcomed with open arms—or the new TL had to work hard to overcome the bad past impression.

To cope, first-year TLs tried to learn about the school and about library technologies. They tried to find supporters at the site and within the profession. They tried to be more assertive and welcoming. By the second year, TLs felt more self-confident, and balanced school and home more effectively; they were often given more responsibility, but were given more support. In any case, the onus was squarely placed on them.

TLs who decided to leave the profession identified the following reasons:

- feeling of isolation,
- preference to work with a small number of students in more depth rather than deal with all students more superficially,
- feeling of lack of control and self-determination because of other people's demands on library services,
- unrealistic job expectations, either because of heightened expectations raised in pre-service academic preparation or because of principal's determination.

Work Conditions

In terms of working conditions, TLs worked an average of 40 hours weekly. Hong Kong TLs tended to work longer hours, and Canadians tended to work fewer. A quarter of the respondents worked alone; the majority had at least one library clerk or technician who worked half-time or more. Almost a quarter worked with another professional librarian, and one respondent worked with seven other TLs. Usually no adult volunteers worked in the library, but several had multiple parent volunteers (20 at the most, more often in non-U.S.

libraries). The median number of student volunteers was four, with libraries having a range from zero to over a hundred student help (more often in U.S. libraries).

This table shows how often TLs self-reported performing job functions (1 = never, 2 = seldom, 3 = sometimes, 4 = often).

Job Function Frequency

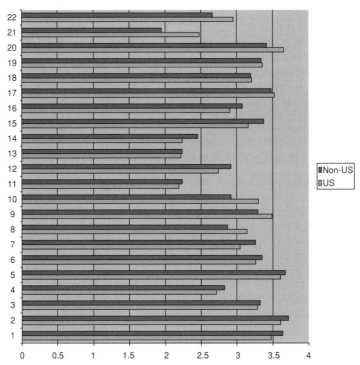

1. **Collection development; 2. Readers' advisory/promotion; 3. Reference/homework support; 4. Reference/research to adults; 5. Library instruction; 6. Curriculum collaboration; 7. Cataloging/database management; 8. Library materials processing/maintenance; 9. Library materials circulation; 10. Sorting/shelving/filing; 11. Textbook management; 12. Library systems/hardware/software; 13. Network management/tech support; 14. Web development/maintenance; 15. Professional development; 16. Personnel supervision; 17. Planning/decision-making; 18. Policy development; 19. Budgeting/finance management; 20. Managing space/facilities; 21. Fund-raising/donor support; 22. Marketing and PR.**

Several differences (at the .05 significance level) in job functions emerged relative to experience, as this chart shows. The symbols indicate frequency relative to the U.S. TLs in the preceding column. For example, second-year TLs did about the same amount of collection development work as did first-year TLS, but less than TLs who had been working in the field for 3–5 years; moreover, National Board certified TLs did more collection development work than all the other TLs. For non-U.S. TLs, similar patterns emerged for collection development and instruction. Less experienced non-U.S. TLs did more materials processing than their more experienced peers.

1st Year TLs	2nd Year TLs	3–5 Year TLs	Natl. Bd. Certf. TLs
Collection development	=	<	<
Readers' advisory	=	<	=
Instruction	<	<	<
Reference	=	>	=
Collaboration	=	=	<
Circulation	<	<	>
Shelving	=	<	>
Textbooks	=	>	>
Web development	<	>	<
Professional development	=	=	<
Personnel supervision	=	=	<
Planning/decision-making	<	=	<
Policy development	<	=	=
Marketing/PR	=	=	<

In terms of the relative importance of each of these job functions, TLs responded according to this scale: 1 = no importance, 2 = of little importance, 3 = important, 4 = vital.

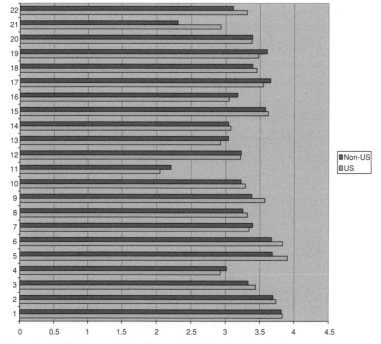

1. Collection development; 2. Readers' advisory/promotion; 3. Reference/homework support; 4. Reference/research to adults; 5. Library instruction; 6. Curriculum collaboration; 7. Cataloging/database management; 8. Library materials processing/maintenance; 9. Library materials circulation; 10. Sorting/shelving/filing; 11. Textbook management; 12. Library systems/hardware/software; 13. Network management/tech support; 14. Web development/maintenance; 15. Professional development; 16. Personnel supervision; 17. Planning/decision-making; 18. Policy development; 19. Budgeting/finance management; 20. Managing space/facilities; 21. Fund-raising/donor support; 22. Marketing and PR.

In terms of valuing library functions, National Board certified TLs valued collaboration, professional development, planning/decision-making, policy development, and fund-raising significantly more (at the .05 level) than the other TLs.

About 20% of the TLs had no other jobs. More experienced TLs either had few extra duties or many extra duties; they reflected the extremes. Some of the nonlibrary jobs that TLs performed included:

- textbooks (particularly by beginning U.S. TLs)
- club/activity supervision
- technology-related work (mainly in Hong Kong and Australia)
- mentoring (mainly by experienced TLs)

Work Satisfaction

How satisfied were TLs relative to aspects of school librarianship at their site? In general, those TLs with master's degrees were more satisfied with their jobs than non-degree owners. Overall, the most satisfying aspects were intellectual challenge and autonomy; second most satisfying were safety and professional development issues. The least satisfying factor was district support. There was no significant difference in perceptions relative to country. Several aspects of the job were significantly positively correlated (at the .01 level). Besides the overall work conditions correlating with job satisfaction, the following significant correlations were identified:

- intellectual challenge satisfaction with TL influence, professional development, recognition;
- autonomy and technology expectations;
- teacher collegiality and satisfaction with intellectual challenge, prestige, information literacy expectations, professional development, recognition;
- prestige and higher expectations for information literacy, technology, and reading.
- Significant (at the .01 level) *negative* correlations existed between satisfaction with parent support and satisfaction with library tasks, library influence, reading expectations, student behavior. Satisfaction with higher expectations also correlated negatively with satisfaction with student behavior.

Satisfaction with the intellectual challenge and autonomy was reported for all TLs. However, TLs reported different degrees of satisfaction of site factors depending on the length of time in this profession.

- First-year TLs were least satisfied with resources, student motivation, and information literacy expectations.
- Second-year TLs were least satisfied with equipment, student motivation, professional development, and parent support.
- Third- to fifth-year TLs were, on the majority, very satisfied with the professional caliber of the teachers, but were least satisfied with district administration support, and to a lesser degree with workload and equipment.
- Sixth- to tenth-year TLs were least satisfied with administrators, information literacy expectations, and library size.
- Eleventh- to fifteenth-year TLs were, on the majority, very satisfied with their tasks and school safety, and were least satisfied with school expectations and district support.

- Long-term TLs were, on the majority, very satisfied with their job security and professional development.

In terms of the relative importance of work conditions, all were rated highly.

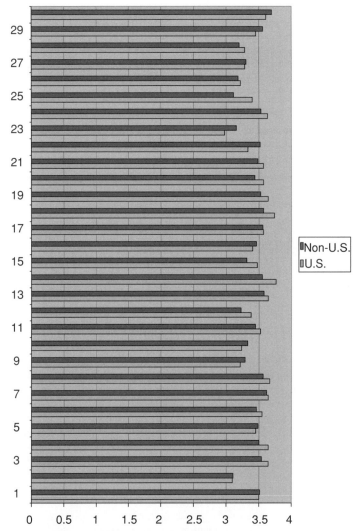

1 Overall job satisfaction; 2. Job security; 3. Benefits; 4. Salary; 5. Support from parents; 6. Support from district administrators; 7. Recognition and support from site administrators; 8. Procedures for performance evaluation; 9. Opportunities for professional development; 10. Safety of school environment; 11. Student discipline and behavior; 12. Student motivation to learn; 13. School learning environment; 14. Collegiality of classroom teachers; 15. Professional caliber of colleagues; 16. Expectations and norms about the school; 17. Expectations and norms about the library; 18. Expectations and norms about reading; 19. Expectations and norms about technology; 20. Expectations and norms about information literacy; 21. Professional prestige; 22. Your influence over school policies and practices; 23. Autonomy or control over the school library; 24. Intellectual challenge; 25. Type of tasks you perform; 26. Work load; 27. Availability of resources and materials/equipment for the school library; 28. Library size; 29. General work conditions.

All respondents thought that intellectual challenge, autonomy, site administration support/recognition, and the school learning environmental were vital. However, significant differences in relative importance emerged, depending on how long the respondent had been a TL.

- First-year TLs rated the following aspects as vital: information literacy and library expectations, student discipline, and safety.

- Second-year TLs rated the following aspects as vital: resources, kinds of tasks performed, information literacy and reading expectations, collegiality, student motivation, and job security.

- Third- to fifth-year TLs rated the following aspects as vital: district support and job security; the majority considered the following as vital aspects: kinds of tasks performed, reading and library expectations, collegiality and professional caliber of counterparts, safety, professional development.

- Sixth- to tenth-year TLs rated the following as vital: resources; the majority considered the following as vital aspects: workload and tasks to be done, reading and library expectations, collegiality and professional caliber of counterparts, safety, and professional development.

- Eleventh- to fifteenth-year TLs rated the following as vital: reading expectation and overall work conditions; the majority considered the following as vital aspects: resources, workload and tasks to be done, prestige, library and information literacy expectations, collegiality and professional caliber of counterparts, professional development, student motivation and behavior, administrative support (both site and district), and job satisfaction.

- The majority of long-term TLs rated the following aspects as vital: resources, reading and library expectations, collegiality, student motivation, safety, and job security.

The degree of satisfaction with some site factors were found to be significantly correlated (at the .01 level) with several important aspects of the job: the types of tasks performed, intellectual challenge, influence, school expectations, student behavior, performance evaluation procedures, and parent support. For example, when TLs were happier about school and library expectations, resource availability becomes more important. Likewise, when TLs were satisfied with professional development opportunities, collegiality and library size become more important. For workload and parental support, there was a negative significant correlation; that is, when TLs liked the tasks they performed or have satisfying intellectual challenge, the workload, salary, and amount of parent support was not as important.

Respondents were asked what would motivate them to perform better. Regardless of county or experience, the main issues were resources, funding, time, availability of library staff, and administrative support/recognition. Europeans wanted more school emphasis on information literacy, and Hong Kong TLs wanted more collaboration. Beginning TLs focused on need for more collaboration. National Board certified TLs wanted more policymaking opportunities, and wished that students were more motivated.

In responding to job changes over the past five years, the majority of TLs strongly agreed that their jobs become more interesting, challenging, enjoyable, and rewarding; they are more motivated to do their jobs. Over two-thirds of the respondents agreed that their job currently requires more skill and incorporates a wider variety of tasks, that they perform more management and leadership functions, and that they needed to learn more new tasks including high-tech functions.

All TLs noted some kinds of challenges in their work. As with motivation, overall challenges for all segments of the study population included time, money, staffing, and workload. Many mentioned conflicting teaching loads, as well as the difficulty of balancing work and personal life. In Hong Kong one theme was the fact that other people controlled their job decisions. In Australia, it appeared that the library situation is in great transition: new sites and mergers, new curriculum, more technologies, uneven workloads. Challenges also differed according to the length of time that the respondent had served as a TL.

- First-year TLs sometimes had to clean up after a prior TL, entice people to use the library (particularly if the past TL was not outgoing), and deal with incoming books from prior-year orders. They sometimes felt overwhelmed because they were learning a new job, often at a new site. Some TLs felt isolated because they did not have their usual support group (e.g., other teachers at the same grade or within the same discipline). Some lacked clarity about their job functions and budget details. Some did not have a positive or clear working relationship with their principals. In general, the source of challenge was outside the library: the TL had to respond to others' demands or behaviors.

- Second-year TLs were challenged by textbook management, dealing with student behavior—while trying to encourage more students to use the library, updating technology, and dealing with new administrators.

- Veteran TLs were trying to keep current, and were frustrated with increased testing that resulted in less library-based instruction.

- National Board certified TLs were frustrated by nonsupportive administrators, and were asked to do more nonlibrary functions such as accreditation and special program coordination.

When asked how they met those challenges, beginning TLs tended to mention administrators, classroom teachers, and mentors. Expert TLs identified many more sources of help; they had established a strong support system.

While over time, TLs tended to become more satisfied with their jobs, those TLs who were identified as expert TLs did not necessarily have more positive job satisfaction or job status than nonexperts. They were more satisfied than beginning TLs with the resources available, but were less satisfied with their workload, influence, and professional development opportunities. They valued equipment availability, autonomy, performance evaluation procedures, and benefits more than beginning TLs, but were less concerned about parental support. While they all self-reported a more in-depth understanding of their role, especially in terms of instruction, their role did not necessarily align with their status. In some cases, expert TLs were asked to do more work or assume greater responsibility without commensurate authority. In other cases, their status did not change and other faculty felt more threatened by their national certification. Relative to beginning TLs, expert TLs had a greater support system, used a greater repertoire of coping techniques, and took a longer-term perspective, including effective work-arounds for current practice.

DISCUSSION

Initial findings from the local research indicate that academic preparation has some impact on TL hiring. Furthermore, first- and second-year TLs have different experiences, expectations, and challenges; how they address those issues impact their immediate future.

Additionally, expert TLs share some of the same issues as beginning TLs, have some different issues, and resolve these issues in acceptable ways. Unsuccessful TLs also shared some factors that led to the decision of leaving the field.

The experiences of TLs and principals are more closely aligned than experiences of teachers for three main reasons: (1) likelihood of having prior work experience; (2) extent of administrative tasks; and (3) school-wide perspective and clientele. As such, as both parties moved into their career position, they followed predictable patterns, substantiated by the theoretical models noted above. Furthermore, these models were considered from an ecological perspective (Barab & Roth, 2006) that recognized the particular network of opportunities, intentions, and "life-world" perspectives of the individual.

While no one institution had a "lock" on successful TLs, those TLs whose academic preparation melded theory and practice factors had more satisfying work experiences. Those students who pursued a master's degree had a deeper understanding of the profession, and were more able to weather temporary setbacks and use a longer-term perspective. Generally, service learning and field experience provided reality checks for professional expertise and matches for individual success. As much as possible, academic preparation should prepare TLs for technological expectations. Pre-service programs should also prepare beginning TLs for the possibility that the school community might not be ready to embrace information literacy and other current professional standards, and provide advocacy techniques to help beginning TLs educate their prospective school communities. Academic programs should also alert new TLs that they will need to negotiate their duties and sense of control.

The degree of change from prior job experience to the workings of the TL sometimes impacted the individual's ultimate career success. If it was easy to make the transition, then fewer surprises occurred, which facilitated the new job (Skinner, 1969). On the other hand, less change required less commitment; it was easier to slip back to the prior job. Most TLs who left their library positions did so in their first year; moreover, most of them worked at the same site as they had before, and returned to their previous duties. In some cases, being at the same location makes that reassignment easier; in other cases, a change in site may be in order, particularly if the beginning TL has not had a good experience in the new position. Change in job title and site requires more commitment—and a greater leap of faith. Additionally, coercion into a TL position seems to be a counterproductive measure. If the potential TL did not self-identify him/herself in that position, it was more likely that the person would not be successful and would try to be transferred to another position. On the other hand, if individuals identify peers as good potential TLs, then this action can be a way to recruit TLs; the key is whether the identified person goes from the awareness status to self-appreciation/acceptance status. Administrators need to handpick potential TLs carefully, and facilitate their change in job affiliation.

Induction activities should support new TLs explicitly address the unique tasks of beginning TLs even though few governmental or educational expectations or standards exist. First-year TLs, in particular, felt isolated, overwhelmed, and unclear about their job or school expectations. The most effective training involved library-savvy mentors or subject-specific training. Beginning TLs needed to feel comfortable about site-specific resources such as the library's automation system and related administrative systems. While activities to facilitate social relationships help beginning TLs feel more accepted, it did not automatically lead to greater job satisfaction. TLs also liked having a choice in their training activities, which might account for the fact that independent reading was a preferred professional development method. School systems and regional or national capacity also impacted the type of professional development available; distance to learning sites, lack of technology and other resources, lack of mentorship training, and underdeveloped professional associations all constitute possible barriers to further education.

Of particular interest was the occasional mismatch of expectations relative to information literacy and collaboration; current beginning TLs may well expect that the school community will value these notions, but few teacher and administrative preparation programs address these issues. The beginning TL sometimes found him/herself in the unenviable position of being considered a neophyte while being more highly trained in collaboration and information literacy strategies. Those with a strong professional reputation had an easier time educating their faculty regarding library program potential. Nevertheless, administrators would do well to acknowledge the beginning TL's current expertise, and find venues for these new professionals to share their recent academic training with the rest of the school community. Such practices would help newcomers feel more recognized for their learning, and would foster a sense of a learning community, which is a significant factor for job satisfaction.

The experiences of first- and second-year TLs differed significantly from more experienced TLs. In general, beginning TLs were more involved with daily operations such as textbook management (particularly in the United States). First-year TLs were trying to sort out their job functions and balance work with personal life. Second-year TLs understood their own jobs better so they could focus more attention on their professional relationships with the rest of the school community. More experienced TLs did more planning (including collection development), instruction, and readers' advisory; they demonstrated a more long-term perspective and collaborative attitude.

Although most job functions and their relative importance were universal, a few differences existed between countries: money-raising was less typical and less valued among non-U.S. TLs, probably because of state funding. The main reason for differences among cultures depended on administrative issues: hiring practices and job assignments. Additionally, when TLs experienced support and recognition from administrators and other school personnel, they felt less resentment about workload, and complied more easily with resource constraints.

In terms of job satisfaction, first-year TLs sometimes experienced a "honeymoon" attitude of idealism and staff openness. By the end of that first year, they were less hopeful; if they felt that they "survived," they felt successful; they focused on their own activity and felt that the rest of the school should provide appropriate structures and support. Second-year TLs had sufficient time to reflect upon their first-year experience and make appropriate adjustments so that they felt more self-confident and outgoing the following year; they focused more on effective working relationships. With competence and a sense of belonging, experienced TLs expected more district support and recognition; they reached a plateau of competence and so wanted accompanying recognition, be it in terms of influence or allocation of resources. Expert TLs accurately identified what they could control or influence, and what needed to be accepted or sidestepped; in either case, their goal was student and library program success. Generally, with time TLs become increasingly happy with their job; they had invested the time and had made accommodations that led to comfortable workload and accepted relationships with the rest of the school community. They did not expect others to "make" their job.

Experienced TLs either were satisfied with their job as is (and focused on job security), or they sought opportunities for expansions of tasks or influence. The transition from experienced TL to expert TL seemed to require a mind-set of lifelong learning and risk-taking. This transition was site-independent, depending primarily on the TL. Formal professional development was usually needed to make that transition, be it an external incentive such as National Board certification or self-initiated professional development/recognition opportunities.

CONCLUSIONS

This study provides a model for future investigation, and can be replicated in additional settings both in the United States and globally. Constraints in classroom visitation and videotaping rights limited this study; including those experiences would strengthen the reliability of the self-reporting. Another important limitation was the identification of non-U. S. expert TLs; the only criteria was longevity. Professional awards might be one filter, though flawed, to determine expertise status.

Nevertheless, the findings from this research provide a richer picture of the experiences and needs of first- and second- year TLs. Of particular interest is the potential differentiation among beginning, competent, and expert TLs. Thus, the study's findings can inform TL-preparation graduate programs and site induction programs. Furthermore, longitudinal data can determine if the TL program modifications impact the success rate of these TLs.

The international aspect advances study on determining the universal and culture-specific experiences of TLs in their academic preparation, induction period, and eventual long-term success. Amazingly, most content knowledge and practices are universal. Culturally defined aspects tend to focus on hiring practices, job functions, and decision-making. Additionally, gender- and age-linked factors were not identified as significant.

What kinds of candidates should TL preparation program coordinators and school administrators look for? Extroverted or service-oriented individuals who are self-confident risk-takers or at least open-minded, lifelong learners, and flexible. Candidates are more likely to be successful if they are good communicators and collaborators. In terms of "good fit" with the function of a TL, those who value intellectual challenge and autonomy, and those who like reading and research processes, are more likely to feel comfortable. While having these pre-existing dispositions can facilitate beginning TL experiences, some of the behaviors (e.g., independent learning skills, communication, and collaboration) can be taught in pre-service programs.

In terms of its impact on academic TL preparation programs, the assessment instruments can be used in the field experience to ascertain to what extent those candidates are prepared for their first professional position. Data collected from the use of the instruments can also be examined to modify programs in order to optimize TL candidates' professional success. Candidates need to understand underlying theories of librarianship as well as apply those principles and best practices in real-life situations, with an intention of educational management and leadership. They also need to be able to explore current library technologies in order to develop valued expertise at the future work sites. Furthermore, explicitly addressing professional dispositions should constitute part of academic recruitment and socialization.

Reflecting expert TLs' high regard for continuing education, TL preparation programs should give serious consideration to offering advanced and refresher courses for TL practitioners. Potentially, such programs could provide mentoring opportunities, combining pre- and in-service TLs. Another promising practice is to provide two-tiered TL licensure: (1) a preliminary credential to enable individuals to begin work within a school setting, perhaps as a part-time intern; and (2) a "clear" credential, which would require additional academic preparation. This latter tier could involve an induction partnership between the school system and the university.

In terms of dispositions and career motivation, whatever the motivation (e.g., activist vs. idealist), the match between personal and school expectations should be optimized. Field experience can be an effective "filter" or reality check to make sure that the anticipated expectation reflects real job functions. Additionally, pre-service faculty should explain change theory and issues of job transitioning in order to help candidates deal with possible stressful situations. Academic advisors should alert potential TLs that the job will not be less stressful or demanding, but rather the pacing and interaction with the school community will be different from their prior jobs. They should also be alerted that they will likely not be able to read on the job.

The contingency theory of socialization provided a framework to explain the relative success of beginning TLs, and reinforced the impact that administrators have on the success of TLs. Indeed, academic faculty should remind their students that the hiring process is as much about interviewing and sizing up the school and its administration as much as the school interviewing the potential TL. Several recommendations for administrators emerged from the data analysis. For example, administrators need to clarify job expectations, including budget issues. They should also be sensitive to first-year workload, and provide professional development opportunities for new functions such as technology expert. To ensure TL retention and success, administrators should provide targeted professional development opportunities throughout TLs' career paths. Greater attention needs to be given to earlier professional development, particularly to close transfer of learning. Administrators should make sure that beginning TLs have subject-expert mentors and opportunities to see TL best practice. While general/site orientations are useful, more social connections should be the focus in the second year. To that end, administrators need to demonstrate explicit encouragement for collaboration and information literacy incorporation. Additionally, they need to explicitly encourage reading, information literacy, and technology competencies through curriculum development and allocation for time and recognition for collaborative planning and implementation. Fostering a learning community could optimize such efforts. Administrations also need to make sure to acknowledge and publicly recognize TLs' efforts beyond their identified job descriptions; their public support will gain them acceptance when they ask TLs to do more with no additional remuneration. Administrators also need to make sure that all TLs, regardless of their tenure, have opportunities to network, to voice their needs, and to contribute to the school's mission based on their abilities.

The findings reinforce the identified theoretical constructs of competency theory, change theory, and contingency theory of socialization. Based on the data collected and analyzed, the main conclusion drawn is that librarians grow developmentally in their job:

- growing from outside control to inner control,
- growing from concerns about self-centric actions to impact on student achievement,
- moving from self-survival to school-wide improvement,
- moving from absolutist to realistic expectations,
- focusing from daily operations to long-term influence,
- focusing from skills development to a deep understanding of information literacy and the role of information, moving from self-control to schoolwide leadership.

Reflecting competency theory, significant differences existed between first- and second-year TLs, and between second- and third-year TLs and more experienced TLs. Additionally, significant differences existed between veteran TLs and National Board certified TLs. In general, first-year TLs focused on their own practice and their transition to their new role. Second-year TLs tended to focus on fitting into the school culture as they impact student achievement; they also put more attention on the resources they had in contributing to the school's purpose. By the time that TLs reached their third year, they focused on their working relationship with other school personnel as well as other TLs. National Board certified and other expert TLs were self-motivated, and found ways to improve library programs by optimizing school factors and finding ways to advance one's own knowledge and application for influencing school improvement. Administrators and library service supervisors would do well to check the process of TLs from one year to the next to determine if satisfactory progress is being made. They should also encourage and facilitate tenured TLs to advance from a competent status quo to an expert status.

Several research questions remain to be explored. Replicating the study in other geographic areas would extend the conclusions' reliability, and more fully determine the universality or culturally embeddedness of TL experiences and success.

The present study did not see age- or gender-linked perceptions, mainly due to the small number of the population. Larger populations may lead to correlations due to these demographics.

Tying motivation for entering the TL profession to Chin and Young's personnel clusters could provide insights into eventual success and job retention.

Few pre-service teacher and administration programs address TLs or library issues. Further study on incorporation of such knowledge and determining the impact of such pre-service coverage on induction activities and library program impact would be insightful.

Examining how pre- and in-service TLs experience and cope with change might also lead to predictions about TL success, including the conditions for work success. The Concerns-Based Adoption Model is a promising assessment approach.

Similarly, studying how beginning TLs and the rest of the school community negotiate current expectations about information and technology literacies as well as collaborative practices could lead to beneficial practices that could be woven into pre-service training for TLs and other school personnel. Additionally, discovering how TLs, both beginning and expert, are perceived by the rest of the school community could help facilitate socialization and eventual success/satisfaction.

Focusing on the differences between competent and expert TLs could also inform pre- and in-service learning experiences as well as career ladder development.

In summary, this area of research is ripe for study and could well advance future TL preparation, induction, and ultimate effectiveness.

REFERENCES

Achinstein, B., Ogawa, R., & Speiglman, A. (2004, Fall). Are we creating separate and unequal tracks of teachers? The effects of state policy, local conditions, and teacher characteristics on new teacher socialization. *American Educational Research Journal, 41*(3), 557–603.

Ambrose, S. & Bridges, M. (2005). Becoming a master teacher. *Advocate, 22*(3), 5–8.

American Association of School Librarians. (2002). *ALA/AASL standards for initial preparation programs: School library media specialists.* Chicago: American Library Association.

Australian Library and Information Association. (2005). Mentoring programs in librarianship. Kingston, NSW: Australian Library and Information Association. Available at http://www.alia.org.ua/groups/mentoringnsw/

Bandura, A. (1997). *Self-efficacy.* New York: Freeman.

Barab, S. & Roth, W. (2006). Curriculum-based ecosystems: Supporting knowing from an ecological perspective. *Educational Researcher, 35*(5), 3–13.

Belenky, M. & Stanton, A. (2000). Inequality, development, and connected knowing. In J. Mezirow (Ed.), *Learning as transformation* (pp. 71–201). San Francisco: Jossey-Bass.

Berliner, D. (1994). Expertise: The wonder of exemplary performance. In J. Mangieri & C. Block (Eds.), *Creating powerful thinking in teachers and students* (Chapter 7). Fort Worth, TX: Holt, Rinehart and Winston.

Bourke, M. (2003). *First year library media teachers' perceptions of challenges and support systems.* Unpublished paper. Long Beach, CA: California State University.

Brindley, R., Morton, M., & Williams, N. (2006). Colliding cultures: Career-switchers' transition to elementary school classrooms. *Action in Teacher Education, 28*(1), 40–50.

Canadian Library Human Resource Study. (2005). *Individual survey instrument.* Edmonton: University of Alberta.

Charter, J. (1982). Case study profiles of six exemplary public high school library media programs. Doctoral dissertation, Florida State University. *Dissertation Abstracts International, 43*(02), 293.

Chin, E. & Young, J. (2007). A person-oriented approach to characterizing beginning teachers in alternative certification programs. *Educational Researcher, 36*(2), 74–83.

Clagg, M. (2002). Why beginning teachers stay in the profession: Views in a Kansas school district. Doctoral dissertation, Wichita State University. *Dissertation Abstracts International, 63*(04), 1197.

Cochran-Smith, C. (2004, November). Stayers, leavers, lovers, and dreamers: Insights about teacher retention. *Journal of Teacher Education, 55*(5), 387–392.

Collins, J. (2005). *Good to great and the social sectors.* New York: HarperCollins.

Cunningham, J. (1998, February). *The workplace: A learning environment.* Paper delivered at the First Annual Conference of the Australian Vocational Education and Training Research Association, Sydney.

Dall-Alba, G. & Sandberg, J. (2006). Unveiling professional development: A critical review of stage models. *Review of Educational Research, 76*(3), 383–412.

Domeracki, D. (2002). *Maturing perceptions of school building climate by first-year teachers: The role of evolving perceptions in optimizing instruction success.* Doctoral dissertation, Northern Illinois University.

Dreyfus, S. (2004). The five-stage model of adult skill acquisition. *Bulletin of Science, Technology & Society, 24*(3), 177–181.

Dumas, J. (1994). Continuing education and job performance of school library media specialists. Doctoral dissertation, Georgia State University. *Dissertation Abstracts International, 55*(05), 1169.

Dweck, Carol. (2006). *Mindset: The new psychology of success.* New York: Random House.

Ericsson, K. & Charness, N. (1994). Expert performance: Its structure and acquisition. *American Psychologist, 49*, 725–747.

Farmer, L. (2001, February). Survey of library media teacher candidates. *CLA Newsletter, 6.*

Feldman, D. (1976). A contingency theory of socialization. *Administrative Science Quarterly, 21*, 433–452.

Fieman-Nemser, S. (2003). What new teachers need to learn. *Educational Leadership, 60*(8), 23–29.

Fisher, C. (1986). Organizational socialization: An integrative review. In K. Roland & G. Ferris (Eds.), *Research in personnel and human resource management: A research annual* (Vol. 4, pp. 101–145). Greenwich, CT: JAI Press.

Fiske, M. (1980). Changing hierarchies of commitment in adulthood. In N. Smelser & E. Erikson (Eds.), *Themes of work and love in adulthood* (pp. 238–264). Cambridge, MA: Harvard University Press.

Gagnon, D. (2004). Influencing factors that foster first-year teacher success (Doctoral dissertation, Cardinal Stritch University). *Dissertation Abstracts International*, *65*(05), 1667.

George, L. (1980). *Role transitions in later life.* Monterey, CA: Brooks/Cole.

Gott, S. (1989). Apprenticeship instruction for real world tasks: The coordination of procedures, mental models, and strategies. *Review of Research in Education*, *15*, 97–169.

Graziano, C. (2005, February). School's out. *Edutopic*, 39–44.

Guarino, C., Santibanez, L., & Daley, G. (2006). Teacher recruitment and retention: A review of the recent empirical literature. *Review of Educational Research*, *76*(2), 173–208.

Gwatney, M. (2001, May). Reality versus the ideal. *Knowledge Quest*, *29*(5), 36–40.

Hein, K. (2006). Information uncommon: Public computing in the life of reference. *Reference Services Review*, *34*(1), 33–42.

Hook, S., Bracke, M., Greenfield, L., & Mills, V. (2003). In-house training for instruction librarians. *Research Strategies*, *19*, 99–127

Hord, S., Rutherford, W., & Hall, G. (1987). *Taking charge of change.* Alexandria, VA: Association for Supervision and Curriculum Development.

Ingram, E. (2002). An analysis of principals' behavior that support beginning teachers in the emotional, instrumental, informational and appraisal domains (Doctoral dissertation, East Carolina University). *Dissertation Abstracts International*, *63*(10), 3432.

International Federation of Library Associations and Institutions. (2000). *Guidelines for professional library/information educational programs.* The Hague, Belgium: International Federation of Library Associations and Institutions. Available at http://www.ifla.org/VII/s23/bulletin/guidelines.htm.

Johnson, L. (2002). The effect of supportive interventions on first-year teacher efficacy (Doctoral dissertation, Indiana State University). *Dissertation Abstracts International*, *64*(08), 2846.

Johnson, S. & Birkeland, S. (2003, Fall). Pursuing a sense of success: New teachers explain their career decisions. *American Educational Research Journal*, *40*(3), 581–617.

Jones, G. (1986). Socialization tactics, self-efficacy, and newcomers' adjustments to organizations. *Academy of Management Journal*, *29*(2), 262–279.

Kardos, S. (2004). Supporting and sustaining new teachers in schools: The importance of professional culture and mentoring (Doctoral dissertation, Harvard University). *Dissertation Abstracts International*, *65*(05), 1609.

Kinard, B. (1991). An evaluation of the actual and preferred role of library media specialists in a major urban public school system (Doctoral dissertation, University of Maryland). *Dissertation Abstracts International*, *52*(06), 2116.

Kram, K. (1985). *Mentoring at work: Developmental relationships in organizational life.* Glenview, IL: Scott, Foresman & Co.

Kuhlthau, C. (1993). Implementing a process approach to information skills: A study identifying indicators of success in library media programs. *SLMQ*, *22*(1), http://www.ala.org/ala/aasl/aaslpubsandjournals/slmrb/editorschoiceb/infopower/selectkuhlthau1.cfm

Louis, M. (1980). Surprise and sense making: What newcomers experience in entering unfamiliar organizational settings. *Administrative Science Quarterly*, *25*(2), 226–251.

Macmillan, R. (1998). Approaches to leadership: What comes with experience? *Educational Management & Administration*, *26*(2), 173–84.

Manuel, K., Beck, S., & Molloy, M. (2005). An ethnographic study of attitudes influencing faculty collaboraiotn in library instruction. *Reference Librarian, 89/90*, 139–161.

McCoy, B. (2001). A survey of practicing school library media specialists to determine the job competencies that they value most (Doctoral dissertation, Georgia State University). *Dissertation Abstracts International, 62*(03), 821.

McCracken, A. (2000). Perceptions of school library media specialists regarding their roles and practices (Doctoral dissertation, George Mason University). *Dissertation Abstracts International, 61*(04), 1369.

Mezirow, J. (1991). *Transformative dimensions of adult learning*. San Francisco, CA: Jossey -Bass.

Monsour, F. (1998, January). Twenty recommendations for an administrative mentoring program. *NASSP Bulletin, 82*(594), 96–100.

Nahl, D. (2005). Affective and cognitive information behavior: Interaction effects in internet use. In A. Grove (Ed.), *Proceedings 68th Annual Meeting of the American Society for Information Science and Technology (ASIST)* 42, Charlotte, NC.

National Center for Education Statistics. (2005). Schools and staffing survey. Washington, DC: National Center for Education Statistics.

Nelson, D. (1987). Organizational socialization: A stress perceptive. *Journal of Occupational Behaviour, 8*, 311–324.

Nicholson, N. (1984). A theory of work role transitions. *Administrative Science Quarterly, 29*, 172–292.

Oberg, D. (1991). *Learning to be a teacher-librarian: A research report*. Edmonton: University of Alberta.

———. (1995a). Principal support: What does it mean to teacher-librarians? Available at http://www.ualberta.ca/~doberg/prcsup.htm.

———. (1995b). *Sustaining the vision: A selection of conference papers*. 24th International Association of School Librarianship Conference July 1995 (pp. 17–25). Worcester, England: Worcester College of Higher Education.

Perrone, V. (2004). *Librarians and the nature of expertise*. LIANZA Conference paper. Auckland, New Zealand November 2004. Online: http://opac.lianza.org.nz/cgi-bin/koha/opac-detail.pl?bib=248.

Person, D. (1993). A comparative study of role perceptions of school library media specialists and information power guidelines (Doctoral dissertation, New York University). *Dissertation Abstracts International, 54*(07), 2368.

Peterson, K. & Deal, T. (2002). *The shaping school culture fieldbook*. San Francisco: Jossey-Bass.

Pierce, G. (2004.). Mentoring junior faculty. *NEA Higher Education Advocate, 22*(1), 5–8.

Richardson, M. (2003). Mentoring and keeping new teachers (Doctoral dissertation, Cappella University). *Dissertation Abstracts International, 64*(05), 1485.

Roys, N. & Brown, M. (2004). The ideal candidate for school library media specialist: Views from school administrators, library school faculty, and MLS students. *School Library Media Research, 7*, http://www.ala.org/ala/aasl/aaslpubsandjournals/slmrb/slmrcontents/volume72004/candidate.cfm.

Schmidt, L., Kosmoski, G., & Pollack, D. (1998). Novice administrators: Psychological and physiological effects. *ERIC Digest* (Syracuse, NY: ERIC).

Shannon, D. (2002). The education and competencies of school library media specialists: A review of the literature. *School Library Media Research* (Online), *5*.

Short, B. (2003). How do beliefs and other factors such as prior experience influence the decision-making of new teachers during their first year teaching experience? (Doctoral dissertation, Illinois State University). *Dissertation Abstracts International, 64*(12), 4346.

Skinner, B. (1969). *Contingencies of reinforcement: A theoretical analysis.* New York: Appleton-Century-Crofts.

Slygh, G. (2000). Shake, rattle, and role! The effects of professional community on the collaborative role of the school librarian (Doctoral dissertation, University of Wisconsin-Madison). *Dissertation Abstracts International, 61*(08), 2969.

Smith, P. (2003). Workplace learning and flexible delivery. *Review of Educational Research, 73*(1), 53–88.

Smith, T. & Ingersoll, R. (2004, Fall). What are the effects of induction and mentoring on beginning teacher turnover. *American Educational Research Journal, 41*(3), 681–714.

Toffler, B. (1981). Occupational role development: The changing determinants of outcomes for the individual. *Administrative Science Quarterly, 26*(3), 396–418.

Van Manen, M. (1977). Linking ways of knowing with ways of being practical. *Curriculum Inquiry, 6,* 208–225.

Vereen, A. (2002). A study of professional development school program graduates through their first year as urban school teachers (Doctoral dissertation, Old Dominion University). *Dissertation Abstracts International, 64*(01), 115.

Weiner, B. (1986). *An attributional theory of motivation and emotion.* New York: Springer-Verlag.

Williamson, J., Pemberton, A., & Lounsbury, L. (2005). An investigation of career and job satisfaction in relations to personality traits of information professionals. *Library Quarterly, 75*(2), 122–141.

Yontz, E. & McCook, K. (2003). Service-learning and LIS education. *Journal of Education for Library and Information Science, 44*(1), 58–67.

Zhang, A., Vertegen, D., & Fan, X. (2006, April). *Teacher job satisfaction and teacher retention.* Paper delivered at the Annual Meeting of American Educational Research Association, San Francisco.

Using Organizational Culture to Frame Discussions of the Disciplinary Field of School Library Media

Susan L. Stansberry
Oklahoma State University

I absolutely loved my job as a school library media specialist (LMS)! Through my own experience and observation of other school library media specialists, I have seen the following:

- designing and delivering lessons to preschoolers one hour and twelfth graders the next;

- delivering professional development for teachers on a regular basis;

- building a video production studio and courses to go with it;

- involvement in curriculum planning and delivery in all content areas and at all levels across the district;

- leading the technology planning committee and administrative search committees;

- testing of new instructional technologies and then introducing these to the rest of the faculty;

- shopping for wonderful books and resources such as new and classic literature, educational software, and even a staging area for student presentations;

- helping students develop multimedia projects for state and national competitions and traveling with them to receive their awards;

- learning the reading preferences of many of the students and teachers and actually encouraging some students to read who never had;

- guiding other students into learning when they thought they were just having fun with computer games and simulations;

- learning all about digital phone systems, media retrieval systems, and computerized lighting and sound for auditorium productions;

- encouraging teachers toward innovative and effective practices and supporting them in their professional growth;

- helping write and administer grants; and

- telling everyone—students, teachers, administrators, and community members—who walked in the door that the library media center was *their place*—surprising, since most had never been told that before.

What an absolutely fabulous job! To my surprise, I heard a woman say the other day that she could not imagine a more boring job in the world than that of a school librarian! Clearly, my experience was vastly different. Immersed in the research culture of higher education as a professor of library media and educational technology, I realize that the particular organizational culture of my school helped facilitate my opportunity to meet national and state standards for my job; the school expected nothing less from me. The superintendent was well-versed in the concepts set forth in *Information Power* (1988, 1998), and the principals in the district provided teamwork and support in creating an excellent school library media program integrated across an elementary, middle, and high school.

The teachers looked to me for instructional leadership. I assumed this was the norm across all school districts.

Now as a professor, I have learned there are *school library media programs* in districts of all shapes, sizes, and types. Unfortunately, some administrators may be unaware as to the advantages of having a school library media program that meets national guidelines. Perhaps this is the reason that many superintendents petition the state to not pay the salary of a certified LMS. Do classroom teachers not want a curriculum planning and instructional partner who is an expert in information and technology resources? Research demonstrates that principals, teachers, and even some school library media specialists have inaccurate perceptions of the role of an LMS (Dorrell & Lawson, 1995; Horton, 1989; Naylor & Jenkins, 1988; Ceperley, 1991; McCracken, 2001; Haycock, 1995; O'neal, 2004; Alexander, Smith, & Carey, 2003).

The standards and defined roles of the person who functions as a school librarian have changed drastically as the world has advanced into a global, information-based society. However, there is a great disconnect between these guidelines that are understood and taught in library education programs and what is actually practiced in schools on a daily basis (Shannon, 2002; Hartzell, 2002; Roys, 2004; Neuman, 2004). This chapter will explore theoretical issues and practical solutions related to this disconnect at this particular point in the history of the field. The field of school library media has come to a crossroads of sorts: professional organizations are taking on the task of crafting the next generation of national standards that will serve to carry the field forward, and states and school districts are facing a critical shortage of certified candidates emerging from the academic discipline.

THE LENS OF ORGANIZATIONAL CULTURE

Each academic discipline is a cultural entity with its own socially constructed realities (Valimaa, 1998). Harris (2005) noted that "culture ultimately defines the essence of the school and gives meaning to human endeavor. It encompasses the entire educational process, specifically the values, beliefs, norms, and social patterns of all members of the school community" (p. 32). A school library media program is comprised of all the services performed by the LMS, who is a teacher, administrator, and information specialist; the library media center (LMC), which houses the school's collection of print and nonprint curriculum resources; and all processes, social patterns, values and beliefs associated with services provided. Therefore, when discussing the discipline of school library media, it is most helpful to consider a cultural perspective. Each school library media program is set within the context of its particular school and community—a cultural frame that reflects the unique program as well as the discipline of the field. Theoretically, we can examine an individual school library media program as a culture, but we can also consider the discipline, or field of study, a culture. Regarding the culture of a discipline, Becher (1994) quoted Clifford Geertz: "to be a Shakespearean scholar, absorb oneself in black holes, or attempt to measure the effect of schooling on economic achievement—is not just to take up a technical task but to place oneself inside a cultural frame that defines and even determines a very great part of one's life" (p. 153). Harris (2005) describes the holistic approach to studying the culture of an educational organization:

> Every school organization consists of cultural members, including educators, students and community members, who share a history in the school. These cultural members visualize and interpret the world around them, organize themselves, conduct their activities, and have particular roles in the field. The holistic view attempts to capture the complex nature of culture. It explains how the historically derived values and ideas of people affect their actions, attitudes, and labor in organizations. (p. 29)

In applying this holistic approach to the field of school library media studies, we can assume that the disciplinary field consists of cultural members, including researchers, theorists, practitioners, and students, who all share a history in the field, have roles that they play, choose actions, reflect attitudes, and conduct activities in a complex way. In order to examine culture, researchers have used sports (Lingenfelter, 1996 1998; Stansberry & Harris, 2005) or theatre (Lightfoot, 1983; Harris, 2005) metaphors to explain observations. In this chapter, I will use the theatre imagery to discuss the complex culture of school library media studies. By giving a lens to discussions of the field, this contributes to furthering the opportunities for schools to experience school library media programs.

STAGE: THE SPACE IN WHICH WORK OCCURS

In describing the stage, one must consider all aspects of the physical environment, or the context in which action takes place. What kinds of behavior does the setting promote or prevent? What props are used? How is the physical environment maintained? What values are conveyed through the organization of space? (Harris 2005).

School library media centers have been described as unimportantly as circulation depots and as gloriously as the heartbeat of instruction in a school. The "Colorado" research studies conducted by Keith Curry Lance and similar studies by colleagues in Alaska, Massachusetts, North Carolina, Pennsylvania, Oregon, Texas, Iowa, and California (Burgin & Bracy, 2003) found that variables related to *stage*—size, use, computing facilities, and per-pupil expenditures—were the most powerful predictors of the library media program's impact on student achievement. For many school library media specialists, their stage has expanded far beyond books and buildings to include the bits and bytes of the Internet (Martrell, 2000a). As funding for school library media programs continues to erode, and the growth of electronic information continues to explode, building a stage that emphasizes access to information rather than ownership of it (Martrell, 2000a) is highly critical. Even a school library that is sorely lacking in *owned* resources can still offer *access* to resources through the use of technology. To do this, however, the LMS must be well-prepared to facilitate the construction, maintenance, and use of digital library resources. In the past, discussions have centered on making the school library the *hub of the school*, ideally locating it in the actual center of the facility. Now, these same discussions need to focus on the school library as portal to the world. It is no longer a question of whether the Internet is a space that can be used in schools; the question is how well are schools using it? Martrell (2000a) challenges librarians to enter this new space:

> We need to remake ourselves to avoid becoming obsolete. We need to create
> a range of services unthinkable in the twentieth century, but mandatory in the
> twenty-first century, if we are to provide society with the value-added services
> it will need from its professionals. (p. 13)

If students and teachers *think* they can get everything they need from the Internet and not have to make the trek down to the library, there is no incentive for doing otherwise. When students, teachers, and administrators enter the stage of the library media program, they must be able to recognize and access all program resources, whether they are physical or virtual.

Every stage is decorated with props. What props define the setting of your school library media center? A center with print materials only is clearly staging outdated services. Likewise, a center with state-of-the-art technology that sits unused or misused is a staging problem as well. In our instruction for future school library media specialists, we must be prepared to lead them through construction of a stage that offers both physical and virtual learning spaces.

Ask yourselves these questions: What behaviors are taking place on our stage? Are we seeing information literacy played out at all grade levels, throughout all content areas, and with a wide variety of print and digital resources? Is it clear from looking at our stage that we value open access to information over ownership of information? Are players on this stage using "props" appropriately? Does this stage exist only within the school building?

On the stage of the discipline of school library media, important action in the field takes place on the stages of professional conferences and on the pages of professional journals. The American Association of School Librarians (AASL) and the International Association of School Librarianship (IASL) offer conferences and publications focused entirely on the field. However, there are many more organizations also performing with the best interests of the field in mind: the Association of Educational Communications and Technology (AECT), the Association of Library and Information Science Educators (ALISE), the International Society of Technology in Education (ISTE), the Association for Supervision and Curriculum Development (ASCD), and the Institute of Museum and Library Services (IMLS). These organizations also offer conferences and publications as well as collaborative audiences; therefore, they are important stages to attend to as well. Additionally, all professional organizations concerned with the improvement of education should be aware of issues of the field of school library media. Organizations focusing on educational leadership, school administration, curriculum and supervision, teacher education, and educational technology should all have representation from the field of school library media. It should be recognized that multiple stages presenting issues of the field can only be of benefit to the field. We need to ask ourselves where other stages might be on which the voices of our field should be heard.

CAST: THE PARTICIPANTS

Examining the stage carefully takes us next to the theatre participants—the cast. In any theatre, there are producers, directors, set designers, costume designers, stage hands, bit players, and stars of the show. Each school is made up of a very unique cast, and each cast reflects a distinctive balance of power, responsibilities, collaboration, and ownership of resources. In examining the organizational culture of a school library media program, we can ask the following questions:

Who are the players, the characters?
How many are there?
What are their roles?
What are the rules they go by?
What are their relationships?
Who else is in the scene?
What brings them together?
Who is allowed and not allowed here? (Harris, 2005, pp. 69–70)

In a school library media program, the central players are the LMS, the staff, and those they serve directly—teachers and students. However, administrators, fellow teachers, and community resources are also extremely important players. An effective program will manage a large, diverse cast made up of players who *all* have a vested interest in the vitality of the program. Green (2007) quotes actor Harvey Fierstein: "When people come into the theater, it's an act of faith no different from a sacrament in a church. They are willing to go where you take them, and you have the duty to take them where it will do the absolute best." School library media programs must be able to draw people to their physical and virtual stages and faithfully lead them through the optimal services to improve teaching and learning. Martrell (2000a) noted that it's not WHAT you have in your library; rather, it is WHO you have. Each program should carefully examine the cast, making sure *all* players understand the field, the program, and the audience they are there to serve.

The discipline of school library media needs to expand its cast to embrace those in ancillary organizations. It is no longer a viable option to have only school library media specialists understanding, studying, and advocating for the field. School administrators, educational technology specialists, teachers, and educators of all of these groups, must be eagerly embraced and brought into the cast to strengthen the field.

PLOT: THE ACTIVITIES AND INTERACTIONS

In examining the plot and subplots of an organization, Harris (2005) recommends focusing on the following questions:

> What are the activities?
> What is going on?
> What might be a definable sequence of activities?
> How do people interact with the activity and with one another?
> How are people and activities connected and interrelated?
> What is being acted out but not said?
> How many stories (subplots) coexist in the same drama? (p. 70)

In education's current climate of high-stakes assessment and outcomes-based accreditation, the activities and interactions in a school library media program have broadened far beyond the original scope of school library services, which may help insure the vitality of individual programs in schools as well as in the disciplinary field. The original coauthors of the *Information Power* national standards, AECT and AASL, are both currently updating standards to shape the actions and purposes of the field. These activities have tended in the past to focus inwardly to the library media center itself. It is time, however, to look far beyond the individual center itself to the larger plot of improving education hand-in-hand with administrators, technology specialists, fellow teachers, and educators of all these groups. This improvement must move beyond traditional information literacy instruction to fully embrace twenty-first-century skills, use and development of educational technology, innovative and effective pedagogy, and critical thinking about traditional content knowledge. The activities of developing standards, arriving at common understandings, identifying shared values and goals, and forging powerful new identities are the basis for the exciting plot taking place on the stage of school library media studies.

TIME: THE TIME FRAME IN WHICH ACTIVITIES AND INTERACTIONS OCCUR

One very important aspect of plot is the time frame in which action occurs. Regarding time in libraries, Martrell (2000b) noted:

> The time and space considerations of librarians are defined and circumscribed by the libraries in which they work. The library is a highly formalized physical operation. Discontinuities of time and space have rarely been allowed to intrude on the library environment. Things are fixed in space in a linear pattern. Time is carefully structured in order to optimize the use of the library's

resources. Library and unit hours and a wide array of policies and procedures impose limits on the user. (p. 104)

In school library media centers, this imposition of limits based on scheduled classes, traditional times the "school day" encompasses, and the role of the LMS as a teacher has fueled a debate centered on three issues: flexible vs. fixed scheduling (Johnson, 2001; van Deusen, 1999), time spent on tasks set forth in guidelines (Miller, 2005; van Deusen, 1996; Everhart, 1992), and not having enough time to implement the roles set forth in national guidelines (McCracken, 2001; McCarthy, 1997).

Harris (2005) offers the following questions for structuring the discussion of time in organizational culture:

What value is placed on time?
What parameters define the school calendar? Is it detailed and followed fervently or is it vague and moderately adhered to?
Are daily work activities regulated by specific rules, routines, and/or bells?
Is time allotted for meaningful professional development? (p. 70)

When answered through thoughtful reflection on one's library media program, each of these questions can assist in solving the three issues of time. It is time for the debate over the value of flexible vs. fixed schedule to end; what works in the organizational culture of one school may not work in another. The importance is the match between the implementation plan and the existing culture; a mismatch of implementation plan and organizational culture will undoubtedly result in failure (Harris, 2005; Stansberry & Harris, 2005). If an LMS is not achieving the tasks set forth in guidelines due to time constraints, it is the responsibility of that LMS to gather together the stakeholders (or cast, in the theatre metaphor) and carefully examine the existing program in relation to guidelines.

Like the theatre, a disciplinary field has boundaries (Becher, 1994). In the theatre, there is an expectation that the performers will not deviate from the script, that the audience will stay in their seats and off the stage, and that the curtain will come down when the performance has reached its ending. While some are speculating that the curtain may be closing on the job of the school media specialist (Loertscher, 2004), it may, rather, be the perfect time for our field to redesign sets and rewrite scripts. Why are the boundaries of our discipline where they are? Who has decided this group or those groups are the only ones allowed to be part of the cast? Why would the stage be limited only to physical space and the performance only be delivered at specific times?

Haycock (1995) suggested that we are aware of what makes effective library media programs and services (and it is clear from the research that we are), but the trouble is actually putting effective programs into place. I suggest that to know what is effective in an individual school library media program and in the field of school library media as a whole, we must carefully examine the existing organizational culture and then broaden our audience, invite a whole host of cast members to participate, and set a stage that truly reflects the opportunities that abound in teaching and learning today.

EXPLORING THE ORGANIZATIONAL CULTURE OF SCHOOL LIBRARY MEDIA

This set of open-ended questions will guide you in thinking critically about your own program or your perceptions of the field as a whole.

I. Stage: The Space in which Work Occurs

    A.   Describe all aspects of the physical environment, or the context in which action takes place.

    B.   What kinds of behavior does the setting promote or prevent?

    C.   What props are used?

    D.   How is the physical environment maintained?

    E.   What values are conveyed through the organization of space?

    F.   What other aspects of the stage can you think of that weren't covered by the above questions?

II. Cast: The Participants

    A.   Who are the players, the characters?

    B.   How many are there?

    C.   What are their roles?

    D.   What are the rules they go by?

    E.   What are their relationships?

    F.   Who else is in the scene?

    G.   What brings them together?

    H.   Who is allowed and not allowed here?

    I.   What other aspects of the cast can you think of that weren't covered by the above questions?

III. Plot: The Activities and Interactions

    A.   What are the activities?

    B.   What is going on?

    C.   What might be a definable sequence of activities?

    D.   How do people interact with the activity and with one another?

    E.   How are people and activities connected and interrelated?

    F.   What is being acted out but not said?

    G.   How many stories (subplots) coexist in the same drama?

    H.   What other aspects of the plot can you think of that weren't covered by the above questions?

IV. Time: The Time Frame in which Activities and Interactions Occur

    A.   What value is placed on time?

    B.   What parameters define the school calendar? Is it detailed and followed fervently or is it vague and moderately adhered to?

    C.   Are daily work activities regulated by specific rules, routines, and/or bells?

    D.   Is time allotted for meaningful professional development?

    E.   What other aspects of time can you think of that weren't covered by the above questions?

RESOURCES

Alexander, L. B., Smith, R. C., & Carey, J. O. (2003, November–December). Education reform and the school library media specialist: Perceptions of principals. *Knowledge Quest, 32*(2), 10–13.

American Association of School Librarians and Association for Educational Communications and Technology. (1988). *Information power: Guidelines for school library media programs.* Chicago, IL: ALA.

———. (1998). *Information power: Guidelines for school library media programs.* Chicago, IL: ALA.

Becher, T. (1994, June). The significance of disciplinary differences. *Studies in higher education, 19*(2), 151–162.

Burgin, R. & Bracy, P. B. (2003). *An essential connection: How quality school library media programs improve student achievement in North Carolina.* Spring, TX: Hi Willow Research and Publishing.

Ceperley, P. E. (1991). *Information needs 2000: Results of a survey of library media specialists.* Charleston, WV: Appalachia Educational Lab. (ERIC Document Reproduction Service No. ED340393).

Dorrell, L. D. & Lawson, L. V. (1995). What are principals' perceptions of the school library media specialist? *NASSP Bulletin, 79*(2), 72–80.

Everhart, N. (1992). An analysis of the work activities of high-school library media specialists in automated and nonautomated library media centers using work sampling. *School Library Media Annual, 10*, 148–157.

Green, J. (2007, March). The authentics: Harvey Fierstein. *The Oprah Magazine, 8*(3), 217.

Harris, E. L. (2005). *Key strategies to improve schools: How to apply them contextually.* Lanham, MD: Rowan & Littlefield Education.

Hartzell, G. (2002). What's it take? Proceedings from the *White House Conference on School Libraries*, Washington, DC, June 4, 2002, 29. Supplement to the September/October 2002 issue of *Knowledge Quest*.

Haycock, K. (1995, Summer). Research in teacher-librarianship and the institutionalization of change. *School Library Media Quarterly, 23*(4). Retrieved on February 3, 2007, from http://archive.ala.org/aasl/SLMR/slmr_resources/select_haycock.html

Horton, J. A. (1989). Principals' and teachers' attitudes toward Kansas school library media programs. *School Library Media Quarterly, 17*(2), 98–100.

Johnson, D. (2001, November). It's good to be inflexible. *School Library Journal, 47*, 39.

Lightfoot, S. L. (1983). *The good high school: Portraits of character and culture.* New York: Basic Books.

Lingenfelter, S. G. (1996). *Agents of transformation: A guide for effective cross-cultural ministry.* Grand Rapids, MI: Baker Books.

———. (1998). *Transforming culture: A challenge for Christian mission*, 2nd ed. Grand Rapids, MI: Baker Books.

Loertscher, D. V. (2004, November). Extreme makeover: If school librarians plan to survive, it's time to make some tough changes. *School Library Journal, 2004*(11). Retrieved on January 30, 2007, from http://www.schoollibraryjournal.com/article/CA475521.html

Martrell, C. (2000a). The disembodied librarian in the digital age. *College and Research Libraries, 61*(1), 10–28.

———. (2000b). The disembodied librarian in the digital age, part II. *College and Research Libraries, 61*(2), 99–113.

McCarthy, C. A. (1997). A reality check: The challenges of implementing *Information Power* in school library media programs. Research and professional paper presented at the annual conference of International Association of School Librarianship, Vancouver, B.C., July 6–11. (ERIC Document Reproduction Service No. ED412958).

McCracken, A. (2001). School library media specialists' perceptions of practice and importance of roles described in *Information Power. School Library Media Research, 4.* Retrieved on January 30, 2007, from http://www.ala.org/ala/aasl/aaslpubsandjournals/slmrb/slmrcontents/volume42001/volume42001.htm

Miller, N. A. S. (2005). Oklahoma association of school library media specialists time task study. Research paper presented at the Judy Pitts Research Forum, *American Association of School Librarians 12th National Conference*, Pittsburgh, PA. October 7, 2005. Retrieved on November 17, 2006, at http://www.oklibs.org/~oaslms/OKTimeTaskReport.pdf

Naylor, A. P. & Jenkins, K. (1988). An investigation of principals' perceptions of library media specialist performance evaluation terminology. *School Library Media Quarterly, 21*(2), 115–121.

Neuman, D. (2004). The library media center: Touchstone for instructional design and technology in schools. In D. H. Jonassen (Ed.), *Handbook of research on educational communications and technology* (pp. 499–522). Mahwah, NJ: Lawrence Erlbaum Associates.

O'neal, A. J. (2004). Administrators', teachers', and media specialists' perceptions of the roles of media specialists in the schools' instructional programs: Implications for instructional administration. *Journal of Education for Library and Information Science, 45*(4), 286–306.

Roys, N. K. (2004). The ideal candidate for school library media specialist: Views from school administrators, library school faculty, and MLS students. *School Library Media Research, 7.* Retrieved on January 15, 2007, from http://news.ala.org/ala/aasl/aaslpubsandjournals/slmrb/slmrcontents/volume72004/candidate.cfm

Shakespeare, W. (1906). *As You Like It* (II, vii, pp. 139–143). Boston, MA: Ginn and Company.

Shannon, D. (2002). The education and competencies of school library media specialists: A review of the literature. *School Library Media Research, 5.* Retrieved on January 15, 2007, from http://www.ala.org/ala/aasl/aaslpubsandjournals/slmrb/slmrcontents/volume52002/shannon.htm

Stansberry, S. L. & Harris, E. L. (2005, Spring). Understanding the interrelationship of instructional technology use and organizational culture: A case study of a veterinary medicine college. *Journal of Veterinary Medical Education,32*(1), 31–37.

Valimaa, J. (1998). Culture and identity in higher education research. *Higher Education, 36*, 119–138.

Van Deusen, J. D. (1996, Winter). An analysis of the time use of elementary school library media specialists and factors that influence it. *School Library Media Quarterly, 24*(2), 85–92.

———. (1999). Prerequisites to flexible scheduling. In K. Haycock, (Ed.), *Foundations for effective school library media programs* (pp. 223–227). Englewood, CO: Libraries Unlimited.

Part Three
Leadership Profiles

Introduction

The purpose of this section is to profile individuals who have made significant contributions to the field of educational media and communication technology. Leaders profiled in the *Educational Media and Technology Yearbook* have typically held prominent offices, composed seminal works and made significant contributions that have influenced the contemporary vision of the field. The people profiled in this section have often been directly responsible for mentoring individuals, who have themselves become recognized for their contributions in one way or another.

There are special reasons to feature people of national and international renown. This volume of the *Educational Media and Technology Yearbook* profiles an individual who continues to uphold the tradition of leadership in educational media and communication technology. The leader profiled this year is:

David Michael Moore

The following people [alphabetically listed] were profiled in earlier volumes of the *Educational Media and Technology Yearbook*:

John C. Belland	Jean E. Lowrie
Robert K. Branson	Wesley Joseph McJulien
James W. Brown	M. David Merrill
Bob Casey	Michael Molenda
Betty Collis	Robert M. Morgan
Robert E. De Kieffer	Robert Morris
Robert M. Diamond	James Okey
Walter Dick	Ronald Oliver
Frank Dwyer	Tjeerd Plomp
Donald P. Ely	Rita C. Richey
James D. Finn	Paul Saettler
Robert Mills Gagné	Wilbur Schramm
Castelle (Cass) G. Gentry	Charles Francis Schuller
Thomas F. Gilbert	Don Carl Smellie
Kent Gustafson	Howard Sullivan
John Hedberg	William Travers
Robert Heinich	Constance Dorothea Weinman
Stanley A. Huffman	Paul Welliver
Harry Alleyn Johnson	Paul Robert Wendt
Roger Kaufman	David R. Krathwohl

There is no formal survey or popularity contest to determine the persons for whom the profiles are written. People profiled in this section are usually emeritus faculty who may or may not be active in the field. You are welcome to nominate individuals to be featured in this section. Your nomination of someone to be profiled in this section must also be accompanied by the name of the person who agrees to compose the leadership profile. Please direct comments, questions, and suggestions about the selection process to the Senior Editor.

Robert Maribe Branch

Leading the Field of Visual Literacy: David Michael (Mike) Moore

Barbara B. Lockee
Virginia Tech

For those with an interest in visual literacy, the name of David Michael (Mike) Moore is a familiar one. For more than 30 years, Mike has provided leadership in research efforts regarding the use of images for instructional purposes. A review of the relevant literature illustrates that Mike is one of the most prolific and prominent scholars in instructional technology. The following chapter details his professional career and describes his contributions to our field.

DEVELOPING A CAREER AND A FIELD

In 1963, Mike began his academic career as a public school teacher in Shelbyville, Illinois, teaching history in junior high. Because he was the only one who used media, he became de facto "the AV guy." He was given the title of District AV Director, and in addition to his teaching efforts, he assisted other teachers with their technology support issues.

When Mike learned of a well-regarded masters program in AV administration at Eastern Illinois, he enrolled part-time while continuing his teaching and AV director responsibilities. His advisor was Vern Stockman, who was also a pioneer in the field. Mike was the first to do the program on a part-time basis, much to the chagrin of his advisor. During this era (the mid-1960s) the federal government was investing heavily in the use of technology for instruction. The National Defense Education Act was designed to upgrade science and math teaching, with a particular focus on using technology to do so. Mike's school was the beneficiary of such funding. So, while learning about AV administration in his graduate program by night, Mike was informing school AV purchasing decisions by day.

In 1966 Mike attended the Summer Media Institute at Purdue, where he learned about the newly developed concept of instructional design and advanced his knowledge of programmed instruction, all for graduate credit. Guest speakers included the leaders in the field of audiovisual instruction at the time, which was a great source of professional development and motivation for Mike, instigating his interest in doctoral studies.

In 1967, Mike took a job in Charleston, Illinois, to serve as an AV specialist for a 13-school district cooperative. In this role, he conducted workshops for teachers in graphic production and the use of media for instruction. While there, he pursued his interest in doctoral studies and was accepted to Southern Illinois University. In the summer of 1968, he moved to Carbondale, Illinois, and began working on his Ph.D. in educational media and library studies. His dissertation study examined the effect of size and type of image on recall of content, setting the stage for one of the field's most extensive research programs related to the use of images for instruction.

Mike accepted his first faculty position at Southern Illinois at Edwardsville, a sister university to SIU and commuter school serving the St. Louis area. He taught large sections of 300 students, offering courses in AV instruction, photography, instructional design, and library courses for school media personnel. He was there for two years before he received an invitation to interview at the newly established College of Education at Virginia Tech. They wanted him to run a curriculum lab, and also to start a master's and doctoral program in educational media. Upon his hiring, Mike established the Self-Instruction Curriculum Laboratory, which not only served the college but was critical to obtaining a more supportive milieu for research in areas of Mike's interest namely, visual design and visual literacy. He then wrote a federal grant to train community college media personnel in the use of AV for instruction. Through this project, he recruited the first five students of the newly created instructional technology doctoral program at VT.

In the 1980s, federal support for curriculum laboratories declined, but interest in computer-based instruction rapidly increased. At that time Mike and his colleagues, Drs. Norm Dodl and John Burton, reinvented the IT program to incorporate a more high-tech focus. This faculty team took "portable" IBM computers around the state of Virginia to do instructional computing workshops for community college and public school personnel. Those early efforts have led the IT graduate program at VT to become renowned for the application of technological innovations for the advancement of teaching and learning.

During his career at Virginia Tech, Mike provided leadership to the program there, serving for many years as the program area leader until his retirement in 2003. Although retired, this professor emeritus continues to remain actively involved in the program and is often called upon for his expertise and assistance.

RESEARCH EFFORTS

Reflective of his early work on the use of images for instruction, Mike's research efforts consistently focused on visual literacy. A sabbatical during the fall semester of 1990 at Pennsylvania State University launched a significant collegial partnership with Dr. Frank Dwyer, another pioneer in the field of IT. The two experts designed an extensive research program that analyzed the cognitive style of field dependence and its effect on instructional image design. This collaborative effort generated 15 scholarly articles, numerous professional presentations, and an award-winning book entitled, *Visual Literacy: A Spectrum of Visual Learning*. This book won the 1995 James W. Brown Publication Award from the Association for Educational Communications and Technology (AECT), as an outstanding publication in the field of Educational Technology.

Mike has published over 100 research articles related to visual literacy in journals, including *Educational Technology Research and Development*, *Journal of Educational Technology Systems*, *International Journal of Instructional Media*, *British Journal of Educational Technology*, and the *Journal of Educational Computing Research*, to name but a few. Reflective of his excellence in graduate advising, Mike worked closely with doctoral students in the publication of their own dissertation efforts, providing not only expertise in research design, but also guidance through the sometimes tricky waters of scholarly publishing. Some of the most important pieces that he has written, however, are efforts to preserve the history and foundations of the seminal research in IT. Mike has co-written multiple chapters for the *Handbook of Research on Educational Communications and Technology*, including topics on behaviorism, multiple-channel instruction, and programmed technologies. These works are critical reference points for anyone conducting instructional technology. For his contributions to the advancement of research in IT, Mike also won the Lifetime Achievement Award for Research in Instructional Technology, awarded by the Research and Theory Division of AECT in 2003.

PROFESSIONAL ACTIVITIES

Mike began attending AECT in 1969 in Houston as a graduate student and has continued to participate in the association throughout his career. Also, he has been a very active member and supporter of the International Visual Literacy Association since its inception. He was interested in IVLA because of Paul Wendt, who had helped start the organization in Rochester, New York. Mike and his colleagues at Virginia Tech hosted the IVLA conference in Blacksburg, Virginia, in 1998, and he was elected president of the association in 1990. Mike continues to remain engaged in IVLA efforts and activities.

When Indiana University sold the Shawnee Bluffs resort in 1996, Mike was responsible for continuing the informal professional gathering known as the Professors of Instructional Design and Technology (PIDT). Virginia Tech began hosting PIDT at Smith Mountain Lake (Wirtz, VA) in 1998, with Mike at the helm. PIDT continues to be coordinated by Virginia Tech and Mike is still a regular attendee and contributor.

While Mike is known professionally for advancing the field of visual literacy, his true legacy lies in his extraordinary advisement of graduate students. During his career, he successfully graduated 38 doctoral candidates and countless master's students. Six of his graduates received awards for their doctoral research, including the 1992 Outstanding Professional Multimedia Award (Jeanne Gleason) and the AECT Young Researcher Award (Rob Branch). His tremendous efforts in preparing the future professoriate have been recognized at Virginia Tech, as Mike has received the College of Human Resources and Education's Excellence in Graduate Student Advising Award (2002) and the Alumni Award for Excellence in Graduate Academic Advising (2002). A significant cadre of his advisees currently serve as faculty in the field of instructional design and technology, nationally and internationally, working to continue the tradition of professional excellence established by their own mentor and graduate advisor.

Note: Many thanks to Mike for providing the conversations and documents to inform this chapter.

The author is a former graduate advisee and colleague of Dr. Moore in the Instructional Design and Technology Program at Virginia Tech (1993–2003).

Part Four
Organizations and Associations in North America

Introduction

Part four includes annotated entries for associations and organizations, most of which are headquartered in North America, whose interests are in some manner significant to the fields of instructional technology and educational media. For the most part, these organizations consist of professionals in the field or agencies that offer services to the educational media community. This year organizations that we haven't received updates from in over four years were omitted from our listings. Any readers are encouraged to contact the editors with names of unlisted media-related organizations for investigation and possible inclusion in the 2008 edition.

Information for this section was obtained through e-mail directing each organization to an individual Web form through which the updated information could be submitted electronically into a database created by Dr. Mike Orey. Although the section editors made every effort to contact and follow up with organization representatives, responding to the annual request for an update was the responsibility of the organization representatives. The editing team would like to thank those respondents who helped assure the currency and accuracy of this section by responding to the request for an update. So that readers can judge the accuracy of information provided by each entry, a "last updated" date has been provided. Figures quoted as dues refer to annual amounts unless stated otherwise. Where dues, membership, and meeting information is not applicable, such information is omitted.

Jamal Olusesi
Section Editor

Alphabetical List

Agency for Instructional Technology (AIT). Box A, Bloomington, IN 47402-0120, United States. (812)339-2203. Fax: (812)333-4218. E-mail: info@ait.net. Web site: http://www.ait.net. Charles E. Wilson, Executive Director. The Agency for Instructional Technology has been a leader in educational technology since 1962. A nonprofit organization, AIT is one of the largest providers of instructional TV programs in North America. AIT is also a leading developer of other educational media, including online instruction, CDs, videodiscs, and instructional software. AIT learning resources are used on six continents and reach nearly 34 million students in North America each year. AIT products have received many national and international honors, including an Emmy and Peabody award. Since 1970, AIT has developed 39 major curriculum packages through the consortium process it pioneered. American state and Canadian provincial agencies have cooperatively funded and widely used these learning resources. Funding for other product development comes from state, provincial, and local departments of education; federal and private institutions; corporations and private sponsors; and AIT's own resources. No regular public meetings. Updated: 4/21/2006. Cheri Harris charris@ait.net.

American Association of Community Colleges (AACC). One DuPont Circle, NW, Suite 410, Washington, DC 20036-1176, United States. (202)728-0200. Fax: (202)833-9390. E-mail: nkent@aacc.nche.edu. Web site: http://www.aacc.nche.edu. George R. Boggs, President and CEO. AACC is a national organization representing the nation's more than 1,100 community, junior, and technical colleges. Headquartered in Washington, DC, AACC serves as a national voice for the colleges and provides key services in the areas of advocacy, research, information, and professional development. The nation's community colleges serve more than 10 million students annually, almost half (44%) of all U.S. undergraduates. Memberships: 1,151 institutions, 31 corporations, 15 international associates, 79 educational associates, 4 foundations. Vary by category. Annual Convention, April of each year; 2003: April 5–8, Dallas, Texas. Publications: *Community College Journal* (bimonthly); *Community College Times* (biweekly newspaper); *College Times*; *Community College Press* (books, research and program briefs, and monographs). Updated: 7/7/04. Mary Latif, Director of Administrative Services.

American Association of School Librarians (AASL). 50 E. Huron St., Chicago, IL 60611-2795, United States. (312)280-4386, (800)545-2433, ext. 4386. Fax: (312)664-7459. E-mail: aasl@ala.org. Web site: http://www.ala.org/aasl. Julie A. Walker, Exec. Dir. A division of the American Library Association, AASL is interested in the general improvement and extension of school library media services for children and youth. Activities and projects of the association are divided among 30 committees and 3 sections. Membership: 9,500. Personal membership in ALA (1st yr., $50; 2nd yr., $75; 3rd and subsequent yrs., $100) plus $40 for personal membership in AASL. Inactive, student, retired, unemployed, and reduced-salary memberships are available. Meetings: National conference every two years; next national conference to be held in 2003. Publications: *School Library Media Research* (electronic research journal, http://www.ala.org/aasl/SLMR/), *Knowledge Quest* (print journal; online companion at http://www.ala.org/aasl/kqweb/), *AASL Hotlinks* (e-mail newsletter), Nonserial publications (http://www.ala.org/aasl/pubs_menu.html). Updated: 2/27/03. Robin Ely, rely@ala.org, 312-280-4382.

American Educational Research Association (AERA). 1230 17th St. NW, Washington, DC 20036-3078, United States. (202)223-9485. Fax: (202)775-1824. E-mail: outreach@aera.net. Web site: http://www.aera.net. Marilyn Cochran-Smith, President of the Board, 2004–2005, cochrans@bc.edu. AERA is an international professional organization with the primary goal of advancing educational research and its practical application. Its members include educators and administrators; directors of research, testing, or evaluation in federal, state, and local agencies; counselors; evaluators; graduate students; and behavioral scientists. The broad range of disciplines represented includes education, psychology, statistics, sociology, history, economics, philosophy, anthropology, and political science. AERA has more than 145 Special Interest Groups, including Advanced Technologies for Learning, Computer Applications in Education, Electronic Networking, Instructional Systems and Intelligent Tutors, Instructional Technology, and Text, Technology, and Learning Strategies. Mebbership: 23,000, charges vary by category, ranging from $20 for students to $45 for voting members, for one year. See AERA Web site for complete details: www.aera.net. Meetings: 2005 Annual Meeting, April 11–15, Montreal, Canada. Publications: *Educational Researcher*; *American Educational Research Journal*; *Journal of Educational and Behavioral Statistics*; *Educational Evaluation and Policy Analysis*; *Review of Research in Education*; *Review of Educational Research*. Books: *Handbook of Research on Teaching*, 2001. (revised, 4th edition) *Ethical Standards of AERA, Cases and Commentary*, 2002; *Standards for Educational and Psychological Testing* (resived and expanded, 1999). Copublished by AERA, American Psychological Association, and the National Council on Measurement in Education. Updated: 7/7/04. Marilyn Cochran-Smith, cochrans@bc.edu.

American Foundation for the Blind (AFB). 11 Penn Plaza, Suite 300, New York, NY 10001, United States. (212)502-7600, (800)AFB-LINE (232-5463), (212)502-7777. E-mail: afbinfo@afb.net. Web site: http://www.afb.org. Carl R. Augusto, Pres.; Kelly Parisi, Vice Pres. of Communications. AFB is a national nonprofit that expands possibilities for people with vision loss. AFB's priorities include broadening access to technology; elevating the quality of information and tools for the professionals who serve people with vision loss; and promoting independent and healthy living for people with vision loss by providing them and their families with relevant and timely resources. In addition, AFB's Web site serves as a gateway to a wealth of vision loss information and services. AFB is also proud to house the Helen Keller Archives and honor the over forty years that Helen Keller worked tirelessly with AFB. For more information visit us online at www.afb.org., Publications: *AFB News* (free); *Journal of Visual Impairment & Blindness*; *AFB Press Catalog of Publications* (free) *AccessWorld*™. Subscriptions. Tel: (800) 232-3044 or (412) 741-1398.

American Library Association (ALA). 50 E. Huron St., Chicago, IL 60611, United States. (800) 545-2433. Fax: (312) 440-9374. E-mail: ala@ala.org. Web site: http://www.ala.org. Keith Michael Fiels, Exec. Dir. The ALA is the oldest and largest national library association. Its 68,000 members represent all types of libraries: state, public, school, and academic, as well as special libraries serving persons in government, commerce, the armed services, hospitals, prisons, and other institutions. The ALA is the chief advocate of achievement and maintenance of high-quality library information services through protection of the right to read, educating librarians, improving services, and making information widely accessible. See separate entries for the following affiliated and subordinate organizations: American Association of School Librarians, American Library Trustee Association, Association for Library Collections and Technical Services, Association for Library Service to Children, Association of College and Research Libraries, Association of Specialized and Cooperative Library Agencies, Library Administration and Management Association, Library and Information Technology Association, Public Library Association, Reference and User Services Association, Young Adult Library Services Association, and Continuing Library Education Network and Exchange Round Table. Membership: 68,000 members at present; everyone who cares about libraries is allowed to join the American Library Association. Professional rate: $50, first year; $75, second year; third year & renewing: $100, Library Support Staff: $35, Student members: $25, Retirees: $35 International librarians: $50, first year;

$60, second year, Trustees: $45 Associate members (those not in the library field): $45. Meetings: Annual Conference: June 22–28, 2006, New Orleans, LA; June 21–27, 2007, Washington, DC; Midwinter Meeting: January 19–24, 2007, Seattle, WA; January 25–30, 2008, Philadelphia, PA. Publications: *American Libraries*; *Booklist*; *Choice*; *Book Links*. Updated: 4/21/2006. Karen Muller; library@ala.org.

American Montessori Society (AMS). 281 Park Ave. S, New York, NY 10010, United States. (212)358-1250. Fax: (212)358-1256. E-mail: mimi@amshq.org. Web site: http://www.amshq.org. Eileen Roper Ast, Executive Director. Dedicated to promoting better education for all children through teaching strategies consistent with the Montessori system. Membership is composed of schools in the private and public sectors, teacher education programs, Montessori credentialed teachers, parents and other individuals. It serves as a resource center and clearinghouse for information and data on Montessori education, prepares teachers in different parts of the country, and conducts a consultation service and accreditation program for school members. The mission of the AMS is to promote high quality Montessori education for all children by providing service to parents, teachers and schools. Membership includes schools, teachers, parents, school heads, and friends of Montessori. This total is approximately 11,000. Dues vary based on membership. Membership is available for Certified Montessori Teachers, Montessori School and General Members (includes those who are not Certified Montessori Teachers, parents, friends of AMS). Three regional and four professional development symposia under the auspices of the AMS Teachers' Section. Meetings: 42nd Annual Conference, Apr 25–28, 2002, Crystal City, VA; Regional Conferences, August 11–13,2001, Breckenridge, CO; October 19–21, Atlanta. Publications: *AMS Montessori LIFE* (quarterly); *Schoolheads* (newsletter); *Montessori in Contemporary American Culture*, Margaret Loeffler, Editor; *Authentic American Montessori School*; *AMS The Montessori School Management Guide*; AMS position papers; and the following AMS Publications: *Montessori Teaching A Growth Profession*; *The Elemenary School Years 6-12*; *Your Child Is In An Accredited School*; *Some Considerations in Starting a Montessori School*; *Montessori Education Q&A*; *The Early Childhood Years, 3-6*; *Attracting and Preparing Montessori Teacher for the 21st Century*; *Adolescent Programs*; *The Kindergarten Experience*; *Some Comparisons of Montessori Education with Traditional Education*; *Helping Children Become All They Can Become*; *The Montessori Family: A Parent Brochure*; *Tuition and Salary Surveys*. Updated: 5/13/03. Carol Monroe, Dir.Fin & Admin, 212-358-1250, Ext. 203.

American Society for Training and Development (ASTD). 1640 King St., Box 1443, Alexandria, VA 22313, United States. (703)683-8100. Fax: (703)683-1523. E-mail: customercare@astd.org. Web site: http://www.astd.org. Tony Bingham, President and CEO. Founded in 1944, ASTD is the worlds premiere professional association in the field of workplace learning and performance. ASTDs membership includes more than 70,000 people in organizations from every level of the field of workplace performance in more than 100 countries. Its leadership and members work in more than 15,000 multinational corporations, small and medium-sized businesses, government agencies, colleges, and universities. ASTD is the leading resource on workplace learning and performance issues, providing information, research, analysis, and practical information derived from its own research, the knowledge and experience of its members, its conferences and publications, and the coalitions and partnerships it has built through research and policy work. ASTD has a board membership of 16 and staff of 90 to serve member needs. 70,000 National and Chapter members. The Classic Membership ($150.00) is the foundation of ASTD member benefits. Publications, newsletters, research reports, discounts and services and much more, are all designed to help you do your job better. Here is what you have to look forward to when you join: Training and Development—Monthly publication of the Industry. Stay informed on Trends, successful practices, public policy, ASTD news, case studies and more.

Performance in Practice—Quarterly newsletter offers articles written by members for members. *Hot Topics*—ASTDs online reading list gets you up to speed on leading edge issues in the training and performance industry. Database and Archive Access—FREE online access to Trainlit, ASTDs searchable database featuring products reviews, book and article summaries and archived articles. *Learning Circuits*—Monthly Webzine features articles, departments and columns that examine new technologies and how they're being applied to workplace learning. *Human Resource\ Development Quarterly*— in-depth studies and reports on human resource theory and practice give you a scholarly look at the training profession. HRDQ is available ONLY online with archives dating back to 1998. *ASTD News Briefs*—weekly news briefs relating to the training and performance industry. Special Reports and Research—*Trends Report, State of the Industry, Learning Outcomes and International Comparison Report. Training Data Book*—an annual publication, now online, draws on ASTD research and highlights the nature and magnitude of corporate investment in employer-provided training. Research Assistance—ASTD provides an Information Center that can provide you with the research you're looking for while you're on the phone. You can also send you research request through the Web site. Just provide your member number! Membership Directory—online directory and searchable by a variety of criteria. Access to the Membership Directory is for Members Only, and is being enhanced for future networking capabilities. Buyers Guide & Consultants Directory—a one-stop resource for information on over 600 suppliers of training and performance products and services. We also have several segments that you can add on to your Classic Membership: Membership Plus : Your choice of 12 info lines or four prechosen ASTD books $79.00. Training Professionals : Includes an annual subscription to *Info-lines, Pfeiffers Best of Training* and the *ASTD Training and Performance Yearbook.*

$130.00. Organizational Development/Leadership Professionals : Includes *Pfeiffers Consulting Annual, Leader to Leader* and *Leadership in Action* $200.00 Consulting : Includes annual subscription to *C2M* (quarterly journal), and *Pfeiffers Consulting Annual.* $75.00 E-Learning: Includes *Training Media Review Online* (Database and newsletter that evaluates audio,video,software, and online products 6/year e-mail newsletters yr.) and *ASTD Distance Learning Yearbook.* $175.00. *Training & Development Magazine; Info-Line; The American Mosaic: An In-depth Report of Diversity on the Future of Diversity at Work; ASTD Directory of Academic Programs in T&D/HRD; Training and Development Handbook;* Quarterly publications: *Performance in Practice; National Report on Human Resources; Washington Policy Report.* ASTD also has recognized professional forums, most of which produce newsletters. Meetings: International Conference 2002, New Orleans, Louisiana, May 31–June 6: International Conference 2003, San Diego, CA, May 17–22. Updated: 7/7/04. CustomerCare@astd.org, 703.683.8100.

American Society of Educators (ASE). 1429 Walnut St., Philadelphia, PA 19102, United States. (215)563-6005. Fax: (215)587-9706. E-mail: tatjana@media-methods.com. Web site: http://www.media-methods.com. Michele Sokolof, Publisher & Editorial Director. American Society of Educators publishes *Media & Methods* magazine, the recognized authoritative publication dedicated to exemplary teaching practices and resource materials for K-12 educators. Full of pragmatic articles on how to use todays instructional technologies and teaching tools, *Media & Methods* is the flagship magazine of practical educational applications specifically for school district technology coordinators, media specialists, school librarians, administrators and teachers. A long-respected and treasured magazine focusing on how to integrate todays tools for teaching as well as for administrative and library management in K-12 schools. Individuals subscribe to *Media & Methods* magazine. Meetings occur at national education conferences. Media & Methods magazine is published 7 times a year. Cost: $33.50 per year. Updated: 7/7/04. Tatjana Miloradovic, tatjana@media-methods.com.

American Women in Radio and Television (AWRT). 8405 Greensboro Drive, Suite 800, McLean, VA 22102, United States (703)506-3290. Fax: (703)506-3266. E-mail: info@awrt.org. Web site: www.awrt.org. Maria E. Brennan. American Women in Radio and Television is a national, nonprofit organization that extends membership to qualified professionals in the electronic media and allied fields. AWRT's mission is to advance the impact of women in the electronic media and allied fields by educating, advocating, and acting as a resource to its members and the industry. Founded in 1951, AWRT has worked to improve the quality of broadcast programming and the image of women as depicted in radio and television. 40 chapters. Membership: Student memberships available.$125. Annual Leadership Summit, Annual Gracie Allen Awards. Publications: *News and Views*; *Resource Directory*; *Careers in the Electronic Media*; *Sexual Harassment*; Mentoring Brochure (pamphlet). Updated: 5/19/03. info@awrt.org.

Anthropology Film Center (AFC). #5 Paseo Sin Nombre, Valencia, NM 87535-9635, United States (505)757-2219. E-mail: info@anthrofilm.org. Web site: http://www. anthrofilm.org. Carroll Williams, Dir. Offers the Ethnographic/Documentary Film Program, a 32-week full-time course for 16mm film, CD and DVD production and theory. Workshops are offered as well. AFC also provides consultation, research facilities, and a specialized library. Workshops in Visual Anthropology are offered. September and June starts. Mailing address is HC70 Box 3209, Glorieta, NM 87535-9635. We have no memberships. No dues. –No annual meeting scheduled further until 2005. A filmography for American Indian Education. Updated: 3/6/04. Carroll Warner Williams, 505-757-2219.

AEL, Inc. (AEL). P.O. Box 1348-Charleston, WV 25325-1348, United States. (304)347-0400, (800)624-9120. Fax: (304)347-0487. E-mail: aelinfo@ael.org. Web site: http://www.ael.org. Dr. Doris L. Redfield, President and CEO. AEL is a catalyst for schools and communities to build lifelong learning systems that harness resources, research, and practical wisdom. To contribute knowledge that assists low-performing schools to move toward continuous improvement, AEL conducts research, development, evaluation, and dissemination activities that inform policy, affect educational practice, and contribute to the theoretical and procedural knowledge bases on effective teaching, learning, and schooling. Strategies build on research and reflect a commitment to empowering individuals and building local capacity. AEL serves Kentucky, Tennessee, Virginia, and West Virginia. The AEL Electronic Library contains links to free online tools and information created by staff on a wide array of education-related topics. In addition there are the online versions of AELs newsletters. *The Link* is a free quarterly publication that provides helpful information to practitioners about trends in education, while *Transformation* is written for those interested in policy related to education. Updated: 4/27/04. Carla McClure, mcclurec@ael.org, 800-614-9120.

Association for Childhood Education International (ACEI). 17904 Georgia Ave., Suite 215, Olney, MD 20832, United States (301)570-2111. Fax: (301)570-2212. E-mail: ACEIHQ@aol.com. Web site: http://www.udel.edu/bateman/acei/. Anne W. Bauer, Ed. and Dir. ACEI publications reflect careful research, broad-based views, and consideration of a wide range of issues affecting children from infancy through early adolescence. Many are media-related in nature. The journal (*Childhood Education*) is essential for teachers, teachers-in-training, teacher educators, day care workers, administrators, and parents. Articles focus on child development and emphasize practical application. Regular departments include book reviews (child and adult); film reviews, pamphlets, software, research, and classroom idea-sparkers. Six issues are published yearly, including a theme issue devoted to critical concerns. Membership: 12,000. $45, professional; $26, student; $23, retired; $80, institutional. Meetings: 1999 Annual International Conference and Exhibition, Apr 7–11, San Antonio; 2000, Baltimore. Publications: *Childhood Education* (official journal) with *ACEI Exchange* (insert newsletter); *Journal of Research in Childhood Education*; professional division newsletters (*Focus on Infants and Toddlers, Focus on Pre-K and K, Focus on Elementary, and Focus on Middle School*); *Celebrating Family Literacy Through Intergenerational Programming*; *Selecting Educational Equipment for School and Home*; *Developmental Continuity Across Preschool and Primary Grades*; *Implications for Teachers*; *Developmentally Appropriate Middle Level Schools*; *Common Bonds: Antibias Teaching in a Diverse Society*; *Childhood 1892–1992*; *Infants and Toddlers with Special Needs and Their Families* (position paper); and pamphlets. Updated: 6/6/03. Marilyn Gardner, Director of IT, Membership & Mark.

Association for Computers and the Humanities (ACH)-[Address]-[City]-ON-[Zip Code]- [Country]-[phone number-[fax number]. E-mail: ach@digitalhumanities.org. Web site: http://www.ach.org/. Executive Secretary, ACH. ACH is an international professional organization. Since its establishment, it has been the major professional society for people working in computer-aided research in literature and language studies, history, philosophy, and other humanities disciplines, and especially research involving the manipulation and analysis of textual materials. The ACH is devoted to disseminating information among its members about work in the field of humanities computing, as well as encouraging the development and dissemination of significant textual and linguistic resources and software for scholarly research. Membership: 300. Individual regular member, US $65 Student or Emeritus Faculty member, US $55 Joint membership (for couples), Add US $7. Meetings: Annual meetings held with the Association for Literary and Linguistic Computing. ACH Publications: *Literary & Linguistic Computing*; *Humanist*. Updated: 3/14/2006. Executive Secretary, ach@digitalhumanities.org.

Association for Continuing Higher Education (ACHE). Trident Technical College, P.O. Box 118067, CE-M-Charleston, SC 29423-8067, United States (803)574-6658. Fax: (803)574-6470. E-mail: irene.barrineau@tridenttech.edu. Web site: http://www.acheinc. org/. Dr. Jerry Hickerson, President, Dr. Pamela R.Murray, President Elect. ACHE is an institution-based organization of colleges, universities, and individuals dedicated to the promotion of lifelong learning and excellence in continuing higher education. ACHE encourages professional networks, research, and exchange of information for its members and advocates continuing higher education as a means of enhancing and improving society. Membership: 1,622 individuals in 674 institutions. $60, professional; $240, institutional. Meetings: For a list of Annual and Regional Meetings, see http://www.acheinc.org/ calendar_of_events.html. Publications: *Journal of Continuing Higher Education* (3/yr.); *Five Minutes with ACHE* (newsletter, 10/yr.); *Proceedings* (annual). Updated: 4/26/04. Irene Barrineau.

Association for Educational Communications and Technology (AECT). 1800 N Stonelake Dr., Suite 2, Bloomington, IN 47404, United States. (812) 335-7675. Fax: (812) 335-7678. E-mail: aect@aect.org. Web site: http://www.aect.org. Phillip Harris, Executive Director; Ward Cates, Board President. AECT is an international professional association concerned with the improvement of learning and instruction through media and technology. It serves as a central clearinghouse and communications center for its members, who include instructional technologists, library media specialists, religious educators, government media personnel, school administrators and specialists, and training media producers. AECT members also work in the armed forces, public libraries, museums, and other information agencies of many different kinds, including those related to the emerging fields of computer technology. Affiliated organizations include the International Visual Literacy Association (IVLA), Minorities in Media (MIM), New England Educational Media Association (NEEMA), SICET (the Society of International Chinese in Educational Technology), and KSET (the Korean Society for Educational Technology). The ECT Foundation is also related to AECT. Each of these affiliated organizations has its own listing in the Yearbook. AECT Divisions include: Instructional Design & Development, Information & Technology Management, Training & Performance, Research & Theory, Systemic Change, Distance Learning, Media & Technology, Teacher Education, and International, and Multimedia Productions. Membership: 2500 members in good standing from K-12, college and university and private sector/government training. Anyone interested can join. There are different memberships available for students, retirees, corporations and international parties. We also have a new option for electronic membership for international affiliates. $99.00 standard membership discounts are available for students and retirees. Additional fees apply to corporate memberships or international memberships. Meetings: Summer Leadership Institute held each July. In 2007 it will be in Chicago, IL. AECT holds an annual Conference each year in October. In 2007, it will be held in Anaheim, CA. Publications: *TechTrends* (6/yr., free with AECT membership; available by subscription through Springer at www.springeronline.com); *Educational Technology Research and Development* (6/yr. $46 members; available by subscription through Springer at www.springeronline.com); *Quarterly Review of Distance Education* (quarterly, $55 to AECT members); many books; videotapes. Updated: 4/4/2007. Phillip Harris by e-mail at pharris@aect.org

(AECT) Division of School Media and Technology (DSMT). 1800 N. Stonelake Dr., Suite #2, Bloomington, IN 47404, United States. (812) 335-7675. Fax: (812) 335-7678. E-mail: aect@aect.org. Web site: http://www.aect.org/Divisions/mt.asp and http://www.coe.ecu. edu/aect/dsmt/Default.htm. Lois Wilkins, Pres., lwilkins@tapnet.net, and Nancy Reicher, Sec., nreichkc@pei.edu. The School Media and Technology (K-12) Division provides leadership in educational communications and technology by linking professionals holding a common interest in the use of instructional technology and its applicaton to the learning process in the school environment. This division of AECT is of special interest to School Library Media Specialists and others who work with technology in a K-12 environment. Membership: One division membership included in the basic AECT membership which is $95 for regular status and $130 for comprehensive status; additional division memberships $10. Meetings: DSMT meets in conjunction with the annual AECT National Convention. Publication: DSMT Update is now published in electronic format. The Update editors are Mary Alice Anderson and Mary Ann Fitzgerald. Please direct all content questions and comments to them. E-mail to: mfitzger@coe.uga.edu or maryalic@wms.luminet.net. In addition, *TechTrends* is published 6 times annually. Updated: 6/9/03. Phillip Harris, pharris@aect.org.

(AECT) Division of Design and Development (D&D). 1800 N. Stonelake Dr., Suite 2, Bloomington, IN 47408, United States. +1 315 443 1362. Fax: +1 315 443 1218. E-mail: martindalee@mail.ecu.edu. Web site: http://reusability.org/blogs/dd/. Trey Martindale, President. D&D is composed of individuals from business, government, and academic settings concerned with the systematic design of instruction and the development of solutions to performance problems. Members interests include the study, evaluation, and refinement of design processes; the creation of new models of instructional development; the invention and improvement of techniques for managing the development of instruction; the development and application of professional ID competencies; the promotion of academic programs for preparation of ID professionals; and the dissemination of research and development work in ID. Membership: Approximately 750—membership is open to any AECT member. Division membership can be indicated when joining or renewing AECT membership or any time thereafter and has no additional cost associated. Meetings: held in conjunction with the annual AECT Convention. Publications: D&D listserv with an occasional D&D newsletter and papers; members regularly contribute to and read *Educational Technology Research & Development* and *TechTrends*. Division news can be found at: http://reusability.org/blogs/dd/. Updated: 5/15/04. Trey Martindale martindalee@mail.ecu.edu.

(AECT) Division of Learning and Performance Environments (DLPE). 1025 Vermont Ave. NW, Suite 820, Washington, DC 20005, United States. (202)347-7834. Fax: (928) 523-7624. E-mail: sschaff@purdue.edu. Web site: http://www.aect.org/T&P/index.htm. Scott Schaffer, President; Pam Loughner, President-Elect. DLPE supports human learning and performance through the use of computer-based technology; design, development, evaluation, assessment, and implementation of learning environments and performance systems for adults. A Division of AECT. See www.aect.org for membership information. Membership: One division membership included in the basic AECT membership; additional division memberships $10. Meetings: Held in conjunction with the annual AECT Convention. Publication: *TechTrends* in coordination with AECT. Updated: 5/22/03.

(AECT) School Media and Technology Division (SMT). 1800 N. Stonelake Dr., Suite 2, Bloomington, IN 47408, United States. 877-677-AECT. Fax: (912) 267.4234. E-mail: susan.stansberry@oksate.edu. Web site: http://www.aect-members.org/smt/. Dr. Susan Stansberry, President; Dr. Bruce Spitzer, President-elect; Mary Beth Jordan, Board representative; Heidi Blair, Secretary. The School Media and Technology (K-12) Division provides leadership in educational communications and technology by linking professionals holding a common interest in the use of instructional technology and its application to the learning process in the school environment. Members of this division are primarily School Library Media Specialists, Instructional Technology Coordinators in K-12 school districts, and Higher Ed faculty preparing educators to serve as School Library Media Specialist or Technology Coordinators. Membership: Division membership included in the basic AECT membership. Meetings: Held in conjunction with the annual AECT Convention. Publications: *Information Power* is a landmark guide to promoting student achievement through collaborative partnerships within the learning community. Information Literacy Standards for Student Learning is a major component in developing information literate, socially responsible independent learners. *Information Power* was developed by a committee of instructional, technology and information science experts of the American Association of School Librarians (AASL) and the Association for Educational Communications and Technology (AECT). *Information Power* serves as a model for collaborative planning between classroom teachers and library media specialists, teachers and students, library media specialists and students, parents and students with other individuals within the broader learning community. All library media specialists are heartily encouraged to introduce and incorporate the guidelines and activities of *Information Power* within their local schools and learning communities. To access more information and to purchase your copy of *Information Power* and the companion Information Literacy Standards for Student Learning, please visit The AECT Online Bookstore at http://www.aect.org/store/default.asp. To read more about *Information Power*, go to http://www.ala.org/ala/aasl/aaslpubsandjournals/informationpowerbook/informationpowerbooks.htm. For an on-line list of resources from ALA related to *Information Power*, go to http://www.ala.org/ala/aasl/aaslproftools/informationpower/informationpower.htm. For a video series based upon Information Literacy Standards, go to www.gpn.unl.edu. Updated: 4/22/2006. Susan Stansberry, susan.stansberry@okstate.edu.

AECT Training & Performance (T&P). 1800 North Stonelake Drive, Suite 2, Bloomington, IN 47408, United States. (812) 335-7675. Fax: (812) 335-7678. E-mail: sschaff@purdue.edu. Web site: http://www.aect.org/T&P/. Scott Schaffer, President; Pam Loughner, President-Elect; Sheila Christy, Past-President; Nada Dabbagh, Board Representative; Cynthia Conn, VP-Communications; Jim Ellsworth, Brice Jewell, and Angela Benson, Members-at-Large. AECT's Training & Performance (T&P) Division serves members from government, business and industry, and academic communities. Its members are training, performance, and education professionals interested in applying current theory and research to training and performance improvement initiatives. Topics of interest to T&P Division members are real-world solutions that intersect the use of hard technologies

(e.g., computers, the Internet), soft technologies (e.g., instructional design and performance technology processes and models), and current learning and instructional theories
(e.g., Constructivism, Problem-based learning). The Training & Performance Division resulted from the 2000 merger of the former Industrial Training and Education Division
(ITED) and the Division for Learning and Performance Environments (DLPE). If you're a
training, performance, or education professional who values the application of theory and
research to practice, join Association for Educational Communications and Technology
(http://www.aect.org/Membership/) and be sure to specify Training & Performance as one
of the divisions you'd like to join. Training & Performance Division membership is free
with your AECT membership. Meetings are held in conjunction with the annual AECT
Conference. Updated: 5/29/03. Cynthia Conn, Cynthia.Conn@nau.edu, 928-523-7624.

(AECT) Research and Theory Division (RTD). 1800 N. Stonelake Dr., Suite 2, Bloomington, IN 47404, United States. 812-335-7675. Fax: 812-335-7678. E-mail: aect@aect.org.
Web site: www.aect.org. Phil Harris, AECT Executive Director. Seeks to improve the design,
execution, utilization, and evaluation of educational technology research; to improve the
qualifications and effectiveness of personnel engaged in educational technology research;
to advise the educational practitioner as to the use of the research results; to improve
research design, techniques, evaluation, and dissemination; to promote both applied and
theoretical research on the systematic use of educational technology in the improvement of
instruction; and to encourage the use of multiple research paradigms in examining issues
related to technology in education. Membership: 452. One division membership included
in the basic AECT membership; additional division memberships $10. Meetings: held in
conjunction with annual AECT Convention. Publication: Newsletter. Updated: 2/27/03.
Phil Harris, aect@aect.org.

(AECT) Systemic Change in Education Division (CHANGE). 1800 N. Stonelake Dr.,
Suite 2, Bloomington, IN 47408, United States. 877-677-AECT. Fax: 812-335-7675. E-
mail: frick@indiana.edu. Web site: http://ide.ed.psu.edu/change/. Roberto Joseph, President. CHANGE advocates fundamental changes in educational settings to dramatically improve the quality of education and to enable technology to achieve its potential. Members
of the Association for Educational Communications and Technology (AECT) are welcome
to join the CHANGE Division. In March, 2004, there are approximately 2,500 members
of AECT and of those about 150 are members of CHANGE. Membership in AECT (the
Association for Educational Communications and Technology) is required. Once an AECT
member, one can join the CHANGE Division at no extra cost. Meetings: held in conjunction
with annual AECT Convention. See the Web site: http://ide.ed.psu.edu/change/. Updated:
3/5/04. Theodore W. Frick (frick@indiana.edu).

AECT Archives (AECT).   University of Maryland, Hornbake Library, College Park,
MD 20742, United States. (301)405-9255. Fax: (301)314-2634. E-mail: tc65@umail.umd.
edu. Web site: http://www.library.umd.edu/UMCP/NPBA/npba.html. Thomas Connors,
Archivist, National Public Broadcasting Archives. A collection of media, manuscripts,
and related materials representing important developments in visual and audiovisual education and in instructional technology. The collection is housed as part of the National
Public Broadcasting Archives. Maintained by the University of Maryland in cooperation with AECT. Open to researchers and scholars. Updated: 2/27/03. Tom Connors,
tc65@umail.umd.edu.

Association for Experiential Education (AEE). 3775 Iris Avenue, Ste 4, Boulder, CO
80301-2043, United States. (303)440-8844. Fax: (303)440-9581. E-mail: info@aee.org.
Web site: http://www.aee.org. Patricia Hammond, Executive Director. AEE is a nonprofit,
international, professional organization committed to the development, practice, and evaluation of experiential education in all settings. AEE's vision is to be a leading international

organization for the development and application of experiential education principles and methodologies with the intent to create a just and compassionate world by transforming education. Membership: Nearly 1,500 members in over 30 countries including individuals and organizations with affiliations in education, recreation, outdoor adventure programming, mental health, youth service, physical education, management development training, corrections, programming for people with disabilities, and environmental education.-$55–$115, individual; $145, family; $275–$500, organizational. Meetings: AEE Annual Conference in November. Regional Conferences in the Spring. Publications: *The Journal of Experiential Education* (3/yr.); *Experience and the Curriculum*; *Adventure Education*; *Adventure Therapy*; *Therapeutic Applications of Adventure Programming*; *Manual of Accreditation Standards for Adventure Programs*; *The Theory of Experiential Education*, Third Edition; *Experiential Learning in Schools and Higher Education*; *Ethical Issues in Experiential Education*, Second Edition; *The K.E.Y. (Keep Exploring Yourself) Group: An Experiential Personal Growth Group Manual*; *Book of Metaphors*, Volume II; *Women's Voices in Experiential Education*; bibliographies, directories of programs, and membership directory. New publications since last year: *Exploring the Boundaries of Adventure Therapy*; *A Guide to Women's Studies in the Outdoors*; *Administrative Practices of Accredited Adventure Programs*; *Fundamentals of Experience-Based Training*; *Wild Adventures: A Guidebook of Activities for Building Connections with Others and the Earth*; *Truth Zone: An Experimental Approach to Organizational Development*; *Exploring the Power of Solo, Silence, and Solitude.* Updated: 4/21/2006. Patricia Hammond, executive@aee. org.

Association for Library and Information Science Education (ALISE). 11250 Roger Bacon Drive, Suite 8, Reston, VA 20190-5202, United States. 703-234-4146. Fax: 703-435-4390. E-mail: alise@drohanmgmt.com. Web site: http://www.alise.org. Louise Robbins, Professor and Director. Seeks to advance education for library and information science and produces annual Library and Information Science Education Statistical Report. Open to professional schools offering graduate programs in library and information science; personal memberships open to educators employed in such institutions; other memberships available to interested individuals. Membership: 500 individuals, 73 institutions. Institutional, sliding scale, $325–600; $200 associate; $125 international; personal, $90 full-time; $50 part-time, $40 student, $50 retired. Meetings: 1999, Jan 26–29, Philadelphia; 2000, Jan 11–14, San Antonio; 2001, Jan 9–12, Washington, DC. Publications: *Journal of Education for Library and Information Science*; *ALISE Directory and Handbook*; *Library and Information Science Education Statistical Report.* Updated: 5/21/03.

Association for Library Collections & Technical Services (ALCTS). 50 E. Huron St., Chicago, IL 60611, United States. (312)280-5038. Fax: (312)280-5033. E-mail: alcts@ala.org. Web site: www.ala.org/alcts. Charles Wilt, Executive Director; Bruce Johnson, President (2006–2007); Rosann Bazirjian, Past President (2006–2007). A division of the American Library Association, ALCTS is dedicated to acquisition, identification, cataloging, classification, and preservation of library materials; the development and coordination of the country's library resources; and aspects of selection and evaluation involved in acquiring and developing library materials and resources. Sections include Acquisitions, Cataloging and Classification, Collection Management and Development, Preservation and Reformatting, and Serials. Membership: 4,800. Membership is open to anyone who has an interest in areas covered by ALCTS.-$55 plus membership in ALA. Meetings: ALA Annual Conference; Washington, DC, June 21–27, 2007, Anaheim, June 26-July 2, 2008; Chicago, July 9–15, 2009: ALA Midwinter Meeting; Seattle, January 19–24, 2007; Philadelphia, January 11–18, 2008, Denver, January 23–28, 2009. Publications: *Library Resources & Technical Services* (quarterly); *ALCTS Newsletter Online* (6/yr.). Updated: 4/21/2006. Charles Wilt, cwilt@ala.org, phone: 312-280-5030.

Association for Library Service to Children (ALSC).   50 E. Huron St., Chicago, IL 60611, United States. (312)280-2163. Fax: (312)944-7671. E-mail: alsc@ala.org. Web site: http://www.ala.org/alsc. Malore I. Brown. ALSC: Who We Are. The Association for Library Service to Children develops and supports the profession of children's librarianship by enabling and encouraging its practitioners to provide the best library service to our nations children. The Association for Library Service to Children is interested in the improvement and extension of library services to children in all types of libraries. It is responsible for the evaluation and selection of book and nonbook library materials and for the improvement of techniques of library service to children from preschool through the eighth grade or junior high school age, when such materials and techniques are intended for use in more than one type of library. Committee membership is open to ALSC members. Membership: 3,600. $45 plus membership in ALA. Meetings: Annual Conference and Midwinter Meeting with ALA National Institutes, next is October 2002, site to be announced. Publications: *Children and Libraries: The Journal of the Association for Library Service to Children* (3x per year); *ALSConnect* (quarterly newsletter). Updated: 3/4/04. Laura Schulte-Cooper, 312-280-2165 or lschulte@ala.

Association of American Publishers (AAP). 50 F Street, NW, Suite 400, Washington, DC 20001, United States. (202)347-3375. Fax: (202)347-3690. E-mail: kblough@publishers. org. Web site: http://www.publishers.org. Patricia S. Schroeder, Pres. and CEO (DC); Judith Platt, Dir. of Communications/Public Affairs. The Association of American Publishers is the national trade association of the U.S. book publishing industry. AAP was created in 1970 through the merger of the American Book Publishers Council, a trade publishing group, and the American Textbook Publishers Institute, a group of educational publishers. AAPs approximately 300 members include most of the major commercial book publishers in the United States, as well as smaller and nonprofit publishers, university presses, and scholarly societies. AAP members publish hardcover and paperback books in every field and a range of educational materials for the elementary, secondary, postsecondary, and professional markets. Members of the Association also produce computer software and electronic products and services, such as online databases and CD-ROMs. AAPs primary concerns are the protection of intellectual property rights in all media, the defense of free expression and freedom to publish at home and abroad, the management of new technologies, development of education markets and funding for instructional materials, and the development of national and global markets for its members' products. Membership: Regular Membership in the Association is open to all U.S. companies actively engaged in the publication of books, journals, loose leaf services, computer software, audiovisual materials, databases and other electronic products such as CD-ROM and CD-I, and similar products for educational, business, and personal use. This includes producers, packagers, and co-publishers who coordinate or manage most of the publishing process involved in creating copyrightable educational materials for distribution by another organization. "Actively engaged" means that the candidate must give evidence of conducting an ongoing publishing business with a significant investment in it. Each Regular Member firm has one vote, which is cast by an official representative or alternate designated by the member company. Associate Membership (nonvoting) is available to U.S. not-for-profit organizations that otherwise meet the qualifications for regular membership. A special category of associate membership is open to nonprofit university presses. Affiliate Membership is a nonvoting membership open to paper manufacturers, suppliers, consultants, and other nonpublishers directly involved in the industry. Dues are assessed on the basis of annual sales revenue from the print and electronic products listed above (under Regular Membership), but not from services or equipment. To maintain confidentiality, data is reported to an independent agent. Meetings: Annual Meeting (February), Small and Independent Publishers Meeting (February), School Division Annual Meeting (January), PSP Annual Meeting (February).

Publications: *AAP Monthly Report*. Updated: 7/7/04. K.Blough, kblough@publishers.org, 212/255-0200 ex.

Association of College and Research Libraries (ACRL). 50 E. Huron St., Chicago, IL 60611-2795, United Sates. (312)280-2523. Fax: (312)280-2520. E-mail: acrl@ala.org. Web site: http://www.ala.org/acrl. Camila Alire, President; Mary Ellen Davis, Executive Director. The Association of College and Research Libraries (ACRL), the largest division of the American Library Association, is a professional association of academic librarians and other interested individuals. It is dedicated to enhancing the ability of academic library and information professionals to serve the information needs of the higher education community and to improve learning, teaching, and research. ACRL is the only individual membership organization in North America that develops programs, products, and services to meet the unique needs of academic and research librarians. Committees include the AASL/ACRL Interdivisional Committee on Information Literacy, Academic/Research Librarian of the Year Award, ACRL/Harvard Leadership Institute Advisory, Advocacy Coordinating, Hugh C. Atkinson Memorial Award, Budget and Finance, Colleagues, Bylaws, Copyright, Council of Liaisons, Doctoral Dissertation Fellowship, Effective Practices Review, Ethics, Excellence in Academic Libraries Award, Government Relations, Information Literacy Advisory, Institute for Information Literacy Executive, Intellectual Freedom, International Relations, (Dr. E.J.) Josey Spectrum Scholar Mentor, Samuel Lazerow Fellowship Award, Marketing Academic and Research Libraries, Membership Advisory, National Conference Executive, Professional Development Coordinating, Publications Coordinating, Racial and Ethnic Diversity, Research, Scholarly Communication, Standards and Accreditation, Statistics, and Status of Academic Librarians committees. The association administers 19 different awards in three categories: Achievement and Distinguished Service Awards, Research Awards/Grants, and Publications. With over 13,000 members, is a national organization of academic and research libraries and librarians working with all types of academic libraries—community and junior college, college, and university—as well as comprehensive and specialized research libraries and their professional staffs. Membership: $45, $35 for students and retirees (in addition to ALA membership). Meetings: 2007 ACRL National Conference, March 29–April 1, Baltimore, MD. Publications: *Academic Library Trends & Statistics* (annually). Statistics data for all academic libraries reporting throughout the U.S. and Canada. Trends data examines a different subject each year. Available from ALA Order Fulfillment, P.O. Box 932501, Atlanta, GA 31193-2501 and online (www.ala.org/ala/acrl/acrlpubs/acadlibrarystats). *Choice* (monthly, 11 issues a yr., combined July–Aug. issue and any special issues or supplements): $285 a yr. ($335 international surface rate; $415 international airmail rate); single copies, $30. *Choice Reviews-on-Cards*: $370 a yr. ($430 international surface rate; $500 international airmail rate); card stack, $40. *ChoiceReviews.online:* Password Edition (one yr. Password access for up to 20 designated users): $325; fee for each block of 10 additional users in excess of 20 provided above, $135. *ChoiceReviews.online* Site License Edition (1 simultaneous user): $325; each additional simultaneous user, $135. Ed. and publisher, Irving Rockwood. *College & Research Libraries* (6 bimonthly journal issues). Sent to all ACRL members. Subscriptions, $65 a yr. (PUAS countries, $70; other countries, $75); single copies, $14. Ed., William Gray Potter; bk. review ed., Fred J. Hay. *College & Research Libraries News* (11 monthly issues, July–Aug. combined). Sent to all ACRL members. Subscriptions, $44 a yr. (PUAS countries, $50; other countries, $55); single copies, $6.50. Ed., Stephanie D. Orphan. *Publications in Librarianship* (ACRL monograph series) (occasional). Available from ALA Order Fulfillment, P.O. Box 932501, Atlanta, GA 31193-2501 and online (www.ala.org/ala/acrl/acrlpubs/booksmonographs). Ed., Charles Schwartz. *RBM: A Journal of Rare Books, Manuscripts, and Cultural Heritage*. (2 issues). Subscriptions, $40 a yr. (PUAS countries, $45; other countries, $55); single copies, $15. Ed.,

Richard Clement. ACRL also sponsors an open discussion listserv, ACRL-FRM@ala.org. Updated: 4/21/2006. David Connolly, dconnolly@ala.org.

Association of Independent Video and Filmmakers/Foundation for Independent Video and Film (AIVF/FIVF). 304 Hudson St., 6th Floor, New York, NY 10013, United States. (212)807-1400. Fax: (212)463-8519. E-mail: info@aivf.org. Web site: http://www.aivf.org. Beni Matias, Interim Executive Director. AIVF-AIVF is the national trade association for independent video and filmmakers, representing their needs and goals to industry, government, and the public. Programs include screenings and seminars, insurance for members and groups, and information and referral services. Recent activities include seminars in filmmaking technology, meets with distributors, and regular programs on related topics. AIVF also advocates public funding of the arts, public access to new telecommunications systems, and monitoring censorship issues.

Membership includes: annual subscription to the Independent magazine; avid trade discounts; online and phone information service; Web members-only area; discounted admission to events, etc.-$55, indiv.; $75, library; $100, nonprofit organization; $150, business/industry; $35, student. Meeting: annual membership meeting. Publications: *The Independent Film and Video Monthly*; *The AIVF Guide to International Film and Video Festivals*; *The AIVF Guide to Film and Video Distributors*; *The Next Step: Distributing Independent Films and Videos*; the *AIVF Self Distribution Toolkit & the AIVF Film & Video Exhibitors Guide*. Updated: 7/7/04. Sonya Malfa, sonia@aivf.org

Association of Specialized and Cooperative Library Agencies (ASCLA). 50 E. Huron St., Chicago, IL 60611, United States. (800)545-2433, ext. 4398. Fax: (312)944-8085. E-mail: ascla@ala.org. Web site: http://www.ala.org/ascla. Cathleen Bourdon, Exec. Dir. A division of the American Library Association, ASCLA represents state library agencies, multitype library organizations, independent libraries and libraries serving special populations to promote the development of coordinated library services with equal access to information and material for all persons. The activities and programs of the association are carried out by 21 committees, 4 sections, and various discussion groups. Membership: 917. Join ALA and ASCLA new member $90; student member $40 ($25 for ALA plus $15 for ASCLA); trustee and associate member $85 ($45 for ALA plus $40 for ASCLA; add ASCLA to current ALA membership $40; renew ALA and ASCLA membership $140 ($100 for ALA plus $40 for ASCLA). Meetings: ASCLA meets in conjunction with the American Library Association. Publication: *Interface* (quarterly); see Web site http://www.ala.org/ascla for list of other publications. Updated: 4/27/04. Eileen Hardy, ehardy@ala.org

Natural Science Collections Alliance (NSC Alliance). P.O. Box 44095, Washington, DC 20026-4095, United States. (202)633-2772. Fax: (202)633-2821. E-mail: general@nscalliance.org. Web site: http://www.nscalliance.org. Executive Director. Fosters the care, management, and improvement of biological collections and promotes their utilization. Institutional members include free-standing museums, botanical gardens, college and university museums, and public institutions, including state biological surveys and agricultural research centers. The NSC Alliance also represents affiliate societies, and keeps members informed about funding and legislative issues. Membership: 80 institutions, 30 affiliates, 120 individual and patron members. Dues: depend on the size of collections. Meeting: Annual Meeting (May or June) Publications: *Guidelines for Institutional Policies and Planning in Natural History Collections*; *Global Genetic Resources*; *A Guide to Museum Pest Control*. Updated: 3/29/2006. Karen Kajiwara, phone (202) 633-2772.

Cable in the Classroom (CIC). 1724 Massachusetts Avenue, NW, Washington, DC 20036, United States. 202.775.1040. Fax: 202.775.1047. E-mail: cic@ciconline.org. Web site: http://www.ciconline.org. Peggy OBrien, Ph.D., Executive Director. Cable in the Classroom represents the cable telecommunications industry's effort to use cable content and new technologies to improve teaching and learning for children in schools, at home, and in their communities. By focusing on five essential elements of a good education in the 21st century—visionary and sensible use of technologies, engagement with rich content, community with other learners, excellent teaching, and the support of parents and other adults—the cable industry works for positive change in education locally and nationally. Cable in the Classroom is a consortium of more than 8,500 local cable companies and 40 national cable programming networks. Local cable companies provide free basic cable service to all accredited K-12 schools passed by cable. Cable networks offer free educational programming with no commercials or viewing requirements and with extended copyright clearances so teachers can tape for classroom use. In addition, cable companies and networks create print and online resources to help teachers use the resources effectively in the classroom. Publication: *Cable in the Classroom Magazine* (monthly). Updated: 7/7/04. Windy Wiener, wwiener@ciconline.org.

American Telecommunications Group (ATG). 1400 E. Touhy, Suite 260, Des Plaines, IL 60018-3305, United States. (847)390-8700. Fax: (847)390-9435. E-mail: gerie@atgonline. org. Web site: http://www.itmonline.com/Marketplace/atg.htm. James A. Fellows, President. The American Telecommunications Group serves as am umbrella framework for six entities that are organized to provide and support educational and programming services, professional development and policy development for public broadcasting, educational telecommunications and related public service media: American Center for Children and Media—a professional development and resource center for people who create, commission, distribute and study children's TV and digital media; Center for Education Initiatives—Supports distance learning, adult training, and evaluation of new technology initiatives in education; Central Educational Network—a non-profit executive-level association of public broadcasting licensees that undertakes joint activities and services, administers program funds and awards, and conducts leadership exchanges; Continental Program Marketing—distributes quality programming to U.S. public television stations; The Hartford Gunn Institute—assists in developing fundamental plans for building the second generation of public telecommunications; The Higher Education Telecommunications Consortium—assists colleges and universities in managing telecommunications operations and advances the expansion and development of higher education-based telecommunication services. Membership in the CEN component of ATG is available to public television and telecommunications organizations and agencies. Membership in The Higher Education Telecommunications Consortia is available to public television stations that are licensed to colleges and universities. "Close Up Online" is a periodic briefing that keeps readers informed about the various services and activities of the organizations that are a part of the ATG. Close Up Online also reports on noteworthy people and activities throughout our nationwide constituency. Updated: 7/7/04. Marilyn Price, marilyn@atgonline.org.

Children's Television International (CTI)/GLAD Productions, Inc.(CTI/GLAD). PO BOX 87723, SAN DIEGO, CA 92138, United States. (619)445-4647. Fax: (619)445-2813. E-mail: CTI GLADPROD@WORLDNET.ATT.NET. Web site: WORLDNET.ATT.NET. Tim Gladfelter, Pres. and Dir. of Customer Services. An educational organization that develops, produces, and distributes a wide variety of color television and video programming and related publications as a resource to aid the social, cultural, and intellectual development of children and young adults. Programs cover language arts, science, social studies, history, and art for home, school, and college viewing. Publication: Teacher guides for instructional series; *The History Game: A Teachers Guide*; complimentary catalog for educational videos. Updated: 5/13/03. Tim Gladfelter by phone or e-mail.

Close Up Foundation (CUF). 44 Canal Center Plaza, Alexandria, VA 22314, United States. (703)706-3300. Fax: (703)706-0000. E-mail: alumni@closeup.org. Web site: http://

www.closeup.org. Stephen A. Janger, CEO. A nonprofit, nonpartisan civic education organization promoting informed citizen participation in public policy and community service. Programs reach more than a million participants each year. Close Up brings 25,000 secondary and middle school students and teachers and older Americans each year to Washington for week-long government studies programs and produces television programs on the C-SPAN cable network for secondary school and home audiences. Any motivated 10th–12th grade or 6th–8th grade student who wants to learn about government and American history is eligible to come on program. There are no "dues." Tuition is required to participate on Close Up educational travel programs. A limited amount of tuition assistance is available to qualified students through the Close Up Fellowship program. With a designated number of students, teachers receive a fellowship that covers the adult tuition and transportation price. Please contact 1-800-CLOSE UP (256-7387), ext. 606 for more information. Meetings are scheduled most weeks during the academic year in Washington, DC, all with a government, history, or current issues focus. Publication: *Current Issues*; *The Bill of Rights: A Users Guide*; *Perspectives*; *International Relations*; *The American Economy*; documentary videotapes on domestic and foreign policy issues. Updated: 3/5/03 Kimberly Ash, ashk@closeup.org.

Computer Assisted Language Instruction Consortium (CALICO). 214 Centennial Hall, Texas State University, 601 University Dr., San Marcos, TX 78666, United States. (512)245-1417. Fax: (512)245-9089. E-mail: info@calico.org. Web site: http://calico.org. Robert Fischer, Exec. Dir. CALICO is devoted to the dissemination of information on the application of technology to language teaching and language learning. Membership: 1,000 members from the United States and 20 foreign countries. Anyone interested in the development and use of technology in the teaching/learning of foreign languages are invited to join., $65 annual/individual. Meetings: 2007, Texas State University, San Marcos; 2008, University of San Francisco. *CALICO Journal* (three times a year), *CALICO Monograph Series* (Monograph V, 2006; Monograph VI, 2007). Updated: 3/26/2007. Esther Horn (info@calico.org).

Consortium of College and University Media Centers (CCUMC). 1200 Communications Bldg., Iowa State University, Ames, IA 50011-3243, United States. (515)294-1811. Fax: (515)294-8089. E-mail: ccumc@ccumc.org. Web site: www.ccumc.org. Executive Director (currently vacant). CCUMC is a professional group of higher education media personnel whose purpose is to improve education and training through the effective use of educational media. Assists educational and training users in making films, video, and educational media more accessible. Fosters cooperative planning among university media centers, Gathers and disseminates information on improved procedures and new developments in instructional technology and media center management. Membership: 750 individuals at 325 institutions/corporations:

Institutional Memberships—Individuals within an institution of higher education who are associated with the support of instruction and presentation technologies in a media center and/or technology support service. Corporate Memberships—Individuals within a corporation, firm, foundation, or other commercial or philanthropic whose business or activity is in support of the purposes and objectives of CCUMC. Associate Memberships— Individuals from a public library, religious, governmental, or other organization not otherwise eligible for other categories of membership. Student Memberships—Any student in an institution of higher education who is not eligible for an institutional membership. Institutional or Corporate Membership:

$325 for 1–2 persons,
$545 for 3–4 persons,
$795 for 5–6 persons,
$130 each additional person beyond six

Student Membership: $55 per person
Associate Membership: $325 per person
Meetings: 2007 Conference, Gainesville Florida, October 18–22, 2007. Publications: *College & University Media Review* (journal—semi-annual)
Leader (newsletter—3 issues annually in electronic format). Updated: 3/20/2007. Aileen Scales, President-Elect, 812-855-2064.

Copyright Clearance Center, Inc. (CCC). 222 Rosewood Drive, Danvers, MA 01923, United States. (978)750-8400. Fax: (978)750-0347. E-mail: marketing@copyright.com. Web site: http://www.copyright.com. Joseph S. Alen, Pres. Copyright Clearance Center, Inc. (CCC) is the world's largest licenser of text reproduction rights and provider of many licensing services for the reproduction of copyrighted materials in print and electronic formats. Formed in 1978 to facilitate compliance with U.S. copyright law, CCC manages the rights relating to more than 1.75 million textbooks, newspapers, magazines, and other copyrighted works. CCC-licensed customers in the U.S. number over 10,000 corporations and subsidiaries (including most of the Fortune 100 companies), as well as thousands of government agencies, law firms, document suppliers, libraries, academic institutions, copy shops and bookstores. CCC's licensing services include: Annual Authorizations Service (AAS)—a blanket annual photocopy license for companies with more than 750 employees, as well as law firms of any size. Their employees can photocopy content for distribution in-house. Photocopy Authorizations License (PAL) – the same as the AAS license, but for companies with fewer than 750 employees. Digital Repertory Amendment – a blanket annual license that provides companies with the rights to copy copyrighted content for distribution in-house via e-mail, intranet sites, and other digital formats. Multinational Repertory License—a blanket annual photocopy license that covers U.S. companies' employees working in other countries. Multinational Digital Repertory Amendment—a license similar to the Digital Repertory Amendment, but for U.S. companies with employees working outside of the U.S. Transactional Reporting Service (TRS)—an online "pay as you go" service that enables customers to acquire photocopy permissions on an as-needed basis for library reserves, inter-library loans, as well as general photocopy needs. Customers also use TRS to report their photocopying activity. Republication Licensing Service (RLS)—an online service that provides customers with permissions to reproduce copyrighted materials for the purpose of republishing that content into a variety of formats, such as Web sites, brochures, books, ads, etc. Academic Permissions Service (APS)—an online permissions service that colleges and universities can use to get the rights to photocopy copyrighted content for use in coursepacks. Electronic Course Content Service (ECCS)—an online service that colleges and universities can use to acquire permissions to reproduce copyrighted content for use in electronic coursepacks and reserves, as well as for distance learning. Digital Permissions Service (DPS)—a transactional service that customers can use to order permissions to reproduce and distribute copyrighted content electronically either in-house or outside of their organizations. Rightslink—a digital rights management service that licenses, packages and delivers digital content from publishers' Web sites. Foreign Authorizations Service (FAS)—authorizes photocopying of U.S. copyrighted materials in foreign countries and distributes royalties collected by foreign reproduction rights organizations to U.S. publishers, authors and other rightsholders. Federal Government Photocopy Licensing Service—a blanket annual license that provides rights for federal government employees to photocopy content for in-house use. Updated: 3/19/03.Christine Corcoran ccorcoran@copyright.com

Corporation for Public Broadcasting (CPB). 401 9th St., NW, Washington, DC 20004-2037, United States. (202)879-9600. Fax: (202)879-9700. E-mail: info@cpb.org. Web site:http://www.cpb.org. Patricia Harrison, Pres. and CEO. A private, nonprofit corporation created by Congress in 1967 to develop noncommercial television, radio, and online services for the American people. CPB created the Public Broadcasting Service (PBS) in

1969 and National Public Radio (NPR) in 1970. CPB distributes grants to over 1,000 local public television and radio stations that reach virtually every household in the country. The Corporation is the industry's largest single source of funds for national public television and radio program development and production. In addition to quality educational and informational programming, CPB and local public stations make important contributions in the areas of education, training, community service, and application of emerging technologies. CPB has over 100 employees. Publications: *Annual Report*; *CPB Public Broadcasting Directory*. Updated: 4/21/2006. Carolyn Wapnick; cwapnick@cpb.org

Council for Basic Education (CBE). 1319 F St. NW, Suite 900, Washington, DC 20004-1152, United States. (202)347-4171. Fax: 202-347-5047. E-mail: jkeiser@c-b-e.org. Web site: http://www.c-b-e.org-A. Graham Down, Acting CEO, gdown@c-b-e.org. CBE's mission is to strengthen teaching and learning of the core subjects (mathematics, English, language arts, history, government, geography, the sciences, foreign languages, and the arts) in order to develop the capacity for lifelong learning and foster responsible citizenship. As an independent, critical voice for education reform, CBE champions the philosophy that all children can learn, and that the job of schools is to achieve this goal. CBE advocates this goal by publishing analytical periodicals and administering practical programs as examples to strengthen content in curriculum and teaching. CBE is completing a kit of Standards for Excellence in Education, which includes a CD-ROM; guides for teachers, parents, and principals, and a book of standards in the core subjects. Publications: *Basic Education: A Journal of Teaching and the Liberal Arts*. The publication of *Basic Education* has been suspended as of September 2003. Copies of past issues are still available for ordering. (Single copy $10 which includes shipping and handling; contact CBE for bulk orders; issues of BE before September 2002 are only $4 a copy; change price on order form.) Each issue contains analyses, opinions, and reviews of the key issues in K-12 education. Updated: 7/7/04. J. Keiser, jkeiser@c-b-e.org

Council for Exceptional Children (CEC). 1110 N. Glebe Rd. #300, Arlington, VA 22201, United States. (703)620-3660. TTY: (703)264-9446. Fax: (703)264-9494. E-mail: cec@cec.sped.org. Web site: http://www.cec.sped.org. Nancy Safer, Exec. Dir. CEC is the largest international organization dedicated to improving the educational success of students with disabilities and/or gifts and talents. CEC advocates for governmental policies supporting special education, sets professional standards, provides professional development, and helps professionals obtain conditions and resources necessary for high quality educational services for their students. Teachers, administrators, professors, related services providers (occupational therapists, school psychologists . . .), and parents. Membership: CEC has approximately 50,000 members-$89 a year. Meeting: Annual Convention & Expo attracting approximately 6,000 special educators. Publications: Journals, newsletters books, and videos with information on new research findings, classroom practices that work, and special education publications. (See also the ERIC Clearinghouse on Disabilities and Gifted Education.). Updated: 3/12/03. Lynda Van Kuren, lyndav@cec.sped.org, 703-264-9478.

Council on International Non-Theatrical Events (CINE). 1112 16th Street, N.W., Suite 510, Washington, DC 20036, United States. (202)785-1136. Fax: (202)785-4114. E-mail: info@cine.org. Web site: http://www.cine.org. Carole L. Feld, President. CINE's mission is to discover, reward, educate and support professional and new emerging talent in the film and video fields. It accomplishes its mission through major film and video competitions that recognize and celebrate excellence, and through various educational programs. CINE is best known for its prestigious CINE Golden Eagle competitions, culminating annually in a gala Awards Ceremony in Washington, D.C. Awards are given in 20 major categories, encompassing all genres of professional and pre-professional film and video production. CINE also facilitates entry into worldwide film festivals for its own competition winners;

at the same time, it has reciprocal arrangements whereby distinguished works from outside the United States achieve CINE recognition and viewership in the United States. CINE is not at this time a membership organization. CINE Showcase and Awards held annually in Washington, DC. Publications: *CINE Annual Yearbook of Film and Video Awards*; *Worldwide Directory of Film and Video Festivals and Events*. Updated: 7/7/04. David L. Weiss

East-West Center 1601 East-West Rd., Honolulu, HI 96848-1601, United States. (808) 944-7111. Fax: (808)944-7376. E-mail: ewcinfo@EastWestCenter.org. Web site: http://www.eastwestcenter.org/. Dr. Charles E. Morrison, Pres. The U.S. Congress established the East-West Center in 1960 with a mandate to foster mutual understanding and cooperation among the governments and peoples of Asia, the Pacific, and the United States. Officially known as the Center for Cultural and Technical Interchange Between East and West, it is a public, nonprofit institution with an international board of governors. Funding for the center comes from the U.S. government, with additional support provided by private agencies, individuals, and corporations, and several Asian and Pacific governments, private agencies, individuals, and corporations. The center, through research, education, dialog, and outreach, provides a neutral meeting ground where people with a wide range of perspectives exchange views on topics of regional concern. Scholars, government and business leaders, educators, journalists, and other professionals from throughout the region annually work with Center staff to address issues of contemporary significance in such areas as international economics and politics, the environment, population, energy, the media, and Pacific islands development. Updated: 3/4/04.

Educational Communications, Inc., Environmental and Media Projects of P.O. Box 351419, Los Angeles, CA, 90035, United States. (310)559-9160. Fax: (310)559-9160. E-mail: ECNP@aol.com. Web site: www.ecoprojects.org. Nancy Pearlman, Executive Director and Producer, Educational Communications is dedicated to enhancing the quality of life on this planet and provides radio and television programs about the environment. Serves as a clearinghouse on ecological issues. Programming is available on 100 stations in 25 states. These include: ECONEWS television series and ENVIRONMENTAL DIRECTIONS radio series. ECO-TRAVEL Television shows focus on ecotourism. Services provided include a speaker's bureau, award-winning public service announcements, radio and television documentaries, volunteer and intern opportunities, and input into the decision-making process. Its mission is to educate the public about both the problems and the solutions in the environment. Other projects include the Ecology Center of Southern California (a regional conservation group), Project Ecotourism, Humanity and the Planet, Earth Cultures (providing ethnic dance performances), and more, $20.00 for yearly subscription to the *Compendium Newsletter*, $20 for regular. All donations accepted. Publications: *Compendium Newsletter* (bi-monthly newsletter) Environmental Directions radio audio cassettes, (1550 produced to date) ECONEWS and ECO-TRAVEL television series (over 550 shows in the catalog available on 3/4", VHS, and DVD). Update: 3/31/2007. Nancy Pearlman, ECNP@aol.com

ECT Foundation (ECT). c/o AECT, 1800 N. Stonelake Drive, Suite 2, Bloomington, IN 47404, United States. 812-335-7675. Fax: 812-335-7678. E-mail: aect@aect.org. Web site: www.aect.org. Addie Kinsinger, President. The ECT Foundation is a nonprofit organization whose purposes are charitable and educational in nature. Its operation is based on the conviction that improvement of instruction can be accomplished, in part, by the continued investigation and application of new systems for learning and by periodic assessment of current techniques for the communication of information. In addition to awarding scholarships, internships, and fellowships, the foundation develops and conducts leadership training programs for emerging professional leaders. Its operations are closely allied to AECT program goals, and the two organizations operate in close conjunction with each other. No membership. No annual dues. Meetings: The Board meets monthly. Does not publish books or other items. Updated: 3/9/2006. Phillip Harris Exec.Dir.pharris@aect.org.

Education Development Center, Inc. (EDC). 55 Chapel St., Newton, MA 02458-1060, United States. (617)969-7100. Fax: (617)969-5979. E-mail: comment@edc.org. Web site: http://www.edc.org. Dr. Luther S. Luedtke, President and CEO, Education Development Center, Inc. (EDC) is an international, nonprofit organization that conducts and applies research to advance learning and to promote health. EDC currently manages 325 projects in 50 countries. Our award-winning programs and products, developed in collaboration with partners around the globe, address nearly every critical need in society, including early child development, K-12 education, health promotion, workforce preparation, community development, learning technologies, basic and adult education, institutional reform, medical ethics, and social justice. Publications:

(1) *Annual Report*

(2) *Mosaic*, an EDC Report Series

(3) *EDC Update*, an EDC Newsletter

(4) *EDC Online Report*

(5) Detailed Web site with vast archive of publications, technical reports, and eval-uation studies. Updated: 3/26/2007, Eric Marshall, emarshall@edc.

Educational Products Information Exchange (EPIE Institute). 103 W. Montauk High-way, Hampton Bays, NY 11946, United States. (516)728-9100. Fax: (516)728-9228. E-mail: kkomoski@optonline.net. Web site: http://www.epie.org-P. Kenneth Komoski, Exec. Dir. Assesses educational materials and provides consumer information, product descrip-tions, and citations for virtually all educational software and curriculum-related Web sites. All of EPIEs services are available to schools and state agencies as well as parents and individuals. Online access is restricted to states with membership in the States Consortium for Improving Software Selection (SCISS).The Educational Software Selector Database (TESS), available to anyone. All publication material now available on CD-ROM. Up-dated: 5/27/03. Kenneth Komoski, kkomoski@optonline.net

ACCESS ERIC, **Aspen Systems Corp**.   2277 Research Blvd., Mailstop 4M, Rockville, MD 20850, United States. 1-800-LET-ERIC [538-3742] Fax: (301)519-6760. E-mail: ac-cesseric@accessiceric.org. Web site: http://www.eric.ed.gov/. ACCESS ERIC coordinates ERIC's outreach and systemwide dissemination activities, develops new ERIC publications, and provides general reference and referral services. Publications: *A Pocket Guide to ERIC*; *All About ERIC*; *The ERIC Review*; *ERIC Annual Report*; *ERICNews* (online monthly newsletter). Databases: ERIC Digests Online (EDO); Education Resource Organizations Directory (EROD); ERIC Resource Collections; ERIC Calendar of Education-Related Conferences. (The databases are available through the Internet: http://www.eric.ed.gov/) Updated: 5/2/02. Heather Starcher (1-800-538-3742).

70-ERIC Clearinghouse for Community Colleges (JC). JC-University of California at Los Angeles (UCLA), 3051 Moore Hall, P.O. Box 951521, Los Angeles, CA 90095-1521, United States. (310)825-3931, (800)832-8256. Fax: (310)206-8095. E-mail: er-iccc@ucla.edu. Web site: http://www.gseis.ucla.edu/ERIC/eric.html. Arthur M. Cohen, Dir. Selects, synthesizes, and distributes reports and other documents about two-year pub-lic and private community and junior colleges, technical institutes, and two-year branch university programs, and outcomes of these institutions; linkages between two-year colleges and business, industrial, and community organizations; and articulation between two-year colleges and secondary and four-year postsecondary institutions. Publication: *EdInfo Summaries* are one-page reports of important research in the field. *ERIC Bibliographies*. These bibliographies are lists of current ERIC literature on popular community college topics. *ERIC Digests* are two-page summaries of current trends and practices in the field. *Information Bulletins* published quarterly; *Information Bulletins* provide citations of ERIC documents on current topics, as well as up-to-date information on ERIC products and services. The online versions of our bulletins are now enhanced to provide links to related sites across the Web. *Key Resources in Community Colleges* is the complete collection of bibliographies originally compiled for New Expeditions, a W.K. Kellogg Foundation initiative sponsored by the American Association of Community Colleges and the Association of Community College Trustees. One bibliography is updated each quarter. *New Directions for Community Colleges*, the NDCC journal, which has been published quarterly since 1973, addresses issues of interest to community college researchers and practitioners. Copies of the journals can be obtained from Jossey-Bass by calling 800-956-7739. Updated: 3/21/03. Daphne Lu, (310) 825-3931.

ERIC Clearinghouse for Social Studies/Social Science Education.   SO, Indiana University, Social Studies Development Center, 2805 East 10th St., Suite 120, Bloomington, IN 47408-2698, United States. (812)855-3838, (800)266-3815. Fax: (812)855-0455. E-mail: ericso@indiana.edu. Web site: http://ericso.indiana.edu/. John Patrick, Director. All levels of social studies, social science, art, and music education; the contributions of history, geography, and other social science disciplines; applications of theory and research to social science education; education as a social science; comparative education (K-12); content and curriculum materials on social topics such as law-related education, ethnic studies, bias and discrimination, aging, and women's equity. Includes input from the Adjunct Clearinghouses for United States. Japan Studies, for Service Learning, and for International Civics. Listed in ERIC/Chess catalog; contact to obtain a free copy. Updated: 3/12/03-Laura Pinhey; e-mail lpinhey@indiana.edu

Edvantia, Inc.   (formerly AEL, Inc.), Edvantia, P.O. Box 1348, Charleston, WV 25325-1348, United States. (304)347-0400, (800)624-9120. Fax: (304)347-0487. E-mail: info@edvantia.org. Web site: http://www.edvantia.org. Dr. Doris L. Redfield, President and CEO. Edvantia is a nonprofit education research and development corporation, founded in 1966, that partners with practitioners, education agencies, publishers, and service providers to improve learning and advance student success. Edvantia provides clients with a range of services, including research, evaluation, professional development, and consulting. The Edvantia Electronic Library contains links to free online tools and information created by staff on a wide array of education-related topics. Visitors to the Edvantia Web site can also access archived webcasts and webinars and sign up for a free monthly newsletter. Updated: 3/12/2007. Carla McClure, carla.mcclure@edvantia.org

National Clearinghouse for United States-Japan Studies-(NC United States JS).   1021 East Third Street, #211, Bloomington, IN 47405-7005, United States. (800)441-3272. E-mail: japan@indiana.edu. Web site: http://www.indiana.edu/~japan. Anne Prescott, Director. Provides educational information on topics concerning Japan and U.S.-Japan relations. Anybody interested in teaching or learning about Japan may contact the Clearinghouse for an information packet in drum form. The entire information packet is also available to download from our Web site. No dues. No meetings. Publications: *Guide to Teaching Materials on Japan*; *Teaching About Japan: Lessons and Resources*; *The Constitution and Individual Rights in Japan: Lessons for Middle and High School Students*; *Internationalizing the U.S. Classroom: Japan as a Model*; *Tora no Maki II*: *Lessons for Teaching About Contemporary Japan*; *The Japan Digest Series* (complimentary, concise discussions of various Japan-related topics): Fiction About Japan in the Elementary Curriculum; *Daily*

Life in Japanese High Schools; *Rice: It's More Than Food in Japan*; *Ideas for Integrating Japan into the Curriculum*; *Japanese Popular Culture in the Classroom*; *An Introduction to Kabuki*; *Building a Japanese Language Program from the Bottom Up*; *Teaching Primary Children about Japan through Art*; *The History and Artistry of Haiku*; *Learning from the Japanese Economy*; *Teaching about Japanese-American Internment*; *Using Museums to Teach about Japan*; *Lessons on the Japanese Constitution*; *Using Film to Explore History*; *Shinbun* (project newsletter). Updated: 4/26/2006. Patricia Tennen, japan@indiana.edu

ERIC Clearinghouse on Adult, Career, and Vocational Education (ERIC/ACVE). The Ohio State University, Center on Education and Training for Employment, 1900 Kenny Rd., Columbus, OH 43210-1090, United States. (614)292-7069, (800)848-4815, ext. 2-7069. Fax: (614)292-1260. E-mail: ericacve@postbox.acs.ohio-state.edu. Web site: http://ericacve.org. Susan Imel, Dir. Judy Wagner, Assoc. Dir. All levels and settings of adult and continuing, career, and vocational/technical education. Adult education, from basic literacy training through professional skill upgrading. Career awareness, career decision making, career development, career change, and experience-based education. Vocational and technical education, including new subprofessional fields, industrial arts, corrections education, employment and training programs, youth employment, work experience programs, education and business partnerships, entrepreneurship, adult retraining, and vocational rehabilitation for individuals with disabilities. Includes input from the Adjunct ERIC Clearinghouse on Consumer Education. Membership: There is no membership. Anyone can use the products and services of the clearinghouse. Publications: *ERIC Digests*; *Trends and Issues Alerts*; *Practice Application Briefs*; *Myths and Realities*; *ERIC File* (newsletter); *Practitioner File*; major publications. Updated: 5/14/02. Judy Wagner wagner.6@osu.edu.

ERIC Clearinghouse on Assessment and Evaluation (ERIC/AE). The University of Maryland, 1129 Shriver Lab-College Park, MD 20742-5701, United States. (301)405-7449, (800)464-3742. Fax (301)405-8134. E-mail ericae@ericae.net. Web site http://ericae.net. Lawrence M. Rudner, Dir. Tests and other measurement devices; methodology of measurement and evaluation; application of tests, measurement, or evaluation in educational projects and programs; research design and methodology in the area of assessment and evaluation; and learning theory. Includes input from the Adjunct Test Collection Clearinghouse. Updated 4/23/02. Lawrence Rudner.

ERIC Clearinghouse on Counseling and Student Services (ERIC/CASS). University of North Carolina at Greensboro, School of Education, 201 Ferguson Building, P.O. Box 26170, Greensboro, NC 27402-6170, United States. (336)334-4114, (800)414-9769. Fax: (336)334-4116. E-mail: ericcass@uncg.edu. Web site: http://ericcass.uncg.edu/. Garry R. Walz, Co-Dir.; Jeanne C. Bluer, Co-Dir. The ERIC Counseling and Student Services Clearinghouse (ERIC/CASS), one of the original clearinghouses, was established in 1966 by Dr. Garry R. Walz at the University of Michigan. Its scope area includes school counseling, school social work, school psychology, mental health counseling, marriage and family counseling, career counseling, and student development. Topics covered by ERIC/CASS include: Preparation, practice, and supervision of counselors and therapists at all educational levels and in all settings; theoretical development of counseling and student services; assessment and diagnosis procedures such as testing and interviewing and the analysis and dissemination of the resultant information; outcomes analysis of counseling interventions; groups and case work; nature of pupil, student, and adult characteristics; identification and implementation of strategies that foster student learning and achievement; personnel workers and their relation to career planning, family consultations, and student services activities; identification of effective strategies for enhancing parental effectiveness; and continuing preparation of counselors and therapists in the use of new technologies for professional renewal and the implications of such technologies for service provision. Meeting: Annual

Assessment Conference. Family Counseling for All Counselors; Thriving in Challenging and Uncertain Times; Building Stronger School Counseling Programs: Bringing Futuristic Approaches Into the Present; Helping People Cope with Tragedy & Grief: information, Resources & Linkages; Addressing school Violence: Practical Strategies & Interventions; Substance Abuse and Counseling; Implementing Comprehensive School Guidance Programs: Critical Leadership Issues and Successful Responses; Counseling for High Skills: Responding to the Career Needs of All Students; Proven Strategies for Learning and Achievement; Assessment: Issues & Challenges for the Millennium; Career Transitions in Turbulent Times; Saving the Native Son; Cultural and Diversity Issues in Counseling; Safe Schools, Safe Students; many others. Call for catalog. Dozens of free, full-text ERIC/CASS Digests available. Updated: 2/27/03. Jillian Jonas, contact by phone, mail or e-mail.

ERIC Clearinghouse on Disabilities and Gifted Education (ERIC EC). 1110 N. Glebe Rd., Arlington, VA 22201-5704, United States. (703)264-9474, (800)328-0272. Fax: (703) 620-4334. E-mail: ericec@cec.sped.org. Web site: http://ericec.org. Associate Director. ERIC EC is part of the U.S. Department of Education's information network. ERIC EC collects the professional literature on disabilities and gifted education for inclusion in the ERIC database. ERIC EC also responds to requests for information on disabilities and gifted education; serves as a resource and referral center for the general public; conducts general information searches; and publishes and disseminates free or low-cost materials on disability and gifted education research, programs, and practices. Please visit the Web site for a complete list of publications. Updated: 2/27/03. Jean Smith. Contact info above.

ERIC Clearinghouse on Educational Management (ERIC/CEM). University of Oregon (Dept. 5207), 1787 Agate St., Eugene, OR 97403-5207, United States. (541)346-5043, (800)438-8841. Fax: (541)346-2334. E-mail: ppiele@uoregon.edu. Web site: http://eric. uoregon.edu/. Philip K. Piele, Dir. The governance, leadership, management, and structure of K–12 public and private education organizations; local, state, and federal education law and policy-making; practice and theory of administration; preservice and inservice preparation of administrators; tasks and processes of administration; methods and varieties of organization and organizational change; and the social context of education organizations. Updated 6/7/03.

ERIC Clearinghouse on Elementary and Early Childhood Education (ERIC/EECE). University of Illinois, Children's Research Center, 51 Gerty Dr., Champaign, IL 61820-7469, United States. (217)333-1386, (800)583-4135. Fax: (217)333-3767. E-mail: ericeece@uiuc.edu. Web site: http://ericeece.org. Lilian G. Katz and Dianne Rothenberg, co-directors. The ERIC Clearinghouse on Elementary and Early Childhood (ERIC/EECE) provides information and resources in the areas of child development, the education and care of children from birth through early adolescence, the teaching of young children, and parenting and family life. These resources relate to the physical, cognitive, social, educational, and cultural development of children from birth through early adolescence; prenatal factors; parents, parenting, and family relationships that impinge on education; learning theory research and practice related to the development of young children, including the preparation of teachers for this educational level; interdisciplinary curriculum and mixed-age teaching and learning; educational, social, and cultural programs and services for children; the child in the context of the family and the family in the context of society; theoretical and philosophical issues pertaining to children's development and education. ERIC/EECE publishes: *ERIC Digests*, books and monographs, newsletters, *Early Childhood Research & Practice*, a scholarly peer-reviewed Internet journal and *Parent News* an online parenting magazine. For details see: http://ericeece.org/eecepub.html. Updated 4/17/02. Laurel Preece; e-mail at l-preece@uiuc.edu.

Adjunct ERIC Clearinghouse for Child Care (NCCIC). National Child Care Information Center, 243 Church Street, NW, 2nd Floor, Vienna, VA 22180, United States. (703)938-6555, (800)516-2242. Fax: 800-716-2242. E-mail: jmascia@nccic.org. Web site: http://nccic.org/. Janet Mascia, Exec. Dir. Adjunct to the ERIC Clearinghouse on Elementary and Early Childhood Education. Works with Bureau, Administration for Children and Families (ACF), of DHHS, to complement, enhance, and promote child care linkages and to serve as a mechanism for supporting quality, comprehensive services for children and families. NCCIS's activities include: dissemination of child care information in response to requests from States, Territories and Tribe, other policymakers, child care organizations, providers, business communities, parents, and the general public; outreach to ACF child care grantees and the boarder child care community; publication of the child care Bulletin and development and dissemination of other publications on key child care issues; and coordination of National Leadership Forums, which provide an opportunity for experts from across the country to participate in one-day conferences on critical issues affecting children and families. Working closely with ACF Regional offices, the NCCIC also provides technical assistance to states through a network of state technical assistance specialists. Many materials produced and distributed by NCCIC are available in Spanish. NCCIC is the Adjunct ERIC Clearinghouse for Child Care. Updated: 5/21/03. info@nccic.org.

ERIC Clearinghouse on Higher Education (ERIC-HE). George Washington University, One DuPont Circle, NW, Suite 630, Washington, DC 20036-1183, United States. (202)296-2597, (800)773-3742. Fax: (202)452-1844. E-mail: eric-he@eric-he.edu-Web site: http://www.eriche.org. Elaine El-Khawas, Director. Topics relating to college and university conditions, problems, programs, and students. Curricular and instructional programs, and institutional research at the college or university level. Federal programs, professional education (medicine, law, etc.), professional continuing education, collegiate computer-assisted learning and management, graduate education, university extension programs, teaching and learning, legal issues and legislation, planning, governance, finance, evaluation, interinstitutional arrangements, management of institutions of higher education, and business or industry educational programs leading to a degree. Free Government-funded Service. Membership: No membership required. Meeting: Annual Advisory Board Meeting. Publications: *Spring-Higher Education Leadership*: *Analyzing the Gender Gap*; *The Virtual Campus: Technology and Reform in Higher Education*; *Early Intervention Programs: Opening the Door to Higher Education*; *Enriching College with Constructive Controversy*; *A Culture for Academic Excellence: Implementing the Quality Principles in Higher Education*; *From Discipline to Development: Rethinking Student Conduct in Higher Education*; *Proclaiming and Sustaining Excellence: Assessment as a Faculty Role*; *The Application of Customer Satisfaction Principles to Universities*; *Saving the Other Two-Thirds: Practices and Strategies for Improving the Retention and Graduation of African American Students in Predominately White Institutions*; *Enrollment Management: Change for the 21st Century*; *Faculty Workload: States Perspectives*.
New Ashe-Eric Reports:

Kezar, A. J. (2001) Understanding and Facilitating Organizational Change in the 21st Century: Recent Research and Conceptualizations. *ASHE-ERIC Higher Education Report* (Volume 28, No. 4). San Francisco: Jossey-Bass Publishers.

Weidman, J. C., Twale, D. J. & Stein, E. L. (2001) Socialization of Graduate and Professional Students in Higher Education: A Perilous Passage? ASHE-ERIC Higher Education Report (Volume 28, No. 3). San Francisco: Jossey-Bass Publishers.

Sutton, T. & Bergerson, P. (2001) Faculty Compensation Systems: Impact on the Quality of Higher Education. ASHE-ERIC Higher Education Report (Volume 28, No. 2). San Francisco: Jossey-Bass Publishers. Updated: 4/10/02. Shannon Loane; sloane@eric-he.edu.

ERIC Clearinghouse on Information & Technology. IR, Syracuse University, 621 Skytop Rd., Suite 160, Syracuse, NY 13244-5290, United States. (315)443-3640, (800)464-9107. Fax: (315)443-5448. E-mail eric@ericir.syr.edu;askeric@ericir.syr.edu. Web site: www.ericit.org. R. David Lankes, Dir. Educational technology and library and information science at all levels. Instructional design, development, and evaluation within educational technology, along with the media of educational communication: computers and microcomputers, telecommunications, audio and video recordings, film, and other audiovisual materials as they pertain to teaching and learning. The focus is on the operation and management of information services for education-related organizations. Includes all aspects of information technology related to education. Membership: not a membership organization. Updated 4/12/02. Joan Laskowski, jmlaskow@syr.edu.

85-ERIC Clearinghouse on Languages and Linguistics (ERIC/CLL). Center for Applied Linguistics, 4646 40th St., NW Washington, DC 20016-1859, United States. (202) 362-0700. Fax: (202) 362-3740. E-mail: eric@cal.org. Web site: http://www.cal.org/ericcll/. Joy Peyton, Dir. Dr. Craig Packard, User Services Coordinator, contact person. Languages and language sciences. Aspects of second language instruction and learning in commonly and uncommonly taught languages, including English as a second language. Bilingualism and bilingual education. Cultural education in the context of second language learning, including intercultural communication, study abroad, and international education exchange. Areas of applied linguistics within an educational context. Includes input from the National Clearinghouse for ESL Literacy Education (NCLE). Membership: not a membership organization. Updated: 5/13/03. Craig Packard (800) 276-9834 or Craig@cal.org.

ERIC Clearinghouse on Reading, English, and Communication (CS). Indiana University, Smith Research Center, Suite 140, 2805 E. 10th St.,Bloomington, IN 47408-2698, United States. (812)855-5847, (800)759-4723. Fax: (812)856-5512. E-mail: ericcs@indiana.edu-Web site: http://eric.indiana.edu/. Dr. Carl B. Smith, Director; Stephen Stroup, Co-Director. Reading, English, and communication (verbal and nonverbal), preschool through college; research and instructional development in reading, writing, speaking, and listening; identification, diagnosis, and remediation of reading problems; speech communication (including forensics), mass communication; interpersonal and small group interaction; interpretation; rhetorical and communication theory; speech sciences; and theater. Preparation of instructional staff and related personnel. All aspects of reading behavior with emphasis on physiology, psychology, sociology, and teaching; instructional materials, curricula, tests and measurement, and methodology at all levels of reading; the role of libraries and other agencies in fostering and guiding reading; diagnostics and remedial reading services in schools and clinical settings. Preparation of reading teachers and specialists. The Web site makes available a wealth of information pertaining to the full gamut of language arts topics enumerated above. Membership: There is no membership. There are no dues. Meetings: There are no formal meetings. Parents and Children Together Online Magazine (PCTO), at http://eric.indiana.edu/www/indexfr.html Publications: *Parent Talk*, Updated: 3/30/03. Stephen Stroup, Codirector, sstroup@indiana.edu.

ERIC Clearinghouse on Rural Education and Small Schools (Closed Dec. 31, 2003) (ERIC/CRESS). No longer in operation. No longer in operation. WV. No longer in operation. United States. (800) 624-9120. Fax: No longer in operation. E-mail: No longer in operation@nomore. Web site: http://www.ael.org/eric/. No longer in operation. No longer in operation. No longer in operation. No longer in operation. No longer in operation. Updated: 3/4/04. No longer in operation.

ERIC Clearinghouse on Science, Mathematics, and Environmental Education (SE). The Ohio State University, 1929 Kenny Road, Columbus, OH 43210-1080, United States. (614)292-6717, (800)276-0462. Fax: (614)292-0263. E-mail: ericse@osu.edu. Web site:

http://www.ericse.org. David L. Haury, Director; Linda A. Milbourne, Associate Director. The Clearinghouse acquires, produces, and distributes information about science, mathematics, and environmental education at all levels. Within these three broad subject areas, the following topics are covered: development of curriculum and instructional materials; teachers and teacher education; learning theory and outcomes, including the influences of interest level, attitudes, values, classroom experiences, and concept development upon learning in these fields. The Clearinghouse is particularly interested in educational programs; research and evaluative studies; media applications; computer applications, and Internet applications relating to teaching and learning in science, mathematics, technology, and environmental education. Anyone is eligible, there is no membership. No dues required. Meetings: Attend various meetings throughout the year: NCTM, NSTA, etc. Publications: In addition to producing at least ten ERIC Digests each year, the Clearinghouse regularly produces books such as the following: *Proceedings of Annual Meetings for the North American Chapter of the International Group for the Psychology of Mathematics Education*; *Developing Teacher Leaders: Professional Development in Science and Mathematics*; *Elementary Teachers Do Science: Guidelines for Teacher Preparation Programs*; *Rethinking Portfolio Assessment: Documenting the Intellectual Work of Learners in Science and Mathematics*; *Creative Childhood Experiences in Mathematics and Science*; *Trends in Science Education Research*; etc. Updated: 3/12/03. David L. Haury, Director, haury.2@osu.edu.

ERIC Clearinghouse on Teaching and Teacher Education (ERIC-SP). American Association of Colleges for Teacher Education (AACTE), 1307 New York Avenue, N.W., Suite 300, Washington, DC 20005, United States. (202)293-2450, (800)822-9229. Fax: (202)457-8095. E-mail: query@aacte.org-Web site: http://www.ericsp.org. Mary E. Dilworth, Dir. An information clearinghouse funded by the Department of Education, Institute of Education Sciences. The Clearinghouse serves school personnel at all levels. The scope area covers teacher recruitment, selection, licensing, certification, training, preservice and in-service preparation, evaluation, retention, and retirement. The theory, philosophy, and practice of teaching. Curricula and general education not specifically covered by other clearinghouses. Organization, administration, finance, and legal issues relating to teacher education programs and institutions. All aspects of health, physical, recreation, and dance education. Publications: Monographs, digests, information cards and bookmarks. Updated: 2/27/03. Catalina Boggio, cboggio@aacte.org.

American Association of Colleges for Teacher Education (AACTE). 1307 New York Ave., N.W., Suite 300, Washington, DC 20005-4701, United States. 202/293-2450. Fax 202/457-8095. E-mail not@available-Web site http://www.aacte.org/. David G. Imig, President and Chief Executive Officer. Adjunct to the ERIC Clearinghouse on Teaching and Teacher Education, the American Association of Colleges for Teacher Education (AACTE) provides leadership for the continuing transformation of professional preparation programs to ensure competent and caring educators for all Americas children and youth. It is the principal professional association for college and university leaders with responsibility for educator preparation. It is the major voice, nationally and internationally, for American colleges, schools, and departments of education, and is a locus for discussion and decision-making on professional issues of institutional, state, national and international significance. Membership: over 2,400 members; membership in AACTE is institutional and there are three categories: regular, affiliate, and candidate. Regular membership is available to four-year degree-granting colleges and universities with significant commitment to the preparation of education personnel, which meet all the criteria for regular or candidate membership. Affiliate membership is available to not-for-profit two-year or four-year degree-granting foreign institutions of higher education; not-for-profit two-year domestic degree-granting institutions of higher education; and not-for-profit organizations, state education associations, regional education laboratories, university-based research or policy centers, and other not-for-profit education associations as identified by the AACTE Board of Directors. Meetings: Many meetings including the New Deans Institute. See: http://www.aacte.org/Events/default.htm. Publications: AACTE publishes books and other publications in a range of areas that address key issues related to teacher education. We have over 70 titles available on a variety of subject areas. Updated: 5/22/03.

ERIC Clearinghouse on Urban Education (ERIC/CUE). Teachers College, Columbia University, Institute for Urban and Minority Education, Main Hall, Rm. 303, Box 40, 525 W. 120th St, New York, NY 10027-6696, United States. (212)678-3433, (800)601-4868. Fax: (212)678-4012. E-mail: eric-cue@columbia.edu. Web site: http://eric-web.tc. columbia.edu. Erwin Flaxman, Dir. Programs and practices in public, parochial, and private schools in urban areas and the education of ethnic minority children and youth in various settings; the theory and practice of educational equity; urban and minority experiences; and urban and minority social institutions and services. Please see our Web site: http://eric-web. tc.columbia.edu. Updated: 3/3/03, James Lonergan, 212 678-8179, jml118@columbia.edu.

ERIC Document Reproduction Service (EDRS). 7420 Fullerton Rd., Suite 110, Springfield, VA 22153-2852, United States. (800)443-ERIC (3742). Fax: (703)440-1408. E-mail: service@edrs.com. Web site: http://www.edrs.com. Peter M. Dagutis, Dir. Provides subscription services for ERIC document collections in electronic format (from 1993 forward) and on microfiche (from 1966 forward). Links to the full text at EDRS are incorporated into a number of ERIC search products. On-demand delivery of ERIC documents is also available in formats including paper, electronic PDF image, fax, and microfiche. Delivery methods include shipment of hard copy documents and microfiche, document fax-back, and online delivery. Back collections of ERIC documents, annual subscriptions, and other ERIC-related materials are also available. ERIC documents can be ordered by toll-free phone call, fax, mail, or online through the EDRS Web site. Document ordering also available from EBSCO, OVID, DIALOG and OCLC. Updated: 2/27/03. Pete Dagutis. 703-440-1400.

ERIC Processing and Reference Facility (ERIC). 4483-A Forbes Blvd., Lanham, MD 20706, United States. (301)552-4200,(800)799-ERIC(3742). Fax: (301)552-4700. E-mail: info@ericfac.piccard.csc.com. Web site: http://www.ericfacility.org. Donald Frank, Dir. A central editorial and quality control office that coordinates document processing and database building activities for ERIC, the U.S. Department of Education's database on education research; performs acquisition, lexicographic, and reference functions; and maintains systemwide quality control standards. NONE; we are a contract held by the Computer Sciences Corporation (CSC)with the United States Department of Education. The ERIC Facility also prepares *Resources in Education* (RIE); *Current Index to Journals in Education* (CIJE); *The Thesaurus of ERIC Descriptors*; *The ERIC Identifier Authority List* (IAL); *ERIC Ready References*; the *ERIC Processing Manual*; and other products. Updated: 5/16/02. Sarah Pugh, spugh@csc.com.

Penn State Media Sales (PSMS). 118 Wagner Building, University Park, PA 16802, United States. (800)770-2111, (814)863-3102. Fax: (814)865-3172. E-mail: MediaSales@outreach.psu.edu. Web site: http://www.MediaSales.psu.edu. Robin P Guillard, Coordinator. Distributor of educational video with a primary audience of postsecondary education. One of Americas largest collections on historic psychology, including Stanley Milgrams experiments, psychosurgery, and early mental illness treatments. Other catogories are anthropology, including the Mead/Bateson studies, primatology, sciences, agriculture, and training. Closed circuit television, broadcast and footage use available on many titles. Call for more information. No dues. Unlimited. No meetings. Product catalog. Updated: 4/26/04. Roberta Stover, rls46@psu.edu or 814-865-3333 ×250.

Eisenhower National Clearinghouse for Mathematics and Science Education (ENC). 1929 Kenny Road, Columbus, OH 43210-1079, United States. (800)621-5785, (614)292-7784. Fax: (614)292-2066. E-mail: info@enc.org. Web site: http://www.enc.org. Dr. Len Simutis, Director. The Eisenhower National Clearinghouse for Mathematics and Science Education (ENC) is located at The Ohio State University and funded by the U.S. Department of Education's Office of Elementary and Secondary Education (OESE). ENC provides K–12 teachers and other educators with a central source of information on mathematics and science curriculum materials, particularly those that support education reform. Among ENCs products and services are *ENC Online*; 12 demonstration sites located throughout the nation; and a variety of publications, including the *Guidebook of Federal Resources for K–12 Mathematics and Science*, a listing of federal resources in mathematics and science education, *ENC Focus*, a free online and print magazine on topics of interest to math and science educators, and professional development CD-ROMs. Users include K–12 teachers, other educators, policymakers, and parents. Magazine subscriptions are free and there are no fees for any ENC services. *ENC Focus* magazine has more than 130,000 subscribers, mostly K-12 math and science teachers. *ENC Focus* (an online and print magazine on selected topics); *Guidebook of Federal Resources for K–12 Mathematics and Science* (federal programs in mathematics and science education); CD-ROMs on professional development topics. *ENC Online* is available online (http://www.enc.org). Updated: 3/11/04. Melanie Shreffler, mshreffler@enc.org.

Federal Communications Commission (FCC). 445, 12th St. S.W., Washington, DC 20554, United States. 1-888-225-5322. Fax: (202)418-1232. E-mail: fccinfo@fcc.gov. Web site: http://www.fcc.gov. Michael Powell, Chairman. The Federal Communications Commission (FCC) is an independent United States government agency, directly responsible to Congress. The FCC was established by the Communications Act of 1934 and is charged with regulating interstate and international communications by radio, television, wire, satellite and cable. The FCCs jurisdiction covers the 50 states, the District of Columbia, and U.S. possessions. Updated: 3/17/04 fccinfo@fcc.gov.

Film Arts Foundation (Film Arts). 145 9th St. #101, San Francisco, CA 94103, United States. (415)552-8760. Fax: (415)552-0882. E-mail: info@filmarts.org. Web site: http://www.filmarts.org. Service organization that supports and promotes independent film and video production. Services include low-cost 16mm, Super-8, and dV equipment rental; on and off-line editing including AVID, Final Cut, 16mm flatbeds, VHS & S-VHS, as well as a Pro Tools sound room and Optical Printer; resource library; group legal and production insurance plans; monthly magazine; seminars; grants program; annual film and video festival; nonprofit sponsorship; exhibition program; and advocacy and significant discounts on film- and video-related products and services. Membership: 3500 +–$45 for "supporter" level benefits including monthly magazine, and access to libraries and online databases $65 for full "filmmaker" benefits including above plus: access to equipment and post production facilities, discounts on seminars, nonprofit fiscal sponsorship, group legal and Delta Dental plans. Meetings: Annual Festival, Annual membership meeting,and Network events. Publications: *Release Print* (magazine)- Updated: 4/26/04. Eric, erich@filmarts.org

100-Film/Video Arts (F/VA). 462 Broadway, suite 520, New York, NY 10013, United States. (212)941-8787. Fax: (212)219-8924. E-mail: education@fva.com. Web site: www.fva.com. Eileen Newman, Exec. Dir. Film/Video Arts has come a long way since its founding in 1968 when educators Rodger Larson and Lynne Hofer in collaboration with filmmaker Jaime Barrios introduced 16mm motion picture equipment to Latino youth on the Lower East Side. Operating out of a storefront just off the Bowery, the teenagers were soon making highly personal films, mostly concerned with growing up in the neighborhood.

In 1968, the organization was officially incorporated as the Young Filmakers Foundation, to encourage filmmaking as an artistic, educational, and vocational experience for young people. A major grant in 1970 made it possible for Young Filmakers to stabilize and expand its programs citywide. In 1971, in collaboration with the New York State Council on the Arts, Young Filmakers established the first public media equipment access center in a basement on West 53rd Street. Known as Media Equipment Resource Center (MERC), this program served film and video makers of all ages with production and postproduction services free of charge. In 1973, the activities of the organization were consolidated in a loft building at 4 Rivington Street. By 1978, Young Filmakers had introduced modest fees and redirected its focus to adults. In 1985, Young Filmakers changed its name to Film/Video Arts and relocated to 817 Broadway. The new location and major equipment upgrades enabled the organization to evolve from a set of experimental programs to an established service institution. In 1997, Film/Video Arts built the Digital Studio and initiated the Digital Arts Certificate Program. Consequently, a new generation of digital media producers was emerging from Film/Video Arts with the benefit of having equal access to necessary resources. In 2001, Film/Video Arts relocated to its present address at 462 Broadway (corner of Grand Street). The future of the Film/Video Arts at its new location holds forth many possibilities as the organization continues to grow with the emergence of newer technologies.

Drawing from its rich history Film/Video Arts has steadily evolved, all the time maintaining its staunch commitment to supporting the needs of independent film, video, and digital media producers. The founder's mission, to make the tools and skills of the media arts available to those who might otherwise not have access to them, remains the guiding force behind all Film/Video Arts activities and programs. Join Film/Video Arts today and become a part of a thriving community of independent film, video, and multimedia producers. A Film/Video Arts membership allows one to take courses, receive fiscal sponsorship and mentorship, and receive access to the postproduction facilities at affordable rates. Membership contributions help support Film/Video Arts equipment purchases and low service fees. Memberships are valid for one year from the date of issue. Contributions are tax-deductible to the full extent of the law.

To become a member fill out the Membership Application and submit it to Film/Video Arts (with membership payment) via e-mail or regular mail. Membership: Individual $75/Organization $95.

Access to Film/Video Arts courses, production equipment rentals, and postproduction services at affordable rates. Fiscal Sponsorship Referrals for affordable premiums on General Liability and Production Insurance. Opportunities to exhibit work in Members Screenings. A subscription to *Film/Video Arts Email* Newsletter. Enrollment in Film/Video Arts Membership Discount Program that entitles F/VA members to savings at several film and video service providers. **Note**: Individual membership is for one person only. An organizational membership is for two authorized individuals. Fiscal sponsorship program. This program serves the independent producer who is seeking funding for projects. Film/Video Arts will act as a fiscal sponsor for independent producers in cases where a donor (such as a governmental body, nonprofit organization, an individual or other entity) stipulates in their funding guidelines that the recipient have nonprofit status under 501(c)3 of the Internal Revenue Code. In such cases Film/Video Arts can use its nonprofit status to receive and administer grants, gifts or donations that are made in the name of the producers project. As a Fiscal Sponsor, Film/Video Arts does not supervise the actual production of projects, but is responsible for monitoring their progress. In order to apply to the program, individuals must complete and send in the Fiscal Sponsor Application accompanied by a project proposal which includes a detailed description/treatment of the project, fundraising and distribution plan, résumés of key personnel, a list of project advisors (as applies), a budget and a sample reel. A nonrefundable membership fee of $75 is required for review of the project proposal. The proposal will be reviewed by a Film/Video Arts screening committee. The review process takes approximately two weeks.

Once a project is accepted into Film/Video Arts Fiscal Sponsor Program, Film/Video Arts will then administer and turn over all funding raised by the producer after deducting a 6% administrative fee. Updated: 3/5/04. Guil Parreiras.

Freedom of Information Center (FOI Center). 127 Neff Annex, University of Missouri, Columbia, MO 65211-0012, United States. (573)882-4856. Fax: (573)882-9002. E-mail: FOI@missouri.edu. Web site: http://www.missouri.edu/~foiwww. Dr. Charles N. Davis, Director; Kathleen Edwards, Manager; Robert W. Anderson, Web Manager. Located in the Missouri School of Journalism, the Freedom of Information Center is an academic research facility specializing in educational advocacy. The collection focuses on the centrality of open government to its role in fostering democracy. The Center's staff assists the public with requests or questions about freedom of information with the help of an extensive archive of materials dating from the FOI movements inception. The Center's operating hours are Monday through Friday, 8:00 a.m. to 5:00 p.m., excluding University holidays. Membership: The FOI Center does not offer memberships. The Center serves approximately 23,000 researchers annually through its Web page and through individual contacts. No dues charged. Minimal fees may be charged for research. Meetings: The Center meets annually with the National Freedom of Information Coalition. Publications: Access to Public Information: A Resource Guide to Government in Columbia and Boone County, Missouri, a directory of public records, and the *FOI Advocate*, a periodic electronic newsletter. Both publications are linked to the Centers Web page. Some older publications are available for sale by contacting the Center. Updated: 7/7/04. K. Edwards, edwardsm@missouri.edu.

George Eastman House International Museum of Photography and Film (GEH). 900 East Ave., Rochester, NY 14607, United States. (585)271-3361. Fax: (585)271-3970. E-mail: tbannon@geh.org. Web site: http://www.eastman.org. Anthony Bannon, Dir. World-renowned museum of photography and cinematography established to preserve, collect, and exhibit photographic art and technology, film materials, and related literature, and to serve as a memorial to George Eastman. Services include archives, traveling exhibitions, research library, school of film preservation, center for the conservation of photographic materials, and photographic print service. Educational programs, exhibitions, films, symposia, music events, tours, and internship stipends offered. Eastman's turn-of-the-century mansion and gardens have been restored to their original grandeur. Membership: 13,000-$40, library; $50, family; $40, indiv.; $36, student; $30, senior citizen; $75, Contributor; $125, Sustainer; $250, Patron; $500, Benefactor; $1,000, George Eastman Society. Publications: newsletter; *Annual Report: The George Eastman House and Gardens*; *Masterpieces of Photography from the George Eastman House Collections*; *Index to American Photographic Collections*; and exhibition catalogs. Updated: 4/26/04. Dresden Engle, PR Mgr., dengle@geh. org.

The George Lucas Educational Foundation (GLEF). P.O. Box 3494, San Rafael, CA 94912, United States. (415)662-1600. Fax: (415)662-1619. E-mail: edutopia@glef.org. Web site: http://edutopia.org. Milton Chen, PhD. Exec. Dir. Mission: The George Lucas Educational Foundation (GLEF) is a nonprofit operating foundation that documents and disseminates models of the most innovative practices in our nation's K-12 schools. We serve this mission through the creation of media—from films, books, and magazine to CD-ROMS and DVDs. GLEF works to provide its products as tools for discussion and action in conferences, workshops, and professional development settings. Audience: A successful educational system requires the collaborative efforts of many different stakeholders. Our audience includes teachers, administrators, school board members, parents, researchers, and business and community leaders who are actively working to improve teaching and learning. Vision: The Edutopian vision is thriving today in our country's best schools: places where students are engaged and achieving at the highest levels, where skillful educators are energized by the excitement of teaching, where technology brings outside resources and expertise into the classroom, and where parents and community members are partners in educating our youth. All online content and the Edutopia magazine are offered free of charge to educators. Free subscription to Edutopia magazine for those working in education., no public meetings; advisory council meets annually; board of directors meets quarterly. Publications: *Edutopia Online*. The Foundation's Web site, Edutopia (www.edutopia.org) celebrates the unsung heroes who are making Edutopia a reality. All of GLEF's multimedia content dating back to 1997 is available on its Web site. A special feature, the Video Gallery, is an archive of short documentaries and expert interviews that allow visitors to see these innovations in action and hear about them from teachers and students. Detailed articles, research summaries, and links to hundreds of relevant Web sites, books, organizations, and publications are also available to help schools and communities build on successes in education. *Edutopia: Success Stories for Learning in the Digital Age*. This book and CD-ROM include numerous stories of innovative educators who are using technology to connect with students, colleagues, the local community, and the world beyond. The CD-ROM contains more than an hour of video footage. Published by Jossey-Bass. *Teaching in the Digital Age* (TDA) Videocassettes. This video series explores elements of successful teaching in the Digital Age. The project grows out of GLEFs belief that an expanded view is needed of all our roles in educating children and supporting teachers. The series explores school leadership, emotional intelligence, teacher preparation, and project-based learning and assessment. *Learn & Live*. This documentary film and 300-page companion resource book showcases innovative schools across the country. The film, hosted by Robin Williams, aired on public television stations nationwide in 1999 and 2000. The *Learn & Live* CD-ROM includes digital versions of the film and book in a portable, easy-to-use format. *Edutopia Magazine*, a free magazine which shares powerful examples of innovative and exemplary learning and teaching. *Edutopia Newsletter*. This free, semiannual print newsletter includes school profiles, summaries of recent research, and resources and tips for getting involved in public education, instructional modules, free teaching modules developed by education faculty and professional developers. They can be used as extension units in existing courses, or can be used independently in workshops. Includes presenter notes, video segments, and discussion questions. Topics include project-based learning, technology integration, and multiple intelligences. Updated: 3/8/2007, Jennifer Celonit, jen@glef.org.

Graphic Arts Technical Foundation (GATF). 200 Deer Run Road, Sewickley, PA 15143-2600, United States. (412)741-6860. Fax: (412)741-2311. E-mail: info@gatf.org. Web site: http://www.gain.net. George Ryan, Executive Vice President and Chief Operating Officer. GATF is a member-supported, nonprofit, scientific, technical, and educational organization dedicated to the advancement of graphic communications industries worldwide. For 77 years GATF has developed leading-edge technologies and practices for printing, and each year the Foundation develops new products, services, and training programs to meet the evolving needs of the industry. GATF consolidated its operations with the Printing Industries of America (PIA) in 1999. Membership: 13,000 corporate members, 520 teachers, 100 students. $45, teachers; $30, students; corporations pay dues to regional printing organizations affiliated with GATF/PIA. See www.gain.net. GATF publishes books relating to graphic communications. GATFs Publications Catalogs promotes 320 books, 100 of which are published by GATF. Recent publications include: *Customer Service in the Printing Industry, What the Printer Should Know About Ink, Total Production Maintenance, Managing Mavericks: The Official Printing Industry Guide to Effective Sales Management, Print Production Scheduling Primer, Paper Buying Primer, and Print Production Management Primer*. Updated: 3/12/03-Deanna M. Gentile, dgentile@gatf.org.

Great Plains National ITV Library (GPN). P.O. Box 80669, Lincoln, NE 68501-0669, United States. (402)472-2007, (800)228-4630. Fax: (800)306-2330. E-mail: gpn@unl.edu. Web site: http://gpn.unl.edu. Stephen C. Lenzen, Executive Director. Produces and distributes educational media, video, CD-ROMs and DVDs, prints and Internet courses. Available for purchase for audiovisual or lease for broadcast use. Membership: Membership not required. There are no dues required. Meetings: There are no meetings. We do attend subject-specific conventions to promote our products. GPN Educational Video Catalogs by curriculum areas; periodic brochures. Complete listing of GPN's product line is available via the Internet along with online purchasing. Free previews available. Updated: 7/7/04-Connie Hoerle, E-Mail Address: gpn@unl.edu.

Health Sciences Communications Association (HeSCA). One Wedgewood Dr., Suite 27, Jewett City, CT 06351-2428, United States. (203)376-5915. Fax: (203)376-6621. E-mail: keven@hesca.org. Web site: http://www.hesca.org/. Ronald Sokolowski, Exec. Dir. An affiliate of AECT, HeSCA is a nonprofit organization dedicated to the sharing of ideas, skills, resources, and techniques to enhance communications and educational technology in the health sciences. It seeks to nurture the professional growth of its members; serve as a professional focal point for those engaged in health sciences communications; and convey the concerns, issues, and concepts of health sciences communications to other organizations that influence and are affected by the profession. International in scope and diverse in membership, HeSCA is supported by medical and veterinary schools, hospitals, medical associations, and businesses where media are used to create and disseminate health information. Membership: 150. $150, indiv.; $195, institutional ($150 additional institutional dues); $60, retiree; $75, student; $1,000, sustaining. All include subscriptions to the journal and newsletter. Meetings: Annual meetings, May–June. Publications: *Journal of Biocommunications*; *Feedback* (newsletter). Updated: 3/7/2006. Keven, keven@hesca.org

Hollywood Film Archive (HFA). 8391 Beverly Blvd., #321, Hollywood, CA 90048, United States. 323/655-4968. Fax: 323/555-4321. E-mail: info@hfa.com. Web site: www. hfa.com. D. Richard Baer, Dir. Archival organization for information about feature films produced worldwide, from the early silents to the present. Comprehensive movie reference works for sale, including *Variety Film Reviews* (1907–1996) and the *American Film Institute Catalogs* (1893–1910,1911–1920, 1921–1930, 1931–1940, 1941–1950, 1961–1970), as well as the *Film Superlist* (1894–1939, 1940–1949, 1950–1959) volumes, which provide information both on copyrights and on motion pictures in the public domain; *Harrisons Reports and Film Reviews* (1919–1962). Updated: 5/23/03. Richard Baer; by phone 323/655-4968.

HOPE Reports-owner. 58 Carverdale Dr.,Rochester, NY 14618-4004, United States. (585)442-1310. Fax: (585)442-1725. E-mail: hopereport@aol.com-hope. Thomas W. Hope, Owner. Mabeth S. Hope, Administrator. Supplies statistics, marketing information, trends, forecasts, salary and media studies to the visual communications industry through printed reports, custom studies, consulting, and by telephone. Clients and users in the United States and abroad include schools and colleges, manufacturers, dealers, producers of media, and media users in business, government, health sciences, religion, education, and community agencies. Large Screen Presentation Systems; Media Market Trends; Overhead Projection System; Presentation Slides-Electronic & Film; Producer & Video Post Wages & Salaries; Corporate Media Salaries; Hotel AV Personnel Compensation; Americas Top 100 Industrial Contract Producers; Contract Production; Executive Compensation; Media Production; Outsource or Insource; Audience Response Business and Evaluating A Media Production Company. Updated: 5/19/03. Tom Hope, Tel. 585-442-1310, e-mail hopereport@aol.

Institute for the Future (IFTF). 124 University Avenue, 2nd Floor, Palo Alto, CA 94301, United States. (650)854-6322. Fax: (650)854-7850. E-mail: info@iftf.org. Web site:

http://www.iftf.org. Dale Eldredge, COO. The Institute for the Future (IFTF) is an independent nonprofit research group. We work with organizations of all kinds to help them make better, more informed decisions about the future. We provide the foresight to create insights that lead to action. We bring a combination of tools, methodologies, and a deep understanding of emerging trends and discontinuities to our work with companies, foundations, and government agencies. We take an explicitly global approach to strategic planning, linking macro trends to local issues in such areas as: Work and daily life, Technology and society, Health and health care, Global business trends, and Changing consumer society. The Institute is based in California's Silicon Valley, in a community at the crossroads of technological innovation, social experimentation, and global interchange. Founded in 1968 by a group of former RAND Corporation researchers with a grant from the Ford Foundation to take leading-edge research methodologies into the public and business sectors, the IFTF is committed to building the future by understanding it deeply. Become a Member. Membership: To become a member of IFTF, companies and organizations can join one or more of our membership programs or contract with us for private work. Each membership program offers a distinct set of deliverables at different membership prices and enrollment terms. Please visit the individual program sites for more detailed information on a particular program. For more information on membership contact Sean Ness at sness@iftf.org or 650-854-6322. Ten-Year Forecast Program, Technology Horizons Program, Health Horizons Program, Custom Private Work. Corporate-wide memberships are for one year periods: Ten-Year Forecast—$15,000/year, Technology Horizons—$65,000/year, Health Horizons—$65,000/year. At present, we do not have university, individual, or small-company programs set up. For those companies that support our research programs, we will often conduct custom research. Several a year, for supporting members. IFTF blogs. *Future Now* (http://future.iftf.org)—emerging technologies and their social implications. *Virtual China* (http://www.virtual-china.org)—an exploration of virtual experiences and environments in and about China. *Future of Marketing* (http://fom.iftf.org)—emerging technology, global change, and the future of consumers and marketing. *Ten-Year Forecast* (members only) (http://blogger.iftf.org/tyf)—a broad scan of the leading edge of change in business, government, and the global community. *Technology Horizons* (members only) (http://blogger.iftf.org/tech!@)—emerging technologies and their implications for business, society and family life. Updated: 3/7/2006. Sean Ness, sness@iftf.org

Instructional Technology Council (ITC). One DuPont Cir., NW, Suite 410, Washington, DC 20036-1176, United States. (202)293-3110. Fax: (202)833-2467. E-mail: cdalziel@ aacc.nche.edu. Web site: http://www.itcnetwork.org. Christine Dalziel, Executive Director. An affiliated council of the American Association of Community Colleges established in 1977, the Instructional Technology Council (ITC) provides leadership, information, and resources to expand access to, and enhance learning through, the effective use of technology. ITC represents higher education institutions in the United States and Canada that use distance learning technologies. ITC members receive a subscription to the *ITC News* and ITC listserv with information on what's happening in distance education, participation in ITC's professional development audio conference series, distance learning grants information, updates on distance learning legislation, discounts to attend the annual Telelearning Conference that features more than 80 workshops and seminars, discounts to downlink PBS/ALS videoconferences, and a free copy of ITC publications and research. Members include single institutions and multicampus districts; regional and statewide systems of community, technical and two-year colleges; for-profit organizations; four-year institutions; and nonprofit organizations that are interested or involved in instructional telecommunications. Members use a vast array of ever-changing technologies for distance learning. They often combine different systems according to students' needs. The technologies they use and methods of teaching include: audio and video conferences, cable television, compressed and full-motion video, computer networks, fiber optics, interactive videodisc, ITFS, microwave, multimedia, public television, satellites, teleclasses, and telecourses. Membership: $450, Institutional; $750, Corporate. Meetings: Annual Telelearning Conference. Quality Enhancing Practices in Distance Education: Vol. 2, Student Services; *Quality Enhancing Practices in Distance Education: Vol. 1, Teaching and Learning*; *New Connections: A Guide to Distance Education* (2nd ed.); *New Connections: A College President's Guide to Distance Education*; *Digital Video: A Handbook for Educators*; *Faculty Compensation and Support Issues in Distance Education*; *ITC News* (monthly publication/newsletter); ITC Listserv. Updated: 5/13/03. Christine Dalziel, 202/293-3110.

International Association for Language Learning Technology (IALLT). Instr. Media Svcs, Concordia Coll., Moorhead, MN 56562, United States. (218) 299-3464. Fax: (218) 299-3246. E-mail: business@iallt.org. Web site: http://iallt.org. Claire Bartlett, President; Ron Balko, Treasurer. IALLT is a professional organization whose members provide leadership in the development, integration, evaluation, and management of instructional technology for the teaching and learning of language, literature, and culture. Membership: 400 members. Membership/Subscription Categories. Educational Member: for people working in an academic setting such as a school, college or university. These members have voting rights. Full-time Student Member: for full-time students interested in membership. Requires a signature of a voting member to verify student status. These members have voting rights. Commercial Member: for those working for corporations interested in language learning and technology. This category includes, for example, language laboratory vendors, software and textbook companies. Library Subscriber: receive our journals for placement in libraries. 1 year: $50, voting member; $25, student; $60, library subscription; $75, commercial. 2 year: $90, voting member; $140, commercial. Meetings: Biennial IALLT conferences treat the entire range of topics related to technology in language learning as well as management and planning. IALLT also sponsors sessions at conferences of organizations with related interests, including CALICO and ACTFL. Publications: *IALLT Journal of Language Learning Technologies* (2 times annually); materials for language lab management and design, language teaching, and technology. Visit our Web site for details. http://iallt.org. Updated: 3/7/2006. Ron Balko, business@iallt.org

International Association of School Librarianship (IASL). PO Box 83, Zillmere, QLD 4034, AUSTRALIA. 61 7 3216 5785. Fax: 61 7 3633 0570. E-mail: iasl@kb.com.au. Web site: www.iasl-slo.org/. Peter Genco-President; Karen Bonanno-Executive Secretary. Seeks to encourage development of school libraries and library programs throughout the world; promote professional preparation and continuing education of school librarians; achieve collaboration among school libraries of the world; foster relationships between school librarians and other professionals connected with children and youth and to coordinate activities, conferences, and other projects in the field of school librarianship. Membership: 550 plus. $50 Zone A (e.g., United States, Canada, Western Europe, Japan); $35 Zone B (e.g., Eastern Europe, Latin America, Middle East); $20 Zone C (e.g., Angola, India, Bulgaria, China). Zone based on GNP. Meetings: Annual Conference, Lisbon, Portugal, July 2006. Publications: *IASL Newsletter* (3/yr.); *School Libraries Worldwide* (semiannual); *Conference Professionals and Research Papers* (annual). Updated: 4/20/2006. Karen Bonanno.

International Center of Photography (ICP). 1114 Avenue of the Americas at 43rd Street, New York, NY 10036, United States. (212)857-0045. Fax: (212)857-0090. E-mail: info@icp.org. Web site: http://www.icp.org. Willis Hartshorn, Dir.; Phyllis Levine, Dir. of Communications. Located on a dynamic two-part campus in midtown Manhattan, the International Center of Photography (ICP) stands amongst the nation's foremost museums dedicated to preserving the past and ensuring the future of the art of photography. One of the largest facilities of its kind, ICP presents changing exhibitions of the finest works of some of the most talented photographers in the world. With over 20 exhibitions each year, ICP presents an extensive array of historical and contemporary photographs, revealing the power and diversity of the medium from documentary photography to digital imaging. The School of the International Center of Photography fosters study of the history, techniques, aesthetics, and practices of photography in a wide range of programs: continuing education classes; two full-time certificate programs; a Master of Fine Arts program in collaboration with Bard College, Master of Arts and Master of Fine Arts degree programs in conjunction with NYU; Digital Media Program; lectures; and symposia. Membership: 4,430. Current levels available on request. Meetings: The ICP Infinity Awards (annual—2007 is the 23rd), Martin Munkacsi; Ecotopia; Atta Kim: ON-AIR; Snap Judgments: New Positions in Contemporary African Photography; African American Vernacular Photography: Selections from the Daniel Cowin Collection; Modernist Photography: Selections from the Daniel Cowin Collection; Young America. The Daguerreotypes of Southworth and Hawes; and others! Updated: 4/6/2007. David Appel, 212-857-0045 or info@icp.org

International Council for Educational Media (ICEM). Postfach 114, Vienna, A-1011, Austria, +43 660 5113241. E-mail: lylt@a1.net. Web site: www.icem-cime.org. John Hedberg, President; Ray Laverty, Secretary General. Welcome to ICEM. Our purposes are: To provide a channel for the international exchange and evaluation of information, experience and materials in the field of educational media as they apply to preschool, primary and secondary education, to technical and vocational, industrial and commercial training, teacher training, continuing and distance education. To foster international liaison among individuals and organizations with professional responsibility in the field of educational media. To cooperate with other international organizations in the development and application of educational technology for practice, research, production, and distribution in this field. What are the main advantages of ICEM membership?

ICEM membership enables those professionally involved in the production, distribution, and use of media in teaching and learning to establish a broad network of contacts with educators, researchers, managers, producers, and distributors of educational media from around the world. It also provides opportunities to discuss topics of mutual concern in an atmosphere of friendship and trust, to plan and carry out coproductions, to compare and exchange ideas and experiences, to keep abreast of the latest developments, and to work together toward the improvement of education on an international level. Membership in ICEM includes a subscription to the ICEM quarterly journal, *Educational Media International*, an entry in the Whose Who on the ICEM Webpage, registration at ICEM events and activities either free of charge or at reduced rates, eligibility to engage in working groups or become a member of the Executive Committee, participate at the General Assembly and numerous other advantages. Membership: Who can be a member of ICEM? Members are organizations and individuals who are involved in educational technology in any one of a variety of ways. There are several different types and categories of ICEM members, Individual Members, National Representatives, Deputy Representatives, and Coordinators. Individual Members may join ICEM by paying individual membership fees. National Representatives are appointed by their Ministry of Education. National Coordinators are elected by other ICEM members in their country. Regional Representatives and Coordinators represent a group of several countries. ICEM Secretariat, c/o Ray Laverty SGPf 114 1011 WIEN AUSTRIA E-mail: lylt-at-a1.net. Meetings: Annual General Assembly in autumn; Executive Committee meeting in spring; Locations Vary. Publications: *Educational Media International* (quarterly journal) http://www.icem-cime.org/emi/issues.asp

Aims & Scope

Educational media has made a considerable impact on schools, colleges, and providers of open and distance education. This journal provides an international forum for the exchange of information and views on new developments in educational and mass media. Contributions are drawn from academics and professionals whose ideas and experiences come from a number of countries and contexts.

Abstracting & Indexing

Educational Media International is covered by the British Education Index; *Contents Pages in Education*; *Educational Research Abstracts* online (ERA); *Research into Higher Education Abstracts*; *ERIC*; *EBSCOhost*; and *Proquest Information and Learning*. Updated: 3/16/2007. Raymond Laverty, lylt@a1.net 00436605113241.

International Graphics Arts Education Association (IGAEA). 1899 Preston White Drive, Reston, VA 20191-4367, United States. 703-758-0595. E-mail: gcc@teched.vt.edu. Web site: http://www.igaea.org. Mark Sanders, gcc@teched.vt.edu. IGAEA is an association of educators in partnership with industry, dedicated to sharing theories, principles, techniques, and processes relating to graphic communications and imaging technology. Teachers network to share and improve teaching and learning opportunities in fields related to graphic arts, imaging technology, graphic design, graphic communications, journalism, photography, and other areas related to the large and rapidly changing fields in the printing, publishing, packaging, and allied industries. Membership: Approx. 600 members. Open to educators, middle school through college and university, who teach graphic arts, graphic communications, printing and publishing, desktop publishing, multimedia, and photography. $20, regular; $12, associate (retired); $5, student; $10, library; $50–$200; sustaining membership based on number of employees. See Web site for info: http://www.igaea. org. Publications: *The Communicator*; *Visual Communications Journal* (annual). Updated: 7/7/04. Mark Sanders, gcc@teched.vt.edu.

The Association for Information and Image Management (AIIM International). 1100 Wayne Avenue, Suite 1100, Silver Spring, MD 20910, United States. 301-587-8202. Fax: 301-587-2711. E-mail: pwinton@aiim.org. Web site: http://www.aiim.org/. John Mancini, President. AIIM International is the industry's leading global organization. We believe that at the center of an effective business infrastructure in the digital age is the ability to capture, manage, store, preserve, and deliver enterprise content to support business processes. The requisite technologies to establish this infrastructure are an extension of AIIM's core document and content technologies. These Enterprise Content Management (ECM) technologies are key enablers of e-Business and include: Content/Document Management, Business Process Management, Enterprise Portals, Knowledge Management, Image Management, Data Warehousing, and Data Mining. AIIM is a neutral and unbiased source of information. We produce educational, solution-oriented events and conferences, provide up-to-the-minute industry information through publications and our online ECM Resource Center, and are an ANSI/ISO-accredited standards developer. Membership: Trade Membership; Professional Membership; Trade Membership: $1,000/yr; New Professional Membership: $62.50; Renewal Professional Membership: $125. Meetings: AIIM Content Management Solutions Seminars, AIIM Service Company Executive Forum. Publications: *AIM E-DOC Magazine*; *DOC.1 e* (Newsletter). Updated: 5/13/03. Beth Mayhew; bmayhew@aiim.org.

International Society for Technology in Education (ISTE). 480 Charnelton Street, Eugene, OR 97401, United States. 800.336.5191 (U.S. & Canada) 541.302.3777 (Intl.). Fax: 541.302.3780. E-mail: iste@iste.org. Web site: http://www.iste.org. Don Knezek, CEO; Cheryl Williams, Copresident; Cathie Norris, Copresident. As the leading organization for educational technology professionals, the International Society for Technology in Education is a professional organization that supports a community of members through research, publications, workshops, symposia, and inclusion in national policymaking through

ISTE-DC. Home of the National Center for Preparing Tomorrows Teachers to Use Technology (NCPT3), ISTE works in conjunction with the U.S. Department of Education and various private entities to create and distribute solutions for technology integration. ISTE's National Educational Technology Standards (NETS) for students and teachers have been adopted by hundreds of districts nationwide. ISTE is also the home of NECC, the premier U.S. educational technology conference, is a forum for advancing educational philosophies, practices, policies, and research that focus on the appropriate use of current and emerging technologies to improve teaching and learning in K-12 and teacher education. ISTE members are leaders. ISTE members contribute to the field of educational technology as classroom teachers, lab teachers, technology coordinators, school administrators, teacher educators, and consultants. ISTE provides leadership and professional development opportunities for its members. In addition to other benefits, ISTE members can participate in ISTE-sponsored invitational events at the National Educational Computer Conference (NECC), join one of ISTE's many Special Interest Groups (SIGs), and test and evaluate the latest in educational technology products and services through the ISTE Advocate Network. ISTE members also enjoy subscriptions to *ISTE Update* and *Learning & Leading with Technology* or the *Journal for Research on Technology in Education*. In the member's areas of the ISTE Web site, ISTE members can join discussion lists and other online forums for participation, review a database of educational technology resources, network with a cadre of education professionals, and review online editions of ISTE publications. Membership: Annual dues for individual ISTE members are $58. Membership to SIG communities is $20 for ISTE members. Contact iste@iste.org to become a member. Annual dues for ISTE 100 members are $50,000. Contact iste100@iste.org for more information. Group discounts are available. To see if you qualify, contact groupdiscounts@iste.org. National Educational Computing Conference (NECC). Publications: ISTEs publications include *ISTE Update* (online member newsletter); *Learning & Leading with Technology*; the *Journal of Research on Technology in Education* (quarterly; formerly *Journal of Research on Computing in Education*); and books about incorporating technology in the K16 classroom. Updated: 5/21/03. Leslie Conery, Deputy CEO, lconery@iste.org.

International Society for Performance Improvement (ISPI). 1400 Spring Street, Suite 260, Silver Spring, MD 20910, United States. 301-587-8570. Fax: 301-587-8573. E-mail: info@ispi.org. Web site: http://www.ispi.org. Richard D. Battaglia, Exec. Dir. The International Society for Performance Improvement (ISPI) is dedicated to improving individual, organizational, and societal performance. Founded in 1962, ISPI is the leading international association dedicated to improving productivity and performance in the workplace. ISPI represents more than 10,000 international and chapter members throughout the United States, Canada, and 40 other countries. ISPI's mission is to develop and recognize the proficiency of our members and advocate the use of Human Performance Technology. This systematic approach to improving productivity and competence uses a set of methods and procedures and a strategy for solving problems for realizing opportunities related to the performance of people. It is a systematic combination of performance analysis, cause analysis, intervention design and development, implementation, and evaluation that can be applied to individuals, small groups, and large organizations. Membership: 10,000. Performance technologists, training directors, human resources managers, instructional technologists, human factors practitioners, and organizational consultants are members of ISPI. They work in a variety of settings including business, academia, government, health services, banking, and the armed forces. Membership Categories: Active Membership ($145 annually)—this is an individual membership receiving full benefits and voting rights in the Society. Student Membership ($60 annually)—this is a discounted individual full membership for full-time students. Proof of full-time enrollment must accompany the application. Retired Membership ($60 annually)—this is a discounted individual full membership for individuals who are retired from full-time employment. Special Organizational Membership Categories: these groups support the Society at the top level. Sustaining Membership ($950 annually)—this is an organizational membership and includes five active memberships and several additional value-added services and discounts. Details available upon request. Patron Membership ($1400 annually)—this is an organizational membership and includes five active memberships and several additional value-added services and discounts. Details available upon request. Meetings: Annual International Performance Improvement Conference, Fall Symposiums, Professional Series Workshops, Human Performance Technology Institutes. Publications: *Performance Improvement Journal* (10/yr)—the common theme is performance improvement practice or technique that is supported by research or germane theory. *PerformanceXpress* (12/yr)—monthly newsletter published online. *Performance Improvement Quarterly* (PIQ) is a peer-reviewed journal created to stimulate professional discussion in the field and to advance the discipline of HPT through publishing scholarly works. ISPI Bookstore, the ISPI online bookstore, is hosted in partnership with John Wiley & Sons. Updated: 4/24/2006. April Davis, Associate Exec. Dir., april@ispi.org.

Media Communications Association—International (MCA-I). 7600 Terrace Avenue, Suite 203, Middleton, WI 53562, United States. 608-827-5034. Fax: 608-831-5122. E-mail: info@mca-i.org. Web site: http://www.mca-i.org. Susan Rees, Executive Director. The Rees Group. Formerly the International Television Association. Founded in 1968, MCA-I's mission is to provide media communications professionals opportunities for networking, forums for education, and resources for information. MCA-I also offers business services, such as low-cost insurance, buying programs, etc., to reduce operating costs. MCA-I also confers the highly acclaimed Media Festival awards (The Golden Reel is back!) on outstanding multimedia productions. Visit MCA-I's Web site for full details. Membership: Over 3000 individual and corporate members. Membership programs also are available to vendors for relationship and business development. $160, individual; $455, organizational; PLATINUM—$7,500; GOLD—$5,500; SILVER—$2,500; BRONZE—$1250; Various Partnerships with Association Conferences. Publications: *MCA-I News* (quarterly newsletter); *MCA-I Member2Member E-News* (6/yr.); *Membership Directory* (annual). Updated: 4/25/04. Kenan Branam, Webmaster, (713) 426-5854, kenan@bra.

International Visual Literacy Association, Inc. (IVLA). Darrell Beauchamp, IVLA Treasurer, Navarro College, 3200 W. 7th Ave., Corsicana, TX 75110, United States. 903-875-7441. Fax: 903-874-4636. E-mail: darrell.beauchamp@navarrocollege.edu. Web site: www.ivla.org. Darrell Beauchamp. IVLA provides a multidisciplinary forum for the exploration, presentation, and discussion of all aspects of visual learning, thinking, communication, and expression. It also serves as a communication link bonding professionals from many disciplines who are creating and sustaining the study of the nature of visual experiences and literacy. It promotes and evaluates research, programs, and projects intended to increase effective use of visual communication in education, business, the arts, and commerce. IVLA was founded in 1968 to promote the concept of visual literacy and is an affiliate of AECT. Membership of 500 people, mostly from academia and from many disciplines. Anyone interested in any visual-verbal area should try our organization: architecture, engineering, dance, the arts, computers, video, design, graphics, photography, visual languages, mathematics, acoustics, physics, chemistry, optometry, sciences, literature, library, training, education, etc. Membership: $40 regular; $20 student and retired; $45 outside United States; corporate memberships available; $500 lifetime membership. Meetings: We are an international organization and have conferences abroad once every third year. Yearly conference usually Oct./Nov. in selected locations. Publications: *The Journal of Visual Literacy* (biannual—juried research papers); *Selected Readings from the Annual Conference*; and *The Visual Literacy Review* (newsletter—4 times per year). Updated: 7/7/04. darrell.beauchamp@navarrocollege.edu.

International Recording Media Association (IRMA). 182 Nassau St., Suite 204, Princeton, NJ 08542-7005, United States. (609)279-1700. Fax: (609)279-1999. E-mail: info@ recordingmedia.org. Web site: http://www.recordingmedia.org. Charles Van Horn, President; Guy Finley, Associate Exec. Director. IRMA, the content delivery and storage association, is the worldwide forum on trends and innovation for the delivery and storage of entertainment and information. Founded in 1970, this global trade association encompasses organizations involved in every facet of content delivery. Beginning with the introduction of the audiocassette, through the home video revolution, and right up to today's digital delivery era, IRMA has always been the organization companies have turned to for news, networking, market research, information services, and leadership. Membership: Over 400 corporations, IRMAs membership includes raw material providers, manufacturers, replicators, duplicators, packagers, copyright holders, logistics providers, and companies from many other related industries. Corporate membership includes benefits to all employees. Corporate membership dues based on gross dollar volume in our industry. Meetings: Annual Recording Media Forum (Palm Springs, CA); December Summit (New York, NY). Publications: *Mediaware Magazine*; *Annual International Source Directory*, *Quarterly Market Intelligence*. Updated: 3/20/2007. Guy Finley, gfinley@recordingmedia.org.

Library Administration and Management Association (LAMA). 50 E. Huron St., Chicago, IL 60611, United States. (312)280-5032. Fax: (312)280-5033. E-mail: lama@ ala.org. Web site: http://www.ala.org/lama. Lorraine Olley, Executive Director; Catherine Murray-Rust, President. MISSION: The Library Administration and Management Association encourages and nurtures current and future library leaders, and develops and promotes outstanding leadership and management practices. VISION: LAMA will be the foremost organization developing present and future leaders in library and information services. IMAGE: LAMA is a welcoming community where aspiring and experienced leaders from all types of libraries, as well as those who support libraries,come together to gain skills in a quest for excellence in library management, administration, and leadership. Sections include: Buildings and Equipment Section (BES); Fundraising & Financial Development Section (FRFDS); Library Organization & Management Section (LOMS); Human Resources Section (HRS); Public Relation and Marketing Section (PRMS); Systems & Services Section (SASS); and Measurement, Assessment and Evaluation Section (MAES). Membership: 4,800. $50, regular(in addition to ALA membership); $65, organizations and corporations; $15, library school students. Meetings: ALA Annual Conference 2006, New Orleans, June 22–27; Midwinter Meeting 2007, San Diego, Jan 9–14. Publications: *Library Administration & Management* (quarterly); *LEADS from LAMA* (electronic newsletter, irregular). Updated: 3/13/2006. Fred Reuland, e-mail: freuland@ala.org.

Library and Information Technology Association (LITA). 50 E. Huron St, Chicago, IL 60611, United States. (312)280-4270, (800)545-2433, ext. 4270. Fax: (312)280-3257. E-mail: lita@ala.org. Web site: http://www.lita.org. Mary C. Taylor, Exec. Dir., mtaylor@ala.org. An affiliate of the American Library Association, LITA is concerned with library automation; the information sciences; and the design, development, and implementation of automated systems in those fields, including systems development, electronic data processing, mechanized information retrieval, operations research, standards development, telecommunications, video communications, networks and collaborative efforts, management techniques, information technology, optical technology, artificial intelligence and expert systems, and other related aspects of audiovisual activities and hardware applications. LITA's members come from all types of libraries and institutions focusing on information technology in libraries. They include library decision-makers, practitioners, information professionals and vendors. Membership: Approximately 5,400 members. $35 (first time) plus membership in ALA; $25, library school students; $35, first year; renewal memberships $45 plus ALA cost. Meetings: National Forum, fall. Publications: *LITA*

Newsletter (electronic only; see Web site). *Information Technology and Libraries* (*ITAL*): Contains the table of contents, abstracts and some full-text of *ITAL*, a refereed journal published quarterly by the Library and Information Technology Association. *Technology Electronic Reviews* (*TER*): *TER* is an irregular electronic serial publication that provides reviews and pointers to a variety of print and electronic resources about information technology. LITA Publications List: Check for information on LITA Guides and Monographs. Updated: 6/10/03, lita@ala.org.

Library of Congress (LOC). James Madison Bldg., 101 Independence Ave., SE, Washington, DC 20540, United States. (202)707-5000. Fax: (202)707-1389. E-mail: pao@loc.gov. Web site: http://www.loc.gov. Dr. James Billington, Librarian of Congress. The Library of Congress is the major source of research and information for the Congress. In its role as the national library, it catalogs and classifies library materials in some 460 languages, distributes the data in both printed and electronic form, and makes its vast collections available through interlibrary loan, on-site to anyone over high school age, and through its award-winning Web site at www.loc.gov. The Library is the largest library in the world, with more than 126 million items on 532 miles of bookshelves. The collections include nearly 19 million cataloged books, 2.6 million recordings, 12 million photographs, 4.8 million maps, and 56 million manuscripts. It contains the worlds largest television and film archive, acquiring materials through gift, purchase, and copyright deposit. In 2002, some 23 million items (discs, cassettes, braille materials) produced by the Library in Braille and recorded formats for persons who are blind or physically challenged were circulated to a readership of more than 500,000. The collections of the Motion Picture, Broadcasting and Recorded Sound Division include nearly 900,000 moving images. The Library's public catalog, as well as other files containing copyright and legislative information, are available on the Library's Web site. In 2000, the Library launched the Americas Library Web site for children and families. This easy-to-use, interactive site (www.americaslibrary.gov) allows children to "have fun with history." The site receives more than 150 million hits annually. See list on Librarys Web site. Updated: 5/23/03. Audrey Fischer, 202-707-2905, afis@loc.gov.

Lister Hill National Center for Biomedical Communications (LHNCBC). National Library of Medicine, 8600 Rockville Pike, Bethesda, MD 20894, United States. (301)496-4441. Fax: (301)402-0118. E-mail: lhcques@lhc.nlm.nih.gov. Web site: http://lhncbc. nlm.nih.gov/. Clement J. McDonald, MD, Director, ClemMcDonald@mail.nih.gov. The Lister Hill National Center for Biomedical Communications is a research and development division of the National Library of Medicine (NLM). The Center conducts and supports research and development in the dissemination of high-quality imagery, medical language processing, and high-speed access to biomedical information, intelligent database systems development, multimedia visualization, knowledge management, data mining, and machine-assisted indexing. The Lister Hill Center also conducts and supports research and development projects focusing on educational applications of state-of-the-art technologies including the use of microcomputer technology incorporating stereoscopic imagery and haptics, the Internet, and videoconferencing technologies for training health care professionals and disseminating consumer health information. The Center's Collaborator for High Performance Computing and Communication serves as a focus for collaborative research and development in those areas, cooperating with faculties and staff of health sciences educational institutions. Health profession educators are assisted in the use and application of these technologies through periodic training, demonstrations and consultations. High-Definition (HD) video is a technology area that has been explored and developed within the Center, and is now used as the NLM standard for all motion imaging projects considered to be of archival value. Advanced three-dimensional animation and photo-realistic rendering techniques have also become required tools for use in visual projects within the Center. Fact sheet (and helpful links to other publications) at: http://www.nlm.nih.gov/pubs/factsheets/lister_hill.html. Updated: 3/27/2007. Melanie Modlin, 301-496-7771, mm354i@nih.gov.

Magazine Publishers of America (MPA). 919 Third Ave., 22nd Floor, New York, NY 10022, United States. (212)872-3700. Fax: (212)888-4217. E-mail: infocenter@magazine. org. Web site: http://www.magazine.org. Nina Link, Pres. MPA is the trade association of the consumer magazine industry. MPA promotes the greater and more effective use of magazine advertising, with ad campaigns in the trade press and in member magazines, presentations to advertisers and their ad agencies, and magazine days in cities around the United States. MPA runs educational seminars, conducts surveys of its members on a variety of topics, represents the magazine industry in Washington, DC, and maintains an extensive library on magazine publishing. Membership: 230 publishers representing more than 1,200 magazines. Meetings: 2002 American Magazine Conference, The Arizona Biltmore Resort & Spa, Phoenix, AZ, Oct 20–23; 2003, The Westin Mission Hills Resort & Spa Rancho Mirage (Palm Springs), CA, Oct 19–22. Publications: *Newsletter of Consumer Marketing*; *Sales Edge*; *Newsletter of International Publishing*; *Washington Newsletter*. Updated: 5/8/02.

Medical Library Association (MLA). 65 E. Wacker Pl., Ste. 1900, Chicago, IL 60601-7246, United States. (312)419-9094. Fax: (312)419-8950. E-mail: info@mlahq.org. Web site: http://www.mlanet.org. Carla J. Funk, MLS, MBA, CAE, Executive Director. MLA, a nonprofit, educational organization, comprises health sciences information professionals with more than 4,500 members worldwide. Through its programs and services, MLA provides lifelong educational opportunities, supports a knowledgebase of health information research, and works with a global network of partners to promote the importance of quality information for improved health to the health care community and the public. Membership categories: Regular Membership, Institutional Membership, International Membership, Affiliate Membership, Student Membership. $165, regular; $110, introductory; $255–600, institutional, based on total library expenditures, including salaries, but excluding grants and contracts; $110, international; $100, affiliate; $40, student. Meetings: National annual meeting held every May; most chapter meetings are held in the fall. Publications: *MLA News* (newsletter, 10/yr.); *Journal of the Medical Library Association* (quarterly scholarly publication.); *MLA DocKit* series, collections of representative, unedited library documents from a variety of institutions that illustrate the range of approaches to health sciences library management topics); *MLA BibKits*, selective, annotated bibliographies of discrete subject areas in the health sciences literature; standards; surveys; and copublished monographs. Updated: 4/21/2006. Tomi Gunn, mlams@mlahq.org, 312.419.9094 ×11.

Mid-continent Research for Education and Learning (McREL). 2550 S. Parker Rd., Suite 500, Aurora, CO 80014, United States. (303)337-0990. Fax: (303)337-3005. E-mail: info@mcrel.org. Web site: http://www.mcrel.org. J. Timothy Waters, Exec. Dir. McREL is a private, nonprofit organization whose purpose is to improve education through applied research and development. McREL provides products and services, primarily for K-12 educators, to promote the best instructional practices in the classroom. McREL houses one of 10 regional educational laboratories funded by the U.S. Department of Education, Institute for Educational Science. The regional laboratory helps educators and policymakers work toward excellence in education for all students. It also houses one of 10 Eisenhower Regional Consortia for Mathematics and Science Education. McREL has particular expertise in standards-based education systems, leadership for school improvement, effective instructional practices, teacher quality, mathematics and science education improvement, early literacy development, and education outreach programs. Membership: not a membership organization. No dues. Meetings: Annual conference. Publications: *Changing Schools* (quarterly newsletter); *Noteworthy* (annual monograph on topics of current interest in education reform). Numerous technical reports and other publications. Check Web site for current listings. Updated: 4/26/04. Linda Brannan, Info. Resource Mgr., info@mcrel.org.

Minorities in Media (MIM). New England Educational Media Association (NEEMA), SICET (the Society of International Chinese in Educational Technology), and KSET (the Korean Society for Educational Technology). The ECT Foundation is also related to AECT. Each of these affiliated organizations has its own listing in the Yearbook. AECT Divisions include: Instructional Design & Development, Information & Technology Management, Training & Performance, Research & Theory, Systemic Change, Distance Learning, Media & Technology, Teacher Education, and International, and Multimedia Productions., 2500 members in good standing from K-12, college and university and private sector/government training. Anyone interested can join. There are different memberships available for students, retirees, corporations and international parties. We also have a new option for electronic membership for international affiliates. $99.00 standard membership discounts are available for students and retirees. Additional fees apply to corporate memberships or international memberships. Summer Leadership Institute held each July. In 2007 it will be in Chicago, IL. AECT holds an annual Conference each year in October. In 2007, it will be held in Anaheim, CA., Tec Trends (6/yr., free with AECT membership; available by subscription through Springer at www.springeronline.com); Educational Technology Research and Development (6/yr. $46 members; available by subscription through Springer at www.springeronline.com); Quarterly Review of Distance Education (q., $55 to AECT members); many books; videotapes., 4/4/2007, Phillip Harris by email at pharris@aect.org

Museum Computer Network (MCN). 65 Enterprise, Aliso Viejo, CA 92656, United States. (877) 626-3800. Fax: (949) 330-7621. E-mail: membership@mcn.edu. Web site: http://www.mcn.edu. Leonard Steinbach, Pres. 2001–2002; Fred Droz, Admin. MCN is a nonprofit organization of professionals dedicated to fostering the cultural aims of museums through the use of computer technologies. We serve individuals and institutions wishing to improve their means of developing, managing and conveying museum information through the use of automation. We support cooperative efforts that enable museums to be more efficient at creating and disseminating cultural and scientific knowledge as represented by their collections and related documentation. MCN members are interested in building databases complete with images and multimedia components for their collections, in using automated systems to tract membership, manage events and design exhibits, in discovering how multimedia systems can increase the effectiveness of educational programs, and in developing professional standards to ensure the investment that information represents. Membership: MCN's membership includes a wide range of museum professionals representing more than 600 major cultural institutions throughout the world. The primary job duties of our membership include 33% Registrar/Collection Managers; 33% IT professionals; and the remaining third comprised of administrator, curators, and education professionals. Our membership comes from all sorts of cultural heritage organizations, including art, historical and natural history museums and academia. Each member receives a complimentary issue of *Spectra* (published three times a year), a discount on conference fees, can subscribe to MCN-L, the online discussion list, and can join, at no additional cost, any of our Special Interest Groups which focus on such topics as intellectual property, controlled vocabulary, digital imaging, IT managers, and data standards. $300, corporate; $200, institution; $60, individual. Meetings: Annual Conference, held in the fall; educational workshops. Publications: *Spectra* (newsletter), published three times a year. Subscription to *Spectra* is available to libraries only for $75 plus $10 surcharge for delivery. *eSpectra* is a monthly electronic magazine featuring online links to information of interest to the museum computing community, job openings, and a calendar of museum-related events, such as workshops, conferences, or seminars. Updated: 6/12/02. fred.droz@mcn.edu.

Museum of Modern Art, Circulating Film and Video Library (MoMA). 11 W. 53rd St., New York, NY 10019, United States. (212)708-9530. Fax: (212)708-9531. E-mail: circfilm@moma.org. Web site: http://www.moma.org. William Sloan, Libr. Provides film and video rentals and sales of over 1,300 titles covering the history of film from the 1890s to the present. It also includes an important collection of work by leading video artists and is the sole distributor of the films of Andy Warhol. The Circulating Film and Video Library continues to add to its holdings of early silents, contemporary documentaries, animation, avant-garde, independents and video and to make these available to viewers who otherwise would not have the opportunity to see them. The Circulating Film and Video Library has 16mm prints available for rental, sale, and lease. Some of the 16mm titles are available on videocassette. The classic film collection is not. The video collection is available in all formats for rental and sale. The Library also has available a limited number of titles on 35mm, including rare early titles preserved by the Library of Congress. They also now distribute some films on art and artists formally handled by the American Federation of the Arts as well as the film work of contemporary artists such as Richard Serra and Yoko Ono. Membership: Not a membership organization. Publications: Information on titles may be found in the free Price List, the Documentaries on the Arts brochure and the Films of Andy Warhol brochure, all available from the Library. Circulating *Film and Video Catalog Vols. 1 and 2*, a major source book on film and history, is available from the Museum's Mail Order Dept. (To purchase by mail order, a form is included in the Price List.). Updated: 4/27/04. Kitty Cleary, Kitty_Cleary@moma.org.

National Aeronautics and Space Administration (NASA). NASA Headquarters, 300 E Street SW, Washington, DC 20546, United States. (202)358-0103. Fax: (202)358-3032. E-mail: shelley.canright@nasa.gov. Web site: http://education.nasa.gov. Angela Phillips Diaz, Assistant Administrator for Education. From elementary through postgraduate school, NASA's educational programs are designed to inspire the next generation of explorers by capturing students' interest in science, mathematics, and technology at an early age; to channel more students into science, engineering, and technology career paths; and to en-hance the knowledge, skills, and experiences of teachers and university faculty. NASAs educational programs include NASA Spacelink (an electronic information system); video-conferences (60-minute interactive staff development videoconferences to be delivered to schools via satellite); and NASA Television (informational and educational television pro-gramming). Additional information is available from the Office of Education at NASA Headquarters and counterpart offices at the nine NASA field centers. Further informa-tion may be obtained from the NASA Education Homepage (education.nasa.gov) and also accessible from the NASA Public Portal at www.nasa.gov. See learning in a whole new light! Publications and Products can be searched and downloaded from the follow-ing URL: http://www.nasa.gov/audience/foreducators/5-8/learning/index.html. Updated: 3/7/2006. Shelley Canright (see above).

National Alliance for Media Arts and Culture (NAMAC). 145 Ninth Street, Suite 250, San Francisco, CA 94103, United States. (415)431-1391. Fax: (415)431-1392. E-mail: na-mac@namac.org. Web site: http://www.namac.org. Helen DeMichel, Codirector. NAMAC is a nonprofit organization dedicated to increasing public understanding of and support for the field of media arts in the United States. Members include media centers, cable access cen-ters, universities, and media artists, as well as other individuals and organizations providing services for production, education, exhibition, distribution, and preservation of video, film, audio, and intermedia. NAMACs information services are available to the general public, arts and nonarts organizations, businesses, corporations, foundations, government agen-cies, schools, and universities. Membership: 300 organizations, 75 individuals. $75–$450, institutional (depending on annual budget); $75, indiv. Meetings: Biennial Conference. Publications: *Media Arts Information Network*; *The National Media Education Directory*, annual anthology of case-studies, *A Closer Look*; periodic White Paper reports; *Digital Directions: Convergence Planning for the Media Arts*. Updated: 3/29/2006. Daniel Schott, namac@namac.org.

National Association for the Education of Young Children (NAEYC). 1509 16th St., Washington, DC 20036-1426, United States. (202)232-8777. Fax: (202)328-1846. E-mail: naeyc@naeyc.org. Web site: http://www.naeyc.org. Mark R. Ginsberg, Ph.D., Exec. Dir.; Alan Simpson, Communications. Dedicated to improving the quality of care and education provided to young children (birth–8 years). Membership: NAEYC has over 100,000 members, including teachers and directors in child care, preschool and Head Start programs and in classrooms from kindergarten through third grade. Other members include researchers, professional development experts and parents. Anyone who is interested in improving early childhood education is welcome to join NAEYC. Most members join NAEYC as well as state and local Affiliates in their area, and the dues vary according to which Affiliates you join. Generally, dues range between $45 and $75 annually, with lower rates for full-time students. Meetings: 2003 Annual Conference, Chicago, IL; 2004 Annual Conference, Anaheim, CA. Publications: *Young Children* (journal); more than 100 books, posters, videos, and brochures. Updated: 3/5/03. Alan Simpson, ext 11605.

National Association for Visually Handicapped (NAVH). 22 West 21st St., 6th Floor, New York, NY 10010, United States. (212) 889-3141. Fax: (212) 727-2931. E-mail: navh@navh.org. Web site: http://www.navh.org. Dr. Lorraine H. Marchi, Founder/CEO; Cesar Gomez, Executive Director. NAVH ensures that those with limited vision do not lead limited lives. We offer emotional support; training in the use of visual aids and special lighting; access to a wide variety of optical aids, electronic equipment and lighting; a large print, nationwide, free-by-mail loan library; large print educational materials; free quarterly newsletter; referrals to eye care specialists and local low vision resources; self-help groups for seniors and working adults; and educational outreach to the public and professionals. Membership: It is not mandatory to become a member in order to receive our services. However, your membership helps others retain their independence by allowing NAVH to provide low-vision services to those who cannot afford to make a donation. In addition, members receive discounts on visual aids, educational materials and our catalogs. Corporations and publishers may also join to help sponsor our services. Please contact us for more information. Membership is $50 a year for individuals. Publishers and corporations interested in membership should contact NAVH. Meetings: Seniors support group 2 times a month; Seminar on low vision for ophthalmology residents; yearly showcase of the latest in low vision technology, literature and services. Publications: Free quarterly newsletter distributed throughout the English-speaking world; *Visual Aids Catalog*; *Large Print Loan Library Catalog*; informational pamphlets on vision, common eye diseases and living with limited vision; booklets for professionals who work with adults and children with limited vision. Updated: 3/9/2007. Janet Handy, (212) 889-3141.

National Association of Media and Technology Centers (NAMTC). NAMTC, 7105 First Ave. SW, Cedar Rapids, IA 52405, United States. 319 654 0608. Fax: 319 654 0609. E-mail: bettyge@mchsi.com. Web site: www.namtc.org. Betty Gorsegner Ehlinger, Executive Director. NAMTC is committed to promoting leadership among its membership through networking, advocacy, and support activities that will enhance the equitable access to media, technology, and information services to educational communities. Membership is open to regional, K-12, and higher education media centers that serve K-12 students as well as commercial media and technology centers. Membership: Institutional and corporate members numbering approximately 225. $100 institutions; $300, corporations. Meetings: Regional meetings are held throughout the United States annually. A national Leadership Summit is held in the spring. Publications: Membership newsletter is *ETIN*, a quarterly publication. Updated: 3/24/2006. Betty Gorsegner Ehlinger, bettyge@mchsi.com.

National Association of State Textbook Administrators (NASTA). 120 S. Federal Place, Room 206, Santa Fe, NM 87501, United States. 505.827.1801. Fax: 505.827.1826. E-mail: president@nasta.org. Web site: http://www.nasta.org. David P. Martinez, President. NASTA's purposes are to (1) foster a spirit of mutual helpfulness in adoption, purchase, and distribution of instructional materials; (2) arrange for study and review of textbook specifications; (3) authorize special surveys, tests, and studies; and (4) initiate action leading to better quality instructional materials. Services provided include a working knowledge of text construction, monitoring lowest prices, sharing adoption information, identifying trouble spots, and discussions in the industry. The members of NASTA meet to discuss the textbook adoption process and to improve the quality of the instructional materials used in the elementary, middle, and high schools. NASTA is not affiliated with any parent organization and has no permanent address. Textbook administrators from each of the 21 states that adopt instructional material at the state level on an annual basis. Membership: $25 annually per individual. Meetings: NASTA meets annually during the month of July. Publications: *Manufacturing Standards and Specifications for Textbooks* (*MSST*). Updated: 6/9/03. Ali Ahmed, ali.ahme@uwlax.edu.

NCTI (NCTI). 8022 Southpark Circle, Suite 100, Littleton, CO 80120, United States. (303)797-9393. Fax: (303)797-9394. E-mail: info@ncti.com. Web site: http://www.ncti. com. Tom Brooksher, President and CEO; Alan Babcock, Chief Learning Officer. Located in the Denver area, NCTI provides workforce performance products, services, and education to the cable and broadband industry. NCTI offers extensive and up-to-date training in electronic, instructor-led, paper-based and Web-delivery formats; services such as customized curriculum development, performance assessment and testing; and professional development through college credit and industry certification. Since 1968, system operators, contractors, and industry vendors have turned to NCTI to train more than 250,000 industry professionals. By creating innovative products that develop and improve skills; services that evaluate, identify, and improve workforce competencies; and education that advances careers, NCTI remains committed to providing individuals and their employers the knowledge they need to succeed in the broadband industry. For more information, please visit www.ncti.com. Updated: 5/20/03. Michael Guilfoyle, michaelg@ncti.com.

National Center to Improve Practice (NCIP). Education Development Center, Inc., 55 Chapel St., Newton, MA 02458-1060, United States. (617)969-7100 ext. 2387TTY (617)969-4529. Fax: (617)969-3440. E-mail: jzorfass@edc.org. Web site: http://www.edc. org/FSC/NCIP. Judith Zorfass, Project Dir. NCIP, a project funded by the U.S. Department of Education's Office for Special Education Programs (OSEP), promoted the effective use of technology to enhance educational outcomes for students (preschool to grade 12) with sensory, cognitive, physical, social, and emotional disabilities. NCIP's award-winning Web site offers users online discussions (topical discussions and special events) about technology and students with disabilities, an expansive library of resources (text, pictures, and video clips), online workshops, "guided tours" of exemplary classrooms, "spotlights" on new technology, and links to more than 100 sites dealing with technology and/or students with disabilities. NCIP also produces a series of videos illustrating how students with disabilities use a range of assistive and instructional technologies to improve their learning. Membership: Membership and dues are not required. NCIP presented sessions at various educational conferences around the country. Publications: *Video Profile Series: Multimedia and More: Help for Students with Learning Disabilities; Jeff with Expression: Writing in the Word Prediction Software*; *Tools for Angie: Technology for Students Who Are Visually Impaired*; *Telling Tales in ASL and English: Reading, Writing and Videotapes*; *Welcome to My Preschool: Communicating with Technology*. Excellent for use in training, workshops, and courses, videos may be purchased individually or as a set of five by calling (800)793-5076. A new video to be released this year focuses on standards, curriculum, and assessment in science.

National Clearinghouse for Bilingual Education (NCBE). The George Washington University, 2011 “ I” Street NW, Suite 200, Washington, DC 20006. (202)467-0867. Fax: (800)531-9347, (202)467-4283. E-mail: askncbe@ncbe.gwu.edu. Web site: http://www.ncbe.gwu.edu. Dr. Minerva Gorena, Interim Dir. NCBE is funded by the U.S. Department of Education's Office of Bilingual Education and Minority Languages Affairs (OBEMLA) to collect, analyze, synthesize, and disseminate information relating to the education of linguistically and culturally diverse students in the United States. NCBE is operated by The George Washington University Graduate School of Education and Human Development, Center for the Study of Language and Education in Washington, DC. Online services include the NCBE Web site containing an online library of hundreds of cover-to-cover documents, resources for teachers and administrators, and library of links to related Internet sites; an e-mail-based, biweekly news bulletin, Newsline; an electronic discussion group, NCBE Roundtable; and an e-mail-based question answering service, AskNCBE. Publications: short monographs, syntheses, and reports. Request a publications catalog for prices. The catalog and some publications are available at no cost from the NCBE and other Web sites. Updated: 5/23/02. Judy Zorfass, jzorfass@edc.org.

National Clearinghouse for English Language Acquisition and Language Instruction Educational Programs (National Clearinghouse). The George Washington University, 2121 K Street NW, Suite 260, Washington, DC 20037, United States. (800) 321-6223, (202)467-0867, (800)531-9347. Fax: (202)467-4283. E-mail: askncbe@ncbe.gwu.edu. Web site: http://www.ncbe.gwu.edu. Dr. Minerva Gorena, Director. The National Clearinghouse for English Language Acquisition and Language Instruction Educational Programs is funded by the U.S. Department of Education's Office of English Language Acquisition, Language Enhancement and Academic Achievement for Limited English Proficient Students (OELA) to collect, analyze, synthesize, and disseminate information relating to the education of linguistically and culturally diverse students in the United States. Online services include a Web site containing an online library of hundreds of cover-to-cover publications, resources for teachers and administrators; links to related Web sites; a weekly e-mail news bulletin, *Newsline*; a monthly e-mail magazine, *Outlook*; and an e-mail question answering service. The National Clearinghouse is operated by The George Washington University Graduate School of Education and Human Development, Center for the Study of Language and Education in Washington, DC. The National Clearinghouse is funded by the U.S. Department of Education. Membership: There is no membership, and services are provided at no cost. Publications: Short monographs, syntheses, and reports. Request a publications catalog for prices. The catalog and most publications are available at no cost from the National Clearinghouse Web site. Updated: 4/11/02. Anneka Kindler, akindler@ncbe.gwu.edu.

National Commission on Libraries and Information Science (NCLIS). 1800 M Street, NW, Suite 350, North Tower, Washington, DC 20036-5841, United States. (202)606-9200. Fax: (202)606-9203. E-mail: info@nclis.gov. Web site: http://www.nclis.gov. C. Beth Fitzsimmons, Chairman, A permanent independent agency of the U.S. government charged with advising the executive and legislative branches on national library and information policies and plans. The Commission reports directly to the president and Congress on the implementation of national policy; conducts studies, surveys, and analyses of the nation's library and information needs; appraises the inadequacies of current resources and services; promotes research and development activities; conducts hearings and issues publications as appropriate; and develops overall plans for meeting national library and information needs and for the coordination of activities at the federal, state, and local levels. The Commission provides general policy advice to the Institute of Museum and Library Services (IMLS) director relating to library services included in the Library Services and Technology Act (LSTA). Membership: 16 commissioners (14 appointed by the president and confirmed by the Senate, the Librarian of Congress, and the Director of the IMLS). Meetings: Average 2–3 meetings a year. Updated: 3/27/2007. Kim Miller, kmiller@nclis.gov.

National Communication Association (NCA). 1765 N Street, NW, Washington, DC 22003, United States. 202-464-4622. Fax: 202-464-4600. E-mail: dwallick@natcom.org. Web site: http://www.natcom.org. Roger Smitter, Exec. Dir. A voluntary society organized to promote study, criticism, research, teaching, and application of principles of communication, particularly of speech communication. Founded in 1914, NCA is a nonprofit organization of researchers, educators, students, and practitioners, whose academic interests span all forms of human communication. NCA is the oldest and largest national organization serving the academic discipline of Communication. Through its services, scholarly publications, resources, conferences and conventions, NCA works with its members to strengthen the profession and contribute to the greater good of the educational enterprise and society. Research and instruction in the discipline focus on the study of how messages in various media are produced, used, and interpreted within and across different contexts, channels, and cultures. Membership: 7,700. From $60 (Student) to $300 (Patron). Life membership also available. Meetings: Four regional conferences (ECA, ESCA SSCA, WSCA) and 1 Annual National Conference. Publications: *Spectra Newsletter* (monthly); *Quarterly Journal of Speech*; *Communication Monographs*; *Communication Education*; *Critical Studies in Mass Communication*; *Journal of Applied Communication Research*; *Text and Performance Quarterly*; *Communication Teacher*; *Index to Journals in Communication Studies through 1995*; *National Communication Directory of NCA and the Regional Speech Communication Organizations* (CSSA, ECA, SSCA, WSCA). For additional publications, request brochure. Updated: 3/7/2006. Dennis Wallick, dwallick@natcom.org.

National Council for Accreditation of Teacher Education (NCATE). 2010 Massachusetts Ave. NW, Suite 500, Washington, DC 20036, United States. (202)466-7496. Fax: (202)296-6620. E-mail: ncate@ncate.org. Web site: http://www.ncate.org. Arthur E. Wise, Pres. NCATE is a consortium of professional organizations that establishes standards of quality for and accredits professional education units in schools, colleges, and departments of education. Membership: Members include 34 National Professional organizations. NCATE accredits colleges of education in over 550 higher education institutions and over 100 institutions are in candidacy. See http://www.ncate.org/accred/fees.htm. See http://www.ncate.org/partners/meetings.htm. Publications: *Standards*; *Quality Teaching* (newsletter, twice yearly; online resources for institutions and the public); *NCATE Speakers Guide*; *Handbook for Accreditation Visits*. Check our Web site for the complete publications list. Updated: 2/27/03. ncate@ncate.org.

National Council of Teachers of English: Commission on Media, Assembly on Media Arts (NCTE). 1111 W. Kenyon Rd., Urbana, IL 61801-1096, United States. (217)328-3870. Fax: (217)328-0977. E-mail: public_info@ncte.org. Web site: http://www.ncte.org. Kent Williamson, NCTE Executive Director; David Bruce, Commission Director; Mary Christel, Assembly Chair. The NCTE Commission on Media is a deliberative and advisory body that each year identifies and reports to the NCTE Executive Committee on key issues in the teaching of media; reviews what the Council has done concerning media during the year; recommends new projects and persons who might undertake them. The commission monitors current and projected NCTE publications (other than journals), suggests topics for future NCTE publications on media, and performs a similar role of review and recommendation for the NCTE Annual Convention program. Occasionally, the commission undertakes further tasks and projects as approved by the Executive Committee. The NCTE Assembly on Media Arts promotes communication and cooperation among all individuals who have a special interest in media in the English language arts; presents programs and special projects on this subject; encourages the development of research, experimentation, and investigation in the judicious uses of media in the teaching of English; promotes the extensive writing of articles and publications devoted to this subject; and integrates the efforts of those with an interest in this subject. Membership: The National Council of Teachers of English, with 50,000 individual and institutional members worldwide, is dedicated to improving the teaching and learning of English and the language arts at all levels of education. Members include elementary, middle, and high school teachers; supervisors of English programs; college and university faculty; teacher educators; local and state agency English specialists; and professionals in related fields. The members of the NCTE Commission on Media are NCTE members appointed by the director of the group. Membership in the Assembly on Media Arts is open to members and nonmembers of NCTE. Membership in NCTE is $40 a year; adding subscriptions to its various journals adds additional fees. Membership in the Assembly on Media Arts is $15 a year. http://www.ncte.org/conventions/. Meetings: 96th NCTE Annual Convention, November 20–25, 2003, San Francisco, California; 94th NCTE Annual Convention, November 16–21, 2006, Nashville, Tennessee. Publications: NCTE publishes about 20 books a year. Visit http://www.ncte.org/pubs/books/ and http://www.ncte.org/store. NCTEs journals include *Language Arts, English Journal, College English, College Composition and Communication, English Education, Research in the Teaching of English, Teaching English in the Two-Year College, Voices from the Middle, Primary Voices, K-6 Talking Points, Classroom Notes Plus, English Leadership Quarterly, The Council Chronicle* (included in NCTE membership). Journal information is available at http://www.ncte.org/pubs/journals/. The Commission on Media doesn't have its own publication. The Assembly on Media Arts publishes *Media Matters*, a newsletter highlighting issues, viewpoints, materials, and events related to the study of media. Assembly members receive this publication. Updated: 4/14/2006. Lori Bianchini, public_info@ncte.org.

National Council of the Churches of Christ in the USA (NCC). Communication Commission, 475 Riverside Dr., New York, NY 10115, United States. (212)870-2574. Fax: (212)870-2030. E-mail: dpomeroy@ncccusa.org. Web site: http://www.ncccusa.org. Wesley M. "Pat" Pattillo, Director of Communication. Ecumenical arena for cooperative work of Protestant and Orthodox denominations and agencies in broadcasting, film, cable, and print media. Offers advocacy to government and industry structures on media services. Services provided include liaison to network television and radio programming; film sales and rentals; information about telecommunications; and news and information regarding work of the National Council of Churches, related denominations, and agencies. Works closely with other faith groups in the Interfaith Broadcasting Commission. Online communication Web site: www.ncccusa.org. Thirty-six denominations. Twice a year. Publications: *EcuLink*. Updated: 4/12/02. Dave Pomeroy, dpomeroy@ncccusa.org.

National Education Knowledge Industry Association (NEKIA). 1718 Connecticut Avenue, NW, Suite 700, Washington, DC 20009-1162, United States. 202-518-0847. Fax: (202)785-3849. E-mail: info@nekia.org. Web site: http://www.nekia.org. James W. Kohlmoos, Pres. Founded in 1997, NEKIA is a nonpartisan, nonprofit trade association representing the emerging knowledge industry. In the same way that research and development are crucial to the sciences, manufacturing, and agriculture, research and development is vital to the field of education. In recent years, a new field—the education knowledge industry—has emerged to provide structure, quality, and coherence to education practices, policies, and products. The members of this industry include researchers, educational developers, service providers, and a rapidly increasing number of entrepreneurs. Together, they work across the education spectrum from research to development to dissemination to practice. NEKIA brings educational innovation and expertise to all communities while providing its members with leadership, policy development, advocacy, professional development, and the promotion of quality products and services.

NEKIA's mission is to advance the development and use of research-based knowledge for the improvement of the academic performance of all children. The association's members are committed to finding new and better ways to support and expand high-quality education research, development, dissemination, technical assistance, and evaluation at the federal, regional, state, tribal, and local levels. Membership: 28. Meetings: Annual Legislative and Policy Conference; Annual Meeting. Publications: *Plugging In: Choosing and Using Educational Technology*; *Probe: Designing School Facilities for Learning*; *Education Productivity*; *Technology Infrastructure in Schools*. Updated: 5/12/03. John Waters may be reached using info above.

National Endowment for the Humanities (NEH). Division of Public Programs, Media Program, 1100 Pennsylvania Ave., NW, Room 426, Washington, DC 20506, United States. (202)606-8269. Fax: (202)606-8557. E-mail: publicpgms@neh.gov. Web site: http://www. neh.gov. Tom Phelps, Acting Director, Division of Public Programs. The NEH is an independent federal grant-making agency that supports research, educational, and public programs grounded in the disciplines of the humanities. The Division of Public Program's Media Program supports film and radio programs in the humanities for public audiences, including children and adults. All programs in the Division of Public Program support various technologies, specifically Web sites both as stand-alone projects and as extensions of larger projects such as museum exhibitions. Nonprofit institutions and organizations including public television and radio stations. Visit the Web site (http://www.neh.gov) for application forms and guidelines as well as the Media Log, a cumulative listing of projects funded through the Media Program. Updated: 3/9/2007. Margaret Scrymser, mscrymser@ neh.gov.

National Federation of Community Broadcasters (NFCB). 1970 Broadway, Ste. 1000, Oakland, CA 94612, United States. 510 451-8200. Fax: 510 451-8208. E-mail: nfcb@ aol.com. Web site: http://www.nfcb.org. Carol Pierson, President and CEO. NFCB represents non-commercial, community-based radio stations in public policy development at the national level and provides a wide range of practical services, including technical assistance. Membership: 250. Noncommercial community radio stations, related organizations, and individuals. Range from $200 to $3500 for participant and associate members. Meetings: 2002 Charlottesville, VA; 2003 San Francisco; 2004 Albuquerque; 2005 Baltimore; 2006 Portland, OR; 2007 New Orleans. Publications: *Public Radio Legal Handbook*; *AudioCraft*; *Community Radio News*; *Let a Thousand Voices Speak: A Guide to Youth in Radio Projects*; *Guide to Underwriting*. Updated: 3/26/2007. Ginny Z. Berson, ginnyz@ nfcb.org.

National Film Board of Canada (NFBC). 350 Fifth Ave., Suite 4820, New York, NY 10118, United States. (212)629-8890. Fax: (212)629-8502. E-mail: j.sirabella@nfb.ca. Web site: www.nfb.ca. John Sirabella, U.S. Marketing Mgr./Nontheatrical Rep. The National Film Board of Canada has been producing and distributing films for over sixty years, and has become particularly well known for its insightful point-of-view documentaries and creative auteur animation. The NFBC has made more than 10,000 original films, which have won more than 4,000 prizes including ten Academy Awards. Updated: 2/27/03. Lisa Malcolm, l.malcolm@nfb.ca.

National Film Information Service (NFIS). Center for Motion Picture Study, 333 So. La Cienega Blvd.,Beverly Hills, CA 90211, United States. (310)247-3000. Fax: (310) 657-5597. E-mail: nfis@oscars.org. Web site: http://www.oscars.org/mhl/nfis.html. The fee-based National Film Information Service of the Margaret Herrick Library can answer queries from patrons outside of a 150-mile radius from the Fairbanks Center for Motion Picture Study. N.F.I.S. can accept inquiries via e-mail, fax or letter but all work undertaken by N.F.I.S. requires payment in advance. Requests for information should be as specific as possible. Updated: 6/5/03.

National Gallery of Art (NGA). Department of Education Resources, 2000B South Club Drive, Landover, MD 20785, United States. (202)842-6273. Fax: (202)842-6935. E-mail: EdResources@nga.gov. Web site: http://www.nga.gov/education/classroom/loanfinder/. Leo J. Kasun, Education Resources Supervisory Specialist. This department of NGA is responsible for the production and distribution of 120+ educational audiovisual programs, including interactive technologies. Materials available (all loaned free to individuals, schools, colleges and universities, community organizations, and noncommercial television stations) range from videocassettes and color slide programs to CD-ROMs, and DVDs. All videocassette and DVD programs are closed captioned. A free catalog of programs is available upon request. All CD-ROMs, DVDs, utilizing digitized images on the galleries collection are available for long-term loan. Our free-loan lending program resembles that of a library and because we are a federally funded institution we have a membership system. Last year we lent programs directly to over one million borrowers. Our programs are available to anyone who requests them and they range from individuals to institutions. Extension Programs Catalogue. Updated: 3/9/2007. Leo Kasun, (202) 842-6280 or L-Kasun@ nga.gov.

National ITFS Association (NIA). 77 W. Canfield, Detroit, MI 48201, United States. (313) 577-2085. Fax: (313) 577-5577. E-mail: p.gossman@wayne.edu. Web site: http:// www.itfs.org. Patrick Gossman, Chair, Bd. of Dirs.; Don MacCullough, Exec. Dir. Established in 1978, NIA is a nonprofit, professional organization of Instructional Television Fixed Service (ITFS) licensees, applicants, and others interested in ITFS broadcasting. ITFS is a very high frequency television broadcast service that is used to broadcast distance learning classes, two-way internet service and data service to schools and other locations where education can take place. The goals of the association are to gather and exchange information about ITFS, gather data on utilization of ITFS, act as a conduit for those seeking ITFS information, and assist migration from video broadcast to wireless, broadband Internet services using ITFS channels. The NIA represents ITFS interests to the FCC, technical consultants, and equipment manufacturers. The association uses its Web site and Listserv list to provide information to its members in areas such as technology, programming content, FCC regulations, excess capacity leasing, and license and application data. Membership: The current membership consists of Educational Institutions and nonprofit organizations that hold licenses issued by the Federal Communications Commission for Instructional Television Fixed Service (ITFS). We also have members that have an interest in ITFS and members such as manufacturers of ITFS-related equipment and law firms that represent licensees. We have two main types of memberships: Voting memberships for ITFS licensees only, and nonvoting memberships for other educational institutions and sponsors. See the Web site http://www.itfs.org for details. Meetings: Annual Member Conference, January/February. http://www.itfs.org. Updated: 5/13/03. Orville Thein, VP of the NIA, 319-398-5663.

National PTA (National PTA). 541 North Fairbanks Ct, Ste. 1300, Chicago, IL 60611, United States. (312)670-6782. Fax: (312)670-6783. E-mail: info@pta.org. Web site: http:// www.pta.org. Anna Weselak, President (2005–2007); Warlene Gary, Chief Executive Officer. Advocates the education, health, safety, and well-being of children and teens. Provides parenting education and leadership training to PTA volunteers. National PTA partners with the National Cable & Telecommunications Association on the "Taking Charge of Your TV" project by training PTA and cable representatives to present media literacy workshops. The workshops teach parents and educators how to evaluate programming so they can make informed decisions about what to allow their children to see. The National PTA in 1997 convinced the television industry to add content information to the TV rating system. Membership: 6.2 million. Membership open to all interested in the health, welfare, and education of children and who support the PTA mission. http://www.pta.org/aboutpta/mission_en.asp. Vary by local unit—national dues portion is $1.75 per member annually. Meetings: National convention, held annually in June in different regions of the country, is open to PTA members; convention information available on the Web site. Publications: *Our Children* (magazine) plus electronic newsletters and other Web-based information for members and general public. Updated: 4/21/2006. Information Center, info@pta.org.

National Press Photographers Association, Inc. (NPPA). 3200 Croasdaile Dr., Suite 306, Durham, NC 27705, United States. 919-383-7246. Fax: (919)383-7261. E-mail: president@nppa.org. Web site: http://www.nppa.org. Todd Stricker, President. An organization of professional news photographers who participate in and promote photojournalism in publications and through television and film. Sponsors workshops, seminars, and contests; maintains an audiovisual library of subjects of media interest. Membership: 9,000. $90, domestic; $120, international; $55, student. Meetings: An extensive array of conferences, seminars, and workshops are held throughout the year. Publications: *News Photographer* (magazine, monthly); *The Best of Photojournalism* (annual book). Updated: 3/5/04.

National Public Broadcasting Archives (NPBA). Hornbake Library, University of Maryland, College Park, MD 20742, United States. (301)405-9255. Fax: (301)314-2634. E-mail: tc65@umail.umd.edu. Web site: http://www.library.umd.edu/UMCP/NPBA/npba.html. Thomas Connors, Archivist. NPBA brings together the archival record of the major entities of noncommercial broadcasting in the United States. NPBAs collections include the archives of the Corporation for Public Broadcasting (CPB), the Public Broadcasting Service (PBS), and National Public Radio (NPR). Other organizations represented include the Midwest Program for Airborne Television Instruction (MPATI), the Public Service Satellite Consortium (PSSC), Americas Public Television Stations (APTS), Children's Television Workshop (CTW), and the Joint Council for Educational Telecommunications (JCET). NPBA also makes available the personal papers of many individuals who have made significant contributions to public broadcasting, and its reference library contains basic studies of the broadcasting industry, rare pamphlets, and journals on relevant topics. NPBA also collects and maintains a selected audio and video program record of public broadcastings national production and support centers and of local stations. Oral history tapes and transcripts from the NPR Oral History Project and the Televisionaries Nal History Project are also available at the archives. The archives are open to the public from 9 A.M. to 5 P.M., Monday through Friday. Research in NPBA collections should be arranged by prior appointment. For further information, call (301)405-9988. Updated: 2/27/03. Tom Connnors tc65@umail.umd.edu.

National Religious Broadcasters (NRB). 9510 Technology Dr., Manassas, VA 20110, United States. (703)330-7000. Fax: (703)330-7100 E-mail: atower@nrb.org. Web site: http://www.nrb.org. Dr. Frank Wright, President, fwright@nrb.org. National Religious Broadcasters is a Christian international association of radio and TV stations, Web casters, program producers, consultants, attorneys, agencies, and churches. NRB maintains rapport with the FCC, the broadcasting industry, and government bodies. NRB encourages growth of Christian communications through education, professional training, publications, and networking opportunities. The association maintains relationships with other media associations to promote cutting-edge technology and practice. NRB fosters high professional standards through its Code of Ethics and Statement of Faith. Membership: 1,500 members who are organizations and individuals representing Christian TV, radio and internet stations and broadcasters, program producers, churches, agencies, consultants, attorneys, and companies who are directly or indirectly related to Christian broadcasting. Intercollegiate Religious Broadcasters (IRB) is a chapter of NRB for colleges and universities who have a student run broadcast. Membership is open for both faculty and students. Based on broadcast-related expenses. Associate members have fixed rates. Meetings: Annual NRB Convention and Exhibition, 5 regional conventions held during summer and fall. Publications: *NRB* magazine (10 issues a year); *Directory of Religious Media and CD Rom*; *Inside NRB* (for members only), an e-mail broadcast; *Convention News*, a daily newspaper at national convention. Updated: 6/10/03. Anne Tower, VP of Membership, atower@nrb.org.

National School Boards Association/ITTE: Education Technology Programs (NSBA/ITTE). 1680 Duke St, Alexandria, VA 22314, United States. (703)838-6722. Fax: (703)548-5516. E-mail: itte@nsba.org. Web site: http://www.nsba.org/itte. Ann Lee Flynn, Director, Education Technology. ITTE was created to help advance the wise uses of technology in public education. ITTE renders several services to state school boards associations, sponsors conferences, publishes, and engages in special projects. The Technology Leadership Network, the membership component of ITTE, is designed to engage school districts nationwide in a dialogue about technology in education. This dialogue is carried out via newsletters, meetings, special reports, projects, and online communications. The experience of the Network is shared more broadly through the state associations' communications with all school districts. Membership: Approximately 400 school districts in 47 states and Canada. Membership includes mostly public school districts, though private schools are eligible as well. Contacts include technology directors, superintendents, board members, curriculum directors, library/media specialists, teachers. Based upon the school district's student enrollment. Meetings: T+L2: Leading Learning to a Higher Level Conference, Oct. 27–29, 2004, CO. Publications: *Virtual Realities: A School Leaders Guide to Online Education*; *Connecting Schools and Communities through Technology*; *Technology Professional Development for P-12 Educators*; *Legal Issues and Education Technology: A School Leader's Guide*, 2nd edition; *Education Leadership Toolkit: A Desktop Companion*; *Plans and Policies for Technology in Education: A Compendium*, 2nd edition; *Models of Success: Case Study of Technology in Schools*; *Investing in School Technology: Strategies to Meet the Funding Challenge/School Leader's Version*; *Leadership and Technology: What School Board Members Need to Know*; *Technology Leadership Newsletter*; *Technology & School Design: Creating Spaces for Learning*. Updated: 3/8/04. Ann Flynn, itte@nsba.org, 703-838-6764.

National Science Foundation (NSF). 4201 Wilson Blvd., Arlington, VA 22230, United States. 703-292-5111. E-mail: lboutchy@nsf.gov. Web site: http://www.nsf.gov/start.htm. Mary Hanson, Chief, Media Relations and Public Affairs. Linda Boutchyard, Contact Person. NSF, an independent federal agency, funds research and education in all fields of science, mathematics, and engineering. With an annual budget of about $5 billion, NSF funds reach all 50 states, through grants, contracts, and cooperative agreements to more than 2,000 colleges, universities, and other institutions nationwide. NSF receives more than 50,000 requests for funding annually, including at least 30,000 new proposals. Applicants should refer to the NSF Guide to Programs. Scientific material and media reviews are available to help the public learn about NSF-supported programs.

NSF news releases and tipsheets are available electronically via *NSFnews*. To subscribe, send an e-mail message to listmanager@nsf.gov; in the body of the message, type "subscribe nsfnews" and then type your name. Also see NSF news products at http://www.nsf.gov/od/lpa/news/start.htm, http://www.eurekalert.org/, and http://www.ari.net/newswise. In addition, NSF has developed a Web site that offers information about NSF directorates, offices, programs, and publications at http://nsf.gov. Updated: 5/8/02. Linda Boutchyard, Contact Person.

National Telemedia Council Inc. (NTC). 1922 University Ave., Madison, WI 53726, United States. (608)218-1182. Fax: (608)218-1183. E-mail: NTelemedia@aol.com. Web site: http://www.nationaltelemediacouncil.org and www.journalofmedialiteracy.org. Karen Ambrosh, President; Marieli Rowe, Exec. Dir. The NTC is a national, nonprofit professional organization dedicated to promoting media literacy, or critical media viewing and listening skills. This is done primarily through the *Journal of Media Literacy*, the publication of the National Telemedia Council, as well as work with teachers, parents, and caregivers. NTC activities include publishing the *Journal of Media Literacy*, the *Teacher Idea Exchange* (T.I.E.), and the Jessie McCanse Award for individual contribution to media literacy, assistance to media literacy educators and professionals. Member/subscribers to the *Journal of Media Literacy*, currently over 500, including individuals, organizations, schools and university libraries across the globe including Asia, Australia, Europe, North and South America. Membership: Our membership is open to all those interested in media literacy. Individuals: $35, basic; $50, contributing; $100, patron. Organizations/Library: $60. Corporate sponsorship: $500. (Additional Postage for Overseas). Meetings: No major meetings scheduled this year. Publications: The Journal of Media Literacy. Updated: 3/30/2007. Marieli Rowe.

Native American Public Telecommunications (NAPT). 1800 North 33rd Street, Lincoln, NE 68503, United States. (402)472-3522. Fax: (402)472-8675. E-mail: native@unl.edu. Web site: http://nativetelecom.org. Shirley K. Sneve, Exec. Dir. Native American Public Telecommunications (NAPT) supports the creation, promotion, and distribution of Native public media. We accomplish this mission by:

- Producing and developing educational telecommunication programs for all media, including public television and public radio.

- Distributing and encouraging the broadest use of such educational telecommunications programs.

- Providing training opportunities to encourage increasing numbers of American Indians and Alaska Natives to produce quality public broadcasting programs.

- Promoting increased control and use of information technologies by American Indians and Alaska Natives.

- Providing leadership in creating awareness of and developing telecommunications policies favorable to American Indians and Alaska Natives.

- Building partnerships to develop and implement telecommunications projects with tribal nations, Indian organizations, and native communities. Membership: No Membership. Publications: *The Vision Maker* (e-newsletter). Updated: 3/26/2007. Rebecca Fauver, rfauver1@unl.edu.

The NETWORK, Inc. (NETWORK). 136 Fenno Drive, Rowley, MA 01969-1004, United States. 800-877-5400. Fax: (978)948-7764, (978)948-7836. E-mail: davidc@ thenetworkinc.org. Web site: www.thenetworkinc.org. David Crandall, President. A nonprofit research and service organization providing training, research and evaluation, technical assistance, and materials for a fee to schools, educational organizations, and private sector firms with educational interests. The NETWORK has been helping professionals manage and learn about change since 1969. Our Leadership Skills series of computer-based simulations extends the widely used board game versions of *Making Change*^{TM} and *Systems Thinking/Systems Changing*^{TM} with the addition of *Improving Student Success: Teachers, Schools and Parents* to offer educators a range of proven professional development tools. Available in 2007, *Networking for Learning*, originally developed for the British Department for Education and Skills, offers schools considering forming or joining a network a risk-free means of exploring the many challenges. Membership: None required, no dues, fee for service. Call. Publications: *Making Change: A Simulation Game* [board and computer versions]; *Systems Thinking/Systems Changing: A Simulation Game* [board and computer versions]; *Improving Student Success: Teachers, Schools and Parents* [computer-based simulation]; *Systemic Thinking: Solving Complex Problems*; *Benchmarking: A Guide for Educators*; *Networking for Learning*; *Check Yourself into College: A Quick and Easy Guide for High School Students*. Updated: 3/9/2007. David Crandall, davidc@thenetworkinc.org.

New England Educational Media Association (NEEMA). c/o Charles White, Executive Director, 307 Cumberland Terrace, 5C, Myrtle Beach, SC 29572, United States. (843) 497-4630. Fax: (617) 559-6191. E-mail: nadeau@ccsu.edu. Web site: www.neema.org. Charles White, Executive Director. An affiliate of AECT, NEEMA is a regional professional association dedicated to the improvement of instruction through the effective utilization of school library media services, media, and technology applications. For over 75 years, it has represented school library media professionals through activities and networking efforts to develop and polish the leadership skills, professional representation, and informational awareness of the membership. The Board of Directors consists of departments of education as well as professional leaders of the region. An annual conference program and a Leadership Program are offered in conjunction with the various regional state association conferences. NEEMA focuses on school library media issues among the six New England states, consequently, membership is encouraged for school library media specialists in this region. Membership: Regular membership $20. Student /retired membership $10. Meetings: Annual Leadership Conference and Business Meeting. Publications: *NEEMS Views*. Updated: 3/12/03. Fran Zilonis, fran_zilonis@newton.mec.edu.

New York Festivals (NYF). 260 West 39th Street, 10th Floor, New York, NY 10018, United States. 212-643-4800. Fax: 212-643-0170. E-mail: info@newyorkfestivals.com. Web site: http://www.newyorkfestivals.com. Alisun Armstrong, Executive Director. New York Festivals (NYF) is an international awards company founded in 1957. Recognizing The World's Best Work™ in advertising, programming, design, and marketing, NYF honors creativity and effectiveness in global communications through six different annual competitions. New York Festivals International Film & Video Awards is one of the oldest extant international festivals in the world. Known best for honoring informational, educational, and industrial film production, the New York Festivals Film & Video Awards is entering its 50th year of recognizing The Worlds Best Work™ in categories including documentaries, business theatre, short and feature-length films, home video productions, distance learning, slide productions, and multiscreen productions. Winners are honored in a black-tie event in Manhattan in January. The 2007 International Film & Video Awards will open for entry on July 5. The discount deadline is August 23 (enter online by that date and get a 10% discount off the entry total), and the final deadline will be September 22. For more information and fees, plus a full list of categories and the rules and regulations, please visit www.newyorkfestivals.com. Membership: No membership feature. The competition is open to any nonbroadcast media production. Winners are posted on our Web site at www.newyorkfestivals.com. Updated: 4/24/2006. Alisun, Mkt Cor., aarmstrong@newyorkfestivals.com.

North Central Regional Educational Laboratory (NCREL). 1120 E. Diehl Road Suite 200, Naperville, IL 60563-1486, United States. (630)649-6500, (800)356-2735. Fax: (630)649-6700. E-mail: info@ncrel.org. Web site: http://www.ncrel.org. Gina Burkhardt,

Executive Director. NCREL's work is guided by a focus on comprehensive and systemic school restructuring that is research-based and learner-centered. One of ten Office of Educational Research and Improvement (OERI) regional educational laboratories, NCREL disseminates information about effective programs, develops educational products, holds conferences, provides technical assistance, and conducts research and evaluation. A special focus is on technology and learning. In addition to conventional print publications, NCREL uses computer networks, videoconferencing via satellite, and video and audio formats to reach its diverse audiences. NCREL's Web site includes the acclaimed Pathways to School Improvement. NCREL operates the Midwest Consortium for Mathematics and Science Education, which works to advance systemic change in mathematics and science education. Persons living in Illinois, Indiana, Iowa, Michigan, Minnesota, Ohio, and Wisconsin are encouraged to call the NCREL Resource Center with any education-related questions. NCREL also hosts the North Central Regional Technology in Education Consortium that helps states and local educational agencies successfully integrate advanced technologies into K–12 classrooms, library media centers, and other educational settings. Staff of 100, region covers Michigan, Minnesota, Wisconsin, Illinois, Ohio, Indiana and Iowa. Meetings: Annual conference. Publications: *Learning Point* (three times a year). Updated: 5/14/03. Arlene Hough, arlene.hough@ncrel.org.

Northwest College and University Council for the Management of Educational Technology (NW/MET). c/o WITS, Willamette University, 900 State St., Salem, OR 97301, United States. (503)370-6650. Fax: (503)375-5456. E-mail: mmorandi@willamette.edu. Web site: http://www.nw-met.org. Kees Hof, Director; Marti Morandi, Membership Chair. NW/MET is a group of media professionals responsible for campus-wide media services. Founded in 1976, NW/MET is comprised of members from three provinces of Canada and four northwestern states. Is restricted to information technology managers with campus-wide responsibilities for information technology services in the membership region. Corresponding membership is available to those who work outside the membership region. Current issues include managing emerging technologies, distance education, adaptive technologies, staff evaluation, course management, faculty development, copyright, and other management/administration issues. Organizational goals include identifying the unique status problems of media managers in higher education. Membership: approx. $35. Meetings: An annual conference and business meeting are held each year, rotating through the region. Publications: An annual Directory and Web site. Updated: 3/8/2007. Marti Morandi by e-mail at mmorandi@willamette.edu.

Northwest Regional Educational Laboratory (NWREL). 101 SW Main St., Suite 500, Portland, OR 97204, United States. (503)275-9500. Fax: (503)275-0448. E-mail: info@nwrel.org. Web site: http://www.nwrel.org. Dr. Carol Thomas, Exec. Dir. One of 10 Office of Educational Research and Improvement (OERI) regional educational laboratories, NWREL works with schools and communities to improve educational outcomes for children, youth, and adults. NWREL provides leadership, expertise, and services based on the results of research and development. The specialty area of NWREL is school change processes. It serves Alaska, Idaho, Oregon, Montana, and Washington. Membership: 856 organizations. Publications: *Northwest Education* (quarterly journal). Updated: 3/8/2007. Jennifer Klump Resource Advisor, 503 275 0454.

Online Audiovisual Catalogers (OLAC). United States. E-mail: neumeist@buffalo.edu. Web site: http://www.olacinc.org/. In 1980, OLAC was founded to establish and maintain a group that could speak for catalogers of audiovisual materials. OLAC provides a means for exchange of information, continuing education, and communication among catalogers of audiovisual materials and with the Library of Congress. While maintaining a voice with the bibliographic utilities that speak for catalogers of audiovisual materials, OLAC works toward common understanding of AV cataloging practices and standards. Membership: 700. United States and Canada.

Personal Memberships	One year	$20.00
	Two years	$38.00
	Three years	$55.00
Institutional Memberships	One year	$25.00
	Two years	$48.00
	Three years	$70.00
Other Countries		
All Memberships	One year	$25.00
	Two years	$48.00
	Three years	$70.00

Publications: OLAC Newsletter (bi-annual). Updated: 4/21/2006. Sue Neumeister, neumeist@buffalo.edu.

Online Computer Library Center, Inc. (OCLC). 6565 Frantz Rd., Dublin, OH 43017-3395, United States. (614)764-6000. Fax: (614)764-6096. E-mail: oclc@oclc.org. Web site: http://www.oclc.org. Jay Jordan, President and CEO. Founded in 1967, OCLC On-line Computer Library Center is a nonprofit, membership, computer library service and research organization dedicated to the public purposes of furthering access to the world's information and reducing information costs. More than 45,000 libraries in 84 countries and territories around the world use OCLC services to locate, acquire, catalog, lend, and preserve library materials. Researchers, students, faculty, scholars, professional librarians, and other information seekers use OCLC services to obtain bibliographic, abstract, and full-text information. OCLC and its member libraries cooperatively produce and main-tain WorldCat—the OCLC Online Union Catalog. OCLC FOREST PRESS, a division of OCLC since 1988, publishes the Dewey Decimal Classification. Digital Collection and Preservation Services, a division of OCLC since 1994, provides digitizing, microfilming, and archiving services worldwide. OCLCs netLibrary provides libraries with eContent solutions that support Web-based research, reference, and learning. OCLC welcomes in-formation organizations around the world to be a part of our unique cooperative. A variety of participation levels are available to libraries, museums, archives, historical societies, and professional associations. Membership: OCLC membership represents more than 45,000 li-braries in 84 countries and territories around the world. OCLC also has 60 Members Council delegates who are elected by and represent the OCLC member libraries in their respective regions. Meetings: OCLC Members Council (3/yr.) Held in Dublin, Ohio. Publications: An-nual Report (1/yr.); *OCLC Newsletter* (4/yr.); *OCLC Abstracts* (1/week, electronic version only). Updated: 5/5/04. Carrie Lauer, OCLC Communications: lauerc@oclc.org.

Pacific Film Archive (PFA). University of California, Berkeley Art Museum, 2625 Du-rant Ave., Berkeley, CA 94720-2250, United States. (510)642-1437 (library); (510)642-1412 (general). Fax: (510)642-4889. E-mail: pfalibrary@uclink.berkeley.edu. Web site: http://www.bampfa.berkeley.edu. Susan Oxtoby, Senior Curator of Film; Nancy Goldman, Head, PFA Library and Film Study Center. Sponsors the exhibition, study, and preservation of classic, international, documentary, animated, and avant-garde films. Provides on-site research screenings of films in its collection of over 7,000 titles. Provides access to its collections of books, periodicals, stills, and posters (all materials are noncirculating). Of-fers BAM/PFA members and University of California, Berkeley, affiliates reference and research services to locate film and video distributors, credits, stock footage, etc. Library hours are 1 P.M. to 5 P.M. Mon. to Thurs. Membership: Membership is through our parent organization, the UC Berkeley Art Museum and Pacific Film Archive, and is open to anyone. The BAM/PFA currently has over 3,000 members. Members receive free admission to the Museum; reduced-price tickets to films showing at PFA; access to the PFA Library & Film Study Center; and many other benefits. Applications and more information is available at http://www.bampfa.berkeley.edu/membership/index.html. $40 indiv. and nonprofit departments of institutions. Publications: *BAM/PFA Calendar* (6/yr.). Updated: 3/13/03. Nancy Goldman, e-mail: NLG@uclink.berkeley.edu.

Pacific Resources for Education and Learning (PREL). 900 Fort Street Mall, Suite 1300, Honolulu, HI 96813, United States. (808) 441-1300. Fax: (808) 441-1385. E-mail: askprel@prel.org. Web site: http://www.prel.org/. Thomas W. Barlow, Ed.D., President and Chief Executive Officer. Pacific Resources for Education and Learning (PREL) is an independent, nonprofit 501(c)(3) corporation that serves the educational community in the United States. Affiliated to Pacific islands, the continental United States, and countries throughout the world. PREL bridges the gap between research, theory, and practice in education and works collaboratively to provide services that range from curriculum development to assessment and evaluation. PREL serves the Pacific educational community with quality programs and products developed to promote educational excellence. We work throughout school systems, from classroom to administration, and collaborate routinely with governments, communities, and businesses. Above all, we specialize in multicultural and multilingual environments. From direct instruction to professional development to creation of quality educational materials, PREL is committed to ensuring that all students, regardless of circumstance or geographic location, have an equal opportunity to develop a strong academic foundation. PREL brings together in the Center for Information, Communications, and Technology (CICT) an experienced cadre of specialists in Web site development and design, educational technology, distance and online learning, multimedia production, interactive software development, writing and editing, graphics, and print production. By combining tested pedagogy with leading edge technology, PREL can create learning materials encompassing a wide variety of subject matter and delivery methods. PREL partners with researchers, schools, evaluators, publishers, and leaders in the learning technology industry to develop state-of-the-art learning tools and technology solutions. There are vast disparities across the Pacific when it comes to school resources, technology access, and bandwidth. PREL's goal is to work effectively in any type of setting in which an application is needed. With routine travel and a staff presence throughout the northern Pacific, PREL has resolved to reach underserved communities, determine their needs, and meet their requirements with the appropriate delivery and dissemination methods. Multimedia, software, and Web site conception, design, and delivery have become critical components of many learning programs. Our projects include development of teacher and student resources and resource kits, learning games, software solutions, and complex interactive database design. Distance learning content and delivery extend educational resources to audiences and individuals outside the classroom setting. Distance options both enhance and exponentially increase learning opportunities. The CICT is a premier provider of distance education, integrating curriculum and technology. High-quality publications are a PREL hallmark. PREL produces and distributes numerous high-quality publications for educators, including its research compendium, *Research into Practice*; *Pacific Educator* magazine; educational books and videos; and briefs and reports on research findings and current topics of interest.

-PREL serves teachers and departments and ministries of education in American Samoa, Commonwealth of the Northern Mariana Islands, Federated States of Micronesia (Chuuk, Kosrae, Pohnpei, and Yap) Guam, Hawaii, the Republic of the Marshall Islands, and the Republic of Palau. In addition, we work with the educational community on the continental United States and countries throughout the world. Membership: We are not a membership organization. We are grant-funded with grants from the United States Departments of Education, Labor, Health and Human Services, and other federal funding agencies such as the Institute of Museum and Library Services and the National Endowment for the Arts. In addition we have projects in partnership with regional educational institutions. Internationally we have worked with the International Labor Organization and the World Health Organization and are currently working with Save the Children on a US AID project in the Philippines. Meetings: PREL supports the annual Pacific Educational Conference (PEC), held each July. Publications: Publications are listed on the PREL Web site at http://ppo.prel.org/. Most are available in both PDF and HTML format. Some recent publications are described below: *Focus on Professional Development,* (Research-Based Practices in Early Reading Series). *A Focus on Professional Development* is the fourth in the Research-Based Practices in Early Reading Series published by the Regional Educational Laboratory (REL) at Pacific Resources for Education and Learning (PREL). Because reading proficiency is fundamental to student achievement across all subjects and grades, the preparation of the teachers and administrators who are responsible for providing early reading instruction is of special importance. This booklet examines what research tells us about professional development and about the role that effective professional development plays in improving both teacher performance and student achievement. http://www.prel.org/products/re_/prodevelopment.pdf (902K) *Look and See: Using the Visual Environment as Access to Literacy* (Research Brief) This paper describes how the visual environment—what we see when we look—can be used to develop both visual and verbal literacy, including aesthetic appreciation, comprehension, and vocabulary. http://www.prel.org/products/re_/look_see.pdf (1M) *Measuring the Effectiveness of Professional Development in Early Literacy: Lessons Learned* (Research Brief). This Research Brief focuses on the methodology used to measure professional development (PD) effectiveness. It examines the needs that generated this research, what PREL did to meet those needs, and lessons that have been learned as a result. In particular, it discusses the development of a new instrument designed to measure the quality of PD as it is being delivered. http://www.prel.org/products/re_/effect_of_pd.pdf (730K). *Pacific Early Literacy Resource Kit* CD-ROM (Early Literacy Learning Resources). The *Pacific Early Literacy Resource Kit* was developed from PRELs research-based work performed with early literacy teachers in US-affiliated Pacific islands. The contents of the Resource Kit represent information, products, and processes we found beneficial as we worked to support literacy teachers in their efforts to improve student literacy achievement. http://www.prel.org/toolkit/index.htm. *Research Into Practice 2006* (PREL Compendium). This 86-page volume of PRELs annual research compendium brings together articles detailing research conducted during 2005 by PREL. The six articles in this issue focus on putting research findings to work to improve education. http://www.prel.org/products/pr_/compendium06/tableofcontents.asp Updated: 4/13/2006. Jackie Burniske, askprel@prel.org.

Photographic Society of America (PSA). 3000 United Founders Blvd., Suite 103, Oklahoma City, OK 73112, United States. (405)843-1437. Fax: (405)843-1438. E-mail: hq@psa-photo.org. Web site: http://www.psa-photo.org. Linda Lowery, operations manager. A nonprofit organization for the development of the arts and sciences of photography and for the furtherance of public appreciation of photographic skills. Its members, largely advanced amateurs, consist of individuals, camera clubs, and other photographic organizations. Divisions include electronic imaging, color slide, video motion picture, nature, photojournalism, travel, pictorial print, stereo, and techniques. Sponsors national, regional, and local meetings, clinics, and contests. Membership: 5500. $42, North America; $48 elsewhere. Meetings: 2002 International Conference of Photography, Pittsburg, PA, Sept 2–7, 2002. Publications: PSA Journal. Updated: 4/24/02. Linda Lowery, Operations manager, PSA.

Professors of Instructional Design and Technology-PIDT-Instructional Technology Dept., 220 War Memorial Hall, Virginia Tech-Blacksburg-VA-24061-0341-USA-(540)231-5587-Fax (540)231-9075-moorem@VT.EDU-https://www.conted.vt.edu/ssl/pidt-reg.htm-Dr. Mike Moore, or Dr. Ed Caffarella, contact persons.-An informal organization designed to encourage and facilitate the exchange of information among members of the instructional design and technology academic and corporate communities. Also serves to promote excellence in academic programs in instructional design and technology and to encourage research and inquiry that will benefit the field while providing leadership in the public and private sectors in its application and practice.-Faculty employed in higher education institutions whose primary responsibilities are teaching and research in instructional technology, their corporate counterparts, and other persons interested in the goals and activities of the PIDT. No formal membership. Contact either Dr. Mike Moore (moorem@vt.edu), or Dr. Ed Caffarella (CAFFAREL@unco.edu) to be added to listserv for announcements of meeting times, location and conferecnce registration. Cohosts alternate between Virginia Tech and University of Northern Colorado and meetings alternate annually between Virginia and Colorado. Meeting usually is around the middle of May and usually runs from Friday pm to Monday am. e.g., 2002 Virginia, 2003 Colorado-There are no dues, officers, bylaws or formal organization. Contact Dr. Mike Moore (moorem@vt.edu), or Dr. Ed Caffarella Dr. Mike Moore, or Dr. Ed Caffarella (CAFFAREL@unco.edu) for information.-Annual conference alternates between Virginia and Colorado; see above e-mail address for information and registration-none-5/8/02-Mike Moore, moorem@vt.edu or 540-231-5 87

PBS Adult Learning Service-ALS-1320 Braddock Place-Alexandria-VA-22314-1698-US-(800)257-2578-(703)739-8471-als@pbs.org-http://www.pbs.org/als/-Clinton OBrien, Senior Director-The PBS Adult Learning Service is a provider of course content to colleges and universities nationwide. Offerings include Web-based online courses and video-basesd telecourses. Content is developed by prominent educators and producers and designed for college-credit use. Public television stations nationwide cooperate with colleges that offer PBS courses to reach local populations of adult learners. A pioneer in the widespread use of video in college-credit learning, PBS first began distributing telecourses in 1981. Since that time, more than 3 million students have earned college credit through telecourses from PBS. -Nearly 500 institutions are PBS Associate Colleges. These members save on licensing and acquisition fees for PBS courses and are entitled to discounts on related services such as Web-based scheduling, master broadcast tape duplication, and educational videotape purchase. Non–members still have access to the same content and services; they simply pay higher fees.-$1,500. Multi-college and consortium rates are available-n/a-PBS Adult Learning Service Course Catalog. PBS Course Bulletin (monthly e-mail update for course faculty and administrators) -5/29/02-Kathy Dunne, kdunne@pbs.org

PBS VIDEO-PBS VIDEO-1320 Braddock Pl.-Alexandria-VA-22314-US-(703)739-5380; (800)344-3337-(703)739-5269-jcecil@pbs.org-http://shop2.org/pbsvideo/.-Jon Cecil, Dir.-PBS VIDEO Marketing. Markets and distributes PBS television programs for sale on videocassette and DVD to colleges, public libraries, schools, governments, and other organizations and institutions.-N/A-N/A-N/A-PBS VIDEO Catalogs of New and Popular Video (4/yrs). Website: PBS VIDEO Online Catalog at http://shopPBS.com/teachers.-5/13/03-Jon Cecil, 703-739-5157 or jcecil@pbs.org

Public Library Association-PLA-50 E. Huron St.-Chicago-IL-60611-US-(312)280-5PLA-(312)280-5029-pla@ala.org-www.pla.org-Greta Southard, Exec. Dir.-An division of the American Library Association, PLA is concerned with the development, effectiveness, and financial support of public libraries. It speaks for the profession and seeks to enrich the professional competence and opportunities of public librarians. -PLA has 9,940 members as of 2/2002. Any member of the American Library Association is eligible to join PLA.-$50, open to all ALA members-Spring Symposium March 3–6, 2003 Chicago IL; 10th National Conference Feburary 24–28, 2004 Seattle WA-Public Libraries (bi-monthly); electronic newsletter sent to members-4/10/02-Greta Southard 800-545-2433×5028

Puppeteers of America, Inc.-POA-PO Box 29417-Parma-OH-44129-0417-US-888-568-6235-440-843-7867-PofAjoin@aol.com-http://www.puppeteers.org-Joyce and Chuck Berty, Membership Officers-Formed in 1937, POA holds festivals for puppetry across the country, supports local guilds, presents awards, sponsors innovative puppetry works, provides consulting, and provides research materials through the Audio-Visual Library. A National Festival is held in the odd number years and Regional Festivals are held in the even number years at various locations around the United States. The group supports a National Day of Puppetry the last Saturday in April. Local celebrations of the Art of Puppetry are held throughout the United States. The Puppetry Store is an invaluable source of books and miscellaneous printed materials for Puppeteers or anyone interested in Puppetry. The Puppetry Journal is the magazine published quarterly for the members of the organization and Playboard is the Bi-Monthly newletter.-Our current membership is over 2,200 memberships from people around the world interested in the art of puppetry. Our Membership consists of Performing Professionals to librarians, storytellers or someone just interested in the art of puppetry. We offer subscription memberships to Libraries and discounted memberships to Seniors and Youths. −$40, Single Adult; $50, couple; $20, youth (17–6); $25 Full-time Student; $25 Senior (65 and over); $60, family; $70 Company or Business; $35, Journal subscription available to libraries. -Great Lakes Regional Festival July 26–28,2002; Great Plains June 27–30,2002;NE-MidAtl July 11–14,2002; Pac.NW &SW 23–26 2002-The Puppetry Journal (q) A quarterly magazine published only for our membership. It is the only publication in the United States dedicated to Puppetry in America. Playboard bi-monthly newsletter published to up-date the voting membership on the business of the organization.-4/10/02-Joyce Berty e-mail pofajoin@aol.com or phone

Recording for the Blind and Dyslexic-RFB&D-20 Roszel Road-Princeton-NJ-08540-US-(609)452-0606. Customer Service (800)221-4792-(609)987-8116-information@rfbd.org-http://www.rfbd.org.-Richard Scribner, Pres.-Recording for the Blind & Dyslexic (RFB&D), a national nonprofit volunteer organization founded in 1948, is the nations educational library serving people who cannot read standard print effectively because of a learning disability, visual impairment or other physical disability. RFB&D operates 32 recording studios and offices across the country. Our more than 90,000 volume library contains a broad selection of titles, from literature & history to math and the sciences, at all academic levels, from kindergarten through postgraduate and professional. RFB&D offers individual and institutional Learning Through Listening emberships, scholarship programs, a reference service and a custom recording service. RFB&D also offers for nonprofit sale a variety of playback devices and accessories. -RFB&DS MATERIALS ARE FOR PEOPLE WHO CANNOT READ STANDARD PRINT BECAUSE OF VISUAL IMPAIRMENT, LEARNING DISABILITY OR PHYSCICAL DISABILITY. Potential individual members must complete an application form, which contains a "disability verification" There are 102,000 Individuals Members and 4200 Institutions Members.-The cost of an individual membership is $25 per year, plus a one time $50 registration fee for qualified individuals. Fees for institutional membership vary based on level of membership chosen. (Contact Customer Service)-NONE-RFB&D LEARNING THROUGH LISTENING IMPACT NEWLETTER-5/14/02-Paula Whitcomb-pwhitcomb@rfbd.org

Recording Industry Association of America, Inc.-RIAA-1330 Connecticut Ave. NW #300-Washington-DC-20036-US-(202)775-0101-(202)775-7253-aweiss@riaa.com-http://www.riaa.com/.-Hilary Rosen, Chairman and CEO.-Founded in 1952, RIAA's mission is to promote the mutual interests of recording companies, as well as the betterment of the industry overall through successful government relations (both federal and state), intellectual property protection, and international activities; evaluating all aspects of emerging technologies and technology-related issues; and promoting an innovative and secure online marketplace. RIAA represents the recording industry, whose members create and/or distribute approximately 90 percent of all legitimate sound recordings produced and sold in the United States. RIAA is the official certification agency for gold, platinum, and multi-platinum record awards.-Over 250 recording companies-d-d-Consumer Profile-5/24/02-Amanda Collins 202-775-0101

Reference and User Services Association-RUSA-50 E. Huron St.-Chicago-IL-60611-US-(800)545-2433, ext. 4398.-Fax (312)944-8085-cbourdon@ala.org-http://www.ala.org/rusa-Cathleen Bourdon, Exec. Dir-A division of the American Library Association, RUSA is responsible for stimulating and supporting in every type of library the delivery of reference information services to all groups and of general library services and materials to adults.-4,900-Join ALA and RUSA $95; RUSA membership $45(added to current ALA membership); student member $45 ($25 for ALA and $20 for RUSA).-Meetings are held in conjunction with the American Library Association.-RUSQ (q.), information provided on RUSA website at www.ala.org/rusa, select publications.-4/27/04-Eileen Hardy, ehardy@ala.org

Research for Better Schools, Inc.-RBS-112 North Broad Street-Philadelphia-PA-19102-1510-US-(215)568-6150-(215)568-7260-info@rbs.org-http://www.rbs.org/-Keith M. Kershner & Louis Maguire, Co-Executive Directors-Research for Better Schools is a non-profit education organization that has been providing services to teachers, administrators, and policy makers since 1966. Our mission is to help students achieve high learning standards by supporting improvement efforts in schools and other education environments. The staff are dedicated to and well experienced in providing the array of services that schools, districts, and states need to help their students reach proficient or higher learning standards: 1) technical assistance in improvement efforts; 2) professional development that is required for the successful implementation of more effective curricula, technologies, or instruction; 3) application of research in the design of specific improvement efforts; 4) evaluation of improvement efforts; 5) curriculum implementation and assessment; and 6) effective communication with all members of the school community. RBS has worked with a wide range of clients over the years, representing all levels of the education system, as well as business and community groups.-There is no membership in Research for Better Schools. The Mid-Atlantic Eisenhower Consortium for Mathematics and Science Education, which RBS operates, does encourage regional educators to become members. Information is available online at http://www.rbs.org/eisenhower/membership.shtml. The Mid-Atlantic Eisenhower Consortium currently has over 18,000 members, who include teachers, school administrators, representatives from higher education, state department of education staff, professional association representatives, business persons, and other community members interested in mathematics and science education.-N/A-The Mid-Atlantic Eisenhower Consortium sponsors an annual regional conference and state team meetings throughout the year.-RBS publishes the Currents newsletter, available in print, online, and delivered via e-mail (http://www.rbs.org/currents/index.shtml). The Consortium also publishes the electronic newsletter, Riptides (http://www.rbs.org/archives/riptides.html).The catalog for RBS Publications is online (visit our homepage at http://www.rbs.org).-5/19/03-Debra Gingerich, gingerich@rbs.org

Society for Applied Learning Technology-SALT-50 Culpeper St.-Warrenton-VA-20186-US-(540)347-0055-(540)349-3169-info@lti.org.-http://www.salt.org-Raymond G. Fox, Pres.-The society is a nonprofit, professional membership organization that was founded in

1972. Membership in the society is oriented to professionals whose work requires knowledge and communication in the field of instructional technology. The society provides members with a means to enhance their knowledge and job performance by participation in society-sponsored meetings, subscription to society-sponsored publications, association with other professionals at conferences sponsored by the society, and membership in special interest groups and special society-sponsored initiatives. In addition, the society offers member discounts on society-sponsored journals, conferences, and publications.-350-$55.-Orlando Learning Technologies 2004, February 18–20, 2004, Orlando, FL; 2004 Interactive Technologies, August 18-20, 2004, Arlington, VA-Journal of Educational Technology Systems; Journal of Instruction Delivery Systems; Journal of Interactive Instruction Development. Send for list of available publications.-5/14/03-Yvonne Beichner yvonne@lti.org

Society for Photographic Education, SPE, 126 Peabody Hall, The School of Interdisciplinary Studies, Miami University, Oxford, OH, 45056, US, (513) 529-8328, (513) 529-9301, speoffice@spenational.org, www.spenational.org, Richard Gray, Chairperson of SPE Board of Directors, An association of college and university teachers of photography, museum photographic curators, writers, publishers and students. Promotes discourse in photography education, culture, and art., 1,800 Membership dues are for the calendar year, January through December.

Membership Dues:
$90-Regular Membership
$50-Student Membership
$600-Corporate Member
$380-Collector Member (with print)
$150-Sustaining Member
$65-Senior Member, Denver, CO, March 13–16, 2008, -Exposure (Photographic Journal) - biannual
-Quarterly Newsletter
-Membership Directory
-Conference Program Guide, 3/29/2007, Kelly OMalley, speoffice@spenational.org

Society of Cable Telecommunications Engineers-SCTE-140   Philips Rd-Exton-PA-19341-1318-US-(610)363-6888-(610)363-5898-info@scte.org-http://www.scte.org-John Clark, Pres. & CEO-The Society of Cable Telecommunications Engineers is a non-profit professional organization committed to advancing the careers of cable telecommunications professionals and serving their industry through excellence in professional development, information and standards. SCTE currently has approximately 14,000 members from the U.S. and 70 countries worldwide and offers a variety of programs and services for the industry's educational benefit. SCTE has more than 70 chapters and meeting groups and has technically certified more than 3,000 employees of the cable telecommunications industry. Visit www.scte.org.-14,000 worldwide-$58 Individual $350 Sustaining Members $29 Full-time Student, Unemployed or Retired (one-year)-Conference on Emerging Technologies: January 11–13, 2005 Los Angeles; Cable-Tec Expo, Orlando, FL, June 15–18, 2004; Cable-Tec Expo, San Antonio, TX, June 14–17, 2005.-Interval Membership Directory SCTE Monthly Credentials Standards Bulletin Leadership Forum-5/4/04-Sandra L. Ray, e-mail: sray@scte.org

Society of Photo Technologists-SPT-11112   S. Spotted Rd.-Cheney-WA-99004-US-(888)662-7678 or (509)624-9621-(509)624-5320-cc5@earthlink.net-http://www.spt.info/-Chuck Bertone, Executive Director-An organization of photographic equipment repair technicians, which improves and maintains communications between manufacturers and repair shops and technicians. We publish Repair Journals, Newsletters, Parts & Service Directory and Industry Newsletters. We also sponsor SPTNET (a technical email group), Remanufactured parts and residence workshops.-1,000 shops and manufactures world wide, eligible people or businesses are any who are involved full or part time in the camera repair field.-$97.50-$370. Membership depends on the size / volumn of the business. Most one man shops are Class A / $170 dues. Those not involved full time in the field is $95.50 / Associate Class.-SPT Journal; SPT Parts and Services Directory; SPT Newsletter; SPT Manuals—Training and Manufacturer's Tours.-Journals & Newsletters-4/26/04-Chuck Bertone. cc5@earthlink.net or 1-800-624-9621

SouthEastern Regional Vision for Education-SERVE-SERVE   Tallahassee Office, 1203 Governor's Square Blvd., Suite 400-Tallahassee-FL-32301-US-(800)352-6001, (904)671-6000-(904)671-6020-wmccolsk@serve.org-http://www.serve.org/-Wendy Mc-Colskey, Program Director-SERVE is a regional educational research and development laboratory funded by the U.S. Department of Education to help educators, policymakers, and communities improve schools so that all students achieve their full potential. The laboratory offers the following services: field-based models and strategies for comprehensive school improvement; publications on hot topics in education, successful implementation efforts, applied research projects, and policy issues; database searches and information search training; a regional bulletin board service that provides educators electronic communication and Internet access; information and assistance for state and local policy development; and services to support the coordination and improvement of assistance for young children and their families. The Eisenhower Mathematics and Science Consortium at SERVE promotes improvement of education in these targeted areas by coordinating regional resources, disseminating exemplary instructional materials, and offering technical assistance for implementation of effective teaching methods and assessment tools.——For dates and topics of conferences and workshops, contact Gladys Jackson, (800)755-3277-Reengineering High Schools for Student Success; Schools for the 21st Century: New Roles for Teachers and Principals (rev. ed.); Designing Teacher Evaluation Systems That Promote Professional Growth; Learning by Serving: 2,000 Ideas for Service-Learning Projects; Sharing Success: Promising Service-Learning Programs; Future Plans (videotape, discussion guide, and pamphlet); Future Plans Planning Guides.-5/22/03–

Southwest Educational Development Laboratory-SEDL-211 East Seventh St.-Austin-TX-78701-US-(512) 476-6861-(512) 476-2286-info@sedl.org-http://www.sedl.org-Dr. Wesley A. Hoover, Pres. and CEO-The Southwest Educational Development Laboratory (SEDL) is a private, not-for-profit education research and development corporation based in Austin, Texas. SEDL has worked in schools to investigate the conditions under which teachers can provide student-centered instruction supported by technology, particularly computers alone with other software. From that field-based research with teachers, SEDL has developed a professional development model and modules, which resulted in the production of Active Learning with Technology (ALT) portfolio. ALT is a multimedia training program for teachers to learn how to apply student-centered, problem-based learning theory to their instructional strategies that are supported by technologies. Copies of Active Learning with Technology Portfolio and other products used to integrate technology in the classroom can be viewed and ordered online at http://www.sedl.org/pubs/category_technology.html from SEDLs Office of Institutional Communications. SEDL operates the Southeast Comprehensive Center (SECC), funded by the U.S. Department of Education, which provides high-quality technical assistance in the states of Alabama, Georgia, Louisiana, Mississippi and South Carolina. The goals of the SECC are to build the capacities of states in its region to implement the programs and goals of the No Child Left Behind Act of 2001 (NCLB) and to build states capacity to provide sustained support of high-needs districts and schools. SECC works closely with each state in its region to provide access and use of information, models, and materials that facilitate implementation of and compliance with NCLB. SEDLs Texas Comprehensive Center provides technical assistance and support to the Texas Education Agency to assure Texas has an education system with the capacity and commitment to eliminate achievement gaps and enable all students to achieve at high levels. -Not applicable.-Not applicable.-Not applicable-SEDL LETTER and other newsletters and documents are available for free general distribution in print and online. Topic-specific publications related to educational change, education policy, mathematics, language arts, science, and disability research and a publications catalog are available at http://www.sedl.org/pubs on the SEDL Web site.-3/7/2006-Nancy Reynolds (nreynold@sedl.org)

Special Libraries Association-SLA-331 South Patrick Street-Alexandria-VA-22314-US-703-647-4900-703-647-4901-sla@sla.org-http://www.sla.org-The Honorable Janice R. Lachance, CEO-The Special Libraries Association (SLA) is a nonprofit global organization for innovative information professionals and their strategic partners. SLA serves more than 11,000 members in 75 countries in the information profession, including corporate, academic and government information specialists. SLA promotes and strengthens its members through learning, advocacy, and networking initiatives. For more information, visit us on the Web at www.sla.org.-11,500-Full Membership: USD 160.00 (members earning greater than USD 35,000 in annual salary); USD 99.00 (members earning USD 35,000 or less in annual salary). Student/Retired Membership: USD 35.00-2006 Annual Conference and Exposition: 11–14 June, Baltimore; 2007 Annual Conference and Exposition: 3–6 June, Denver-Information Outlook (monthly glossy magazine that accepts advertising). SLA Connections (monthly electronic newsletter for members and stakeholders.-4/21/2006-John Crosby, Chief Marketing Officer; 703=647-4916

Teachers and Writers Collaborative, T&W, 520 Eighth Avenue, Suite 2020, New York, NY, 10018, US, (212)691-6590, Toll-free (888)266-5789, (212)675-0171, info@twc.org, http://www.twc.org and http://www.writenet.org, Amy Swauger, Dir., T&W brings the joys and pleasures of reading and writing directly to children. As an advocate for the literary arts and arts education, we support writers and teachers in developing and implementing new teaching strategies; disseminate models for literary arts education to local, national, and international audiences; and showcase both new and established writers via publications and literary events held in our Center for Imaginative Writing. T&W was founded in 1967 by a group of writers and educators who believed that professional writers could make a unique contribution to the teaching of writing and literature. Over the past 40 years, 1,500 T&W writers have taught writing workshops in New York City's public schools. Approximately 700,000 New York City students have participated in our workshops, and we have worked with more than 25,000 teachers. Our wealth of experience, which is reflected in T&W's 80 books about teaching writing, led the National Endowment for the Arts to single out T&W as the arts-in-education group "most familiar with creative writing/literature in primary and secondary schools." The American Book Review has written that T&W "has created a whole new pedagogy in the teaching of English." T&W has over 1,000 members across the country. The basic membership is $35; patron membership is $75; and benefactor membership is $150 or more. Members receive a free book or T-shirt; discounts on publications; and a free one-year subscription to Teachers & Writers magazine. (Please see http://www.twc.org/member.htm.), T&W is seeking general operating support for all of our programs and program support for specific projects, including: 1) T&W writing residencies in New York City area schools; 2) T&W publications, books and a quarterly magazine, which we distribute across the country; 3) T&W events, including readings for emerging writers and small presses; and 4) T&W's Internet programs for teachers, writers, and students. Grants to T&Ws Endowment support the stability of the organization and help to guarantee the continuation of specific programs. T&W offers year-round public events in our Center for Imaginative Writing in New York City. For a list of events, please see http://www.twc.org/events.htm., T&W has published over 80 books on the teaching of imaginative writing, including The T&W Handbook of Poetic Forms; The Dictionary of Wordplay; The Story in History; Personal Fiction Writing; Luna, Luna: Creative Writing from Spanish and Latino Literature; The Nearness of You: Students and Teachers Writing On-Line. To request a free publications catalog, please send email to info@twc.org or call 888-BOOKS-TW. (Please see http://www.twc.org/pubs), 3/9/2007, Bruce Morrow, bmorrow@twc.org

USA Toy Library Association-USA-TLA-1326 Wilmette Ave., Ste. 201-Wilmette-IL-60091-US-(847)920-9030-(847)920-9032-usatla@aol.com-http://usatla.deltacollege.org-Judith Q. Iacuzzi, Exec. Dir.-The mission of the USA-TLA is to provide a networking system answering to all those interested in play and play materials to provide a national resource to toy libraries, family centers, resource and referrals, public libraries, schools, institutions serving families of special need, and other groups and individuals involved with children; to support and expand the number of toy libraries; and to advocate for children and the importance of their play in healthy development. Individuals can find closest toy libraries by sending an e-mail or written inquiry in a self-addressed stamped envelope.-80 institutions, 150 individuals. Members receive a subscription to the quarterly newsletter Childs Play, reduced fees on conferences, workshops, books, videos and other publications and products sold by the USA Toy Library Association. Comprehensive members receive a bonus gift each year.-$165, comprehensive; $55, basic; $15, student.-Regional workshops in the spring and fall.-Childs Play (q. newsletter); How to Start and Operate a Toy Library; Play Is a Childs Work (videotape); other books on quality toys and play.-4/22/02-Judith Iacuzzi - usatla@aol.com

University Continuing Education Association-UCEA-One DuPont Cir. NW, Suite 615-Washington-DC-20036-US-(202)659-3130-(202)785-0374-shirley@ucea.edu-http://www.ucea.edu/-Kay J. Kohl, Executive Director, kjkohl@ucea.edu-UCEA is an association of public and private higher education institutions concerned with making continuing education available to all population segments and to promoting excellence in continuing higher education. Many institutional members offer university and college courses via electronic instruction.-425 institutions, 2,000 professionals.-vary according to membership category; see: http://www.ucea.edu/membership.htm-UCEA has an annual national conference and several professional development seminars throughout the year. See: http://www.ucea.edu/page02.htm-monthly newsletter; quarterly; occasional papers; scholarly journal, Continuing Higher Education Review; Independent Study Catalog. With Peterson's, The Guide to Distance Learning; Guide to Certificate Programs at American Colleges and Universities; UCEA-ACE/Oryx Continuing Higher Education book series; Lifelong Learning Trends (a statistical fact book on continuing higher education); organizational issues series; membership directory.-5/22/03–

WestEd. 730 Harrison St., San Francisco, CA 94107-1242, United States. (415)565-3000. Fax: (415)565-3012 E-mail: lcardin@wested.org. Web site: http://www.WestEd.org. Glen Harvey, CEO; Richard Whitmore, Chief Financial Officer; Sri Ananda, Chief Development Officer. WestEd is a nonprofit research, development, and service agency dedicated to improving education and other opportunities for children, youth, and adults. Drawing on the best from research and practice, WestEd works with practitioners and policymakers to address critical issues in education and other related areas, including accountability and assessment; early childhood intervention; curriculum, instruction, and assessment; the use of technology; career and technical preparation; teacher and administrator professional development; science and mathematics education; safe schools and communities. WestEd was created in 1995 to unite and enhance the capacity of Far West Laboratory and Southwest Regional Laboratory, two of the nation's original education laboratories. In addition to its work across the nation, WestEd serves as the regional education laboratory for Arizona, California, Nevada, and Utah. A publications catalog is available and WestEd.org has a comprehensive listing of services offered. Various, relating to our work, plus quarterly board meetings. See Resources at www.WestEd.org. Updated: 4/27/04. Liza Cardinal lcardin@wested.org or 415.615.3219.

Young Adult Library Services Association (YALSA)   50 E. Huron St., Chicago, IL 60611, United States. (312)280-4390. Fax: (312)280-5276. E-mail: yalsa@ala.org. Web site: http://www.ala.org/yalsa. Beth Yoke, Executive Director; Judy T. Nelson, President. A division of the American Library Association (ALA), the Young Adult Library Services Association (YALSA) seeks to advocate, promote, and strengthen service to young adults as part of the continuum of total library services. Is responsible within the ALA to evaluate and select books and media and to interpret and make recommendations regarding their use with young adults. Selected List Committees include Best Books for Young Adults, Popular Paperbacks for Young Adults, Quick Picks for Reluctant Young Adult Readers, Outstanding Books for the College Bound, Selected Audio Books for Young Adults, Great Graphic Novels for Teens and Selected Films for Young Adults. To learn more about our literary awards, such as the Odyssey Award for best audio book production, and recommended reading, listening, and viewing lists go to www.ala.org/yalsa/booklists. YALSA celebrates Teen Tech Week, the first full week of March each year. To learn more go to www.ala.org/teentechweek. Membership: 5,500. YALSA members may be young adult librarians, school librarians, library directors, graduate students, educators, publishers, or anyone for whom library service to young adults is important. $50; $20 students; $20 retirees (in addition to ALA membership). Meetings: 2 ALA conferences yearly, Midwinter (January) and Annual (June); one biennial Young Adult Literature Symposium (beginning in 2008). Publications: *Young Adult Library Services*, a quarterly print journal; *Attitudes*, a quarterly electronic newsletter for members only. Updated: 3/26/2007. Esther Murphy, 1-800-545-2433, ext. 4390.

Association for Media and Technology in Education in Canada (AMTEC).   3, 1750 The Queensway, Suite 1318, Etobicoke, ON M9C 5H5, Canada. (403)220-3721. Fax: (403)282-4497. E-mail: wstephen@ucalgary.ca. Web site: http://www.amtec.ca. Bob Brandes, Past President; Christine Shelton, Pres.; Wendy Stephens, Sec./Treas. AMTEC is Canada's national association for educational media and technology professionals. The organization provides national leadership through annual conferences, publications, workshops, media festivals, and awards. It responds to media and technology issues at the international, national, provincial, and local levels, and maintains linkages with other organizations with similar interests. AMTEC members represent all sectors of the educational media and technology fields. Membership: $101.65, Canadian regular; $53.50, student and retiree. Meetings: Annual Conferences take place in late May or early June. 1999, Ottawa; 2000, Vancouver. Publications: *Canadian Journal of Learning and Technology* (a scholarly journal published three times a year); *Media News* (3/yr.); Membership Directory (with membership). Updated: 4/26/04, Wendy Stephens, 403-220-3721, wstephen@ucalgary.ca.

Canadian Education Association/Association comedienne déducation (CEA)   317 Adelaide Street West, suite 300, Toronto, ON M5V 1P9, Canada. (416) 591-6300. Fax: (416) 591-5345. E-mail: cea-ace@acea.ca. Web site: http://www.acea.ca. Penny Milton, Executive Director, Valérie Pierre-Pierre, Research Officer. CEA is a national, bilingual, charitable organization that advances public commitment to education by engaging diverse perspectives in finding common ground on issues that affect the learning of all children and youth in our society. Current issues include ICT and learning; social equity; school improvement. Membership: Sustaining Members—provincial, territorial departments of education, and federal government. Organization Members—nonprofit: educational institutions, research organizations, stakeholder associations: for profit: firms with interests in the education sector. Individuals—educators, researchers. $120, indiv.; $360, not-for-profit organizations; $500, for-profit organizations; school boards, based on enrollment. Publications: *Technology Summit*; *National Education Forum*; *Superintendents Forum*; *CEA Handbook*; *Education Canada* (quarterly); *CEA Newsletter* (8/yr.); *Connections Series*. Updated: 4/11/02. Penny Milton, pmilton@acea.ca.

Canadian Library Association (CLA). 328 Frank Street, Ottawa, ON K2P 0X8, Canada. (613)232-9625. Fax: (613)563-9895. E-mail: info@cla.ca. Web site: http://www.cla.ca. Linda Sawden Harris, Manager of Financial Services. The mission of the Canadian Library Association is to provide leadership in the promotion, development, and support of library and information services in Canada for the benefit of Association members, the profession, and Canadian society. In the spirit of this mission, CLA aims to engage the active, creative participation of library staff, trustees, and governing bodies in the development and management of high-quality Canadian library service; to assert and support the right of all Canadians to the freedom to read and to free universal access to a wide variety of library materials and services; to promote librarianship and to enlighten all levels of government as to the significant role that libraries play in educating and socializing the Canadian people; and to link libraries, librarians, trustees, and others across the country for the purpose of providing a unified nationwide voice in matters of critical concern. Membership: 2,300 individuals, 700 institutions, 100 Associates and Trustees. $50–$300. Meetings: 2006 Annual Conference in Ottawa (June 14–17), 2007 Annual Conference in St Johns (May 23–26, 2007). Publications: *Feliciter* (membership magazine, 6/yr.). Updated: 4/21/2006. Judy Green, jgreen@cla.ca.

Canadian Museums Association/Association des musées canadiens (CMA/AMC). 280 Metcalfe St., Suite 400, Ottawa, ON, K2P 1R7, Canada. (613)567-0099. Fax: (613)233-5438. E-mail: info@museums.ca. Web site: http://www.museums.ca. John G. McAvity, Exec. Dir. The Canadian Museums Association is a nonprofit corporation and registered charity dedicated to advancing public museums and museum works in Canada, promoting the welfare and better administration of museums, and fostering a continuing improvement in the qualifications and practices of museum professionals. Membership: 2,000 museums and individuals, including art galleries, zoos, aquariums, historic parks, etc. Individual ($75): For those who are or have been associated with a recognized museum in Canada. Affiliate ($100): For those outside the museum community who wish to support the aims and programs of the Association. Foreign ($100): For individuals and institutions, residing or based outside Canada. Institutional/Association: For all recognized Canadian museums that are non-profit, have a collection, and are open to the public. Fee is 0.001 (one tenth of one percent) of operating budget (i.e., if your budget is $150,000, you would pay $150). The minimum fee payable is $100, and the maximum, $2,500. Corporate ($250): For corporations wishing to support the aims and programs of the Association while developing opportunities within the museum community. Student ($50): Special rate for students. Please enclose a photocopy of your student ID Senior ($50): For those who are retired and have been associated with a recognized museum in Canada. Meetings: CMA Annual Conference, spring. Publications: *Muse* (bimonthly magazine, colour; Canada's only national, bilingual, magazine devoted to museums; it contains museum-based photography, feature articles, commentary, and practical information); *The Official Directory of Canadian Museums and Related Institutions* (online directory) lists all museums in Canada plus information on government departments, agencies, and provincial and regional museum associations. Updated: 5/20/03. L. McConnell, lmcconnell@museums.ca.

Canadian Publishers Council (CPC). 250 Merton St., Suite 203, Toronto, ON M4S 1B1, Canada. (416)322-7011. Fax: (416)322-6999. E-mail: pubadmin@pubcouncil.ca. Web site:

http://www.pubcouncil.ca. Jacqueline Hushion, Exec. Dir. CPC members publish and distribute an extensive list of Canadian and imported learning materials in a complete range of formats from traditional textbook and ancillary materials to CDs and interactive video. The primary markets for CPC members are schools, universities and colleges, bookstores, and libraries. CPC also provides exhibits throughout the year and works through a number of subcommittees and groups within the organization to promote effective book publishing. CPC was founded in 1910. Membership: 27 companies, educational institutions, or government agencies that publish books as an important facet of their work. To be assessed when a membership application form is submitted for consideration. Please visit the CPC Web site at www.pubcouncil.ca for various publications. Updated: 3/13/03. Lydia Pencarski, 416-322-7011 ext. 221.

National Film Board of Canada (NFBC). 350 Fifth Ave., Suite 4820, New York, NY 10118, United States. (212)629-8890. Fax: (212)629-8502. E-mail: NewYork@nfb.ca. Web site: www.nfb.ca. John Sirabella, U.S. Marketing Mgr./Nontheatrical Rep. Established in 1939, the NFBCs main objective is to produce and distribute high-quality audiovisual materials for educational, cultural, and social purposes. Updated: 3/12/03. Tim Sheehy, through e-mail contact above.

Ontario Film Association, Inc.   (also known as the Association for the Advancement of Visual Media/Lassociation pour lavancement des médias visuels) (OLA). 50 Wellington St East Suite 201, Toronto, ON M5E 1C8, Canada. (416)363-3388, 1-800-387-1181. E-mail: info@accessola.com. Web site: www.accessola.com. Lawrence A. Moore, Exec. Dir. A membership organization of buyers, and users of media whose objectives are to promote the sharing of ideas and information about visual media through education, publications, and advocacy. Membership: 112. $120, personal membership; $215, associate membership. Meetings: OFA Media Showcase, spring; Publications: No publication. Updated: 3/30/2007. Tanya Farr.

The Learning Team (TLT). Suite 204 84, Business Park Drive, Armonk, NY 10504, United States. 914-273-2226. Fax: 914-273-0936 E-mail: NMcLaren@LearningTeam.org. Web site: http://www.learningteam.org. Executive Director, Tom Laster. The Learning Team is a not-for-profit company that is focused on publishing inquiry-based, supplementary, technology resources for science education. The multimedia resources include: Science, mathematics, and utilities software and videos. Science subjects include : physics, physical sciences, biology, earth sciences (geosciences), environmental sciences, general science, chemistry, energy use, and culture and technology. Software includes inquiry-based student resources, teacher resources, and professional development. Resources available include *High School Geography Product (HSGP), Intermediate Science Curriculum Study (ISCS), Man: A Course of Study (MACOS)* and *Human Sciences Project (HSP)*. Most of the resources come from National Science Foundation (NSF) funding and have been done in conjunction with institutions such as the American Association of Physics Teachers (AAPT), the American Institute of Physics (AIP), American Geological Institute (AGI). Although the term membership does not apply specifically to our organization, it loosely applies to the range of licensors, collaborators, and colleagues that cooperate with us and are active in the area of science education. Publications: *Physics InfoMall, CPU—Constructing Physics Understanding, Exploring the Nardoo, Investigating Lake Iluka, The Dynamic Rainforests, Insects—Little Creatures in a Big World, Culture & Technology, Enhanced Science Helper, Enhanced Science Helper Videos, The Green Home, The Sun's Joules, Whelmers, EarthView Explorer, GETIT—Geosciences Education Through Interactive Technology, Crossword Wizard, Cloze word Wizard, Maths Worksheet Wizard*. Updated: 5/6/02. Neil McLaren, Ph. 914-273-2226 ext. 585.

Adaptech Research Network. Dawson College, 3040 Sherbrooke St. West, Montreal, QC H3Z 1A4, Canada. 514-931-8731 #1546. Fax: 514-931-3567 Attn: Catherine Fichten. E-mail: catherine.fichten@mcgill.ca. Web site: http://www.adaptech.org. Catherine Fichten, Ph.D., codirector; Jennison V. Asuncion, M.A., codirector; Maria Barile, M.S.W., codirector. Based at Dawson College (Montreal), we are a Canada-wide, grant-funded team, conducting bilingual empirical research into the use of computer, learning, and adaptive technologies by postsecondary students with disabilities. One of our primary interests lies in issues around ensuring that newly emerging instructional technologies are accessible to learners with disabilities. Our research team is composed of academics, practitioners, students, consumers, and others interested in the issues of access to technology by students with disabilities in higher education. Publications: Fossey, M.E., Asuncion, J.V., Fichten, C.S., Robillard, C., Barile, M., Amsel, R., Prezant, F. & Morabito, S. (2005). Development and validation of the Accessibility of Campus Computing for Students with Disabilities Scale (ACCSDS). *Journal of Postsecondary Education and Disability*, 18(1), 23–33. Jorgensen, S., Fichten, C.S., Havel, A., Lamb, D., James, C. & Barile, M. (2005). Academic performance of college students with and without disabilities: An archival study. *Canadian Journal of Counselling*, 39(2), 101–117. Fichten, C.S., Asuncion, J.V., Barile, M., Fossey, M.E., Robillard, C., Judd, D., Wolforth, J., Senécal, J., Généreux, C., Guimont, J.P., Lamb, D. & Juhel, J-C. (2004). Access to information and instructional technologies in higher education I: Disability service providers' perspective. *Journal of Postsecondary Education and Disability*, 17(2), 114– 133. Updated: 3/26/2007. Catherine Fichten, catherine.fichten@mcgill.ca.

Multimedia Education Group, University of Cape Town (MEG). Hlanganani Building, Upper Campus University of Cape Town, Rondebosch, Cape Town, 7700, South Africa. 27 21 650 3841. Fax: 27 21 650 3841. E-mail: lcz@its.uct.ac.za. Web site: www.meg.uct.ac.za. Director Laura Czerniewicz. MEG aims to research and harness the potential of interactive computer-based technologies and approaches (ICBTA) to support effective learning and teaching. Our work focuses on meeting the needs of South African students from diverse backgrounds, particularly those at the University of Cape Town. We employ multimedia researchers and developers with strong educational interests in diversity, redress, and accesss. See our Web site www.meg.uct.ac.za. Updated: 5/20/03. Laura Czerniewicz, lcz@ched.uct.ac.za.

The Institute for the Advancement of Emerging Technologies in Education (IAETE) at AEL, IAETE, PO Box 1348, Charleston, WV 25325-1348, United States. 304-347-1848. Fax: 304-347-1847. E-mail: info@iaete.org. Web site: www.iaete.org. Dr. John D. Ross, Associate Director. The mission of the Institute for the Advancement of Emerging Technologies in Education (IAETE) is to support the purposeful use of new and emerging technologies to improve teaching, learning, and school management. IAETE is committed to providing unbiased, research-based information to the education community as well as to product developers. Meetings: Annual National Conference. Publications: IAETE publishes several white papers, briefs, and reports annually in both print and electronic format. All address new and emerging technologies and their impact on teaching, learning, and school management. For more information, please visit www.iaete.org. Updated: 4/26/04. John Ross (rossj@iaete.org).

Consortium for Consumers in the Humanities/Consortium pour Ordinateurs en Sciences Humaines (COCH/COSH). Arts 200, UofA, Edmonton, AB T6G 2E6, Canada. 780.492.6768. Fax: 780.492.9106. E-mail: ss@huco.ualberta.ca. Web site: http://coch-coch.ca/. Ray Siemens (President-English), Jean-Claude Guédon (President-French), Geoffrey Rockwell (Vice President), Stéfan Sinclair (Secretary). The Consortium for Computers in the Humanities is a Canada-wide association of representatives from Canadian colleges and universities that began in 1986. Our objective is to foster communications about, and sharing of, information technology developed by Canadian institutions for the betterment of postsecondary education across Canada. Membership: 120. Annual, $65 CDN. Meetings: May, annually, with the HSSFC Congress. Publications: COCH/COSH has formal affiliation with the journals *Text Technology*, *Computing in the Humanities Working Papers* and Surfaces, and is pleased to have also enjoyed publications relationships with Early Modern Literary Studies. Updated: 3/4/04. Stéfan Sinclair, e-mail given above.

Part Five
Graduate Programs in North America

Introduction

Robert Maribe Branch

This directory describes graduate programs in Instructional Technology, Educational Media and Communications, School Library Media, and closely related programs in the United States. Master's, specialist, and doctoral degrees are combined into one unified list.

Entries provide as much of the following information as furnished by respondents: (1) name and address of the institution; (2) chairperson or other individual in charge of the program; (3) types of degrees offered and specialization, emphases, or tracks, including information on careers for which candidates are prepared; (4) special features of the degree program; (5) admission requirements; (6) degree requirements; (7) number of full-time and part-time faculty; (8) number of full-time and part-time students; (9) types of financial assistance available; and (10) the number of degrees awarded by type in 2004. All grade-point averages (GPAs), test scores, and degree requirements are minimums unless stated otherwise. The Graduate Record Examination, Miller Analogies Test, National Teacher's Examination, and other standardized tests are referred to by their acronyms. The Test of English as a Foreign Language (TOEFL) appears in many of the admission requirements, and in most cases this test is required only for international students. Although some entries explicitly state application fees, most do not. Prospective students should assume that most institutions require a completed application, transcripts of all previous collegiate work, and a nonrefundable application fee.

Directors of advanced professional programs for instructional technology or media specialists should find this degree program information useful as a means of comparing their own offerings and requirements with those of institutions offering comparable programs. This listing should also assist individuals in locating institutions that best suit their interests and requirements. In addition, a comparison of degree programs across several years may help scholars with historical interests trace trends and issues in the field over time.

Information in this section can be considered current as of early 2005 for most programs. Information for this section was obtained by e-mail directing each institution to an individual Web form through which the updated information could be submitted electronically. Although the section editor made every effort to contact and follow up with program representatives, it is up to the program representatives to respond to the annual request for an update. The editing team would like to thank those respondents who helped assure the currency and accuracy of this section by responding to the request for an update.

Additional information on the programs listed, including admission procedure instructions, may be obtained by contacting individual program coordinators. General or graduate catalogs and specific program information usually are furnished for a minimal charge. In addition, most graduate programs now have e-mail contact addresses and Web sites that provide a wealth of descriptive information.

Again, we are greatly indebted to those individuals who responded to our requests for information. Although the editors expended considerable effort to ensure currency and completeness of the listings, there may be institutions within the United States that now have programs of which we are unaware. This year organizations that we haven't received updates from in over four years were omitted from our listings. Any readers are encouraged to furnish new information to the publisher who, in turn, will contact the program for inclusion in the next edition of *EMTY*.

Alphabetical List

Alabama State University. Department of Instructional Support Programs. 915 South Jackson Street, Montgomery, AL 36101-0271, United States. (334)229-6829. Fax: (334)229-6904. Web site: http://www.alasu.edu. Dr. Agnes Bellel, Coord., Instructional Technology and Media. abellel@asunet.alasu.edu. School media specialist preparation (K-12) only; master's and specialist degrees. The applicant must hold a bachelor's degree from an accredited institution. All admission requirements for graduate programs in education should be completed prior to registration for courses. Application forms should be secured from and returned to the School of Graduate Studies. Full admission status should be granted to persons who meet all applicable admission requirements prior to enrollment. Under extraordinary circumstances, a student may be considered as conditionally admitted, but in all circumstances, the requirements for admission to graduate program in education must be met during the First Enrollment Period. When such requirements are met, the student's status will be changed from conditional to full admission, retroactive to the beginning of the enrollment period. A special status may be granted to those persons who do not wish to pursue a degree program but who wish to enroll in a limited number of graduate classes.

Admission Requirements: Admission to a master's degree program requires that the applicant: hold a Class B Certificate, general counseling does not require a teachers certificate; take and attain satisfactory scores on specified national tests (Graduate Record Examination [GRE] or Miller Analogy Test [MAT]. For all graduate programs, the applicant must submit two letters of recommendation from persons who are qualified to evaluate an applicant's ability to do graduate work; hold a Class A Certificate in a teaching field (for admission to a certification program in Administration and Supervision only).

Master's degree in library/media education: Admission to an Education Specialist degree program requires that the applicant: (1) hold professional certification and a master's degree in the area they want to pursue an Education Specialist degree; (2) have at least two years of successful work experience; (3) must have a 3.25 G.P.A. on master's degree; (4) make a satisfactory score on the Graduate Record Examination (GRE) or Miller Analogy Test (MAT); (5) AA Certification Programs require a 3.25 graduate G.P.A., appropriate Class A Certification, and approval of the major department. Degree Requirements: Master's: 33 semester hours with 300 clock-hour internship. Specialist: 36 semester hours in 600-level courses. Students: Master's, 50 part-time; Specialist, 8 part-time. Financial Assistance: student loans and scholarships. Degrees Awarded: 15 M.Ed., 1 Ed.S. Updated: 7/7/04. abellel@asunet.alasu.edu.

Auburn University. Educational Foundations, Leadership, and Technology, 3402 Haley Center, Auburn, AL 36849-5216, United States. (334)844-4291. (334)844-4292. Web site: http://www.auburn.edu/academic/college_of_education/academics/departments/eflt.html. Susan H. Bannon, Associate Professor and Program Coordinator. bannosh@auburn.edu. Specialization: M.Ed. (nonthesis) and Ed.S. for school library media certification. Features: The Department of Educational Foundations, Leadership & Technology (EFLT) prepares exemplary educational practitioners and develops cooperative partnerships with university departments, schools, community agencies, and business and industry to provide high-quality educators, trainers, and leaders. Faculty are committed to guiding students toward becoming competent and professional educational leaders. This department ensures that students will participate in theoretical, applied and practitioner-based research enhancing the fields of Adult Education, Educational Leadership, Educational

Media/Technology and Educational Psychology. Outreach partnerships are continually established in these respective fields to provide students with an informative and experiential curriculum. All programs emphasize interactive technologies and computers. Admission Requirements: All programs: graduate school admission; GRE test scores less than 5 years old; 3 letters of recommendation; bachelor's degree from accredited institution; and teacher certification at least a bachelor's level. Degree Requirements: Library Media Masters: 33 sem. hours. Specialist: 30 sem. hours. Faculty: 3 full-time. Students: 2 full-time, 15 part-time. Financial Assistance: graduate assistantships. Updated: 6/10/03. Susan H. Bannon, bannosh@auburn.edu.

Jacksonville State University. Educational Resources, 700 Pelham Road N, Jacksonville, AL 36265, United States. (256)782-5096. (256)782 5872. Web site: www.jsu.edu. Dr.Martha Merrill, Coord., Instructional Media Program. mmerrill@jsucc.jsu.edu. Specialization: M.S. in Education with emphasis in Library Media. Add-on Certification in Library Media-Technology, Management, Literature, Reference. Admission Requirements: Bachelor's degree in Education. Degree Requirements: 36–39 semester hours including 24hours in library media. Students: 2 full-time, 30 full- and part-time. Updated: 4/1/04. Dr. Martha Merrill, (256)782-5011.

University of Alabama. School of Library and Information Studies, Box 870252, Tuscaloosa, AL 35487-0252, United States. (205)348-4610. (205)348-3746. Web site: http://www.slis.ua.edu. Joan Atkinson, Director; Gordy Coleman, Coordinator of School Media Program. jatkinso@slis.ua.edu; gcoleman@slis.ua.edu. Specialization: M.L.I.S. degrees in a varied program including school, public, academic, and special libraries. Ph.D. in the larger College of Communication and Information Sciences; flexibility in creating individual programs of study. Also a Master of Fine Arts Program in Book Arts (including history of the book). M.L.I.S. is one of 56 accredited programs in the United States and Canada. Admission Requirements: M.L.I.S.: 3.0 GPA; 50 MAT or 1000 GRE and an acceptable score on Analytical Writing. Doctoral: 3.0 GPA; 60 MAT or 1200 GRE and acceptable score on Analytical Writing. Degree Requirements: Master's: 36 semester hours. Doctoral: 48–60 semester hours plus 24 hours dissertation research. Faculty: 10 full-time; 5 part-time. Students: Master's, 45 full-time, 140 part-time; doctoral, 1 full-time, 3 part-time. Financial Assistance: assistantships, grants, student loans, scholarships, work assistance, campus work. Degrees Awarded: 88 M.L.I.S; 4 educational specialist; 3 MFA in Book Arts. Updated: 6/9/03. Joan Atkinson, jatkinso@slis.ua.edu.

University of South Alabama. Department of Behavioral Studies and Educational Technology, College of Education, University Commons 3700, Mobile, AL 36688, United States. (251)380-2861. (251)380-2713. Web site: http://www.southalabama.edu/coe/bset/. Daniel W. Surry, IDD Program Coord.; Mary Ann Robinson, Ed Media Program Coord. dsurry@usouthal.edu. Specialization: M.S. and Ph.D. in Instructional Design and Development. M.Ed. in Educational Media (Ed Media). Online master's degrees in ED Media and IDD are available for qualified students. For information about online master's degree programs, http://usaonline.southalabama.edu. Features: The IDD master's and doctoral programs emphasize extensive education and training in the instructional design process, human performance technology, and multimedia- and online-based training. The IDD doctoral program has an additional emphasis in research design and statistical analysis. The Ed Media master's program prepares students in planning, designing, and administering library/media centers at most levels of education, including higher education. Admission Requirements: For the ED Media & IDD Masters: undergraduate degree in appropriate academic field from an accredited university or college; admission to Graduate School; satisfactory score on the GRE. ED Media students must have completed requirements for a certificate at the baccalaureate or master's level in a teaching field. For IDD Ph.D.:

Master's degree, all undergraduate & graduate transcripts, 3 letters of recommendations, written statement of purpose for pursuing Ph.D. in IDD, satisfactory score on GRE. Degree Requirements: Ed Media masters: satisfactorily complete program requirements (minimum 33 semester hours), 3.0 or better GPA, satisfactory score on comprehensive exam. IDD masters: satisfactorily complete program requirements (minimum 40 semester hours), 3.0 or better GPA; satisfactory complete comprehensive exam. Ph.D.: satisfactory complete program requirements (minimum 82 semester hours of approved graduate course), one-year residency, satisfactory score on examinations (research & statistical exam and comprehensive exam), approved dissertation completed. Any additional requirements will be determined by students' doctoral advisory committee. Faculty: 17 full-time in department; 8 part-time faculty. Students: IDD Masters, 68, Ph.D., 100; Ed Media Masters 44, Ed Media Certificate 26. Financial Assistance: 10 graduate assistantships. Degrees Awarded: Ed Media masters = 12; IDD masters = 10; IDD doctoral = 5. Updated: 5/19/04. Daniel W. Surry, dsurry@usouthal.edu.

Arizona

Arizona State University; Educational Technology Program. Division of Psychology in Education. Box 870611, Tempe, AZ 85287-0611, United States. (480)965-3384. (480)965-0300. Web site: http://coe.asu.edu/psyched. Dr. Willi Savenye, Associate Professor; Nancy Archer, Admissions Secretary. dpe@asu.edu. Specialization: The Educational Technology program at Arizona State University offers M.Ed. degree and Ph.D. degrees that focus on the design, development, and evaluation of instructional systems and educational technology applications to support learning. Features: The program offers courses in a variety of areas such as instructional design technology, media development, technology integration, performance improvement, evaluation, and distance education. The doctoral program emphasizes research using educational technology in applied settings. Admission Requirements: Requirements for admission to the M.Ed. program include a 4-year undergraduate GPA of 3.0 or above and a score of either 500 or above on verbal section of the GRE or 50 or above on the MAT. A score of 550 or above on the paper-based TOEFL (or 213 on the computer-based test) is also required for students who do not speak English as their first language.

Requirements for admission to the Ph.D. program include a 4-year undergraduate GPA of 3.20 or above and a combined score of 1200 or above on the verbal and quantitative sections of the GRE. A score of 600 or above on the paper-based TOEFL (or 250 on the computer-based test) is also required for students who do not speak English as their first language. Degree Requirements: The M.Ed. degree requires completion of a minimum of 30 credit hours including 18 credit hours of required coursework and a minimum of 12 credit hours of electives. M.Ed. students also must complete an internship and a comprehensive examination. The Ph.D. degree requires a minimum of 84 semester hours beyond the bachelor's degree. At least 54 of these hours must be taken at ASU after admission to the program. Ph.D. students must fulfill a residence requirement and are required to be continuously enrolled in the program. Students also take a comprehensive examination and must satisfy a publication requirement prior to beginning work on their dissertation. Faculty: The Educational Technology program at ASU has 6 full-time faculty. Students: 30 M.Ed. and 20 Ph.D. students are currently enrolled in the program. Financial Assistance: Financial assistance such as scholarships, fellowships, graduate assistantships, loans, and professional work opportunities are available to qualified applicants. Degrees Awarded: 10 M.Ed. degrees and 3 Ph.D. degrees were awarded in 2005. Updated: 3/7/2006. James D. Klein, james.klein@asu.edu.

University of Arizona. School of Information Resources and Library Science. 1515 E. First St, Tucson, AZ 85719, United States. (520)621-3565. Fax: (520)621-3279. Web site: http://www.sir.arizona.edu. Susan Irwin. sirwin@u.arizona.edu. Specialization: The School of Information Resources and Library Science offers courses focusing on the study of information and its impact as a social phenomenon. Features: The school offers a virtual education program via the Internet. Between two and three courses are offered per semester. Admission Requirements: Very competitive for both degrees. Minimum criteria include: undergraduate GPA of 3.0 or better; competitive GRE scores; two letters of recommendation reflecting the writers opinion of the applicants potential as a graduate student; a resume of work and educational experience; written statement of intent. The school receives a large number of applications and accepts the best qualified students. Admission to the doctoral program may require a personal interview and a faculty member must indicate willingness to work with the student. Degree Requirements: M.A.: a minimum of 36 units of graduate credit. Students may elect the thesis option replacing 6 units of coursework. Ph.D.: at least 48 hours of coursework in the major, a substantial number of hours in a minor subject supporting the major, dissertation. The university has a 6-unit residency requirement that may be completed in the summer or in a regular semester. More detailed descriptions of the program are available at the school's Web site. Faculty: 8 full-time. Students: 220 total; M.A.: 51 full-time; Ph.D.: 12 full-time. Financial Assistance: Scholarships, Teaching Assistantships, Tuition Fee Waivers. Degrees Awarded: 75. Updated: 4/27/04. Susan Irwin, sirwin@u.arizona.edu.

Arkansas

Arkansas Tech University. Curriculum and Instruction. 308 Crabaugh, Russellville, AR 72801-2222, United States. (501)968-0434. Fax: (501)964-0811. Web site: http://education.atu.edu/. Connie Zimmer, Assoc. Professor of Secondary Education, Coord. Connie.Zimmer@mail.atu.edu. Specialization: Master of Education in Instructional Technology with specializations in library media education, instructional design, and instructional technology. Features: NCATE accredited institution. A standards-based program meeting the Arkansas State Department of Educations licensure requirements for school library media specialist. Classrooms have the latest technology available. Admission Requirements: GRE or MAT, 2.5 undergraduate GPA, bachelor's degree. Teaching Licensure required for the school library media specialization. Degree Requirements: 36 semester hours, B average in major hours, action research project. Faculty: 2 full-time. Students: 5 full-time, 72 part-time. Financial Assistance: graduate assistantships, work-study, student loans. Degrees Awarded: 45. Updated: 3/4/04. Connie Zimmer@mail.atu.edu or 501-968-0434.

University of Central Arkansas. Middle/Secondary Education and Instructional Technologies. 201 Donaghey, Conway, AR 72035, United States. (501)450-5463. Fax: (501)450-5680. Web site: http://www.coe.uca.edu/. Stephanie Huffman, Program Director of the Library Media and Information Technologies Program. steph@uca.edu. Specialization: M.S. in Library Media and Information Technologies Tracks: School Library Media and Public Information Agencies. Admission Requirements: Specialization in school library media: transcripts, GRE scores, and a copy of the candidates teaching certificate (if enrolled in School Library Media Track). Degree Requirements: 36 semester hours, practicum (for School Library Media), and a professional portfolio. Faculty: 3 full-time, 3 part-time. Students: 40 full-time, 30 part-time. Financial Assistance: 3 to 4 graduate assistantships each year. Degrees Awarded: 30. Updated: 3/7/2006. Stephanie Huffman, steph@uca.edu.

California

Alliant University. School of Education. 10455 Pomerado Rd., San Diego, CA 92131-1799, United States. (619)635-4715. Fax: (619)635-4714. Web site: http://www.alliant.

edu/gsoe/. Karen Schuster Webb System wide Dean for the Graduate School of Education. lbanerjee@alliant.edu. Specialization: Master's in Designing Technology for Learning, Planning Technology for Learning, and Technology Leadership for Learning. Ed.D. in Technology and Learning offers three specializations: Designing Technology for Learning, Planning Technology for Learning, and Technology Leadership for Learning. Features: Interactive multimedia, cognitive approach to integrating technology and learning. Admission Requirements: Masters: English proficiency, interview, 3.0 GPA with 1900 GRE or 2.0 GPA with satisfactory MAT score. Degree Requirements: Ed.D.: 88 graduate qtr. units, dissertation. Faculty: 2 full-time, 4 part-time. Students: Masters, 32 full-time, 12 part-time; doctoral, 6 full-time, 1 part-time. Financial Assistance: Internships, graduate assistantships, grants, student loans, scholarships. Updated: 6/6/03.

Azusa Pacific University. EDUCABS, Advanced Studies. 901 E. Alosta, Azusa, CA 91702, United States. (626)815-5355. Fax: (626)815-5416. Web site: http://www.apu.edu. Kathleen Bacer, Online program; Joanne Gilbreath, site-based program. kbacer@apu.edu. Specialization: Educational Technology, site-based and online program. Master of Arts in Educational Technology and Learning Program offered at 5 different locations (Azusa, Inland, Menifee, Orange, Ventura). Admission Requirements: Online Master of Arts in Educational Technology program: undergraduate degree from accredited institution with at least 12 units in education, 3.0 GPA, ownership of a designated laptop computer and software. Degree Requirements: 36 unit program. Faculty: 2 full-time, 16 part-time. Students: 180 part-time. Financial Assistance: student loans. Degrees Awarded: 89. Updated: 4/28/04. Dr. Kathleen Bacer, Director, Ed Tech.

California State University—Dominguez Hills. Graduate Education. 1000 E. Victoria St., Carson, CA 90747, United States. (310)243-3524. Fax: (310)243-3518. Web site: http://www.csudh.soe.edu. Peter Desberg, Prof., Coord., Technology-Based Education Program. pdesberg@csudh.edu. Specialization: M.A. and Certificate in Technology-Based Education. Admission Requirements: 2.75 GPA. Degree Requirements: M.A.: 30 semester hours including project. Certificate: 15 hours. Faculty: 2 full-time, 2 part-time. Students: 60 full-time, 40 part-time. Financial Assistance: Available. Degrees Awarded: 30. Updated: 3/5/04. Peter Desberg, pdesberg@earthlink.net.

California State University—Los Angeles. Division of Educational Foundations and Interdivisional Studies. 5151 State University Drive, Los Angeles, CA 90032, United States. (323)343-4330. Fax: (323)343-5336. Web site: http://www.calstatela.edu/dept/efis/. Dr. Fernando A. Hernandez, Division Chairperson. efis@calstatela.edu. Specialization: Our four major programmatic areas include: Educational Foundations, which offers a graduate degree in Educational Foundations focusing on Educational Sociology, Educational Psychology, Urban Education, or the Philosophy of Education. Instructional Technology and Computer Education that offers graduate degrees in Instructional Technology and Computer Education. TESOL that offers a graduate degree in Teaching as a Secondary Language. (For more information see the TESOL homepage.) Educational Research, Evaluation, and Statistics, which offers service courses to other Education degree programs in statistics, educational research, and evaluation. Features: M.A. degree in Education, option in New Media Design and Production; Computer Education and Leadership; Joint Ph.D. in Special Education with UCLA. Admission Requirements: Not listed. Degree Requirements: 2.75 GPA in last 90 qtr. units, 45 qtr. units, comprehensive written exam or thesis or project. Must also pass Writing Proficiency Examination (WPE), a California State University—Los Angeles requirement. Faculty: 7 full-time. Updated: 3/25/03. Betty C. Lee, efis@calstatela.edu.

California State University—San Bernardino. Dept. of Science, Mathematics, and Technology Education. 5500 University Parkway, San Bernardino, CA 92407, United States. (909)880-5290, (909)880-5688. Fax: (909)880-7040. Web site: http://soe.csusb.edu/etec/

index.html. Olga E. Cordero, Administrative Support Coordinator. ocordero@csusb.edu. Specialization: Technology integration, online instruction, instructional design. Features: Preparing educators in K-12, corporate, and higher education. Admission Requirements: Bachelor's degree, appropriate work experience, 3.0 GPA, completion of introductory computer course and expository writing course. Degree Requirements: 48 units including a Master's project (33 units completed in residence); 3.0 GPA; grades of "C" or better in all courses. Faculty: 6 full-time, 9 part-time. Students: 106. Financial Assistance: Contact Office of Graduate Studies. Updated: 7/7/04. ocordero@csusb.edu

San Diego State University. Educational Technology. 5500 Campanile Dr., San Diego, CA 92182-1182, United States. (619)594-6718. Fax: (619)594-6376. Web site: http://edtec.sdsu.edu/. Dr. Marcie Bober, Assoc. Prof., Chair. bober@mail.sdsu.edu. Specialization: Certificate in Instructional Technology. Advanced Certificate in Distance Learning and Software Design. Master's degree in Education with an emphasis in Educational Technology. Doctorate in Education with an emphasis in Educational Technology (a joint program with the University of San Diego). Features: Focus in design of intervention to improve human performance via strategies that combine theory and practice in relevant, real-world experiences. Offer both campus and online programs. Please refer to SDSU Graduate bulletin at http://libweb.sdsu.edu/bulletin/.

Admission Requirements: Requirements include a minimum score of 950 on the GRE (verbal + quantitative) and 4.5 on the analytical. See our Web site at http://edtec.sdsu.edu for more information. Degree Requirements: 36 semester hours for the masters (including 6 prerequisite hours) 15 to 18 semester hours for the certificates. Faculty: 9 full-time, 5 part-time. Students: 80 in campus program; 100 in online program. Financial Assistance: Graduate assistantships, and other university- and college-level scholarships/loan programs. Degrees Awarded: 40. Updated: 3/8/2006. etapi@mail.sdsu.edu.

San Francisco State University. College of Education, Department of Instructional Technology. 1600 Holloway Ave., San Francisco, CA 94132, United States. (415)338-1509. Fax: (415)338-0510. Web site: www.itec.sfsu.edu. Dr. Kim Foreman, Chair; Anna Kozubek, Office Coord. kforeman@sfsu.edu. Specialization: Master's degree with emphasis on Instructional Multimedia Design, Training and Designing Development, and Instructional Computing. The school also offers an 18-unit Graduate Certificate in Training Systems Development that can be incorporated into the master's degree. Features: This program emphasizes the instructional systems approach, cognitive principles of learning design, practical design experience, and project-based courses. Admission Requirements: Bachelors degree, appropriate work experience, 2.5 GPA, purpose statement, 2 letters of recommendation, interview with the department chair. Degree Requirements: 30 semester hours, field study project, or thesis. Three to nine units of prerequisites, assessed at entrance to the program. Faculty: 4 full-time, 16 part-time. Students: 250–300. Financial Assistance: Contact Office of Financial Aid. Degrees Awarded: 60. Updated: 3/4/04. kforeman@sfsu.edu.

San Jose State University. Instructional Technology. One Washington Square, San Jose, CA 95192-0076, United States. (408) 924-3620. Fax: (408) 924-3713. Web site: http://sweeneyhall.sjsu.edu/depts/it. Dr. Robertta Barba, Program Chair. rbarba@email.sjsu.edu. Specialization: Master's degree. Features: MA in Education with an emphasis on Instructional Technology. Admission Requirements: Baccalaureate degree from approved university, appropriate work experience, minimum GPA of 2.5, and minimum score of 550 on TOEFL (Test of English as a Foreign Language). Degree Requirements: 36 semester hours (which includes 6 prerequisite hours). 30 units of approved graduate studies. Faculty: 4 full-time, 12 part-time. Students: 50 full-time master's students, 260 part-time. Financial Assistance: Assistantships, grants, student loans and scholarships. Degrees Awarded: 42. Updated: 3/7/2006. Robertta H. Barba, rbarba@email.sjsu.edu.

University of Southern California, Rossier School of Education. Educational Psychology & Instructional Technology. 3470 Trousdale Parkway, Los Angeles, CA 90089-4036, United States. (213)740-3465. Fax:(213)740-2367. Web site: http://www.usc.edu/dept/education/academic/masters/index.htm. For Admissions Info (soeinfo@usc.edu), For general program info (rsoemast@usc.edu), For specific program info (rueda@usc.edu). rsoemast@usc.edu. Specialization: The Educational Psychology/Instructional Technology program focuses on learning and motivation, emphasizing the study of new information and performance technologies used to improve instruction among diverse student populations. To understand human learning, educational psychologists study areas such as: motivation; developmental and individual differences; social, cultural, and group processes; instructional technology; and the evaluation of instruction. Students will be prepared to apply a wide range of computer and telecommunications technologies in achieving educational goals within school, community, corporate and public settings.

Distinctive Features: Focus on learning and motivation with a strong emphasis on technology and a major concern with urban education settings. Major objective is to learn how to diagnose and solve learning and motivation problems, especially those characteristic of urban learning settings. Faculty are well-known in the field and are active researchers. Special emphasis upon instructional design, human performance at work, systems analysis, and computer-based training. Admission Requirements: Bachelor's degree, 1000 GRE. Program of Study: 28 Units. 7 core courses and 2 elective courses.

Core Courses:
EDPT 576 Technology in Contemporary Education and Training
EDPT 550 Statistical Inference
EDPT 502 Learning and Individual Differences
EDPT 510 Human Learning
EDPT 540 Introduction to Educational Measurement and Evaluation
EDPT 571 Instructional Design
CTSE 593A & B Master's Seminar

Electives (2 classes):
EDPT 511 Human Motivation in Education
EDPT 520 Human Lifespan Development
EDPT 570 Language and Cultural Diversity in Learning
CTSE 573 Management of Instructional Resources
EDPA 671 The Computer and Data Processing Education

Faculty: 6 full-time, variable adjunct part-time. Financial Assistance: Part-time, instructional technology-related work available in the Los Angeles area and on campus, some scholarship monies available. Full support for Ph.D. students. Degrees Awarded: 15. Updated: 3/27/2006. Robert Rueda, rueda@usc.edu.

Colorado

University of Colorado at Denver and Health Sciences Center. School of Education and Human Development. Campus Box 106, P.O. Box 173364, Denver, CO 80217-3364, United States. (303)556-4478. Fax: (303)556-4479. Web site: http://www.cudenver.edu/ilt. Brent Wilson, Program Coordinator, Information and Learning Technologies. brent.wilson@cudenver.edu. Specialization: M.A. in Information & Learning Technologies; Certificate and M. A. in eLearning Design and Implementation; Ph.D. in Educational Leadership and Innovation with emphasis in Instructional Design and Technology. Features: The ILT program focuses on design and use of digital learning resources. Ph.D. students complete 12 semester hours of doctoral labs (small groups collaborating with faculty on difficult problems of practice). Throughout the program, students complete a product portfolio of research, design, teaching, and applied projects. The program is cross-disciplinary, drawing on expertise in technology, adult learning, systemic change, research methods, reflective practice, and cultural studies. Admission Requirements: M.A. and Ph.D.: satisfactory GPA, GRE, writing sample, letters of recommendation, transcripts. See Web site for more detail. Degree Requirements: M.A.: 36 semester hours including 28 hours of core coursework; professional portfolio; field experience. Ph.D.: 50 semester hours of coursework and labs, plus 20 dissertation hours; portfolio; dissertation. Faculty: 5 full-time, several part-time (see Web). Students: M.A., 15 full-time, 60 part-time; Ph.D., 3 full-time, 10 part-time. Financial Assistance: assistantships, internships. Degrees Awarded: 2005: 42. Updated: 3/7/2006. Brent Wilson, brent.wilson@cudenver.edu.

University of Northern Colorado. Educational Technology, College of Education. Greeley, CO 80639, United States. (970)351-2816. Fax: (970)351-1622. Web site: http://www.coe.unco.edu/edtech/. Kay Persichitte, Professor, Department Chair, Educational Technology. kay.persichitte@unco.edu. Specialization: M.A. in Educational Technology; M.A. in Educational Media; Nondegree endorsement for school library media specialists; Ph.D. in Educational Technology with emphases in Distance Education, Instructional Development/Design, Interactive Technology, and Technology Integration. Features: Graduates are prepared for careers as instructional technologists, course designers, trainers, instructional developers, media specialists, and human resource managers. Graduates typically follow employment paths into K-12 education, higher education, business, industry, and, occasionally the military. Admission Requirements: M.A.: bachelor's degree, 3.0 undergraduate GPA, 1000 GRE verbal and quantitative and 3.5 on the written/analytical, 3 letters of recommendation, statement of career goals. Endorsement: Same as M.A. but no GRE. Ph.D.: 3.2 GPA in last 60 hours of coursework, three letters of recommendation, congruency between applicants statement of career goals and program goals, 1100 GRE verbal and quantitative and 3.5 on the written/analytical, interview with faculty. Degree Requirements: M.A.-Ed Tech: 30 semester hours (min); M.A.-Ed Media: 36–39 semester hours (min); Endorsement: 30–33 semester hours (min); Ph.D.: 67 semester hours (min). Faculty: 6 full-time. Students: M.A., 20 full-time, 130 part-time; Ph.D., 20 full-time, 25 part-time. Financial Assistance: Assistantships, grant development, student loans, fellowships, scholarships through the Graduate School. Very competitive with first consideration to full-time doctoral students. Degrees Awarded: >30 M.A.; 3 Ph.D.. Updated: 3/5/03. Kay A. Persichitte, kay.persichitte@unco.

Connecticut

Central Connecticut State University. Educational Technology. 1615 Stanley St., New Britain, CT 06050, United States. (860)832-2139. Fax: (860)832-2109. Web site: http://www.ccsu.edu. Farough Abed, Director, Educational Technology Program. abedf@ccsu.ctstateu.edu. Specialization: M.S. in Educational Technology. Features: Curriculum emphases include instructional technology, instructional design, message design, and computer technologies. Degree applies to: Public school, Business-Training and Development, and College teaching position. The program supports the Center for Innovation in Teaching and Technology to link students with client-based projects. Hands-on experience with emphasis on design, production, and evaluation. Students work as teams in their second year. Admission Requirements: Bachelor's degree, 2.7 undergraduate GPA. Degree Requirements: 36 semester hours, optional thesis or master's final project (3 credits). Bachelor, two letters of reference, and goal statement. Faculty: 2 full-time, 4 part-time. Students: Full-time 3, part-time 45. Financial Assistance: graduate assistant position. Degrees Awarded: 28. Updated: 7/7/04. abedf@ccsu.edu.

Fairfield University. Educational Technology. N. Benson Road, Fairfield, CT 06824, United States. (203)254-4000. Fax: (203)254-4047. Web site: http://www.fairfield.edu. Dr. Ibrahim M. Hefzallah, Prof., Chair., Educational Technology Department; Dr. Justin Ahn, Assistant Professor of Educational Technology. ihefzallah@mail.fairfield.edu; jahn@mail.fairfield.edu. Specialization: M.A. and a certificate of Advanced Studies in Educational Technology in one of five areas of concentrations: Computers-in-Education, Instructional Development, School Media Specialist, Applied Educational Technology in Content Areas, and Television Production; customized course of study also available. Features: emphasis on theory, practice, and new instructional developments in computers in education, multimedia, school/media, and applied technology in education. Admission Requirements: Bachelor's degree from accredited institution with 2.67 GPA. Degree Requirements: 33 credits. Faculty: 2 full-time, 8 part-time. Students: 4 full-time, 74 part-time. Financial Assistance: assistantships, student loans. Degrees Awarded: 12. Updated: 5/15/03. Dr. Hefzallah, contact by email.

Southern Connecticut State University. Information and Library Science. 501 Crescent St., New Haven, CT 06515, United States. (203)392-5781. Fax: (203)392-5780. Web site: http://www.southernct.edu/. Arlene Bielefield, JD, Chairperson; Edward Harris, Ph.D.., Dean. mckayl1@southernct.edu. Specialization: M.S. in Instructional Technology; Sixth-Year Professional Diploma Library—Information Studies (student may select area of specialization in Instructional Technology). Features: Courses in instructional design and technology and in corporate training and development. Admission Requirements: Bachelor's degree from an institution accredited by a recognized regional accrediting agency in the United States. Degrees from outside the United States must be evaluated by an accredited evaluating agency. Undergraduate cumulative average of at least 2.5 on a scale of A = 4. Initial teacher certification programs require a minimum of 2.7. Recommendation of the graduate program coordinator. Degree Requirements: for Instructional Technology only, 36 semester hours. For sixth-year: 30 credit hours with 6 credit hours of core requirements, 9–15 credit hours in specialization. Faculty: 1 full-time; 4 part-time. Students: 3 full-time and 38 part-time in M.S./IT program. Financial Assistance: graduate assistantship (salary $1,800 per semester; assistants pay tuition and a general university fee sufficient to defray cost of student accident insurance). Updated: 3/5/04. Please contact Arlene Bielefield, bielefielda1@sou.

University of Connecticut. Educational Psychology. 249 Glenbrook Rd, Unit, 2064, Storrs, CT 06269-2064, United States. (860)486-0182. Fax: (860)486-0180. Web site: http://www.epsy.uconn.edu/. Michael Young, program coordinator. myoung@UConnvm.UConn.edu. Specialization: M.A. in Educational Technology (portfolio or thesis options), 1-year partially online Masters (summer, fall, spring, summer), 6th Year certificate in Educational Technology, and Ph.D. in Learning Technology. Features: M.A. can be on-campus or 2 Summers (on campus) and Fall–Spring (Online) that can be completed in a year. The Ph.D. emphasis in Learning Technology is a unique program at UConn. It strongly emphasizes Cognitive Science and how technology can be used to enhance the way people think and learn. The program seeks to provide students with knowledge of theory and applications regarding the use of advanced technology to enhance learning and thinking. Campus facilities include $2 billion twenty-first-century UConn enhancement to campus infrastructure, including a new wing to the Neag School of Education. Faculty research interests include interactive video for anchored instruction and situated learning, telecommunications for cognitive apprenticeship, technology-mediated interactivity for learning by design activities, and in cooperation with the National Research Center for Gifted and Talented, research on the use of technology to enhance cooperative learning and the development of gifted performance in all students. Admission Requirements: admission to the graduate school at UConn, GRE scores (or other evidence of success at the graduate level). Previous experience in a related area of technology, education, or experience in education or training. Degree Requirements: completion of plan of study coursework, comprehensive exam (portfolio-based with multiple requirements), and completion of an approved dissertation. Faculty: The program in Cognition and Instruction has 7 full-time faculty; 3 full-time faculty administer the emphasis in Educational Technology. Students: M.A. 8, Ph.D., 10. Financial Assistance: graduate assistantships, research fellowships, teaching assistantships, and federal and minority scholarships are available competitively. Degrees Awarded: 4 M.A., 2 Ph.D. Updated: 5/19/03. m. young, myoung@uconn.edu.

Florida

Barry University. Department of Educational Computing and Technology, School of Education. 11300 N.E. Second Ave., Miami Shores, FL 33161, United States. (305)899-3608. Fax: (305)899-3718. Web site: http://www.barry.edu/ed/programs/masters/ect/default.htm. Donna Lenaghan, Dir. dlenaghan@bu4090.barry.edu. Specialization: M.S. and Ed.S. in Educational Technology Applications and Ph.D. degree in Educational Technology Leadership. Features: These programs and courses prepare educators to integrate computer/technologies in their disciplines and/or train individuals to use computers/technologies. The focus is on improving the teaching and learning process thought integration of technologies into curricula and learning activities. Admission Requirements: GRE scores, letters of recommendation, GPA, interview, achievements. Degree Requirements: M.S. or Ed.S.: 36 semester credit hours. Ph.D.: 54 credits beyond the Masters including dissertation credits. Faculty: 5 full-time, 10 part-time. Students: M.S., 8 full-time, 181 part-time; Ed.S., 5 full-time, 44 part-time; Ph.D., 3 full-time, 15 part-time. Financial Assistance: assistantships, student loans. Degrees Awarded: 75. Updated: 5/19/03. Dr. Donna Lenaghan, (305) 899-3740.

Florida Institute of Technology. Science Education Department. 150 University Blvd., Melbourne, FL 32901-6975, United States. (321)674-8126. Fax: (321)674-7598. Web site: http://www.fit.edu/catalog/sci-lib/comp-edu.html#master-info. Dr. David Cook, Dept. Head. dcook@fit.edu. Specialization: Master's degree options in Computer Education and Instructional Technology; Ph.D. degree in Science Education with options for research in Computer Science, Computer Education, and Instructional Technology. Features: Flexible program depending on student experience. Admission Requirements: Masters: 3.0 GPA for regular admission; 2.75 for provisional admission. Ph.D.: Master's degree and 3.2 GPA. Degree Requirements: Masters: 33 semester hours (15 in computer or and technology education, 9 in education, 9 electives); practicum; no thesis or internship required or 30 semester hrs. for thesis option. Ph.D.: 48 semester hours (12 in computer and technology education, 12 in education, 24 dissertation and research). Faculty: 4 full-time. Students: 1 full-time, 4 part-time. Financial Assistance: loans, limited graduate student assistantships (full tuition plus stipend) available. Degrees Awarded: 1. Updated: 4/4/2006. David Cook, dcook@fit.edu.

Florida State University. Educational Psychology and Learning Systems. 305 Stone Bldg., Tallahassee, FL 32306, United States. (850)644-4592. Fax: (850)644-8776. Web site: http://www.epls.fsu.edu/is/index.htm. Mary Kate McKee, Program Coordinator. MMcKee@oddl.fsu.edu. Specialization: M.S., Ed.S., Ph.D. in Instructional Systems with specializations for persons planning to work in academia, business, industry, government, or military, both in the United States and in international settings. Features: Core courses include systems and materials development, development of multimedia, project management, psychological foundations, current trends in instructional design, and research and statistics. Internships are recommended. Admission Requirements: M.S.: 3.0 GPA in last two years of undergraduate program, 1000 GRE (verbal plus quantitative), 550 TOEFL (for international applicants). Ph.D.: 1100 GRE (V+Q), 3.5 GPA in last two years; international students, 550 TOEFL. Degree Requirements: M.S.: 36 semester hours, 2–4 hour internship, comprehensive exam preparation of professional portfolio. Faculty: 7 full-time, 4 part-time. Students: M.S., 50; Ph.D., 50. Financial Assistance: Graduate research and teaching assistantships on faculty grants and contracts; Program, college, and university fellowships. Updated: 3/5/04. Robert Reiser, rreiser@mailer.fsu.edu.

Nova Southeastern University—Fischler Graduate School of Education and Human Services. Programs in Instructional Technology and Distance Education (ITDE). 1750 NE 167th Street, North Miami Beach, FL 33162, United States. 954-262-8572, (800)986-3223, ext. 8572. Fax: (954)262-3905. itde.nova.edu. Marsha L. Burmeister, Recruitment Coordinator & Program Professor ITDE. itdeinfo@nova.edu. Specialization: M.S. and Ed.D. in Instructional Technology and Distance Education. Features: M.S. 21 months (M.S. ITDE program graduates may continue with the Ed.D. program as second year students). Ed.D. 36 months. M.S. and Ed.D. combined: 4+ years. Blended/hybrid delivery model with limited face-to-face and via instruction at-a-distance using Web-based technologies. Active employment in the field of instructional technology/distance education. Admission Requirements: Completion of bachelor's degree for M.S. program (2.5 minimum GPA); master's degree required for admission to Ed.D. program (3.0 minimum GPA). Miller Analogies Test (MAT) score (test taken within last 5 years). Submission of application/supplementary materials, approval of Skills Checklist (application),three letters of recommendation, official copies of transcripts for all graduate work, resume and oral interview (via telephone). Demonstrated potential for successful completion of the program via acceptance of application, Internet Service Provider, Laptop computer. Degree Requirements: 21 months and 30 semester credits. Ed.D. 3 years and 65 semester credits. M.S. Program: 3 "extended weekends": one extended weekend in the fall (5 days), one extended weekend in the spring (4 days), one summer instructional session (4–5 days; July), final term online delivery. Ed.D. program: same as above, continues throughout the 3 years (3 sessions in first year, 2 sessions in the second year, and 1 instructional session in the third year for a total of 6 face-to-face sessions) Faculty: 6 full-time and 20 adjuncts. Students: 300 full time. Financial Assistance: Student loans; apply to Nova Southeastern University Office of Student Financial Assistance: http://www.nova.edu/cwis/finaid/index.html. All ITDE students are considered full-time students for the purposes of financial aid. Degrees Awarded: 100. Updated: 3/19/03. Marsha L. Burmeister, Ed.D., burmeist@nova.edu.

University of Central Florida. College of Education. ERTL, 4000 Central Florida Blvd., Orlando, FL 32816-1250, United States. (407)823-4835. Fax: (407)823-4880. Web site: http://pegasus.cc.ucf. edu/~instsys/. http://pegasus.cc.ucf.edu/~edmedia. http://pegasus.cc.ucf.edu/~edtech. Gary Orwig, Instructional Systems; Judy Lee, Educational Media; Glenda Gunter, Educational Technology. orwig@mail.ucf.edu; jlee@pegasus.cc.ucf.edu; ggunter@pegasus.cc.ucf.edu. Specialization: M.A. in Instructional Technology/Instructional Systems, http://pegasus.cc. ucf.edu/~instsys/; M.Ed. in Instructional Technology/Educational Media (entirely Web-based), http://pegasus.cc.ucf.edu/~edmedia/; M.A. in Instructional Technology/Educational Technology, http://pegasus.cc.ucf. edu/~edtech; Ph.D. and Ed.D. with specialization in Instructional Technology, http://www. graduate.ucf.edu. Features: There are approximately 18 Ed.D. students and 22 Ph.D. students in the doctoral programs. All programs rely heavily on understanding of fundamental competencies as reflected by ASTD, AECT, AASL, and ISTE. There is an emphasis on the practical application of theory through intensive hands-on experiences. Orlando and the surrounding area is home to a plethora of high-tech companies, military training and simulation organizations, and tourist attractions. UCF, established in 1963, now has in excess of 36,000 students, representing more than 90 countries. It has been ranked as one of the leading "most-wired" universities in North America. Admission Requirements: Interviews (either in person or via e-mail); GRE score of 840 if last 60 hours of undergraduate degree is 3.0 or above, 1000 if less; TOEFL of 550 (270 computer-based version) if English is not first language; three letters of recommendation; resume, statement of goals; residency statement; and health record. Financial statement if coming from overseas. Degree Requirements: M.A. in Instructional Technology/Instructional Systems, 39–42 semester hours; M.Ed. in Instructional Technology/Educational Media, 39–45 semester hours; M.A. in Instructional Technology/Educational Technology, 36–45 semester hours. Practicum required in all three programs; thesis, research project, or substitute additional coursework. Ph.D. and Ed.D. require between 58–69 hours beyond the master's for completion. Faculty: 4 full-time, 12 part-time. Students: Inst Sys, 70; Ed Media, 35; Ed Technology, 50. Full-time, 120; part-time, 35. Financial Assistance: Competitive graduate assistantships in department and college, numerous paid internships, limited number of doctoral fellowships. Degrees Awarded: 65. Updated: 5/22/03. Gary Orwig, orwig@mail.ucf.edu.

University of Florida. School of Teaching and Learning. 2403 Norman Hall, Gainesville, FL 32611-7048, United States. 352-392-9191 X261. Fax: 352-392-9193. Web site: http://www.coe.ufl.edu/school/edtech/index.htm (Hybrid programs); http://www.coe.ufl.edu/online/edtech/index.html (Online programs). Kara Dawson. dawson@coe.ufl.edu. Specialization: Hybrid Program: Educational technology students may earn M.Ed., Ed.S., Ed.D., or Ph.D. degrees and have an opportunity to specialize in one of two tracks: (1) Teaching and teacher education or (2) Design and Production of educational materials. Many students merge these tracks. Teacher education students and students in other degree programs may also elect to specialize in Educational Technology. Online Programs: We offer online Masters and Ed.S. degrees in "Teaching, learning & facilitating change with educational technology." http://www.coe.ufl.edu/online/edtech/index.html. Features: Students take core courses listed on our Educational Technology Web site and then select an area of specialization. Opportunities to collaborative research, write, and design with faculty members. Strong community of graduate students. Admission Requirements: Please see the Educational Technology Web site for the most up-to-date information. Current admission requirements are as follows: Obtain a GRE score of 1000 or more on the verbal and quantitative components of the GRE. Applicants must have a score of 450 or higher for each component (verbal and quantitative). Submit a written document outlining (1) your career goals and (2) the track you wish to specialize in the Educational Technology program. Degree Requirements: Please see the Educational Technology website for the most up-to-date information. Program and college requirements must be met but there is considerable flexibility for doctoral students to plan an appropriate program with their advisors. Faculty: 2 full-time faculty members; 2 faculty members teach part-time within the program. Students: approximately 53 students are enrolled in our Educational Technology. Financial Assistance: A limited number of graduate assistantships are available. Interested students should submit an assistantship application with their admissions application. Students should also check the Web site for information about available assistantships. Updated: 3/7/2006. Kara Dawson, dawson@coe.ufl.edu.

University of South Florida. Instructional Technology Program, Secondary Education Department, College of Education. 4202 E. Fowler Avenue, EDU162, Tampa, FL 33620-5650, United States. (813)974-3533. Fax: (813)974-3837. Web site: http://www.coedu.usf.edu/it. Dr. William Kealy, Graduate Certificates; Dr. Frank Breit, Master's program; Dr. Ann Barron, Education Specialist program; Dr. James White, Doctoral program. See@http://www.coedu.usf.edu/it. Specialization: Graduate Certificates in Web Design, Instructional Design, Multimedia Design, School Networks, and Distance Education. M.Ed., Ed.S., and Ph.D. in Curriculum and Instruction with emphasis in Instructional Technology. Features: Many students gain practical experience in the Florida Center for Instructional Technology (FCIT), which provides services to the Department of Education and other grants and contracts; the Virtual Instructional Team for the Advancement of Learning (VITAL), which provides USF faculty with course development services; and Educational Outreach. The College of Education is one of the largest in the United States in terms of enrollment and facilities. As of Fall 1997, a new, technically state-of-the-art building was put into service. The University of South Florida has been classified by the Carnegie Foundation as a Doctoral/Research University—Extensive. Admission Requirements: See http://www.coedu.usf.edu/it. Degree Requirements: See http://www.coedu.usf.edu/it. Faculty: 4 full-time, 6 part-time. Students: 120 full-time, 255 part-time. Financial Assistance: some assistantships, grants, loans, scholarships, and fellowships. Degrees Awarded: 60+. Updated: 5/20/03. James A. White, jwhite@tempest.coedu.usf.edu.

Georgia

Georgia Southern University. College of Education. Box 8131, Statesboro, GA 30460-8131, United States. (912)681-5307. Fax: (912)486-7104. Web site: http://coe. georgiasouthern.edu/eltr/tech/inst_tech/index.htm. Rlizabeth Downs, Associate Professor, Dept. of Leadership, Technology, and Human Development. EDowns@georgiasouthern. edu. Specialization: M.Ed. and GA certification for School Library Media Specialist. An Instructional Technology strand is available in the Ed.S. in Teaching and Learning Program and in the Ed.D. program in Curriculum Studies. Features: GA Special Technology Certification course available; strong emphasis on technology. Admission Requirements: BS (teacher certification *not* required), MAT score of 44 or GRE score of 450 verbal and 450 quantitative for regular admission. Provisional admission requires lower scores but also requires letters of intent/reference. Degree Requirements: 36 semester hours, including a varying number of hours of media for individual students. Faculty: 3 full-time. Students: 100 part-time. Financial Assistance: See graduate catalog for general financial aid information. Degrees Awarded: 20. Updated: 3/24/2006. Elizabeth Downs, edowns@georgiasouthern.edu.

Georgia State University. Middle–Secondary Education and Instructional Technology. Box 3976, Atlanta, GA 30302-3976, United States. (404)651-2510. Fax: (404)651-2546. Web site: http://edtech.gsu.edu. Dr. Stephen W. Harmon, contact person. swharmon@gsu.edu. Specialization: M.S., Ed.S., and Ph.D. in Instructional Technology or Library Media. Features: -Focus on research and practical application of instructional technology in educational and corporate settings. Admission Requirements: M.S.: Bachelor's degree, 2.5 undergraduate GPA, 800 GRE, 550 TOEFL. Ed.S.: Master's degree, teaching certificate, 3.25 graduate GPA, 48 MAT or 900 GRE. Ph.D.: Master's degree, 3.30 graduate GPA, 53 MAT or 500 verbal plus 500 quantitative GRE or 500 analytical GRE. Degree Requirements: M.S.: 36 sem. hours, internship, portfolio, comprehensive examination. Ed.S.: 30 sem. hours, internship, and scholarly project. Ph.D.: 66 sem. hours, internship, comprehensive examination, dissertation. Faculty: 10 full-time, 3 part-time. Students: 100 M.S., 40 Ph.D. Financial Assistance: assistantships, grants, student loans. Degrees Awarded: 25 M.S., 4 Ed.S., 4 Ph.D. Updated: 3/14/2006. Steve Harmon, swharmon@gsu.edu.

State University of West Georgia. Department of Media and Instructional Technology. 138 Education Annex, Carrollton, GA 30118, United States. 678-839-6558 or 839-6149. Fax: 678-839-6153. Web site: http://coe.westga.edu/mit/index.html. Dr. Barbara K. McKenzie, Professor and Chair. bmckenzi@westga.edu. M.Ed. with specializations in School Library Media and Instructional Technology and Add-On certification in School Library Media for students with Master's degrees in other disciplines. The department also offers an Ed.S. program in Media with two options, Media Specialist or Instructional

Technology. The program strongly emphasizes technology integration in the schools. Features: Master's degree students and initial certification students are required to complete a practicum. Admission Requirements: M.Ed.: 800 GRE, 44 MAT, 550 NTE Core, 2.7 undergraduate GPA. Ed.S.: 900 GRE, 48 MAT, or 575 NTE and 3.25 graduate GPA. Degree Requirements: 36 semester hours for M.Ed.; 27 semester hours for Ed.S. Faculty: 7 full-time in Media/Technology; 3 full-time instructors in Instructional Technology; 2 part-time in Media/Instructional Technology. Students: Approximately 450, part-time. Financial Assistance: two graduate research assistantships for the department. Degrees Awarded: Approximately 80 across both levels. Updated: 3/11/2006. Dr. Barbara K. McKenzie, bmckenzi@westga.edu.

University of Georgia. Department of Educational Psychology and Instructional Technology, College of Education. 604 Aderhold Hall, Athens, GA 30602-7144, United States. (706)542-3810. Fax: (706)542-4032. Web site: http://www.coe.uga.edu/epit/. Dr. Thomas Reeves, IT Program Leader. treeves@uga.edu. Specialization: M.Ed. and Ed.S. in Instructional Technology with two emphasis areas: Instructional Design & Development and School Library Media; Ph.D. for leadership positions as specialists in instructional design and development and university faculty. The program offers advanced study for individuals with previous preparation in instructional media and technology, as well as a preparation for personnel in other professional fields requiring a specialty in instructional systems or instructional technology. Representative career fields for graduates include designing new courses, educational multimedia (especially Web-based), tutorial programs, and instructional materials in state and local school systems, higher education, business and industry, research and nonprofit settings, and in instructional products development. Features: Minor areas of study available in a variety of other departments. Personalized programs are planned around a common core of courses and include practica, internships, or clinical experiences. Research activities include grant-related activities and applied projects, as well as dissertation studies. Admission Requirements: All degrees: application to graduate school, satisfactory GRE score, other criteria as outlined in Graduate School Bulletin and on the program Web site. Degree Requirements: M.Ed.: 36 semester hours with 3.0 GPA, portfolio with oral exam. Ed.S.: 30 semester hours with 3.0 GPA and project exam. Ph.D.: three full years of study beyond the Master's degree, two consecutive semesters full-time residency, comprehensive exam with oral defense, internship, dissertation with oral defense. Faculty: 12 full-time, 4 part-time. Students: M.Ed. 158; Ed.S. 72; Ph.D. 52. Financial Assistance: Graduate assistantships available. Degrees Awarded: degrees in 2003: 60. Updated: 3/7/2006. Thomas C. Reeves, treeves@uga.edu.

Valdosta State University. Curriculum & Instructional Technology. 1500 N. Patterson St., Valdosta, GA 31698, United States. (229)333-5927. Fax: (229)333-7167. Web site: http://education.valdosta.edu/info/cait/. Gayle Brooks. gbrooks@valdosta.edu. Specialization: M.Ed. in Instructional Technology with two tracks: Library/Media or Technology Applications; Online Ed.S. in Instructional Technology; Ed.D. in Curriculum and Instruction. Features: The program has a strong emphasis on systematic design and technology in M.Ed., Ed.S., and Ed.D. Strong emphasis on change leadership, reflective practice, applied research in Ed.S. and Ed.D. Admission Requirements: M.Ed.: 2.5 GPA, 800 GRE. Ed.S.: Master's degree, 3 years of experience, 3.0 GPA, 850 GRE, MAT 390 and less than 5 years old. Ed.D.: Master's degree, 3 years of experience, 3.50 GPA, 1000 GRE. Degree Requirements: M.Ed.: 33 semester hours. Ed.S.: 27 semester hours. Ed.D.: 54 semester hours. Faculty: 6 full-time, 6 part-time. Students: 64 Masters, 87 Specialist, 35 Doctoral students. Financial Assistance: graduate assistantships, student loans, scholarships. Degrees Awarded: M.Ed., Ed.S., Ed.D. Updated: 3/7/2006. Jane Zahner, Professor/Acting Dept. Head.

Hawaii

University of Hawaii—Manoa. Department of Educational Technology. 1776 University Ave., Honolulu, Hawaii 96822-2463, United States. (808)956-7671. Fax: (808)956-3905. Web site: http://www.hawaii.edu/edtech. Geoffrey Z. Kucera, Prof., Chair. edtechdept@hawaii.edu. Speci: M.Ed. in Educational Technology. Features: min. 39 semester hours, including 3 in practicum, 3 in internship; thesis and nonthesis available. Admission Requirements: Bachelor's degree in any field, B average (3.0 GPA). Degree Requirements: 39 sem. hours (plus 6 sem. hrs of prerequisites if needed). Faculty: 6 full-time, 1 part-time. Students: 13 full-time, 35 part-time students. Financial Assistance: Consideration given to meritorious second-year students for tuition waivers and scholarship applications. Degrees Awarded: 12 (2003), 16 (2002), 11 (2001). Updated: 5/12/03. Geoffrey Z. Kucera, (808) 956-7671, Fax: (808) 956.

Idaho

Boise State University. Instructional & Performance Technology. 1910 University Drive, ET-327, Boise, ID 83725, United States. (208)424-5135;(800)824-7017 ext. 61312. Fax: (208)426-1970. Web site: http://ipt.boisestate.edu/. Dr. Don Stepich, IPT Program Chair.; Jo Ann Fenner, IPT Program Developer and distance program contact person. bsuipt@boisestate.edu. Specialization: The Master of Science in Instructional & Performance Technology (IPT) degree is intended to prepare students for careers in the areas of instructional technology, performance technology, instructional design, performance improvement, training, education and training management, e-learning, human resources, organizational development, and human performance consulting. Features: Leading experts in learning styles, evaluation, e-learning, performance improvement, and leadership principles serve as adjunct faculty in the program via computer and modem from their various remote locations. For details, visit our faculty Web page at http://ipt.boisestate.edu/faculty.htm. Admission Requirements: undergraduate degree with 3.0 GPA, one-to-two page essay describing why you want to pursue this program and how it will contribute to your personal and professional development, and a resume of personal qualifications and work experience. For more information, visit http://ipt.boisestate.edu/application_admission.htm. Degree Requirements: 36 semester hours in instructional and performance technology and related coursework; and four options for a culminating activity; project, thesis, portfolio or oral comprehensive exam (included in 36 credit hours). Faculty: 6 full-time, 10 part-time. Students: 190 part-time. Financial Assistance: DANTES funding for some military personnel, low-interest loans to eligible students, graduate assistantships for on-campus enrollees. *Note*: All active military are eligible for the resident rate of $295 per credit. Degrees Awarded: 45. Updated: 3/14/2006. Jo Ann Fenner, contact me by e-mail or phone.

Illinois

Governors State University. College of Arts and Sciences. University Drive. University Park, IL 60466, United States. (708)534-4051. Fax: (708)534-7895. Web site: http://faculty.govst.edu/users/glanigan/homepage.htm. Mary Lanigan, Associate Prof., Human Performance and Training. m-lanigan@govst.edu. Specialization: M.A. in Communication and Training with HP&T major. Program concentrates on building instructional design skills. Features: Instructional Design overview; front-end analysis including both needs and task; design and delivery using various platforms; evaluation skills and how to predict behavior transfer; various technologies; consulting; project management; systems thinking; principles of message design; and more. Admission Requirements:

Undergraduate degree in any field. Degree Requirements: 36 credit hours (trimester), all in instructional and performance technology; internship or advanced field project required. Metropolitan Chicago area based. Faculty: 2 full-time and 2 to 4 adjuncts depending on the semester. Students: 30 part-time. Financial Assistance: Contact Student Assistance. Degrees Awarded: 10. Updated: 3/25/2006. Mary Lanigan, m-lanigan@govst.edu.

Northern Illinois University. Educational Technology, Research and Assessment. 208 Gabel Hall, DeKalb, IL 60115, United States. (815)753-9339. Fax: (815)753-9388. Web site: http://www.cedu.niu.edu/etra. Dr. Jeffrey B. Hecht, Department Chair., etra@niu.edu. Specialization: M.S.Ed. in Instructional Technology with concentrations in Instructional Design, Distance Education, Educational Computing, and Media Administration; Ed.D. in Instructional Technology, emphasizing instructional design and development, computer education, media administration, and preparation for careers in business, industry, and higher education. In addition, Illinois state certification in school library media is offered in conjunction with either degree or alone. Features: Program is highly individualized. All facilities remodeled and modernized in 2002–2003 featuring five smart classrooms and over 110 student use desktop and laptop computers. Specialized equipment for digital audio and video editing, Web site and CD creation, and presentations. All students are encouraged to create portfolios highlighting personal accomplishments and works (required at Masters). Masters program started in 1968, doctorate in 1970. Admission Requirements: M.S.Ed.: 2.75 undergraduate GPA, GRE verbal and quantitative scores, two references. Ed.D.: 3.25 M.S. GPA, writing sample, three references, interview. Degree Requirements: M.S.Ed.: 39 hours, including 30 in instructional technology; portfolio. Ed.D.: 63 hours beyond Master's, including 15 hours for dissertation. Faculty: 8 full-time, 18 part-time. Students: M.S., 185 part-time; Ed.D., 135 part-time. Financial Assistance: Assistantships available at times in various departments, scholarships, and minority assistance. Degrees Awarded: 2001 degrees awarded: M.S.Ed. in I.T.=93; Ed.D. in I.T.=11. Updated: 5/27/03. Jeffrey B. Hecht, jbhecht@niu.edu.

Southern Illinois University at Carbondale. Department of Curriculum and Instruction. 625 Wham Drive, Mailcode 4610, Carbondale, IL 62901, United States. (618)4534218. Fax: (618)4534244. Web site: http://ci.siu.edu/. Sharon Shrock, Coord., Instructional Design/Instructional Technology. sashrock@siu.edu. Specialization: M.S. in Education with specializations in Instructional Design and Instructional Technology. Ph.D. in Education including specialization in Instructional Technology. Features: All specializations are oriented to multiple education settings. The ID program emphasizes nonschool (primarily corporate) learning environments, human performance technology, and criterion-referenced performance assessment. The IT program include two mini-tracks: (a) e-Learning and (b) instructional gaming. Admission Requirements: M.S.: Bachelor's degree, 2.7 undergraduate GPA, transcripts. Ph.D.: Master's degree, 3.25 GPA, GRE scores, 3 letters of recommendation, transcripts, writing sample. International students without a degree from a U.S. institution must submit TOEFL score. Degree Requirements: M.S., 32 credit hours with thesis; 36 credit hours without thesis; Ph.D., 40 credit hours beyond the masters degree in courses, 24 credit hours for the dissertation. Faculty: 4 full-time. Students: 20 full-time, 23 part-time. Financial Assistance: some graduate assistantships and scholarships available to qualified students. Degrees Awarded: 13 graduates. Updated: 3/27/2006. Christian S. Loh, csloh@siu.edu.

Southern Illinois University at Edwardsville. Instructional Design and Learning Technologies Program. School of Education. Edwardsville, IL 62026-1125, United States. (618)650-3277. Fax: (618)650-3808. Web site: http://www.siue.edu/EDUCATION/ ed_leadership/tech.html. Dr. Yuliang Liu, Dir., Dept. of Educational Leadership. yliu@siue.edu. Specialization: (1) Educational Technologies—enables teachers and other school personnel to plan, implement, and evaluate technology-based instruction and learning activities in P-12 settings. Students interested in leadership roles in educational technology, such as technology coordinators in schools or school districts, can work toward meeting the standards for the Illinois State Board of Educations Technology Specialist certificate through this program. (2) Instructional Design & Performance Improvement— focuses on skills necessary for careers in instructional technology, performance improvement, instructional design, and training in nonschool settings. (3) Interactive Multimedia Technologies—appropriate for people wishing to pursue the design and development of various interactive multimedia and Web-based learning experiences. Several unique features of the program provide students with opportunities for important practical experiences that complement coursework. Juried presentations provide students with an opportunity to share their work with a jury of professors and peers and defend their work in light of their own goals and the content of their degree program. Design Studios provide students with opportunities to work on real-world projects for a variety of real clients in order to develop skills in collaboration, design, development tools and techniques, and project management. Admission Requirements: The requirements for admission are a bachelor's degree and a GPA of 3.0 or above during their last two years of undergraduate work. Applicants are also required to take the Miller Analogies Test or the Graduate Record Examination, and an interview may be requested. Degree Requirements: 36 semester hours; Thesis or Final Project options. Faculty: 3 full time, 1 part time. Students: 125. Financial Assistance: Assistance may be available through the university. Degrees Awarded: 15. Updated: 4/7/2006. Wayne Nelson, wnelson@siue.edu.

Indiana

Indiana University. School of Education. W. W. Wright Education Bldg., Rm. 2276, 201 N. Rose Ave., Bloomington, IN 47405-1006, United States. (812)856-8451. Fax: (812)856-8239. Web site: http://education.indiana.edu/~ist/. Elizabeth Boling, Chair, Dept. of Instructional Systems Technology. istdept@indiana.edu. Specialization: M.S. and Ed.S. degrees designed for individuals seeking to be practitioners in the field of Instructional Technology. M.S. degree also offered in Web-based format with instructional product and portfolio requirements. Offers Ph.D. degree with four program focus areas: Foundations; Instructional Analysis, Design, and Development; Instructional Development and Production; and Implementation and Management. Features: Requires computer skills as a prerequisite and makes technology utilization an integral part of the curriculum; eliminates separation of various media formats; and establishes a series of courses of increasing complexity integrating production and development. The latest in technical capabilities have been incorporated, including teaching, computer, and laptop-ready laboratories, a multimedia laboratory, and video and audio production studios. Admission Requirements: M.S.: Bachelor's degree from an accredited institution, 1350 GRE (3 tests required) or 900 plus 3.5 analytical writing (new format), 2.75 undergraduate GPA. Ed.S. and Ph.D.: 1650 GRE (3 tests required) or 1100 plus 4.5 analytical writing (new format), 3.5 graduate GPA. Degree Requirements: M.S.: 36 credit hours (including 15 credits in required courses); colloquia; an instructional product; and 9 credits in outside electives, and portfolio. Ed.S.: 65 hours, capstone project with written report and a portfolio. Ph.D.: 90 hours, portfolio, and thesis. Faculty: 11 full-time, 2 part-time. Students: 240 (includes full time, part time, and ABDs). Financial Assistance: assistantships, fellowships. Degrees Awarded: 48 M.S.; 2 Ed.S.; 10 Ph.D. (2002). Updated: 2/28/03. Susan Sloffer, ssloffer@indiana.edu.

Purdue University. College of Education, Department of Curriculum and Instruction. 100 N. University St., West Lafayette, IN 47907-2098, United States. (765)494-5669. Fax: (765)496-1622. Web site: http://www.edci.purdue.edu/et/. Dr. Tim Newby, Prof. of Educational Technology. edtech@education.purdue.edu. Specialization: Master's degree and Ph.D. in Educational Technology. Master's program started in 1982; Ph.D. in 1985. Features: Vision Statement. The Educational Technology Program at Purdue University nurtures graduates who are effective designers of learning experiences and environments that incorporate technology to engage learners and improve learning. Admission Requirements: Master's and Ph.D: 3.0 GPA, three letters of recommendation, statement of personal goals. A score of 550 (paper-based) or 213 (computer-based) or above on the Test of English as a Foreign Language (TOEFL) for individuals whose first language is not English. Ph.D. Additional Requirement: 1000 GRE (V+Q); Verbal score of at least 500 preferred. Degree Requirements: Masters: minimum of 32 semester hours (17 in educational technology, 6–9 in research, development, and exit requirements, 6–9 electives); thesis optional. Ph.D.: 60 semester hours beyond the Master's degree (15–18 in educational technology, 27–30 in education and supporting areas; 15 dissertation research hours). Faculty: 5 full-time; 1 part-time. Students: M.S., 25; Ph.D., 33. Financial Assistance: assistantships and fellowships. Degrees Awarded: 3. Updated: 3/8/2006. Aggie Ward, aggie@purdue.edu.

Iowa

Clarke College. Graduate Studies. 1550 Clarke Drive, Dubuque, IA 52001, United States. (563)588-8180. Fax: (563)584-8604. Web site: http://www.clarke.edu. Margaret Lynn Lester. llester@clarke.edu. Specialization: M.A.E. (Two tracks: Instructional Leadership and Literacy). The "Instructional Leadership" track of this program offers hybrid courses in educational technology. Courses are offered through WEB-ST and face to face. Outcomes are aligned with the National Educational Technology Standards for Educators. Admission Requirements: Completed graduate application, official transcripts, photocopy of all teaching certificates and licenses, 2.75 GPA (4 point scale), two letters of reference, interview, statement of goals, ad $25 application fee. (Minimum TOEFL score of 550 if English is not first language.) Degree Requirements: 9 hours in Research Core; 9 hour in Instructional Core; and 18 hours in Instructional Leadership Track. Faculty: 1 full-time, 1–2 part-time. Students: Total M.A.E. program: 10 full-time, 12 part-time. Financial Assistance: No financial aid is available without acceptance to program. Special rates or forgivable loan program for Archdiocese of Dubuque teachers. Degrees Awarded: New program. Updated: 3/24/2006. Margaret Lynn Lester, 588-8180, llester@clarke.edu.

Iowa State University. College of Education. E262 Lagomarcino Hall, Ames, IA 50011, United States. (515)294-7021. Fax: (515)294-6260. Web site: http://www.educ. iastate.edu/. Niki Davis, Director, Center for Technology in Learning and Teaching. nedavis@iastate.edu. Specialization: M.Ed., M.S., and Ph.D. in Curriculum and Instructional Technology. Features: Prepares candidates as practitioners and researchers in the field of curriculum and instructional technology. All areas of specialization emphasize appropriate and effective applications of technology in teacher education. M.Ed. program also offered at a distance (online and face-to-face learning experiences). Practicum experiences related to professional objectives, supervised study, and research projects tied to long-term studies within the program, development and implementation of new techniques, teaching strategies, and operational procedures in instructional resources centers and computer labs, program emphasis on technologies for teachers. Admission Requirements: M.Ed. and M.S.: Bachelor's degree, top half of undergraduate class, official transcripts, three letters, autobiography. Ph.D.: top half of undergraduate class, official transcripts, three letters, autobiography, GRE scores, scholarly writing sample. Degree Requirements: M.Ed. 32 credit hours (7 research, 12 foundations, 13 applications and leadership in instructional technology); and action research project. M.S. 36 credit hours (16 research, 12 foundations, 8 applications and leadership in instructional technology); and thesis. Ph.D. 78 credit hours (minimum of 12 research, minimum of 15 foundations, additional core credits in conceptual, technical, and advanced specialization areas, minimum of 12 dissertation); portfolio, and dissertation. Faculty: 5 full-time, 2 part-time. Students: M.Ed. and M.S.: 80. Ph.D.: 45. Financial Assistance: Assistantships and fellowships. Updated: 7/7/04. Denise Schmidt, dschmidt@iastate.edu.

University of Northern Iowa. Educational Technology Program. 618 Schinder Education Center. Cedar Falls, IA 50614-0606, United States. (319)273-3250. Fax: (319)273-5886. Web site: http://ci.coe.uni.edu/edtech/index.html. Sharon E. Smaldin. - Sharon.Smaldino@UNI.edu. Specialization: M.A. in Curriculum & Instruction: Educational Technology, M.A. in Performance and Training Technology. Features: The master's degrees are designed to meet the AECT/ECIT standards and are focused on addressing specific career choices. The Educational Technology master's is designed to prepare educators for a variety of professional positions in educational settings, including: school building level, school district level, vocational-technical school, community college, and university. The Performance and Training Technology master's is designed for persons planning to work in nonschool settings. Majors in this area will complete a basic core of coursework applicable to all preparing for work as media specialists, trainers in industry and business, or communications designers. Specific areas of interest will determine the supporting electives. Licensure as a teacher is not required for admission to either master's in Iowa. The bachelor's degree may be in any field. Admission Requirements: Bachelors degree, 3.0 undergraduate GPA, 500 TOEFL. Degree Requirements: 38 semester credits, optional thesis worth 6 credits or alternative research paper of project, comprehensive exam. Faculty: 4 full-time, 6 part-time. Students: 120. Financial Assistance: assistantships, grants, student loans, scholarships, student employment. Degrees Awarded: 32. Updated: 6/9/03. Sharon Smaldino, sharon.smaldino@uni.edu.

Kansas

Emporia State University. Instructional Design & Technology. 1200 Commercial St., Campus Box 4037, Emporia, KS 66801, United States. 620-341-5829. Fax: 620-341-5785. Web site: http://idt.emporia.edu. Dr. Marcus D. Childress, Chair. marcus.childress@emporia.edu. Specialization: distance education, Web-based education, corporate education, P-12 technology integration. Features: Emporia State University's IDT department has the largest graduate instructional technology program in the state and is the only program in Kansas that grants a Master of Science Degree in Instructional Design and Technology. ESUs Instructional Design and Technology program prepares individuals for leadership in the design, development, and integration of technology and online learning into teaching and private sector training. All program courses are completely available online. Forms and application materials available at the Web site, http://idt.emporia.edu. Admission Requirements: 2.75 undergrad. GPA; resume; 2 recommendations; writing competency. Two admission approval dates each year—September 15 (for spring semester admission) and February 15 (for fall semester admission). Only applicants with completed admission packets will be considered. An IDT admission committee will meet to review admission materials. Applicants will be admitted to the IDT graduate program based upon the selection process. Those applicants who are not admitted may request that their names be placed on a waiting list for the next semester. Degree Requirements: 36 semester hours: 19 cr. core, 6 cr. research, 11 cr. electives. Faculty: 5.5 FTE. Students: 20 full-time; 150 part-time. Financial Assistance: 4 graduate teaching assistant positions with tuition waiver. Degrees Awarded: 30. Updated: 3/10/2006. Marcus Childress, marcus.childress@emporia.edu.

Emporia State University. School of Library and Information Management. 1200 Commercial, P.O. Box 4025, Emporia, KS 66801, United States. 800/552-4770. Fax: 620/341-5233. Web site: http://slim.emporia.edu. Daniel Roland, Director of Communications. slim-info@emporia.edu. Specialization: Master's of Library Science (ALA accredited program);

Master's in Legal Information Management—in partnership with the University of Kansas School of Law. Features: 50 semester hours or 15 hour certificate. School Library Certification program, which includes 27 hours of the M.L.S. program; Ph.D. in Library and Information Management B.S. in Information Resource Studies Information Management Certificate—18 hours of MLS curriculum Library Services Certificates—6 separate 12-hour programs of undergraduate work available for credit or noncredit. Areas include Information Sources and Services; Collection Management; Technology; Administration; Youth Services; and Generalist. The Master of Library Science program is also delivered to satellite campus sites in Denver, Salt Lake City, Portland, Oregon. New programs tend to start every three years in each location. New programs include Denver, Summer 2004; Portland, Spring 2005; Salt Lake City, Fall 2005. Admission Requirements: Undergrad GPA of 3.0 or better for master's degrees, 3.5 or better for Ph.D. GRE score of 1,000 points combined in Verbal and Analytical sections for master's degrees, 1,100 for Ph.D. GRE can be waived for students already holding a graduate degree in which they earned a 3.75 GPA or better. Admission interview. Degree Requirements: M.L.S.: 42 semester hours. Ph.D.: total of 55–59 semester hours beyond the masters. Faculty: 10 full-time, 25 part-time. Students: 71 full-time, 297 part-time. Financial Assistance: assistantships, grants, student loans, scholarships, doctoral fellowships. Degrees Awarded: in 2003: 127 master's degrees, 2 doctoral degrees. Updated: 3/4/04. Daniel Roland, rolandda@emporia.edu.

Kansas State University. Secondary Education. 364 Bluemont Hall, Manhattan, KS 66506, United States. 541-757-4890. Fax: (785)532-7304. Web site: http://coe.ksu.edu/ ecdol. Dr. Diane McGrath. dmcgrath@ksu.edu. Specialization: M.S. in Curriculum & Instruction with a specialization in Educational Computing, Design, and Online Learning; Ph.D. and Ed.D. in Curriculum & Instruction with a specialization in Educational Computing, Design, and Online Learning. Master's program started in 1982; doctoral in 1987. Features: Coursework focuses on research, theory, practice, ethics, and design of learning environments. Students work in a project-based learning environment much of the time, but also read, discuss, and write and present papers. The program does not focus on how to do particular applications, but rather on how and why one might use technology to improve the learning environment. Some courses focus on the K-12 learning environment (generally MS coursework) and others on lifelong learning. Admission Requirements: M.S.: B average in undergraduate work, one programming language, 590 TOEFL. Ed.D. and Ph.D.: B average in undergraduate and graduate work, one programming language, GRE, three letters of recommendation, experience or course in educational computing. Degree Requirements: M.S.: 31 semester hours (minimum of 15 in Educational Computing); thesis, internship, or practicum not required, but all three are possible. Master's portfolio project is required. Ed.D.: 94 semester hours (minimum of 18 hours in Educational Computing or related area approved by committee, 16 hours dissertation research, 12 hours internship); thesis. Ph.D.: 90 semester hours (minimum of 21 hours in Educational Computing, Design, and Online Learning or related area approved by committee, 30 hours for dissertation research); thesis; internship or practicum not required but available. Faculty: 1 full-time, 1 part-time, 1 adjunct, other faculty available to serve on committees. Students: M.S., 0 full-time, est. 8 part-time; doctoral, 6 full-time, 10 part-time. Financial Assistance: 2–3 assistantships typically go to people associated with the program; occasional assistantships on grant projects; other assistantships sometimes available in other departments. Degrees Awarded: 2005: 11 M.S. degrees and 4 Ph.Ds. Updated: 4/3/2006. Diane McGrath, dmcgrath@ksu.edu.

Kentucky

University of Louisville. College of Education and Human Development. Belknap Campus, Louisville, KY 40292, United States. (502)852-6667. Fax: (502)852-4563. Web site:

http://www.louisville.edu/edu. Carolyn Rude-Parkins, Chair of Leadership, Foundations, Human Resource Education. cparkins@louisville.edu. Specialization: Masters in Instructional Technology (appropriate for K-12 teacher and for trainers/adult educators), Post Masters/Rank 1 in Instructional Technology (K-12 teachers). Doctoral strand in Instructional Technology Leadership. Technology Leadership Institute Cohort for Jefferson County Schools offered onsite. Features: Appropriate for business or school audiences. Program is based on ISTE and ASTD standards, as well as Kentucky Experienced Teacher Standards. Admission Requirements: 2.75 GPA, 800 GRE, 2 letters of recommendation, application fee. Degree Requirements: 30 semester hours, internship. Faculty: 2 full-time, 6 part-time. Students: 75 part-time students. Financial Assistance: graduate assistantships. Degrees Awarded: 20 M.Ed. Updated: 3/3/03. Carolyn Rude-Parkins, cparkins@louisville.edu.

Louisiana

Louisiana State University. School of Library and Information Science. 267 Coates Hall, Baton Rouge, LA 70803, United States. (225)578-3158. Fax: (225)578-4581. Web site: http://slis.lsu.edu. Beth Paskoff, Dean, Assoc. Prof., School of Library and Information Science. bpaskoff@lsu.edu. Specialization: M.L.I.S., C.L.I.S. (post-Master's certificate), Louisiana School Library Certification. An advanced certificate program is available. Admission Requirements: Bachelors degree, with 3.00 average. Degree Requirements: M.L.I.S.: 40 hours, comprehensive exam, one semester full-time residence, completion of degree program in five years. Faculty: 10 full-time. Students: 84 full-time, 86 part-time. Students: A large number of graduate assistantships are available to qualified students. Deg.: 90. Updated: 7/7/04. Bert Boyce, lsboyc@lsu.edu.

Maryland

McDaniel College (formerly Western Maryland College). Department of Education. 2 College Hill, Westminster, MD 21157, United States. (410)857-2507. Fax: (410)857-2515. Web site: http://www.mcdaniel.edu. Dr. Ramona N. Kerby, Coord., School Library Media Program, Dept. of Education. rkerby@mcdaniel.edu. Specialization: M.S. in Education with an emphasis in School Library Media. Features: School librarianship. Admission Requirements: 3.0 Undergraduate GPA, 3 reference checklist forms from principal and other school personnel, acceptable application essay, acceptable Praxis test scores. Degree Requirements: 36 credit hours, including professional digital portfolio. Faculty: 1 full-time, 7 part-time. Students: 140, most part-time. Updated: 3/25/2006. Mona Kerby, by e-mail.

The Johns Hopkins University. Graduate Division of Education, Technology for Educators Program. Columbia Gateway Park, 6740 Alexander Bell Drive, Columbia, MD 21046, United States. (410)309-9537. Fax: (410)312-3868. Web site: http://www.spsbe.jhu.edu. Dr. Linda Tsantis, Program Coordinator; Dr. John Castellani, Program Coordinator. tsantis@jhu.edu. Specialization: The Department of Technology for Education offers programs leading to the M.S. degree in Education, the M.S. in Special Education, and four specialized advanced Graduate Certificates: Technology for Multimedia and Internet-Based Instruction; Instructional Technology for Online Professional Development and Training; Data-Driven Decision-Making; and Assistive Technology for Communication and Social Interaction. Features: Focuses on training educators to become decision makers and leaders in the use of technology, with competencies in the design, development, and application of emerging technologies for teaching and learning. Incorporates basic elements that take into account the needs of adult learners, the constantly changing nature of technology, and the need for schools and universities to work together for schoolwide change. The Center for Technology in Education works in partnership with the graduate program linking research and teaching of the university with the leadership and policy direction of the Maryland State Department of Education. Admission Requirements: Bachelors degree with strong background in teaching, curriculum and instruction, special education, or a related service field. Degree Requirements: 36 Credit hour part-time program, Electronic Portfolio in place of comprehensive exams. Faculty: 2 full-time, 30 part-time. Students: 300 part-time. Financial Assistance: grants, student loans, scholarships. Degrees Awarded: 48. Updated: 6/16/03. John Castellani, jcastellani@jhu.edu.

Towson University. College of Education. Hawkins Hall, Towson, MD 21252, United States (410)704-4226. Fax: (410)704-4227. Web site: http://wwwnew.towson.edu/coe/rset/insttech/. Dr. Jeffrey M. Kenton, Assistant Professor. Dept.: Reading, Special Education, and Instructional Technology. jkenton@towson.edu. Specialization: M.S. degrees in Instructional Development, Educational Technology and School Library Media. Ed.D. degrees in Instructional Technology. Features: Excellent labs. Strong practical hands-on classes. Focus of M.S. program. Students produce useful multimedia projects for use in their teaching and training. Many group activities within courses. Innovative Ed.D. program with online hybrid courses and strong mix of theory and practical discussions. Admission Requirements: Bachelor's degree from accredited institution with 3.0 GPA. (Conditional admission granted for many applicants with a GPA over 2.75.) Degree Requirements: M.S. degree is 36 graduate semester hours without thesis. Ed.D. is 63 hours beyond the M.S. degree. Faculty: 10 full-time, 5 adjunct. Students: 20 full-time, 190 part-time (approximately). Financial Assistance: graduate assistantships, work study, scholarships, loans. Degrees Awarded: ~25 in master's degree program. Updated: 3/14/2006. Jeff Kenton, jkenton@towson.edu.

University of Maryland Baltimore County (UMBC). Department of Education. 1000 Hilltop Circle, Baltimore, MD 21250, United States. (410)455-2310. Fax: (410)455-3986. Web site: http://www.research.umbc.edu/~eholly/ceduc/isd/. Greg Williams, Ed.D., Program Director. isd-td@umbc.edu. Specialization: M.A. degrees in School Instructional Systems, Post-Baccalaureate Teacher Certification, Training in Business and Industry, Experienced Teacher—Advanced Degree, ESOL/Bilingual. Features: Programs are configured with evening courses to accommodate students who are changing careers. Maryland teacher certification is earned two thirds of the way through the post-baccalaureate program. Admission Requirements: 3.0 undergraduate GPA, GRE scores. Degree Requirements: 36 semester hours (including 18 in systems development for each program); internship. Faculty: 18 full-time, 25 part-time. Students: 59 full-time, 254 part-time. Financial Assistance: assistantships, scholarships. Degrees Awarded: 75. Updated: 7/7/04. story1@umbc.edu.

Massachusetts

Boston University. School of Education. Two Sherborn St., Boston, MA 02215-1605, United States. (617)353-3181. Fax: (617)353-3924. Web site: http://web.bu.edu/EDUCATION. David B. Whittier, Asst. Professor and Coord., Program in Educational Media and Technology. whittier@bu.edu. Specialization: Ed.M., CAGS (Certificate of Advanced Graduate Study) in Educational Media and Technology; Ed.D. in Curriculum and Teaching, Specializing in Educational Media and Technology; preparation for Massachusetts public school certificates as Instructional Technology Specialist. Features: The Master's program prepares graduates for professional careers as educators, instructional designers, developers of educational materials, and managers of the human and technology-based resources necessary to support education and training with technology. Graduates are employed in K-12 schools, higher education, industry, medicine, government, and publishing. Students come to the program from many different backgrounds and with a wide range of professional goals. The doctoral program sets the study of Educational Media and

Technology within the context of education and educational research in general, and curriculum and teaching in particular. In addition to advanced work in the field of Educational Media and Technology, students examine and conduct research and study the history of educational thought and practice relating to teaching and learning. Graduates make careers in education as professors and researchers, technology directors and managers, and as developers of technology-based materials and systems. Graduates also make careers in medicine, government, business, and industry as instructional designers, program developers, project managers, and training directors. Graduates who work in both educational and noneducational organizations are often responsible for managing the human and technological resources required to create learning experiences that include the development and delivery of technology-based materials and distance education. Admission Requirements: Ed.M.: recommendations, minimum 2.7 undergraduate GPA, graduate test scores are required and either the GRE or MAT must be completed within past five years. CAGs: Ed.M., recommendations, 2.7 undergraduate GPA, graduate test scores are required and either the GRE or MAT must be completed within past five years. Ed.D.: 3 letters of recommendation, MAT or GRE scores, transcripts, writing samples, statement of goals and qualifications, analytical essay, minimum 2.7 GPA. Degree Requirements: Ed.M.: 36 credit hours (including 24 hours from required core curriculum, 12 from electives). CAGs: 32 credits beyond Ed.M., one of which must be a curriculum and teaching course and a mini-comprehensive exam. Ed.D.: 60 credit hours of courses in Educational Media and Technology, curriculum and teaching, and educational thought and practice with comprehensive exams; coursework and apprenticeship in research; dissertation. Faculty: 1 full-time, 1 half-time, 10 part-time. Students: 20 full-time, 25 part-time. Financial Assistance: U.S. government-sponsored work study, assistantships, grants, student loans, scholarships. Degrees Awarded: EdM = 17; Ed D = 2. Updated: 5/21/03. David Whittier, whittier@bu.edu.

Fitchburg State College. Division of Graduate and Continuing Education. 160 Pearl Street, Fitchburg, MA 01420, United States. (978) 665-3544. (978) 665-3055. Web site: http://www.fsc.edu. Dr. Randy Howe, Chair. rhowe@fsc.edu. Specialization: M.S. in Applied Communication with specializations in Applied Communication, Instructional Technology, and Library Media. Features: Collaborating with professionals working in the field both for organizations and as independent producers, Fitchburg offers a unique M.S. program. The objective of the Master of Science in Applied Communication is to develop in candidates the knowledge and skills for the effective implementation of communication within business, industry, government, not-for-profit agencies, health services, and education. Admission Requirements: MAT or GRE scores, official transcript(s) of a baccalaureate degree, two or more years of experience in communications or media, department interview and portfolio presentation, three letters of recommendation. Degree Requirements: 36 semester credit hours. Faculty: 2 full-time, 7 part-time. Students: 30 part-time. Financial Assistance: assistantships, student loans, scholarships. Degrees Awarded: 10 M.S. in Applied Communication. Updated: 3/8/2006. Randy Howe, 978-665-3544 or rhowe@fsc.edu.

Harvard University. Graduate School of Education. Appian Way, Cambridge, MA 02138, United States. (617)495-3541. Fax: (617)495-3626. Web site: http://www.gse.harvard.edu/tie. Joseph Blatt, director, Technology, Innovation, and Education Program; Kristen DeAmicis, program coordinator, Technology, Innovation, and Education Program. deamickr@gse.harvard.edu. Available degrees: Ed.M. in Technology, Innovation, and Education; Ed.D. in various fields, with research focus in technology in education. Features: Courses in design, technology policy and leadership, research and evaluation. Access to other courses throughout Harvard University and at MIT. Internship opportunities. Admission Requirements: Bachelor's degree, MAT or GRE scores, 600 TOEFL, 3 letters of recommendation. Students interested in further information about the TIE Program should visit the Web site, address above, which includes a link to the Harvard Graduate School of Education online application. Degree Requirements: 32 semester credits. Faculty: 4 full-time, 5 part-time. Students: approx. 40: 35 full-time, 5 part-time. Financial Assistance: Determined by Harvard policies. Degrees Awarded: 40. Updated: 3/7/2006. Joe Blatt, joe_blatt@harvard.edu.

Lesley University. Technology In Education. 29 Everett St., Cambridge, MA 02138-2790, United States. (617)349-8419. Fax: (617)349-8169. Web site: -http://www.lesley.edu/soe/111tech.html. Dr. George Blakeslee, Division Director. gblakesl@lesley.edu. Specialization: M.Ed. in Technology in Education CAGS/Ed.S. in Technology in Education Ph.D. in Educational Studies with specialization in Technology in Education. Features: M.Ed. program is offered off-campus at 70+ sites in 21 states; contact 617-349-8311 for information. The degree is also offered completely online. Contact Maureen Yoder, myoder@lesley.edu or (617)348-8421 for information. Or check our Web site. Admission Requirements: Completed bachelor's Teaching certificate. Degree Requirements: M.Ed.: 33 semester hours in technology, integrative final project in lieu of thesis, no internship or practicum. C.A.G.S.: 36 semester hours. Ph.D. requirements available on request. Faculty: 12 full-time and 1 part time core, approximately 200 part-time adjuncts on the Master's and doctorate levels. Students: 1000+ part-time. Financial Assistance: Information available from Admissions Office. Degrees Awarded: Approximately 375. Updated: 3/29/2006. See above for contact person.

University of Massachusetts Lowell. Graduate School of Education. 255 Princeton Street, North Chelmsford, MA 01863, United States. (508)934-4601. Fax: (508)934-3005. Web site: http://gse.uml.edu/. Vera Ossen, Coordinator, Graduate Program in Teaching. vera_ossen@uml.edu. Specialization: M.Ed., CAGS, and Ed.D. concentrations in Educational Technology may be pursued in the context of any degree program area (Leadership, Administration & Policy; Curriculum & Instruction; Math & Science Education; Reading, Language Arts & Literacy). The M.Ed. program in Curriculum & Instruction has a specialization strand in educational technology. The Certificate of Advanced Graduate Study (CAGS), equivalent to 30 credits beyond a M.Ed., is also offered. Features: As part of the U Mass Lowell "CyberEd" online learning initiative, a new Web-based M.Ed./state certification program in educational administration was launched in 2001 and is now in full swing. The School also manages an extensive video network that links the University with other campuses in the state higher education system, and with area public schools. Technology is heavily infused into the teacher preparation and school support programs, where new initiatives have been supported by grants from several federal and nonfederal sources. Admission Requirements: For admission at the Master's level, a bachelor's degree from an accredited institution in an academic discipline is required, along with a completed application form, recent GRE scores, a narrative statement of purpose, and three written recommendations. Additional admission requirements and conditions are described in the UMass Lowell Graduate Catalog. Degree Requirements: M.Ed. 30 credits beyond Bachelor's; Ed.D. 60 credits beyond Master's plus dissertation based on original research and demonstration of comprehensive mastery in relevant fields of inquiry. Faculty: Various full-time and part-time faculty members teach educational technology courses in the School. Students: full-time approximately 500. Financial Assistance: Assistantships; work-study; student loans; occasional scholarships. Degrees Awarded: Approximately 75. Updated: 7/7/04. Professor John LeBaron, John_Lebaron@uml.edu.

Michigan

Eastern Michigan University. Teacher Education. 313 John W. Porter Building, Ypsilanti, MI 48197, United States. (734)487-3260. Fax: (734)487-2101. Web site: http://www.

emich.edu. Toni Stokes Jones, Ph.D., Assistant Professor/Graduate Coordinator. tsjones@online.emich.edu. Specialization: M.A. in Educational Psychology with concentration in Educational Technology. The mission of this program is to prepare professionals who are capable of facilitating student learning in a variety of settings. The program is designed to provide students with both the knowledge base and the application skills that are required to use technology effectively in education. Focusing on the design, development, utilization, management, and evaluation of instructional systems moves us toward achieving this mission. Students who complete the educational technology concentration will be able to: (a) provide a rationale for using technology in the educational process; (b) identify contributions of major leaders in the field of educational media technology and instructional theory, and the impact that each leader has had on the field; (c) assess current trends in the area of educational media technology and relate the trends to past events and future implications; (d) integrate technology into instructional programs; (e) teach the operation and various uses of educational technology in instruction; (f) act as consultants/facilitators in educational media technology; (g) design and develop instructional products to meet specified needs; and (h) evaluate the effectiveness of instructional materials and systems. Features: Courses in our 30 credit hour Educational Media & Technology (EDMT) program include technology and the reflective teacher, technology and student-centered learning, technology-enhanced learning environments, issues and emerging technologies, instructional design, Internet for educators, advanced technologies, psychology of the adult learning, principles of classroom learning, curriculum foundations, research seminar, and seminar in educational technology. Effective Spring 2003, all of the EDMT courses will be taught online. In some EDMT courses, students may be asked to come to campus only 3 times during the semester. Students who do not want to receive a master's degree can apply for admission to our 18 credit hour Educational Media and Technology certificate. The EDMT courses for the certificate are also offered online. Admission Requirements: Individuals seeking admission to this program must: (1) Comply with the Graduates School admission requirements. (2) Score 550 or better on the TOEFL and 5 or better on TWE, if nonnative speaker of English. (3) Have a 2.75 undergraduate grade point average or a 3.30 grade point average in 12 hours or more of work in a master's program. (4) Solicit three letters of reference. (5) Submit a statement of professional goals. Degree Requirements: In order to graduate, each student is expected to: (1) Complete all work on an approved program of study (30 semester hours). (2) Maintain a "B" (3.0 GPA) average or better on coursework taken within the program. (3) Get a recommendation from the faculty adviser. (4) Fill out an application for graduation and obtain the advisers recommendation. (5) Meet all other requirements for a master's degree adopted by the Graduate School of Eastern Michigan University. (5) Complete a culminating experience (research, instructional development, or evaluation project) as determined by the student and faculty adviser. Faculty: 5 full-time; 3 part-time. Students: 75. Financial Assistance: graduate assistantship. Degrees Awarded: 10. Updated: 3/31/03. Toni Stokes Jones, Ph.D., toni.jones@ emich.edu.

Michigan State University. College of Education. 513E Erickson, East Lansing, MI 48824, United States. (517)353-0637. Fax: (517)353-6393. Web site: http://edutech.educ. msu.edu/masters/TLTEL.htm. Susan Way. ways@msu.edu. Specialization: M.A. in Educational Technology with Learning, Design, and Technology specialization. Features: Extensive opportunities to work with faculty in designing online courses and online learning environments. Several courses available online. Admission Requirements: Bachelor's degree, two letters of recommendation, goal statement. Degree Requirements: 30 semester hours, Web-based portfolio. Faculty: 14 full-time. Students: approximately 60. Financial Assistance: some assistantships for highly qualified students. Degrees Awarded: 6. Updated: 3/21/03. Professor Patrick Dickson, pdickson@msu.edu.

University of Michigan. Department of Educational Studies. 610 East University, Ann Arbor, MI 48109-1259, United States. (734) 763-7500. Fax: (734) 615-1290. Web site: http://www.soe.umich.edu/learningtechnologies/. Barry J. Fishman. fishman@umich.edu. Specialization: M.A., M.S., Ph.D. in Learning Technologies. Features: The Learning Technologies Program at the University of Michigan integrates the study of technology with a focus in a substantive content area. A unique aspect of the program is that your learning and research will engage you in real-world educational contexts. You will find that understanding issues related to a specific content area provides an essential context for meaningful research in learning. Your understanding of technology, school contexts, and a content area will place you among the leaders who design and conduct research on advanced technological systems that change education and schooling. The Doctoral specialization in Learning Technologies must be taken in conjunction with a substantive concentration designed in consultation with your advisor. Current active concentrations include: Science, Literacy, Culture and Gender, Teacher Education, Design and Human-Computer Interaction, Policy, and Social Studies. Other areas are possible. The Master's Degree in Learning Technologies at the University of Michigan prepares professionals for leadership roles in the design, development, implementation, and research of powerful technologies to enhance learning. Our approach to design links current knowledge and research about how people learn with technological tools that enable new means of organizing and evaluating learning environments. Course and project work reflects the latest knowledge and practice in learning, teaching, and technology. Core courses prepare students to use current understandings about learning theory, design principles, research methodologies, and evaluation strategies in educational settings ranging from classrooms to Web-based and distributed learning environments. Faculty work with students to shape programs that meet individual interests. Practical experience is offered through internships with area educational institutions. Admission Requirements: GRE, B.A. for M.A., M.S., or Ph.D.; TOEFL for students from countries where English is not the primary language. Degree Requirements: M.A. and M.S.: 30 hours beyond B.A. Ph.D.: 60 hours beyond B.A. or 30 hours beyond Master's plus research paper/qualifying examination, and dissertation. Faculty: 3 full-time, 6 part-time. Students: 35 full-time. Financial Assistance: assistantships, grants, student loans, scholarships, internships. Degrees Awarded: 7. Updated: 3/7/2006. Barry Fishman, fishman@umich.edu.

Minnesota

Minnesota State University. Educational Leadership, College of Education. MSU 313 Armstrong Hall, Mankato, MN 56001, United States. (507)389-1965. Fax: (507)389-5751. Web site: http://www.coled.mnsu.edu/coled_new_home/coe_new.htm. Dr. P. Gushwa. prudence.gushwa@mnsu.edu. Specialization: M.S. in Educational Technology with three tracks; M.S. in Library Media Specialist; SP in Library Media Education. Features: Educational Technology certificates Licensure program in Library Media. Admission Requirements: Bachelor's degree, 2.75/4.0 for last 2 years of undergraduate work. Degree Requirements: 32 semester hour credits, comprehensive exam. Faculty: 4 full-time. Students: About 75. Financial Assistance: Contact Financial Aid Office. Updated: 5/28/03. Dr. Prudence Gushwa, Chair, Educational Leadership.

Missouri

Northwest Missouri State University. Department of Computer Science/Information Systems. 800 University Ave., Maryville, MO 64468, United States. (660)562-1600. Fax: 660-562-1963. Web site: http://www.nwmissouri.edu/csis. Dr. Phillip Heeler, Chairperson.

pheeler@nwmissouri.edu. Specialization: M.S.Ed. in Instructional Technology. Certificate Program in Instructional Technology. Features: These degrees are designed for industry trainers and computer educators at the elementary, middle school, high school, and junior college level. Admission Requirements: 3.0 undergraduate GPA, 700 GRE (V+Q). Degree Requirements: 32 semester hours of graduate courses in computer science, education,and instructional technology courses. Fifteen hours of computer education and instructional technology courses for the Certificate. Faculty: 12 full-time. Students: 5 full-time, 20 part-time. Financial Assistance: assistantships, grants, student loans, and scholarships. Degrees Awarded: 10. Updated: 3/26/2006. Dr. Heeler, pheeler@mail.nwmissouri. edu.

Southwest Missouri State University. School of Teacher Education. 901 S. National, Springfield, MO 65804, United States. (417)836-5280. Fax: (417)836-6252. Web site: http://www.smsu.edu/. Dr. Roger Tipling. RogerTipling@smsu.edu. Specialization: M.S. in Education Emphasis areas: Technology Coordinator strand, Building Level Technology Specialist strand, School Library Media Specialist strand, Business/Industrial/Medical strand, Production, Administration, Instructional Design, Selection, and Utilization Networking, Web Based Education, Hardware and Software Troubleshooting, Library Certification Courses, Building Level Technology Specialist Certificate, Research Practicum. Admission Requirements: Graduate College Admission Standards, three letters of reference, autobiography. Degree Requirements: Minimum of 33 hrs. in Instructional Design and Technology Major research paper or project. Comprehensive Exam Practicum (dependent upon emphasis). Faculty: Three full-time faculty, two part-time faculty. Students: Five to ten full-time students, more than 50 part-time students. Financial Assistance: Graduate Assistantships. Degrees Awarded: Six. Updated: 4/28/04. Dr. Roger Tipling, RogerTipling@smsu.edu/.

University of Missouri—Columbia. School of Information Science & Learning Technologies. 303 Townsend Hall, Columbia, MO 65211, United States. (573)882-4546. Fax: (573)884-2917. Web site: http://sislt.missouri.edu. John Wedman. wedmanj@missouri.edu. Specialization: The Educational Technology program takes a theory-based approach to designing, developing, implementing, and researching computer-mediated environments to support human activity. We seek individuals who are committed to lifelong learning and who aspire to use advanced technology to improve human learning and performance. Graduates of the program will find opportunities to use their knowledge and competencies as classroom teachers, media specialists, district technology specialists, and coordinators, designers and developers of technology-based learning and information systems, training specialists for businesses, medical settings, and public institutions, as well as other creative positions. The curriculum at the Masters and Specialist levels has two focus areas: Technology in Schools and Learning Systems Design and Development; with coursework tailored to each focus area. For information regarding our Ph.D., see http://sislt.missouri.edu/phd. Features: Both focus areas are available online via the Internet or on the MU campus. The Technology in Schools focus area is based on the ISTE competencies and culminates in an online portfolio based on these competencies. Several courses are augmented by technical resources developed at MU, including a technology integration knowledge repository and online collaboration tools. The Learning Systems Design and Development focus area links to business, military, and government contexts. This focus area offers challenging balance of design and development coursework, in addition to coursework dealing with needs assessment and evaluation. For information regarding our Ph.D., see http://sislt.missouri.edu/phd. Admission Requirements: Master: Bachelor's degree, GRE (V>500; A>500; W>3.5) EdS.: Master's degree, GRE (V>500; A>500; W>3.5) Ph.D.: 3.5 graduate GPA, 1GRE (V>500; A>500; W>3.5). See Web site for details. Degree Requirements: Masters and EdS: Minimum of 30 graduate credit hours required for the degree; 15 hours of upper division coursework. Maximum of 6 hours of transfer credit. Ph.D.: See Web site for details. Faculty: 9 full time; ~5 part-time. Students: Masters ~ 200; Ph.D., 55. Financial Assistance: Masters: assistantships, grants, student loans, scholarships. Ph.D.: graduate assistantships with tuition waivers; numerous academic scholarships ranging from $200 to $18,000. Degrees Awarded: ~55. Updated: 3/8/2006. John Wedman.

Webster University. Learning and Communication Arts, College of Education. St. Louis, MO 63119, United States. (314)968-7490. Fax: (314)968-7118. Web site: http://www. webster.edu/gradcatalog/ed_tech.html. Dr. Phyllis Wilkinson. wilkinsp@webster.edu. Specialization: Master's degree (M.A.T.); State Certification in Media Technology is a program option. Admission Requirements: Bachelor's degree with 2.5 GPA. Degree Requirements: 33 semester hours (including 24 in media); internship required. Faculty: 5. Students: 7 full-time, 28 part-time. Financial Assistance: partial scholarships, minority scholarships, government loans, and limited state aid. Updated: 5/28/03.

Montana

University of Montana. School of Education. 32 Campus Drive, Missoula, MT 59812, United States. (406)243-2163. Fax: (406)243-4908. Web site: http://www.umt.edu. Dr. Sally Brewer, Associate Professor of Library/Media. sally.brewer@mso.umt.edu. Specialization: M.Ed. and Specialist degrees; K-12 School Library Media specialization with School Library Media Certification endorsement. Features: 25 credits online, school endorsement. Combined program with University of Montana-Western in Dillon, MT. Admission Requirements: (both degrees): GRE, letters of recommendation, 2.75 GPA. Degree Requirements: M.Ed.: 37 semester credit hours (18 overlap with library media endorsement). Specialist: 28 semester hours (18 overlap). Faculty: 2 full-time. Students: 25 full-time, 70 part-time. Financial Assistance: assistantships; contact the University of Montana Financial Aid Office. Degrees Awarded: Endorsements 15. Updated: 3/9/2006. Carolyn Lott, carolyn.lott@mso.umt.edu.

Nebraska

University of Nebraska at Kearney. Teacher Education. 905 West 25th Street, Kearney, NE 68849-5540, United States. (308)865-8833. Fax: (308)865-8097. Web site: http://www.unk.edu/departments/pte. Dr. Scott Fredrickson, Professor and Chair of the Instructional Technology Graduate Program. fredricksons@unk.edu. Specialization: M.S.ED in Instructional Technology, M.S.ED in Educational Media. Features: Four emphasis areas—Instructional Technology; Multimedia Development; Educational Media; Assistive Technology. Admission Requirements: M.S. GRE (or electronic portfolio meeting dept. requirements), acceptance into graduate school, approval of Instructional Technology Committee. Degree Requirements: M.S.: 36 credit hours, Instructional technology project or field study. Faculty: 4 full-time, 11 part-time. Students: 150 full-time. Financial Assistance: assistantships, grants, student loans. Degrees Awarded: 27. Updated: 3/7/2006.

University of Nebraska—Omaha. Department of Teacher Education. College of Education, Kayser Hall 208D, Omaha, NE 68182, United States. (402)554-2119. Fax: (402)554-2125. Web site: www.unomaha.edu/~edmedia. Dr. R. J. Pasco. rpasco@mail.unomaha.edu. Specialization: -Library Media Endorsement (undergraduate and Graduate); M.S. in Secondary and Elementary Education, M.A. in Secondary and Elementary Education, both with Library Media concentration; M.S. in Reading with Library Media concentration; M.S. in Educational Administration with Library Media concentration; Masters in Library Science Program (Cooperative program with University of Missouri at Columbia); Instructional Technology Certificate—Graduate program only. Admission Requirements: As per

University of Nebraska at Omaha undergraduate and graduate requirements. Degree Requirements: Library Media Endorsement (Undergraduate and Graduate)—33 hours; M.S. in Secondary and Elementary Education, M.A. in Secondary and Elementary Education, both with Library Media concentration—36 hours; M.S. in Reading with Library Media concentration—45 hours; M.S. in Educational Administration, with Educational Media concentration Masters in Library Science Program (Cooperative program with University of Missouri at Columbia)—42 hours. Faculty: 1 full-time, 4 part-time (adjunct). Students: 21 undergraduates; 157 graduate students (mix of part-time and full-time). Financial Assistance: Contact Financial Aid Office. Degrees Awarded: 23. Updated: 4/26/04. Dr. R. J. Pasco, rpasco@mail.unomaha.edu.

New Jersey

Montclair State University. Department of Curriculum & Teaching. 1 College Avenue, Montclair, NJ 07043, United States. (973)655-5187. Fax: (973)655-7084. Web site: http://cehs.montclair.edu. Dr. Vanessa Domine, Professor of Educational Technology. dominev@mail.montclair.edu. Specialization: MSU offers (1) an M.Ed. degree program in Educational Technology (EDTC); (2) a post-doc certification program for Associate School Library Media Specialists (ALMS); and (3) an advanced certification program for School Library Media Specialists (SLMS). Features: All three programs draw from the same pool of educational technology courses and can be completed together in a carefully assembled program of approximately 46 graduate credits. Three areas comprise coursework: Philosophical foundations, Pedagogical design and integration, and Practical design and application. In the M.Ed. program, students can choose to emphasize in one of three areas: (A) Administration, Policy, and Leadership; (B) Organizational Planning and Development; and (C) Curriculum and Technology Integration. Admission Requirements: Students can apply in person or online to the Graduate School (http://www.montclair.edu/graduate). The M.Ed. program requires submission of GRE scores, letters of recommendation, and a project sample. The ALMS program requires a bachelor's degree and standard NJ teaching license. The SLMS program requires a master's degree, a standard NJ teaching license, and at least one year of successful teaching as an associate school library media specialist. Degree Requirements: The M.Ed. program requires 33 credits of coursework and field experience. The ALMS program requires 18–21 credits of coursework and field experience. The SLMS program requires 36 credits of coursework and field experience. Faculty: 14 full-time, 3 part-time. Students: A majority of students are working professionals attending 1/2 time. Financial Assistance: Scholarship and Graduate Assistants are available. Updated: 3/24/2006. Dr. Domine, dominev@mail.montclair.edu.

Rutgers—The State University of New Jersey. School of Communication, Information and Library Studies. 4 Huntington Street, New Brunswick, NJ 08901-1071, United States. (732)932-7500, ext 8955. Fax: (732)932-2644. Web site: http://www.scils.rutgers.edu/. Dr. Ross J Todd, Director, Master of Library and Information Science, Dept. of Library and Information Studies, School of Communication, Information and Library Studies. Dr. Michael Lesk, Chair. rtodd@scils.rutgers.edu. Specialization: The Master of Library and Information Science (M.L.I.S.) program provides professional education for a wide variety of service and management careers in libraries, information agencies, the information industry, and in business, industry, government, research, and similar environments where information is a vital resource. Specializations include: school library media; services for children and youth; digital libraries; information retrieval/information systems; knowledge management (http://www.scils.rutgers.edu/programs/lis/Curriculum.jsp). Features: The M.L.I.S. program, available both on campus and online, is organized around six themes in the field of library and information science: human-information interaction;

information access; information and society; information systems; management; and organization of information. Six lead courses, one in each area, form the foundation of the curriculum and offer general knowledge of the major principles and issues of the field. Two or more central courses in each theme offer basic understanding and competencies in important components of the field. Specialization courses in each theme allow students to develop expertise in preparation for specific career objectives. All students on campus in the New Brunswick M.L.I.S. program work with an advisor to plan a course of study appropriate for their interests and career objectives. Admission Requirements: A bachelor's degree or its equivalent from a recognized institution of higher education with a B average or better; GRE scores; personal statement that presents a view of the library and information science profession and applicants aspirations and goals in the library and information science professions; 3 letters of recommendation that focus on the applicant's academic capacity to undertake a rigorous program of graduate study. Degree Requirements: A minimum of thirty-six credits, or twelve courses, is required to earn the M.L.I.S. degree. All students are required to enroll in two noncredit classes, 501–Introduction to Library and Information Professions in their first semester and 502–Colloquium in a later semester. There are no language requirements for the M.L.I.S. degree, and there is no thesis or comprehensive examination. Faculty: 23 full-time, 20 adjunct. Students: 180 full-time, 180 part-time. Financial Assistance: scholarships, fellowships, and graduate assistantships. Updated: 3/31/2006. Dr Ross J Todd, rtodd@scils.rutgers.edu.

William Paterson University. College of Education. 300 Pompton Rd., Wayne, NJ 07470, United States. (973)720-2140. Fax: (973)720-2585. Web site: http://pwcweb.wilpaterson. edu/wpcpages/library/default.htp. Dr. Amy G. Job, Librarian, Assoc. Prof., Coord., Program in Library/Media, Elementary and Early Childhood Dept. joba@wpunj.edu. Specialization: M.Ed. for Educational Media Specialist, Associate Media Specialist, Ed.S. Features: Provides training for New Jersey certified Educational Media Specialists and Associate Media Specialists. Admission Requirements: teaching certificate, 2.75 GPA, MAT or GRE scores, 1-year teaching experience. Assoc. Ed.S.: certificate, 2.75 GPA. Degree Requirements: M.Ed.: 33 semester hours, including research projects and practicum. Assoc. Ed.S.: 18 sem. hours. Faculty: 6 full-time, 2 part-time. Students: 30 part-time. Financial Assistance: limited. Degrees Awarded: 6. Updated: 6/30/04. Amy G. Job, joba@wpunj.edu.

New York

Buffalo State College. CIS Department. 1300 Elmwood Ave., Buffalo, NY 14222-1095, United States. (716)878-3531. Fax: (716)878-6677. Web site: http://www.buffalostate.edu/ depts/edcomputing/. Dr. John Thompson, Program Coordinator. thompsjt@buffalostate. edu. Specialization: M.S. in Education in Educational Computing. Features: This program is designed for educators who wish to develop and expand their skills in the educational application of computers. Emphasis is given to the use of computers in the instructional process. Admission Requirements: Bachelor's degree from accredited institution, undergraduate 3.0 GPA, 3 letters of recommendation, one letter from applicant. Degree Requirements: 36 semester hours. See http://www.buffalostate.edu/depts/edcomputing/ for full details. Faculty: 2 full-time, 5 part-time. Students: 5 full-time, 120 part-time. Financial Assistance: As qualified. Degrees Awarded: approx. 50. Updated: 3/8/2006. John Thompson, Ph.D.

Fordham University. Department of Communication and Media Studies. Rose Hill Campus, 441 E. Fordham Rd., Bronx, NY 10458, United States. (718)817-4860. (718)817-4868. Web site: http://www.fordham.edu. Robin Andersen, Department Chair; James Capo, Director of Graduate Studies. andersen@fordham.edu. Specialization: M.A. in Communications. Features: Internship or thesis option; full-time students can complete program in twelve months. Admission Requirements: 3.0 undergraduate GPA. Degree Requirements:

10 courses plus internship or thesis. Faculty: 8 full-time, 2 part-time. Students: 8 full-time, 22 part-time. Financial Assistance: assistantships, student loans, scholarships. Updated: 6/6/03.

Ithaca College. School of Communications. Park Hall, Ithaca, NY 14850, United States. (607)274-1025. Fax: (607)274-7076. Web site: http://www.ithaca.edu/ocld. Gordon Rowland, Professor, Chair, Graduate Program in Communications; Roy H. Park, School of Communications. rowland@ithaca.edu. Specialization: M.S. in Communications. Students in this program find employment in such areas as instructional design/training, multimedia/Web development, corporate/community/public relations and marketing, and employee communication. The program can be tailored to individual career goals. Features: Program is interdisciplinary, incorporating organizational communication, instructional design, management, and technology. Admission Requirements: 3.0 GPA, recommendations, statement of purpose, resume, application forms and transcripts, TOEFL 550 (or 213 computer-scored) where applicable. Degree Requirements: 36 semester hours including capstone seminar. Faculty: 8 full-time. Students: approx. 25 full-time, 10 part-time. Financial Assistance: graduate assistantships, research fellowships (for continuing students). Degrees Awarded: 15. Updated: 3/24/2006. Gordon Rowland, 607/274-1031, rowland@ithaca.edu.

New York University. Educational Communication and Technology Program, Steinhardt School of Education. 239 Greene St., Suite 300, New York, NY 10003, United States. (212)998-5520. Fax: (212)995-4041. Web site: http://www.nyu.edu/education/alt/ectprogram. Francine Shuchat-Shaw, Assoc. Prof. (MA Advisor), Dir.; W. Michael Reed, Prof., (Doctoral Advisor). sm24@nyu.edu. Specialization: M.A., Ed.D., and Ph.D. in Education—for the preparation of individuals as instructional media designers, developers, media producers, and/or researchers in education, business and industry, health and medicine, community services, government, museums and other cultural institutions; and to teach or become involved in administration in educational communications and instructional technology programs in higher education, including instructional television, microcomputers, multimedia, Internet, and telecommunications. The program also offers a post-M.A. 30-point Certificate of Advanced Study in Education. Features: emphasizes theoretical foundations, especially a cognitive science perspective of learning and instruction, and their implications for designing media-based learning environments and materials. All efforts focus on video, multimedia, instructional television, Web-based technology, and telecommunications; participation in special research and production projects and field internships. Web site: http://create.alt.ed.nyu.edu. CREATE—Consortium for Research and Evaluation of Advanced Technologies in Education—uses an apprenticeship model to provide doctoral students and advanced M.A. students with research opportunities in collaboration with faculty. Admission Requirements: M.A.: 3.0 undergraduate GPA, responses to essay questions, interview related to academic and professional goals. Ph.D.: 3.0 GPA, 1000 GRE, responses to essay questions, interview related to academic or professional preparation and career goals. For international students, 600 TOEFL and TWE. Degree Requirements: M.A.: 36 semester hours including specialization, elective courses, thesis, English Essay Examination. Ph.D.: 57 semester hours beyond M.A., including specialization, foundations, research, content seminar and elective coursework; candidacy papers; dissertation; English Essay Examination. Faculty: 4 full-time, 6 part-time. Students: M.A.: 40 full-time, 35 part-time. Ph.D.: 14 full-time, 20 part-time. Financial Assistance: graduate and research assistantships, student loans, fellowships, scholarships, and work assistance programs. Degrees Awarded: M.A., Ph.D. Updated: 3/8/04. Jan L. Plass, Associate Professor and Chair.

Pace University. School of Education. 861 Bedford Road, Pleasantville, NY 10570, United States. (914) 773-3200, (914) 773-3870. Fax: (915) 773-3871. Web site:

http://www.pace.edu. Janet McDonald, Dean and Professor of Education. jmcdonald@pace.edu. Specialization: M.Ed. in Educational Technology (leads to New York State Certification as an Educational Technology Specialist.). Advanced Certificate in Educational Technology leads to New York State Certification as an Educational Technology Specialist.) Pace certificate in Computing for Teachers. Features: Results in New York State Educational Technology Specialist Certification (2/2004). Program is individualized to meet the needs of two distinct populations: those with an education background or those with a technology background. Some courses are delivered through a distance learning platform. Admission Requirements: Bachelor's degree or higher from an accredited institution, minimum GPA of at least 3.0. (Upon the recommendation of the Dean, Graduate Faculty Admissions Committee or the Director of Student Support Services, candidates whose GPA is less than 3.0 may be admitted on a conditional basis, provided that it is determined that the candidate has the necessary knowledge and skills to complete the program successfully.) A Transcript review is required of all candidates to determine if any Arts & Sciences content knowledge required for certification are unmet. If unmet requirements exist, they must be met during the course of the program; however, the credit hours earned completing them may not be counted toward the graduate degree. Transcript review demonstrating Arts & Sciences and Content Area background comparable to New York State requirements including preparation to teach to the New York State Learning Standards. Completion of the application process, including an essay, two letters of recommendation, personal statement and, in some cases, an interview. Degree Requirements: 36–39semester hours. Faculty: 8 full-time, 50 part-time. Students: 60–70 part-time. Financial Assistance: assistantships, internships, scholarships. Degrees Awarded: Program is new and was implemented as of 9/01. Updated: 7/7/04. Anna Fishman, Assistant to the Dean, afishman@pace.

St. Johns University. Division of Library and Information Science. 8000 Utopia Parkway, Jamaica, NY 11439, United States. (718)990-6200. Fax: (718)990-2071. http://www.stjohns.edu/libraryscience. Elizabeth B. Pollicino, Associate Director. libis@stjohns.edu. Specialization: M.L.S. with specialization in School Media. The school also offers a 24-credit Advanced Certificate program in which students may also take School Media and Technology courses. Features: small class size, personal advisement, student lounge and computer lab, high-tech classrooms. Admission Requirements: 3.0 GPA, 2 letters of reference, statement of professional goals. GRE (General) required for assistantships. Degree Requirements: 36 semester hours, comprehensive exam, practicum. Faculty: 6 full-time, 10 part-time. Students: 30 full-time, 77 part-time. Financial Assistance: 4 assistantships in DLIS; others available in University Library Rev. Brian J. OConnell, CM Library Studies Scholarships (for incoming students with superior academic records). Degrees Awarded: 29. Updated: 6/11/03. Elizabeth Pollicino, pollicie@stjohns.edu.

State University College of Arts and Science at Potsdam. Information and Communication Technology. 302 Satterlee Hall, Potsdam, NY 13676, United States. (315)267-2525. Fax: (315)267-2987. Web site: http://www.potsdam.edu/EDUC/gradpages/MSEdPrograms/ICTHome.html. Dr. Anthony Betrus, Chair, Information and Communications Technology. betrusak@potsdam.edu. Specialization: M.S. in Education in Instructional Technology with concentrations in: Educational Technology Specialist, Human Performance Technology, Information Technology, and Organizational Leadership. Features: A progressive, forward-looking program with a balance of theoretical and hands-on practical coursework. Admission Requirements: (1) Submission of an official transcript of an earned baccalaureate degree from an accredited institution. (2) A minimum GPA of 2.75 (4.0 scale) in the most recent 60 credit hours of coursework. (3) Submission of the Application for Graduate Study (w/$50 nonrefundable fee). (4) For students seeking the Educational Technology Specialist Certification, a valid NYS Teaching Certificate is required. Degree Requirements: 36–39 semester hours, including internship or practicum; culminating project required. Faculty: 3 full-time, 3 part-time. Students: 33 full-time, 92 part-time. Financial Assistance: student loans, student work study, graduate assistantship. Degrees Awarded: 28. Updated: 4/27/04. Anthony Betrus, betrusak@potsdam.edu.

State University of New York at Stony Brook. Technology & Society. College of Engineering & Applied Sciences, SUNY at Stony Brook. Stony Brook, NY 11794-3760, United States. Carole (631)632-8765, (631)632-8770, (631)632-8765; Rita (631)632-1057. Fax: (631)632-7809. Web site: http://www.stonybrook.edu/est/. Carole Rose. Carole.Rose@stonybrook.edu. Specialization: Master's Degree in Technological Systems Management with concentration in Educational Computing (30 credits). Students may simultaneously earn an Advanced Graduate Certificate (ACG) in Educational Computing (18 credits). Students develop the skills to be effective educational leaders and decision makers. Graduates manage technology-based learning environments and integrate technology into education in meaningful and innovative ways. Our program emphasizes the: (a) design of standard-based learning modules, (b) research and evaluation of educational technologies, and (c) development of prototype learning technologies and learning activities. Admission Requirements: bachelor's degree in engineering, natural sciences, social sciences, mathematics, or closely related area; 3.0 undergraduate GPA, have taken the GRE, experience with computer applications or computer applications or use of computers in teaching. Degree Requirements: 30 semester credits, including two general technology core courses, 5 required educational computing courses, and 3 eligible electives. Faculty: 5 full-time, 8 part-time. Students: 15 full-time, 30 part-time. Financial Assistance: assistantships, grants, student loans. Degrees Awarded: 14. Updated: 6/9/03. Glenn Smith, glenn.smith@stonybrook.edu.

Syracuse University. Instructional Design, Development, and Evaluation Program, School of Education. 330 Huntington Hall, Syracuse, NY 13244-2340, United States. (315)443-3703. Fax: (315)443-1218. Web site: http://idde.syr.edu. Nick Smith, Professor. lltucker@syr.edu. Specialization: Certificates in Educational Technology and Adult Lifelong Learning, M.S., C.A.S., and Ph.D. degree programs in Instructional Design, Educational Evaluation, Human Issues in Instructional Development, Technology Integration, and Educational Research and Theory (learning theory, application of theory, and educational media research). Graduates are prepared to serve as curriculum developers, instructional designers, program and product evaluators, researchers, resource center administrators, technology coordinators, distance learning design delivery specialists, trainers and training managers, and higher education faculty. Features: The courses and programs are typically project-centered. Collaborative project experience, field work and internships are emphasized throughout. There are special issues seminars, as well as student- and faculty-initiated mini-courses, seminars, and guest lecturers, faculty-student formulation of department policies, and multiple international perspectives. International collaborations are an ongoing feature of the program in IDD&E. The graduate student population is highly diverse. Admission Requirements: M.S.: undergraduate transcripts, recommendations, personal statement, interview recommended; TOEFL for international applicants; GRE recommended. Doctoral: Relevant Master's degree from an accredited institution or equivalent, GRE scores, recommendations, personal statement, TOEFL for international applicants; interview strongly encouraged. Degree Requirements: M.S.: 36 semester hours, comprehensive exam and portfolio required. Ph.D.: 90 semester hours, research apprenticeship, portfolio, qualifying exams and dissertation required. Faculty: 4 full-time, 4 part-time. Students: Masters: 15 full-time, 25 part-time; CAS: 1 full-time, 8 part-time; doctoral: 21 full-time, 20 part-time. Financial Assistance: Fellowships, scholarships, and graduate assistantships entailing either research or administrative duties in instructional technology. Degrees Awarded: 2005: M.S.—21; CAS—2; Ph.D.—7. Updated: 3/8/2006. Philip Doughty, pldought@syr.edu.

North Carolina

Appalachian State University. Department of Curriculum and Instruction. College of Education. Boone, NC 28608, United States. 828-262-2277. Fax: 828-262-2686. Web site: http://edtech.ced.appstate.edu. Robert Muffoletto. muffoletto@appstate.edu. Specialization: M.A. in Educational Media and Technology with three areas of concentration: Computers, Media Literacy, and Media Production. A plan of study in Internet distance teaching is offered online. Two certificate programs: (1) Distance Learning—Internet delivered and (2) Media Literacy. Features: Business, university, community college, and public school partnership offer unusual opportunities for learning. The programs are focused on developing learning environments over instructional environments. Admission Requirements: Undergraduate degree. Degree Requirements: 36 graduate semester hours. We also have certificates in (1) Distance Learning and (2) Media Literacy. Faculty: 6 full-time faculty. Students: 35. Financial Assistance: assistantships, grants, student loans. Degrees Awarded: 5. Updated: 5/13/03. Robert Muffoletto.

East Carolina University. Department of Library Science and Instructional Technology. 1105 Joyner Library, Greenville, NC 27858-4353, United States. (252)328-6621. Fax: (252)328-4368. lsit.coe.ecu.edu. Dr. William Sugar, M.S. Program Coordinator and Dr. Carol Brown, M.A.Ed. Program Coordinator. sugarw@coe.ecu.edu. Specialization: Master of Library Science; Certificate of Advanced Study (Library Science); Master of Arts in Education (North Carolina Instructional Technology Specialist licensure); Master of Science in Instructional Technology; Certificate in Distance Education; Certificate in Virtual Reality in Education and Training; Certificate in Performance Improvement; Certificate for Special Endorsement in Computer Education. Features: M.L.S. graduates are eligible for North Carolina School Media Coord. certification and for NC Public Library Certification; C.A.S. graduates are eligible for North Carolina School Media Supervisor certification; M.A.Ed. graduates are eligible for North Carolina Instructional Technology certification; Cert. for Special Endorsement in Computer Education for North Carolina Licensure as Technology Facilitator. All programs available 100 percent online. Admission Requirements: M.S., M.A.Ed., and M.L.S.: Bachelor's degree; C.A.S.: M.L.S. or equivalent degree. Admission to Graduate School. Degree Requirements: M.L.S.: 39 semester hours; M.A.Ed.: 39 semester hours; M.S.: 36 semester hours; C.A.S.: 30 semester hours. Faculty: 16 full-time; 14 part-time. Students: 27 full-time, 293 part-time. Financial Assistance: Graduate assistantships. Degrees Awarded: M.L.S: 62; M.A.Ed.: 26; M.S.: 15. Updated: 3/15/2006. William Sugar, sugarw@coe.ecu.edu, 252-328-1546.

North Carolina State University. Department of Curriculum and Instruction. P.O. Box 7801, Raleigh, NC 27695-7801, United States. (919)515-1779. Fax: (919)515-6978. Web site: http://www.ncsu.edu/ced/ci/. Dr. Ellen Vasu, Professor. Ellen_Vasu@ncsu.edu. M.Ed. and M.S. in Instructional Technology (program track within one Master's in Curriculum and Instruction). Ph.D. in Curriculum and Instruction with focus on Instructional Technology as well as other areas. Admission Requirements: Master's: undergraduate degree from an accredited institution, 3.0 GPA in major or in latest graduate degree program; transcripts; GRE or MAT scores; 3 references; goal statement. Ph.D.: undergraduate degree from accredited institution, 3.0 GPA in major or latest graduate program; transcripts; recent GRE scores, writing sample, three references, vita, research, and professional goals statement (see http://www2.acs.ncsu.edu/grad/prospect.htm). Degree Requirements: Master's: 36 semester hours, internship, thesis optional; Ph.D.: 72 hours beyond bachelors (minimum 33 in Curriculum and Instruction core, 27 in Research); other information available upon request. Faculty: 2 full-time, 2 part-time. Students: Master's, 15 part-time; Ph.D., 4 part-time, 1 full-time. Financial Assistance: some assistantships available on a limited basis. Degrees Awarded: 5 master's degrees. Updated: 3/13/2006. Ellen Vasu, Ellen_Vasu@ncsu.edu.

University of North Carolina. School of Information and Library Science. CB#3360, Chapel Hill, NC 27599-3360, United States. (919)962-8062, 962-8366. Fax: (919)962-8071. Web site: http://www.ils.unc.edu/. Evelyn H. Daniel, Prof., Coord., School Media Program. daniel@ils.unc.edu. Specialization: Master of Science Degree in Library Science (M.S.L.S.) with specialization in school library media work. Post-Master's certification program. Features: Rigorous academic program plus teaching practicum requirement; excellent placement record. Many courses offered online. Admission Requirements: Competitive admission based on all three GRE components (quantitative, qualitative, analytical), undergraduate GPA (plus graduate work if any), letters of recommendation, and student statement of career interest and school choice. Degree Requirements: 48 semester hours, practicum, comprehensive exam, Master's paper. Faculty: 22 full-time, 10 part-time. Students: 300 full-time, 50 part-time (about 20 students specialize in SLMC). Financial Assistance: Grants, assistantships, student loans. Degrees Awarded: 130 degrees awarded—20 for school library media certification. Updated: 4/24/04. Evelyn Daniel (see contact information above).

North Dakota

Minot State University. Graduate School. 500 University Ave. W., Minot, ND 58707, United States. (701)858-3250. Fax: (701)839-6933. Web site: www.minotstateu.edu. Dr. Jack L. Rasmussen, Dean of the Graduate School. butler@minotstateu.edu. Specialization: M.S. in Elementary Education (including work in educational computing); M.S. in Special Education with Specialization in Severe Multiple-Handicaps, Early Childhood Special Education, Education of the Deaf, and Learning Disabilities; M.S. in Communication Disorders, Specializations in Audiology and Speech Language Pathology. Features: All programs include involvement in computer applications appropriate to the area of study, including assistive technologies for persons with disabilities. Computer laboratories are available for student use in the library and various departments. Some courses are offered through the Interactive Video Network, which connects all universities in North Dakota. All programs have a rural focus and are designed to offer a multitude of practical experiences. Admission Requirements: $35 fee, three letters of recommendation, 300-word autobiography, transcripts, GRE in Communication Disorders or GMAT for M.S. in Management. Degree Requirements: 30 semester hours (hours in computers, education, and outside education vary according to program); written comprehensive exams; oral exams; thesis or project. Faculty: 10 full-time. Students: 61 full-time, 63 part-time. Financial Assistance: loans, assistantships, scholarships. Degrees Awarded: 60. Updated: 4/9/02. Phyllis Butler, Secretary Graduate School.

Ohio

Kent State University. Instructional Technology. 405 White Hall, Kent, OH 44242, United States. (330) 672-2294. Fax: (330) 672-2512. Web site: http://itec.educ.kent.edu. Dr. Albert L. Ingram, Coord., Instructional Technology Program. aingram@kent.edu. Specialization: M.Ed. or M.A. in Instructional Technology, Computing/Technology, and Library/Media Specialist; Ph.D. in Educational Psychology with emphasis in Instructional Technology. Features: Programs are planned individually to prepare students for careers in elementary, secondary, or higher education, business, industry, government agencies, or health facilities. Students may take advantage of independent research, individual study, practica, and internships. Admission Requirements: Master's: Bachelor's degree with 2.75 undergraduate GPA. Degree Requirements: Master's: 37–42 semester hours. Faculty: 5 full-time, 5 part-time. Students: 60, most part-time. Financial Assistance: Graduate assistantships, John Mitchell and Marie McMahan Awards, some teaching fellowships. Degrees Awarded: 20. Updated: 3/7/2006. Albert L. Ingram, aingram@kent.edu.

Ohio University. Educational Studies. 313D McCracken Hall, Athens, OH 45701-2979, United States. (740)593-4561. Fax: (740)593-0477. Web site: http://www.ohio.edu/education/dept/es/it/index.cfm. Teresa Franklin, Instructional Technology Program Coordinator. franklit@ohio.edu. Specialization: M.Ed. in Computer Education and Technology. Ph.D. in Curriculum and Instruction with a specialization in Instructional Technology also available; call for details (740-593-4561) or visit the Web site: http://www.ohio.edu/education/dept/es/it/index.cfm. Features: Master's program is a blended online delivery. Admission Requirements: Bachelor's degree, 2.5 undergraduate GPA, 35 MAT, 420 GRE (verbal), 400 GRE (quantitative), 550 TOEFL, three letters of recommendation. Degree Requirements: Master's—54 qtr. credits, electronic portfolio or optional thesis worth 2–10 credits or alternative seminar and paper. Students may earn two graduate degrees simultaneously in education and in any other field. Ph.D.—109 hours with 20 hours being dissertation work. Faculty: 3 full-time, 1 part-time. Students: M.Ed.: 42, Ph.D.: 17. Financial Assistance: assistantships. Degrees Awarded: 24 M.Ed., 4 Ph.D. Updated: 3/7/2006. Teresa Franklin, franklit@ohio.edu.

University of Cincinnati. College of Education. 401 Teachers College, ML002, Cincinnati, OH 45221-0002, United States. (513)556-3579. Fax: (513)556-1001. Web site: http://www.uc.edu/. Richard Kretschmer. richard.kretschmer@uc.edu. Specialization: M.Ed. or Ed.D. in Curriculum and Instruction with an emphasis on Instructional Design and Technology; Educational Technology degree programs for current professional, technical, critical, and personal knowledge. Features: Contact division for features. Admission Requirements: Bachelor's degree from accredited institution, 2.8 undergraduate GPA; GRE 1500 or better 54 qtr. hours, written exam, thesis or research project. Degree Requirements: 12–15 credit hours college core; 12–15 C&I; 18–27 credit hours specialization; 3-6 credit hours thesis or project. Faculty: 3 full-time. Students: In C&I there are 74 doctoral students and 25 Masters' students. Financial Assistance: scholarships, assistantships, grants. Degrees Awarded: C&I Degrees 26 M.Ed. and 12 Ed.D. Updated: 3/24/2006.

University of Toledo. Curriculum & Instruction. MS 924, Carver Education Center, Toledo, OH 43606, United States. (419)530-2837. Fax: (419)530-2466. Web site: http://www.utoledo.edu/~rsulliv/. Robert F. Sullivan, Ph.D. Robert.Sullivan@utoledo.edu. Specialization: Technology Using Educator/Technology Coordinator, Instructional Designer, and Performance Technologist. Features: Graduate students may concentrate in one of the three primary "roles," or may choose a blended program of study. Program was completely redesigned in 2004. Admission Requirements: Master's: 3.0 undergrad. GPA, GRE (if undergrad. GPA < 2.7), recommendations; Doctorate: Master's degree, GRE, TOEFL (as necessary), recommendations, entrance writing samples, and interview. Degree Requirements: Master's: 36 semester hours, culminating project; Doctorate: 76 sem. hours (after M.S.), major/minor exams, dissertation. Faculty: 4 full-time, 1 part-time (Fall 2004). Students: Master's, 12 full-time, 50 part-time; Doctoral, 4 full-time, 25 part-time (approximate). Financial Assistance: assistantships, scholarships, fellowships, and fee waivers (extremely competitive); student loans. Degrees Awarded: approximately 15 (graduate) awarded in 2003. Updated: 4/27/04. Robert F. Sullivan, Ph.D.

Wright State University. College of Education and Human Services, Dept. of Educational Leadership. 421 Allyn Hall, 3640 Colonel Glenn Highway, Dayton, OH 45435, United States. (937)775-2509 or (937)775-2821. Fax: (937)775-4485. Web site: http://www.ed.wright.edu. Dr. Bonnie K. Mathies, Associate Dean; Dr. Roger Carlsen, Program Coordinator. bonnie.mathies@wright.edu. Specialization: M.Ed. in Computer/Technology, Library Media; M.A. in Educational Media or Computer Education; Specialist degree in Curriculum and Instruction with a focus on Educational Technology; Specialist degree in Higher Education with a focus on Educational Technology. Features: Ohio licensure available in Multi-age library media (ages 3–21) Computer/technology endorsement. Above licensure only available on a graduate basis and with teaching credentials. Admission Requirements: Completed application with nonrefundable application fee, Bachelor's degree from accredited institution, official transcripts, 2.7 overall GPA for regular status (conditional acceptance possible), statement of purpose, satisfactory scores on MAT or GRE. Degree Requirements: M.Ed. requires a comprehensive portfolio; M.A. requires a 6-hour thesis. Faculty: 2 full-time, 10 part-time, including other university full-time faculty and staff. Students: approx. 2 full-time, approx. 180 part-time. Financial Assistance: 2 graduate assistantships in the College's Educational Resource Center; plus graduate fellowships for full-time students available; limited number of small graduate scholarships. Degrees Awarded: 15; we also work with numerous students who are seeking Ohio licensure. Updated: 3/27/2006. Bonnie Mathies, 937-775-2509.

Oklahoma

The University of Oklahoma. Instructional Psychology and Technology, Department of Educational Psychology. 321 Collings, Hall, Norman, OK 73019, United States. (405)325-5974. Fax: (405)325-6655. Web site: http://www.ou.edu/education/edpsy/iptwww/. Dr. Raymond B. Miller, Area Head. rmiller@ou.edu. Specialization: Master's degree with emphases in Instructional Technology, Design & Development of Instructional Software, Instructional Design, Instructional Psychology & Technology, Teaching with Technology. Doctoral degree in Instructional Psychology and Technology. Features: Strong interweaving of principles of instructional psychology with instructional design and development. Application of IP&T in K-12, vocational education, higher education, business and industry, and governmental agencies. Admission Requirements: Master's: acceptance by IPT program and Graduate College based on minimum 3.00 GPA for last 60 hours of undergraduate work or last 12 hours of graduate work; written statement that indicates goals and interests compatible with program goals. Doctoral: 3.25 GPA, GRE scores, written statement that indicates goals and interests compatible with program goals. Degree Requirements: Master's: approx. 36 hours coursework (specific number of hours dependent upon Emphasis) with 3.0 GPA; successful completion of thesis or comprehensive exam. Doctorate: see program description from institution or http://www.ou.edu/education/edpsy/iptwww/. Faculty: 10 full-time. Students: Master's, 6 full-time, 24 part-time; doctoral, 10 full-time, 16 part-time. Financial Assistance: assistantships, grants, student loans, scholarships. Degrees Awarded: 13 masters; 4 Ph.D. Updated: 3/8/2006. Raymond B. Miller, rmiller@ou.edu.

Oregon

Western Oregon State College. Teacher Education. 345 N. Monmouth Ave., Monmouth, OR 97361, United States. (503)838-8471. Fax: (503)838-8228. Web site: http://www.wou.edu/education/elms/msed.html. Dr. Dana Ulveland, Coordinator for Information Technology. ulvelad@wou.edu. Specialization: M.S. in Information Technology. Features: offers advanced courses in library management, instructional development, multimedia, and computer technology. Additional course offerings in distance delivery of instruction and computer-interactive video instruction. Admission Requirements: 3.0 GPA, GRE or MAT. Degree Requirements: 45 qtr. hours; thesis optional. Faculty: 3 full-time, 6 part-time. Students: 6 full-time, 131 part-time. Financial Assistance: assistantships, grants, student loans, scholarship, work assistance. Updated: 6/30/03.

Pennsylvania

Bloomsburg University. Institute for Interactive Technologies—Instructional Technology. 1210 McCormick Bldg., Bloomsburg, PA 17815, United States. (717)389-4506. Fax:

(717)389-4943. Web site: http://iit.bloomu.edu. Dr. Timothy L. Phillips, contact person. tphillip@bloomu.edu. Specialization: M.S. in Instructional Technology with emphasis on preparing for careers as interactive media specialists. The program is closely associated with the Institute for Interactive Technologies. Features: instructional design, authoring languages and systems, media integration, managing multimedia projects. Admission Requirements: Bachelor's degree. Degree Requirements: 33 semester credits (27 credits + 6 credit thesis, or 30 credits + three credit internship). Faculty: 4 full-time. Students: 53 full-time, 50 part-time. Financial Assistance: assistantships, grants, student loans. Updated: 5/28/03.

Clarion University of Pennsylvania. Library Science. 209 Carlson Library Building, Clarion, PA 16214, United States. (814)393-2271. Fax: (814)393-2150. Web site: www.clarion.edu/libsci. Dr. Andrea L. Miller, Chair. amiller@clarion.edu. Specialization: Master of Science in Library Science; Master of Science in Library Science with Pennsylvania School Library Media Certification; Certificate of Advanced Studies. Students may specialize in various areas of library science as determined by program of study. Clarion has a Rural Libraries program and began an online cohort program with a focus on rural and small libraries in January of 2004. In January of 2005, an online cohort program with a Master's of Library Science with Pennsylvania School Library Media Certification will begin. Features: The graduate program in library science provides professional study encompassing the principles and techniques common to all types of libraries and information centers with the opportunity for advanced work in areas of special interest. The curriculum reflects today's applications of information technology in libraries and information centers. The master's program at Clarion University was initiated in 1967 and has the distinction of being the first graduate library science program offered within the State System of Higher Education. The program has been accredited by the American Library Association since 1976. As part of its commitment to meeting the needs of all residents of the Commonwealth of Pennsylvania, the Department of Library Science offers a variety of distance education programs. These programs utilize various delivery techniques, including on-site instruction, interactive television (ITV), and Web-based delivery. ITV delivery involves two or more sections of the same course that are taught simultaneously by the same instructor from a central location. Students at remote sites participate in the class via two-way audio and video. Courses offered via the World Wide Web may, at the instructors discretion, require some on-campus meetings. Clarion presently offers the program at the Dixon Center in Harrisburg, PA and at the Free Library in Philadelphia. In January of 2004, Clarion began offering a Web-based online cohort program with a focus on rural and small libraries. In January of 2005, Clarion will offer a Web-based online cohort program, Master of Science in Library Science with Pennsylvania School Library Media Certification. Admission Requirements: Applicants for admission to the Master of Science in Library Science degree program must meet Division of Graduate Studies admission requirements with the following additions: M.S.L.S. 1.an overall quality-point average for the baccalaureate degree of at least 3.00 on a 4.00 scale; or 2.a 3.00 quality-point average for the last 60 credits of the baccalaureate degree with an overall quality-point average of at least 2.75; or 3.a 2.75 to 2.99 overall quality-point average for the baccalaureate degree with a score of at least 50 on the Miller Analogies Test or a combined score of at least 1,000 on the quantitative and verbal sections of the Graduate Record Examination; or 4.a graduate degree in another discipline with an overall quality-point average of at least 3.00 and an overall undergraduate quality-point average of at least 2.75. International students are required to achieve a minimum score of 550 on the TOEFL. M.S.L.S. with Pennsylvania School Library Media Certification In addition to the above, students who begin their M.S.L.S. with Pennsylvania School Library Media Certification program in spring 2002 or later must meet the following additional requirements: 1.completion of at least six credits of college-level mathematics; and 2.completion of at least six credits of college-level English composition and literature.

Applicants without valid teacher certification must also pass the Praxis I pre-professional skills tests. State law limits the number of applicants with an overall quality-point average for the baccalaureate degree of less than 3.00 on a 4.00 scale who can be admitted to the School Library Media Certification program. Procedure Degree Requirements: The degree of Master of Science in Library Science is conferred upon the candidate who has met the following requirements: The completion of 36 hours of approved graduate study, including five required core courses (LS 500, 501, 502, 504, and 550), one management course (LS 530, 531, 532, 533, or 569), and six elective courses. The maintenance of a cumulative average of 3.00 or higher. A student who receives a grade of "C" or lower in two or more courses is disqualified as a candidate in the degree program unless special permission to continue is obtained from the dean of the College of Education and Human Services and the coordinator of Graduate Studies. The completion of all degree requirements within a six-year period. Coursework over six years old may not be applied toward the degree. Master of Science in Library Science Degree with Pennsylvania School Library Media Certification Program Requirements.

A student wishing to obtain Pennsylvania School Library Media Certification, K-12, must hold a valid teaching certificate (or meet the requirements for preliminary certification by taking required undergraduate courses); complete 36 semester hours of an approved curriculum in library science; and complete three semester hours of internship in a school library media center. Students without prior certification will substitute twelve semester hours of student teaching for the internship requirement; students with emergency Pennsylvania School Library Media Certification may petition the department to substitute a site visit and portfolio for the internship requirement. Required courses for the Master of Science in Library Science degree with Pennsylvania School Library Media Certification, K-12, include: LS 459g, 490g, 500, 501, 502, 504, 532, 550, 555/577, 570, 583, 589, and one elective course. Praxis Series: Professional Assessments for Beginning TeachersR, The Commonwealth of Pennsylvania requires that all candidates for teacher certification take and pass specified tests in the Praxis Series, which is administered by the Educational Testing Service (ETS). Students without prior certification take the Praxis I, Academic Skills Assessments, to qualify for entry into teacher certification programs administered by the College of Education and Human Services. Tests in the Praxis II Series, Subject Assessments, are required of all students for licensure. These include Elementary Education, Content Knowledge (10014) and, for Pennsylvania School Library Media Certification, K-12, Library Media Specialist (10310). Students must pass the latter test with a minimum score of 620. Starting in spring 2004, students without prior certification must pass these tests prior to student teaching. The departments certification curricula are designed to cover topics found on this test. Click on the following link for a list of topics and the courses in which they are covered. Master of Science in Library Science/Juris Doctor Program The department offers a joint M.S.L.S./J.D. program in cooperation with Widener University School of Laws Harrisburg, Pennsylvania, campus. Students must be admitted to both programs separately. Any six credits of coursework taken as part of a students J.D. program may be applied to that students M.S.L.S. program, and vice versa. These courses will be chosen in consultation with the students' faculty advisors. Effective spring 2002. Certificate of Advanced Studies. The Certificate of Advanced Studies program is designed to provide the post-master's student an opportunity to expand and update professional skills and competencies through a structured pattern of continuing education. Study may be either full- or part-time. On a full-time basis, the certificate may be completed in two semesters. Requirements include a written statement of personal/professional goals, completion of a program of 24 graduate credits within a four-year period, and maintenance of a 3.00 (B) quality-point average. Faculty: 6 full-time and a large number of professional part-time faculty. Students: 45 full-time and 175 part-time. Financial Assistance: Assistantships and various scholarships and Awards. Degrees Awarded: 55. Updated: 4/26/04. Barbara Reed, 814-393-2271.

Drexel University. College of Information Science and Technology. 3141 Chestnut Street, Philadelphia, PA 19104-2875, United States. (215)895-2474. Fax: (215)895-2494. Web site: http://www.ischool.drexel.edu. David E. Fenske, Dean. info@ischool.drexel.edu. Specialization: M.S. Master of Science (Library and Information Science; M.S.I.S. Master of Science in Information Systems; M.S.S.E. Master of Science in Software Engineering; Ph.D. Features: On campus and online degree programs for M.S., M.S.I.S., and M.S.S.E. Admission Requirements: GRE scores; applicants with a minimum 3.2 GPA in last half of undergraduate credits may be eligible for admission without GRE scores. Degree Requirements: 15 courses. Faculty: 32 full-time, 25–30 active adjuncts per term. Students: Graduate, 112 full-time; 568 part-time. Financial Assistance: The IST Web site currently lists all IST scholarships available in the academic year. IST offers many different types of scholarships including, graduate assistantships for Ph.D. students, endowed scholarships, deans and doctoral fellowships, and IST. Degrees Awarded: 174 Graduate degrees (2004/2005 academic year). Updated: 4/20/2006. Peg Fallis, 215-895-2053, peg.fallis@ischool.drexel.

Lehigh University. Teaching, Learning, and Technology. 111 Research Drive, Bethlehem, PA 18015, United States. (610)758-3249. Fax: (610)758-6223. Web site: http://www.lehigh.edu/collegeofeducation/degree_programs/ed_technology/index.htm. Ward Cates, Interim Associate Dean. ward.cates@LEHIGH.EDU. Specialization: M.S. in Instructional Technology: Emphasizes implementation, integration, and evaluation of technology in school settings. The degree is well suited to both classroom teachers and technology specialists. Graduate certificate in Technology Use in the Schools: This twelve-credit grad certificate focuses on integrating technology into daily practice in the schools. Ph.D. in Learning Sciences and Technology: Emphasizes cognitive processes and their implications for the design, implementation, and evaluation of technology-based teaching and learning products in a variety of settings. Involves university-wide coursework in departments in all four colleges of the university. Features: High level of integration with teacher education and certification, leading to a practical and quickly applicable program of study. Our Integrated Professional Development School approach offers further opportunities to get into the schools and work on solving meaningful teaching and learning problems, not just "tech support." Both masters and doctoral students collaborate with faculty on projects and studies (including national presentation and publication). Admission Requirements: M.S. (competitive): 3.0 undergraduate GPA or 3.0 graduate GPA, GREs recommended, transcripts, at least 2 letters of recommendation, statement of personal and professional goals, application fee. Application deadlines: July 15 for fall admission, Dec 1 for spring admission, Apr 30 for summer admission. Ph.D. (highly competitive): 3.5 graduate GPA, GREs required. Copy of two extended pieces of writing (or publications); statement of future professional goals; statement of why Lehigh best place to meet those goals; identification of which presentations, publications, or research by Lehigh faculty attracted applicant to Lehigh. Application deadline: February 1 (admission only once per year from competitive pool). Degree Requirements: M.S.: 30 credits; thesis option. Ph.D.: 72 credits past bachelors or 48 credits past masters (including dissertation). Qualifying Research Project (publication quality) + Comprehensive Exams (written and oral) + dissertation. Faculty: 2.0 full-time, 1 part-time. Students: M.S.: 6 full-time, 30 part-time; Ph.D.: 4 full-time, 10 part-time. Financial Assistance: University graduate and research assistantships, graduate student support as participants in funded projects. Degrees Awarded: 10. Updated: 3/13/2006. Ward Cates, ward.cates@lehigh.edu; 610/758-3249.

Pennsylvania State University. Instructional Systems. 314 Keller Bldg., University Park, PA 16802, United States. (814)865-0473. Fax: (814)865-0128. Web site: http://www.ed.psu.edu/insys/. Alison Carr-Chellman, Associate Professor of Education, Professor in Charge of Instructional Systems. ali.carr@psu.edu. Specialization: M.Ed., M.S., D.Ed, and Ph.D. in Instructional Systems. Current teaching emphases are on Corporate Training, Interactive Learning Technologies, and Educational Systems Design. Research interests include multimedia, visual learning, educational reform, emerging technologies, constructivist learning, open-ended learning environments, scaffolding, technology integration in classrooms, technology in higher education, change and diffusion of innovations. Features: A common thread throughout all programs is that candidates have basic competencies in the understanding of human learning; instructional design, development, and evaluation; and research procedures. Practical experience is available in mediated independent learning, research, instructional development, computer-based education, and dissemination projects. Exceptional opportunities for collaboration with faculty (30%+ of publications and presentations are collaborative between faculty and students). Admission Requirements: D.Ed., Ph.D.: GRE (including written GRE), TOEFL, transcript, three letters of recommendation, writing sample, vita or resume, and letter of application detailing rationale for interest in the degree, match with interests of faculty. Degree Requirements: M.Ed.: 33 semester hours; M.S.: 36 hours, including either a thesis or project paper; doctoral: candidacy exam, courses, residency, comprehensives, dissertation. Faculty: 9 full-time, 1 joint appointment in Information Sciences, 4 affiliate and 1 adjunct. Students: Master's, approx. 46; doctoral, 103. Financial Assistance: assistantships, graduate fellowships, student aid loans, internships; assistantships on grants, contracts, and projects. Degrees Awarded: Ph.D., D.Ed., M.S., M.Ed. Updated: 7/7/04. Alison Carr-Chellman, ali.carr@psu.edu.

Rosemont College. Graduate Studies in Education. 1400 Montgomery Ave., Rosemont, PA 19010-1699, United States. (610)526-2982; (800)531-9431. Fax: (610)526-2964. Web site: http://www.rosemont.edu/root/grad_studies/gs_education.html. Dr. Robert Siegfried, Director of Technology and Education. rsiegfried@rosemont.edu. Specialization: M.Ed. in Technology in Education, Certificate in Professional Study in Technology in Education. Admission Requirements: GRE or MAT scores. Degree Requirements: Completion of 12 units (36 credits) and comprehensive exam. Faculty: 7 full-time, 10 part-time. Students: 110 full- and part-time. Financial Assistance: graduate student grants, assistantships, Federal Stafford Loan Program. Updated: 5/28/03.

Temple University. Department of Psychological Studies in Education. 1301 Cecil B. Moore Avenue, Philadelphia, PA 19122, United States. (215)204-4497. Fax: (215)204-6013. Web site: http://www.temple.edu/education/. Susan Miller, Ph.D. susan.miller@temple.edu. Specialization: Instructional and Learning Technology (ILT) is a new master's program within the Educational Psychology Program in the Department of Psychological Studies in Education. As such, ILT is designed to address conceptual as well as technical issues in using technology for teaching and learning. Program areas include (a)instructional theory and design issues, (b) application of technology, and (c) management issues. Features: Instructional Theory and Design topics includes psychology of the learner, cognitive processes, instructional theories, human development, and individual differences as well as psychological and educational characteristics of technology resources, and identification of strengths and weaknesses of instructional technology resources. The Application of Technology area focuses on clarification of instructional objectives, identification of resources to facilitate learning, operation and application of current and emergent technologies, facility using graphic design, multimedia, video, distributed learning resources, WWW, and print publishing. Management and Consultation is structured around defining instructional needs, monitoring progress, and evaluating outcomes, designing technology delivery systems, preparing policy statements, budgets, and facility design criteria, managing skill assessment and training, understanding legal and ethical issues, and managing and maintaining facilities. Admission Requirements: Bachelor's degree from an accredited institution, GRE(MAT)scores, 3 letters of recommendation, transcripts from each institution of higher learning attended (undergraduate and graduate), goal statement. Degree Requirements: Coursework (33 hours: 5 core courses, 3 technology electives, 3 cognate area courses) Practicum in students area of interest Comprehensive

Exam Portfolio of Certification Competencies (for students interested in PA Dept. of Ed Certification as Instructional Technology Specialist). Faculty: 2 full-time, 1 part- time (plus educational psychology faculty). Financial Assistance: Presidential, Russell Conwell, and University Fellowships, Graduate School Tuition and Fellowship Funds, Graduate Teaching Assistantships and Assistantships in Administrative Offices, CASHE (College Aid Sources for Higher Education National comput. Updated: 3/1/2006.

Rhode Island

The University of Rhode Island. Graduate School of Library and Information Studies. Rodman Hall, 94 W. Alumni Ave., Kingston, RI 02881-0815, United States. (401)874-2947. Fax: (401)874-4964. Web site: http://www.uri.edu/artsci/lsc. W. Michael Havener, Ph.D., Director. mhavener@uri.edu. Specialization: M.L.I.S. degree with specialties in School Library Media Services, Information Literacy Instruction, Youth Services Librarianship, Public Librarianship, Academic Librarianship, and Special Library Services. Features: Fifteen-credit Post-Baccalaureate Certificate in Information Literacy Instruction. Admission Requirements: undergraduate GPA of 3.0, score in 50th percentile or higher on SAT or MAT, statement of purpose, current resume, letters of reference. Degree Requirements: 42 semester-credit program offered in Rhode Island and regionally in Worcester, MA, and Durham, NH. Faculty: 8 full-time, 30 part-time. Students: 200. Financial Assistance: graduate assistantships, some scholarship aid, student loans. Degrees Awarded: 80. Updated: 3/24/2006. W. Michael Havener, mhavener@uri.edu.

South Carolina

University of South Carolina Aiken and University of South Carolina Columbia. Aiken: School of Education; Columbia: Department of Educational Psychology. 471 University Parkway, Aiken, SC 29801, United States. 803.641.3489. Fax: 803.641.3720. Web site: http://edtech.usca.edu. Dr. Thomas Smyth, Professor, Program Director. smyth@usca.edu. Specialization: Master of Education in Educational Technology (A Joint Program of The University of South Carolina Aiken and Columbia). Features: The master's degree in Educational Technology is designed to provide advanced professional studies in graduate level coursework to develop capabilities essential to the effective design, evaluation, and delivery of technology-based instruction and training (e.g., software development, multimedia development, assistive technology modifications, web-based development, and distance learning). The program is intended (1) to prepare educators to assume leadership roles in the integration of educational technology into the school curriculum and (2) to provide graduate-level instructional opportunities for several populations (e.g., classroom teachers, corporate trainers, educational software developers) that need to acquire both technological competencies and understanding of sound instructional design principles and techniques.

Several course offerings will be delivered from only one campus, though students on both campuses will enroll in the courses. These will include Web-based courses, two-way video courses, and courses that include a combination of Web-based, two-way video, and face-to-face meetings. Admission Requirements: Application to the Educational Technology Program can be made after completion of at least the bachelor's degree from a college or university accredited by a regional accrediting agency. The standard for admission will be based on a total profile for the applicant. The successful applicant should have an undergraduate grade point average of at least 3.0, a score of 45 on the Miller's Analogies Test or scores of 450 on both the verbal and quantitative portions of the Graduate Record Exam, a well-written letter of intent that matches the objectives of the program and includes a description of previous technology experience, and positive letters of recommendation from individuals who know the professional characteristics of the applicant. Any exceptions for students failing to meet these standards shall be referred to the Admissions Committee for review and final decision. Degree Requirements: 36 semester hours, including instructional theory, computer design, and integrated media. Faculty: 2 full-time, 4 part-time. Students: 45. Financial Assistance: -Graduate Assistantships are available. Degrees Awarded: 8. Updated: 3/10/2006. Tom Smyth, smyth@usca.edu; 803-641-3527.

Tennessee

East Tennessee State University. College of Education, Dept. of Curriculum and Instruction. Box 70684, Johnson City, TN 37614-0684, United States. (423)439-7843. Fax: (423)439-8362. Web site: http://coe.etsu.edu/department/cuai/meda.htm. Harold Lee Daniels. danielsh@etsu.edu. Specialization: (1) M. Ed. in School Library Media, (2) M.Ed. in Educational Technology, (3) 24 hour School Library media specialist add on for those with current teaching license and a master's degree, (4) M.Ed. in Classroom Technology for those with teaching license. Features: Two(MAC &PC)dedicated computer labs (45+ computers) Online and evening course offerings for part-time, commuter, and employed students. Student pricing/campus licensing on popular software (MS, Adobe, Macromedia, etc.) Off site cohort programs for classroom teachers. Extensive software library (900 + titles) with review/checkout privileges. Admission Requirements: Bachelor's degree from accredited institution, transcripts, personal essay; in some cases, GRE and/or interview. Degree Requirements: 36 semester hours, including 12 hours in common core of instructional technology and media, 18 professional content hours and 5 credit hour practicum (200 field experience hours). Faculty: 2 full-time, 4 part-time. Students: 15 full-time, 50 part-time. Financial Assistance: Scholarships, assistantships, aid for disabled. Degrees Awarded: 12. Updated: 4/3/2006. Harold Lee Daniels, danielsh@mail.etsu.edu.

University of Memphis. Instruction and Curriculum Leadership/Instructional Design & Technology. 406 Ball Hall, Memphis, TN 38152, United States. 901-678-2365. Fax: 901-678-3881. Web site: http://idt.memphis.edu. Dr. Richard Van Eck. rvaneck@memphis.edu. Specialization: Instructional Design, Web-based instruction, Computer-based instruction, Digital Video, K-12 NTeQ technology integration model, Instructional Games, Pedagogical Agents. Features: The Advanced Instructional Media (AIM) lab, staffed and run by IDT faculty and students, serves as an R&D space for coursework and research involving technologies such as digital media, WBT/CBT (Dreamweaver, Flash, Authorware, WebCT, DV cameras, DV editing, DVD authoring, etc.), pedagogical agents, gaming and simulation. The AIM lab and IDT program is connected to the Center for Multimedia Arts in the FedEx Institute of Technology. The AIM lab brings in outside contract work from corporate partners to provide real-world experience to students. We have also partnered with the Institute for Intelligent Systems and the Tutoring Research Group (www.autotutor.org) to work on intelligent agent development and research. Admission Requirements: Minimum standards that identify a pool of masters level applicants from which each department selects students to be admitted: An official transcript showing a bachelor's degree awarded by an accredited college or university with a minimum GPA of 2.0 on a 4.0 scale, competitive MAT or GRE scores, GRE writing test, two letters of recommendation, graduate school and departmental application. Doctoral students must also be interviewed by at least two members of the program. Degree Requirements: M.S.: 36 hours, internship, masters project or thesis, 3.0 GPA. Ed.D: 54 hours, 45 in major, 9 in research; residency project; comprehensive exams; dissertation. Faculty: 4 full-time, 6 part-time. Students: 10 full-time, 50 part-time. Financial Assistance: Teaching Assistantships (Two classes, full tuition waiver plus stipend). Graduate Assistantships (20 hours per week, full tuition plus stipend). Degrees Awarded: 2002/2003: 8 doctoral, 10 masters. 2003/2004: 5 doctoral, 10 masters. Updated: 3/4/04. Richard Van Eck, 901-678-2869, rvaneck@memphis.edu.

University of Tennessee-Knoxville. Instructional Technology and Educational Studies, College of Education. A535 Claxton Addition, Knoxville, TN 37996-3456, United States. 865-974-5037. Web site: http://ites.tennessee.edu/. Jay Pfaffman. pfaffman@utk.edu. Specialization: M.S., Ed.S., and Ph.D. in Ed. Concentrations in Curriculum/Evaluation/ Research and Instructional Technology; M.S. and Ph.D. in Ed. Concentration in Cultural Studies in Education coursework in media production and management, advanced software production, utilization, research, theory, instructional computing, and instructional development. Features: See Graduate Catalog for current program requirements. Admission Requirements: See Graduate Catalog for current program requirements. Degree Requirements: 12 full-time. Students: M.S., 80; Ed.S., 30; Ed.D., 40; Ph.D., 20. Financial Assistance: Provided for most doctoral students. Many students are also supported in various other IT positions across campus. Degrees Awarded: approximately 20 across all levels. Updated: 3/8/2006. Jay Pfaffman, pfaffman@utk.edu.

Texas

Texas A&M University. Educational Technology Program, Dept. of Educational Psychology. College of Education & Human Development. College Station, TX 77843-4225, United States. (979)845-7276. Fax: (979)862-1256. Web site: http://educ.coe.tamu.edu/~edtc. Ronald D. Zellner, Assoc. Prof., Coord. Program information/Carol Wagner for admissions materials. zellner@tamu.edu/c-wagner@tamu.edu. Specialization: M.Ed. in Educational Technology; EDCI Ph.D. program with specializations in Educational Technology and in Distance Education; Ph.D. in Educational Psychology Foundations: Learning & Technology. The purpose of the Educational Technology Program is to prepare educators with the competencies required to improve the quality and effectiveness of instructional programs at all levels. A major emphasis is placed on multimedia instructional materials development and techniques for effective distance education and communication. Teacher preparation with a focus on field-based instruction and school to university collaboration is also a major component. The program goal is to prepare graduates with a wide range of skills to work as professionals and leaders in a variety of settings, including education, business, industry, and the military. Features: Program facilities include laboratories for teaching, resource development, and production. Computer, video, and multimedia development are supported in a number of facilities. The college and university also maintain facilities for distance education materials development and fully equipped classrooms for course delivery to nearby collaborative school districts and sites throughout the state. Admission Requirements: M.Ed.: Bachelors degree, (range of scores, no specific cut-offs) 400 GRE Verbal, 550 (213 computer version) TOEFL; Ph.D.: 3.0 GPA, 450 GRE Verbal. Composite score from GRE verbal & Quantitative and GPA, letters of recommendation, general background, and student goal statement. Degree Requirements: M.Ed.: 39 semester credits, oral exam; Ph.D.: coursework varies with student goals; degree is a Ph.D. in Educational Psychology Foundations with specialization in educational technology. Faculty: 4 full-time, 1 lecturer; several associated faculty from related programs in EPSY. Students: M.Ed., 25 full-time, 15 part-time; Ph.D., 12 full-time, 10 part-time. Financial Assistance: several graduate assistantships and teaching assistantships. Degrees Awarded: M.Ed. 20, Ph.D. 3. Updated: 3/24/03. Ron Zellner, zellner@tamu.edu.

Texas A&M University—Commerce. Department of Secondary and Higher Education. PO Box 3011, Commerce, TX 75429-3011, United States. (903)886-5607. Fax: (903)886-5603. Web site: http://www.tamu-commerce.edu/. Dr. Sue Espinoza, Associate Professor, Program Coordinator. Sue_Espinoza@tamu-commerce.edu. Specialization: M.S. or M.Ed. degree in Learning Technology and Information Systems with emphases in Educational Computing, Educational Media and Technology, and Library and Information Science. Certifications offered—School Librarian and Technology Applications, both approved by the Texas State Board for Educator Certification. Features: Courses are offered in a variety of formats, including traditional classroom/lab based, and distance ed, via video teleconferencing and/or online. Most courses are taught in only one of these, but some include multiple delivery methods. Degree Requirements: 36 hours for each Master's Degree; Educational Computing includes 30 hours of required courses, and 6 hours of electives; Media & Technology includes 21 hours of required courses, and 15 hours of electives, selected in consultation with advisor; Library includes courses in Library, Educational Technology, and Education. Faculty: 3 full-time, 5 part-time. Students: 30 full-time, 150 part-time. Financial Assistance: graduate assistantships in teaching and research, scholarships, federal aid program. Degrees Awarded: 15. Updated: 6/10/03. Sue_Espinoza@tamu-commerce.edu.

Texas Tech University. College of Education. Box 41071,TTU, Lubbock, TX 79409, United States. (806)742-1997, ext. 287. Fax: (806)742-2179. Web site: http://www.educ.ttu.edu/edit. Dr. Nancy Maushak, Program Coordinator, Instructional Technology. nancy.maushak@ttu.edu. Specialization: M.Ed. in Instructional Technology; completely online M.Ed. in Instructional Technology; Ed.D. in Instructional Technology. Features: Program is NCATE accredited and follows ISTE and AECT guidelines. Admission Requirements: holistic evaluation based on GRE scores, GPA, student goals and writing samples. Degree Requirements: M.Ed.: 39 hours (30 hours in educational technology, 6 hours in education, 3 hours electives). Ed.D.: 93 hours (60 hours in educational technology, 21 hours in education or resource area, 12 hours dissertation. Faculty: 5 full-time, 1 part-time, 6 Teaching assistants. Students: M.Ed.:10 full-time, 30 part-time; Ed.D.:15 full-time, 15 part-time. Financial Assistance: teaching and research assistantships available ($9,000 for 9 months); small scholarships. Degrees Awarded: 6 M.Ed, 2 Ed.D. Updated: 5/29/03. Nancy Maushak, nancy.maushak@ttu.edu.

University of Houston. Curriculum & Instruction. 256 Farish, Houston, TX 77204, United States. 713-743-4950. Fax: 713-743-4990. Web site: http://www.it.coe.uh.edu/. Bernard Robin, Program Area Director. brobin@uh.edu. Specialization: urban community partnerships enhanced by technology integration of technology in teaching visual representation of information collaborative design teams innovative uses of technology in instruction. Features: The IT Program at the University of Houston can be distinguished from other IT programs at other institutions through our unique philosophy based on a strong commitment to the broad representations of community, the individual, and the collaboration that strengthens the two. We broadly perceive community to include our college, the university, and the local Houston environment. The community is a rich context and resource from which we can solicit authentic learning tasks and clients, and to which we can contribute new perspectives and meaningful products. Our students graduate with real-world experience that can only be gained by experience with extended and coordinated community-based projects, not by contrived course requirements. Our program actively seeks outside funding to promote and continue such authentic projects because we so strongly believe it is the best context in which our students can develop expertise in the field.

We recognize that each student brings to our program a range of formal training, career experience, and future goals. Thus, no longer can we be satisfied with presenting a single, static curriculum and still effectively prepare students for a competitive marketplace. Our beliefs have led us to develop a program that recognizes and celebrates student individuality and diversity. Students work with advisors to develop a degree plan that begins from their existing knowledge and strives toward intended career goals. We aim to teach not specific software or hardware operations, but instead focus on transferable technical skills couched in solid problem-solving experiences, theoretical discussions, and a team-oriented atmosphere. Students work throughout the program to critically evaluate their own work for the purpose of compiling a performance portfolio that will accurately and comprehensively portray their individual abilities to themselves, faculty, and future employers.

Completing our philosophical foundation is a continuous goal of collaboration. Our faculty operates from a broad collaborative understanding that recognizes how everyone involved in any process brings unique and valuable experiences and perspectives. Within the IT program, faculty, staff, and students rely on each other to contribute relevant expertise. Faculty members regularly seek collaboration with other faculty in the College of Education, especially those involved with teacher education, as well as with faculty in other schools across campus. Collaboration is a focus that has been infused through the design of our courses and our relationships with students.

Admission Requirements: Admission information for graduate programs: http://www.it.coe.uh.edu/. Masters program: 3.0 grade point average (GPA) for unconditional admission or a 2.6 GPA or above for conditional admission over the last 60 hours of coursework attempted. GRE or MAT scores: The 30th percentile on each section (Verbal, Quantitative, and Analytic) of the GRE serves as the minimum guideline for admission to all masters programs in the College of Education. A score of 35 on the MAT serves as the minimum guideline for admissions to all masters programs in the College of Education. The GRE or the MAT must have been taken within five (5) years of the date of application for admission to any Graduate program in the College of Education. Doctoral program: Each applicant must normally have earned a master's degree or have completed 36 semester hours of appropriate graduate work with a minimum GPA of 3.0 (A = 4.0). GRE: The 35th percentile on each section (Verbal, Quantitative, and Analytic) of the GRE serves as the minimum guideline for admission to all doctoral programs in the College of Education. The GRE or the MAT must have been taken within five (5) years of the date of application for admission to any Graduate program in the College of Education. Degree Requirements: Master's: Students with backgrounds in educational technology can complete the masters program with 36 hours of coursework. For the typical student, the M.Ed. in Instructional Technology consists of 9 semester hours of core courses required by the College of Education, and an additional 18 hour core in Instructional Technology as well as 9 hours that are determined by the students' career goals (K-12, higher education, business, and industry). Students take a written comprehensive examination over the program, coursework, and experiences. Doctoral: The minimum hours required in the doctoral program is 66. More details about the courses and requirements can be found on the IT Web site: http://www.it.coe.uh.edu/. Faculty: 5 full-time, 5 part-time. Students: 20 full-time, 120 part-time. Financial Assistance: Graduate Assistantships (20 hours week); University and College Scholarships. Degrees Awarded: approximately 30. Updated: 3/22/03. Sara McNeil, smcneil@uh.edu, 713-743-4975.

University of North Texas. Technology & Cognition (College of Education). Box 311337, Denton, TX 76203-1337, United States. (940)565-2057. Fax: (940)565-2185. Web site: http://www.cecs.unt.edu. Dr. Mark Mortensen & Mrs. Donna Walton, Computer Education and Cognitive Systems. Dr. Jon Young, Chair, Dept. of Technology and Cognition. coeinfo@coefs.coe.unt.edu. Specialization: M.S. in Computer Education and Cognitive Systems—two emphasis areas: Instructional Systems Technology & Teaching and Learning with Technology. Ph.D. in Educational Computing. See www.cecs.unt.edu. Features: Unique applications of theory through research and practice in curriculum integration of technology, digital media production, and Web development. See www.cecs.unt.edu. Admission Requirements: Toulouse Graduate School Requirements, 18 hours in education, acceptable GRE: 405 V, 489 A, 3 Analytical Writing for M.S. Degree. Increased requirements for Ph.D. program. Degree Requirements: 36 semester hours (12 hour core, 12 hour program course requirement based on M.S. track, 12 hour electives. See www.cecs.unt.edu. Faculty: 8 full-time, 1 part-time. Students: 300+ actively enrolled students in M.S. Highly selective Ph.D. program. Financial Assistance: Please see http://essc.unt.edu/finaid/index.htm. Degrees Awarded: 10–30. Updated: 5/12/03. Dr. Mark Mortensen, markmort@unt.edu.

The University of Texas at Austin. Curriculum & Instruction. 406 Sanchez Building, Austin, TX 78712-1294, United States. (512)471-5211. Fax: (512)471-8460. Web site: http://jabba.edb.utexas.edu/it/. Min Liu, Ed.D., Associate Professor and IT Program Area Coordinator/Graduate Advisor. Mliu@mail.utexas.edu. Specialization: The Instructional Technology Program at the University of Texas—Austin is a graduate program and offers degrees at the master's and doctoral levels. This comprehensive program prepares professionals for various positions in education and industry. Master's degrees (M.A. and M.Ed.) in Instructional Technology focus upon the processes of systematic planning, design. and development of instruction. Since IT requires more than skill in the production of instructional materials and use of machines, the instructional technologist emerging from our program uses knowledge of learning theory, curriculum development, instructional systems, communications theory, and evaluation to support appropriate uses of instructional resources.

The doctoral programs in Instructional Technology are comprehensive and research-oriented, providing knowledge and skills in areas such as instructional systems design, learning and instructional theories, instructional materials development, and design of learning environments using various technology-based systems and tools. Graduates assume academic, administrative, and other leadership positions such as instructional evaluators, managers of instructional systems, and professors and researchers of instructional design and performance technology. Features: The program is interdisciplinary in nature, although certain competencies are required of all students. Programs of study and dissertation research are based on individual needs and career goals. Learning resources include a model Learning Technology Center, computer labs and classrooms, a television studio, and interactive multimedia lab. Students can take courses offered by other departments, including Radio-TV Film, school of information, Computer Science, and Educational Psychology. Admission Requirements: 95% of the current students and recent graduates admission materials included the following: Master's: 3.5 GPA; 450 GRE Verbal, 1150 GRE Verbal + Quantitative; strong letters of recommendation; statement of study goals that can be satisfied with existing program offerings and resources Doctoral: 3.5 GPA; 500 GRE Verbal, 1250 GRE Verbal + Quantitative; strong letters of recommendation; statement of study goals that can be satisfied with existing program offerings and resources. Degree Requirements: see http://jabba.edb.utexas.edu/it/ for details. Faculty: 3 full-time, 1 part-time. Students: 16 Masters, 38 doctoral. Financial Assistance: Different forms of financial aid are often available to develop instructional materials, supervise student teachers in local schools, and assist with research/service projects. Degrees Awarded: (in fall 2004–summer 2005) 5 masters; 4 doctoral. Updated: 4/18/2006. Min Liu, mliu@mail.utexas.edu.

Utah

Brigham Young University. Department of Instructional Psychology and Technology. 150 MCKB, BYU, Provo, Utah 84602, United States. (801)422-5097. Fax: (801)422-0314. Web site: http://www.byu.edu/ipt. Russell Osguthorpe, Prof., Chair. russ_osguthorpe@byu.edu. Specialization: M.S. degrees in Instructional Design, Research and Evaluation, and Multimedia Production. Ph.D. degrees in Instructional Design and Research and Evaluation. Features: Course offerings include principles of learning, instructional design, assessing learning outcomes, evaluation in education, empirical inquiry in education, project management, quantitative reasoning, microcomputer materials production, multimedia production, naturalistic inquiry, and more. Students participate in internships and projects related to development, evaluation, measurement, and research. Admission Requirements: both degrees: transcript, 3 letters of recommendation, letter of intent, GRE scores. Apply by Feb 1. Students agree to live by the BYU Honor Code as a condition for admission. Degree Requirements: Master's: 38 semester hours, including prerequisite (3 hours), core courses

(14 hours), specialization (12 hours), internship (3 hours), thesis or project (6 hours) with oral defense. Ph.D.: 94 semester hours beyond the bachelor's degree, including: prerequisite and skill requirements (21 hours), core course (16 hours), specialization (18 hours), internship (12 hours), projects (9 hours), and dissertation (18 hours). The dissertation must be orally defended. Also, at least two consecutive 6-hour semesters must be completed in residence. Faculty: 10 full-time, 1 half-time. Students: Master's, 25 full-time, 2 part-time; Ph.D., 47 full-time, 3 part-time. Financial Assistance: internships, tuition scholarships, loans, and travel to present papers. Degrees Awarded: 18. Updated: 2/28/03. Michele_Bray@byu.edu.

Utah State University. Department of Instructional Technology, College of Education. 2830 Old Main Hill, Logan, Utah 84322-2830, United States. (435)797-2694. Fax: (435)797-2693. Web site: http://www.coe.usu:edu/it/. Dr. Byron R. Burnham, Prof., Chair.byron.burnham@usu.edu. Specialization: M.S. and Ed.S. with concentrations in the areas of Instructional Development, Multimedia, Educational Technology, and Information Technology/School Library Media Administration. Ph.D. in Instructional Technology is offered for individuals seeking to become professionally involved in instructional development in corporate education, public schools, community colleges, and universities. Teaching and research in higher education is another career avenue for graduates of the program. Features: M.S. and Ed.S. programs in Information Technology/School Library Media Administration and Educational Technology are also delivered via an electronic distance education system. The doctoral program is built on a strong Master's and Specialists program in Instructional Technology. All doctoral students complete a core with the remainder of the course selection individualized, based upon career goals. Admission Requirements: M.S. and Ed.S.: 3.0 GPA, a verbal and quantitative score at the 40th percentile on the GRE or 43 MAT, three written recommendations. Ph.D.: Master's degree in Instructional Technology, 3.0 GPA, verbal and quantitative score at the 40th percentile on the GRE, three written recommendations. Degree Requirements: M.S.: 39 sem. hours; thesis or project option. Ed.S.: 30 sem. hours if M.S. is in the field, 40 hours if not. Ph.D.: 62 total hours, dissertation, 3-sem. residency, and comprehensive examination. Faculty: 11 full-time, 7 part-time. Students: M.S., 70 full-time, 119 part-time; Ed.S., 6 full-time, 9 part-time; Ph.D., 50. Financial Assistance: approx. 18 to 26 assistantships (apply by April 1). Degrees Awarded: Awarded 2003: 36 M.S., 42 M.Ed., 4 Ph.D. Updated: 3/31/04. Byron R. Burnham, (435) 797-2694, byron.burnham@us.

Virginia

George Mason University. Instructional Technology Programs. Mail Stop 5D6, 4400 University Dr., Fairfax, VA 22030-4444, United States. (703)993-3798. Fax: (703)993-2722. Web site: http://it.gse.gmu.edu/. Dr. Eamonn Kelly, Coord. of Instructional Technology Academic Programs. akelly1@gmu.edu. Specialization: Ph.D. specializations in Instructional Design & Development Integration of Technology in Schools; Assistive Technology Master's Degrees Curriculum and Instruction with emphasis in Instructional Technology; Track I—Instructional Design & Development; Track II—Integration of Technology in Schools; Track III—Assistive Technology Graduate Certificates eLearning Integration of Technology in Schools; Assistive Technology. Features: The Instructional Technology program promotes the theory-based design of learning opportunities that maximize the teaching and learning process using a range of technology applications. Program efforts span a range of audiences, meeting the needs of diverse learners—school-aged, adult learners, and learners with disabilities—in public and private settings. Within this framework, the program emphasizes research, reflection, collaboration, leadership, and implementation and delivery models. The Instructional Technology (IT) program provides professionals with the specialized knowledge and skills needed to apply today's computer and telecommunications technologies to educational goals within school, community, and corporate settings. The IT program serves professional educators as well as those involved in instructional design, development, and training in government and private sectors. Master's degrees and certificates can be earned in each of three program tracks. Refer to the IT Web site (http://it.gse.gmu.edu/) for detailed information on admissions.

Track 1: Instructional Design and Development (IDD)—Students are prepared to craft effective solutions within public, private, and educational contexts to instructional challenges by using the latest information technologies in the design and development of instructional materials.

Track II: Integration of Technology in Schools (ITS)—Students are prepared to effectively integrate technology in the K-12 learning environment. Graduates frequently become the local expert and change agent for technology in schools.

Track III: Assistive/Special Education Technology (A/SET)—Graduates will use technology to assist individuals to function more effectively in school, home, work, and community environments. Graduates are prepared to incorporate technology into the roles of educators, related service providers, Assistive Technology consultants, hardware/software designers, and school-based technology coordinators.

Admission Requirements: Teaching or training experience, undergrad GPA of 3.0, TOEFL of 575(written)/230(computer), three letters of recommendation, goal statement. Degree Requirements: M.Ed. in Curriculum and Instruction: 39 hours; practicum, internship, or project. M.Ed. in Special Education: 36–42 hours. Ph.D.: 56–62 hours beyond master's degree for either specialization. Certificate programs: 12–15 hours. Faculty: 8 full-time, 15 part-time. Students: M.Ed. full-time 75, M.Ed. part-time 150, certificate programs 300. Financial Assistance: Information on assistantships, fellowships, loans, and other types of financial aid is available through the Office of Student Financial Aid at 703-993-2353 or at apollo.gmu.edu/finaid. The IDD cohort offers tuition assistance. Degrees Awarded: 130. Updated: 3/24/2006. Brenda Mueller, bmueller@gmu.edu.

Radford University. Educational Studies Department, College of Education and Human Development. P.O. Box 6959, Radford, VA 24142, United States. (540)831-5302. Fax: (540)831-5059. Web site: http://www.radford.edu. Dr. Martin S. Aylesworth, Acting Dept. Chair. mayleswo@radford.edu. Specialization: M.S. in Education with Educational Media/Technology emphasis. Features: School Library Media Specialist licensure. Admission Requirements: Bachelor's degree, 2.7 undergraduate GPA. Degree Requirements: 33 semester hours, practicum; thesis optional. Faculty: 2 full-time, 3 part-time. Students: 2 full-time, 23 part-time. Financial Assistance: assistantships, grants, student loans, scholarships. Updated: 5/28/03.

University of Virginia. Department of Leadership, Foundations, and Policy, Curry School of Education. Ruffner Hall, Charlottesville, VA 22903, United States. (434)924-7471. Fax: (434)924-0747. Web site: http://curry.edschool.virginia.edu/curry/dept/edlf/instrtech/. John B. Bunch, Assoc. Prof., Coord., Instructional Technology Program, Dept. of Leadership, Foundations and Policy Studies. jbbunch@virginia.edu. Specialization: M.Ed., Ed.S., Ed.D, and Ph.D. degrees with focal areas in Media Production, Interactive Multimedia, e-Learning/Distance learning, and K-12 Educational Technologies. Features: The IT program is situated in a major research university with linkages to multiple disciplines. Graduate Students have the opportunity to work with faculty across the Curry School and the University. Admission Requirements: undergraduate degree from accredited institution in any field, undergraduate GPA 3.0,1000 GRE (V+Q), 600 TOEFL. Financial aid application deadline is March 1st of each year for the fall semester for both master's and doctoral degrees; admission is rolling. Degree Requirements: M.Ed.: 36 semester hours, comprehensive examination. Ed.S.: 60 semester hours beyond undergraduate degree. Ed.D.: 54 semester hours, dissertation, at least one conference presentation or juried publication, comprehensive examination, residency; Ph.D.: same as Ed.S. with the addition of 18 semester hours. For specific degree requirements, see Web site, write to the address above, or refer to the UVA. Faculty: 5 full-time, 2 part-time. Students: M.Ed., 7/11; Ed.D, 2/6; Ph.D., 12/18. Financial Assistance: Graduate assistantships and scholarships are available on a competitive basis. Degrees Awarded: 5 M.Ed., 3 Ph.D. Ed.D. Updated: 4/26/04. John Bunch.

Virginia Polytechnic Institute and State University. College of Liberal Arts and Human Sciences. 220 War Memorial Hall, Blacksburg, VA 24061-0341, United States. (540)231-5587. Fax: (540)231-9075. Web site: http://www.soe.vt.edu/idt/. Katherine Cennamo, Program Area Leader, Instructional Design & Technology, Dept. of Learning Sciences & Technologies. cennamo@vt.edu. Specialization: M.A., Ed.S., Ed.D., and Ph.D. in Instructional Design and Technology. Features: Graduates of our Masters and Educational Specialist programs find themselves applying their expertise in a variety of rewarding, professional venues; for example, as instructional designers, trainers, or performance consultants in industrial settings and as teachers or technology coordinators in preK-12. Graduates of our doctoral program typically assume exciting roles as faculty in higher education, advancing research in the field and preparing the next generation of instructional technologists for the profession. Areas of emphasis are Instructional Design, Distance Education, and Multimedia Development. Facilities include two computer labs, extensive digital video and audio equipment, distance education classroom, and computer graphics production areas. Admission Requirements: Ed.D. and Ph.D.: 3.3 GPA from Master's degree, GRE scores, writing sample, three letters of recommendation, transcripts. M.A.: 3.0 GPA Undergraduate. Degree Requirements: Ph.D.: 96 hrs above B.S., 2 year residency, 12 hrs. research classes, 30 hrs. dissertation; Ed.D.: 90 hrs. above B.S., 1 year residency, 12 hrs. research classes; MA.: 30 hrs. above B.S. Faculty: 5 full-time, 2 part-time. Students: 30 full-time and 5 part-time, doctoral level. 15 full-time and 200 part-time (online), Masters. Financial Assistance: 10 assistantships. Degrees Awarded: 9 Ph.D. and 50 M.S. Updated: 3/7/2006. Katherine Cennamo, cennamo@vt.edu.

Virginia State University. School of Graduate Studies, Research and Outreach. 1 Hayden Drive, Box 9402, Petersburg, VA 23806, United States. (804)524-5377. Fax: (804)524-5104. Web site: http://www.vsu.edu. Vykuntapathi Thota, Chair, Dept. of Education. Specialization: M.S., M.Ed. in Educational Technology Video Conferencing Center and PLATO Laboratory, internship in ABC and NBC channels. Admission Requirements: See http://www.vsu.edu/catalogweb/graduate/admission/requirement.htm. Degree Requirements: 30 semester hours plus thesis for M.S.; 33 semester hours plus project for M.Ed.; comprehensive exam. Faculty: 1 full-time, 2 part-time. Students: 8 full-time, 50 part-time. Financial Assistance: Scholarships through the School of Graduate Studies. Updated: 5/19/03.

Washington

Eastern Washington University. Department of Computer Science. 202 Computer Science Building, Cheney, WA 99004-2412, United States. (509) 359-6260. Fax: (509) 359-2215. Web site: http://acm.ewu.edu/csd/. Ray O Hamel, Ph.D., Linda Kieffer, Ph.D. compsci@mailserver.ewu.edu. Specialization: M.Ed. in Computer and Technology Supported Education; M.S. Interdisciplinary. Master's program started in 1983. Features: Many projects involve the use of high-level authoring systems to develop educational products, technology driven curriculum, and Web projects. Admission Requirements: 3.0 GPA for last 90 graded undergraduate qtr. Credits. Degree Requirements: M.S Interdisciplinary.: 52 qtr. hours (30 hours in computers, 15 hours outside education; the hours do not total to 52 because of freedom to choose where Methods of Research is taken, where 12 credits of supporting courses are taken, and where additional electives are taken); research project with formal report. M.Ed.: 52 qtr. hours (28 hours in computer education, 16 hours in education, 8 hours outside education). Faculty: 1 full-time. Students: approx. 25. Financial Assistance: some research and teaching fellowships. Updated: 5/30/03. Margo Dalager Stanzak, (509) 359-4734, mdalager@ewu.

University of Washington. College of Education. 115 Miller Hall, Box 353600, Seattle, WA 98195-3600, United States. (206)543-1847. Fax: (206)543-1237. Web site: http://www.educ.washington.edu/COE/c-and-i/c_and_i_med_ed_tech.htm. William Winn, Prof. of Education. billwinn@u.washington.edu. Specialization: M.Ed., Ed.D, and Ph.D. for individuals in business, industry, higher education, public schools, and organizations concerned with education or communication (broadly defined). Features: Emphasis on design of materials and programs to encourage learning and development in school and nonschool settings; research and related activity in such areas as interactive instruction, Web-based learning, virtual environments, use of video as a tool for design and development. Close collaboration with program in Cognitive Studies. Admission Requirements: M.Ed.: goal statement (2–3pp.), writing sample, 1000 GRE (verbal plus quantitative), undergraduate GPA indicating potential to successfully accomplish graduate work. Doctoral: GRE scores, letters of reference, transcripts, personal statement, master's degree or equivalent in field appropriate to the specialization with 3.5 GPA, two years of successful professional experience and/or experience related to program goals desirable. Degree Requirements: M.Ed.: 45 qtr. hours (including 24 in technology); thesis or project recommended, exam optional. Ed.D.: see http://www.educ.washington.edu/COEWebSite/programs/ci/EdD.html. Ph.D.: http://www.educ.washington.edu/COEWebSite/students/prospective/phdDescrip.html. Faculty: 4 full-time, 3 part-time. Students: 12 full-time, 32 part-time; 26 M.Ed., 18 doctoral. Financial Assistance: Assistantships awarded competitively and on basis of program needs; other assistantships available depending on grant activity in any given year. Degrees Awarded: 5. Updated: 3/7/2006. Bill Winn.

Wisconsin

Edgewood College. Department of Education. 1000 Edgewood College Drive, Madison, WI 53711-1997, United States. (608)663-2293. Fax: (608)663-6727. Web site: http://www.edgewood.edu. Dr. Joseph E. Schmiedicke, Chair, Dept. of Education. schmied@edgewood.edu. Specialization: M.A. in Education with emphasis on Instructional Technology. Master's program started in 1987. Features: classes conducted in laboratory setting with emphasis on applications and software. Admission Requirements: 2.75 GPA. Degree Requirements: 36 semester hours. Faculty: 2 full-time, 3 part-time. Students: 5 full-time, 150 part-time. Financial Assistance: grants, student loans. Degrees Awarded: 8. Updated: 2/27/03. Joseph E. Schmiedicke.

University of Wisconsin—-La Crosse. Educational Media Program. Rm. 235C, Morris Hall, La Crosse, WI 54601, United States. (608)785-8121. Fax: 608)785-8128. Web site: http://www.uwlax.edu/mediaservices/soe/html/soe-about.htm. Ronald Rochon, Ph. D., Interim Associate Dean, Director of School of Education. rochon.rona@uwlax.edu. Specialization: M.S. in Professional Development with specializations in Initial Instructional Library Specialist, License 901; Instructional Library Media Specialist, License 902 (39 credits). Degree Requirements: 30 semester hours, including 15 in media; no thesis. Faculty: 2 full-time, 4 part-time. Students: 21. Financial Assistance: guaranteed student loans, graduate assistantships. Updated: 6/7/03. Ali Ahmed O, ali.ahme@uwlax.edu.

University of Wisconsin—Madison. Curriculum and Instruction, School of Education. 225 North Mills Street, Madison, WI 53706, United States. (608)263-4670.

Fax: (608)263-9992. Web site: http://www.education.wisc.edu/ci/. Michael J. Streibel. streibel@education.wisc.edu. Specialization: M.S. and Ph.D. degree programs to prepare college and university faculty. Ongoing research in photography and visual culture in education as well as educational game design and design experiments in education. Features: Traditional instructional technology courses are processed through social, cultural, and historical frames of reference. Current curriculum emphasizes new media theories, critical cultural and visual culture theories, and constructivist theories of instructional design and development. Many courses offered in the evening. Admission Requirements: Master's and Ph.D.: previous experience in Instructional Technology preferred, previous teaching experience, 3.0 GPA on last 60 undergraduate credits, acceptable scores on GRE, 3.0 GPA on all graduate work. Degree Requirements: M.S.: 24 credits plus thesis and exam (an additional 12 credits of Educational Foundations if no previous educational background); Ph.D.: 1 year of residency beyond the bachelor's, major, minor, and research requirements, preliminary exam, dissertation, and oral exam. Faculty: 2 full-time, 1 part-time. Students: M.S., 14; Ph.D., 10. Financial Assistance: TA and PA positions are available. Degrees Awarded: 2 Ph.D., 4 M.S. Updated: 4/12/04. Michael J. Streibel, streibel@education.wisc.edu.

Foreign Institutions

Universiti Sains Malaysia. Centre for Instructional Technology and Multimedia. Centre for Instructional Tech and Multimedia, Universiti Sains Malaysia, Minden, Pg 11800, Malaysia. 604-6533222. Fax: 04-6576749. Web site: http://www.ptpm.usm.my. Assoc. Prof. Wan Mohd. Fauzy Wan Ismail, Director. Fauzy@usm.my. Specialization: Instructional Design, Web/Internet Instruction and Learning,Educational Training/Resource Management, Instructional Training Technology/Evaluation, Instructional System Development, Design and Development of Multimedia/Video/Training materials, Instructional and Training Technology, Constructivism in Instructional Technology, E-Learning Systems, Learning Management Systems Masters in Instructional Technology. Features: entering its third academic year 2004–2005 (full-time—1–2 years, part-time—2–4 years). Teaching Programs—Postgraduate programs and research Consultancy—services on the application of educational/Instructional Design technology in teaching and learning training and diffusion, continuing education in support of lifelong learning. Academic Support Services—services to support research, teaching, and learning activities and centres within the university. Admission Requirements: Bachelor's and master's degree from accredited institution or relevant work experience. Faculty: Part-time, full-time—11. Students: full time Postgraduate students 30 full time, 60 part time. Financial Assistance: None. Degrees Awarded: Ph.D. in Instructional Technology and M.Ed. in Instructional Technology, MIM. Updated: 3/29/2006. Assoc. Prof. Wan Mohd. Fauzy Wan Ismail, Director.

Part Six
Mediagraphy—Print and Non-Print Resources

Introduction

Chad Galloway

CONTENTS

This resource lists journals and other resources of interest to practitioners, researchers, students, and others concerned with educational technology and educational media. The primary goal of this section is to list current publications in the field. The majority of materials cited here were published in 2006 or mid-2007. Media-related journals include those listed in past issues of EMTY, as well as new entries in the field. A thorough list of journals in the educational technology field has been updated for the 2007 edition using Ulrich's Periodical Index Online and journal Web sites. This chapter is not intended to serve as a specific resource location tool, although it may be used for that purpose in the absence of database access. Rather, readers are encouraged to peruse the categories of interest in this chapter to gain an idea of recent developments within the field. For archival purposes, this chapter serves as a snapshot of the field of instructional technology publications in 2005. Readers must bear in mind that technological developments occur well in advance of publication and should take that fact into consideration when judging the timeliness of resources listed in this chapter.

SELECTION

Items were selected for the Mediagraphy in several ways. The EBSCO Host Databases were used to locate most of the journal citations. Others were taken from the journal listings of large publishing companies. Items were chosen for this list when they met one or more of the following criteria: reputable publisher, broad circulation, coverage by indexing services, peer review, and coverage of a gap in the literature. The author chose items on subjects that seem to reflect the instructional technology field as it is today. Because of the increasing tendency for media producers to package their products in more than one format and for single titles to contain mixed media, titles are no longer separated by media type. The author makes no claims as to the comprehensiveness of this list. It is, instead, intended to be representative.

OBTAINING RESOURCES

Media-related periodicals: The author has attempted to provide various ways to obtain the resources listed in this Mediagraphy, including telephone and fax numbers, Web and postal addresses, as well as e-mail contacts. Prices are also included for individual and institutional subscriptions. The information presented reflects the most current information available at the time of publication.

ERIC documents: As of December 31, 2003, ERIC was no longer funded. However, ERIC documents can still be read and copied from their microfiche form at any library holding an ERIC microfiche collection. The identification number beginning with ED (for example, ED 332 677) locates the document in the collection. Document delivery services and copies of most ERIC documents also continue to be available from the ERIC Document

Reproduction Service. Prices charged depend on format chosen (microfiche or paper copy), length of the document, and method of shipping. Online orders, fax orders, and expedited delivery are available.

To find the closest library with an ERIC microfiche collection, contact: ACCESS ERIC, 1600 Research Blvd., Rockville, METHOD 20850-3172; (800) LET-ERIC (538-3742); e-mail: acceric@inet.ed.gov.

To order ERIC documents, contact:

ERIC Document Reproduction Services (EDRS)
7420 Fullerton Rd., Suite 110, Springfield, VA 22153-2852
(800) 433-ERIC (433-3742); (703) 440-1400
Fax: (703) 440-1408
E-mail: service@edrs.com

Journal articles: Photocopies of journal articles can be obtained in one of the following ways: (1) from a library subscribing to the title, (2) through interlibrary loan, (3) through the purchase of a back issue from the journal publisher, or (4) from an article reprint service such as UMI.

UMI Information Store, 500 Sansome St., Suite 400
San Francisco, CA 94111
(800) 248-0360 (toll-free in United States and Canada); (415) 433-5500 (outside United States and Canada)
E-mail: orders@infostore.com

Journal articles can also be obtained through the Institute for Scientific Information (ISI).

ISI Document Solution
P.O. Box 7649
Philadelphia, PA 19104-3389
(215) 386-4399
Fax: (215) 222-0840 or (215) 386-4343
E-mail: ids@isinet.com

ARRANGEMENT

Mediagraphy entries are classified according to major subject emphasis under the following headings:

- Artificial Intelligence, Robotics, and Electronic Performance Support Systems
- Computer-Assisted Instruction
- Distance Education
- Educational Research
- Educational Technology
- Information Science and Technology
- Instructional Design and Development
- Libraries and Media Centers

- Media Technologies
- Professional Development
- Simulation, Gaming, and Virtual Reality
- Special Education and Disabilities
- Telecommunications and Networking

Mediagraphy

ARTIFICIAL INTELLIGENCE, ROBOTICS, AND ELECTRONIC PERFORMANCE SUPPORT SYSTEMS

Artificial Intelligence Review. Springer Science+Business Media, 333 Meadowlands Pkwy, Seacaucus, NJ 07094. www.springer.com/journal/10462, tel: 800-777-4643, fax: 201-348-4505, journals-ny@springer.com [8/yr; $249 indiv, $732 inst]. Publishes commentary on issues and development in artificial intelligence foundations and current research.

AI Magazine. Association for the Advancement of Artificial Intelligence, 445 Burgess Dr, Suite 100, Menlo Park, CA 94025. www.aaai.org/Magazine, tel: 650-328-3123, fax: 650-321-4457, aimagazine07@aaai.org [4/yr; $35 student, $95 indiv, $190 inst; free with AAAI membership]. Proclaimed "journal of record for the AI community," this magazine provides full-length articles on research and new literature, but is written to allow access to those reading outside their area of expertise.

International Journal of Robotics Research. Sage Publications, 2455 Teller Rd, Thousand Oaks, CA 91320. www.sagepub.co.uk/journalsProdDesc.nav?prodId=Journal201324, tel: 800-818-7243, fax: 800-583-2665, journals@sagepub.com [12/yr; $186 indiv, $1356 inst (online), $1477 inst (print), $1507 inst (online + print)]. Interdisciplinary approach to the study of robotics for researchers, scientists, and students. The first scholarly publication on robotics research.

Journal of Intelligent and Robotic Systems. Springer Science+Business Media, 333 Meadowlands Pkwy, Seacaucus, NJ 07094. www.springer.com/journal/10846, tel: 800-777-4643, fax: 201-348-4505, journals-ny@springer.com [12/yr; $693 indiv, $1450 inst]. Main objective is to provide a forum for the fruitful interaction of ideas and techniques that combine systems and control science with artificial intelligence and other related computer science concepts. It bridges the gap between theory and practice.

Journal of Interactive Learning Research. Association for the Advancement of Computing in Education, P.O. Box 1545, Chesapeake, VA 23327-1545. www.aace.org/pubs/jilr, tel: 757-366-5606, fax: 703-997-8760, info@aace.org [4/yr; $95 for AACE members (discount available for ordering multiple AACE journals), $175 inst]. Publishes articles on how intelligent computer technologies can be used in education to enhance learning and teaching. Reports on research and developments, integration, and applications of artificial intelligence in education.

Knowledge-Based Systems. Elsevier, Inc., Customer Service Dept, 6277 Sea Harbor Dr, Orlando, FL 32887-4800. www.elsevier.com/locate/knosys, tel: 800-654-2452, fax: 800-225-6030, elspcs@elsevier.com [8/yr; $179 indiv, $1108 inst]. Interdisciplinary applications-oriented journal on fifth-generation computing, expert systems, and knowledge-based methods in system design.

Minds and Machines. Springer Science+Business Media, 333 Meadowlands Pkwy, Seacaucus, NJ 07094. www.springer.com/journal/11023, tel: 800-777-4643, fax: 201-348-4505, journals-ny@springer.com [4/yr; $232 indiv, $620 inst]. Discusses issues concerning machines and mentality, artificial intelligence, epistemology, simulation, and modeling.

COMPUTER-ASSISTED INSTRUCTION

AACE Journal. Association for the Advancement of Computing in Education, P.O. Box 1545, Chesapeake, VA 23327-1545. www.aace.org/pubs/aacej, tel: 757-366-5606, fax: 703-997-8760, info@aace.org [4/yr; $175 inst; free to AACE members]. Publishes articles dealing with issues in instructional technology.

CALICO Journal. Computer Assisted Language Instruction Consortium, 214 Centennial Hall, Texas State Univ, San Marcos, TX 78666. calico.org, tel: 512-245-1417, fax: 512-245-9089, info@calico.org [3/yr; $50 indiv, $35 K–12 or community college teacher, $30 students, $30 senior citizen, $85 inst]. Provides information on the applications of technology in teaching and learning languages.

Children's Technology Review. Active Learning Associates, 120 Main St, Flemington, NJ 08822. www.childrenstechnology.com, tel: 800-993-9499, fax: 908-284-0405, lisa@childrenssoftware.com [12/yr; $96 online, $144 online + print]. Provides reviews and other information about software to help parents and educators more effectively use computers with children.

Computers and Composition. Elsevier, Inc., Customer Service Dept, 6277 Sea Harbor Dr, Orlando, FL 32887-4800. www.elsevier.com/locate/compcom, tel: 800-654-2452, fax: 800-225-6030, elspcs@elsevier.com [4/yr; $66 indiv, $328 inst]. International journal for teachers of writing that focuses on the use of computers in writing instruction and related research.

Computers & Education. Elsevier, Inc., Customer Service Dept, 6277 Sea Harbor Dr, Orlando, FL 32887-4800. www.elsevier.com/locate/compedu, tel: 800-654-2452, fax: 800-225-6030, elspcs@elsevier.com [8/yr; $328 indiv, $1638 inst]. Presents technical papers covering a broad range of subjects for users of analog, digital, and hybrid computers in all aspects of higher education.

Computers in Education Journal. American Society for Engineering Education, Computers in Education Division, P.O. Box 68, 68 Port Royal Sq, Port Royal, VA 22535. www.asee.org/about/publications/divisions/coed.cfm, tel: 804-742-5611, fax: 804-742-5030, ed-pub@crosslink.net [4/yr; $45]. Covers transactions, scholarly research papers, application notes, and teaching methods.

Computers in Human Behavior. Elsevier, Inc., Customer Service Dept, 6277 Sea Harbor Dr, Orlando, FL 32887-4800. www.elsevier.com/locate/comphumbeh, tel: 800-654-2452, fax: 800-225-6030, elspcs@elsevier.com [6/yr; $257 indiv, $1283 inst]. Scholarly journal dedicated to examining the use of computers from a psychological perspective.

Computers in the Schools. Haworth Press, Inc., 10 Alice St, Binghamton, NY 13904-1580. www.haworthpress.com/web/CITS, tel: 800-429-6784, fax: 800-429-6784, getinfo@haworthpress.com [4/yr; $75 indiv, $535 inst]. Features articles that combine theory and practical applications of small computers in schools for educators and school administrators.

Converge. e.Republic, Inc., 100 Blue Ravine Rd, Folsom, CA 95630. www.convergemag. com, tel: 800-940-6039, fax: 916-932-1470, subscriptions@govtech.net [4/yr; free]. Explores the revolution of technology in education.

Dr. Dobb's Journal. CMP Media, P.O. Box 56188, Boulder, CO 80321. www.ddj.com, tel: 800-456-1215, fax: 902-563-4807, drdobbsjournal@halldata.com [12/yr; $11.99; free to qualified applicants]. Articles on the latest in operating systems, programming languages, algorithms, hardware design and architecture, data structures, and telecommunications; indepth hardware and software reviews.

eWEEK. Ziff Davis Media, Inc., 28 E 28th St, New York, NY 10016-7930. www.eweek. com, tel: 888-663-8438, fax: 847-564-9453, eweek@ziffdavis.com [51/yr; $195 (print), free online]. Provides current information on the IBM PC, including hardware, software, industry news, business strategies, and reviews of hardware and software.

Information Technology in Childhood Education Annual. Association for the Advancement of Computing in Education, P.O. Box 1545, Chesapeake, VA 23327-1545. www.aace.org/pubs/itce, tel: 757-366-5606, fax: 703-997-8760, info@aace.org [1/yr]. Scholarly trade publication reporting on research and investigations into the applications of instructional technology.

Instructor. Scholastic, Inc., 557 Broadway, 5th Floor, New York, NY 10012. teacher. scholastic.com/products/instructor, tel: 866-436-2455, fax: 386-447-2321, instructor@ palmcoastd.com [8/yr; $8 (8 issues), $14.95 (16 issues)]. Features articles on applications and advances of technology in education for K-12 and college educators and administrators.

Interactive Learning Environments. Taylor & Francis Group, Customer Services Dept, 325 Chestnut St, Suite 800, Philadelphia, PA 19106. www.tandf.co.uk/journals/titles/ 10494820, tel: 800-354-1420, fax: 215-625-8914, customerservice@taylorandfrancis.com [3/yr; $119 indiv, $353 inst (online), $371 inst (print + online)]. Explores the implications of the Internet and multimedia presentation software in education and training environments.

Journal of Computer Assisted Learning. Blackwell Publishing, Journal Customer Services, 350 Main St, Malden, MA 02148. www.blackwellpublishing.com/journals/JCA, tel: 800-835-6770, fax: 781-388-8232, customerservices@blackwellpublishing.com [6/yr; $184 indiv (print + online), $969 inst (online), $1001 inst (print + online)]. Articles and research on the use of computer-assisted learning.

Journal of Educational Computing Research. Baywood Publishing Co., Inc., 26 Austin Ave, Box 337, Amityville, NY 11701-0337. www.baywood.com/journals/previewjournals. asp?id=0735-6331, tel: 800-638-7819, fax: 631-691-1770, baywood@baywood.com [8/yr; $163 indiv, $432 inst]. Presents original research papers, critical analyses, reports on research in progress, design and development studies, article reviews, and grant award listings.

Journal of Educational Multimedia and Hypermedia. Association for the Advancement of Computing in Education, P.O. Box 1545, Chesapeake, VA 23327-1545. www. aace.org/pubs/jemh, tel: 757-366-5606, fax: 703-997-8760, info@aace.org [4/yr; $95 for AACE members (discount available for ordering multiple AACE journals), $175 inst]. A multidisciplinary information source presenting research about and applications for multimedia and hypermedia tools.

Journal of Research on Technology in Education. International Society for Technology in Education, 175 West Broadway, Suite 300, Eugene, OR 97401-3003. www.iste.org/jrte, tel: 800-336-5191, fax: 541-302-3778, iste@iste.org [4/yr]. Contains articles reporting on the latest research findings related to classroom and administrative uses of technology, including system and project evaluations.

Language Resources and Evaluation. Springer Science+Business Media, 333 Meadowlands Pkwy, Seacaucus, NJ 07094. www.springer.com/journal/10579, tel: 800-777-4643, fax: 201-348-4505, journals-ny@springer.com [4/yr; $189 indiv, $600 inst]. Contains papers on computer-aided studies, applications, automation, and computer-assisted instruction.

Learning and Leading with Technology. International Society for Technology in Education, 175 West Broadway, Suite 300, Eugene, OR 97401-3003. www.iste.org/LL, tel: 800-336-5191, fax: 541-302-3778, iste@iste.org [8/yr]. Focuses on the use of technology, coordination, and leadership; written by educators for educators. Appropriate for classroom teachers, lab teachers, technology coordinators, and teacher educators.

MacWorld. Mac Publishing, Macworld Subscription Services, P.O. Box 37781, Boone, IA 50037. www.macworld.com/magazine, tel: 800-288-6848, fax: 515-433-1013, mcwcustserv@cdsfulfillment.com [12/yr; $19.97]. Describes hardware, software, tutorials, and applications for users of the Macintosh microcomputer.

OnCUE. Computer-Using Educators, Inc., 387 17th St, Suite 208, Oakland, CA 94612. www.cue.org/oncue, tel: 510-814-6630, fax: 510-444-4569, cueinc@cue.org [4/yr; free to CUE members; not sold separately]. Contains articles, news items, and trade advertisements addressing computer-based education.

PC Magazine. Ziff Davis Media, Inc., 28 E 28th St, New York, NY 10016-7930. www. pcmag.com, tel: 212-503-3500, fax: 212-503-4399, pcmag@ziffdavis.com [50/yr; $39.94]. Comparative reviews of computer hardware and general business software programs.

Social Science Computer Review. Sage Publications, 2455 Teller Rd, Thousand Oaks, CA 91320. www.sagepub.com/journal.aspx?pid=198, tel: 800-818-7243, fax: 800-583-2665, journals@sagepub.com [4/yr; $112 indiv (print), $498 inst (online), $542 inst (print), $553 inst (online + print)]. Interdisciplinary peer-reviewed scholarly publication covering social science research and instructional applications in computing and telecommunications; also covers societal impacts of information technology.

Wireless Networks. Springer Science+Business Media, 333 Meadowlands Pkwy, Seacaucus, NJ 07094. www.springer.com/journal/11276, tel: 800-777-4643, fax: 201-348-4505, journals-ny@springer.com [6/yr; $548 inst]. Devoted to the technological innovations that result from the mobility allowed by wireless technology.

DISTANCE EDUCATION

American Journal of Distance Education. Taylor & Francis Group, Customer Services Dept, 325 Chestnut St, Suite 800, Philadelphia, PA 19106. www.ajde.com, tel: 800-354-1420, fax: 215-625-8914, customerservice@taylorandfrancis.com [4/yr; $60 indiv (online + print), $195 inst (online), $235 inst (online + print)]. Created to disseminate information and act as a forum for criticism and debate about research on and practice of systems, management, and administration of distance education.

Journal of Distance Education. Canadian Network for Innovation in Education, BCIT Learning & Teaching Centre, British Columbia Institute of Technology, 3700 Willingdon Ave, Burnaby, BC, V5G 3H2, Canada. www.jofde.ca, tel: 613-241-0018, fax: 604-431-7267, jde@bcit.ca [at least 2/yr; $40 (print); free online]. Aims to promote and encourage scholarly work of empirical and theoretical nature relating to distance education in Canada and throughout the world.

Journal of Library & Information Services in Distance Learning. Haworth Press, Inc., 10 Alice St, Binghamton, NY 13904-1580. www.haworthpress.com/web/JLISD, tel: 800-429-6784, fax: 800-429-6784, getinfo@haworthpress.com [4/yr; $48 indiv, $150 inst]. Contains peer-reviewed articles, essays, narratives, current events, and letters from distance learning and information science experts.

Journal of Research on Technology in Education. International Society for Technology in Education, 175 West Broadway, Suite 300, Eugene, OR 97401-3003. www.iste.org/jrte, tel: 800-336-5191, fax: 541-302-3778, iste@iste.org [4/yr]. This peer-reviewed publication presents communications technology, projects, research findings, publication references, and international contact information in instructional technology.

Open Learning. Taylor & Francis Group, Customer Services Dept, 325 Chestnut St, Suite 800, Philadelphia, PA 19106. www.tandf.co.uk/journals/titles/02680513, tel: 800-354-1420, fax: 215-625-8914, customerservice@taylorandfrancis.com [3/yr; $92 indiv, $274 inst (online), $289 inst (print + online)]. Academic, scholarly publication on aspects of open and distance learning anywhere in the world. Includes issues for debate and research notes.

EDUCATIONAL RESEARCH

American Educational Research Journal. Sage Publications, 2455 Teller Rd, Thousand Oaks, CA 91320. aer.sagepub.com, tel: 800-818-7243, fax: 800-583-2665, journals@sagepub.com [4/yr; $49 indiv (print + online), $274 inst (print), $252 inst (online), $280 inst (print + online)]. Reports original research, both empirical and theoretical, and brief synopses of research.

Educational Research. Taylor & Francis Group, Customer Services Dept, 325 Chestnut St, Suite 800, Philadelphia, PA 19106. www.tandf.co.uk/journals/titles/00131881, tel: 800-354-1420, fax: 215-625-8914, customerservice@taylorandfrancis.com [4/yr; $155 indiv, $434 inst (online), $457 inst (print + online)]. Reports on current educational research, evaluation, and applications.

Educational Researcher. Sage Publications, 2455 Teller Rd, Thousand Oaks, CA 91320. edr.sagepub.com, tel: 800-818-7243, fax: 800-583-2665, journals@sagepub.com [9/yr; $49 indiv (print + online), $294 inst (print), $270 inst (online), $300 inst (print + online)]. Contains news and features of general significance in educational research.

Journal of Interactive Learning Research. Association for the Advancement of Computing in Education, P.O. Box 1545, Chesapeake, VA 23327-1545. www.aace.org/pubs/jilr, tel: 757-366-5606, fax: 703-997-8760, info@aace.org [4/yr; $95 for AACE members (discount available for ordering multiple AACE journals), $175 inst]. Publishes articles pertaining to theory, implementation, and overall impact of interactive learning environments in education.

Learning Technology. IEEE Computer Society, Technical Committee on Learning Technology. lttf.ieee.org/learn_tech, tel: (+64) 6-350-5799 (x2090), fax: (+64) 6-350-5725, kinshuk@ieee.org [4/yr; free]. Online publication that reports developments, projects, conferences, and findings of the Learning Technology Task Force.

Meridian. North Carolina State University, College of Education, Poe Hall, Box 7801, Raleigh, NC 27695-7801. www.ncsu.edu/meridian, meridian_mail@ncsu.edu [2/yr; free]. Online journal dedicated to research in middle school educational technology use.

Research in Science & Technological Education. Taylor & Francis Group, Customer Services Dept, 325 Chestnut St, Suite 800, Philadelphia, PA 19106. www.tandf.co.uk/journals/titles/02635143, tel: 800-354-1420, fax: 215-625-8914, customerservice@taylorandfrancis.com [3/yr; $293 indiv, $1411 inst (online), $1486 inst (print + online)]. Publication of original research in the science and technological fields. Includes articles on psychological, sociological, economic, and organizational aspects of technological education.

EDUCATIONAL TECHNOLOGY

Appropriate Technology. Research Information Ltd., Grenville Court, Britwell Rd, Burnham, Bucks, SL1 8DF, United Kingdom. www.researchinformation.co.uk/apte.php, tel: 44 (0) 1628 600499, fax: 44 (0) 1628 600488, info@researchinformation.co.uk [4/yr; $315]. Articles on less technologically advanced, but more environmentally sustainable, solutions to problems in developing countries.

British Journal of Educational Technology. Blackwell Publishing, Journal Customer Services, 350 Main St, Malden, MA 02148. www.blackwellpublishing.com/journals/BJET, tel: 800-835-6770, fax: 781-388-8232, customerservices@blackwellpublishing.com [6/yr; $176 indiv, $922 inst (online), $970 inst (print + online)]. Published by the National Council for Educational Technology, this journal includes articles on education and training, especially theory, applications, and development of educational technology and communications.

Canadian Journal of Learning and Technology. Canadian Network for Innovation in Education (CNIE), 1102 Education Tower, 2500 University Dr NW, Calgary, AB, T2N 1N4, Canada. www.cjlt.ca, tel: 403-220-4123, fax: 403-282-8479, cjlt@ucalgary.ca [3/yr; $50 student or retiree, $100 indiv, $350 inst (all in Canadian dollars; does not include tax)]. Concerned with all aspects of educational systems and technology.

Educational Technology. Educational Technology Publications, Inc., 700 Palisade Ave, P.O. Box 1564, Englewood Cliffs, NJ 07632-0564. www.bookstoread.com/etp, tel: 800-952-2665, fax: 201-871-4009, edtecpubs@aol.com [6/yr; $159]. Covers telecommunications, computer-aided instruction, information retrieval, educational television, and electronic media in the classroom.

Educational Technology Abstracts. Taylor & Francis Group, Customer Services Dept, 325 Chestnut St, Suite 800, Philadelphia, PA 19106. www.tandf.co.uk/journals/titles/02663368, tel: 800-354-1420, fax: 215-625-8914, customerservice@taylorandfrancis.com [1/yr; $527 indiv, $1352 inst (online), $1424 inst (print + online)]. An international publication of abstracts of recently published material in the field of educational and training technology.

Educational Technology Research & Development. Springer Science+Business Media, 333 Meadowlands Pkwy, Seacaucus, NJ 07094. www.springer.com/journal/11423, tel: 800-777-4643, fax: 201-348-4505, journals-ny@springer.com [6/yr; $95 indiv, $233 inst]. Focuses on research, instructional development, and applied theory in the field of educational technology.

International Journal of Technology and Design Education. Springer Science+Business Media, 333 Meadowlands Pkwy, Seacaucus, NJ 07094. www.springer.com/journal/10798, tel: 800-777-4643, fax: 201-348-4505, journals-ny@springer.com [3/yr; $141 indiv, $262 inst]. Publishes research reports and scholarly writing about aspects of technology and design education.

Journal of Computing in Higher Education. Norris Publishers, P.O. Box 2593, Amherst, MA 01004-2593. www.jchesite.org, tel: 413-549-5150, fax: 413-253-9525, carolb.macknight@verizon.net [2/yr; $46 indiv, $86 inst]. Publishes scholarly essays, case studies, and research that discuss instructional technologies.

Journal of Educational Technology Systems. Baywood Publishing Co., Inc., 26 Austin Ave, Box 337, Amityville, NY 11701-0337. www.baywood.com/journals/previewjournals. asp?id=0047-2395, tel: 800-638-7819, fax: 631-691-1770, baywood@baywood.com [4/yr; $300 inst]. Deals with systems in which technology and education interface; designed to inform educators who are interested in making optimum use of technology.

Journal of Interactive Media in Education. Open University, Knowledge Media Institute, Milton Keynes MK7 6AA United Kingdom. www-jime.open.ac.uk, jime@open.ac.uk [Irregular; free]. A multidisciplinary forum for debate and idea sharing concerning the practical aspects of interactive media and instructional technology.

Journal of Science Education and Technology. Springer Science+Business Media, 333 Meadowlands Pkwy, Seacaucus, NJ 07094. www.springer.com/journal/10956, tel: 800-777-4643, fax: 201-348-4505, journals-ny@springer.com [6/yr; $154 indiv, $835 inst]. Publishes studies aimed at improving science education at all levels in the United States.

MultiMedia & Internet@Schools. Information Today, Inc., 143 Old Marlton Pike, Medford, NJ 08055-8750. www.mmischools.com, tel: 800-300-9868, fax: 609-654-4309, custserv@infotoday.com [6/yr; $42.95]. Reviews and evaluates hardware and software. Presents information pertaining to basic troubleshooting skills.

Science Communication. Sage Publications, 2455 Teller Rd, Thousand Oaks, CA 91320. www.sagepub.com/journal.aspx?pid=144, tel: 800-818-7243, fax: 800-583-2665, journals@sagepub.com [4/yr; $145 indiv (print), $586 inst (online), $638 inst (print), $651 inst (online + print)]. An international, interdisciplinary journal examining the nature of expertise and the translation of knowledge into practice and policy.

Social Science Computer Review. Sage Publications, 2455 Teller Rd, Thousand Oaks, CA 91320. www.sagepub.com/journal.aspx?pid=198, tel: 800-818-7243, fax: 800-583-2665, journals@sagepub.com [4/yr; $112 indiv (print), $498 inst (online), $542 inst (print), $553 inst (online + print)]. Interdisciplinary peer-reviewed scholarly publication covering social science research and instructional applications in computing and telecommunications; also covers societal impacts of information technology.

TechTrends. Springer Science+Business Media, 333 Meadowlands Pkwy, Seacaucus, NJ 07094. www.springer.com/journal/11528, tel: 800-777-4643, fax: 201-348-4505, journals-ny@springer.com [6/yr; $55 indiv, $98 inst]. Targeted at leaders in education and training; features authoritative, practical articles about technology and its integration into the learning environment.

T.H.E. Journal. 1105 Media, P.O. Box 2170, Skokie, IL 60076. www.thejournal.com, tel: 866-293-3194, fax: 847-763-9518, THE@1105service.com [12/yr; $29, free to those in K-12, free online]. For educators of all levels; focuses on a specific topic for each issue, as well as technological innovations as they apply to education.

INFORMATION SCIENCE AND TECHNOLOGY

Canadian Journal of Information and Library Science. University of Toronto Press, Journals Division, 5201 Dufferin St, Toronto, ON, M3H 5T8, Canada. www.utpjournals. com/cjils/cjils.html, tel: 416-667-7810, fax: 800-221-9985, journals@utpress.utoronto.ca [4/yr; $75 indiv, $109 inst]. Published by the Canadian Association for Information Science to contribute to the advancement of library and information science in Canada.

EContent. Information Today, Inc., 143 Old Marlton Pike, Medford, NJ 08055-8750. www.econtentmag.com, tel: 800-300-9868, fax: 609-654-4309, custserv@infotoday.com [10/yr; $115]. Features articles on topics of interest to online database users; includes database search aids.

Information Processing & Management. Elsevier, Inc., Customer Service Dept, 6277 Sea Harbor Dr, Orlando, FL 32887-4800. www.elsevier.com/locate/infoproman, tel: 800-654-2452, fax: 800-225-6030, elspcs@elsevier.com [6/yr; $299 indiv, $1656 inst]. International journal covering data processing, database building, and retrieval.

Information Services & Use. IOS Press, Nieuwe Hemweg 6B, 1013 BG Amsterdam, The Netherlands. www.iospress.nl/html/01675265.php, tel: 31-20-688-3355, fax: 31-20-620-3419, info@iospress.nl [4/yr; $105 indiv (online), $300 inst (online), $405 inst (print + online)]. An international journal for those in the information management field. Includes online and offline systems, library automation, micrographics, videotex, and telecommunications.

The Information Society. Taylor & Francis Group, Customer Services Dept, 325 Chestnut St, Suite 800, Philadelphia, PA 19106. www.tandf.co.uk/journals/titles/01972243, tel: 800-354-1420, fax: 215-625-8914, customerservice@taylorandfrancis.com [5/yr; $145 indiv, $375 inst (online), $395 inst (print + online)]. Provides a forum for discussion of the world of information, including transborder data flow, regulatory issues, and the impact of the information industry.

Information Technology and Libraries. American Library Association, Subscriptions, 50 E Huron St, Chicago, IL 60611-2795. www.lita.org/ital, tel: 800-545-2433, fax: 312-944-2641, subscription@ala.org [4/yr; $55]. Articles on library automation, communication technology, cable systems, computerized information processing, and video technologies.

Information Today. Information Today, Inc., 143 Old Marlton Pike, Medford, NJ 08055-8750. www.infotoday.com/it, tel: 800-300-9868, fax: 609-654-4309, custserv@infotoday. com [11/yr; $79.95]. Newspaper for users and producers of electronic information services. Includes articles and news about the industry, calendar of events, and product information.

Information Technology Newsletter. Idea Group Publishing, 701 E Chocolate Ave, Suite 200, Hershey, PA 17033-1240. www.idea-group.com/journals/details.asp?id=201, tel: 866-342-6657, fax: 717-533-7115, cust@idea-group.com [2/yr; $40 indiv, $55 inst]. Designed for library information specialists, this biannual newsletter presents current issues and trends in information science presented by and for specialists in the field.

Internet Reference Service Quarterly. Haworth Press, Inc., 10 Alice St, Binghamton, NY 13904-1580. www.haworthpress.com/web/IRSQ, tel: 800-429-6784, fax: 800-429-6784, getinfo@haworthpress.com [4/yr; $40 indiv, $125 inst]. Discusses multidisciplinary aspects of incorporating the Internet as a tool for reference service.

Journal of Access Services. Haworth Press, Inc., 10 Alice St, Binghamton, NY 13904-1580. www.haworthpress.com/web/JAS, tel: 800-429-6784, fax: 800-429-6784, getinfo@haworthpress.com [4/yr; $45 indiv, $150 inst]. Explores topics and issues surrounding the organization, administration, and development of information technology on access services and resources.

Journal of the American Society for Information Science and Technology. John Wiley & Sons, Ltd., Subscription Dept, 111 River St, Hoboken, NJ 07030-5774. www.asis.org/Publications/JASIS/jasis.html, tel: 800-825-7550, fax: 201-748-5915, subinfo@wiley. com [14/yr; $1799 inst (print), $1979 inst (online), $2159 inst (print + online)]. Provides an overall forum for new research in information transfer and communication processes, with particular attention paid to the context of recorded knowledge.

Journal of Database Management. Idea Group Publishing, 701 E Chocolate Ave, Suite 200, Hershey, PA 17033-1240. www.idea-group.com/journals/details.asp?id=198, tel: 866-342-6657, fax: 717-533-7115, cust@idea-group.com [4/yr; $105 indiv, $345 inst (online), $395 inst (print + online)]. Provides state-of-the-art research to those who design, develop, and administer DBMS-based information systems.

Journal of Documentation. Emerald Group Publishing Limited, 875 Massachusetts Ave, 7th Floor, Cambridge, MA 02139. www.emeraldinsight.com/jd.htm, tel: 888-622-0075, fax: 617-354-6875, subscriptions@emeraldinsight.com [6/yr; $849]. Focuses on theories, concepts, models, frameworks, and philosophies in the information sciences.

Journal of Internet Cataloging. Haworth Press, Inc., 10 Alice St, Binghamton, NY 13904-1580. www.haworthpress.com/web/JIC, tel: 800-429-6784, fax: 800-429-6784, getinfo@haworthpress.com [4/yr; $48 indiv, $165 inst]. Gives library cataloging experts a system for managing Internet reference resources in the library catalog.

Resource Sharing & Information Networks. Haworth Press, Inc., 10 Alice St, Binghamton, NY 13904-1580. www.haworthpress.com/web/RSIN, tel: 800-429-6784, fax: 800-429-6784, getinfo@haworthpress.com [4/yr; $50 indiv, $275 inst]. A forum for ideas on the basic theoretical and practical problems faced by planners, practitioners, and users of network services.

INSTRUCTIONAL DESIGN AND DEVELOPMENT

Human-Computer Interaction. Taylor & Francis Group, Customer Services Dept, 325 Chestnut St, Suite 800, Philadelphia, PA 19106. www.tandf.co.uk/journals/titles/07370024, tel: 800-354-1420, fax: 215-625-8914, customerservice@taylorandfrancis.com [4/yr; $65 indiv (online + print), $510 inst (online), $590 institution (online + print)]. A journal of theoretical, empirical, and methodological issues of user science and of system design.

Instructional Science. Springer Science+Business Media, 333 Meadowlands Pkwy, Seacaucus, NJ 07094. www.springer.com/journal/11251, tel: 800-777-4643, fax: 201-348-4505, journals-ny@springer.com [6/yr; $241 indiv, $599 inst]. Promotes a deeper understanding of the nature, theory, and practice of the instructional process and the learning resulting from this process.

International Journal of Human-Computer Interaction. Taylor & Francis Group, Customer Services Dept, 325 Chestnut St, Suite 800, Philadelphia, PA 19106. www.tandf.co.uk/journals/titles/10447318, tel: 800-354-1420, fax: 215-625-8914, customerservice@taylorandfrancis.com [6/yr; $90 indiv (online + print), $620 inst (online), $680 inst (online + print)]. Addresses the cognitive, social, health, and ergonomic aspects of work with computers. It also emphasizes both the human and computer science aspects of the effective design and use of computer interactive systems.

Journal of Educational Technology Systems. Baywood Publishing Co., Inc., 26 Austin Ave, Box 337, Amityville, NY 11701-0337. www.baywood.com/journals/previewjournals. asp?id=0047-2395, tel: 800-638-7819, fax: 631-691-1770, baywood@baywood.com [4/yr; $300 inst]. Deals with systems in which technology and education interface; designed to inform educators who are interested in making optimum use of technology.

Journal of Instructional Delivery Systems. Learning Technology Institute, 50 Culpeper St, Warrenton, VA 20186. www.salt.org/salt.asp?ss=1&pn=jids, tel: 540-347-0055, fax: 540-349-3169, info@lti.org [4/yr; $45 indiv, $40 lib]. Devoted to the issues, problems, and applications of instructional delivery systems in education, training, and job performance.

Journal of Interactive Instruction Development. Learning Technology Institute, 50 Culpeper St, Warrenton, VA 20186. www.salt.org/salt.asp?ss=1&pn=jiid, tel: 540-347-0055, fax: 540-349-3169, jiid@lti.org [4/yr; $45 indiv, $40 lib]. A showcase of successful programs that will heighten awareness of innovative, creative, and effective approaches to courseware development for interactive technology.

Journal of Technical Writing and Communication. Baywood Publishing Co., Inc., 26 Austin Ave, Box 337, Amityville, NY 11701-0337. www.baywood.com/journals/ previewjournals.asp?id=0047-2816, tel: 800-638-7819, fax: 631-691-1770, baywood@ baywood.com [4/yr; $75 indiv, $300 inst]. Essays on oral and written communication for purposes ranging from pure research to needs of business and industry.

Journal of Visual Literacy. International Visual Literacy Association, Darrell Beauchamp, IVLA, Executive Treasurer, c/o Navarro College, 3200 W 7th Ave, Corsicana, TX 75110. plato.ou.edu/~jvl, tel: 903-875-7441, fax: 903-874-4636, cassityc@nsuok.edu [2/yr]. Explores empirical, theoretical, practical, and applied aspects of visual literacy and communication.

Performance Improvement Journal. John Wiley & Sons, Inc., 989 Market St, 5th Floor, San Francisco, CA 94103. www.ispi.org/publications/pij.htm, tel: 888-378-2537, fax:

888-481-2665, jbsubs@jbp.com [10/yr; $75 indiv (print), $275 inst (print), $303 (print + online)]. Promotes performance science and technology. Contains articles, research, and case studies relating to improving human performance.

Performance Improvement Quarterly. International Society for Performance Improvement, 1400 Spring St, Suite 260, Silver Spring, MD 20910. www.ispi.org/publications/piq. htm, tel: 301-587-8570, fax: 301-587-8573, pubs@ispi.org [4/yr; $50]. Presents the cutting edge in research and theory in performance technology.

Training. V N U Business Publications, P.O. Box 2104, Skokie, IL 60076-7804. www. trainingmag.com, tel: 612-333-0471, fax: 612-333-6526, edit@trainingmag.com [12/yr; $79]. Covers all aspects of training, management, and organizational development, motivation, and performance improvement.

LIBRARIES AND MEDIA CENTERS

Collection Building. Emerald Group Publishing Limited, 875 Massachusetts Ave, 7th Floor, Cambridge, MA 02139. www.emeraldinsight.com/cb.htm, tel: 888-622-0075, fax: 617-354-6875, subscriptions@emeraldinsight.com [4/yr; $1379]. Provides well-researched and authoritative information on collection maintenance and development for librarians in all sectors.

Computers in Libraries. Information Today, Inc., 143 Old Marlton Pike, Medford, NJ 08055-8750. www.infotoday.com/cilmag/default.shtml, tel: 800-300-9868, fax: 609-654-4309, custserv@infotoday.com [10/yr; $99.95]. Covers practical applications of microcomputers to library situations and recent news items.

The Electronic Library. Emerald Group Publishing Limited, 875 Massachusetts Ave, 7th Floor, Cambridge, MA 02139. www.emeraldinsight.com/el.htm, tel: 888-622-0075, fax: 617-354-6875, subscriptions@emeraldinsight.com [6/yr; $619]. International journal for minicomputer, microcomputer, and software applications in libraries; independently assesses current and forthcoming information technologies.

Government Information Quarterly. Elsevier, Inc., Customer Service Dept, 6277 Sea Harbor Dr, Orlando, FL 32887-4800. www.elsevier.com/locate/govinf, tel: 800-654-2452, fax: 800-225-6030, elspcs@elsevier.com [4/yr; $159 indiv, $485 inst]. International journal of resources, services, policies, and practices.

Information Outlook. Special Libraries Association, Information Outlook Subscriptions, 331 S Patrick St, Alexandria, VA 22314-3501. www.sla.org/content/Shop/Information/index.cfm, tel: 703-647-4900, fax: 703-647-4901, magazine@sla.org [12/yr; $125; free to SLA members]. Discusses administration, organization, and operations. Includes reports on research, technology, and professional standards.

The Journal of Academic Librarianship. Elsevier, Inc., Customer Service Dept, 6277 Sea Harbor Dr, Orlando, FL 32887-4800. www.elsevier.com/locate/jacalib, tel: 800-654-2452, fax: 800-225-6030, elspcs@elsevier.com [6/yr; $113 indiv, $295 inst]. Results of significant research, issues, and problems facing academic libraries, book reviews, and innovations in academic libraries.

Journal of Librarianship and Information Science. Sage Publications, 2455 Teller Rd, Thousand Oaks, CA 91320. www.sagepub.com/journal.aspx?pid=105829, tel: 800-818-7243, fax: 800-583-2665, journals@sagepub.com [4/yr; $84 indiv (print), $485 inst (online), $528 inst (print), $539 inst (online + print)]. Deals with all aspects of library and information work in the United Kingdom and reviews literature from international sources.

Journal of Library Administration. Haworth Press, Inc., 10 Alice St, Binghamton, NY 13904-1580. www.haworthpress.com/web/JLA, tel: 800-429-6784, fax: 800-429-6784, getinfo@haworthpress.com [8/yr; $75 indiv, $320 inst]. Provides information on all aspects of effective library management, with emphasis on practical applications.

Library & Information Science Research. Elsevier, Inc., Customer Service Dept, 6277 Sea Harbor Dr, Orlando, FL 32887-4800. www.elsevier.com/locate/lisres, tel: 800-654-2452, fax: 800-225-6030, elspcs@elsevier.com [4/yr; $134 indiv, $367 inst]. Research articles, dissertation reviews, and book reviews on issues concerning information resources management.

Library Hi Tech. Emerald Group Publishing Limited, 875 Massachusetts Ave, 7th Floor, Cambridge, MA 02139. www.emeraldinsight.com/lht.htm, tel: 888-622-0075, fax: 617-354-6875, subscriptions@emeraldinsight.com [4/yr; $399]. Concentrates on reporting on the selection, installation, maintenance, and integration of systems and hardware.

Library Hi Tech News. Emerald Group Publishing Limited, 875 Massachusetts Ave, 7th Floor, Cambridge, MA 02139. www.emeraldinsight.com/lhtn.htm, tel: 888-622-0075, fax: 617-354-6875, subscriptions@emeraldinsight.com [10/yr; $519]. Supplements Library Hi Tech and updates many of the issues addressed in depth in the journal; keeps the reader fully informed of the latest developments in library automation, new products, network news, new software and hardware, and people in technology.

Library Journal. Reed Business Information, P.O. Box 5655, Harlan, IA 51593. www.libraryjournal.com, tel: 800-588-1030, fax: 712-733-8019, ljlcustserv@cdsfulfillment.com [20/yr; $149.99, $52.17 student or educator]. A professional periodical for librarians, with current issues and news, professional reading, a lengthy book review section, and classified advertisements.

Library Media Connection. Linworth Publishing, Inc., 480 E Wilson Bridge Rd, Suite L, Worthington, OH 43085. www.linworth.com/lmc, orders@linworthpublishing.com [7/yr; $69]. Journal for junior and senior high-school librarians; provides articles, tips, and ideas for day-to-day school library management, as well as reviews of audiovisuals and software, all written by school librarians.

The Library Quarterly. University of Chicago Press, Journals Division, Journals Division, P.O. Box 37005, Chicago, IL 60637. www.journals.uchicago.edu/LQ, tel: 877-705-1878, fax: 877-705-1879, subscriptions@press.uchicago.edu [4/yr; $23 students (online), $40 indiv (print or online), $45 (online), inst prices vary]. Scholarly articles of interest to librarians.

Library Resources & Technical Services. American Library Association, Subscriptions, 50 E Huron St, Chicago, IL 60611-2795. www.ala.org/alcts/lrts, tel: 800-545-2433, fax: 312-944-2641, subscription@ala.org [4/yr; $75]. Scholarly papers on bibliographic access and control, preservation, conservation, and reproduction of library materials.

Library Trends. Johns Hopkins University Press, 1325 S Oak St, Champaign, IL 61820-6903. www.press.jhu.edu/journals/library_trends, tel: 800-548-1784, fax: 410-516-6968, jlorder@jhupress.jhu.edu [4/yr; $45 indiv (print), $75 inst (print or online)]. Each issue is concerned with one aspect of library and information science, analyzing current thought and practice and examining ideas that hold the greatest potential for the field.

Public Libraries. American Library Association, Subscriptions, 50 E Huron St, Chicago, IL 60611-2795. www.ala.org/ala/pla/plapubs/publiclibraries/publiclibraries.cfm, tel: 800-545-2433, fax: 312-944-2641, subscription@ala.org [6/yr; $50]. News and articles of interest to public librarians.

Public Library Quarterly. Haworth Press, Inc., 10 Alice St, Binghamton, NY 13904-1580. www.haworthpress.com/web/PLQ, tel: 800-429-6784, fax: 800-429-6784, get-info@haworthpress.com [4/yr; $60 indiv, $265 inst]. Addresses the major administrative challenges and opportunities that face the nation's public libraries.

Reference and User Services Quarterly. American Library Association, Subscriptions, 50 E Huron St, Chicago, IL 60611-2795. www.ala.org/rusa/rusq, tel: 800-545-2433, fax: 312-944-2641, subscription@ala.org [4/yr; $65]. Disseminates information of interest to reference librarians, bibliographers, adult services librarians, those in collection development and selection, and others interested in public services.

The Reference Librarian. Haworth Press, Inc., 10 Alice St, Binghamton, NY 13904-1580. www.haworthpress.com/web/REF, tel: 800-429-6784, fax: 800-429-6784, get-info@haworthpress.com [4/yr; $75 indiv, $400 inst]. Each issue focuses on a topic of current concern, interest, or practical value to reference librarians.

Reference Services Review. Emerald Group Publishing Limited, 875 Massachusetts Ave, 7th Floor, Cambridge, MA 02139. www.emeraldinsight.com/rsr.htm, tel: 888-622-0075, fax: 617-354-6875, subscriptions@emeraldinsight.com [4/yr; $419]. Dedicated to the enrichment of reference knowledge and the advancement of reference services. It prepares its readers to understand and embrace current and emerging technologies affecting reference functions and information needs of library users.

School Library Journal. Reed Business Information, P.O. Box 5655, Harlan, IA 51593. www.slj.com, tel: 800-595-1066, fax: 712-733-8019, sljcustserv@cdsfulfillment.com [12/yr; $129.99, $45.88 student or educator]. For school and youth service librarians. Reviews about 4,000 children's books and 1,000 educational media titles annually.

School Library Media Activities Monthly. Libraries Unlimited, Inc., 88 Post Road W, Westport, CT 06881. www.schoollibrarymedia.com, tel: 888-371-0152, fax: 203-454-8662, Deborah.Levitov@lu.com [10/yr; $55]. A vehicle for distributing ideas for teaching library media skills and for the development and implementation of library media skills programs.

School Library Media Research. American Library Association and American Association of School Librarians, Subscriptions, 50 E Huron St, Chicago, IL 60611-2795. www.ala.org/aasl/SLMR, ahanshaw@ala.org [annual compilation; free online]. For library media specialists, district supervisors, and others concerned with the selection and purchase of print and nonprint media and with the development of programs and services for preschool through high-school libraries.

Teacher Librarian. The Scarecrow Press, Inc., 15200 NBN Way, Blue Ridge Summit, PA 17214. www.teacherlibrarian.com, tel: 717-794-3800, fax: 717-794-3833, editor@teacherlibrarian.com [5/yr; $54 prepaid, $59 billed]. "The journal for school library professionals"; previously known as Emergency Librarian. Articles, review columns, and critical analyses of management and programming issues.

MEDIA TECHNOLOGIES

Broadcasting & Cable. Reed Business Information, P.O. Box 5655, Harlan, IA 51593. www.broadcastingcable.com, tel: 800-554-5729, fax: 712-733-8019, bcbcustserv@cdsfulfillment.com [51/yr; $199.99]. All-inclusive newsweekly for radio, television, cable, and allied business.

Communication Abstracts. Sage Publications, 2455 Teller Rd, Thousand Oaks, CA 91320. www.sagepub.com/journal.aspx?pid=168, tel: 800-818-7243, fax: 800-583-2665, journals@sagepub.com [6/yr; $323 indiv (print), $1442 inst (print)]. Abstracts communication-related articles, reports, and books. Cumulated annually.

Educational Media International. Taylor & Francis Group, Customer Services Dept, 325 Chestnut St, Suite 800, Philadelphia, PA 19106. www.tandf.co.uk/journals/titles/09523987, tel: 800-354-1420, fax: 215-625-8914, customerservice@taylorandfrancis.com [4/yr; $114 indiv, $423 inst (online), $446 inst (print + online)]. The official journal of the International Council for Educational Media.

Historical Journal of Film, Radio and Television. Taylor & Francis Group, Customer Services Dept, 325 Chestnut St, Suite 800, Philadelphia, PA 19106. www.tandf.co.uk/journals/titles/01439685, tel: 800-354-1420, fax: 215-625-8914, customerservice@taylorandfrancis.com [4/yr; $333 indiv, $909 inst (online), $957 inst (print + online)]. Articles by international experts in the field, news and notices, and book reviews concerning the impact of mass communications on political and social history of the twentieth century.

International Journal of Instructional Media. Westwood Press, Inc., 116 E 16th St, New York, NY 10003-2112. www.adprima.com/ijim.htm, tel: 212-420-8008, fax: 212-353-8291, PLSleeman@aol.com [4/yr]. Focuses on quality research of ongoing programs in instructional media for education, distance learning, computer technology, instructional media and technology, telecommunications, interactive video, management, media research and evaluation, and utilization.

Journal of Educational Multimedia and Hypermedia. Association for the Advancement of Computing in Education, P.O. Box 1545, Chesapeake, VA 23327-1545. www.aace.org/pubs/jemh, tel: 757-366-5606, fax: 703-997-8760, info@aace.org [4/yr; $95 for AACE members (discount available for ordering multiple AACE journals), $175 inst]. Presents research and applications on multimedia and hypermedia tools that allow the integration of images and sound into educational software.

Journal of Popular Film and Television. Heldref Publications, 1319 18th St NW, Washington, DC 20036-1802. www.heldref.org/jpft.php, tel: 800-365-9753, fax: 202-296-5149, jpft@heldref.org [4/yr; $56 indiv (online), $59 (print + online), $123 inst (print or online), $148 (print + online)]. Articles on film and television, book reviews, and theory. Dedicated to popular film and television in the broadest sense. Concentrates on commercial cinema and television, film and television theory or criticism, filmographies, and bibliographies. Edited at the College of Arts and Sciences of Northern Michigan University and the Department of Popular Culture, Bowling Green State University.

Learning, Media & Technology. Taylor & Francis Group, Customer Services Dept, 325 Chestnut St, Suite 800, Philadelphia, PA 19106. www.tandf.co.uk/journals/titles/17439884, tel: 800-354-1420, fax: 215-625-8914, customerservice@taylorandfrancis.com [4/yr; $372 indiv, $1324 inst (online), $1394 inst (print + online)]. This journal of the Educational Television Association serves as an international forum for discussions and reports on developments in the field of television and related media in teaching, learning, and training.

Media & Methods. American Society of Educators, 1429 Walnut St, Philadelphia, PA 19102. www.media-methods.com, fax: 215-587-9706, info@media-methods.com [5/yr; $35]. The only magazine published for the elementary school library media and technology specialist. A forum for K-12 educators who use technology as an educational resource, this journal includes information on what works and what does not, new product reviews, tips and pointers, and emerging technologies.

Multichannel News. Reed Business Information, P.O. Box 5655, Harlan, IA 51593. www.multichannel.com, tel: 888-343-5563, fax: 712-733-8019, mulcustserv@cdsfulfillment.com [52/yr; $169.99]. A newsmagazine for the cable television industry. Covers programming, marketing, advertising, business, and other topics.

MultiMedia & Internet@Schools. Information Today, Inc., 143 Old Marlton Pike, Medford, NJ 08055-8750. www.mmischools.com, tel: 800-300-9868, fax: 609-654-4309, custserv@infotoday.com [6/yr; $42.95]. This educational magazine offers practical information regarding instructional technologies.

Multimedia Systems. Springer Science+Business Media, 333 Meadowlands Pkwy, Seacaucus, NJ 07094. www.springer.com/journal/00530, tel: 800-777-4643, fax: 201-348-4505, journals-ny@springer.com [6/yr; $552 inst]. Publishes original research articles and serves as a forum for stimulating and disseminating innovative research ideas, emerging technologies, state-of-the-art methods and tools in all aspects of multimedia computing, communication, storage, and applications among researchers, engineers, and practitioners.

Telematics and Informatics. Elsevier, Inc., Customer Service Dept, 6277 Sea Harbor Dr, Orlando, FL 32887-4800. www.elsevier.com/locate/tele, tel: 800-654-2452, fax: 800-225-6030, elspcs@elsevier.com [4/yr; $125 indiv, $1094 inst]. Publishes research and review articles in applied telecommunications and information sciences in business, industry, government, and educational establishments. Focuses on important current technologies, including microelectronics, computer graphics, speech synthesis and voice recognition, database management, data encryption, satellite television, artificial intelligence, and the ongoing computer revolution.

PROFESSIONAL DEVELOPMENT

Journal of Computing in Teacher Education. International Society for Technology in Education, Special Interest Group for Teacher Educators, 1710 Rhode Island Ave NW, Suite 900, Washington, DC 20036. www.iste.org/jcte, tel: 202-861-7777, fax: 202-861-0888, eat@iastate.edu [4/yr]. Contains refereed articles on preservice and inservice training, research in computer education and certification issues, and reviews of training materials and texts.

Journal of Technology and Teacher Education. Association for the Advancement of Computing in Education, P.O. Box 1545, Chesapeake, VA 23327-1545. www.aace.org/pubs/jtate, tel: 757-366-5606, fax: 703-997-8760, info@aace.org [4/yr; $95 for AACE members (discount available for ordering multiple AACE journals), $175 inst]. Serves as an international forum to report research and applications of technology in preservice, inservice, and graduate teacher education.

SIMULATION, GAMING, AND VIRTUAL REALITY

Simulation & Gaming. Sage Publications, 2455 Teller Rd, Thousand Oaks, CA 91320. www.sagepub.com/journal.aspx?pid=34, tel: 800-818-7243, fax: 800-583-2665, journals@sagepub.com [4/yr; $127 indiv (print), $558 inst (online), $608 inst (print), $620 inst (online + print)]. An international journal of theory, design, and research focusing on issues in simulation, gaming, modeling, role-playing, and experiential learning.

SPECIAL EDUCATION AND DISABILITIES

Journal of Special Education Technology. Council for Exceptional Children, Technology and Media Division, Q Corporation, 5 Sand Creek Rd, Albany, NY 12205. jset.unlv.edu, tel: 518-436-9686, fax: 518-436-7433, cryan@boydprinting.com [4/yr; $55 indiv, $109 inst; free online]. Provides information, research, and reports of innovative practices regarding the application of educational technology toward the education of exceptional children.

TELECOMMUNICATIONS AND NETWORKING

Canadian Journal of Learning and Technology. Canadian Network for Innovation in Education (CNIE), 1102 Education Tower, 2500 University Dr NW, Calgary, AB, T2N 1N4, Canada. www.cjlt.ca, tel: 403-220-4123, fax: 403-282-8479, cjlt@ucalgary.ca [3/yr; $50 student or retiree, $100 indiv, $350 inst (all in Canadian dollars; does not include tax)]. Concerned with all aspects of educational systems and technology.

Computer Communications. Elsevier, Inc., Customer Service Dept, 6277 Sea Harbor Dr, Orlando, FL 32887-4800. www.elsevier.com/locate/comcom, tel: 800-654-2452, fax: 800-225-6030, elspcs@elsevier.com [18/yr; $1792 inst]. Focuses on networking and distributed computing techniques, communications hardware and software, and standardization.

Connected Newsletter. Harcourt Connected Learning, 6277 Sea Harbor Dr, Orlando, FL 32887. corporate.classroom.com/newsletter.html, tel: 800-638-1639, fax: 888-801-8299, help@classroom.com [9/yr; $62]. Provides pointers to sources of lesson plans for K-12 educators, as well as descriptions of new Web sites, addresses for online "keypals," Internet basics for new users, classroom management tips for using the Internet, and online global projects. Each issue offers Internet adventures for every grade and subject.

EDUCAUSE Review. EDUCAUSE, 4772 Walnut St, Suite 206, Boulder, CO 80301-2536. www.educause.edu/er, tel: 303-449-4430, fax: 303-440-0461, info@educause.edu [6/yr; $30]. Features articles on current issues and applications of computing and communications technology in higher education. Reports on EDUCAUSE consortium activities.

International Journal on E-Learning. Association for the Advancement of Computing in Education, P.O. Box 1545, Chesapeake, VA 23327-1545. www.aace.org/pubs/ijel, tel: 757-366-5606, fax: 703-997-8760, info@aace.org [4/yr; $95 for AACE members (discount available for ordering multiple AACE journals), $175 inst]. Reports on current theory, research, development, and practice of telecommunications in education at all levels.

The Internet and Higher Education. Elsevier, Inc., Customer Service Dept, 6277 Sea Harbor Dr, Orlando, FL 32887-4800. www.elsevier.com/locate/iheduc, tel: 800-654-2452, fax: 800-225-6030, elspcs@elsevier.com [4/yr; $64 indiv, $319 inst]. Designed to reach faculty, staff, and administrators responsible for enhancing instructional practices and productivity via the use of information technology and the Internet in their institutions.

Internet Reference Services Quarterly. Haworth Press, Inc., 10 Alice St, Binghamton, NY 13904-1580. www.haworthpress.com/web/IRSQ, tel: 800-429-6784, fax: 800-429-6784, getinfo@haworthpress.com [4/yr; $40 indiv, $125 inst]. Describes innovative information practice, technologies, and practice. For librarians of all kinds.

Internet Research. Emerald Group Publishing Limited, 875 Massachusetts Ave, 7th Floor, Cambridge, MA 02139. www.emeraldinsight.com/intr.htm, tel: 888-622-0075, fax: 617-354-6875, subscriptions@emeraldinsight.com [5/yr; $2449]. A cross-disciplinary journal presenting research findings related to electronic networks, analyses of policy issues related to networking, and descriptions of current and potential applications of electronic networking for communication, computation, and provision of information services.

Online. Information Today, Inc., 143 Old Marlton Pike, Medford, NJ 08055-8750. www.infotoday.com/online, tel: 800-300-9868, fax: 609-654-4309, custserv@infotoday.com [6/yr; $119]. For online information system users. Articles cover a variety of online applications for general and business use.

Index

About the Editors

MICHAEL OREY is Associate Professor in the Department of Educational Psychology and Instructional Technology at the University of Georgia.

V. J. McCLENDON is a doctoral candidate in the Department of Educational Psychology and Instructional Technology at the University of Georgia. Spanning two decades, her experience includes K–12 teacher, college instructor, and academic librarian. Her research focuses on faculty collaboration online.

ROBERT MARIBE BRANCH is Professor of Instructional Design in the Department of Educational Psychology and Instructional Technology at the University of Georgia.